INDOCHINA
ADMINISTRATIVE
DIVISIONS
JULY 1965

International boundary, demarcated
International boundary, delimited
Autonomous region or special zone boundary (North Vietnam)
Military region boundary (South Vietnam)
Province boundary
National capital
Autonomous region or special zone capital (North Vietnam)
Province capital
Autonomous municipality

Scale 1:3,500,000

VIET CONG

CENTER FOR INTERNATIONAL STUDIES
MASSACHUSETTS INSTITUTE OF TECHNOLOGY

Studies in International Communism

1. *Albania and the Sino-Soviet Rift,* William E. Griffith (1963)

2. *Communism in North Vietnam,* P. J. Honey (1964)

3. *The Sino-Soviet Rift,* William E. Griffith (1964)

4. *Communism in Europe,* Vol. 1, William E. Griffith, ed. (1964)
   "European Communism and the Sino-Soviet Rift," William E. Griffith
   "Yugoslav Communism," Viktor Meier
   "Polish Communism," Hansjakob Stehle
   "Hungarian Communism," François Fejtö
   "Italian Communism," Giorgio Galli

5. *Nationalism and Communism in Chile,* Ernst Halperin (1965)

6. *Communism in Europe,* Vol. 2, William E. Griffith, ed. (1966)
   "European Communism, 1965," William E. Griffith
   "East Germany," Carola Stern
   "Czechoslovakia," Zdeněk Eliáš and Jaromír Netík
   "Sweden," Åke Sparring
   "Norway," Jahn Otto Johansen
   "Finland," Bengt Matti

7. *Viet Cong: The Organization and Techniques of the
   National Liberation Front of South Vietnam,* Douglas Pike (1966)

VIET CONG

The Organization and Techniques of the
National Liberation Front of South Vietnam

Douglas Pike

THE M.I.T. PRESS
Massachusetts Institute of Technology
Cambridge, Massachusetts, and London, England

Foreword

There are many reasons why Americans are confused and concerned about our deepening involvement in the war in Vietnam. Not the least of these is uncertainty about the character and nature of the National Liberation Front, the guiding hand behind the elusive and shadowy enemy popularly known as the Viet Cong. Is the NLF anything more than a classical Communist-front organization? Is it purely an agent of Hanoi or does it have significant support in South Vietnam? How has it gone about building up its following, and what are its methods, tactics, and objectives? Never before has the United States fought a foe about whom so little is known.

In this study Douglas Pike has utilized NLF and other Vietnamese materials to seek answers to the kinds of questions Americans quite properly ask about the other side in Vietnam. He writes primarily of what he terms the "first war," which ended in late 1964 or early 1965. The NLF long had within itself the potential for divisive clashes over policy but, in the course of the "first war," it increasingly became "regularized" as a monolithic Communist organization controlled from Hanoi. This changed character of the NLF, together with heavy North Vietnamese engagement and growing direct American involvement, marked the end of the "first war" and the beginning of the "new war" in which we are engaged at present. Pike believes that, under some circumstances in the event of a settlement of the Vietnam conflict, the divergence of interests that has for the moment been suppressed might again arise, especially between the "North" and "South" elements within the NLF.

The main focus of Mr. Pike's study is on the organization and communication practices of the NLF. He sees the growth of the NLF as rising out of its capacity to bring into a disorganized and incoherent Asian society the political advantages of disciplined organization and manipulated social communication. The principles of effective organization are thus held to be more important than the appeals of Communist ideology or the frustrations of social and economic conditions.

Douglas Pike has served for many years in Asia, six of them in Vietnam as an official of the United States Information Agency. He received a research leave from USIA for 1964/65 to study at the Center for International Studies of the Massachusetts Institute of Technology and brought with him much of the data he had personally collected over the years about the National Liberation Front. During his year in Cambridge he drew upon these materials to prepare this book.

The analyses, interpretations, and conclusions are entirely those of Mr. Pike. This book, like all other publications of the Center, does not reflect an institutional position nor necessarily the views of other Center members. Pike's study is not a polemic for or against a particular policy line but an account of the nature of the National Liberation Front based largely on the Communists' own output.

In publishing this study the Center for International Studies hopes to contribute to greater understanding of specific problems currently being faced in Vietnam and of a more far-reaching challenge of vital importance for American foreign policy. Only as we learn more about the realities behind such insurgency movements in the developing areas will it be possible for the United States to design more enlightened and effective policies. Mr. Pike's study and other volumes on the international Communist movement prepared at the Center help to clarify the complex interweaving of nationalistic, social, political, and ideological elements that characterizes the phenomenon of international communism today and its local partisans.

Max F. Millikan
Director
Center for International Studies

August 1966

Preface

For Americans Vietnam has grown steadily as a crisis in perception, one that began with a failure in definition. It is both symbolic and significant that no appellation coined for the opposing insurgent forces was acceptable to all parties, including the insurgents themselves. In this sense they were never defined. The reader will note that although the title of this book is *Viet Cong* the term is not employed in the text (the explanation for this, hopefully satisfactory to the reader, appears on the page facing page 1). If, as Spinoza once observed, definition "consists in giving the cause or genesis of a thing, that is, stating how the thing originated or was produced," perhaps in this failure to define lies a clue not only to our crisis in perception but to all our subsequent difficulties. Beyond the ontological basis for our misperceptions, perhaps the most basic cause was mistaken fundamental assumptions. We were in much the same predicament as the character in *The People, Yes* who told Carl Sandburg, "I don't know much and come to think about it, what I do know ain't so." We assumed that the Vietnamese, because they were Vietnamese, would know how to defeat Vietnamese guerrillas if they had the means to do so. We assumed a charismatic leader was required. We assumed the solution was simply some combination of military force and welfare work. We assumed there was a high correlation between helping villagers in economic aid programs and their hostility toward the guerrilla. We assumed that methods used in other counterinsurgencies could be put to work in Vietnam. All of these assumptions, we discovered, were partially or wholly wrong. Error continued largely because of lack of information. Vietnam was a Kafka-like nightmare to anyone seeking facts. Even simple data, the population of a province, for example, were unobtainable. Beyond simply the dearth of statistics lay the domain of obfuscated information, or what Marshal Foch called "the fog of war." One came to believe that the struggle in Vietnam had many faces, all of them false. The falsehoods consisted on the one hand of untruths born of events themselves: the partial account, the uncertain rumor, the contradictory report. When an incident took place, an assassination, for example, immediately there was spun around it like a cocoon around a silk worm larva an involved thread of interpretation. Those remote from the event, say, in the United States, were never able to separate fact from speculation, and after a period even the eyewitness in Vietnam began to doubt his memory. On the other hand, there was that honest misperception or misinterpretation, the result of conflicting patterns of thought held by persons, each conditioned by his own cultural frame of reference and moving from his own peculiar national psychological base. One despaired of ever learning the truth, much less The Truth.

Finally, there was the writer's own sense of perceptual inadequacy. It was difficult enough to describe what those years were like even in one's own camp, and infinitely more difficult to do so from the Communist side.

I have served as a foreign service officer with the U.S. Information Agency in Vietnam since October 1960, with the exception of the academic year 1964/65, which I spent at the Center for International Studies, Massachusetts Institute of Technology, while on a grant from USIA to study the international communication of ideas. The Agency made the grant on the basis that it was in the national interest to have one or more of its foreign service officers knowledgeable in the field of communication of ideas in an insurgency.

The book itself was privately written. It began as an effort to record only certain events in Vietnam (the original working title, for example, was "Communication Factors of Revolutionary Guerrilla Warfare Using Vietnam as a Case History"), but gradually it broadened in scope to include virtually everything in the insurgency. The manuscript was read by interested U.S. governmental officials, as well as scholars and numerous Vietnamese, after it was completed. No substantive changes were made subsequently. I wrote without instruction, mandate, or proscription. No one in or out of the government ever told me, or "suggested" to me, what to put in or leave out. I am deeply indebted to the Center for International Studies at the Massachusetts Institute of Technology, its director Max F. Millikan, as well as staff members, chiefly Jean P. S. Clark, William E. Griffith, Donald L. M. Blackmer, Lucian W. Pye, James L. Dorsey, and

Amelia C. Leiss. In terms of indebtedness I owe the most to my very close friend Nguyen Hung Vuong of Saigon.

Obviously the contents of the book are solely and exclusively mine, for which I alone stand responsible. I have tried hard to be objective, honest, and dispassionate. I serve no school of thought on Vietnam. Further, this is not a theoretical book. It has few theses and makes few arguments. Basically it is reportorial. I have tried to follow the very sound advice of a wise academic friend who counseled me to make the book "affectively neutral, maximizing information and minimizing interpretation."

Although the book presents no thesis as such, its orientation is directed toward the insurgents' communication matrix, which is to say the methods and techniques employed in communicating ideas as well as a consideration of the ideas communicated. The Communists in South Vietnam began with only a set of tenuous theories and not with anything that could be described as a full blueprint. They learned as they went, testing, rejecting, improvising, painstakingly building an organizational steamroller. When I first approached the subject of the National Liberation Front, I was struck by the enormous amounts of time, energy, manpower, and money it spent on communication activities. It seemed obsessed with explaining itself to itself, to the other side, and to the world at large. As the study deepened it became evident that *everything* the NLF did was an act of communication. If the essence of the Chinese revolution was *strategy* and the essence of the Viet Minh was *spirit*, the essence of the third-generation revolutionary guerrilla warfare in South Vietnam was *organization*. What the NLF produced was a major, if not necessarily beneficial, contribution to the sociology of revolution.

From this the reader must surmise that I take a communicational view of social change. The fundamental assumption here is that when people, especially those in developing societies, are exposed to new ideas, new methods, new social structures, certain things happen, and neither they nor their society are ever again quite the same. This assumption seems to me to be beyond debate. The Communists have brought to the villages of South Vietnam significant social change and have done so largely by means of the communication process. This process is what this book is about.

The struggle in Vietnam was in fact two wars, one following the other. The first began in 1960, or possibly as early as 1958, and ended in late 1964 or early 1965. After that time, Vietnam was the arena of a new war, with new actors, new ground rules, new tactics and strategy, new definitions of victory and defeat. This book is about the first war, which, if the two-wars contention is accepted, does then have a beginning, middle, and end (which explains why the book is written in past tense). Many

aspects of the Vietnam scene, for example, the relationship between
Hanoi and the apparatus in the South, were developmental, and point in
time is all important; we are concerned here chiefly with events prior to
the spring of 1965, although references are made to events in the summer
of 1966.

The data from which the book was fashioned were of three types: The
first consisted of internal documents of the National Liberation Front
and the People's Revolutionary Party captured by units of the Vietnamese army in field operations and supplied to me by military friends, Vietnamese and American. (A catalog of these documents, which numbered
over 800, has been compiled and is available from the Center for International Studies, Massachusetts Institute of Technology.) In addition I
had access to some 2,000 examples of NLF printed propaganda produced
and distributed in the South as well as daily transcripts of broadcasts by
Radio Liberation, the NLF's clandestine radio station, Radio Hanoi, and
Radio Peking. The second was a series of some 100 interviews with *quy
chanh,* those who voluntarily quit the NLF ranks, while they were in
camps awaiting return to civilian life. The third consisted of information
and judgments on data from knowledgeable Vietnamese friends, in and
out of the government, whose sources about the NLF I did not always
know but whose veracity was tested and proved time and again.

In addition to these direct source materials I have of course consulted
the general and scholarly literature dealing with Vietnam. For a survey
of Vietnam from early times to the present the reader should consult
Joseph Buttinger, *The Smaller Dragon* (New York: Praeger, 1958);
Donald Lancaster, *The Emancipation of French Indo-China* (London,
New York, Toronto: Oxford University Press, 1961); and Robert Shaplen,
*The Lost Revolution: The Story of Twenty Years of Neglected Oppor-
tunities in Vietnam and of America's Failure to Foster Democracy There*
(New York: Harper & Row, 1965). More specialized interests are served
by the following books, all highly recommended: Jack Henry Brimmell,
Communism in South East Asia (London: Oxford University Press,
1959), a good comparative study; Malcolme W. Browne, *The New Face
of War* (New York: Bobbs-Merrill, 1965), an especially good discussion
of the military considerations; Philippe Devillers, *Histoire du Viet-Nam
de 1940 à 1952* (Paris: Editions du Seuil, 1952), for the French view of
the Viet Minh war; Bernard Fall, *The Viet-Minh Regime* (Ithaca, N.Y.:
Cornell University Press, 1956), a good account of the organizational
efforts of the Viet Minh; Gerald C. Hickey, *Village in Vietnam* (New
Haven, Conn.: Yale University Press, 1964), the only recent study of the
Vietnamese village; P. J. Honey, *North Vietnam Today* (New York:
Praeger, 1962) and *Communism in North Vietnam* (Cambridge, Mass.:
The M.I.T. Press, 1963), by the free world's leading authority on North

Vietnam; Robert G. Scigliano, *South Vietnam: Nation under Stress* (Boston: Houghton Mifflin, 1964), which contains much valuable information on the Vietnamese political scene of the early 1960's; I. Milton Sacks, "Marxism in Vietnam," a very good account of this subject, in Frank N. Trager, ed., *Marxism in Southeast Asia* (Stanford, Cal.: Stanford University Press, 1959); and Denis Warner, *The Last Confucian* (New York: Macmillan, 1963), an account of events leading up to the coup d'état that deposed Ngo Dinh Diem. Communist authors have produced a great deal of material on Vietnam but none of any survey value to the American reader. For example, Wilfred G. Burchett's *Vietnam: Inside Story of the Guerrilla War* (New York: International Publishers Associates, 1965) contains valuable material on the author's travels within the NLF-controlled areas but is not to be trusted. The works of Mao Tse-tung, Vo Nguyen Giap, and Truong Chinh are of course basic source materials.

This is largely the NLF's account of itself, a legitimate approach, I feel, but one the reader should bear in mind at all times. We are dealing here for the most part with Communist materials. I have sought to screen the data and separate the more important from the empty sound and fury. I have approached the material with a most skeptical mind. This has resulted in neither a simple chronology of the Communist effort nor an impressionistic interpretation of it. Rather, I have attempted to list those facts and describe those phenomena that I felt were most significant from a developmental standpoint.

Nevertheless the result is far from complete. Like the Irishman's evidence, this book is chock full of omissions. The most serious perhaps concerns internal conflict within the NLF and how it was resolved. We had many indications that conflict did exist, as manifested, for example, by personnel changes. But we knew little of the substance of the conflicts. Nor did we know of the mechanics for resolving differences. And because we did not know these things we had no accurate way of estimating the degree of cohesiveness within the leadership ranks, a significant area of ignorance on our part. The second major omission concerns the state of NLF and Communist morale, especially at the highest levels, at any given moment. Such a measurement is difficult to make even on one's own side. We never were certain that reports in this sphere were not deliberate plants or the result of wishful thinking. Since morale is all-important in a guerrilla war, this too is a serious shortcoming.

Having lived in Vietnam for six years, I have to a degree put down roots there and have come to care very deeply about what happens. The plight of the Vietnamese people is not an abstraction to me, and I have no patience with those who treat it as such. Victory by the Communists would mean consigning thousands of Vietnamese, many of them of course my friends, to death, prison, or permanent exile. Speeches by American leaders saying that the issue is promulgating the Vietnamese people's freedom of choice is reality to me, not a platitude. I am appalled by those who suggest that the Vietnamese are in Communist China's "proper sphere of influence." This kind of dehumanized political thinking, which eliminates the individual man as the measure of all things, is totally alien to me. My heart goes out to the Vietnamese people — who have been sold out again and again, whose long history could be written in terms of betrayal and who, based on this long and bitter experience, can only expect that eventually America too will sell them out. If America betrays the Vietnamese people by abandoning them, she betrays her own heritage.

Douglas Pike

Saigon, South Vietnam
August 1966

Contents

CONTENTS

Glossary

ARVN	Army of (South) Vietnam.
Binh van	the NLF proselyting program; literally, action among the enemy troops (condensed from *binh van* and *chinh van*, the B and C program, which included *chinh*, or civil servants, as well as *binh*, or military personnel). One of the three major NLF programs.
Chieu Hoi	the GVN's surrender or amnesty program; literally, open arms.
Dan van	the NLF program to develop support among the population in areas it controlled; literally, action among the people. One of the three major NLF programs.
Dich van	the NLF program to develop the struggle movement in GVN-controlled areas; literally, action among the enemy (controlled people). One of the three major NLF programs.
DRV	Democratic Republic of Vietnam, i.e., North Vietnam.
FLA	Farmers' Liberation Association (of the NLF).
First, second, and third stages	the three phases of revolutionary guerrilla warfare as outlined by Mao Tsetung, later amended by General Vo Nguyen Giap, and practiced by the

	NLF in South Vietnam beginning in 1960.
GVN	government of (South) Vietnam.
General Uprising (*Khoi Nghia*)	major social myth of the NLF, similar to the early Communist social myth of the general strike.
ICC or ICSC	International Control Commission or International Control and Surveillance Commission, the international organization (Canada, India, and Poland) created by Great Britain and the Soviet Union to supervise the implementing of the 1954 Geneva accords.
Lao Dong (Workers') Party	the Communist party of North Vietnam; full title: Dang Lao Dong Viet Nam.
NLF or NLFSV (sometimes NLFSVN)	National Liberation Front (of South Vietnam).
PAVN	People's Army of Vietnam (North Vietnamese armed forces).
PRP	People's Revolutionary Party, the Communist party in South Vietnam.
Quy chanh	one who returns under *chieu hoi* program; literally, return (to just cause).
Resistance (the)	the French–Viet Minh war, 1946–1954.
RVNAF	Republic of Vietnam Armed Forces (South Vietnamese armed forces).
SLA	Student Liberation Association (of the NLF).
Strategic hamlet	Diem government's program to develop system of defended villages as part of its resources control program. After Diem, became known as the New Life Hamlet and, later, the Revolutionary Development program.
Struggle movement (*dau tranh*)	social disorders created by the NLF throughout South Vietnam after 1960 in an effort to launch the General Uprising.
Viet Cong	commonly employed term to describe the insurgent force in Vietnam.
VNAF	(South) Vietnam Air Force.
WLA	Workers' Liberation Association (of the NLF).
YLA	Youth Liberation Association (of the NLF).

VIET CONG

"The press in Saigon since 1956 has referred to the latter [Vietnamese Communists] as 'Vietcong', *Cong* (an abbreviation of *Cong-san*) standing for 'communists'. The new term is precise and accurate and, contrary to what many foreign correspondents believe, does not have any disparaging meaning." — Hoang Van Chi, *From Colonialism to Communism*.

"*Viet Cong,* a contemptuous appellation which lumps together the Communists and the patriots, the former Resistance members and the advocates of peace and in general all those who are lukewarm toward the pro-U.S. policy, even on details." — *The South Vietnam National Liberation Front*, published (in English) by the Foreign Languages Publishing House, Hanoi, North Vietnam.

"The nickname *Viet Cong* has stuck and now even the Communists themselves use it." — Stanley Karnow, American reporter.

"A Vietnamese can be shot if he uses the term *Viet Cong* in referring to them." — Jim Robinson, NBC correspondent.

"It means *Vietnamese Communist* and for the life of me I can't see, if you *are* a Vietnamese Communist, why you would object to the term." — A leading Vietnamese political scientist.

"I'll say this, if they ever capture you, don't use the term *Viet Cong* or *V C* in talking to them. They don't like it!" — U.S. military briefing officer in Saigon.

"I suggest we name my book *Viet Cong* — not because the term is fully accurate (it is not) but because it will do what a title is supposed to do: tell the reader what the book is about." — Memorandum from author to publisher.

1

Heritage

Only a few currents in the long winding river of Vietnamese history relate to our primary concern and need be noted in passing. First, the spirit of *doc lap* (independence), or, more accurately in this context, the profound resentment against foreign control, is a major element shaping the Vietnamese social scene. The second, Vietnamese regionalism, which is more than provincialism and deeper than parochialism, is a vital factor. *Doc lap* stemmed from Chinese domination, regionalism from the historic march to the south that began in the tenth century and continued sporadically for 800 years. A strong clan instinct wedded to a deep sense of Vietnamese destiny, placed in the setting of foreign control that unfortunately has marked most of Vietnam's early and late history, produced the third current, an extremely significant cluster of attitudes toward social organization, and created what is perhaps the single most important Vietnamese sociological heritage: the clandestine organization. In combination these factors created, as we shall see, a paradoxical individual outlook on life's struggles and society's problems — the coiled-spring attitude, tolerant pacifism surrounding a small hard center of militant fanaticism.

Doc Lap

Doc lap, the Vietnamese legacy of independence, can be traced back to the dawn of their history around 500 B.C., when several clan tribes, called the Viets, living in China south of the Yangtze River came under strong assimilative pressure from the Chinese. The Nam (South) Viets, rather than yield as did many of their tribal Viet neighbors, began a great southward exodus and chose as their new home the delta of the Red River. Thus an ethnically identifiable group was created whose reasonably pure lineage is traceable to the present day, a fact of which all Vietnamese, and Chinese for that matter, are aware.[1]

The Nam Viets' efforts to escape the Chinese, however, were not successful. Soon the Chinese were upon them and by 258 B.C. had conquered all the Nam Viet tribes of the Red River delta.

Chinese rule, from all accounts, was not oppressive and was far more beneficial in the long run to the Viets than to their overlords. From the Chinese the Vietnamese blandly appropriated an entire sociopolitical structure as well as a body of religion, art, and literature — virtually an entire Confucian civilization *in toto*. In particular the Confucian political ethics — harmony of the universe, absolutism tempered by the mandate-of-heaven concept plus certain overtones of xenophobia — came to have great and lasting influence. In the end, when the Chinese left a millennium later, virtually the only Vietnamese cultural survivals were the language and a determination not to be assimilated, and the latter was probably traceable to the influence of the highly ethnocentric Chinese.[2]

---

[1] A truly remarkable example of the durability of the Sino-Vietnamese racial memory is contained in this story told by a Vietnamese refugee living in Tokyo and quoted by Hoang Van Chi:

> During a banquet for Sun Yat-sen in Tokyo in 1911, his host, the Japanese statesman Ki Tsuyoshi Inukai, asked him unexpectedly, seeking to trap him: "What do you think of the Vietnamese?" Caught off guard, Sun replied: "The Vietnamese are slaves by nature. They have been ruled by us and now they are ruled by the French. They can't have a very brilliant future." Inukai said: "I don't agree with you on that point. Though not independent at present, they are the only one of the 'Hundred Yüeh' [Viet tribes] successfully to resist the process of *Han-hwa* [Sinoization]. Such a people must sooner or later gain their political independence." Sun, it is said, blushed but made no reply, realizing that Inukai knew that he was a Cantonese, one of a people regarded as inferior by the Vietnamese because they became so completely Sinified that they lost all their Yüeh cultural identity, considering themselves wholly Chinese.

> Hoang Van Chi, *From Colonialism to Communism: A Case Study of North Vietnam* (New York and London: Praeger, 1964), p. 5.

> Incredible as it may be to a Westerner, in Asia it is possible for a person to blush because of a decision his ancestors made two thousand years ago.

[2] What the Chinese got for their efforts was constant low-grade resistance punctuated by short-lived rebellions. Vietnamese history and folklore are studded with accounts of heroic

The racial memory of the Chinese occupation and Chinese influence lingered on in Vietnam. As late as 1880, for example, the court of Annam in Hué paid a token yearly tribute to the Emperor of China. Several boatloads of Chinese arrived in the Saigon area in the eighteenth century and settled in what is today Saigon's sister city, Cholon (meaning "big market"). Under French rule overseas Chinese in Indochina acted as the middlemen between the French and the Indochinese, dominating transportation, wholesale trade, and rice milling, and were active in moneylending and retail trade. Vietnamese today both admire and resent the Chinese; they also hold them in considerable fear, but this feeling appears to be more reflexive than rational, more personal than nationalistic. Although China has markedly shaped modern Vietnamese character, the propensity to maintain racial identity, present in all men, has certainly manifested itself in the Vietnamese more strongly and over a longer period of time than in most of the world's other racial groups.

Regionalism

The unity ingrained in Vietnamese bones is thus not geographic but tribal. Yet the people's amazing ability to resist centuries of continuous Chinese political-military pressure without being Sinoized by the all-pervasive Chinese culture when "Chinese tribes" all about them were succumbing, and their ability to maintain a national identity despite the internal divisive conflicts and vast geographic distances[3] that characterized their next thousand years, have been so impressive as to obscure the real and vital fact of deeply ingrained regional differences. This is not to diminish in any way Vietnamese coalescence. But the import and

---

rebels, some of whom are venerated today as virtual deities. The sisters Trung Trac and Trung Nhi, mounted on elephants, led a force against the Chinese in A.D. 39. Even today the anniversary of their short-lived victory over the Chinese is a national holiday in both North and South Vietnam. The Trieu siblings, Trieu Quoc and his sister Trieu Au, led a revolt in A.D. 249, which was followed by the Ly Thuong Nam revolt in 484, the Ly By revolt in 541, and finally by the successful Ngo Quyen rebellion that drove out the Chinese in 938. Most of the early revolutionaries were upper class, and in fact the uprisings against the Chinese in the second and third centuries were exclusively upper-class revolutions in which the peasant took no initiative. Later rebellions did involve him and thus created a sense of involvement on his part. Joseph Buttinger (in *The Smaller Dragon* [New York: Praeger, 1958]) noted that in order to survive as a separate people every Vietnamese had to be ready at all times to sacrifice his life in the many wars against the Chinese armies of invasion or occupation.

[3] Vietnam is even longer and thinner than a map would suggest. In the nearly 1,500-mile coastal strip running from China to Cambodia the overwhelming majority of Vietnamese live within a few dozen miles of the sea; the vast acreages in the highlands are either empty or the domain of non-Vietnamese. That unity should be maintained down such a long thin line is even more remarkable; it is, the Vietnamese say, the unity of a chain.

consequence of Vietnamese sectionalism must be understood and appreciated in understanding Vietnam at this juncture of her history, particularly the South, the main concern in this book.

Regionalism derived from Vietnam's expansionism, its 800-year, 1,500-mile march to the south. This was a series of leapfrog moves, some voluntary and some forced, under the supervision of the emperor and his court, which saw the departure of groups of Vietnamese from the more populous and settled areas and the successive establishment farther south of new villages large enough to be economically viable and physically secure.[4]

The thrust began in the tenth century, when the first indigenous dynasty, the Le (A.D. 980–1009), took the throne from the Chinese and began a three-and-a-half-century rule. The dynasty's fourth king, Le Thanh Ton, conquered the Champa Kingdom in the southern portion of the peninsula, utterly destroyed its culture, dispersed its people, and set the scene for southern penetration. The area around Hué was reached in the early 1300's, and all of what was to be Central Vietnam was settled by the late 1400's. After a hiatus, far-south settlement began in about 1600. The northern portion, down to what is now Phan Thiet, was reached by the end of the seventeenth century, and the area south of the present city of Saigon as far as the Bassac River was reached in the first half of the eighteenth century. Settlement of the Mekong delta region, the southernmost part of Cochin China, all the way to the tip of the Camau peninsula, was completed by 1780.[5]

During much of the past three hundred years Vietnam has been divided into halves or thirds: in half after the secession period of circa 1600; in thirds during the reign of the Tay Son brothers (1788–1802); united by Emperor Gia Long in 1802 only to be divided into thirds by the French in 1884; and then again in half by the 1954 Geneva accords. The French divided Indochina into three administrative regions (plus Laos and Cambodia). Tonkin (English spelling frequently Tongking), meaning "Eastern Capital" (from the Chinese), in Northern Vietnam was a direct protectorate with a French *resident supérieur* acting as the official representative or viceroy for the Vietnamese emperor. Central Vietnam,

---

[4] Buttinger (*op. cit.*, pp. 38–40) described the process:

It was a slow advance that lasted over 800 years, carried on primarily by a type of peasant soldiering for which this people seems to have developed an aptitude at a very early time. The peasant became a soldier whenever an enemy approached either for plunder or to drive the Vietnamese from a newly settled territory. . . . Thus the Vietnamese began to march south, looking for new plains behind every new row of mountains, pushing along the narrow flatland between the mountains and the sea, proceeding on water where the mountains went directly into the ocean, and settling in valley after valley with every new delta as a new base until they finally reached the open spaces of the Mekong River delta. . . .

[5] Cochin China in 1882 consisted of six provinces totaling 22,000 square miles and containing about 1,600,000 people.

called Annam[6] by the French, was an indirect protectorate. There, in the capital city of Hué, sat the emperor and his court, but with authority of course vested in the French. Southern Vietnam was called Cochin China, the first word being a corruption of *ke chiem,* which foreigners pronounced *cochin,* adding China to distinguish it from the Port of Cochin in India. *Ke chiem* was the name of the Nguyen dynasty's suzerain in Quang Nam province in the seventeenth century. Cochin China was a French possession and was not under even nominal rule by the Vietnamese emperors; thus the colonial administrator governed in the South while the mandarin remained somewhat more firmly in control in Annam and Tonkin, and consequently Southerners were more markedly affected by the fact of French colonialism than their cousins to the north.

The 1954 partition divided Vietnam at the 17th parallel. The Democratic Republic of Vietnam (DRV), or North Vietnam, included Tonkin and half of Annam; the Republic of Vietnam, or South Vietnam, the lower half of Annam and Cochin China. The North, Center, and South referents became most common in South Vietnam; for instance, a person from Hué would usually say he was "from the Center," confusing foreigners, who considered Hué to be in northern South Vietnam. The 1954 division, with the accompanying shifts of population, if anything increased the Vietnamese sense of regional identification.

The march to the south produced a South Vietnamese who was something of a pioneer, remote from the subtler pleasures of the North, distant from the venerable city of the emperor. Today he is still distinguishable from his more sophisticated cousin in Hanoi and his more traditional cousin in Hué. Because his land is more tropical — two seasons instead of Hanoi's four — he is more apt to demonstrate some of the lackadaisical attitudes common among hot-climate peoples. Such generalizations are dangerous. Yet one cannot completely discount the regional designations that Vietnamese love to dispense: that Southerners are lazy and slow-witted (Northerners), or boorish and unintellectual (Centerites); that Centerites are hidebound and overly traditional (Northerners), or "vague speaking" and "too political" (Southerners); that Northerners are aggressive and warlike (Southerners), or "money hungry" and overly sharp in business deals (Centerites). On the other hand the Northerner tends to regard himself as dynamic and progressive; the Centerite pictures himself as a cultivated individual, the guardian of a treasured cultural legacy; and the Southerner believes he is the possessor of true happiness, whose secret is the leisurely enjoyment of simple pleas-

---

[6] After the tenth century the Chinese referred to all of Vietnam as An Nam, a humiliating term meaning "pacified south." For their part the Vietnamese used the term Dai Co Viet, or Greater Viet State. In 1802, under Emperor Gia Long, the term Viet Nam came into official as well as wide usage.

ures amid the pastoral harmony of a bountiful nature. Even a foreigner cannot live long in the country without being caught up in this sectional bias, and he soon comes to judge a Vietnamese from the fact of his birthplace. The Vietnamese are as conscious of region as an Indian is of caste, but since dialect instantly identifies one's birthplace, even to a foreigner with only a rudimentary knowledge of the language, one need never inquire; thus the consciousness is not so obvious as in India.

Traditional Social Organization

The kinship system, bedrock of the Vietnamese social system, has become less prominent in recent times but remains of front-rank importance. Loyalty, especially to the family, continues to be the primary virtue, a reflection of the Confucian ethic of *hieu,* or filial piety. Centuries of *hieu* indoctrination made the Vietnamese organizational animals in the same way that many Americans are political animals — instinctively so. The most important social institution in traditional Vietnam was the household (*nha* or *gia*), which was the basic political unit of the village; it, not the individual, was the tax base (*nong ho*); the *nha,* not people, was counted in a census. The *nha* assumed responsibility for a child's rearing and education. It was a collective work group and formed a single economic unit — "one fire, one lamp," as the Vietnamese phrased it. And the *nha* was the place of worship. The law never meddled in internal *nha* affairs, although it would enforce certain aspects of the filial piety code; a prisoner would often be paroled on the grounds that he was needed to support his ancient parents.

The major traditional Vietnamese village organizations included the village itself as a protective association, various mutual-aid societies formed for specific purposes, the village guild, and the elderly women's Buddhist association.

The village itself was often a form of cooperative or protective association. It could own property, perform charitable and social welfare work, maintain granaries against years of famine, and in general protect the villagers in a paternalistic if somewhat authoritarian manner. At the very least every village had an emergency relief organization (*nghia tuong*) that acted quasi-officially under village administration. This system, or fund, began as a voluntary relief group in the Red River delta, where yearly flooding was common and losses to farmers often great. It developed into an ever-normal granary. In the 1860's Emperor Tu Duc established uniform regulations governing *nghia tuong* and extended the system to all villages in the kingdom as part of the village administration. Farmers after each harvest would turn over a portion of their crop, usually ten kilos (22 pounds) of paddy (unhusked) rice for each hectare (2.2 acres) farmed, to the village *nghia tuong* committee, an elected six-man group responsible for storing and distributing rice. Once an adequate stockpile was built up (roughly four tons of rice for each thousand persons in the village), the excess was sold and the money used to help the village indigent. In event of a crop failure rice was distributed on an equal basis to all members of the village.

The mutual-aid society (*hoi tu cap*) was usually organized for a specific purpose, the most common being the burial society. (Other societies managed weddings, helped in home building and home repairing, or celebrated Tet, the lunar new year.) When, for example, a death occurred in a family, members of the *hoi tu cap* were canvassed for contributions; and they attended the wake and the burial or cremation.

The village guild (*hoi bach nghe*) was made up of village craftsmen, carpenters, masons, stonecutters, and blacksmiths. It grew out of the early Vietnamese craft system under which a Vietnamese apprentice would go to China, learn a trade, and return to his home village to share his new knowledge with others; after his death he often became the guild's patron saint. The *hoi bach nghe* was a guild in the feudal European sense in that it set standards of craftsmanship and regulated entry into the various trades; the guild, administered by an elected three-man group, also served as a protective association, aiding indigent members and presenting gifts of cash or labor at important moments in the lives of members, such as marriage, birth of children, or death. Many guilds were wealthy, since membership dues were based on income, and large donations from the wealthy were virtually mandatory. As an offshoot form of the *hoi bach nghe* were associations of wrestlers, boatsmen, and devotees of cockfighting. Other associations at the village level preserved literary traditions, protected the interests of the elderly, or acted as what would today be called a mutual-fund investment club, not unlike the Chinese *hui*.

The elderly women's Buddhist association (*hoi chu ba*) was open to women over 50 and sometimes to widows in their 40's who, being fully supported by their children and with no economic worries, were free to devote themselves to the matter of their salvation. Until recent times the *hoi chu ba* was the only lay Buddhist organization in Vietnam. The novitiate, bearing gifts, appeared at her local pagoda and was introduced by her sponsor, a regular member called a *ba vai* or *chu ba*. If accepted, she would appear nightly for several weeks to receive religious lessons from a *ba vai* or possibly a monk. After being admitted to full membership she was expected to appear frequently at the pagoda, and always on the first and fifteenth days of the lunar month, when she would be greeted by the senior *hoi chu ba,* called a *vai thu ho,* and by the pagoda's monks to whom she would be expected to present food or money. In addition to the Buddhist pagoda every village had a *dinh,* the shrine of the village guardian spirit, which was also the center of communal life; the *dinh* often served as the administrative building for the village and was the scene of communal village activities.

The remains of this heritage today act as a cement holding together a social structure based on a broad nationalistic spirit, a sense of identity that predates the modern nation-state concept. Also serving as a bond is the small size of the original Vietnamese tribal groupings; there are less than one hundred family names, such as Nguyen or Ngo. This spirit of identity also stems from the Confucian political concept of unity of power, hierarchic subordination, and the emperor-father image. Finally, it is the result of great South Vietnamese pride in a four-thousand-year unbroken chain of unity, in a language capable of expressing nuances of great complexity and beauty, and in a unique valor and fighting ability that liberated the land first from the Chinese (one of the most awesome military forces on earth) and later from the technologically advanced French. The result, vague in the peasant, stronger in the sophisticated city dweller, is a sense of mission.

The Clandestine Organization

A strong sense of associational linkages combined with feelings of racial superiority and manifest destiny and nourished in the setting of a foreign-power occupation usually yield a collection of blood brotherhoods, militant nationalist organizations, general-purpose clandestine associations, or some combination of all of these. Such was the case in Vietnam. Many of the traditional village groups were, if not clandestine, at least *sub rosa,* the result of native caution. Unless an organization had some reason to be public, for example, a channel of communication, it remained inconspicuous. Such groups were in no way channels of communication — the *nha* or the clan had only nominal communication within the village; the village-court channel was weak and the clan-court channel virtually nonexistent. Therefore the less anyone knew of a group's existence and purpose the better. Buddhist groups became covert or partially so from time to time after the thirteenth century as a result of sporadic official court discrimination against the religion. The influences of the two types, mutual-protective and religious, became reciprocal. The religious organizations took on mutual-protection functions as a requirement for survival. And the protective associations took on the trappings of the religious order and often were headed by a religious figure; Buttinger described this latter type of organization as hierarchic, ritualistic, and doctrinaire, blending religious and political beliefs; they had small or great purposes, could simply be interested in the well-being of their members, or could seek the destruction of the existing governmental structure.[7] In any event, the tradition of clandestinism was established, and the clandestine organization emerged — if that is the correct term to use — to dominate Vietnamese politics and society to this very day.

Its period of greatest refinement came under the French; the clandestine organization became the instrument for dealing with a foreign ruler, a tendency enhanced by the French when they refused to permit the Vietnamese to have political parties and the freedom to engage in political activity. French policy resulted in the creation of a whole new level of clandestine organizations, political and nationalistic, operating in deep secrecy, holding underground meetings, staging apparently leaderless mass demonstrations, disseminating virulently anti-French printed propaganda, and in some cases indulging in assassinations and other forms of violence.

The basis of the Vietnamese clandestine organization, however, ran even deeper. It rested on the Vietnamese assumption that society consisted of a host of dangerous and conflicting social forces with which only enigmatic organization and secret "inness" could cope. Power in old Vietnam was something to be fought for, to be seized and clung to exclusively. No emperor ever willingly shared it. A challenger to the throne hid his hand until he was ready to strike. Neither in the early days nor later under the French was a loyal opposition permitted to exist. Any opposition was a direct threat and was relentlessly crushed wherever attempted or whenever exposed.

Today Vietnamese politics still bear the mark of the clandestine organization. The organization, clandestine and otherwise, is the arena in which the struggle for power takes place. The winner, if he does not take all, takes most, and the stakes are high. The world of organizational infighting is fluid and dynamic, in constant flux. One must keep running simply to hold his own. Daily activity involves negotiation and bargaining, sincere or otherwise, partially or completely in secret, and usually through third parties. The world should never know precisely where one stands; not only should the organization be clandestine but so should its membership. Constantly there are realignments, or revelations as to one's true colors. No position is ever irretrievable, no commitment ever final. It is a system of centrifugal force always tending to fly apart, only to form again. The rule is: Be flexible, be changeable, adapt. No organization is ever competely undisguised. All consist of at least two parts, the overt face and the secret apparatus; but the best, in addition to the covert

---

[7] Buttinger, *op. cit.*, p. 6.

leadership that "clever" Vietnamese eventually penetrate, has a third layer, which is reality. However, because it is a system of mutation, the reality, even if you discover it, does not last long; soon new alliances outdate your discovery. Sometimes an organization is within an organization, with one organization evincing great hostility for a second when actually both are controlled by a third. Most have false patrons; almost certainly the proclaimed leader is not the wielder of maximum influence. Proselyting is common, and no opprobrium is placed on one who changes sides, providing he observes a decent interval. Loyalty may be a virtue, but consistency is not. (Primary kin group loyalty is an exception.) Members assemble around individual leaders rather than around an ideology or a political platform. The best leader is paternalistic, sly, skilled at intrigue, master of the deceptive move, possessor of untold layers of duplicity, highly effective in the world in which he moves. Sagacity in the follower consists in knowing whom to join and when, for timing is all-important. It is no accident that the Vietnamese hold the professional magician in particular awe.

The model of the clandestine organization leader of course is the man now known to the world as Ho Chi Minh, who for five decades played a phantasmagoric role behind perhaps a dozen aliases. Most Vietnamese believe his real or original name was Nguyen Tat Thanh, with Nguyen being the family name. His two most commonly employed appellations, Nguyen Ai Quoc and Ho Chi Minh, were chosen for their significance in Chinese ideographs, the former meaning Nguyen, the Patriot, and the latter, Ho, the Enlightened One. His choice of aliases during the 1920's in Canton apparently was made lightheartedly. He was known then as Ly Thuy, Lee Suei, and Vuong Son Nhi, all ideographic wordplays on each other. Nearly an entire decade of his life, the 1930's, remains unaccounted for, leading to speculation that there has been more than one Ho Chi Minh. Others maintain that he died in a Hong Kong prison in 1933 under the name of Nguyen Ai Quoc[8] or in a Soviet prison, in either case being replaced by an unknown who went on to become the ruler of North Vietnam. No other world leader in modern times is as enigmatic as Ho Chi Minh. And, in the tradition of the best clandestine organization leader, he has done nothing to clear up the mystery. Far from it, he has given journalists and others over the years a series of contradictory explanations, in Vietnamese eyes behaving exactly as a good leader should.

It was wholly in keeping with Vietnamese tradition that the European front organization, in the "popular" sense of a coalition of political groups formed temporarily for some specific purpose with Communist partici-

---

[8] An account of his death, apparently the action of overhasty editors, was carried in the London *Daily Worker*, August 11, 1932.

pation (whether well or slightly known) but of such nature as to benefit both Communist and non-Communist participants, was immediately accepted into the Vietnamese clandestine political realm. The *mat tran,* or front organization, harmonized with both the temperament of the individual Vietnamese and the nature of social relations in Vietnam and was an accepted political tool. The antifascist united front of European politics arrived in Indochina in 1938 as Mat Tran Thong Nhan Dan Chu (Democratic United Front). In 1939 it became Mat Tran Dan Chu Bai Phong Phan De (Anti-Imperialist United Front). Other front groups followed: the United National Front (Mat Tran Quoc Gia Thong Nhut), the Front for National Unity (Mat Tran Doan Ket), the United National People's Front (Mat Tran Quoc Dan Doan Ket), and the Front for Democracy (Mat Tran Dan Chu Hoa).

In 1941 the Indochinese Communist Party (ICP) formed the Viet Minh (a contraction of Viet Nam Doc Lap Dong Minh Hoi), formally known as the League for the Independence of Vietnam. It was a Communist-front organization even though the term *mat tran* did not appear in its title. Vo Nguyen Giap, describing the victory over the French, declared:

The Vietnamese people's war of liberation was victorious because we had a wide and firm *National United Front . . . organised and led by the Party of the working class: the Indochinese Communist Party, now the Viet Nam Workers'* [Lao Dong] *Party.*[9]

The Viet Minh in turn became part of a broader front organization called the National Union of Vietnam, or National Popular Front Association (Hoi Lien Hiep Quoc Dan Viet Nam) — in everyday use the Lien Viet. Formed under the guidance of Ho Chi Minh, the Lien Viet sought to include organizations not just in Vietnam but also in Cambodia, Laos, and even beyond. The Lien Viet in the early 1950's was absorbed into a still broader front, the Fatherland Front (Mat Tran To Quoc), which was apparently set up to attract membership from South Vietnam, but in this it was unsuccessful.

Religious Groups

Religion in Vietnam tends to be a blending of many creeds. Normally there is little fanaticism and a great tolerance for varying beliefs and teachings. Unlike Hindus, the Vietnamese are not fervently religious people preoccupied with a spiritual quest. The foundation of the Vietnamese social system, like the Chinese, rests not on revealed religion but on ethics. Also like the Chinese, the pragmatic Vietnamese concern

[9] Vo Nguyen Giap, *People's War, People's Army* (Hanoi: Foreign Languages Press, 1961); quoted from facsimile edition (New York: Praeger, 1962), p. 35.

themselves less with the hereafter than with the proper conduct of affairs and the attainment of happiness in the here and now. Religion represents a coalescence of many elements, native and foreign, rational and naïve. The main characteristic of religion in Vietnam is that apart from monks the Vietnamese have never considered themselves exclusively Confucianist, Buddhist, or Taoist. Vietnamese literature is filled with references to the harmony of the three religions, calling them "three roads to the same destination." Indeed they do share certain doctrines: the original goodness of man and salvation through the realization of one's essential nature.

Buddhism in Vietnam is represented by both of its great schools. Most common is the Great Vehicle, or Big Wheel, Buddhism (Mahayana), which came from China. Little Wheel (Hinayana) Buddhism holds that Buddha was a teacher, not a god; it is found mainly in Ceylon, Burma, Cambodia, and in the Mekong delta area of South Vietnam. But Buddhism in Vietnam is amorphous and confused, its creeds are formless, and its followers are united only in the belief that Buddha is a sort of presiding deity. Beneath, there is room for all sorts of beliefs, including ancestor worship and simple animism, the worship of local spirits, which is very common in rural Vietnam.

An example of the nonrigid structure of religion is provided by the Vietnamese sect, which may be described as a combination of clandestine nationalist group, militant religious order, and traditionalist movement advocating a return to the old ways.

The Cao Dai say their organization was formed in 1919 on an island in the Gulf of Siam, where the founder Ngo Van Chieu held séances and talked with spirits, one of whom called himself the Supreme Being or Cao Dai. Chieu moved to Saigon, where, as a civil servant, he continued his séances for the benefit of other civil servants, during which the spirit, Cao Dai, again appeared. The group organized formally in November 1926, ostensibly as a religious organization (with Ho Phap as pope) but actually a nationalistic one. By 1930 it had more than a million members, chiefly in the area between Saigon and the Cambodian border. The first of several splinters took place in 1933 over the temporal-religious issue; the parent body, moving toward temporal activities, began informal relations with the Japanese, and when the temporal pope, Le Van Trung, died in 1935, he was succeeded by Pham Cong Tac, who turned the organization into a pro-Japanese group. In 1941 the French cracked down on the Cao Dai and exiled Pham Cong Tac to Madagascar because of his pro-Japanese sentiment.

Theirs is a strange synthesis religion: Cao Dai worship, among others, Confucius, the Buddha, Christ, Mohammed, believing all the world's religious figures to be reincarnations of the same spirit. It had a pantheon that included Joan of Arc, Marcus Aurelius, Victor Hugo, Clemençeau, Thomas Jefferson, and, it announced in 1945, Winston Churchill upon his death. Charlie Chaplin was dropped as a minor spirit candidate in the late 1940's. Its motto is "God is an eye." In its earlier days the Cao Dai was a fanatical and rigidly disciplined organization with a small but efficient fighting force. It had a treaty arrangement with the French that made it virtually an enclave government.

Another sect, the Hoa Hao, was founded on the eve of World War II by a faith healer named Huynh Phu So, who, according to legend, was sent to a lunatic asylum where he converted the psychiatrist treating him. He preached a vague form of independence and social reform, quoting from ancient texts and prophecies. During World War II the movement became a rowdy sect of dissident Buddhists who professed belief in abstinence and prayer. It had its nationalistic overtones, and although Huynh Phu So was interned by the French, and the Hoa Hao worked throughout the war with the Japanese, it was evident afterwards that actually the organization had been crypto-anti-Japanese.

The third esoteric sect of Vietnam, the Binh Xuyen, might be called the Mafia of Vietnam. The Binh Xuyen, a group of bandits and river pirates who wore mustard-colored uniforms, was led by a former river pirate named General Le Van Vien. It controlled both the vice (brothels) and the police in Saigon under an arrangement with the French and later with Bao Dai.

Ethnic Minorities

Although ethnic Vietnamese dominate affairs in Vietnam, the population also includes several ethnic minority groups: the aborigines of the highlands, overseas Chinese, Chams, and Cambodians.

The first group, usually referred to as montagnards,[10] presents a bewildering mixture of racial and linguistic groups and subgroups in varying stages of civilization. Their number — as yet not fully determined, and their classification is far from complete — is estimated at between 800,000 and one million. Their story is almost the reverse of the Vietnamese, whose history is marked by great unity and continuity; with the montagnards it has been confusion and disintegration, arrested development since the dawn of history. The most important tribes today are the Rhade, Jarai, Bahnar, Sedang, Steing, and Nung.

The economy of the tribes is their only common denominator. Com-

---

[10] A French word now almost universally used by Americans in Vietnam to describe the people of the highlands; also used are "highlander" and "mountaineer." Montagnard of course is not an ethnic description but simply a generic term to describe the whole complex of groups of primitive non-Vietnamese living in the highlands of Vietnam.

merce and industry, strictly speaking, do not exist. The montagnards have distinctly limited capabilities as merchants, since few can count; and money until recently was unknown, so everything was subject to barter. To supplement their miserable crops they hunt and fish and search for forest fruits.

French penetration of the highlands was slow, and submission by the montagnards was spasmodic and unorganized. They often resented the presence of the French, particularly of the big planters who started to move into some areas in the 1920's. However, they did not support the Viet Minh effort during 1945–1954 with the fervor of their Vietnamese neighbors, and they tend to look back on the days of French rule as a period when things were better.

From the Vietnamese point of view, the highland area is a new territory; settlers, encouraged by the Vietnamese government, have moved in at an ever-increasing rate. The montagnards fear this influx and bitterly resent the exploitation on the part of the merchants and especially the land grabbing by the new settlers, since land is perhaps the most important single factor in montagnard thinking. A Michigan State University study group in 1957 found that land grabbing and the fear of land grabbing were among the primary causes of montagnard discontent. Their report described Vietnamese governmental policies in this respect as ambivalent, resulting in administrative chaos. Moreover, Vietnamese administrative officials arrived untrained and unskilled in dealing with their charges and were ignorant of montagnard customs and traditions.[11]

Recently the highlands have become strategic in Vietnam's revolutionary guerrilla war. Down the narrow mountain paths from North Vietnam have come Communist agitators, both montagnard and Vietnamese, to spread their seeds of disunion and trouble. The Communists are dedicated and hard working; they live among the montagnards, wear the same clothes, eat the same food. They learn local dialects, marry into the tribes, and aid the montagnards in any way that will also aid the Communist cause. They do all possible to abet the unrest of the people, undermining the government's efforts and attempting to cast doubt on the motives of various governmental programs in the highlands. Communist propaganda stresses the government's lack of interest in the montagnards and its absence of good faith. Another theme is the offer of autonomy for the montagnards when the Communists take over the South; certain semiautonomous arrangements are said to have been made for the montagnards in North Vietnam, and this alleged fact is constantly being exploited.

The overseas Chinese in Vietnam number about one million and are

[11] Michigan State University Group, *Preliminary Research Report on the Pays Montagnard, Sud* (East Lansing, Mich., 1960).

found chiefly in Saigon's sister city of Cholon. As elsewhere in Asia, they have been largely involved in trade, rice marketing, and export-import activities. Although victims of some economic discrimination by the Vietnamese government after 1954, the Chinese community generally works harmoniously with the Vietnamese. The National Liberation Front (NLF) has made serious efforts to penetrate and influence the Chinese community; however, there is no evidence that the effort has come to much. Undoubtedly the NLF received considerable money from wealthy Chinese, especially from those in the transportation business, but this was essentially extracted by coercion.

The Chams are remnants of a highly civilized nation that once dominated the entire Indochinese peninsula, who were conquered and almost exterminated by the Vietnamese. They are not aborigines or montagnards. The present population, estimated at about 80,000, is found mainly on the coastal lowlands between Da Nang and Phan Rang. Chams have a matriarchal organization, and their language is Malayo-Polynesian; some are Moslems, but most practice a degenerate form of Brahmanism.

Ethnic Cambodians number perhaps a half million people, with another half million carrying some Cambodian blood as the result of intermarriage. They are found for the most part in those portions of South Vietnam that were once part of the Khmer or Cambodian Empire. A low level of animosity, one of about the intensity of British-Irish feelings, exists between the two peoples in parts of the Mekong delta, but in general the groups live together in peace. The NLF throughout the period conducted intensive recruiting drives among ethnic Cambodians, using appeals based on real or alleged Vietnamese discrimination, and these were moderately successful.

The French Présence

Saigon's main street, Tu Do (Freedom), formerly named Catinat after the ship that brought the French army to the city, in many ways symbolizes France in Southern Vietnam. Tu Do runs from the Saigon River docks into a square dominated by the largest Catholic cathedral in Indochina. It is only a few blocks long, but it is a pleasant avenue, lined with tamarind trees, full of shops selling imported goods, bookstores, sidewalk cafés, bars, and a few nightclubs. Trade and religion brought the French to Vietnam. They left not only a style of living and the influence of foreign ideas but also a heritage of bitterness and hatred not found in other ex-colonies of Asia, even Indonesia — an ironic fact, for during their brief sojourn in Indochina the French prided themselves on their unique relations with their colonies, those limbs of the mother country, *la France d'outre-mer*. Rapport was closer than in the colonies of other powers. The economies of France and Indochina were meshed; Indochinese manpower, for example, was freely tapped for the mines of France. A doctrine, first of assimilation and then of association, brought education, dual citizenship, and other benefits of French civilization. The wrench, the breakaway, when it did come, was thus proportionately greater.

The South Vietnamese had no great tradition of revolt as did their cousins to the north. The South of course did not exist in the days of Chinese domination; the Vietnamese arrived in the Camau peninsula not much before the French. And even when the surge of anti-French nationalism began in the 1930's, the feeling was stronger among Northerners and Centerites than Southerners. Virginia Thompson describes the social milieu of those early days:

The [Vietnamese] were still preoccupied with the *malaise* which contact with the West inspired in them. They contented themselves with citing abuses for the French to reform, but they did not yet think of taking matters into their own hands by demanding political rights. This was essentially the attitude that dominated the pre-War [World War I] period. Learning, not revolution, was the byword of the great majority before 1914.[12]

Anti-French feelings in Vietnam came in waves, each of greater height and force than the preceding one. From the very start considerable hostility was demonstrated by segments of the society. The Can Vuong, or Monarchist, movement of the late 1800's, for example, was a series of military uprisings instigated by the emperor and his scholar court at Hué. It was confined for the most part to the ruling classes and did not involve the masses, and particularly it did not involve the South Vietnamese. Two decades later, in 1908, came the so-called Scholars' Movement (Dong Kinh Nghia Thuc) in response to the French suppression of private Vietnamese schools, which the French suspected, correctly, were centers of anti-French activity. Anti-French teachers organized peasants into mass demonstrations, not in the name of educational reform but to demand tax reductions (a typical Janus-faced Vietnamese organizational effort). Again the movement saw its great impact in Central and Northern Vietnam and tended to lose steam in the South.

World War I, which altered so much of the world irrevocably, brought profound changes to Indochina. It stimulated the economy, and the value of the piaster rose steadily as did the standard of living. Economically and psychologically, ties with metropolitan France were loosened. Hordes of workers sent to France to work the mines and perform war services returned home with money, a better understanding of

[12] Virginia Thompson, *French Indo-China* (New York: Macmillan, 1937), pp. 478–479.

the French, and new attitudes toward the white man and colonialism; one still encounters village leaders who became prominent as the result of working in French coal mines.

The early years after World War I were quiet. The French allowed the Cochin Chinese greater political and organizational latitude, partly because Cochin China was a colony, a direct appendage of France. (As noted earlier, Tonkin and Annam held French protectorate status.) Elective councils offered at least a semblance of a legal avenue to power. The most attractive of these were the Saigon Municipal Council and the Colonial Council of Cochin China. The latter, whose members were elected under a system of restricted franchise, consisted of 10 Vietnamese, 10 French, and one member each from the Saigon Chamber of Commerce and the Cochin China Chamber of Agriculture. There were exceptions to this aura of placidity, such as the attack by extremists on the Saigon prison in the early 1920's; but in general the great debate among Vietnamese in the 1920's, that is, the 10 per cent or so who thought much about the matter, was between independence through militancy or working for greater freedom within the French community.

As far as can be generalized, the South Vietnamese were more inclined toward collaboration. This attitude maintained itself throughout the intervening years and colors South Vietnamese thinking today. The author knows several thoughtful South Vietnamese who assert that the Viet Minh war was "a mistake," maintaining that "had we displayed a little patience, had we not been led astray by hotheaded Northerners, the French eventually would have left Vietnam without blood being spilled, as the British left India." This epitomizes the Southern attitude.

Nevertheless in the period between the two world wars the Southerners, like all Vietnamese, were caught up in the fires of nationalism, and nationalist organizations proliferated. Three clusters of them emerged during the 1920's and 1930's: the reformists, who favored collaboration with the French, sought greater freedom and eventual self-determination within the French community, and were strongest in the South; the militants, both Communist and non-Communist, who opposed the French and favored some degree of open warfare; and those opposed to both collaboration and open revolution, who counseled working obliquely — often with or through the Japanese.

Nationalist Organizations

The reformists included the Constitutionalist Party, which was formed by Bui Quang Chieu and Nguyen Phan Long in 1923 and had the distinction of being the first legal or authorized political party in the country. Based in Saigon, it was composed of government officials, intellectuals, and wealthy landowners; its existence was inconclusive. Later it became strongly pro–Cao Dai, and eventually most of its membership was absorbed by that organization. A Hué intellectual and mandarin, Pham Quynh, attempted to form a similar group, the Vietnam People's Progressive Party, but after some months of negotiations with the French was refused the necessary authorization. He finally succeeded in forming a political group some 20 years later, only to be killed by the Viet Minh. Also in this organizational category were members of the Pan-Asian, or Journey East (Dong Du), movement, so named because it looked eastward to Canton or sometimes Tokyo for spiritual support. Phan Boi Chau founded the Vietnam Restoration Association (Viet Nam Quang Phuc Hoi), an organization that today would be labeled Communist but was more of an Asian Fabian Socialist league, espousing a more moderate philosophy. He also helped establish one of Asia's first nationalistic regional organizations, the League of East Asian Peoples (Dong A Dong Minh). Phan Boi Chau, a friend of Sun Yat-sen, was a skilled militant defying political classification; he was both radical and moderate, militant and pacifist. At one point the French arrested and condemned him to death, a sentence he received stoically. But later, when freed, he decided to collaborate with the French, giving as his reason the arrival in Indochina of a French socialist as governor-general, Alexandre Varenne.[13]

The second category, the militants, consisted of those organizations opposed to the French and favoring some degree of open warfare. The earliest was a group called Vietnam Restoration (Phuc Viet), formed on Poulo Condore Island off the southern coast, the Devil's Island of Vietnam, by prisoners involved in a 1908 prison break. This was an old-line revolutionary and even anarchist organization, something of a blood brotherhood, linked later, in ways not entirely clear, to Phan Boi Chau. The Pan-Asian movement soon developed a militancy of its own that resulted in the establishment of what was probably the second (after the Communist) most important nationalist organization in Vietnamese history, the Vietnamese Nationalist (or People's) Party (Viet Nam Quoc Dan Dang — VNQDD). It was a replica of Sun Yat-sen's Kuomintang and embraced the same "doctrine of the three people," that is, sovereignty, family, and welfare, or roughly, democracy, nationalism, and socialism. It was founded in Hanoi in 1927 by Nguyen Thai Hoc, a primary-school teacher, and his brother, who supported the organization

[13] Varenne had remanded the death sentence of Phan Boi Chau, who was considered by many as potentially the greatest Vietnamese leader. Hoang Van Chi, *op. cit.*, pp. 17–21, maintains that Ho Chi Minh betrayed him to the French as a means of eliminating a potential rival.

in its early days by running a print shop. Early members were young, few of the organizing group being over 30, and included many Hanoi University students expelled for their part in the 1925–1926 strikes. Those attracted to the organization consisted for the most part of civil servants, small businessmen and tradesmen, and company-grade officers in the armed forces. While this sounds like a bourgeois group, the VNQDD was actually more proletarian than its chief rival, the Communists. Its people, while neither worker nor peasant, were from the lower end of the social spectrum, usually victims of some form of colonialist exploitation; there were few or no rich merchants, landlords, or prominent scholars. The Communist ranks, on the other hand, contained many sons of mandarins and large estate owners, well-to-do and well-educated men who seemed chiefly interested in communism as a "scientific" ideology.

The VNQDD's propaganda messages in about 1930 were directed toward students, workers, and members of the army. The organization also engaged in more incendiary activities, including the throwing of bombs, which of course attracted the attention of the French police, whose agents sought to penetrate the party. The VNQDD leaders, fearing betrayal, decided to strike. The "general uprising" that resulted, although never reaching the proportions its sponsors expected, was a classic example of organizational clandestinism. It began at Yen Bay, an important military post northwest of Hanoi. At Yen Bay on the morning of February 10, 1930, native soldiers led by VNQDD agents mutinied and killed several of their French officers. The mutineers then had second thoughts and returned to their barracks. But the mutiny set off a series of VNQDD uprisings in Hanoi and throughout Northern Vietnam. A bomb was tossed at a government office in Hanoi, a police officer on the Pont Doumer was wounded, a subprefect in Vinh Bao was assassinated. Long lines of demonstrators paraded in impressive silence to the résidents' homes in Hanoi, Hué, and Saigon to present grievances. Nervous résidents several times ordered troops to fire on the demonstrators although the latter were unarmed. At Ben Thuy some 700 workers set fire to their match factory; since they had just received a Tet wage boost, theirs was not simply an economic grievance, and there is reason to believe that the VNQDD was behind this act. The Yen Bay mutiny became a landmark in the mythology of Vietnamese nationalism. The outcome of the episode had a remarkably modern ring to it; the VNQDD leaders fled Hanoi for the Tonkin village of Co Am, where they established themselves as the local government; they drafted young men into their military force, coerced villagers into supplying them with food, and tortured and killed village officials who resisted them. The French launched an air-ground attack on Co Am. The air strikes dislodged some of the rebels but also killed 200 villagers. French troops then stormed the village, driving out the rest of the VNQDD force and, as a final act of ignominy for the people of Co Am, tore down the village's bamboo hedge.

The postuprising investigation astonished the French when it revealed the scope and extent of the plot, although it is probable that the investigators uncovered only a portion of the organization's structure and activities. Later the VNQDD, led by Le Huu Canh, while in the midst of formulating new plans for an uprising to be touched off by the assassination of Governor-General Pierre Pasquier, was betrayed by a Hanoi businessman, a victim of VNQDD blackmail. Wholesale arrests followed. Remnants of the membership fled to Yunnan and Kuomintang protection. The organization became moribund until revived by the Chinese Nationalists in 1942. Early VNQDD operational activities set the pattern for many nationalist groups that came after it, including the NLF. The VNQDD divided itself into two parts — an overt front organization and a covert operational organization. It placed almost total emphasis on youthful membership. It developed army and civil-servant proselyting techniques, pressed for a worker-peasant alliance, and made extensive use of women, often assigning them tasks of great responsibility. It supported itself through banditry. It executed traitors with a great deal of publicity, and its violent acts in general were carefully conceived for their psychological value. For example, the VNQDD's first assassination victim was a Frenchman named René Bazin, who was responsible for recruiting Vietnamese field-hand labor for the plantations of New Caledonia. Bazin was shot down amid exploding firecrackers during the 1929 Tet celebrations; the act itself was virtually without risk, but then the assassin took the desperate chance of pinning a note on Bazin's shirtfront, listing the crimes for which the VNQDD had executed him. This assassination was the French sûreté's first indication of the existence of the organization; during the subsequent investigation the sûreté was amazed to discover that 50 per cent of the VNQDD members served in the French colonial government. The VNQDD came back to Vietnam with the occupying Chinese forces following World War II and was of some importance until mid-1946, when it was purged by the Viet Minh. It then splintered into at least four factions: One segment went back to China with the departing Nationalists; a small group stayed in North Vietnam; a third faction, under Vu Hong Khanh, went south but refused to deal with the Bao Dai government; and the fourth, led by lawyer Tran Van Tuyen, also went south and briefly supported the Ngo Dinh Diem government. The VNQDD never was a mass political party in the Western sense. At its peak of influence it numbered, by estimates of its own leaders, less than 1,500 persons. Nor was it ever particularly strong in either Central or South Vietnam. It had no formal structure and held no conventions or assemblies. Its amorphous nature was its greatest weakness. The VNQDD's failure was due chiefly to its lack of organization and its leaders' lack of organizational talent.

The other major member of this second or militant opposition group was the Communist organization. Significant Communist activities in Vietnam began in 1925 when Ho Chi Minh, then living in Canton, the prewar Mecca for Vietnamese Communists, formed the Association of Vietnamese Revolutionary Young Comrades (his translation of Viet Nam Thanh Nien Cach Mang Dong Chi Hoi), a crypto-Communist organization generally referred to as the Revolutionary Youth Association (RYA). His daily activity was devoted almost exclusively to organizational work. Hoang Van Chi described his effort:

Most of the Vietnamese refugees there [in Canton] already belonged to one of the existing nationalist groups and Ho found it necessary to represent himself as sharing the same aims as the leaders of these groups in order to contact the individual members of their organisations.[14]

Ho Chi Minh's organizational skills even then were in an advanced stage of development. He gathered around him the best potential youth material, taught them how to print hectograph leaflets, conduct mass meetings, provoke strikes, and carry out other agit-prop activities. The best of his recruits were retained in Canton to form the central committee of the Revolutionary Youth Association, and the rest were sent back into Vietnam to organize a nationwide cell structure. Ellen Hammer estimated that at least 250 Vietnamese received revolutionary education in China during the 1920's, of whom at least 200 returned to Indochina; she quotes French police officials as saying that the 1929 Communist *apparat* in Indochina, including sympathizers, totaled about 1,000.[15] While in Canton Ho Chi Minh also formed the League for Oppressed Peoples and was active in all Communist activities. Hoang Van Chi depicts his basic outlook at the time as a belief that the dictatorship of the proletariat must be achieved in two stages, with a bourgeois-democratic revolution; and that only workers make good revolutionaries, peasants being regarded as merely "long-term allies." Ho Chi Minh sided with Moscow on the question of the use of force and violence, an issue that has divided Vietnamese Communists to this day, favoring leaflets,

[14] *Ibid.*, p. 43.
[15] Ellen J. Hammer, *The Struggle for Indochina* (Stanford, Cal.: Stanford University Press, 1954), p. 80.

mass meetings, demonstrations, and labor disputes rather than terror. These and other policy problems that plagued the party[16] led to a crisis in 1929. At the Revolutionary Youth Association's annual meeting in Hong Kong on May 1, 1929[17] three Tonkinese delegates, angered by the "bourgeois habits" (living too opulently) of Chairman Lam Duc Thu, proposed a series of procedural reforms that would have allied the organization more closely with the Stalinist wing of world communism, and against the Trotskyites, and also would have made it somewhat less nationalistic (the suggestion of a name change, for example). Their proposals were voted down; the three Tonkinese walked out, returned to Hanoi, and formed a Communist party. As a countermeasure, Lam Duc Thu and the Revolutionary Youth Association's central committee quickly formed their own Communist party. At the same time the Phuc Quoc set up a new party, which it called Communist Union, actually a party of intellectuals moving along social democratic lines.

Thus in 1929 there were three Communist parties in Indochina: Lam Duc Thu's Annamese Communist Party (formerly the Revolutionary Youth Association), the Indochinese Communist Party (ICP) formed by the three dissident members of the RYA, and the Communist Union. The Comintern naturally disapproved of this fragmentation of the movement and sent Ho Chi Minh, then pamphleteering in Bangkok, back to negotiate a merger. He moved the headquarters to Haiphong and later to Saigon. With Moscow's blessing and a monthly remittance of 5,000 francs, he proceeded to unify the Communists, a feat accomplished before his arrest on June 6, 1931 in Hong Kong. At the same time Ho Chi Minh molded the organizational structure into a network of affiliated groups and associations of farmers, women, and workers and also created the Anti-Imperialist League and a branch of the International Red Aid organization. This internal party arrangement remained essentially unchanged for three decades and closely resembled the one employed by the NLF, that is, a hierarchy of committees pyramiding upward from the village to a central committee directing all activities. Ho Chi Minh's final contribution was the development of fund-raising techniques, partly through banditry but chiefly through appeals to the farmer; his activities in this respect led Virginia Thompson to observe, "This man, mystic and ascetic that he was, not only was a remarkable organizer but he could raise money from the wary and miserable Annamites. . . ."[18]

Active at this same time in Vietnam, particularly in the South, was

---

[16] Ho Chi Minh had gone to Moscow, leaving Ho Tung Mau to head the association; Mau was arrested, and the leadership passed to Lam Duc Thu.

[17] Attended by four representatives from China, two from Siam, and eleven from Indochina, with the Vietnamese clearly dominant.

[18] Thompson, op. cit., p. 491.

a group of Communists organized by a Vietnamese student recently returned from Paris, Ta Thu Thau, who looked to Leon Trotsky and the Fourth International for spiritual guidance. His efforts throughout the 1930's encountered staunch opposition from the Stalinists, led by perhaps the most impressive Communist produced by the South, Tran Van Giau. As the result of Tran Van Giau's strategy of divisiveness — the offer of united-front cooperation — the Trotskyites split into two wings. The Struggle Group (after its publication, *The Struggle*), strongest in Saigon, sought to form a common front with the Stalinists. The other, the October Group (after its publication in Hanoi), or, more officially, the International Communist League, was bitterly opposed to collaboration. A coalition was formed in the South, and three of its candidates, one Stalinist and two Trotskyites, were elected in 1932 to the Saigon Municipal Council.

The Communist movement in Indochina faced a series of crises and troubles in the 1930's. The first year of the decade brought one of the most serious, the failure of the Nghe An soviets. On May Day 1930 Communist-organized nationwide hunger marches got out of hand in some places, and several demonstrators were shot by French troops. A French crackdown on Communist activity followed, during which dozens of cadres fled to Nghe An province, where they attempted to establish a series of village soviets or governing bodies. They were quickly crushed by the French, and the Communists lost considerable prestige among the nationalists. However, the failure served to heighten the movement's popularity among ordinary Indochinese. By the end of 1931 the Party had an estimated 1,500 members and perhaps as many as 100,000 sympathizers; Ho Chi Minh at this time was particularly well regarded in and out of the Party, having been able to maneuver himself out of any responsibility for the unfortunate Nghe An soviets' movement.

The European and especially French popular-front period in the mid-1930's, if not a time of crisis, was a trying period for the Indochinese Communists. Ho Chi Minh had vanished and so was not present to be embarrassed by orders from the Comintern to play down anticolonialism and press the anticapitalism campaign. For Communists in Indochina this was a difficult order and one never successfully filled. Moscow put the ICP under the French Communist Party, a move that contributed to shifting the emphasis from anticolonialism to the proletariat's struggle against capitalism. The failure of the 1936 French Popular Front government, which many Vietnamese had come to believe would grant them some degree of autonomy only to discover that French socialists could accommodate repressive colonial governments as easily as their less liberal predecessors, further tarnished the Communist image. Particularly in the South the Party encountered heavy weather. Tran Van Giau and other Moscow-trained agents arrived back in Saigon in numbers, but their organizational efforts during the 1930's came to little. Tran Van Giau had too few cadres for the organizational task assigned, the population was too indifferent to his cause, and the French were too active in their efforts to keep communism out of Cochin China. The French in the South had an efficient police net with hundreds of informers and part-time agents. Vietnamese were not free to travel, which made organizational work difficult for the Communists. Cadres could not stage public meetings, the soul of Communist activity, and they were required to submit all manuscripts to censorship before publication, which meant that only clandestine written materials could be produced. Always there was the threat of arrest. The political prisoner population in French jails stood at about 10,000 throughout the decade. The Trotskyites, more powerful in the South, tended to sap the vitality of the Indochinese Communist Party. The Cao Dai sect as well as nationalist organizations also impeded Communist progress. Tran Van Giau's first front organization, the Eastern Mutual Assistance Association (Hoi Cuu Te Dong Phuong) was formed in western Cochin China in the early 1930's. Later it merged with the most important of the early Communist organizations in the South, the Vanguard Youth (or Advance Guard Youth — Thanh Nien Tien Phong), formed ostensibly as a non-Communist group by a young doctor, Pham Ngoc Thach (who later announced he had long been a Party member), but actually controlled by Tran Van Giau. The Vanguard Youth in one form or another has been in existence in Vietnam ever since.

Some militancy did exist in the South. Guerrilla forces operated in the western portions of the country under Nguyen An Ninh, a journalist whose paper had been shut down by the French after he wrote a eulogistic obituary for Phan Chu Trinh; later he was betrayed and arrested, and most of his followers joined Tran Van Giau. Throughout the 1930's the Stalinists attempted unsuccessfully to destroy their first enemy — the Trotskyites; but what they were not able to do, the French did for them. Shortly after the outbreak of hostilities in 1939, French police rounded up virtually the entire leadership of the Trotskyite International Communist League, as it was then called, a coup from which the movement never recovered. In a sense the 1930's were successful for the Stalinists in that they survived when other militant organizations did not. This was chiefly due to their skillful organization building and their general conservatism in policies and programs.

The third constellation of prewar nationalist organizations, being pro-Japanese, quite understandably came into their own after the occupation of Indochina by the Japanese army. Included in this cluster of organizations were powerful organizations in the South: the two major militant religious sects, the Cao Dai and Hoa Hao,[19] and the various Dai Viet, or Greater Vietnam, organizations.

The major Dai Viet organization was the Dai Viet Quoc Dan Dang (Greater Vietnam Nationalist Party, sometimes translated as the Greater Vietnam National People's Party), ultranationalistic, totally clandestine, and at one time the most influential political group in Vietnam. It was formed in 1939 by Truong Tu Anh, who was assassinated by the Communists in 1946. Dai Viet membership included leading Vietnamese figures and governmental officials who viewed Japan as a suitable model for Vietnam. The organization never made any particular obeisance either to democracy or to the rank-and-file Vietnamese. It probably never numbered more than 1,000 members and did not consider itself a mass-based organization. It turned away from Western liberalism, although its economic orientation was basically socialist, in favor of authoritarianism and blind obedience. Later the Dai Viet fragmented into four major Dai Viet parties. In addition to the original there were the Dai Viet Duy Dan (Greater Vietnam Association for Advancement of the People), headed by Phan Huy Quat and attorney Le Thang; the Dai Viet Dan Chinh (Greater Vietnam People's Political Association), led by Nguyen Tuong Tam, Dr. Phan Quang Dan, Dr. Dang Van Sung, and Dr. Nguyen Ton Hoan; and the Dai Viet Quoc Xa (Greater Vietnam National Socialism Association). All these names were prominent in the South. Personalities and not ideology split the original organization. The Dai Viets remained influential in South Vietnam and enjoyed something of a resurgence after the end of the Diem government. The forerunner of the Dai Viets was the Vietnam Restoration Association (Viet Nam Phuc Quoc Dong Minh Hoi), usually called the Phuc Quoc, formed prior to World War I by Prince Cuong De and Phan Boi Chau as an ultranationalist, promonarchist group that sought to place exiled Prince Cuong De on the Hué throne. One of its most prominent members, Tran Trung Lap, led an abortive uprising at Lang Son in 1940. It was at all times strongly pro-Japanese. For their part the Japanese naturally encouraged the development of anti-French, pro-Japanese movements during their occupation and found collaborators easily — especially in the South, where "Asia for the Asiatics" had considerable appeal. The Japanese occupational hand rested lighter in the South than in the North; one finds today in South Vietnam that Northerners are more likely than Southerners to have residual anti-Japanese feelings. At any rate, the Japanese occupation was confined to the cities, for at no time were there

---

[19] Evidence after the war, as noted, indicated that the Hoa Hao leadership had actually been crypto-anti-Japanese.

more than 35,000 Japanese troops in all of Indochina, which would average less than one occupation soldier per village.

Nationalism and Communism

In the late 1930's, in the South to great degree but also throughout the country, clandestine organizational activity began to slow down and military opposition to the French began to taper off. The quiescence ended, however, in the social flux of World War II. Then began the final organizational shakedown, nationalist versus Communist, that set the pattern for the next two decades.

In 1941, at the same time that the Indochinese Communist Party formed the Viet Minh, its major rival, the VNQDD, protégé of the Chinese Nationalists, sought to gather into its fold all Vietnamese — at least all non-Communist — revolutionaries.

Three nationalist congresses of revolutionaries followed, during which the polarization became fixed. The first Nationalist congress, held in China, was attended by a host of nationalist groups and by the Viet Minh but not, as such, by the Indochinese Communist Party. It was convened by the Chinese Nationalists and dominated by the VNQDD. The second Nationalist congress at Liuchow, October 1942, saw the birth of the Dong Minh Hoi,[20] a nationalist united front dominated by the VNQDD. The second congress was the high-water mark of the non-Communist nationalist movement in Indochina and a turning point in Vietnamese history. For reasons never made clear the Chinese Nationalists suddenly reversed their position with respect to the Viet Minh and permitted a third Nationalist congress to be called for the purpose of establishing a provisional government for Vietnam. It was dominated by the Viet Minh, which in turn was dominated by Ho Chi Minh. As might have been predicted, it set in motion a train of events that led to Communist emasculation of the non-Communist nationalist organizations in Vietnam, including the Kuomintang's own.

The political structure in Vietnam at that moment, March 1944, thus consisted of a single party, the Indochinese Communist Party, dominating a united-front organization (the Viet Minh) that was part of a nationalist united-front organization (the Dong Minh Hoi) as a subdominant member. As a sop to the Chinese, the Viet Minh took fewer than the majority of seats in the new provisional government. Ho Chi Minh, having evolved this novel transitional structure, set about first to secure the base of the governmental edifice and then to eliminate his

[20] Full name: Viet Nam Cach Mang Dong Hoi (Vietnam Revolutionary Parties' Association).

chief rival, the VNQDD. Events in Indochina, under Japanese occupation, were moving toward a climax. In March 1945 the Japanese interned French colonial officials and military, an act that in effect unleashed the Vietnamese nationalists and Communists in the rural areas, where the French had maintained a degree of authority and Japanese control was virtually nonexistent. Emperor Bao Dai ruled in name only; the cities were administered by the Japanese. The allied powers met at Potsdam and agreed that for the purpose of disarming the Japanese the British would occupy Indochina south of the 16th parallel and the Chinese north of it.

The end of the war caused a sudden political vacuum in Vietnam for which no one was very well prepared. The Japanese hold in Indochina had begun to disintegrate in the spring of 1945. With French officials under detention following the so-called "Japanese coup d'état," both the nationalists and the Communists began to assert their authority throughout the southern area. The Hoa Hao sect virtually ran what was then Can Tho province from March until August, and the Cao Dai administered Tay Ninh province. In March at an organizational congress held in Can Tho, plans were made to bring together, under a united front, all non-Communist nationalist forces in the South, including the sects, pro-Japanese parties, the Trotskyites, and minor political parties. On August 17 the National United Front (Mat Tran Quoc Gia Thong Nhut) was born, but its life was destined to be a short one. At the same time the Viet Minh had embarked on a major effort to assert itself in the South as the new Vietnamese "government" and the power that was to deal with the occupation forces. The provisional executive committee, dominated by Tran Van Giau, that was formed was in effect the southern arm of the Indochinese Communist Party. Employing the time-tested Ho Chi Minh technique of destroying an organization by joining it, Tran Van Giau persuaded the National United Front, then only two weeks old, to merge with the Viet Minh, and on September 7 the Southern National Bloc Committee was formed. Six of the Southern National Bloc Committee's members were Viet Minh; Hoa Hao leader Huynh Phu So was a member, and Trotskyite Phan Van Hum was an alternate. But the Viet Minh did not merge with the National United Front; it swallowed it.

Much of the country was at this moment under at least nominal control of what were called People's Liberation Committees (Ban Nhan Dan Giai Phong), an organizational structure that had been developing during the war and emerged in August as a hierarchic pyramid with Ho Chi Minh as chairman. The committees in the South were known collectively as the People's Committees of South Vietnam (Uy Ban Nhan Dan Nam Bo). In many areas, particularly in the North, these committees became the *de facto* government. Through them, and aided by some judicious political juggling, Ho Chi Minh, in the boldest move of his career, asserted his authority over Vietnam. Bao Dai abdicated in his favor and became the Supreme Adviser to the new government, thus transferring to the emergent regime the mantle of legitimacy. The Democratic Republic of Vietnam (DRV) was proclaimed. Ho Chi Minh hoped the occupying allied powers would treat him as the authentic leader of Vietnam, a hope quickly dashed. The stroke, however, was as wise as it was bold. It gave the Viet Minh a momentum it never lost and that its nationalist opponents could never match. It put Ho Chi Minh and his fellow Communists firmly at the helm of the anticolonialist struggle. It created in reality and in myth the foundation on which the Communist organization's mass base could be built. And it provided the Communists with the instrument to nullify opposition, for they could and did argue that Vietnam must present a united front and speak with a single voice to the occupying foreigners.[21]

The noose tightened. The British arrived in mid-September. General Douglas Gracey arrived in Saigon with orders to disarm the Japanese. Because of poor advance intelligence he was caught by surprise by the chaotic situation that quickly developed. French residents who had been interned in the city armed themselves from a local arsenal and began settling old scores, and Gracey was forced to disarm them. In addition, the Indian division that had been promised him failed to arrive, and the Gracey forces were therefore under strength. General Leclerc arrived on September 23 and announced at Saigon airport, "We have come to reclaim our inheritance." He quickly deposed the Southern National Bloc Committee, ended a series of disorders in Saigon, and put down some resistance from the Cao Dai and Hoa Hao sects.

The Nationalist and the Communist doctrinal clash in Saigon as well as in the North was chiefly over the question of the correct posture toward the French. The Viet Minh, particularly in the South, maintained as pro-French a position as it dared. The Nationalists saw themselves as "bolsheviks" opposing the "Kerensky" Viet Minh government. The critical issue in the first days after the war's end revolved around the question of what to do with the Japanese arms. Nationalist groups as well as the Trotskyite International Communist League held meetings in Saigon demanding "arms for the people." This the Southern National Bloc Committee, which is to say the Communists, opposed, fearing what would develop if arms fell into the hands of the general population. Milton Sacks quotes a Communist Party leaflet circulated in Saigon at the time:

---

[21] The Viet Minh, or Communist, legend of this period is treated in somewhat more detail in Chapter 2.

[The Communist Party and the Viet Minh disapprove of] all actions of provocation and violence among inhabitants of Indochina of every origin and every race; they will enforce by all means at their disposal the repression of disorder from any source. . . .[22]

The Viet Minh position on the matter resulted from a mousetrap play by Moscow and the French Communist Party. Moscow insisted that the Indochinese Communist Party follow the lead of the French Communist Party, which, on orders from Moscow, insisted that the ICP refrain from open hostilities until the go-ahead was received from Moscow; appeals or queries to Moscow were thus directed to the Party in Paris, and appeals to Paris were referred to Moscow. The ban, which appeared to include virtually all forms of violence, had to be stringently enforced, especially in the South, where Party members and even cadres had launched revolutionary activities on their own, including the seizure of land from the wealthy. The Viet Minh response, as reported by Milton Sacks, was:

This agitation was opposed by the Viet Minh, whose representative, Nguyen Van Tao, is quoted as saying: "All those who have instigated the peasants to seize the landowners' property will be severely and pitilessly punished. . . . We have not yet made the Communist revolution which will solve the agrarian problem. This government is only a democratic government. That is why such a task does not devolve upon it. Our government, I repeat, is a bourgeois democratic government, even though the Communists are now in power." [23]

French High Commissioner Admiral d'Argenlieu opposed efforts toward *rapprochement* between his government and Ho Chi Minh and took strong objection to the basic March 6, 1946 agreement on the independence of Vietnam, in which the French government recognized the Republic of Vietnam.[24] He attempted to circumvent it and form a separate Indochina federation; and, the French government being what it was, he was able to torpedo the March agreement. D'Argenlieu perceived the Viet Minh as a small number of dissident intellectuals whose "government" need only be compressed geographically and then strangled economically. He was determined to preserve for France at least the rich rice-growing South. So on June 1 he announced that "in response to popular pressure for autonomy" the government of Cochin China was established. Hoping to separate Cochin China from the rest of Indochina and wall it off from the winds of nationalism, he formed the Cochin Chinese Advisory Council with Dr. Tran Tan Phat as leader. Phat declared to a *Le Monde* reporter on March 14, 1946: "As Vietnamese we

[22] I. Milton Sacks, in Frank N. Trager, ed., *Marxism in Southeast Asia* (Stanford, Cal.: Stanford University Press, 1959), p. 154.

[23] *Ibid.*, p. 326 (note 158).

[24] Text in Marvin E. Gettleman, ed., *Vietnam: History, Documents, and Opinions on a Major World Crisis* (Greenwich, Conn.: Fawcett Publications, 1966).

think like Indochinese but act like Cochin Chinese." He was shot down in the streets of Saigon within a month. Then when the representatives of the DRV and the French government were formally meeting at Fontainebleau for the purpose of arriving at an amicable solution, d'Argenlieu on his own convened the Dalat conference of representatives from Cochin China, Cambodia, and Laos, but not the DRV. This move, so blatant and obvious, left the DRV representative at Fontainebleau with little choice but to walk out of the conference. Thus d'Argenlieu, a mere functionary, scuttled what might have been an arrangement that would have prevented the Viet Minh war.

2

The Viet Minh Legacy

Since several good works are available on the Viet Minh war,[1] commonly referred to in Vietnam as the Resistance (*Khang Chien*), it is necessary here to describe only those aspects, apart from the fact of victory, that strongly influenced the Viet Minh's successor organization, the National Liberation Front, in the 1960's.

Revolutionary Guerrilla Warfare

Revolutionary guerrilla warfare, especially as it developed in the early 1960's in the mangrove swamps, rain forests, and highlands of South

[1] Bernard Fall's *Le Viet Minh, 1945–60* (Paris: Armand Colin, 1960) and *The Viet Minh Regime* (Ithaca, N.Y.: Cornell University Press, 1956) are basic works. George R. Tanham's *Communist Revolutionary Warfare: The Vietminh in Indochina* (New York: Praeger, 1961) is particularly good on doctrine. Donald Lancaster's *The Emancipation of French Indochina* (London, New York, Toronto: Oxford University Press, 1961) tells the story of Indochina and the Viet Minh war in the broadest terms. See also Major Edgar O'Ballance, *The Indo-Chinese War, 1945–54* (London: Faber & Faber, 1964). For the serious reader, The American University, Special Operations Research Office (SORO), especially *Case Studies in Insurgency and Revolutionary Warfare: Vietnam 1941–1954* (Washington, D. C., 1964); the earlier works of Philippe Devillers and those of Ellen Hammer, Hoang Van Chi (*From Colonialism to Communism*); and of course Ho Chi Minh, Le Duan, Truong Chinh, and Vo Nguyen Giap should be consulted for the special materials and approaches they contain.

31

Vietnam was something new not just in degree but in kind. In the opinion of many it is communism's basic blueprint for control of the underdeveloped nations of Asia, Africa, and Latin America. The Communists attempted to raise the techniques employed in the Chinese revolution and in the Viet Minh war against the French to a science, so as to be able to prescribe a formula that, if applied according to directions, would yield inevitable victory. It is precisely its foolproof, do-it-yourself label that makes the package so attractive to dissidents everywhere and at the same time makes destroying the fiction of the formula's infallibility a prime task for those people and nations interested in peace and in helping nations develop along orderly, constructive lines.

Revolutionary guerrilla warfare should not be confused with older concepts of a similar nature, such as irregular troops in wartime disrupting the enemy's rear, or with civil war, which is between two groups in the same nation (revolutionary guerrilla warfare is not indigenous), rebellion (militant opposition to authority with the issue quickly settled), revolution (successful rebellion), bandit warfare (plunder as a way of life), or partisan warfare (armed fighting by light troops). Part of the concept's newness is semantic. Elements of the strategy can be found in early Communist revolutionary activity, for example, in Lenin's minimum-program technique before it was supplanted by Stalin's exportation of armed revolution; nor need it be exclusively Communist, as evidenced by the operations of the Haganah in Palestine, or the Irish Republican Army in the streets of Dublin. Various partisan efforts, some dating back to the time of Christ, have contained elements of the strategy: revolution by means of the guerrilla making war.

Revolutionary guerrilla warfare as practiced in Vietnam was a way of life. Its aim was to establish a totally new social order, thus differing from insurgencies whose objective is either statehood or change of government. In the hands of the Communists it was a form of aggression useful in nations characterized by people without communication, isolated by terrain, psychology, or politics, people inward-turning. Not military but sociopsychological considerations took precedence. Military activities and other forms of violence were conceived as means of contributing to the sociopolitical struggle. The chief effort was communication; the chief medium was the especially created organization; the chief daily activity of the cadres was agitation and propaganda work. Communication facilitated organization, which facilitated mobilization. The unchanging purpose was to turn rural Vietnam into a sea of angry villagers who would rise up simultaneously in the General Uprising and smash all existing social forms. Thus the object was not the ordinary violent social protest, nor the usual revolutionary stirrings we have seen develop around the world with which we sympathize because they reflect inadequate living standards or oppressive and corrupt governments. Revolutionary guerrilla warfare was quite different. It was an imported product, revolution from the outside; its stock in trade, the grievance, was often artificially created; its goal of liberation, a deception. Communist use of revolutionary guerrilla warfare is nowhere better described than by President John F. Kennedy in a speech before a joint session of the House of Representatives and Senate on May 25, 1961:

Yet their aggression is more often concealed than open. They have fired no missiles; and their troops are seldom seen. They send arms, agitators, aid, technicians and propaganda to every troubled area. But where fighting is required, it is usually done by others, by guerrillas striking at night, by assassins striking alone, assassins who have taken the lives of 4,000 civil officers in the last 12 months in Vietnam, by subversives and saboteurs and insurrectionists, who in some cases control whole areas inside of independent nations.

Revolutionary guerrilla warfare is not a Communist term, nor is it used by them. The Communists classify war into three types: general, limited, and national liberation. The latter, resembling revolutionary guerrilla warfare, is also termed category-three war, revolutionary war, people's war, anti-imperialist war, antineocolonial war, and, in South Vietnam after 1962, Special War; all terms are used more or less interchangeably in Communist literature. To the Viet Minh, the war against the French was a long-duration resistance of protracted struggle (*truong ky khang chien*), as had been the Chinese revolution before it. All Vietnamese even to this day do not call the 1945–1954 period a war but refer to it simply as the Resistance.

The concept of revolutionary guerrilla warfare is, we must acknowledge, a superb strategy, efficacious as an antidote to modern arms and in harmony with the world's temper, efficiently harnessing social forces already loosened. It opposes the aspirations of people while apparently furthering them, manipulates the individual by persuading him to manipulate himself. Communists across the world can assert their love for peace and yet see no inconsistency in advocating war as a weapon of social change. In the endless debate as to whether communism's success has been due to its brilliant strategy or to its unresponsive opposition, in the case of Vietnam and revolutionary guerrilla warfare we must side with the former.

The technique as worked out by the NLF was based largely on a mishmash of piecemeal military maxims and semipolitical aphorisms accumulated over the years chiefly from the writings of Chinese and Vietnamese revolutionaries. Foremost was Mao Tse-tung's collection of lectures delivered from May 26 to June 3, 1938 at the Yenan Association for the Study of the War of Resistance Against Japan and published in 1954 in

Peking under the title *On Protracted War.* Of equal importance to the
NLF were the writings of Vo Nguyen Giap published in Vietnamese in
1960 and in English in 1961 under the title *People's War, People's Army;*
also the anthology *A Heroic People: Memoirs from the Revolution*
(Hanoi: Foreign Languages Publishing House, 1956), and Truong
Chinh's *The August Revolution* (Hanoi: Foreign Languages Publishing House, 1958). An examination of some fifty captured diaries and
notebooks containing notes taken by NLF army personnel at indoctrination and training sessions indicates the scope and the dictums of guerrilla warfare that the NLF leadership felt were of prime value in the
revolutionary guerrilla warfare in the South. They were:

To defeat aggressive imperialism in a backward agricultural country we
must first gain the support of the huge rural masses, then turn these unorganized masses into efficiently organized forces, then build a great united
and powerful force out of the disorderly masses, and then convert the decentralized and scattered troops into a well-organized force under a single command. — Author unknown.

To turn weakness into power, we must transform insignificant and rudimentary organizations and forces into large and well-disciplined forces endowed with a high struggle spirit. — Author unknown.

First organize revolts among the peasant masses, then develop guerrilla
warfare from revolutionary bases in the countryside, and [finally] launch
attacks on the towns. — Truong Chinh [explaining Mao Tse-tung].

Our revolutionary armed struggle is essentially the problem of the laboring class overthrowing the state power of the enemy class and setting up and
protecting the people's state power. — Minh Tranh.

Political power grows out of the barrel of the gun. — Mao Tse-tung.

The War of Liberation is a protracted war and a hard war in which we
must rely mainly on ourselves — for we are strong politically but weak materially while the enemy is very weak politically but stronger materially. —
Vo Nguyen Giap.

Guerrilla warfare is the means whereby the people of a weak, badly
equipped country can stand up against an aggressive army possessing better
equipment and techniques. — Vo Nguyen Giap.

The basic principle of war is to preserve oneself and to annihilate the
enemy. — Mao Tse-tung.

If insurrection is an art, its main content is to know how to give the struggle the forms appropriate to the political situation at each stage. At the beginning the political struggle was our main task, the armed struggle secondary.
Gradually both became of equal importance. Later we went forward to the
stage in which the armed struggle occupied the key role. — Vo Nguyen Giap.

In the early years [of the Viet Minh war], when the masses' political movement was not strong and the enemy force was still stable, political mobilization of the masses in preparation for the General Uprising was the main
task. Organization and propagandizing of the masses throughout the coun-

try, but particularly at vital points, was of decisive importance. — Vo Nguyen Giap.

All guerrilla units start from nothing and grow. — Mao Tse-tung.

The most appropriate guiding principle for our early activities was armed propaganda [by armed units]. . . . Political activities were more important than military activities. Fighting was less important than agit-prop work. Armed activities were used to safeguard, consolidate, and develop the political bases. — Vo Nguyen Giap.

Man is the greatest factor in the universe and can do everything. — Mao Tse-tung.

Each man was a soldier, each village a fortress, each Party cadre and Resistance Committee a staff. This was the situation in the free areas. This was also the situation in the enemy's rear. — Vo Nguyen Giap.

Avoid adventurous, dangerous, and subjective actions caused by irritation and precipitancy. — Author unknown.

Guerrilla warfare is a means of fighting a revolutionary war, which relies on the heroic spirit to triumph over modern weapons. — Vo Nguyen Giap.

Quality can be replaced by quantity and morale. — Mao Tse-tung.

Deceive, tempt, and confuse the enemy. — Sun Tzu.

Guerrilla warfare is primary, and war of movement secondary. But the latter becomes increasingly important. In the advanced phase, war of movement occupies the main role, at first only on the battlefield of local counterattack, then over larger and larger areas. Guerrilla warfare is intensified, but it plays a role second to that of the war of movement, again first on selected battlefields and later over larger and larger areas. — Vo Nguyen Giap.

We follow the *Xuan Mai* [named for the training camp that trained many DRV infiltrators to the South] principal: When the enemy masses we disperse. When the enemy passes we harass. When the enemy withdraws we advance. When the enemy disperses we mass. — Author unknown.

Exalt the will to be self-supporting in order to maintain and gradually augment our forces. Nibble at and progressively destroy those of the enemy. Accumulate a thousand small victories to turn into one success. — Vo Nguyen Giap.

Seem to come from the east and attack from the west. Avoid the solid, attack the hollow. Attack. Withdraw. Deliver a lightning blow. Seek a lightning decision. — Mao Tse-tung.

When engaging a stronger enemy: . . . withdraw when he advances; harass him when he stops; strike him when he is weary; pursue him when he withdraws. . . . The enemy must be harassed, attacked, dispersed, exhausted, and annihilated. — Mao Tse-tung.

The main goal of the fighting must be destruction of the enemy manpower. — Vo Nguyen Giap.

Dien Bien Phu moved the People's Resistance War from a series of local counteroffensives to a great counteroffensive, from strategic initiative only on the northern front to initiative on all fronts. — Vo Nguyen Giap.

Recruits memorized these precepts, and cadres discussed them constantly in study meetings and criticism and self-criticism (*kiem thao*) sessions. Some, obviously inappropriate for South Vietnam, probably received only lip service. Others, which had worked elsewhere, failed in South Vietnam. In some ways the NLF leadership was a prisoner of doctrine, for it is obvious from a study of internal NLF documents that a great deal of effort was spent in attempting to fit earlier formulas, particularly the famous "three stages" of revolutionary warfare, to conditions in another place and time. In the end, as we shall see, there were sharp deviations from the original, and a new "third generation" of revolutionary guerrilla warfare emerged, one far more sophisticated than anything that had gone before. But that is what, in effect, this book is about — those techniques of revolutionary guerrilla warfare original with the NLF, unique in South Vietnam, and new to the world scene. However, the NLF's "third generation" was firmly built on the three stages as stated by Mao Tse-tung and redefined by Vo Nguyen Giap. Mao-Giap became to revolutionary guerrilla warfare what Marxism-Leninism is to Communist theory. To the true believer in both cases the dogma was more valuable as an article of faith than as a road map. Nevertheless it is important to understand the three stages if for no other reason than to be at home with Communist public pronouncements on guerrilla warfare.

Mao did not conceive of guerrilla operations as an independent form of warfare but simply as one aspect of the revolutionary struggle. There were, he said, three types of political activities: those toward the enemy (largely efforts to proselyte), those toward the people (agit-prop work), and those toward the guerrilla forces and supporters (organizational and indoctrinational). Within this framework came his three stages of revolutionary warfare. It can be argued that Giap outlined five stages rather than three, or that he used the three stages but preceded them with two preliminary ones. In the first, which might be called the psychological warfare stage, a base is established among the people, using propaganda and political warfare; discontent among the people is converted into channeled activity; cells are formed; most activity is on the individual level and of course is clandestine. In the second preparatory phase, which might be called the small-unit phase, comes the basic organizational work: the formation of vertical and horizontal associations and the creation of armed propaganda guerrilla companies, agit-prop teams with guns who fight only to defend themselves and whose chief tasks are organization and agit-prop work; Giap said these companies prepared the ground, and only when their work was well done could the three stages actually begin. Basically developmental, the three stages are categories expressed mainly in offense-defense, static-dynamic, military-political terms with respect to both the revolutionary and his enemy.

In the first stage the revolutionaries are on the defensive and the enemy on the offensive. The guerrillas hit, run, and hide, mostly the last. The chief goal: survival; the only law: trade all — time, real estate, people, everything — for survival; the theme: hang together at all costs. The firm revolutionary machine is built. It is a time of ordeal by fire in which the best weapons are tempered in the fires of hopeless combat. This is the heroic phase, the time of myth building, like the Long March. To Giap the first stage, called the guerrilla warfare stage, had as its primary objective defense (*phong ve*). The Chinese strategy of trading land for time obviously is appropriate only in a country with vast expanses and a sparse population. The Viet Minh had no room to move and therefore of necessity placed greater emphasis on organizational work and clandestine activity. Cadres built the hard core in a safe area; the hard core then trained recruits who formed small groups of usually three to five men (never more than 50) into operating units. Later in this stage, larger units were created in a coordinated manner, and rear bases, called "liberated areas," were carved out. The basic Viet Minh strategy was to destroy the French power piecemeal while blocking the successive French pacification efforts; to weaken the French infrastructure; and to get and maintain the support of the people. Giap, like Mao, preached that guerrillas should keep their forces intact, avoiding pitched battles. The basic tactic is the ambush, for it allows the guerrilla to select time, place, and enemy, sometimes supplies him with weapons, and serves as a good training exercise. Strategy in general rests on mobility, offensive operations, and constant activity. It requires eternal alertness. It is directly related to terrain and weather, to its communication system, to its relative local strength among the local population and with respect to the enemy. Its strategy cannot be decisive nor its tactics defensive. However, the guerrilla is paramount. Like a swarm of irate hornets surrounding an unprotected man, the guerrillas dart in, deliver a stinging attack, and retreat quickly when a powerful hand is raised against them.

In the Mao thesis the guerrillas themselves are of three types: the elite hard core, who are well trained, disciplined, dedicated, experienced, the Party's future top leaders; the part-time guerrilla (and part-time farmer), recruited early, who fights in his own village area and becomes the rank-and-file military; and the auxiliaries, poorly trained and armed, used as support troops, couriers, runners, and labor units. The pattern followed in South Vietnam, and advocated by Giap, makes use of two types of guerrillas — the paramilitary and full military, which is essentially the fundamental division of the National Liberation Front's Liberation Army. (The buildup of guerrilla forces into such a structure, however, comes in the second stage.)

Great organizational effort marks the first stage. Allies are rallied, organizations formed, alliances forged, usually under the banner of a united-front political party. Heavy political indoctrination and agit-prop work also mark the first phase. The relatively neutral population is slowly convinced by a combination of selective terrorism, intimidation, persuasion, and massive agitation, or, as the French express it, by "intoxication," that the future lies with the rebels and not with the established regime. This is done through the medium of the organization, people formed into a complex of social groups, either specially created or ongoing legitimate mass movements of the country. The central sociopsychological objective is alienation of the people from their government, making them party to the outlaw.

Leadership is never more important than during the first stage. It comes from the inner Communist party (the Party has both an overt and a covert apparatus), and dogma dictates that it be proletarian; but because proletarians generally are not competent leaders, intellectuals and students are recruited and an elite party group built that can withstand all the inevitable vicissitudes. The leadership unit practices "democratic centralism" and shakes itself down periodically to weed out deviationists and maintain purity.

In the second stage the system is more or less in equilibrium (*cam cu*) and is referred to by Vietnamese as the period of mobile warfare (*van dong chien*) or war of movement. To Giap particularly, it is marked by a combined armed and political struggle and is less passive and full of hazard than the first stage. Strategy changes from one based primarily on the need to conserve strength to one of vicious attrition designed to bleed and weaken the enemy. During this phase the enemy government ceases its active pursuit of the hostile forces and attempts to consolidate its position so as to hang on to what is left. This change, when it comes, is a great boost to guerrilla morale. The guerrilla becomes emboldened, increases his hit-and-run raids, and concentrates on smashing the police apparatus. As enemy troops become more defensive and static, he becomes more offensive-minded and dynamic. It is the buildup phase. The guerrilla forces become larger and less guerrilla-like. The regional or territorial guerrilla is paramount, but increasingly there is use of the structured liberation army in the form of regimental and divisional units. It is the time of escalation. Mobile warfare dominates the scene. Giap defined mobile warfare as "a form of fighting in which the principles of regular warfare gradually appear and increasingly develop but still bear a guerrilla character." Mobile warfare, standing between guerrilla warfare and conventional warfare, is tactically a series of widely scattered guerrilla band attacks against such targets as outposts, convoys, and military patrols; strategically it is a series of carefully timed, integrated campaigns. The mobility comes not by means of physical

movement but by opportunistic strikes against an enemy occupied elsewhere. During attacks, more conventional tactics are employed, the
guerrillas following the principle of concentration of forces to outnum-
ber enemy troops locally in chosen actions and operations.

Although the military effort moves from equilibrium to all-out offensive action, political activities are highly dynamic from the beginning and
remain so throughout. The military objective is to break the government's hold on the population, the political objective to break the psychological ties. In South Vietnam this campaign against the population
was more political than military. Tremendous amounts of manpower
were spent in converting, indoctrinating, agitating, and propagandizing
the people. Ample use was made of terror and assassinations of key opposition figures within and outside the government. A major effort was
also made to increase the efficiency of the organizational structure
formed in the first stage. The transformation from the first to the second
stage is imprecise and can be reversible. Giap, when asked by a Cuban
newsman in 1964 about the start of Stage Two during the Viet Minh
war, replied:

It is very difficult to say at what date we switched from guerrilla to mobile
warfare, since there is actually no mechanical demarcation between the two.
Even during the time we were using guerrilla warfare we were also using
independent companies and marshaled battalions, that is to say, we sent part
of our armed forces to operate as independent companies deep in the enemy's
rear and carry out propaganda work and develop guerrilla warfare. At the
same time we were using marshaled battalions to fight somewhat larger
battles. Thus embryo mobile warfare emerged at that time. Subsequently we
fought battles involving first one and then several regiments and in 1950
launched our first major campaign involving brigades. This campaign enabled us to wipe out important enemy military units and liberate vast areas.
The frontier liberation campaign of 1950 may be regarded as the turning
point in the development of the mobile warfare phase.[2]

The third stage, the beginning of the end, is referred to by the Vietnamese variously as the front assault phase, the attack against fortified
positions stage (*cong kien chien*), the counteroffensive stage (*phan cong*)
or, most commonly, conventional warfare stage. Here the struggle loses
much of its ideological cast and becomes less a war of issues and more a
matter of pure military force. Toe to toe, the two sides slug it out. This
period sees the regularization of the sociopolitical organization and increased control over the population in the liberated areas. To the Chinese
particularly, Stage Three means the emergence of the long-hoped-for
full military war. Mao, the pragmatic, made a virtue out of necessity;
his chief contribution to guerrilla warfare was not so much identifying
universal truisms as demonstrating how to adapt irregular warfare tech-

[2] Radio Hanoi, May 15, 1964.

niques to a particular time and circumstance. He was never particularly
enamored of guerrilla warfare as such, and in fact he frequently dep-
recated it, declaring in 1936, for example, that guerrilla warfare is "our
distinguishing feature and strong point, our means for defeating the
enemy . . . but someday it will definitely become a thing to be ashamed
of and therefore to be discarded." To Giap, Stage Three was true military conflict but still a form of civil war in which political values remained important even if the military obviously dominated events. Giap,
viewing the later struggle in South Vietnam, felt that Stage Three would
begin when the only remaining roadblock to victory, the GVN's armed
forces, would be openly challenged; the gauntlet would be thrown down
and the battle joined at brigade and division level, and the most common tactic would be the human-sea assault. He placed great emphasis
on the *binh van* movement (the military proselyting program, which is
described more fully in Chapter 14) as a softening-up measure. The
Chinese, especially with respect to South Vietnam, saw the end as the
NLF army smashing the enemy's main military force and marching into
Saigon. Giap envisioned a possible intervening political step, the coalition
government that would be infiltrated and eventually taken over by nonmilitary, that is infiltrative, means. This possibility led to a major debate
within the NLF ranks, which revolved around the question of whether
the end should be sought through Stage Three, through the General
Uprising, or by means of negotiation; or by some combination or variant
of these.

Viet Minh theoreticians analyzing their success at a much later date
ascribed victory to the fact that they had correctly mixed the three essential elements of the Resistance: the broad-based anti-imperialist united-
front organization that served as the foundation for the struggle, leadership by the working class, and proper use of the armed struggle. To these
three internal factors was added a vital external context, "the victory of
the Soviet Union in World War II and that of the Chinese People's
Resistance War."[3] Indeed, organization, leadership, and violence — plus
outside aid — were the essential reasons for the Viet Minh success.

However, this reasoning makes no allowance for French politics and
French attitudes at home as well as in Indochina. Paris had difficulty
putting its heart in the Viet Minh war, and the successive French governments demonstrated a singular inability to press the war with a will
for victory, to achieve a settlement, or to effect disengagement. The star-
crossed Indochinese colonial government, a combination of relentless

---

[3] Thanh Luong, *A Short History of Vietnam* (Hanoi: Foreign Languages Publishing
House, 1955), p. 50; the reasons for the Viet Minh victory cited here are also drawn from
this work.

logic and endless corruption, was totally unequal to the task it faced. Deeply ingrained in its *fonctionnaire* was the idea that he could enjoy the benefits of power without exercising any of its responsibilities; he was damned out of hand by his own statistics, none more chilling than those published by the governor-general in his *Annual Statistical Report on Indochina, 1943:*

For schools	748,000 piasters
For hospitals	71,000 piasters
For libraries	30,000 piasters
For purchase of opium by state monopoly	4,473,000 piasters

Even in the South, more hospitable to the French, no serious effort was ever made to induce Southern Vietnamese to remain loyal to France. Quite the opposite. As late as 1949 General Carpentier was able to declare that "they must be taught a lesson they will never forget,"[4] indicating that the previous two and a half years of Indochinese history had taught him nothing. The psychological field was left to the enemy, and the Viet Minh were able to arm themselves with more rational and emotional arguments why the Vietnamese should oppose the French than they could possibly use. The Viet Minh strategy first sought to nullify the opposition to itself within the anticolonialist camp and then to build a highly responsive machine that would organize and energize the people, isolating the colonialists. It accomplished its aims chiefly by organizational maneuvers. Controversial domestic issues were avoided. The campaign of denigration against other anticolonialist leaders, whether nationalist or monarchist, was accomplished with a scalpel, not a broadsword. The resultant political mix, palatable to most Vietnamese, won the support of most for the Viet Minh; in Vietnam today, even in the South, the words *Viet Minh* and *patriotism* are virtually interchangeable. But organizational effort cast in abstract terms means little. The Viet Minh genius consisted of uncovering specific truisms — some Ho Chi Minh's insights, some stolen from the experiences of other organizations — all tested by practice and time. These organizational laws, gleaned from Viet Minh history, include:

1. Don't try for too much; don't smash the existing social system, use it; don't destroy opposition organizations, take them over.

2. Use the amorphous united front to attack opposition political forces too large or too powerful for you to take over; then fragment their leadership, using terror if necessary, and drown their followers in the front organization.

[4] *Le Monde*, September 22, 1949.

3. At all times appear outwardly reasonable about the matter of sharing power with rival organizations although secretly working by every means to eliminate them. Don't posture in public.

4. Divide your organization rigidly into overt and covert sections and minimize traffic between the two. The overt group's chief task is to generate broad public support; the covert group seeks to accumulate and manipulate political power.

5. Use communism as dogma, stressing those aspects that are well regarded by the people; don't hesitate to interpret Marxism-Leninism in any way that proves beneficial. Soft-pedal the class-struggle idea except among cadres.

6. Don't antagonize anyone if it can be helped; this forestalls the formation of rival blocs.

7. Bearing in mind that in Vietnam altruism is conspicuous by its absence, blend the proper mixture of the materialistic appeals of communism and the endemic feelings of nationalism. Win small but vital gains through communism, large ones through nationalism. Plan to win in the end not as Communists but as nationalists.

8. Use the countryside as the base and carry the struggle to the cities later; in rural areas political opportunities are greater and risks smaller. Avoid the lure of the teahouse.

9. But forge a city alliance. Mobilization of the farmer must create a strong farmer-worker bond.

10. Work from the small to the large, from the specific to the general; work from small safe areas to large liberated areas and then expand the liberated areas; begin with small struggle movements and work toward a General Uprising during which state power will be seized.

Most of these precepts show the influence of Ho Chi Minh, whose primary genius was clearly in the field of organization. From the earliest days, when he worked under Michael Borodin at Whampoa, he had been fascinated by the social organization, and clearly it was the clandestine cell structure of underground communism rather than, say, dialectical materialism that attracted him to the cause. Most of Ho Chi Minh's political victories in pre-Viet Minh days were the result of his skill in creating, using, and propitiously merging a succession of united-front organizations, each a plateau higher than its predecessor, each increasing the Party's power, broadening its mass base of support, and eliminating its rivals. His technique involved enfolding a rival organization into a broader social community as a means of obscuring its individual identity and as a prelude to amputating its leadership, after which it disintegrated. Such organization-slaying was not new or unique to Vietnam, but no one has ever performed it more skillfully or so successfully over such a long span of time.

However, Ho Chi Minh not only could destroy organizations; he could also build and maintain them. Largely because of his ability the Viet Minh escaped the terrible internal struggles that tore apart other Communist parties, for example, the Chinese Communists in the decade that ended in 1933. Probably it is safe to conclude that the Viet Minh not only survived but flourished in the first year following the end of World War II because of the organizational skills of its leader. Vo Nguyen Giap may have been the genius of violence, Truong Chinh the erudite theoretician, but it was the brilliant organizational maneuvering of Ho Chi Minh that delivered the clear victory.

Organization Building

In the first postwar year Ho Chi Minh proved for all time his unequaled talent for guile and ruthlessness as well as his organizational genius in political infighting. During that crucial first year he was able to maintain an enclave government in portions of the North; keep fairly workable relations with the Chinese Nationalists in Hanoi from whom he received, mostly through bribery, badly needed war materials; and hold back any decisive action by the French, who for the moment were either unable or unwilling to accept him as a permanent fixture, smash him militarily, or provide the Vietnamese with an acceptable alternative to him.

Ho Chi Minh put the year of grace to good use. It began with a series of delicate negotiations marked by a good deal of intrigue with the VNQDD and other nationalists, and it ended with the ruthless trackdown and destruction of all nationalist opposition. Midway in the year came a major organizational victory, the creation of the coalition Government of National Union and Resistance, which was to be the Viet Minh vehicle in the struggle that followed. The government included Marxists, Dong Minh Hoi non-Marxists, members of smaller political and religious groups including Catholics, and prominent Vietnamese sitting as independents. The Indochinese Communist Party was abolished, to remain dormant until 1951. (Its successor, the Marxist Study Club, served as a holding operation and was available as a source of doctrinal material for the faithful during the five ensuing years.) During these decisive twelve months Ho Chi Minh continued to be the man in the middle — caught between the French, who meant to reassert colonialism in Indochina openly or under the guise of union with France, and the militant nationalists, primarily the VNQDD, who wanted complete and immediate independence and were willing to use insurgency to get it. Negotiations with the French resulted in the French taking more or less official note of the DRV. The Viet Minh also benefited from Sino-French negotiations, which led to the withdrawal of the Chinese Nationalist forces and left the VNQDD in a highly vulnerable position. The VNQDD, bereft of its Chinese protection, was at the moment ambitiously carrying on a two-front guerrilla war in the northern part of the country against the Viet Minh and savagely against the French. The task of eliminating the VNQDD as a military threat went to Vo Nguyen Giap. Using Viet Minh troops, and aided indirectly by the independent French military sweep operations, he was able within a few months to crush the VNQDD. By July 1946, all of its top leaders were under arrest or had fled into exile.

Organizationally Ho Chi Minh also moved ahead. The following March he formed another front organization, commonly called the Lien Viet, ostensibly as a broader-based front than previous ones — its platform, for instance, was simply, "independence and democracy" — but actually as a device for destroying the remnants of the nationalist organizations and for achieving greater control over the population. In October 1946 he reorganized his government, eliminating the last of the Dong Minh Hoi.

In the South, as in the North, opposition was hunted down and slain. The last vestiges of the Trotskyites, under the name Vietnam Socialist Workers' Party (Viet Nam Lao Dong Xa Hoi Dang), led by Phan Van Hum, and the Trotskyite Struggle Group, led by Ta Thu Thau and Tran Van Thach, were eliminated when the Viet Minh killed all three leaders. Bui Quang Chieu, leader of the Constitutionalist Party, was killed, as was Ho Van Nga, leader of the National Independence Party. Also killed were two prominent mandarin political figures: Pham Quynh, the pro-French moderate leader of the Tonkin Party, who had been the equivalent of prime minister in the Bao Dai government, and Ngo Dinh Khoi, brother of the future GVN president, who was buried alive. The Viet Minh singled out the Dai Viet, the pro-Japanese organizations, for especially vicious treatment. The party's chief figure, Truong Tu Anh, was slain in Hanoi in 1946, and the new leader, Nguyen Ton Hoan, fled.

In the 1949–1954 period the Dai Viets infiltrated the Bao Dai government, seeking to use it as the base for their own operations. Two of their leading members, Le Thang and Phan Huy Quat, held cabinet posts in the government. Under Le Thang an effort was made to broaden the organizational base, and in June 1950 he formed the National Popular Movement together with an allied youth group, the Young Patriot

Movement (YPM). The YPM was soon forced underground when a young Cao Dai, also carrying a YPM membership card, murdered a French general and the governor of Cochin China. But the main Dai Viet effort was to establish its own insurgency movement, both anti-French and anti-Viet Minh, in Central Vietnam above and below Hué. A stronghold was maintained, "taxes" were levied, and their radio station broadcast liberation movement appeals.

But events of that time were dominated by the Viet Minh, a theme that has repeatedly been drummed into the younger Vietnamese in the generation since. It was a vital time for the Communists, a time for mythology making: the myth of the multifaceted hero, Ho Chi Minh; the Phoenix myth of the Government of National Union and Resistance; the various myths of unity, spontaneity, and monolithism. In the years that followed, these were carefully nurtured and came to flower naturally on the folklore landscape in South Vietnam, serving well the current Communist venture. Documents carefully tailored for the South portray the history of those days for consumption by the young and ignorant, as in the following:

In a short period of less than ten days the Vietnamese revolutionaries, under the leadership of the Indochinese Communist Party, toppled the imperialists and feudalist rulers the length and breadth of the country.

August 19, 1945: Twenty thousand people and youth in Hanoi launch an armed revolt and seize the administrative offices of the government. . . .

August 23, 1945: Ten thousand people and youths in Hué revolt and take over the Royal Palace of the decadent Nguyen Dynasty. . . .

August 25, 1945: Two and a half million persons and youth in Saigon and Cholon revolt and take over the rule of the country.

The Democratic Republic of Vietnam is born. On September 2, 1945 Chairman Ho delivered the Declaration of Independence at Ba Dinh Square in Hanoi before 500,000 people, listened to by 25 million people throughout the country. . . .[5]

People of all social classes were to benefit from democratic liberties. All taxes were abolished or reformed. Private property was respected. On January 6, 1946, for the first time in the nation's history, the people of Vietnam went to the polls and elected a National Assembly. This assembly was charged with the responsibility of establishing an official government and of writing a constitution. . . .

Within a short time compatriots of all strata, led by the Party and President Ho, achieved outstanding results in nation building. However, the Party had

[5] This was the August Revolution, which in Vietnamese Communist history marked the overthrow of the Japanese occupation forces, Japan having just been militarily defeated by the Allies. Specifically these events took place: On August 19 word went out from Ho Chi Minh to begin full guerrilla warfare against the Japanese; on August 26 Bao Dai abdicated in favor of Ho Chi Minh; and on September 2, the Democratic Republic of Vietnam was proclaimed. Vietnamese Communists sharply distinguish between the August Revolution and the Resistance that followed. As Ho Chi Minh declared later, "The Revolution was successful, the Resistance victorious."

foreseen difficulties caused by the reactionaries at home and abroad. . . .
However, thanks to the skillful leadership of the Party's Central Committee
under the direction of Comrade Ho Chi Minh, those dangers of nationalists
were eliminated and the people's government was strengthened day after day.
Democratic countries as well as our neighboring countries showed us increasing sympathy. . . .

In spite of its successes, the Party voluntarily withdrew from activities in
the revolutionary government, although it never reduced its support efforts.
It worked constantly for the interests of the workers and the people and that
is why, despite reactionaries' attacks, its prestige rose steadily. . . .[6]

The myth wrenches time out of joint. What had actually been a bold,
hasty act of seizing power amid chaos, under circumstances in which organizational nimble-footedness counted most, and when time was measured in days and even hours, was presented as a drawn-out period of
unspecified length during which peace and tranquillity flowed back into
the land, and the labor of nation building was well under way, only to
be interrupted by the surprise return of the colonialists. The myth is as
fraudulent as it was unnecessary. For it detracted from the impressive
and unique accomplishments achieved under the flag of the red field
and yellow star. The Viet Minh, led by Ho Chi Minh, in a blaze of organizational activity, breathed life into a native enclave government. It
skillfully conceived and brilliantly created a social force of extraordinary
character. From the start, this sociopolitical arrangement was able to en-
act its own laws, enforce justice, and raise, equip, and maintain both an
army and an internal police force. In the years that followed, it withstood the tensions and strains developed by a relentless band of military
colonialists aided by a ruthless army of mercenaries. The ultimate victory over the French that resulted was victory made possible by the fact
of the organizational weapon.

In the South

The Viet Minh high command during the nine years of war divided
Vietnam into nine interzones, numbering them from north to south.
Roughly, Interzones One, Two, and Three were in Tonkin; Four, Five,
and Six in Annam; and Seven, Eight, and Nine in Cochin China. The
Viet Minh war for the most part was a Northern affair, fought in Inter-
zones One through Five, with comparatively little military activity in
Four and Five except in the area around Hué, the coastal towns of
Tourane (now Da Nang), Tuy Hoa, and Nha Trang, and the thin
coastal strip connecting them — the famed Street Without Joy. Interzone

---

[6] This account appeared in various versions that differed only slightly in NLF clandestine
newspapers throughout South Vietnam.

Four became a sort of rear base for the Viet Minh operating to the north in the Red River delta area. The people of Interzone Five, whose land was poor and sparse, supported the Viet Minh strongly, providing food even when scarce, supplying manpower, and operating crude weapons factories. Viet Minh communiqués lauded the people of Interzone Five for their ingenuity, thrift, and dedication to service. From this same area in 1954 came 90 per cent of the Vietnamese who moved North after the partition. Interzone Seven was the site of well-known military campaigns in Zone D; Interzone Eight, the Plain of Reeds; and Interzone Nine, the Camau liberated area — all familiar to present-day newspaper readers.

The Viet Minh's sociogovernmental structure over the years, although hierarchic, consisted chiefly of a horizontal chain of village-level committees; in all, from 1941 to 1955, there were five successive generations of such village committees: The first, during the Japanese occupation, was called the Liberation Committee. This was followed in the 1945–1946 period by the People's Committee, which was succeeded early in the Viet Minh war by the Committee for the Resistance, itself replaced later in the war by the Committee for Resistance and Administration. Finally, in the 1954 Geneva conference period, came the Military and Administrative Committee. These were strongest in the North. At all times the basic unit was the village, and the basic administrative and judicial organ was the committee, whatever its name. These committees during the Viet Minh war were joined like spokes in a wheel to the provincial-level committee, and the provinces were directly linked in the first years to Minister of the Interior Vo Nguyen Giap. It was a deceptively simple arrangement but one that proved equal to the great burdens placed on it in the chaotic early days of the war. The Liberation Committee, when first established, was a core unit acting mainly as an intelligence gatherer, and later it, or the People's Committee, became the nucleus for overt organizations and the guerrilla bands. During the Viet Minh war the chief problem in the South was not how to kill the French but how to build a tightly knit, loyal, dedicated, and competent administrative organization that would not be easily betrayed or disintegrate when first threatened. The Southern area was operated on a base-network basis, not as a Viet Minh governmental structure as in the North. An estimated two million Southern Vietamese lived under this base system and never saw a Frenchman from one month to the next; another five million lived in what were called the "contested areas."

The village Viet Minh committees established judicial control, set up indoctrination courses, distributed land, reduced rents, took action against usurers (and themselves loaned money). They attempted to solve local land tenure problems and to improve living conditions for the people by increasing agricultural production, opening schools, and liquidating repressive mandarins, notables, and village leaders. Life was hard and the Viet Minh by no means overwhelmingly popular. However, the government administration in many areas was fair and just, taxes were high but rational, corruption was sternly dealt with, and in general a serious effort was made to root the committee's work in the needs of the people. The result was that support was proffered, even if usually unenthusiastically.

Opposing the Viet Minh was the French–Bao Dai regime. Bao Dai, an underrated man, was a far more skillful negotiator and less of a dilettante than is generally believed; but he lacked organizational skill and was far too credulous about the French. At any rate, his administration was never given the authority needed to develop the counterorganization that might have stopped the Viet Minh.

Viet Minh fortunes in the South might best be summed up paradoxically as a successful failure. From the start the Viet Minh alienated the South Vietnamese. Old Communist Tran Van Giau and his successor, Nguyen Binh, dealt too harshly with the easy-going Southerner. The scorched-earth policy, copied from the Chinese revolution, appalled the South and proved unworkable. The Cochin Chinese regarded the Resistance as Northern oriented: The center of the fighting was in the North, the Viet Minh was strongest in the North, most of its leaders were Northerners, and the French were most vulnerable in the Red River delta. The South had less tradition of revolution, and inevitably a variety of North-South policy conflicts arose. The communication channel between Hanoi and Saigon was undependable, and liaison within the South was difficult. The Northern leadership exhibited little knowledge about Southerners and even less patience with Southern lethargy. Finally, the international situation was such as to favor more active pursuit of the Resistance above the 16th parallel. However, the Southern Viet Minh was able to force the French into a defensive and then passive position fairly early in the war and eventually to wrest from them political control in large parts of the South, but this came by default, not through combat.

Most Vietnamese today say that the French in the South were defeated without fighting, which they regard as a greater victory than the one achieved by the forces in the North. But the Communist organization was simply unable to consolidate its position late in the war. Its chief failure in this respect was its inability to achieve a Viet Minh alliance with the Southern nationalists, particularly the sects, for the Resistance and the attendant dislocations had enabled them to grow strong and to develop their own military forces and administrative units. In effect, enclave governments were carved out of the area west of Saigon by the Cao Dai and south of Saigon by the Hoa Hao, and the ex-river pirates, the Binh Xuyen, controlled both Saigon vice and Saigon police activities. All three came to terms with the French.

Military Aspects

Organization of the Viet Minh military was directly related to the kind of warfare it fought. The French, whose force totaled about 380,000 men, tied themselves down — as illustrated by the fact that 15 million tons of concrete were poured in the Red River delta in the first year of the war, a staggering statistic in terms of countering revolutionary guerrilla warfare — inside useless fortresses. Later, when French mechanized mobility was introduced, it was no match for Viet Minh foot mobility. A bitter lesson learned anew in every guerrilla war is that if a guerrilla band does not want to stand and fight it is virtually impossible to force it to do so. France's basic error was failure to grasp the essential Viet Minh techniques of revolutionary guerrilla warfare. By 1948 a political impasse had been reached between the French and the non–Viet Minh Vietnamese. When China went Communist in 1949 the French position became strategically impossible, for the Viet Minh then had a source of supply and a dependable sanctuary. The Korean armistice freed the Chinese to support fully the Indochina struggle. Time worked for the Viet Minh, which is usually not the case in guerrilla wars; the French were involved in a costly, unpopular war, and they needed not just victory but victory quickly. In the end, time probably was the decisive factor. France probably could have smashed the Viet Minh had there been enough time. But time ran out at Dien Bien Phu. France paid dearly. According to French government figures, 92,797 men were killed in action, dead (noncombat), or missing; 76,369 wounded; and 48,673 evacuated for medical reasons.[7] And so did Vietnam. The total dead Viet Minh and Indochinese civilians will never be known, but estimates vary from 450,000 to 1,000,000 persons.

The success of the Chinese revolution and the Viet Minh Resistance resulted in ascribing to the writings of Mao Tse-tung and Vo Nguyen Giap a pretension they do not have. Their tactics, and that is all they offer, can be defeated. The French proved this in Algeria, where militarily they won, largely by applying the lessons learned in Indochina. Nor is Giap the military genius he is frequently made out to be. He is an intelligent, well-educated history teacher who, driven by hatred, put his

[7] The same source stated that total casualties from metropolitan France were 74,068; Foreign Legion, 24,096; Africans, 54,020; Indochinese in the French army, 48,331; Indochinese in native armies, 29,642. (These figures are from a press briefing paper handed out by the French Embassy in Saigon in 1960.)

brains and historical knowledge to work in a pragmatic way to solve the problem: how best to defeat the French. He and others came up with the concept of an organizational weapon keyed to paramilitary guerrilla activities that could prepare the way and weaken the French so that the third stage, that is conventional warfare, could begin. Giap's larger-than-life image comes chiefly from his previously cited book, *People's War, People's Army,* which is nothing more than a collection of four loosely connected articles — turgid, incredibly repetitious, vague at key points — that he wrote over a period of about ten years. From a military standpoint little of what he, or Mao for that matter, said has not been said before. Protracted war, or people's war, when the verbiage is pared away, can be summed up in the single rule: Fight the kind of war you are best prepared to fight. The elaboration of stages could be summed in the rule: Do more when you are able to do more.

One could easily apply the Mao-Giap doctrine to the American Revolution: Stage One began when the Minutemen from Concord and Lexington ambushed the British along the road to Boston, turning their withdrawal into a rout; Stage Two began with the assumption of command by Washington, called — and not facetiously — the master of the retreat, and was characterized by the strikes of the Green Mountain Boys using techniques learned from the Indians, the George Rogers Clark expedition to the West, and the raids by the irregulars of Sumter, Marion, and Pickens in the South; finally Stage Three, in which Washington sought his Dien Bien Phu at Yorktown; throughout there was the organizational activity of the Continental Congress and the grass-roots agit-prop work by Jefferson, Paine, Samuel Adams, and others. Which is to suggest simply that we read into Mao-Giap undeserved universal truisms.

Yet people concerned in a professional way with revolutionary guerrilla warfare, which is to say military officers, government officials, scholars, and newsmen, tend to fall into two major errors: They are tempted almost irresistibly to raise Mao-Giap to a cult; or they allow the flashy guerrilla forays to obscure the less colorful but far more significant organizational work. Contemporary reporting of the Viet Minh war dealt almost entirely with Viet Minh military operations, although the balance was restored in the years that followed with the emergence of works on the political and organizational activities. Likewise with the NLF, virtually nothing has been written on its organizational structure, nor even on its major sociopolitical programs of the *phong trao tranh dau,* the political struggle movement.[8] Yet by any criterion — money, manpower, time expended — these activities dominated the day-to-day

[8] The struggle movement is described in Chapter 5 and in more detail in Chapters 14–16.

life of both the rank and file and the leadership and dwarfed the military aspects.

Just as we overrate the military significance of revolutionary guerrilla warfare, so do we underrate its power as a social force. The contribution of Mao-Giap to sociological theory is a set of instructions on how to mobilize people into a potent force, which includes military force, for political purposes under circumstances in which one does not have the controls ordinarily available to rulers embarked on creating a nationwide political-military establishment. It is one thing for the accepted leaders of a sovereign nation to mobilize the population in the name of some cause and quite another and far more difficult task to do the same thing under hostile and clandestine circumstances. One reason for reading these theoreticians chiefly in military rather than sociopolitical terms is that they never set down either a conceptual framework or the detailed description out of which dogma could grow. Giap in particular treats organization in a most cursory fashion, probably because it was more the domain of Ho Chi Minh. His book is polemical and hortatory, designed as an encouragement to the potential hero and not as a text for insiders. In retrospect, Giap put greater emphasis on the nonmilitary work of the Viet Minh. In 1964, for example, he told a Cuban newsman:

During the Resistance our people under Party leadership continuously consolidated and reinforced the revolutionary government and used this government as a sharp tool for mobilizing and organizing the people to struggle against the French colonialists, . . . to protect national independence, and to safeguard the achievements of the August Revolution. During the period between the August Revolution and the victory of the Resistance, our people's democratic state — actually the revolutionary dictatorship of the workers and peasants — played a decisive role in the thorough fulfillment of the strategic tasks of the people's national democratic revolution.[9]

The Viet Minh Victory

The Viet Minh victory over the French was ratified in the 1954 Geneva accords, which gave Vietnam an independent international identity but at the fearful price of its internal unity. Deliberately, and from the Communist viewpoint quite unnecessarily, the country was once more divided, this time along the most artificial of all its many boundaries, the 17th parallel, and became the Republic of Vietnam in the south and the Democratic Republic of Vietnam (DRV) in the north.

Ironically the agreement written at Geneva benefited all parties except the winners. For its part, France was able to disengage from a ruinous

[9] Radio Hanoi, May 15, 1964.

war with minimum loss of face, considering the circumstances, and maximum hope for continued economic and cultural *présence*. The Soviet Union saw the scuttling of the European Defense Community, in part perhaps a result of a Soviet deal with the French, retained its seniority in the Communist fraternity and its influence in Southeast Asia, and gave a boost to its Chinese protégé. China gained a certain amount of big-power status and further enhanced the image created at Bandung, its mood at the moment being not to frighten the nonaligned nations. Britain maintained its reputation as a wise world-power middleman valued for its good offices. The United States escaped the dilemma of trying to stop communism without serving colonialism; it also saw the salvage of half of Vietnam from Communist control when at the outset of the conference it had no reason to believe that anything could be saved.

Only the Viet Minh, the winners, lost. Or were sold out. Ho Chi Minh somehow was persuaded — apparently by a joint Sino-Soviet effort — to settle for half the country on the grounds that the other half would be his as soon as elections were held, which would be within a year's time. His willingness to accept partition after Dien Bien Phu proves, as nothing else can, his deep loyalty and fidelity to international communism. The shock of understanding that they had been betrayed, when it came a year later to North Vietnamese, must have been great indeed — nine years of sacrifice in the name of independence and unity washed down the river of abstraction. (In 1965 and 1966, Southern Viet Minh cadres in the ranks of the NLF expressed undiminished bitterness over the settlement and were prejudiced against any political settlement of the later struggle for fear it might lead to a second sellout.)

DRV leaders regarded the partition as transitory, apparently the result of naïve overconfidence in French diplomacy's ability to ensure elections. To Ho Chi Minh and his followers the internal situation seemed well under control: The DRV was monolithic, powerful, and a winner, while the South was weak, divided, and under the discredited and in-effectual Bao Dai. The behavior of the DRV leaders in the first year after Geneva suggested that they believed elections would be held, and so their main task in the interim was to keep the South politically off balance. Exactly why they should have believed this is not clear. Certainly no one should have seriously believed that the Southern government — or any government for that matter — would permit elections under an inter-national agreement to which it was not party, elections that it most likely would lose.[10] To paraphrase Churchill, Ngo Dinh Diem did not

---

[10] Neither the United States nor the Republic of Vietnam signed the 1954 Geneva ac-cords, and therefore neither is bound by them. Walter Bedell Smith, U.S. representative to the conference, afterwards made a unilateral declaration in which the United States took note of the accords and then made two points with respect to them: that the United States would refrain from threat or use of force to disturb them and that it would view

become President of Vietnam in order to preside over the communization of his country. For anyone to have believed otherwise would have indicated excessive credulity, and neither Ho Chi Minh nor Mao Tse-tung deserves to be called credulous.

Beyond this, the entire idea of elections for Vietnam seemed alien, obviously Western originated; they were not a Vietnamese way of settling the problem. An acceptable election consists of more than people assembling and dropping into a box slips of paper that are then counted honestly. It involves relating issues to the social context before the balloting; it involves a campaign and thousands of persons doing campaign work. In Vietnam it would mean intimately relating the vote to the affairs of the village, and such was not feasible if even possible.

Thus the Viet Minh and the Communists were denied the fruits of victory that they felt were honestly and morally theirs. And they were denied it by people who knew what communism was from firsthand experience and wanted none of it. In the famous Operation Exodus Northerners left North Vietnam and resettled in the South, seeding the population, at a ratio of about one to ten, with people deeply knowledgeable and strongly opposed both to communism and to the DRV.[11]

Viet Minh and Viet Cong

In many ways the Viet Minh war, or the Resistance, resembled the later struggle in the South: Both had a political essence, both were intimately bound up with the mobilization of the people, both required outside aid. But they differed in three significant ways that make meaningful parallels between them difficult to draw.

First, the later struggle in the South had a distinct imported quality about it that did not characterize either the Viet Minh war or the Communist revolution in China. The alien character was not simply a matter of outside aid or leadership. The struggle was in essence an expansionist drive by the North Vietnamese who asserted, and truly believed, that their goal of reunification was legally and morally justified.[12] However,

---

renewal of fighting as a violation of the accords and therefore a threat to international peace and security, which obviously implied that if aggression took place the United States would be free to act in any way it felt was in her national interest. The South Vietnam government militantly denounced the entire agreement as a "Communist sellout."

[11] Under the provisions of the 1954 Geneva accords, and the creation of the two Vietnams, individual Vietnamese were permitted to migrate; an estimated 800,000 to one million persons moved from North Vietnam to South Vietnam, and from 30,000 to 100,000 from South to North Vietnam.

[12] The North Vietnamese speak of reunification of the two Vietnams; the term unification is more common in the South. Both words are used interchangeably in this volume. The Vietnamese for unification is *thong nhut* and for reunification, *tai thong nhut*.

because unification was stressed, the Southern Vietnamese came to perceive the struggle not as a spontaneous combustion, as the Resistance had been, but as a deliberate creation of Hanoi and the Northern Vietnamese. The perception rested on the fact of Vietnamese regionalism. The Viet Minh war was anticolonial, clearly nationalistic, and concerned *all* Vietnamese — North, Central, and South — whereas the later struggle in the name of reunification was regarded by the Southern Vietnamese as neither nationalistic nor patriotic, nor even very understandable; a rural South Vietnamese, whose sense of national identification was low, could see little in reunification that would benefit him.

The second distinct characteristic, in part an outgrowth of the first, is the fact that sociopolitical factors, including the communication of ideas, loomed far larger than during the Viet Minh war. The guerrilla ambush might get the headlines, but it was the NLF village agit-prop meeting that did the most to move the cause toward victory. And a far greater premium was placed on the organizational route to power; it was war conducted by other means, to reverse von Clausewitz. The indifference of the villager to the abstract cause of reunification forced the NLF to concentrate on local complaints as a means of winning village support, for local grievances and proposals to end them could be understood and evaluated by any villager. When legitimate grievances did exist, and they did under Diem, the villager was inclined to support the NLF. But even under Diem the government accepted the NLF principle that the fight was to be carried on in the social arena for the loyalties of the rural people, something the French never did accept. Even if often misdirected, massive governmental efforts were made in the fields of social welfare, community organization, and communication of ideas. Finally, the NLF at all times publicly fostered the social myth that not by military assaults in the third stage but by means of the General Uprising would victory be delivered.

The third basic difference was the social milieu of the struggle. The great fact of the Viet Minh war was the French *présence*. To the Vietnamese the French colonialist was an assertive and proprietary foreigner who imposed restrictions that added up to a condition of discrimination or second-class citizenry that the Vietnamese was helpless to oppose. This condition was absent later in the South, and efforts by the NLF to pin the neocolonialist label on the United States lacked saliency in rural areas, for the case simply could not be proved to the satisfaction of the skeptical Vietnamese. The general condition in the South was one of confusion. There was, many Vietnamese felt, no clear right or wrong. One could be a patriot and support the NLF, or one could be a patriot and support the GVN. Families were split, individuals were genuinely puzzled. In short, there was no convenient line, like nationalism, that could be drawn to divide the two camps. The social milieu of the NLF was far broader than that employed by the Viet Minh. What struck one most forcibly about the NLF was its totality as a social revolution first and as a war second. It sought drastic change, not a modification of sociopolitical institutions: the implementation of a new system of property relations, new forms under which production would be carried on, and a new legal structure as well as a new political system. By its communication devices it sought to alter basic Vietnamese cultural institutions and to change the dominant beliefs that Vietnamese hold about man and his place in the universe; to change the social group from which the nation's leaders would be recruited; to reorganize and reorient the educational system and eventually Vietnamese religion. In short, it sought to enter into all spheres of life. Even more important, it openly communicated its intentions to the Vietnamese population. Such an ambition far exceeded that of the Viet Minh.

Special War

In 1962 the Communists, in an effort to distinguish between the Viet Minh Resistance and the later insurgency (which they term the Revolution) in the South, coined a new term to describe what was happening in South Vietnam. It was, they said, a Special War, which they described as a form of neocolonialism in which a colonial power, no longer able to use expeditionary forces to assert its control, worked through a clique of compradors whom it "advised," with the rank-and-file military force being supplied by the colonialized nation. Its main characteristic, said Nguyen Van Hieu, speaking in Peking in late 1964, was that "it colludes with local reactionaries to maintain their rule and interests by means of economic and military aid, building military bases, and military alliances." Khanh Phuong, in an article in *Hoc Tap* (July 1963) listed three major characteristics of Special War:

1. It coordinates military and nonmilitary action with the military playing the principal role. . . . The U.S. seeks to deceive the South Vietnamese people with political and economic tricks to win their confidence.
2. It expands the puppet arm and increases mobility. . . . To do this means press-ganging people into the army and giving everyone military training. . . .
3. It uses the strategic hamlet[18] as the mainstay of the nonmilitary program, disguised concentration camps designed to disrupt the brotherly relations between the people's self-defense armed forces and the people.

He went on to describe it as an antiguerrilla guerrilla, or third stage, war, adding:

[18] The strategic hamlet is described in Chapter 3.

In any case this is a war that is part of the U.S. strategy of using elite troops, but who participate directly only to a degree. The United States uses Diem's forces and thus exploits local human and material strengths. This is total warfare and consists of primarily using military force closely coordinated with political, economic, and social planning. Economic warfare, for instance, is part of the U.S. Special War. When the U.S.-Diemists began their Special War, according to statements they have made, they considered military activities as primary, but their objectives were political. Later they conceived of economic activities to help win military victories. Economic warfare does not play a decisive role but according to the U.S.-Diemists has "strategic significance."

Reference to economic warfare meant of course the United States economic aid program for South Vietnam, which the Communists regarded as a new, sizable, and distinctly dangerous factor in the war, for it was an effort of a scope they could not hope to match.

3

The Diem Environment

Government Vulnerability

The GVN [1] was not a democracy, and the fact that Diem in interviews kept insisting that it was irritated Westerners, but neither could it in all fairness be called a tyranny. It was as good as most Asian governments at the time and better than some. If revolutions stemmed directly from absolutism, they would have developed in dozens of countries elsewhere in the world before Vietnam. But three major weaknesses in the Southern situation made the rise of revolutionary guerrilla warfare not only possible but probable. These were a fragmented sociopolitical structure — the government was disorganized; lack of adequate leadership skill, particularly talent for political compromise; and a rigid conservatism within a political climate that for ten years had been oriented toward radical solutions of economic and political problems.

From an organizational standpoint the government of South Vietnam in 1954 was an incredible mess. French bureaucrats who had managed the South and held all key positions in the colonial government panicked after Dien Bien Phu, sold what they could of their personal belongings,

[1] Abbreviation used throughout the text for the government of South Vietnam.

57

and fled. As already noted, much of Cochin China had been controlled for years by the sects, which were not only separatist but virtually enclave governments defended by their own private armies and maintaining only the loosest federated relations with Saigon. The government of South Vietnam was ill prepared for the responsibility thrust upon it, and still less prepared to withstand systematic sabotage and subversion. Northern refugees began arriving, in all nearly a million, adding both a social problem and a new dimension to the political scene. Bao Dai remained the nominal chief of state — surrounded by Francophiles, out of the country much of the time and completely unequal to the organizational task — until deposed by Diem in a national referendum on October 23, 1955. In the countryside there was little government other than the traditional village structure. The new government under Diem began in just about as total an organizational vacuum as is possible. Diem was alien to the bureaucracy of French sycophants and hangers-on, alien to the Bao Dai monarchists, alien to the sects and to some extent to the Buddhists, alien to the remnant nationalist organizations, and, of course, alien to the Communists. He had no party faithful, no corps of loyal political cadres, no trusted organization. Until the army opted for him he had no means of enforcing a governmental order. What Diem did possess was a record as a man untarred by the colonialist brush, a patriot of integrity who opposed the Communists, sects, and other narrow interest groups not for the sake of his own self-interest but because of deep moral and religious beliefs.

The second weakness of the new government, its leadership, arose from the difficulty its leaders had in accumulating sufficient power to govern, a reflection of the first shortcoming. The new establishment lacked organizational skill at the top and administrative skills at lower levels. To succeed in politics in South Vietnam a leader needed to be skilled not only in the creation and manipulation of organizations but also in the destruction of organized opposition. Diem in particular lacked the ability to deal with people in and through groups. The shortage of administrative civil servants was particularly critical. During the long Resistance against the French the more dedicated, enterprising, and efficient Vietnamese had joined the Viet Minh, left the country, or become a member of that special class of Vietnamese, the *attentisme,* the permanent bystander. A large number of talented Southerners had gone North to serve, leaving the less talented or less experienced to man the Southern positions not occupied by the French. For the Diem government the Northern refugee group became a major manpower recruitment pool; many of these people were trained, efficient, dedicated, and, in addition, uninterested in Southern political infighting. The GVN's civil service soon became asymmetrical, too sectarian, too exclusively Northern; Diem was accused of "loading the government with Catholics," which most of the Northerners were, yet the refugees were the only significant source of trained personnel available.

The most serious failing of the GVN leadership, however, was its inability to meet and defeat on their home ground the various contending opposition organizations. Steeped as were all Vietnamese in the tradition of the clandestine organization, Diem knew well that the greatest threat to his government came not from men but from men in organizations. But countering the clandestine organization required abilities he did not have. The chief threat was the remaining Communist apparatus of the Viet Minh, not so much because of its ideology as because of its organization-building prowess. Diem struck bluntly and in two directions, in attacks on key cadres and against the organization itself, his Denunciation of Communism campaign of the 1957–1960 period.[2] Later the attack broadened to include those whose association with the Viet Minh had been minimal, and something of a witch hunt took place. However, the process was not as wholesale as later portrayed.

The test of whether a man was to be arrested basically was the question: Is he a key figure in some *group* hostile to the government? Simple antipathy toward the government, as held by the very vocal but unorganized Saigon teahouse habitué, for example, was tolerated with contempt. One of the writer's strongest memories of Vietnam in 1960 was listening to Vietnamese in public places — a sidewalk café, the street, a cocktail party — proclaim in loud voices, easily overheard, that "this is a dictatorship and we have no freedom of speech here," and then go on to list all the sins of the government. The unwritten law seemed to be that unorganized hostility was tolerated, organized hostility was not. Two Vietnamese could sit for months in a sidewalk café denigrating the government, and no action would be taken; they might be joined by one or two more, and still no action would be taken; but at some point, perhaps a dozen, the group became a critical mass, expressing *group* hostility toward the government, and very likely its members would be arrested or called in for questioning by the police.

But Ngo Dinh Diem was no simple oriental despot, the image he came commonly to hold in the United States. Many writers thought Diem would say in effect: "Here is a liberal who has criticized me, so into the concentration camp with him." Actually, criticizing his actions had not the slightest effect on him. He missed the whole lesson of the aborted November 11, 1960 coup d'état, for instance, not interpreting it as a sign of serious discontent in at least one segment of the society but view-

---

[2] This campaign, launched in June 1957, was responsible for the large-scale dismissal of civil servants considered disloyal to the government; some were Communists, some Bao Dai supporters, some non-Communist nationalists.

ing its failure as evidence of Heaven's approval of his policies, since "the hand of God had reached down" to protect him. What Diem was apt to say was: "Here is a person who commands a sizable following, who is a potential successor to me; into jail with him." A leaflet urging rural Vietnamese to hate Diem meant nothing to him. The Caravelle Manifesto, signed by 18 prominent professional politicians (April 1960), frightened him badly. Diem's operational technique was to nullify organized opposition by removing its leadership. After the 1959 elections only one lone man, Dr. Phan Quang Dan, in the National Assembly of the Republic of Vietnam was avowedly anti-Diem; yet Diem had him barred from his seat on a trumped-up charge of violating the election campaign laws by exceeding his quota of speeches. It was the clumsiness of the act rather than the act itself that most harmed Diem. Had he been cleverer in manipulating organizations, had he not operated from such a weak political base, had he had his own political following, had he been willing to gamble on taking opposition into his government — as had Ho Chi Minh many times over — the stark and violent confrontation that followed might never have taken place; it is one of history's imponderables, fascinating but in the end futile to contemplate.

The third weakness, stemming from the first two, was the highly conservative nature of the government in a political situation calling for liberal and even radical governmental policies. Actually, Diem was not so much conservative as traditional. His dream seemed to be to return Vietnam to the golden days of pre-French mandarinism. He even seemed uninterested in activities that the most conservative leaders would have pursued, such as building up the nation's basic industrial capacity. Diem might have maintained this posture of traditionalism — rural Vietnamese might have accepted his mandarin, or traditional, statement of authority, even his anti-Communist absolutism, for villagers too are traditional — had he encouraged some of the social welfare programs that the Viet Minh had conditioned Southerners to expect. Pushed by the Americans, Diem went through the motions of a leader interested in the living conditions and the opinions of those he led. But his heart was not in social reform. His efforts were too modestly conceived, too soon ended. The land reform program was the classic example: It lasted but three years and aided only about 10 per cent of the landless. In general, Diem fell into the Communist trap of equating Communist and Communist-backed movements with all who desired social reform; and he played into Communist hands by identifying himself with the opponents of change.

Facing opposition at various levels, which involved varying degrees of militancy, Diem had the choice of employing organizational counterthrusts (preferably organization-slaying, the Ho Chi Minh technique) or repression, or some combination thereof, the exact mix being a matter of judgment. In general, successes won by political maneuvering could lead to more effective government while repressive measures would lead to alienation. In any case, balance had to be maintained. While force against one segment might be necessary, other segments had to be won by politicking; for no political leader could go on indefinitely alienating one major social group after another and expect to survive. Yet that was exactly what Diem did.

This study is not concerned with the GVN's efforts or failure to mobilize the population or with its handling of the question of social integration except as they affected the setting in which the Communists operated, particularly in the rural areas.

The primary problem the GVN faced in this respect revolved around the question of how to introduce political participation that would stay within its political system and help maintain law and order. Diem's approach was to give the appearance of political participation by using highly stylized mass organizational meetings designed to drain off psychic energies, allowing a limited degree of decision-making at a low level, and manipulating the system so as to hold out the promise of greater future participation. The strategic-hamlet program established the basis for the re-establishment of local government in the form of advisory hamlet councils. The post-Diem governments increased the efforts to broaden the general base of the government and make it representative if not representational. The Diem political organizations[3] were replaced by "political tendencies," and a certain amount of decision-making shifted to the local level, although often by default rather than design.

The Rural Scene

Government programs with regard to the rural areas, which have included pacification, began in 1954. Specific measures were Ordinance Fifty-Seven, 1957–1960; the agroville, 1959–1961; the land development center; the strategic hamlet, 1962–1963; the New Life Hamlet program, 1964–1966; and the Revolutionary Development program, which began in 1966.

Pacification of the countryside is a traditional term used for centuries in Vietnam to describe periodic efforts on the part of the emperor to restore order following a peasant uprising or a serious outbreak of

[3] The largest of these, the National Revolutionary Movement (NRM — in Vietnamese, Phong Trao Cach Mang Quoc Gia), had a claimed membership of one and a half million persons in 1962. It was actually a social organization of GVN employees rather than a mass political party.

banditry. At the start it was primarily an attempt to extend GVN control in the areas torn by war. The term is a broad one that in common usage refers to all the past and present rural socioeconomic efforts of the government.

In pre-French days individual holdings by rice-farmer families in the Mekong delta ranged from 2 to 12 acres. From 1880 to 1939, cultivated rice land rose from 1,282 to 5,450,000 acres and the yield (polished rice) from an estimated 284 metric tons to 1,454,000 metric tons. The holdings in nearly half of the cultivated areas of Cochin China were more than 250 acres each, with the tenant-farmer unit averaging 8.5 acres. Tenant farmers usually were assisted at transplanting and harvest time by imported seasonal labor. Two thirds of the rural population of Cochin China in the 1930's were tenants, and their average payment to the landlord was 40 per cent of the crop. Borrowing, usually from Chinese, was endemic, and interest rates were high; most tenant farmers were in perpetual debt. The great landowners were generally Vietnamese, but there were a few French; the Chinese dominated both moneylending and the polishing, transshipping, wholesale marketing, and exporting of the rice crop.

The GVN's land reform program, under Ordinance Fifty-Seven, of the 1957–1960 period had three major provisions. First, it sought to regulate landlord-tenant relations. A rent control program was inaugurated, which stipulated that land rents must remain within 15 to 25 per cent of the chief crop yield. A standard five-year government-prepared contract was made available for use by landlords and tenants. The rent control provisions were enforced only sporadically and virtually disappeared after 1962, when the NLF rather than the GVN determined land rent rates. Second, the program purchased from the large landowners rice paddy acreages above 100 hectares (or 247 acres) per person and resold them to tenants. Generally owners received 10 per cent of the indemnification in cash, the remainder in 12-year bonds bearing 3 per cent interest. Tenants paid for the land in six yearly interest-free payments. An estimated 300,000 farm tenant families benefited from this program. By the end of 1960 when the program was phased out, 2,035 landlords had lost 433,463 hectares (about one million acres) of land and had been indemnified at a cost of a little more than one billion piasters (the free market exchange rate at the time was approximately sixty piasters for one American dollar), one tenth of which was in cash and the rest in bonds. Third, the program purchased and redistributed French-owned land. Under the Franco-Vietnamese agreements of September 1958 France granted the GVN about $3,000,000 worth of francs with which to purchase approximately 262,000 hectares (about 665,000 acres) of French-owned rice land.

At the same time the GVN took over 195,738 hectares (about 490,000 acres) of land that had no clear title, had never been registered or surveyed, or whose ownership for some other reason was in doubt; often this land was being farmed, and its seizure created a great deal of ill will among those working it. None of this land or any land received under the French purchase agreement was redistributed to individuals. Some was rented, with the government in effect becoming a landlord; some was farmed by army units; and some, including the remainder of the ex-landlord holdings not redistributed, was converted into communal land, and title was passed to the village councils. The village councils would then sublet plots each season by means of a secret sealed-bid auction, revenues thus raised going into the village coffers. Although on the surface this might appear equitable, in practice the communal land system turned out to be more vicious than the old landlord system. A rice farmer was forced to compete against his fellow farmer and obliged to bid higher and higher each year to ensure that he again got the plot he had worked the year before and into which he had put a great deal of diking work and other labor. The village as landlord thus extracted maximum rents but lacked the one redeeming grace of the old landlord system — the paternalism under which most landlords would carry a tenant through a bad crop year. Beyond these problems, the GVN land tenure programs were successfully sabotaged by the landlords, and in many cases by government officials themselves, who were also landlords. The landlord system as such was never questioned, although of course the NLF challenged the very idea. Further, the GVN never met successfully other land tenure problems: unclear titles, illegal rent devices, land retention rights, poor title transfer systems, and supervision of squatters taking over abandoned land. Diem announced in 1960 that the land reform program in Vietnam had been completed. At that point the NLF stepped forward with its solutions for the multitude of land tenure problems.[4]

The agroville (*khu tru mat*) was conceived in 1959 primarily in socioeconomic rather than in military terms.[5] The original idea, perhaps suggested by the Chinese commune or the Soviet collective farm, was that the agroville would be the tool for the economic development of the rural areas, for the "social revolution of the countryside."

Also socioeconomic but later quasi-military as well, the land development center (*khu dinh dien*) was conceived as a means of opening new lands in the highlands or reclaimed land in the Mekong delta. It was essentially a pioneering-type venture.

---

[4] See Chapter 15.
[5] See Joseph J. Zasloff, "Rural Resettlement in South Viet Nam: The Agroville Program," *Pacific Affairs*, Vol. xxxv, No. 4 (Winter 1962–63), pp. 327–340.

The strategic hamlet (*ap chien luoc*) was formally launched by presidential decree on February 3, 1962. In terms of purpose, it stood between the agroville, which was largely economic, and the fighting hamlet,[6] which was entirely military; it was the basic unit in the Diem government's socioeconomic war against the Communists. It provided minimal security, certain economic opportunities, and a degree of self-determination. It also provided the government with a means of population control. (The program, as noted, was continued after Diem, but its name was changed to New Life Hamlet program. Later the entire rural development program came to be called the Revolutionary Development program.)

While no effort has been made here to write a history of the strategic-hamlet experiment or even to present a comprehensive critique of it, certain features of the program must be understood in order to appreciate the NLF's response. The GVN strategic-hamlet program, after several false starts, began in earnest in February 1962. To the ordinary Vietnamese the strategic hamlet was just a continuation of the pacification effort that the government had pursued in various forms since 1954. To the Diem government the strategic hamlet was an intensified population-control measure to enable it to tighten its hold on rural Vietnamese by grouping them physically into manageable units, separated from guerrilla bands. To the Americans[7] the strategic hamlet was not only a population-control measure but also an opportunity for meaningful systematic social welfare work or "winning the hearts of the people," as it was frequently expressed; the strategic hamlet was to become a safe island in the midst of a sea of insecurity, it was to be the building site on which a good life would be constructed. In NLF eyes the strategic hamlet was a "concentration camp."

The American-British concept was grounded in the assumption that defeating the NLF required getting the rural Vietnamese to defend himself against the guerrilla, that is, that he must actively contribute to the counterinsurgency effort and not simply be regarded as a passive cow to be protected by the Vietnamese armed forces. The permutations of enough soldiers to protect simultaneously all of the 2,500 villages from attack by any possible combination of the 45 known reinforced guerrilla bands were of course astronomical, reaching into the billions of men.

---

[6] The fighting hamlet was a defended village from which wives and children had been evacuated; the husbands continued farming but also engaged in considerable antiguerrilla activity, seeking to make the area more secure so that families could return.

[7] And the British. BRIAM, the British Advisory Mission, worked closely with the Americans on the project and in fact was largely instrumental in shaping the original concept, based on British experiences in Malaya. NLF media sources frequently declared that "the strategic hamlet is a bastard, whose father is American and mother is British."

In order to get the villager to defend himself three simultaneous actions were required:

1. Each of the 2,500 villages must be made physically defensible. This meant arming, equipping, and training local defenders and the construction of defense perimeters around each village. The functional unit would be the strategic hamlet.

2. The villagers must be motivated to defend themselves, especially in the face of the NLF assertion that it was the villager's only friend and protector. Motivation meant governmental programs designed to provide economic opportunities and governmental services (schools, medical care, agricultural assistance, alleviating major socioeconomic grievances existing in a particular village); the establishment of a system of local self-determination (elected village councils); and what was generally lumped under the generic term rule of law — justice, an end to official corruption, and a codified way of conducting government as opposed to government by whim. If these were provided, it was reasoned, a legitimate claim could be made to the loyalty of the rural Vietnamese.

3. The major guerrilla bands must be kept away from the villages. Even a well-defended and highly motivated village could not withstand a sustained attack by such a unit. This was to be the chief task of the army (ARVN), which ideally would engage the guerrilla units day and night, employing unorthodox tactics, so the guerrillas would never be free to harass villagers. Since this could not be completely guaranteed, fast reaction time was needed on the part of nearby ARVN units in the event a village was attacked.

The overriding psychological objective was to cause the village to opt for the GVN, to commit itself publicly against the guerrillas. Once the guerrilla and the people were separated physically, then would come the effort, through various psychological warfare devices, to separate them socially, that is, to turn the guerrilla into a social pariah, a social outcast. Since morale counts for almost all in a guerrilla war, once this ostracism had begun to take place, it would be only a matter of time before the NLF organization disintegrated. This was the American-British concept of the strategic-hamlet program. Its success depended on being able to persuade the rural Vietnamese to want to defend himself against the NLF and on providing him with the reasonable possibility, including physical capability, of doing so.

To the GVN, and particularly to the president's brother and mastermind of the strategic hamlet, Ngo Dinh Nhu, the strategic hamlet was a base from which attacks against the guerrillas could be launched and a control device that would facilitate GVN manipulation of the rural Vietnamese. One can search in vain through governmental directives and the speeches of Diem and his brothers for a listing of the benefits or rights that the rural Vietnamese could expect within the strategic hamlet. Policy was cast in terms of duty.

Ngo Dinh Nhu particularly sought to work almost exclusively in the spiritual domain. For instance, in a significant speech on April 17, 1963 he defined the events of the moment in Vietnam as a struggle "for the salvation of the Fatherland . . . against feudalism, colonialism, and communism, against underdevelopment and disunity." Then he asked the rhetorical question: "To build a new society, a new life with new values, to live by his own means, to work for his own security and with his own strength, starting from the infrastructure of the hamlets and quarters to pervade the superstructure of the State — is not this the profound and real aspiration of our people?" The language was not in terms of the state serving the people, nor of a government acting for its people; it was a declaration that the people must do for themselves what they wanted done.

Later Nhu spoke of "a new life achieved within the framework of personalism[8] . . . and the transformation of strategic hamlets into centers of democratic civilization, into generators of combatants and heroes, whose light will flood the entire country." In listing the "thought foundations" for cadres he cited

(a) a moral foundation with a personality endowed with the necessary virtues for struggle, (b) an intellectual foundation to enable a cadre to grasp a situation and to apply to it the dialectic of the struggle, and (c) a technical foundation with methods appropriate for mobilizing the people in the struggle.

None of this related to the idea that by providing social services and by performing other civic action tasks the government of Vietnam could prove to the rural people that it was worthy of their support, that their interest lay in supporting that government. At best it was a statement that the government must lead the people in doing things for themselves, perhaps a reasonable argument in an industrialized nation but meaningless in a barter economy.

Indeed such was Ngo Dinh Nhu's orientation, and he brushed aside village social welfare requirements. The author attended a dedication of a strategic hamlet at which Ngo Dinh Nhu spoke. Afterwards a delegation of village elders approached Nhu with a request for aid in building a school. He replied "The government's means are stretched now to their limit. Do not rely on outside aid. First build a revolution within yourself. Then build the school with your own hands." After the delegation left, Americans present pointed out to him that he was in a barter-economy

[8] Personalism, the vague and obscurantist philosophy developed by Ngo Dinh Nhu, sought to combine Western individualism with collectivist ideas and translate the whole into the Vietnamese idiom as an answer to communism.

village, that obviously the people did not have the money to build a school, equip it with books and supplies, and hire a teacher. He brushed aside their comments with "You do not understand these villagers. Satisfy one demand and they would return with ten more." Perhaps a philosophic case could be made for such a laissez-faire policy; it obviously played directly into the NLF's hands and enhanced its position as no NLF act could have done.

Under U.S. pressure Ngo Dinh Nhu agreed to go along with efforts to provide social services to villagers, paid for by the United States, although he continued his spiritual exhortation work, chiefly using "personalism" as his doctrinal instrument. In a speech before strategic-hamlet cadres on October 3, 1962 he outlined the governmental structure of a strategic hamlet:

The regime inside the strategic hamlet should be revolutionary, but the revolution should be inside each individual. . . . There will be a system of guerrilla fighters inside the hamlet. Everyone inside will participate in combat except the young, old, and infirm. Participation is considered a citizen's duty. . . . This is in the direct interest of the village. There is no reason for not participating. Contributions will also be necessary, to take the form of five to ten days of labor and from fifty to one thousand piasters from each citizen over the age of 18.

It appeared that he was attempting to sell an imperfect version of the NLF's village program, ignoring the chief benefit that the government was prepared to offer with U.S. help, and which the NLF could in no way match — massive economic programs to improve village life. Nhu declared: "Do not rely on foreign aid, but on our own internal means. Concentrate on self-improvement. Try to improve your own virtue and behavior."

The GVN's official six criteria for a completed strategic hamlet, enunciated on July 19, 1962, made no reference to economic betterment and offered the people little. A hamlet was completed, it said, when the people (1) have cleared Communists from the area, and have coordinated population-control measures with the police committee and hamlet chief; (2) have coordinated control of people and resources with the Vietnamese Information Service, indoctrinated the population, and successfully organized all the people; (3) have instructed and divided work of all people as to their obligations when disaster strikes; (4) have completed defenses — such as fences, spikes, communication trenches, hidden trenches in all houses; (5) have organized two special forces cells in each strategic hamlet; and (6) have held the election of an advisory council.[9]

[9] Which as the name implies were councils that advised but were without actual power. The hamlet chief, appointed by the province chief on the recommendation of the district chief, was in effect an employee of the district chief's office, and, although he might attempt to defer to the wishes of the villagers, in the event of a district-village conflict he was obliged to side with the district chief.

There was little in the strategic-hamlet program for the rural Vietnamese. Not only was he expected to contribute much but he was deprived of his freedom of movement without adequate explanation; during the day when he left the strategic hamlet to work in the fields he was obliged to surrender his identification card at the gate and get it back at night; if he left the village area and was stopped without an I.D. card he was in serious trouble. He was burdened with extra work, required to devote from as much as one day a week in labor to village defenses; the wealthier could buy their way out. He was in many cases deprived of his land without adequate compensation, and the quarters given him in the strategic hamlet were not as adequate as those he had left. Living in the strategic hamlet put him more at the mercy of possibly corrupt officials or of officials who often suffered from an excess of zeal striving to complete at least the physical trappings. The entire program took on a military cast; its goals were largely in military or security terms; and they were implemented chiefly by the Vietnamese armed forces. It was designed not as a police activity but as part of a war. Above all, it did not take into consideration the intense NLF effort to demonstrate in every conceivable way that it was unnecessary and detrimental.

Social Movements

The Cao Dai during the Viet Minh war had seized every opportunity of Viet Minh weakness to occupy large areas of South Vietnam. Pham Cong Tac returned from exile in Madagascar in 1954 and led the Cao Dai into open military defiance of the new Diem government. Although at the peak of its strength, claiming two and a half million members, it was smashed, and Tac fled to Cambodia where he died a few years later. Ten of the eleven subsects had opposed Diem, and their leadership fled to Cambodia or went into hiding. The eleventh, which had backed Diem, was allowed to remain as a legal organization and operate the holy temple in Tay Ninh city. The members of the ten other sects made up the bulk of the early NLF support, although the alliance was at all times an uneasy one. Since Diem had smashed the Cao Dai, it was against him personally that the Cao Dai directed their opposition within the NLF. After his overthrow the post-Diem governments appealed to the Cao Dai to return to the GVN side, an appeal that was largely heeded. Mass defections took place, during which Cao Dai armed units switched sides.

The Hoa Hao sect in 1952 had formed the Social Democratic Party as its political arm. It too challenged Diem, and its armies were smashed by the ARVN in 1956. Like the Cao Dai, it was an early and major participant in the NLF, and like the Cao Dai it defected en masse to the GVN after the overthrow of Diem.

The Binh Xuyen sect was also smashed by Diem, and the blow struck at the organization was so severe that it has never recovered. It also worked with the NLF in its early days.

Dai Viet activity continued after partition, with the Dai Viet element in the Hué area exhibiting great hostility to the new Diem government. Although able and militant, in the end personal jealousies so fragmented the organization that it became no longer viable. A pro-Diem Dai Viet group was formed in Saigon, the Dai Viet Dan Chinh, led by Dr. Phan Quang Dan, later jailed by Diem, after which Pham Huy Co ran the organization from Paris. The Dai Viets, like the VNQDD, also enjoyed something of a resurgence after 1963 with the overthrow of the Diem government, particularly in the area around Hué.

The Military

Military officers felt that Diem played politics in promoting officers and in making assignments; they also felt that he frequently ordered military operations based on political rather than military judgments. In 1962 the South Vietnamese government launched its *Chieu Hoi*, or Open Arms, program, which was essentially an amnesty program that sought to induce defections from the NLF army. Special camps were built to accommodate the *quy chanh*, or returnees; the *quy chanh* received medical care, economic help, and vocational training before being released into civilian society or permitted to enlist in the South Vietnamese army.

The Vietnamese military force was composed of these specific elements:

1. The Republic of Vietnam Armed Forces (RVNAF), comprised of the Army of the Republic of Vietnam (ARVN), including an airborne brigade and several ranger battalions; the Vietnamese Air Force (VNAF); and the Vietnamese Navy, which included the Sea Force, the Junk Force, the River Force, and the Marine Corps.

2. The Civil Guard (*Bao An*, literally, "protecting the security of the people"), a voluntary area-defense force, essentially nonmobile, in units up to battalion size, which during this period was regarded as the province chief's own military force; although its role changed, its primary task remained to protect key civilian installations such as bridges, electric power stations, and governmental administrative offices. Later the Civil

Guard became less of a police force, was integrated more closely with the ARVN, and became a roving strike force.

3. The Self-Defense Corps (*Dan Ve,* literally, "protecting the people"), a paramilitary force responsible for the defense of Vietnamese villages. Its members patrolled the perimeter of the village defenses. It was organized by squad and platoon, without a ranking system or pay differential; salaries averaged about $10.00 a month plus subsistence and family housing; members at this time did not wear uniforms.

4. The Hamlet Militia (*Thanh Nien Bao Ve Huong Thon*), created as a static village defense youth group replacing the Self-Defense Corps, which took on a more offensive role, patrolling beyond the village defense limits; the young members, both men and women, served voluntarily, part time, and without pay.

5. The Civilian Irregular Defense Group (CIDG — in Vietnamese, *Luc Luong Biet Kich*), a generic term used to describe a diversity of unique military forces in Vietnam, including the famed Father Hoa Sea Swallow Army at Binh Hung in the far south of the Mekong delta, the Cinnamon Army of a wealthy Saigon businessman, and the Shrimp Army of another wealthy businessman, whose business interests lay, respectively, in cinnamon and shrimp raising. It also included a variety of special-mission units, primarily utilizing montagnards in the highlands, who were assigned the task of interdicting the Ho Chi Minh trail, or "hunter-killer" teams, in effect, antiguerrilla guerrillas.

Youth

In the Diem era the youth of Vietnam were notoriously apolitical, a genuine puzzle to Americans and others who had experienced student activities in Japan, Korea, and elsewhere in Asia. Students eschewed politics and exhibited interest in only social activities until the Diem-Buddhist clash somehow ignited them. Resentment over Diem's handling of the dispute burst into nationwide student-youth demonstrations and protest meetings, organized chiefly in the universities at Saigon and Hué. A sudden and, at first, essentially spontaneous alliance was formed between the students and the Buddhist leaders, an alliance chiefly responsible for creating the conditions that toppled the Diem regime.

With the Buddhist hierarchy acting as the strategy planners, and its planning was brilliant, and the students serving as the militant activists, the population centers in Vietnam became a sea of seething discontent. The infection of political fever began with the university students, soon spread to secondary-school ranks, and by late August 1963 involved hordes of youth as young as twelve years. The government rounded up hundreds of these and placed them in immense temporary prisons. Many of them were the sons and daughters of high officials in the Diem government, who, when their parents came to secure their release, refused to leave the prison unless all arrested students were also released.

Soon ARVN officers and men discovered that they were standing guard on prisons containing their younger brothers and sisters, their sympathy even publicly veered to the Buddhist-student cause, and the fate of the Diem government was sealed. The young Vietnamese and particularly the Saigon University students considered themselves the heroes of the overthrow of the Diem regime. They felt that they had been the torch that ignited the explosion, that only they had had the courage to take to the streets to openly oppose Diem, and that they therefore deserved a major voice in post-Diem governments. This resulted in the absurd situation of the prime minister seriously negotiating with six-teen-year-olds who demanded that they be permitted to pass on govern-mental decisions and decrees.

Diem had created the Republican Youth Corps earlier, but the year 1964 saw a proliferation of private Vietnamese youth groups, organiza-tions neither aligned directly with the GVN nor supporting the NLF. Dozens of such organizations were formed, merged, abolished, and re-formed. They issued manifestoes, news releases, student newspapers, lists of "demands" that dealt not only with politics but also with school administration, employment problems, and even foreign policy. Un-doubtedly NLF agents infiltrated many of these groups, but it was virtually impossible to trace the degree of influence, so fluid and ephem-eral were the organizations. However, in general it appeared that the NLF efforts were minimal; the students were cocky and militant and not particularly impressed by the NLF; further, the NLF, like the GVN, represented to them an adult organization, and they preferred to keep their groups for students only.

The Diem Record, 1954–1963

The chronological record of alienation is enlightening:

From the start, the Communists, the Viet Minh intimately identified with the Communists, and certain other militants, primarily the Dai Viets in the Hué area.

1956 — certain elements in the armed forces that challenged Diem's right to rule and his very authority.

1955–1956 — the three major sects: the Union of the Binh Xuyen, the Cao Dai, and the Hoa Hao, all three of which had their own armed forces, lucrative vested interests, and special privileges that no government could tolerate.

1955–1956 — the "feudalists," that is, monarchists who supported Bao Dai; also the extreme Francophiles.

1957–1958 — Saigon intellectuals, whom Diem regarded as totally negative and defeatist and for whom he had the greatest contempt but who were influential opinion-makers.

1956–1960 — certain rural Vietnamese, particularly in the Mekong delta, who had received land from the Viet Minh only to have it reclaimed by the GVN on the grounds that an injustice had been done in seizing it from its original owner, often a GVN official.

1959 — persons and families of persons victimized by improper administration of Law 10/59, which provided for "repression of acts of sabotage, of infringements of national security, and of attacks upon the life or property of citizens." Special tribunals from whose verdict there was no appeal heard these cases and could mete out only death or life imprisonment sentences; often the tribunal became a weapon of local vendettas, quite without the knowledge of Saigon.

1960 — professional politicians of almost all groups; their alienation began very early but reached its climax with the arrest of Doctor Phan Quang Dan, the lone National Assembly member who could have been considered true opposition to the Diem government.

1960–1962 — rural villagers, victims of mismanagement of the various resettlement programs — the prosperity zone, the agroville, and the strategic hamlet. These were socioeconomic ventures designed primarily to break the insurgent infrastructure in the village. Insofar as they benefited the villager, these programs were successful; but frequently they were mishandled by overzealous or corrupt local officials or, in later days, successfully sabotaged by the Communists.

May 1963 — the Buddhist hierarchy and then Buddhist laymen (the result of the clash between the ARVN soldiers and Buddhist demonstrators in Hué on May 8, 1963 and subsequent events).

July–August 1963 — students, formerly passive and politically indifferent, who suddenly caught fire, angered by the government's measures against Buddhists; affected first were university students, then high-school students, and finally grade-school students.

August–November 1963 — the field-grade officer corps, the young Turks; their alienation was based partly on more ancient grievances (such as political interference in military operations, politically based promotions) and personal reasons (an army major's twelve-year-old sister arrested on treason charges).

Finally, the General Staff, appalled by the social disintegration, moved as a man; not one general acted to save Diem at the end. The coup d'état, if that is the term — collapse of Diem's authority would be better — came on November 1, 1963.

The alienation cutoff point might have been 1956. Few would deny that it was impossible for Diem to do business with the Communists. Nor could he countenance mutinous officers. The sects had to be stopped, for continuation of an enclave government arrangement would have been intolerable to any national government; however, having smashed them, Diem could have waited a decent interval and then established a rapprochement. The sects represented nearly one of every ten Vietnamese in the South, and permanent alienation would seem unthinkable, yet Diem never made even a gesture of conciliation toward them. A more skillful organization man would have won over at least part of the "feudalist" group and certainly would have wooed and won some of the intellectuals as post-Diem governments did. The injustices resulting from land tenure problems and mismanagement of Law 10/59 need never have happened or could have been easily corrected, but Diem felt that to do so would be to undercut his civil servants whose loyalty to him had placed them in their positions. No leader could afford to alienate his country's professional political leaders; the arrest of Doctor Dan in 1960 probably was the Diem government's point of no return. Disenchantment gained momentum (by this time actively encouraged by the National Liberation Front) in the mismanaged strategic-hamlet program and then among the Buddhists. After May 8, 1963 the whole nation caught fire: bonzes in self-immolation, students in mass rioting, soldiers refusing to fire on crowds and openly encouraging demonstrators. The social pathology spread like a prairie fire. Saigon, those last days of Diem, was an incredible place. One felt that one was witnessing an entire social structure coming apart at the seams. In horror, Americans helplessly watched Diem tear apart the fabric of Vietnamese society more effectively than the Communists had ever been able to do. It was the most efficient act of his entire career.

4

Development of the NLF

In the years immediately after the signing of the Geneva accords, the DRV based its policy goal of unification of Vietnam chiefly on faith in French diplomatic prowess and on the hope or expectation that the Diem government would soon collapse. When it became apparent that neither elections were to be held nor the Diem government was to fail, the DRV embarked on a new and more aggressive course. Lao Dong Party cadres living in North Vietnam, mainly Southerners who had served in the ranks of the Viet Minh, went South and, with dissident elements in South Vietnam, the most numerous of whom were the Cao Dai, began a political-paramilitary organizational effort that culminated on December 20, 1960 in the creation of the National Liberation Front of South Vietnam (Mat Tran Dan Toc Giai Phong Mien Nam Viet Nam),[1] NLFSV, or NLF as abbreviated here.

[1] The most commonly employed form of the term by both sides. Its literal meaning is Front [of] (Mat Tran) Racial Nationals [for] (Dan Toc) Liberation [of] (Giai Phong) Region [in] South (Mien Nam) Vietnam (Viet Nam). Early usage often employed "people" (*nhan dan*) rather than *dan toc*; and sometimes the term *quoc gia* was used in place of *dan toc*. Both mean "national," but *quoc gia* (country-family) connotes national in the "nationalistic" sense, whereas *dan toc* (man-tribe) conveys the idea of ethnic nationality. Since Viet Nam was often dropped in everyday usage, the title became National Liberation Front for the South. It is also frequently found in print as National Front for the Liberation of South Vietnam, or NFLSV.

74

Pre–NLF Days

Communists, the religious sects, and other groups offered resistance to the Diem government in the 1955–1960 period. Violence in the countryside was not uncommon, although until at least mid-1958 there was no guerrilla warfare in South Vietnam in the generally accepted definition of the term. The government ascribed most of the terror and violence to remnants of the Viet Minh,[2] but how could anyone know for sure whether an incident in a remote village was the work of the Viet Minh, the armed sects, bandits, or someone engaged in personal revenge? Considerable weight of logic rests with those who argue that most of the acts were not Communist or even politically inspired, since the general purpose of a political act of terror is to advertise the cause; if the population does not perceive an assassination, for instance, as the work of a specific political group, then much of the value of the act is lost. (The exception to this of course is the elimination of a person who is himself dangerous to the cause.)

The Viet Minh elements in South Vietnam during the struggle against the French had of course included many non-Communist elements, as, for example, the private Catholic armies that operated south of Saigon. After 1954 many Viet Minh entered the ranks of the new Diem government, and even a decade later many of the top military and civilian governmental figures in Saigon were former Viet Minh. Nevertheless the Viet Minh elements, made up chiefly but not entirely of Communists, continued to offer resistance to the Diem government. Their numerical strength during this time is not known with any certainty.[3] In terms of overt activity such as armed incidents or the distribution of propaganda leaflets the period was quiet and the Communists within the remnant Viet Minh organization relatively inactive. In addition, much of the activity that did take place apparently was the work of impatient cadres operating in the South independently of Hanoi's orders.[4]

[2] Remnants of the Viet Minh remained in certain areas as a governing force, chiefly because of the slowness with which the newly formed GVN was able to extend its suzerainty into what was mainly mangrove swamps and waist-deep water. This was the extent of the instability in rural Vietnam. Certainly conditions were no worse than those in the same period in the western hills of South Korea, northern Burma, or vast portions of Indonesia.

[3] Dr. Wesley R. Fishel of Michigan State University in a statement to the author estimated that during the 1954 partition the Communists had left behind a network of about 10,000 persons, which is probably about correct.

[4] This was the thesis of the French, such as Philippe Devillers, who maintained that the Viet Minh Communists in the South had been promised rapid unification by Hanoi, and when it couldn't deliver, Northern leaders

had to listen to the bitter remarks that were made to them about the inability of the North to do anything about the Diem dictatorship. The overriding needs of the world-

Such action on their part and the religious sects is understandable, and the emergence of a clandestine militant opposition group could be expected. Moreover, as our review of clandestine organizations in Vietnam indicated, it is equally understandable that *anyone* opposed to Diem might also form a clandestine and militant opposition group; such an effort would be in complete harmony with Vietnamese social tradition and individual psychology. But there is a vast difference between a collection of clandestine opposition political groups and the organizational weapon that emerged, a difference in kind and not just degree. The National Liberation Front was not simply another indigenous covert group, or even a coalition of such groups. It was an organizational steamroller, nationally conceived and nationally organized, endowed with ample cadres and funds, crashing out of the jungle to flatten the GVN. It was not an ordinary secret society of the kind that had dotted the Vietnamese political landscape for decades. It projected a social construction program of such scope and ambition that of necessity it must have been created in Hanoi and imported. A revolutionary organization must build; it begins with persons suffering genuine grievances, who are slowly organized and whose militancy gradually increases until a critical mass is reached and the revolution explodes. Exactly the reverse was the case with the NLF. It sprang full-blown into existence and then was fleshed out. The grievances were developed or manufactured almost as a necessary afterthought. The creation of the NLF was an accomplishment of such skill, precision, and refinement that when one thinks of who the master planner must have been, only one name comes to mind: Vietnam's organizational genius, Ho Chi Minh.

Khoi Nghia

The initial doctrine of the NLF was *Khoi Nghia,*[5] or the General Uprising. This was a social myth in the Sorelian sense, perhaps traceable back to the Communist myth of the general strike. Essentially it consisted of the belief that the NLF could develop the revolutionary

wide strategy of the Socialist camp meant little or nothing to guerrilla fighters being hunted down in [the South]. . . . It was in such a climate of feeling that, in 1959, responsible elements of the Communist Resistance in Indo-China came to the conclusion that they had to act, whether Hanoi wanted them to or no. They could no longer continue to stand by while their supporters were arrested, thrown into prison and tortured, without attempting to do anything about it as an organisation, without giving some lead to the people in the struggle in which it was to be involved. Hanoi preferred diplomatic notes, but it was to find that its hand had been forced.

Philippe Devillers, "The Struggle for the Unification of Vietnam," *The China Quarterly,* No. 9 (January–March 1962), p. 15.

[5] In Vietnamese, *khoi nghia* literally means "to stand up and fight for a just cause"; it is frequently mistranslated as "armed uprising."

consciousness of the Vietnamese in the nation's 2,500 villages to such a pitch that at some golden moment there would come a spontaneous uprising, and the people would seize political power, led of course by the NLF. The thesis was constantly drummed into the rural Vietnamese by NLF cadres. Again and again in internal documents and public statements one found the assertion:

The Vietnamese Revolution in the South marches forward toward the General Uprising. . . . To seize power through the General Uprising means utilizing the strength of the people of South Vietnam as a principal medium to overthrow the imperialist and feudal ruling clique and set up a people's revolutionary government.

Said another early basic document:

The Revolution, directed toward the goal of the General Uprising, has these five characteristics: . . . It takes place in a very favorable worldwide setting. . . . It is against the neocolonialism of the U.S.A. . . . The government of Vietnam is unpopular and growing weaker. . . . The people have revolutionary consciousness and are willing to struggle. . . . It is led by the Party, which has great experience.

The following quotation is from an April 1961 learning document devoted to the concept of the General Uprising. So far as can be determined, it is the earliest such document to treat the thesis in specific detail:

We must come to comprehend all aspects of [activity] that lead to the General Uprising. There will be several uprisings, fractional, unsuccessful, etc., and the struggle movement must become fierce before we can launch the General Uprising that will yield us final victory. . . . How will the struggle between us and the enemy proceed to the General Uprising? Due to the nonuniform development of the Revolution in the rural areas, the balance of power between us and the enemy varies from area to area. Consequently farmers do not rise up everywhere at the same moment. Even in those areas where there is a partial uprising and enemy control is broken, this [control] is ended only at the hamlet and village levels; the enemy's higher administrative apparatus remains, and he still has strong armed units and he is still safe in the urban areas from which he can send spies and agents with a design to attack us and gain back the rural area he has lost. Consequently the struggle in the rural areas will be fierce and complicated. . . . But in the struggle we have many strong points and advantages, and the enemy has many deficiencies and limitations. The movement toward the General Uprising under the leadership of the Party will grow more fierce and widespread until it finally takes place.

Initial Organization

The initial organizational phase was the period from mid-1959, when the decision was made to begin building an organization, to December

1960, when the new creation was first unveiled. On May 13, 1959 the Lao Dong Party Central Committee, meeting in Hanoi, declared that "the time has come to struggle heroically and perseveringly to smash" the GVN. General Vo Nguyen Giap, DRV Minister of Defense, declared a short time later that "the North has become a large rear echelon of our army. The North is the revolutionary base for the whole country." [6] There are those who argue that this sort of talk was mere window dressing by Northern Communists for the benefit of Southern cadres. They assert that the resumption of hostilities, when it came, was the act of Southern cadres acting on their own, not on Northern instructions.[7]

Whether led or driven, the DRV clearly did involve itself in the South in terms of doctrinal know-how and civilian cadres and, later, in more material ways. What the DRV cadres brought in particular was organizational ability, and through their efforts the insurgency, previously sporadic and patternless, began to take shape. Insurgency efforts in the 1958–1960 period involved violence such as assassinations but few actual armed attacks. This was so partly because the cadres had little military capability but chiefly because doctrine counseled against violence. This period was devoted to preparing the base, and it well exemplified the dictum that once gunfire begins in a guerrilla war, the incumbent side is already three years or so behind the insurgents. By 1959 an over-all directional hand was apparent. The struggle became an imported thing. But it was not military hardware that was imported at this time. It was something more necessary and valuable: expertise, doctrinal guidance, insurgency know-how, and, above all, organizational skill.

For the true believers operating throughout the South this was a time of surreptitious meetings, cautious political feelers, the tentative assembling of a leadership group, and the sounding out of potential cadres whose names went into a file for future reference. It meant working mainly with non-Communists and, in many cases, keeping one's Communist identity a secret. The hunt was for organizational

---

[6] *Hoc Tap*, January 1960.

[7] Philippe Devillers (*op. cit.*, p. 17), for example, states, although without attribution, that the leaders of the DRV agonized over the emergence of militant opposition to Diem because it put them in the middle of the Sino-Soviet dispute. One element in the DRV, he said, sided with the Soviets, who regarded the Southern cadres as adventurists and who counseled prudence, while the pro-Chinese element considered helping the South as a proper form of activism that incidentally would strike a blow against revisionism. He added:

When it decided to take up arms against the Diem régime, the Resistance movement in the South placed the leaders of Communism in Vietnam in an embarrassing situation. In the field of international relations the Democratic Republic of Vietnam had in all essentials kept to the Soviet line of peaceful coexistence, taking great care not to give, through the slightest provocation, any pretext to M. Diem or to the Americans.

talent, and the only credentials demanded were hostility toward the Diem government and personal dependability. That organizational activity had gone on intensively and systematically for several years was obvious from the structure that finally emerged. Such a machine could not have been built without an intensive and extended organizational effort.

With the conjunction of the professional calculator and a welcome environment, at last the time was propitious. The instrument was to be the united front, tried and tested. The first public indication in Communist circles of this decision came at the Third Lao Dong Party Congress in September 1960, when the delegates heard the liberation of the South described as "a two-stage affair: first, the elimination of the U.S. imperialists and the Ngo Dinh Diem clique, . . . then the establishment of a national democratic coalition government . . . that would negotiate with the North for reunification." A Lao Dong Party resolution went on to outline specifically the nature of this united front:

To ensure the complete success of the revolutionary struggle in South Vietnam our people there must strive to establish a united bloc of workers, peasants, and soldiers to bring into being a broad, united national front directed against the U.S.-Diemists and based on the worker-peasant alliance. The front must carry out its work in a very flexible manner in order to rally all forces that can be rallied, win over all forces that can be won over, neutralize all forces that can be neutralized, and draw the masses into the general struggle against the U.S.-Diem clique for the liberation of the South and the peaceful reunification of the Fatherland.[8]

Communists have asserted that the NLF was formed because the repressed and terrorized people of the South needed an organizational base for their General Uprising, and the people created such an organization, the NLF, aided by the Communists but not dominated by them. Devillers and others maintained that the basic reason for the formation of the NLF was not the DRV striking back out of frustration for its failure to unify the country through the Geneva accords but to take advantage of the seething discontent existing in the South. Devillers fixes 1958 as the start of this open, militant, and semiorganized hostility to Diem:

To make good the lack [of village intelligence], they [Diem's police and army] resorted to worse barbarity, hoping to inspire an even greater terror among the villagers than that inspired by the Communists. And in that fateful year of 1958 they overstepped all bounds. The peasants, disgusted to see Diem's men acting in this way, lent their assistance to the Communists, and even to the sects, going so far as to take up arms at their side. . . . In the course of that December [1958] and the following January armed bands sprang into being almost everywhere.

•   •

[8] From a Lao Dong Party leaflet widely distributed in South Vietnam at the time.

And, indeed, in the course of 1959 the battle spread and became more intense. From the stage of scattered guerrilla operations it passed gradually into partisan warfare.

.   .   .   .

It was thus by its *home* policy that the government of the South finally destroyed the confidence of the population, which it had won during the early years, and practically drove them into revolt and desperation.[9]

Vietnamese with whom the author has talked agree that unrest was widespread in the Vietnamese countryside in 1958, but all have insisted that the Diem government was by no means as well organized or as efficient as would have been necessary to have been as repressive as the Communists claimed. They assert that at one point in time, in 1954, Diem controlled little more than a dozen square blocks of downtown Saigon, that he devoted the 1954–1960 period to trying to extend his governmental *présence* farther into the countryside, and that by the time open armed attacks began in 1960 he had only slight political control over most of the country and still no control at all over certain isolated areas.[10]

At any rate, the critical distinction at this juncture was the difference between the "what" of what happened and the "why" of what happened. The "what" was the creation of the National Liberation Front, which was premeditated, planned, organized at length and in detail, and then pushed and driven into existence and operation. Such an effort had to be the child of the North. The "why" of what happened is much less clear, for it raises the question of which came first, repression or support for subversion. It can be argued that while the NLF was not indigenous as an organization, its support was. There can be little doubt that the ground in South Vietnam was fertile for armed revolt; preconditions for insurgency did exist, although not perhaps in the traditional revolutionary sense. Against this background the National Liberation Front was born and flourished.

The NLF was a true Communist-front organization. In late 1960 the Lao Dong Party circulated a memorandum among its members in the South outlining the proposed NLF and announcing itself as an organizational member of the Front. It declared that

[9] Devillers, *op. cit.*, pp. 14–16.

[10] Six former major Viet Minh bases remained areas of extreme insecurity over which Diem was never able to exert firm civilian control; these formed the nuclei for what were to become the NLF's "liberated area" (their term, and therefore used throughout this volume, for what were often isolated areas rather than one homogeneous area largely controlled by the NLF), that is, the Mao-Giap safe base from which the NLF could operate. These were Do Xa, Mang Kim in Quang Ngai province; To Hap in the mountains behind Nha Trang city; Duong Minh Chau in northern Tay Ninh province along the Cambodian border; Zone D. chiefly in Phuoc Thanh and Binh Duong provinces just north of Saigon; Ban O Qua in Kien Phong province in the Mekong delta; and Kien Lam in An Xuyen province in the far south.

the National Liberation Front has been established to unite closely various classes of the South Vietnamese patriotic population in the struggle against the Americans and Diem in accordance with the wishes of the South Vietnamese. This [move] securely guarantees that the Revolution in South Vietnam will quickly and successfully restore peace and carry out the unification of our Fatherland.[11]

The document likened the NLF to the earlier Indochinese Communist-front organizations:

In 1941 the Viet Minh was established to lead all our people so that the August Revolution might be crowned with success. During the Resistance period the Lien Viet Front united all our people in a successful resistance. In the present political struggle the NLFSV is in charge of leading the South Vietnam population in struggling successfully for the liberation of South Vietnam and carrying out the unification of our country. The operational plans of the Front . . . aim at serving the supreme interests of the Fatherland and at meeting the urgent and present aspirations of the South Vietnam population.

On Southern Lao Dong–Front relations the document declared:

Our Party, the Party of Vietnamese workers, laborers, and progressive intellectuals, . . . is very glad to welcome the NLFSV. We approve entirely of the Front's plans. We promise to be loyal and trustworthy members of the Front . . . and [it concludes] let us closely unite and struggle under the flag of the Front.

The Lao Dong Party in the South, however, did not merge its public identity; it continued to issue leaflets and to circulate clandestine publications bearing the imprimatur of the Party. Several of these declared that the Lao Dong Party stood for peace (in the world peace sense); unification; independence (the dissolution of the Diem government); and, in some leaflets but not others, democracy, defined as the "formation of a progressive government in South Vietnam to solve the people's problems . . . and chosen by general elections." [12]

In its formative days the NLF obscured but did not hide the fact of Communist or Lao Dong Party participation; Party members were instructed, if asked directly, not to deny that the Party was a member organization, and except in strongly religious areas NLF members never made a serious effort to hide Lao Dong Party involvement in the Front. When the admittedly Marxist organization, the People's Revolutionary Party (PRP), was formed and joined the NLF in 1962, Communist vanguard leadership within the Front, although not DRV govern-

---

[11] Memorandum dated December 30, 1960, signed by the chairman of the Lao Dong Party provincial committee, Ba Ria (Phuoc Tuy) province.

[12] Specific proposals endorsed in the leaflets signed by the Lao Dong Party included putting an end to the economic exploitation of workers, the population relocation program, the military draft and corvée labor systems, political arrests, and compulsory membership in such GVN organizations as the Republican Youth Corps and the Women's Solidarity Movement.

mental influence, was not only admitted but emphasized. Only in Catholic refugee villages and among certain elements of the religious sects were agit-prop workers and organizers instructed to play down Communist involvement. In all other segments they were instructed to develop as a major task the "vanguardism" idea of the Party leading the Revolution, using the argument that the Party was uniquely capable of doing so because of its deep reservoir of experience and wisdom.

Thus the NLF was not simply an indigenous organization in which Communists played a part. Neither was it simply a robot-like instrument of the DRV. The Communists formed the NLF to establish a single organization around which all anti-Diem activity could cluster and create a bipolar political condition. This met several of their needs. They needed a mass base, since the Lao Dong Party was not a mass-based organization in South Vietnam. They needed a skeletal, standby governmental structure for possible future use. They needed an opportunity to infiltrate non-Communist organizations, and participation in the Front obviously provided good access to these groups. They also needed a divisive wedge, and the NLF organization allowed the Communists to play one group against another, forcing individual members to choose sides against each other rather than against the Communists. Probably this was long clear to non-Communists at higher levels in the NLF, but they were willing to play the Communists' game. The latter, for their part, were quite willing not to discourage the non-Communist who considered himself clever enough to outmaneuver them.

The National Liberation Front was formally organized by a group of about ten persons representing specific organizations and approximately fifty others attending as individuals. Most of the figures involved had been associated with one another for several years. For instance, its chairman-to-be, Nguyen Huu Tho, when interviewed much later, described pre-NLF history thus: "Although formally established in December 1960 the Front had existed as a means of action but without bylaws or program since 1954 when we founded the Saigon-Cholon Peace Committee. . . . Many of the members of the [NLF] Central Committee were also members of the Peace Committee . . . [namely] Huynh Tan Phat, architect, Ho Thu, a pharmacist, and Le Van Tha, a radio engineer." [13] The chief organizer and acting secretary-general (some documents list him as chairman) of the provisional committee established at the initial meeting was Phung Van Cung, a Paris-trained medical doctor who left his practice in Saigon in the fall of 1960 to join the NLF but who had been engaged in organizational work prior to his departure.

[13] Radio Hanoi, June 5, 1964.

Members of the original NLF, and its most ardent supporters in the early years, were drawn from the ranks of the Viet Minh Communists; the Cao Dai and Hoa Hao sects; a scattering of minority group members, primarily ethnic Cambodians and montagnards; idealistic youth, recruited from the universities and polytechnic schools; representatives of farmers' organizations from parts of the Mekong delta, where serious land tenure problems existed; leaders of small political parties or groups, or professionals associated with them; intellectuals who had broken with the GVN (particularly members of a network of Peace Committees that had sprung up in 1954 in both the North and the South); military deserters; refugees of various sorts from the Diem government, such as those singled out by neighbors in the Denunciation of Communism campaign but who fled before arrest.

This original element was soon joined in numbers by Southerners who had gone North during the 1954–1956 exodus and infiltrated back. Some 30,000 to 100,000 Vietnamese from below the 17th parallel moved to the DRV. They were for the most part of two types: Approximately 90 per cent were Vietnamese from the poor areas of Vietnam, primarily the Phu Yen, Binh Dinh, and Quang Ngai coastal plain that contains some of the most desolate land and destitute people in all of Indochina (and was under strict Viet Minh control during the Viet Minh war); others were Viet Minh and Communists who were well known in the South and feared to remain. They buried their arms and printing presses (the GVN recovered 307 caches of arms in the 1955–1960 period) and went North. Left behind were deeply covert agents, those who either were not known to be Viet Minh or Communist by the local peoples or had relocated.

Many of the original participants in the NLF had turned to it because they had been denied participation in South Vietnam's political process, even in the role of loyal opposition; some felt that the NLF was the most promising route to power, believing as did many at the time that the Diem government would not prove viable. They had one thing in common, to bring down the Diem government. The religious sects supported the NLF because they sought both to restore the special arrangements they had enjoyed under the French and to revenge themselves on Diem, who had smashed them in 1956; the ethnic minority groups saw in the NLF the promise of equality and social justice; for the sundry opportunists it was a means of satisfying their personal aims.

As for the Communists, in the most fundamental sense their purpose in the NLF was to achieve political control of the area below the 17th parallel, thus completing the 1945 August Revolution. The Communists had several alternatives but chose the socio-organizational one that had been successful during the Viet Minh Resistance. First they established the front organization. Then they sought to engage as many Vietnamese as possible — but in any case the vast majority — in a revolt against the state. This was to be accomplished by organizing the population, or to be more precise the rural 85 per cent of the population, into manageable units to conduct the revolt. The rural Vietnamese was not regarded simply as a pawn in a power struggle but as the active element in the thrust. He *was* the thrust. He would carry on the struggle movement that would lead to the General Uprising and the Communist take-over.

5

The Road to Power:
The Struggle Movement

The Concept

The English word "struggle," a pale translation of the Vietnamese term *dau tranh,* fails to convey the drama, the awesomeness, the totality of the original. A *quy chanh* told the author that *"dau tranh* is all-important to a revolutionist. It marks his thinking, his attitudes, his behavior. His life, his revolutionary work, his whole world is *dau tranh.* The essence of his existence is *dau tranh."*

Within the generic term "struggle," there were two types of struggle movements: the political struggle (*dau tranh chinh tri*) and the armed, or military, struggle (*dau tranh vu trang*). To the NLF, as to the Viet Minh and Chinese Communists before it, victory would be achieved through the proper balance of political and military activities or, in Communist terms, by the proper combination of the political struggle and the armed struggle. These categorizations are employed throughout this book, with the exception that here the term "violence program" has been substituted for "armed struggle" because it is felt to be a more meaningful term.[1] The political struggle[2] is not considered as such but is broken down, for discussion, into its three action programs — *dich van, dan van,* and *binh van* — which, together with the violence activities, comprised the entire NLF revolutionary effort.

Dich van, literally, "action among the enemy," meaning the rural Vietnamese controlled by the GVN, was the arena of NLF-GVN confrontation. *Dan van,* literally, "action among the people," meant the backbone, the chief support of the Revolution; in practice it denoted Vietnamese living in those parts of the country from which GVN civilian administrative control had been eliminated, the NLF's so-called "liberated area." The deadly *binh van,* literally, "action among the troops," was the immense proselyting campaign conducted against members of the Vietnamese armed forces and the GVN's civil service. The three action program terms derived from Viet Minh days but with altered meaning; during the Viet Minh war *dan van* meant "action among the people," that is, the general population; *dich van* meant "action among the enemy," meaning the enemy's army and civilian administration, including the Bao Dai government; and *binh van* meant "action among the troops," meaning the Viet Minh troops, or what in the American army would roughly be called "troop information and education work." As used later, and as the terms are employed here, *dich van* is the effort of the NLF to gain support among the rural people in general, *dan van* its effort in the liberated areas, and *binh van* its activities among GVN military and civil servants. The three action programs taken together formed the political struggle, one edge of the NLF's double-edged sword; the other edge was the armed struggle, not simply guerrilla military attacks but kidnapings, assassinations, executions, sabotage, or what is termed collectively here the "violence program."

The struggle movement was the route to power. Declared an early PRP document:

By applying creative reasoning of Marxism-Leninism to conditions in Vietnam, the Party, with reality and capability, has set forth the line and direction of the Revolution in South Vietnam, which is the political struggle combined with the armed struggle marching forward toward the General Uprising.

[1] The author discovered that the term "armed struggle" was misleading to Americans, who equated it either with guerrilla warfare or with the more or less conventional small-scale war. Actually, "armed struggle" is far larger, and the actions within it have no common military characteristic; in fact the only thing in common is that all the actions involve violence or the threat of violence.

[2] Appendix A lists the political struggle movements in South Vietnam claimed by NLF elements. Although obviously inflated, the figures give the reader an impression of the importance the leadership attached to the struggle demonstration and other struggle movement efforts.

Vo Nguyen Giap wrote that if an uprising was an art, the chief characteristic of its leadership was the ability to change the struggle form in accordance with changed events. At the beginning, he said, the political struggle dominated and the armed struggle was secondary. Gradually the two assumed equal roles. Then the armed struggle dominated. In the end came the return to the political struggle. Struggle was *the word*. Its goal, toward which the cadres pledged themselves, toward which each Vietnamese was expected daily to contribute a little, was the General Uprising, the nationwide, simultaneous grand struggle movement.

An early NLF document spelled out the scenario in specific terms:

The government of South Vietnam is brutal, reactionary, imperialist, feudal, dictatorial. . . . The people have no means short of revolution to liberate themselves from slavery. That is why we march forward in a Revolution to seize power by means of the General Uprising. Our immediate goal is preparation of the people for the General Uprising. . . . We must utilize the strength of the people as our great force. . . . This is the struggle movement. . . . The enemy relies on its armed forces. We rely on the people . . . , the people strongly bound together in the struggle movement.

As one PRP indoctrination booklet indicated when it asked "what must we do each day to move toward the General Uprising?" the answer was:

We must make a continuous effort to strengthen and develop the Party . . . and promote Party-mass relations to ensure continued Party leadership. . . . We must build up the worker-farmer alliance as the basic force of the Revolution. . . . We must press forward with the struggle movement, develop unity among the masses, and win support among the enemy's military and administrative workers. . . . We must press the *binh van* movement. . . . We must do agit-prop work among the masses. . . .

From the struggle toward the General Uprising came the creation of the myth of the heroic struggle out of which was fashioned the hero-martyr, described in an early Radio Liberation broadcast:

A woman plugged a gun muzzle with her own body, an old woman burned her own house and the enemy with it to resist the strategic-hamlet program. Groups of people stood facing enemy guns to shield the retreat of the people's forces. Such martyrs will go down as heroes in the history of the nation. How I wish talented moviemakers the world over would come and record these heroic deeds on the part of the people of South Vietnam. . . . Thousands of women and old people advance in orderly ranks toward an enemy post. They brave the enemy planes overhead. They ignore enemy warning shots and give no notice when the guns fire into them. Bringing their wounded along with them, they advance until they come to the U.S.-Diem administrative buildings. They demand an end to arson, looting, murder, cannibalism, and raids against the people. Blows rain upon them while these mothers, sisters, and wives tearfully tell their tales of woe to the evildoers. . . .

In order to understand fully the NLF's use of the struggle movement as its chief offensive device, we should take a brief look at the NLF's perception of the GVN's over-all counterinsurgency strategy. The GVN had no national policy or even official attitude toward the NLF's struggle movement, nor was there any systematic effort at the district and village operational levels to develop techniques designed either to head off a struggle movement as it was being launched or to blunt it once under way. The posture of the Diem government was to pretend it did not exist or, if forced to take notice, to characterize it as an insignificant and ineffectual Communist effort to create disorder. District and village officials were left to their own resources when confronted by a struggle movement, and their responses depended largely on their personalities. Some officials attempted to ameliorate the situation if in their power to do so; others simply ordered their police and troops to disperse the crowds. Occasionally an official was politically astute enough to regard the struggle movement as an opportunity to seize the initiative from the NLF and would alleviate a genuine grievance and turn the crowd's attitude from hostility to amity; this was a difficult manipulation, for it involved both acquiescing to a demand without appearing to surrender in the face of force and structuring the solution so as to maneuver the NLF out of credit for the change.

An early NLF document (1961) assessed the GVN's response to a struggle movement as follows:

> In the face of the struggle movement the enemy usually becomes puzzled, panic-stricken, and troubled from the highest to the lowest rank. In many villages the enemy government's machine has deteriorated; even in some districts this has happened. The arrogant attitude of the enemy has abated. This proves two things, . . . that the foundation of the enemy government is not solid . . . and, if we lead the struggle movement properly, it will paralyze the enemy's administrative machine and destroy their schemes and policies.

Another document of the same period outlined some of the uses of confusion:

> After a serious political struggle [at the village level] the enemy is thrown into confusion. Administrative officials, security agents go into hiding or they surrender themselves to the people. Cadres must make use of this state of confusion to further increase enemy dislocation. Officials or soldiers who are confused and frightened because they are in trouble with the government must be guided into supporting the National Liberation Front. . . . Say to them that since they do not want to serve as cannon fodder they must resign their jobs or desert the army. Point out the errors they have made, welcome them for choosing the right path, and praise their progressive spirit.

Nhan Dan, on August 28, 1961, evaluated the over-all potency of the struggle movement as follows:

Starting with struggles against oppression, restrictions, preventing persons from earning a livelihood by wicked village notables, puppet administrative organs, secret agents, and against exploitation, the merging of villages, evicting people from their villages, and the establishment of agrovilles, the movement went forward with such slogans as "Overthrow the U.S.-Diem regime," "Establish a national-democratic coalition government." . . . From small-group complaints, petitions, and small demonstrations, the movement has advanced toward big demonstrations, including thousands of persons . . . and uprisings that exterminated "wicked agents" . . . and smashed agrovilles. . . . University students protest against examinations in which many fail. . . . Merchants, proprietors, and tradesmen protest against high taxes. . . . During the last few months the struggle movement has defeated many major U.S.-Diem schemes . . . such as mopping-up operations and ranger and antiguerrilla tactics.

The NLF considered that during the 1960–1965 period the GVN campaign against it passed through four broad and overlapping phases: first, the Denunciation of Communism campaign of the 1957–1960 period, predating the actual NLF organization and consisting chiefly of police action against vestiges of the Viet Minh remaining in the South; second, the general "pacification" campaign and its various "mopping-up operations," or military sweeps, through the rural areas, which began in earnest in 1961 and continued through 1964; third, the strategic-hamlet building campaign of 1962 and 1963; and finally the highly mechanized and predominantly air war after 1964.[3] The NLF considered that the first was directed primarily against potential opposition leadership to the GVN; the second at the semiautonomous guerrilla bands; the third at the NLF infrastructure; and the last, it held, was a desperate, irrational death convulsion.

Throughout, the NLF assessed the GVN's political base as weak and shaky, requiring constant doses of force and repression:

The Southern authorities use force to rule the people for these reasons:

1. The administration they established was a step backward in history, . . . a country-selling government manned by a group of bureaucratic landlords and the most reactionary pro-American bourgeois compradors and lackeys . . . , standing starkly in distinction with the [DRV], a truly democratic and national salvation government. . . .

2. They had no just cause . . . , were unpopular . . . , unable to establish a strong base among the people. . . .

3. The masses, especially the workers and peasants, had a high degree of political enlightenment as the result of the education and training by the Party during the Resistance . . . and were not tricked, seduced, or deceived by enemy demagogic policies. . . .

4. Their government . . . is run by cruel, reactionary, feudal landlords,

---

[3] By early 1965 air actions were accounting for 70 per cent of the estimated casualties among the NLF army members.

pro-American bourgeois compradors . . . , ruffians, hooligans, and traitors
. . . whom all the people hate and despise.[4]

The NLF leadership sensed the inherent danger that lay in the American efforts in Vietnam to develop various types of civic action work as a
counter to the struggle movement. *Thong Nhat* (Hanoi), in an editorial
dated June 26, 1964, distinguished between the Viet Minh war and the
later struggle, between the French military effort and the later socioeconomic measures, which it termed "political devices and demagoguery."
The editorial said:

> The French colonialists struck at us mainly with military strength and
> military tricks. We struck back with only military strength and military
> tricks. Today with a new type of colonialism and a new type of rapacious
> warfare, Special War, the enemy uses political schemes to deceive the people.
> . . . American imperialists and their lackeys have been forced to use politi-
> cal devices and demagoguery in order to fight the revolutionaries, and they
> have mobilized powerful persons from among the people to combat the Revo-
> lution. They recognized that in today's war political factors have a decided
> significance; the side that can hold the people . . . is the victor. That is why
> the Americans urged Diem to have a political program more attractive than
> the NLFSV program . . . ; that is why the American imperialists (and their
> new lackeys) . . . primarily and ridiculously pretend to be democratic and
> cordially more solicitous with the people than was Diem. . . .

The NLF's extended and vitriolic attack on U.S. economic aid programs indicated a sensitive nerve. However, civic action programs as
such did not necessarily counter the thrust of the struggle movement;
their contribution was in direct proportion to their responsiveness to
the issues involved in a particular struggle movement or to the degree
that the programs indicated serious governmental concern for village
problems. In any case they would have no lasting effect unless coupled
to village social organization work, thereby enhancing both the public
and the private non-NLF infrastructure in the village. The struggle
movement was an organizational effort, and any counter effort also had to
be essentially organizational.

As employed by the NLF the technique of the political struggle movement is neither as strange nor as alien to Americans as might be supposed on first encounter. The efforts by American Negroes and their
supporters in the 1960's to achieve racial equality introduced Americans
to a similar type of activity. The type of struggle that the rural Vietnamese felt was justified and just, the "peaceful struggle movement,"
was akin to what Arthur Waskow has called "creative disorder."[5] In
the American context, Waskow distinguished the politics of order, that
is, the courts, the legislature, the public forum such as the mass media

[4] *Hoc Tap*, July 1964.
[5] In a conversation with the author.

(which were closed to all dissidents in Vietnam until the end of the Diem regime), and the sporadic bombings and clashes of mobs with police or troops (which would correspond to the NLF's violence program) from a third type of activity — "creative disorder," which lies between the two. It is exemplified by the civil rights march, the school boycott, the sit-in, the pray-in, the wade-in, the rent strike and economic boycott, highway blocking, telephone jamming, and other nonviolent action, which most Americans regard, if not with full approval, at least as legitimate activities that deserve legal protection as much as labor's right to strike. Vietnamese, even strongly anti-Communist Vietnamese, saw nothing improper in the struggle movement; they objected to Communist manipulation of such movements just as Americans fighting for racial equality object to communism's efforts to insinuate itself into the civil rights struggle.

The struggle movement had a long and honorable history in Vietnam. During the Yen Bay mutiny of 1930 long lines of unarmed and impressively silent Vietnamese marched past the French governor-general's residence.[6] In earlier days the struggle movement was little more than a technique for riot manufacture or instigating mob violence. But in the hands of the NLF it developed far beyond such crude usage. Combined with the organizational weapon and employing various communication techniques, the struggle movement became a vast effort to organize and direct rural Vietnamese opposition to the GVN to such a degree that the GVN would be unable to withstand the pressure and would collapse, and in such depth that the United States would find its support of repressive GVN measures so costly that it would choose to withdraw.

The NLF initially approached the entire Revolution not as a small-scale war but as a political struggle with guns, a difference real and not semantic. It maintained that its contest with the GVN and the United States should be fought out at the political level and that the use of

---

[6] An account of a March 19, 1950 incident in Saigon was written later, and broadcast by Radio Liberation on March 19, 1964, to provide a struggle movement heritage:

On that date [March 19] in 1950 a heroic example of the struggle movement was raised in Saigon. . . . A half million people went into the streets to shout "Down with the U.S. interventionists who seek an extension of the war." . . . "Down with the puppet traitors." . . . "U.S. imperialists go home." . . . Downtown Saigon was crowded with unsubmissive people. Students, schoolchildren, workers, teachers, writers, artists, doctors, lawyers, merchants, industrialists, civil servants, in other words all the beloved children of Saigon, regardless of political tendency, religion, or social class, closely united in the struggle to defend the Fatherland. Many soldiers and policemen of the colonialist and puppet regime sided with the people. Obeying the U.S. imperialists' orders, the warring French colonialists and their faithful lackeys pitilessly repressed and terrorized the compatriots . . . but despite their violence . . . these vanguard troops of the Fatherland moved forward and overwhelmed the cruel enemies. . . . U.S. cars were burned, U.S.-French colonialist and puppet flags were torn to pieces and trampled underfoot. . . . Roadblocks were set up.

massed military might was in itself illegitimate. Thus one of the NLF's unspoken, and largely unsuccessful, purposes was to use the struggle movement before the onlooking world to force the GVN and the United States to play the game according to its rules: The battle was to be organizational or quasi-political, the battleground was to be the minds and loyalties of the rural Vietnamese, the weapons were to be ideas; therefore military assaults, as opposed to the NLF's self-defense efforts, were beyond permissible limits of the game, and all force was automatically condemned as terror or repression. In such perspective the struggle movement obviously became a powerful weapon.

If the General Uprising was the great NLF social myth, the struggle movement was its great social fantasy. For here, with a backdrop of high drama, every man could fling himself into the hero's role. The young crusader could embark on a great quest and look the dragon Authority in the face with courage. To the timid old man, for all his life the Persevering Tortoise, came the moment of destiny when he could say to himself and all the world: "This one thing I do." Cinderella and all the other fools could still believe there was magic in the mature world if one mumbled the secret incantation: solidarity . . . union . . . concord. The meek, at last, were to inherit the earth; riches would be theirs and all in the name of justice and virtue. So out of their thatch-roofed houses they came, pouring through their villages and onto the highways of Vietnam, gullible, misled people, pawns of a vast and abstract power struggle, turning the countryside into a bedlam, toppling one Saigon government after another, confounding the Americans, a sad and awesome spectacle, a mighty force of people, a river the Communists hoped to use and then dam. This was the struggle movement.

Political Struggle

The political struggle movement operated on two levels. First, it sought intermediate goals. An early NLF document stated: "The struggle movement in rural areas should lessen enemy pressure, oppose military operations and terrorism, oppose the strategic hamlet and extortion, and halt the seizure of land, the corvée labor system, and the army draft." Another document of the same period declared: "The struggle movement in the . . . [people's] terms has four goals: economic betterment, democratic freedom, opposition to the U.S.-Diem warmongering, and unification. . . . Every struggle should attempt to attain these four goals."

The second level was an effort to engage, activate, and immerse the persons involved in the movement in the Revolution. Said the document just cited: "In all struggle movements bear in mind . . . the need to preserve and expand the various revolutionary organizations, train the people, give them struggle experience, draw lessons and learn from each struggle." A widely used cadre handbook entitled *Needs of the Revolution,*[7] dated July 1962, added: "Our [struggle movement] actions should be designed to influence the people in all walks of life in Vietnam and also abroad, thus gaining the support of the world population. All classes of people must be enlisted to take part in the struggle movement . . . , thus building a large resistance movement that includes the entire population and simultaneously indoctrinating the masses in the Front's policies." Still another directive, dated 1963, declared: "The political struggle . . . is the mobilization of the masses and the assertion of the strength of the revolutionary climate . . . with the masses moving deeply into the enemy's rear to struggle directly with enemy officials. . . . The forms and goals are firm, the masses bare-handed opposing the enemy's military force."

Originally the NLF assumed that the weak, chaotic government of Vietnam, already tottering, could be brought down solely by means of the struggle movement, a series of small-scale, deliberately created local anarchies throughout the rural areas. The theoretical base, and the indoctrinational cement that held this belief together, was the myth of the General Uprising. Engaging a rural Vietnamese in a specific struggle movement such as a demonstration or recruiting him into a guerrilla band imposed self-control on him. Commitment led to adherence, public acts developed self-discipline. The violence program played a vital but limited part in this effort. The guerrilla was important (the NLF employed the slogan "Be a guerrilla or support a guerrilla"), but the bulk of the NLF's day-to-day activity was in the political struggle, in the "people's war."

From a functional standpoint the NLF considered their struggle activities in the villages they controlled to be of two types: the coacting group, or what the NLF called the "meeting for propaganda in width," in which individual members were subjected to outside stimulus, and the face-to-face group, or what was called "the meeting for propaganda in depth," in which the members reacted to each other. The coacting group in turn was divided into various types of meetings for specific purposes:

1. The struggle meeting. This could be a village demonstration that began and ended in the village and was known as the "far from the enemy meeting"; or it could be a meeting that culminated in a struggle movement at a GVN administrative office or military post. Ideally it

---

[7] This printed booklet, which was in effect a handbook on the struggle movement, was frequently captured in NLF-controlled areas.

was a means to seize political control of the village, as outlined in this rather simplistic view:

The meeting is the chief device for motivating the people in the villages to throw out enemy control. Cadres and guerrillas go into a village, capture enemy spies, and hold a meeting of thousands of people to denounce the enemy. The people, supporting the move, destroy the enemy's control. At these meetings the cadres may speak only five or ten sentences, which satisfies the desires of the people. The people rise up. The cadres should not stop them or speak further.

However, there is little indication that such meeting results were common if indeed they occurred at all. In practice the struggle meeting did not differ greatly from the demonstration.[8]

2. The denunciation meeting or, as it was often called, the misery-telling meeting. This could be similar to the Chinese denunciation meeting or, as was more common in Vietnam, a meeting at which individuals arose and described their plight in life. A memorandum dated mid-1962 outlined two incidents from a typical denunciation meeting of the first type:

A Cao Dai priest from Tay Ninh lived in the area, and we had a grudge against him from the Resistance period. He was denounced as an enemy of the Revolution and driven out. In another village recently liberated, women stood up and denounced local men who had violated them; they were motivated by hate and wrath and did not feel shame to denounce them in public.

More commonly these consisted of villagers airing personal complaints or "denouncing" the life they led.

3. The ceremonial meeting. This was designed to commemorate an event or celebrate an NLF victory. In January 1962, at the time of the formation of the PRP, a directive went to all district cadres outlining in detail the staging of the village ceremony to commemorate the establish-

---

[8] The technique of the meeting of this type was outlined in *Needs of the Revolution*:

The demonstration [or struggle meeting] must aim at strongly promoting hatred, and this requires an assembly of several hundred people. The person who delivers the main speech must be well prepared and must [so arrange it] that at the end of his speech the masses will shout slogans expressing their determination to struggle. . . . Then leaders of various groups and organizations will come to the platform one by one and call on each of their groups to shout slogans. The atmosphere must be heated. Slogans should concentrate on one subject. Do not drag things on too long. Don't include an entertainment show, as is often done now, because this dilutes the significance of the struggle demonstration. A well-organized demonstration requires meticulous preparation, with objectives kept well in mind. The order of appearance on the platform must be carefully thought out. Also, have a plan to stir up the masses by first holding small group [face-to-face] meetings in hamlets and then staging a larger joint meeting. . . . In areas newly liberated it is necessary to hold continuous meetings to boost the revolutionary spirit. But in areas that have been liberated for a longer period they should be used sparingly. When held, they should be larger, including people from several villages. End these with a parade, which helps express the spirit of the Revolution.

ment of the PRP.[9] Its purpose, it said, was "to cause all people to appreciate the establishment of the PRP . . . and to create in all classes of people a strong image of the PRP. . . ."

4. The people's convention. The exact nature and purpose of this type of meeting is not clear. One document referred to it as "the highest form of democratic life of the people." Another warned cadres not to organize a struggle meeting and call it a people's convention "because a people's convention should include only people of the same social class." It listed the "four revolutionary classes of people: the workers, the peasant-farmers, the petite bourgeoisie [*tieu tu san*], and the national bourgeoisie [*tu san dan toc*]," stating that the people's convention should include either the first or second group but should not mix the two.

The face-to-face meeting actually was a combined indoctrination session and mutual-aid society gathering. Frequently cadres were criticized for making use of only coacting groups and underestimating the face-to-face group, defined as "meetings that assemble a small number of people, usually from three to five families but not more than 30 people, . . . at which there are long and deep political discussions aimed at promoting the struggle movement, . . . which seek to supply the masses with information about the success of the political and armed struggle throughout Vietnam . . . or which promote hate and resentment.[10] Instructions to cadres on the use of the social movement were extremely

[9] First, Party members were to meet privately, coin slogans to be used, and plan the day's events:

> The ceremony should be observed solemnly in a manner worthy of the PRP. . . . Each hamlet will erect a triumphal arch bearing the main slogan. . . . Other banners and slogans will be hung throughout the hamlet. . . . A grandstand will be constructed and various committees set up, such as the organization committee, order and security committee, protocol committee, first-aid committee, etc., . . . but do not display Front flags. . . . One comrade will act as master of ceremonies and read the speech, which will be supplied to you later. . . . When he has finished, representatives of the liberation associations and other groups are to come forward and express their appreciation for the PRP. . . . [Their remarks] should be written in advance, should be short and clear, and should stress faith in Party leadership and determination to pursue the Revolution. . . . After the ceremony a theatrical event or dragon dance may be performed. . . . Warning: At the ceremony keep the initiative and do not allow the people to ask too many questions. For instance, they may ask, "With the formation of the PRP does this mean the Lao Dong [Party] no longer exists?" or "What is the policy of the PRP?" or "What is the flag of the Party?" or "What is its relationship to the Front?" Since no directive on these matters has yet been issued, we are not qualified to answer such questions.

[10] *Needs of the Revolution* also said the face-to-face meeting should

> discuss the personal problems of members and convince members they can rely on the group for help. . . . For instance, provide economic help for the member who is ill or hard up; or, if a member has been arrested, organize a struggle to secure his release. . . . Discussions should also deal with the defense of the members' daily interests in class-consciousness terms. . . . Indulge in criticism and self-criticism to improve members' work. . . . Reward outstanding members and discipline those who neglect their duties. . . . Raise funds and recruit new members.

detailed, and no aspect, however small, was overlooked. For example, one directive even dealt with the matter of dress at a meeting:

People should be asked to wear clothes proper for the meeting, good clothes for a ceremonial meeting, solemn clothes at a struggle meeting, and old torn clothes at a misery-telling or denunciation meeting. . . . In one district women met to discuss the WIDF [Women's International Democratic Federation] resolution regarding colonialist oppression of women. Some women wore their best clothes and some wore poor clothes because they did not understand the purpose of the meeting.

One way of grasping the substance of a struggle demonstration is to inspect specific instructions to NLF cadres on its use. *Needs of the Revolution* directed that the cadres

1. Begin by investigating and studying the enemy situation, as well as our own. Evaluate the power balance between ourselves and the enemy. Bear in mind that the enemy will flatter the people and employ demagogic appeals. Search for contradictions in the enemy camp that may be exploited. Consider the various issues most likely to arouse public interest and cause the people to become militant. At all times evaluate realistically the capacity of the Revolution and the political strength of the people.

2. In preparing for the struggle: Seek to know the target (Who are they? What position do they hold? Whom are they in conflict with? Whom must we isolate?). Set clear purposes and realistic goals for the struggle in terms of the people's interests. Use realistic slogans that reflect the people's demands. Choose the form of struggle most suitable to the degree of enlightenment of the people. Use the correct forces from among the people, that is, those most directly involved. Choose individuals carefully, picking those who have the courage to deal with the enemy or who have the ability to win the sympathy of enemy officials and troops. Build up determination for the struggle. Use hard-core Party members to support the struggle (do not send them [to participate in the actual demonstration]), such as comforting the families of those engaged in the struggle or supplying food to those elements who are actually struggling. Set up a lead group that will be in the midst of the actual struggle (if absolutely necessary, include a covert Party member) to lead the struggle. Set up a guide group, which should be stationed a few hundred meters away from the struggle scene (this may include a Party member), to act as an adviser and to send messages to the lead group leader. Set up a third unit, the front group, made up of local sympathizers with high fighting morale, to meet and negotiate with the enemy. . . . Make plans to have other social groups support the struggle; one class supports the struggle of another class; strong areas support weak areas; cities support rural struggles; etc. This may be manifested by sympathy struggles, spreading rumors, sending gifts or letters, or even making visits. . . . Try to foresee the enemy's response and plan to counter the repressive measures taken by him. In large-scale and protracted struggles make plans to supply food to those who are struggling.

3. Agit-prop work preparing for the struggle. . . . Educate the people to understand the struggle; teach struggle techniques, how to reason with the enemy; also stress discipline, the importance of following the leaders and

avoiding imprudent violence or actions that may provoke the enemy. Make clear-cut assignments of responsibilities (who subverts whom, who does what, who is on the three committees, etc.).

4. When an incident or issue arises, cell leaders and cadres should meet and make plans, which include (a) arousing the people so they realize the necessity of a struggle; (b) gathering all social groups whose interests and aspirations are involved; (c) deciding the date and time of the struggle; (d) coining slogans and determining the forms of struggle (mass meeting, demonstration, petition, etc.); and (e) determining the struggle target (whether village officials, district, provincial, or central government authorities, army camps, etc.). In preparing for a struggle keep in mind that it will be successful when it brings material benefits to the people and at the same time (a) achieves for the Party a deeper influence of the Party with the people; (b) increases faith by the people in the struggle method by demonstrating their strength and making them confident in the struggle methods; (c) causes the enemy difficulties; (d) exposes the true face of the country-selling U.S.-Diemists; and (e) generally promotes the struggle movement, especially in the villages.

The above deals with the struggle where there is time and when conditions are proper for a relatively large-scale struggle. Daily there are opportunities for smaller struggles that may be staged without complete preparations. Party members should be prepared to take advantage of all opportunities to conduct struggles, large and small.

Actual conduct of the struggle movement consisted of clever, well-timed stage managing, the best of them approaching Giap's art form. During the struggle, said *Needs of the Revolution,*

1. Timing is most important. . . . Choose the right moment to launch [it] . . . [such as] that [conjunction of] the enemy committing a mistake and the population being in a state of preparedness . . . or when the people's rights have been endangered . . . by corruption, high taxation, forced money donations, land robbing, building strategic hamlets, forced membership in reactionary organizations, terror or killing, military draft. . . . Struggle movements can also be launched in favor of freedom to travel and work, freedom of trade, freedom to move to a new part of the country, and for village council elections. . . .

2. Use every form of struggle to create public opinion, . . . the demonstration, petition, complaint. The demonstration may use small or large groups, a few persons, several villages, or tens of thousands of people.

3. During the struggle follow the course of events closely. Observe the enemy's reactions and adopt measures to cope with these. Continue agitation among the militants during the struggle. Be flexible, change slogans if necessary, redistribute the struggle forces if required. If certain people on their own take initiative during the struggle, support them. . . .

4. The lead group should maintain full control over the struggle force at all times. It should maintain contact with the guide group. And the guide group must maintain close contact with the front group in the event enemy officials are willing to meet with them and negotiate. Party members should not be members of the front group, and if possible not members of the lead group.

5. Be prepared to withstand enemy violence. Block the enemy's attempt to arrest any of those in the struggle movement. Be alert to loss of morale or to disheartenment among the people. . . . If it develops, terminate the struggle immediately even if only minor successes have been scored.

6. After the struggle, withdraw quickly; do not allow the people to linger at the scene, as they may become victims of the enemy's retaliation.

Cadres were warned repeatedly against organizing a struggle movement for some light purpose, as in a mid-1962 internal document: "Although we must intensify and extend the face-to-face struggle, we should keep in mind the principle that a 'struggle must be justified, profitable, and kept within bounds.' Avoid having people tire, waste time, lose their lives or properties. Only in special circumstances should the struggle be extremely resolute and go as far as bloodshed."

The poststruggle assessment was all-important. After the struggle, said *Needs of the Revolution,*

1. Anticipate the enemy follow-up reaction and make plans to oppose any retaliation. Protect Party members and hard-core [NLF] sympathizers, or anyone whose identity has become known to the enemy during the struggle. Normalize the lives of the people after the struggle by means of some special event, a banquet, a musical program, or some sports competitions.

2. Evaluate the results of the struggle. Analyze the successes and shortcomings. Correct mistakes. Hold a meeting of those involved and discuss the struggle.

3. Within the Party evaluate our internal organization at a criticism and self-criticism session. Commend those who acted well; discipline the weak elements by giving them education and indoctrination. Enlist new members from the ranks of those who behaved well during the struggle.

4. After a large struggle, preserve its benefits and maintain the offensive by launching a series of continuous small-scale struggles.

Mistakes in the conduct of the struggle movement were apparently frequent and serious. A 1961 directive to district-level cadres listed some of the errors, the result of a series of self-criticism meetings:

1. We struggled against the wrong targets and struggled needlessly. . . .

2. We were impatient and venturesome and took precipitous actions. . . . In one struggle movement cadres led the people into tearing up their identity cards, burning government buildings, felling trees across the roads, and digging up roads.

3. In one area cadres caused the people to forbid all vehicles from traveling, . . . [which] shut down a Chinese rice mill and forced the people to husk their own rice. . . .

4. Many Party cadres came out of covert status and became overt . . . , a serious indiscretion. . . .

5. The term "traitor" was too loosely applied during struggles within villages; . . . there was no distinction made between landowners; all were regarded as enemies of the Revolution without taking into account their political concepts, not distinguishing between good and bad landowners. . . .

6. Failure to struggle against military units. . . .

7. In general, the struggle movement was treated too lightly, and cadres tried to cause the guerrilla units to do most of the work. . . .

8. Cadres did not accurately compare our strength with the enemy, . . . and struggles were easily dispersed by the enemy. Cadres did not agitate and propagandize properly, and the masses did not know what was expected of them.

The struggle movement, not the battle, was the payoff, the culmination of carefully nurtured efforts, the fruit of the labor. "Enthusiasm for revolution is not enough," warned one document, "we must know how to get the masses to struggle, for this is the way we conduct the Revolution."

The Violence Program

To the onlooking world Vietnam's agony of the 1960's appeared to result chiefly from guerrilla warfare, a misconception that this book seeks to correct. Guerrilla warfare, or in NLF terminology the "armed struggle," or what in the author's terms is the "violence program," was only that part of the revolutionary iceberg above water. It has been well and frequently described by American news media, and its pattern certainly is now familiar to those who followed events in Vietnam even casually during 1960–1965. Therefore we are not reviewing here guerrilla warfare in Vietnam but only those aspects that concern the general struggle movement and were part of a broader category, the violence program.

The rural Vietnamese climate of opinion, the availability of supplies and manpower, the inherent dangers involved in the use of force, as well as such abstractions as theoretical considerations, historical lessons, and grand strategy — all helped shape the character and dictate the scope of the NLF's violence program. Never treated as a separate entity, never conceived of in exclusively military terms, and at no time the chief prop of the Revolution, the armed struggle or violence program served to reinforce or make possible the other struggle activities — the *dich van, dan van,* and *binh van.* It was the hardener in the formula, the steel in the superstructure. The two hundred to five hundred "guerrilla incidents" per week that went on in Vietnam week after week and month after month for five years had no purpose in themselves — and indeed when viewed in themselves often made no sense — except to serve the political struggle movement. Thus the primary purpose of the violence program was to make possible the political struggle movement. One NLF document, dated October 1961, assessed the previous three months' work by declaring:

The best feature of the period is that we boldly coordinated the military activities with the political struggle. Because of our perseverance and because we used the correct antiterror measures, in many places the masses had the opportunity to stand up and struggle against the enemy. Reality proves that our policy of "pushing forward the political struggle closely and properly coordinated with the military activities" is the correct one.

At the same time the political struggle, especially in the early days, laid the groundwork for the later increased emphasis on the armed struggle movement. Said an early document:

These continual and strong struggles illustrate the indomitability and strong will of our compatriots in South Vietnam, . . . for they have helped mobilize, organize, and educate the masses so that the latter might be trained to increase their combat strength. . . .

The public rationale for the use of force was that the enemy had given the NLF no alternative. Said an early indoctrination booklet:

During the first years following the re-establishment of peace [post-1954] the people of South Vietnam engaged in a peaceful political struggle. But the warlike and terrorist policies of the enemy forced them to take up rifles and begin an armed struggle. . . . The U.S.-Diem clique uses collaborators, villains, spies, Self-Defense Corps members, and secret police agents to carry out fascist policies and to terrorize and suppress the people's political struggle. Thus it is necessary to have an armed force to counterattack the enemy's military units, destroy collaborators, villains, secret police agents, and spies, and efficiently support, preserve, and develop the political struggle. . . . Armed struggle is required (1) because the enemy's political weaknesses have forced him to resort to the force of arms to impose his will, and this must be countered; . . . (2) because armed struggle will enhance the political struggle; . . . and (3) because it prevents the enemy from mingling freely among the village masses, . . . helps isolate him and thins out his ranks. . . .

A later document outlined the three GVN "policies of force" that, it said, caused the NLF to use counterforce:

Since 1954 the U.S. imperialists and their lackeys have adopted the following principal measures with which we must cope . . . : (1) terrorism, including both the Denunciation of Communism [campaign] and anticommunism; (2) mopping-up operations and pacification efforts; (3) the national policy of strategic hamlets. . . .

Later, and chiefly for the benefit of cadres, justification for the use of violence added doctrinal correctness to necessity. Justification was never an easy matter for the NLF. The natural abhorrence by rural Vietnamese of systematic slaughter formed a major and continuing problem that the leadership constantly sought to overcome. Among NLF cadres, especially those recruited locally, unsophisticated and with great faith in the myth of the General Uprising, the use of force seemed both repugnant and unnecessary; even among more sophisticated cadres the belief was widespread that perhaps there was something to the General Uprising notion after all, that perhaps the NLF could win by the political struggle alone.

The response of the leadership to these reactions was to mix thoroughly the armed and political struggles and insist that the result was essentially political; and to administer, especially to cadres, massive doses of indoctrination "proving" that victory could be achieved only by measured use of force and violence. "We have learned," said a 1962 indoctrination booklet,

> that the only correct way to organize revolutionary forces and make preparations in all areas to smash the enemy's machinery of violence is to use the appropriate form of armed struggle. . . . In the beginning the people pursued the legal and illegal political struggle but soon discovered they were not strong enough or effective enough to prevent enemy mopping-up operations and the killing and imprisoning of people. Therefore from the masses' struggle movement there emerged a new struggle form, the armed struggle, and a new organization, the Liberation Army. Emergence of this new struggle form not only met an urgent demand but was an inevitable result of the revolutionary movement. It did not contradict the political struggle but supplemented it and paved the way for the political struggle to develop.

Increasingly and perhaps inevitably after mid-1963, the armed struggle moved to the forefront, tending to dominate the scene and push the political struggle into the background. An internal document of that period declared:

> We should urgently intensify the armed struggle to keep up with the political movement . . . and also intensify the guerrilla movement . . . and intensify combined operations of the three forces and attack the enemy continuously and everywhere. . . . The three forces should be built up proportionately. Only by building up the concentrated forces [NLF army] can we intensify the destruction of the enemy forces. But be careful not to build up the concentrated forces and neglect the guerrilla movement, . . . which means building combat hamlets and training self-defense forces. . . . In leading armed activities, be fully aware of the necessity of combining the military and political struggles to loosen enemy pressure, oppose military operations, oppose the strategic-hamlet program. . . . Organize attacks against the enemy in his rear areas to upset him. . . . Especially communication centers, warehouses, airports, and U.S. offices should be attacked by specialized forces and clandestine units. . . . Public utilities such as electricity producing plants are not to be sabotaged at this stage. . . .

There appeared to be several reasons for this shift. In the first place, armed combat was a GVN-imposed requirement; the NLF was obliged to use counterforce to survive. This resulted in the creation of guerrilla units with an ever-increasing military cast and a correspondingly improved military capability. As the units' military effectiveness increased and they began to deal serious blows to the ARVN, the argument was pressed that larger and more numerous guerrilla bands would mean more victories over the ARVN as well as a quicker ultimate victory. In short, a militarization cycle began. Second, reinterpretation of doctrine — especially by the Northern cadres, veterans of the more militarized Viet Minh war — placed greater stress on the armed struggle than before 1963. This was also a reflection of the increased DRV influence or intervention in the management of the Southern struggle. Reliable GVN intelligence reports indicate that in August and September 1963 at least two generals from Hanoi arrived in the highlands of the South to act as advisers, or possibly commanders, in the NLF's armed struggle movement. They were professional military, and their advice or orders had the effect of militarizing the looser, more self-contained guerrilla units and restructuring them into more traditional armed forces with more orthodox military assignments. The third reason was a general increase in the use of violence throughout the rural areas by the NLF. The bloom of revolution began to fade for the rural Vietnamese at the end of the Diem regime, and sympathy for the NLF diminished. This called for stricter and more forceful control measures by the NLF in its administration of the liberated area. Finally, in revolutionary guerrilla warfare a sort of Gresham's Law appears to be at work, under which violent acts tend to drive out political acts.

At any rate there is no doubt that the historical development of the NLF from 1960 to 1965 was characterized by a growing use of the armed struggle and by increased efforts to make its use more palatable in and out of the NLF ranks. Whereas to the NLF the Revolution during Diem's time had been essentially a political struggle, the Revolution against the post-Diem governments was basically an armed struggle.

Table 5-1 Estimate of NFL Acts of Violence, 1957–1965

Year	Total Number of Incidents	Military Attacks	Kidnapings	Assassinations
1957–1960	n.a.	negligible	2,000	1,700
1961	500	n.a.	n.a.	1,300
1962	19,000	13,000	9,000	1,700
1963	19,500	15,000	7,200	2,000
1964	25,500	15,500	1,500	500
1965	26,500	15,500	1,700	300

NOTE: Statistics of the sort that could yield precise listings of Viet Cong acts of violence have never been available in Vietnam. The figures given here are estimates based on careful study of data from GVN and U.S. sources.

Tables 5-1 and 5-2 provide estimates of NLF acts of violence and of the casualties in Vietnam that resulted from the step-up in the armed struggle.

Through its news media, the NLF constantly poured out statistics on

Table 5-2 Vietnamese Casualties, 1964 and 1965

Army of Vietnam (ARVN) Casualties

	1964	1965
Killed in action	7,064	11,333
Wounded in action	16,700	22,660
Missing in action	5,874	7,880

Viet Cong Casualties

	1964	1965
Killed in action	16,969	36,924
Wounded in action	(unknown — estimated as twice the KIA figure)	
Captured	4,178	5,986
Surrendered	1,982	9,264
Quy chanh	5,417	11,024

Total Casualty Rate

From 1960 to 1966, the total death rate in Vietnam was an estimated 280,000, or about 575 per week.

the armed struggle program, as illustrated by this Eastern Nambo report for the year 1963, broadcast by Radio Liberation on December 29, 1963:

In the first 11 months in Eastern Nambo we launched 2,662 major and minor attacks and put out of action 10,685 enemy, including 68 U.S. advisers killed and 10 wounded . . . , shot down 35 planes and damaged 63 others . . . , damaged seriously or destroyed 58 M-113 and M-118 amphibious vehicles, 15 bulldozers, 21 trucks, 9 boats . . . , and destroyed 88 military posts . . . , [and] seized 1,036 rifles, 74,000 bullets, 880 grenades, 810 mines. . . . Our compatriots rose up 1,342 times and damaged 491 strategic hamlets. . . . We liberated more than 55,000 compatriots . . . ; 1,060,000 compatriots attended meetings . . . ; and a total of 166,280 compatriots participated in 4,655 struggle movements with puppet authorities at all levels. . . . For its part . . . the enemy in 1963 launched 70,000 small and large mopping-up operations, killed 12,000 persons, wounded 81,000 persons, jailed 42,500 persons, and burned 57,000 homes. . . .

Such detailed and obviously inflated figures were poured out by the NLF media in a never-ending stream. They were so astronomically inflated that even percentage discounting became impossible. However, such tabulations as were made indicated an increased tempo in the armed struggle from 1961 to 1965, which actually did take place; they also indicated a certain scale of values and a set of priority interests of the NLF leadership: belief that the armed struggle was big, busy, and impressive; assertions that terrible damage was being inflicted on the GVN's military structure; indication that a primary goal of the program was the seizure of weapons; belief that American casualties deserved separate statistical treatment and were exaggerated,[11] probably for such psychological effect as they might have on the American public; finally,

[11] At least a fourfold exaggeration. U.S. combat deaths in Vietnam from 1960 to 1965 totaled approximately 300.

the NLF's preoccupation with the enemy's machines of war, particularly
the helicopter, by far the most serious military instrument the guerrilla
faced. This was acknowledged by the NLF, which declared in late 1964,
"The enemy now uses the airplane as a substitute for infantry. . . ."

A chief difficulty involved in insurgency and counterinsurgency statistics in Vietnam was that even if accurate they tended to mislead. This
arose from the problem of criteria for comparison. To be meaningful, for
example, the total number of ambushes per week would have to be compared with the total NLF ambush potential, which was obviously unknown, and with the number of ambushes thwarted during the same
period (which also might be unknown, as in the case of the ambush
leader deciding at the last moment that a convoy was too strong to ambush). Further, there would have to be a system for rating or grading
each ambush, for not all ambushes were the same and equal; damage to
either a specific operation or to the total system would have to be fixed.
In other words, not only was it necessary to compute the quantity of ambushes but it was also necessary to take the quality of each ambush into
account. Any attempt to do this immediately raised an infinite number of
imponderables leading to endless differences of opinion on criteria for
comparison. Yet the ambush was one of the more measurable types of
armed struggle incidents. How much more difficult it was, for example,
to extract objective meaning out of a total number of acts of harassment
or assassinations.

Doctrinal Problems

Two doctrinal problems concerning the violence program plagued the
NLF throughout the entire period. One concerned the propriety or the
efficacy of terror.[12] The other dealt with the ultimate role of the armed
struggle and could be framed in the form of a question: Given the special circumstances in South Vietnam and the U.S. response, should the
armed struggle eventually assume the burden of the Revolution, as
dictated by the Giap third-stage thesis, and climax the drive to power;
or should pursuit of the General Uprising continue, under which the
principal instrument would remain the political struggle, with the
armed struggle, although of increased importance, still a reinforcement
of the primary effort, the political struggle movement?

The great debate within the NLF leadership ranks was how to win,
not how to survive or how to deliver serious blows against the enemy but
how to cross the portals of victory. The NLF faced three choices in
writing the last act of the drama: the military ending, or third stage; the

[12] The NLF use of terror is discussed in Chapter 13.

social ending, or General Uprising; and the political-infiltration and take-over ending, or the negotiated settlement. All three were doctrinally acceptable. It was abundantly clear from both the nature of the NLF struggle movement and the priorities employed, as well as from NLF documents, that the early doctrinaires believed the General Uprising and not the Giap third-stage military assault would be the culmination of the action programs and deliver final victory. It is true that the Giap thesis of "first political struggle, then mixed political and armed struggle, then armed struggle, and finally again political struggle" continued as an ikon motif; but within this sort of generalized approach there was room for great latitude of interpretation. Among the earlier theorizers armed struggle was conceived of not as a military effort but as a series of violent actions, some of a military cast, that sought to achieve those goals that the political struggle movement could not achieve alone. The emergence of a military force for the purpose of fighting a more or less conventional war, similar to the final stages of the Viet Minh war, was considered highly risky and quite unnecessary. The Giap armed struggle phase was conceived of not as regiments or divisions openly confronting the enemy but as an explosion of small-unit acts of violence across the country. The end of the struggle then would be marked by a multitude of guerrilla-unit assaults, in unit force of perhaps 500 men, erupting simultaneously and in coordinated fashion throughout the country. ARVN revolts would break out in every unit as the result of the *binh van* movement. GVN officials would be assassinated in numbers. But most of all the people of the country, by the millions, would have taken to the streets in one grand struggle movement that would paralyze what remained of the GVN administrative and military power. This was the General Uprising, which could be accomplished without use of military or paramilitary units larger than a battalion.

Although victory by means of the military route, the third stage, had clear-cut models to follow — the Resistance and the Communist revolution in China — conditions in South Vietnam differed, and the third stage was fraught with danger. A number of internal NLF documents indicated grave doubts among the leaders about going the full route by means of military power. One secret document, dated 1963, after raising the question of whether American involvement meant that the NLF must increase its military activity, declared:

The enemy is carrying out a real war against our people, but we should not change the course of our struggle and shift to an all-out war to achieve our revolutionary task. To do so would not be advantageous to us, for we would then not make full use of our people's strength and capacity for struggle. We must simply intensify the armed struggle as well as the political struggle. In combination these two forms of struggle will be used to repulse the enemy step by step and to develop the conditions as well as enable us to defeat the enemy completely.

The General Uprising was the social myth and was not necessarily inconsistent with either the third stage or the political settlement; in the event of the first, the uprising would of course enhance the final military plunge; in the event of the second, an uprising would improve the NLF position in negotiations. In either case the enemy would be weakened.

The political settlement or negotiated ending of hostilities as a prelude to infiltration and take-over struck most indigenous Southern NLF cadres as far more feasible than the third stage. The author of the document just cited obviously favored such a course, for later in the document he wrote:

Our political struggle is the manifestation of our absolute political superiority and of the enemy's basic weakness. It demonstrates our strength and capacity for initiative. It aggravates the enemy's basic weakness, curtails his military superiority, and strengthens our cause. It is dangerous to underestimate the importance of the political struggle. To do so is to abandon an efficient weapon, a powerful force. The political struggle contributes to producing long-lasting effects. When important developments occur, as the result of the Revolution's strength, the place of the political struggle may transcend all others — for instance, in the case of negotiations, a cease-fire, and so forth.

Publicly the NLF asserted from its earliest days that it favored the formation of a coalition government in which it would participate. The assertion was dismissed by the GVN as insincere. Internal documents, however, insisted this could and should be the NLF goal.[13]

The following, dated March 1963, was typical:

What is the immediate task of the Revolution? It is to unite the entire nation, resolutely struggle against the U.S. aggressive and bellicose imperialism; smash the Ngo Dinh Diem dictatorial ruling clique, servant of U.S. imperialism; set up a democratic national coalition administration in South Vietnam; realize independence, democratic freedoms, and improvement of the people's living conditions; safeguard peace; and achieve national reunification on the basis of independence and democracy. . . .

The NLF originally saw itself primarily as an agency of social control, not as a military force. It sought to channel rural Vietnamese activities in certain directions and in line with its own purposes. Its control instruments were individuals, especially the natural leaders in villages, the so-called influentials; institutionalized organizations, the various liberation associations and special-interest groups; and social pressure, that is, its own social norms and mores. Its social inducements included superiority in the form of praise, flattery, and prestige; and deterrents were in

[13] For a fuller discussion of the NLF coalition government goal see Chapter 19.

the form of punishment, coercion, social ostracism, humiliation, physical injury, or death. The process of social control was suggestion and example, argument, persuasion and exhortation, inducement, deterrence, encouragement, and discouragement. These were the social bases for its efforts. In its revolutionary guerrilla warfare a three-pronged attack was employed: the political, use of the united front; the social, fomenting and instigating class strife; and the violence program, use of paramilitary and military war, assassinations, and various other acts of violence. The instrument throughout was the organization. Now this gigantic effort suggested something far beyond the traditional three stages of revolutionary guerrilla warfare. It suggested strongly that the ultimate objective was not Stage Three but, assisted perhaps by the General Uprising, assumption of power by means of the conference table.

The advent of what the NLF called Special War, which is to say the U.S. military response, raised the question of whether victory could be delivered as it had in the Viet Minh war or by means of a political settlement. The matter split the NLF leadership. We know from *quy chanh* and captured NLF documents that in 1964 an open division occurred at the Central Committee level and perhaps higher, in which the then dominant doctrine of the General Uprising was openly questioned. Defending it were the original NLF founders and the older more indigenous elements from the South; in opposition to it were the regulars from the North. The first group held that an intensification of the *dich van* and *binh van* programs, and perhaps with a step-up in the armed struggle, eventually could completely destroy the GVN's administrative and military apparatus, and thus a frontal assault would never be necessary. The regular cadres from the North held for increased militarization of the effort, a calculated military challenge to the ARVN, and greater emphasis on military assaults, including assaults on exclusively American military installations in Vietnam. For a time, as the debate raged, the armed sruggle took on a schizoid character: NLF activities for a few weeks would be predominantly military, then switch to political approaches, and then back to military actions.

The heart of this debate was whether it would be possible to win through to victory in revolutionary guerrilla warfare by means of the political and armed struggles, whose basic objectives were mobilization of the civilian population and attrition, and immobilization but not physical destruction of the enemy's military establishment. There could be no doubt that the organizational weapon could carry a revolution far, to the gates of victory in fact. But there was great doubt that it could carry the cause over the threshold. A number of recent revolutions have succeeded without involving a full rebel military confrontation with the country's armed forces. Algeria and perhaps Cuba are the chief examples, but the Indonesian and Tunisian revolutions also serve to illustrate the point. In all four cases, to varying degrees, the revolutionaries bypassed the military, negated its effectiveness, and either shunted it off or won it over without a showdown. Both Mao and Giap, of course, adamantly insisted that no revolutionary guerrilla war could end as a guerrilla war, that it must evolve into a more or less conventional war in which the opposing armed forces are defeated or destroyed in direct combat. In the end the Northerners won the NLF debate, and military activities increased in scope, tempo, and nature. The new approach resulted in a new American response: air strikes against North Vietnam and the dispatch of overwhelming numbers of American troops to South Vietnam. The outcome of the NLF doctrinal debate was the fatal decision to slug it out militarily with the United States, a battle that the Liberation Army, even aided by large numbers of regular troops from North Vietnam, could not hope to win.

6

Organization Building

Introduction

The central fact about Vietnam is the village. For two thousand years it has been so, and although the two cities of Saigon and Hanoi may have been regarded abroad as Vietnam, to the Vietnamese the village was his land's heart, mind, and soul. Surrounded by its high bamboo hedge, itself possessing a mystic quality, the village has bound the inhabitants into close communal and kinship relationships and, at the same time, separated them from the rest of the world. It was a haven and a defense. When he left, a villager was expected to return in pilgrimage each lunar new year; and no matter how far he traveled or how long he stayed away, his village was always home, and there he wished to be buried.

Vietnamese villages vary greatly: There is the long narrow village strung out, one house wide, along a canal in the Mekong delta; the village of houses widely scattered through the deep shadows of a rain forest in the Massif Plain; the ancient village of Central Vietnam with its worn paths and closely grouped houses; the sun-baked village in the near-desert country of the west; the fishing village, resolutely turning its back on the land in favor of the South China Sea. Some were rich, a few poor, but almost all enjoyed a basic self-sufficiency. Life within the village may have been simple, but it was good.

To the 2,561 villages of South Vietnam, where live two thirds of the people, came the Communists, openly or behind a front, determined to turn each village into an instrument for revolution, a drive aimed not at the people as individuals so much as at the village as a unit. The Southern village was weak and vulnerable to this kind of assault, and assistance to it was not always dependable or appropriate. But the village showed surprising reserves and unexpected strengths. The village became the battleground in a peculiar kind of struggle, part political, part military, and wholly social.

Forging the Weapon

The NLF reversed the usual order for front formation: Instead of beginning with the organizations and creating the front, it began with the front and created the organizations and then assigned them the task of engaging in revolution through the mechanism of the struggle movement. Unlike the Viet Minh, the NLF did not grow from a small to a large organization; the NLF created on paper a nationwide network of village associations and then proceeded to turn this paper structure into reality. For this reason NLF references to obviously nonexistent organizations in the 1960–1962 period led Vietnamese and Americans in Vietnam to believe that the NLF was only a phantom edifice created for propaganda purposes. But all the while the dephantomizing was going on.

What the NLF created was not just one but a host of nationwide sociopolitical organizations in a country where mass organizations, as opposed to religious movements or elitist political parties, were virtually nonexistent. This is a significant point. Aside from the NLF there has never been a truly mass-based political party in South Vietnam. The two largest political parties — the Greater Vietnam Party (Dai Viet) and the Vietnamese People's Party (Viet Nam Quoc Dan Dang) — have never had more than a thousand members each by admission of their own leaders. (In July 1964 more than 67 "political tendencies" were identifiable in Saigon.) Although even the Communists did not have a mass organization in keeping with Communist organizational theory, they were, as Milton Sacks wrote of the earlier Communist party in Vietnam, "the most persevering, most cohesive, best-disciplined, and most experienced political group in Viet Nam." [1] That heritage was passed on to the National Liberation Front.

[1] I. Milton Sacks, in Frank N. Trager, ed., *Marxism in Southeast Asia* (Stanford, Cal.: Stanford University Press, 1959), p. 166.

Four years of tireless effort, from 1959 through 1962, converted the NLF organizational structure from a loose, disparate collection of dissident groups, often with nothing more in common than hostility for the Diem government, into a tightly knit movement able to demonstrate a coordinated efficiency rare in a developing nation. That this machine was assembled secretively, by night, in the remote back country makes it even more impressive, although it has been argued that its nocturnal, clandestine nature helped to ensure its success. The formative years were lean indeed. The apparatus withstood the threat of constant betrayal in a land where betrayal is the norm. It developed support in the infertile soil of suspicious and cynical rural Vietnamese society. It absorbed a reeling blow to its morale, the announcement in late 1961 that the United States, the most powerful nation on earth, had decided to come to the aid of its enemy, the government of the Republic of Vietnam.

Beginning in 1960 the NLF grew into a structure that reached to some degree into virtually every village in the country. In the NLF-controlled areas it threw a net of associations over the rural Vietnamese that could seduce him into voluntarily supporting the NLF or, failing that, bring the full weight of social pressure to bear on him, or, if both of these failed, could compel his support. It could subject him effectively to surveillance, indoctrination, and exploitation. It could order his life. It could artificially create grievances and develop voluntary support where logically such support ought not to have been forthcoming.

The purpose of this vast organizational effort was not simply population control but to restructure the social order of the village and train the villagers to control themselves. This was the NLF's one undeviating thrust from the start. Not the killing of ARVN soldiers, not the occupation of real estate, not the preparation for some great pitched battle at an Armageddon or a Dien Bien Phu but organization in depth of the rural population through the instrument of self-control — victory by means of the organizational weapon. The Communists in Vietnam developed a sociopolitical technique and carried it to heights beyond anything yet demonstrated by the West working with developing nations. The National Liberation Front was a Sputnik in the political sphere of the Cold War.

The Village Level

It was in the Vietnamese village[2] that the NLF faced its moment of truth. Here organizational theory came starkly against reality, and the

[2] The Vietnamese word for village is *xa* (sometimes *xom*), and the word for hamlet is *ap* (as in strategic hamlet, *ap chien luoc*). Their usage causes considerable confusion to Americans. To a Westerner the word "hamlet" implies a small cluster of houses sur-

neatness of the organization at the higher levels began to give way to the vagaries and flux of village life. It was one thing to set up and control a six-man provincial secretariat and quite another to energize and direct the thrust of a mass movement composed of distrusting and reluctant Vietnamese farmers. To meet the need, two systems of liberation associations were developed, one of which might be called administrative and the other functional.

The Administrative Liberation Association

The administrative liberation association was elite, narrow, and relatively easy for cadres to control. It resembled a vertical governmental organization running from the NLF Central Committee down through a number of intervening administrative levels to the village administrative liberation association,[3] which was also headed by a committee. This was the "shadow" government of Vietnam to which news stories often refer.

The administrative liberation association had its genesis in the Viet Minh experience; its forebears were the administrative and resistance committees conceived and established by Ho Chi Minh. A SORO study describes them:

On various administrative levels, from the small village to larger units, the Viet Minh administered the areas not under French control through "Committees for Resistance and Administration," which tightly controlled all political, economic, and social activities of the Vietnamese population. This cellular structure of the government had the advantage of being decentralized and flexible while at the same time allowing the decisions taken by the Central Committee to be rigidly enforced at all levels down to the smallest village.[4]

Part of the administrative liberation association structure, the key part in fact, was the upward chain of command. Specifically this consisted of the following levels, all part of the administrative liberation association hierarchy:

---

rounded by fields or woods. An *ap chien luoc* was sometimes as large as forty miles in circumference with as many as 75,000 people, which made it more than a hamlet to the Westerner. The Vietnamese hamlet was more like the American "rural precinct," that is, houses and farm buildings dotted across the landscape and separated by open farmland. The village, or *xa*, was two or more hamlets, similar to the American "township." In fact, some Vietnamese translators have tried to employ the terms rural precinct and township for *ap* and *xa*, but this has merely compounded the confusion. Usage here is hamlet for *ap* and village for *xa*, but the reader should bear in mind that these units often were far larger than their English terms connote. (There are currently in South Vietnam 14,023 hamlets combined in 2,561 villages.)

[3] The NLF village administrative system is discussed in more detail in Chapter 12.

[4] The American University, Special Operations Research Office (SORO), *Case Studies in Insurgency and Revolutionary Warfare: Vietnam 1941–1954* (Washington, D. C., 1964), p. 94.

1. At the top, the National Liberation Front Central Committee, the policy formation unit that was also responsible for planning and supervising the organization building.

2. Three interzone headquarters, at which (after 1963) the agit-prop policy was determined, which were responsible for indoctrination and training.

3. Seven zones, in effect suboffices for the interzones, existing mainly because travel and communication barriers did not easily permit administrative directives directly from the interzone headquarters to the provinces.

4. Approximately 30 provincial committees,[5] the chief operational units of the NLF, with the task of administering the liberation associations and assigning military duties to local guerrilla units.

5. The lower echelons — district, village, and town committees and organizations carrying out the political struggle, the military proselyting task, and the armed struggle.

The Functional Liberation Association

The functional liberation association[6] was mass based, more sociopolitical than governmental; it was large, unwieldy, difficult to control once organized, but full of promise. These associations existed only at the village level and, unlike the administrative liberation associations, were horizontal rather than vertical. A hierarchic system of functional liberation associations did exist on paper, theoretically reaching to the national level in the form of congresses, but these congresses never met. Of the six functional liberation associations, the NLF leadership considered three to be of prime importance: the Farmers' Liberation Association (FLA), the Youth Liberation Association (YLA), and the Women's Liberation Association; the others, the liberation associations of students, workers, and intellectuals (the latter usually called the Cultural Liberation Association), were of somewhat less importance. By far the most important was the Farmers' Liberation Association (in Vietnamese, Hoi Nong Dan Giai Phong). Said an early internal FLA document:

> The Farmers' Liberation Association is the most essential organization for revolutionary activities in rural areas, and various echelons must develop and consolidate it. Meanwhile, attention should also be given to youth and women's associations.

All the functional liberation associations had the common objective of binding their members together for two purposes: to help one another

---

[5] At this writing, mid-1966, there are 43 provinces in South Vietnam; not all provinces had provincial committees.

[6] See Chapter 10 for a more detailed discussion of the NLF functional liberation associations.

in the tradition of the Vietnamese protective association and to engage in the political struggle. All associations had a minimum age limit of 16 years. Members were required to participate actively in the struggle movement and accept associational discipline. In return they were granted the right of freedom of discussion and secret vote at association meetings and the use of the association's library and emergency loan fund. The principle of "democratic centralism" prevailed, and the unit of organization at the lowest level was the natural social or occupational group.

The functional liberation association also developed from the Viet Minh, who had, as Donald Lancaster noted, enmeshed the population in a whole series of special associations

based on the possession of a common occupation, profession, or sex, and were again controlled by Communist cadres who arranged for frequent meetings at which the attitude and behavior of individual members were often the subject of debate. The activities of these associations thus completed the mobilization of the physical and moral resources of the community, while the inquisitorial methods employed to discipline members provided the authorities with an additional means of controlling a potentially restive population.[7]

The French called these associations "parallel inventories," and they were ubiquitous, ranging from general types such as farmer or youth groups to organizations as specialized as a flute-players' association, all existing for indoctrination and propaganda work.

Organizational Phases

The organizational approach taken by the NLF leaders probably was the only route open to them that promised much success. One should not suppose, however, that the Communists in Hanoi started with a packaged program; there is no evidence of a *Mein Kampf* for Vietnam. Further, a mass movement like a revolution tends to develop a logic of its own, and much of the NLF organizational decision-making over the years was a reaction to the exigencies of the situation. Nevertheless three phases are clearly discernible in the development of the NLF organization after 1960.

The first phase, the initial organizing period, was discussed in Chapter 4. In general it was characterized by a polarization around the NLF flag of all opposition to the Diem government and by a tremendous growth of the NLF organization. A word might be appropriate here on

[7] Donald Lancaster, *The Emancipation of French Indochina* (London, New York, Toronto: Oxford University Press, 1961), p. 421.

what is known about the growth of the NLF during its first six years of life. By studying NLF documents and by making some educated guesses we can conclude that the membership of the NLF doubled in size between December 1960 and early 1961, doubled again by late 1961, and by early 1962 had doubled once more. Thus its period of most rapid growth was late 1961 and early 1962, a growth that appears to have been the result of intensive organization-building activity rather than any external political factor as, for example, actions by the Diem government. By early 1962, NLF membership strength stood at about 300,000, and it remained at about that level until the fall of the Diem regime, when it dropped by perhaps 50,000 or 100,000. During 1965 and 1966 it stood at between 250,000 and 300,000. (For what it is worth, Radio Hanoi on December 19, 1963 claimed that the NLF comprised 30 organizations and 7,000,000 members.)

Following the initial activities came the growth and expansion phase, which ran from December 1960 — when the NLF organizing congress was convened — to the formation of the admittedly Communist organization, the People's Revolutionary Party, on January 1, 1962. This period saw the creation of the nationwide network of functional liberation associations and a solidifying of the NLF hierarchic chain of command, the administrative liberation association structure. The first major functional organization created under the NLF umbrella was the Farmers' Liberation Association, and on it was concentrated the NLF's effort during most of 1961. Then other major functional liberation associations were created, after which, in late 1961, efforts were focused on the administrative system, in which the leadership of the various functional liberation associations at the village level were combined in the administrative NLF village liberation association central committee. The pattern was to create separate functional liberation associations at the village level, then to create cross-organizations such as special-interest groups, and finally to mold the leadership of the individual organizations together into an administrative NLF village liberation committee.

The internal strengthening phase ran from the formation of the People's Revolutionary Party in January 1962 to the end of the Diem regime[8] (actually to about August 1963, when it became obvious to the Communists and others that the Diem government was disintegrating). By the end of 1961 the basic organizational work was completed, but it was a shaky structure. Then began the refinement process, the attention to detail, that yields perfection. This involved not only weeding out less competent cadres and raising entrance qualifications but also injecting more Marxism into the bloodstream of the organization. The danger that the NLF might succumb to mere reformism grew increasingly with

[8] Diem was overthrown on November 1, 1963.

the prospect of the Diem government's downfall. The leadership there-fore ordered increased indoctrination efforts aimed at offsetting such a result from a change in the Saigon government.

The period also witnessed, in late 1962 and early 1963, a major crisis for the NLF, the growth of the GVN's strategic-hamlet program. This program not only forced NLF village leaders to flee but it offered alter-native social and political organizations to the villagers. It eliminated the village as a base for guerrilla support. Moreover, since the program re-located villagers and thus mixed people from different villages, efforts by NLF agents to rebuild the network inside the strategic hamlet became increasingly complicated and less successful. It was difficult for an agent to get into and operate inside a strategic hamlet, and the leadership could no longer simply send back to a village that was being organized a na-tive whose only recommendation was that he had been born and raised there. Previously this had been the pattern, and even though the agent was untrained he was relatively successful since he dealt mainly with relatives and friends and needed only limited organizational skill. But in a mixed village the organizers faced strangers, and dealing with them required organizational and persuasive talents and skills that most of them did not possess. The drain on organizational and recruiter man-power was great, and the difficulties faced by the NLF grew steadily.

The Northern take-over, or regularization, phase began in mid-1963, when it was obvious to all that the Diem government was doomed, and continued to the end of 1965, when the NLF was taken over by cadres from North Vietnam and managed by them even down to the village level. It began with the clash between Diem and the Buddhist hierarchy, which, as it grew, confronted the NLF leadership with the prospect that its chief propaganda target, Diem, soon would be deposed.

Of course the NLF leadership had anticipated a change of government earlier, at least as early as February 1962, when two pilots from the Vietnamese air force bombed the Presidential Palace in Saigon and nearly killed Diem. Shortly thereafter the NLF leadership quietly began weeding out of key positions those whom they considered unreliable, chiefly members of the Cao Dai sect. Had the attack on Diem's life been successful the NLF probably would have split, Northern cadres versus indigenous Southerners. But, given warning, the leadership was able to regularize the organization so that when Diem was overthrown the NLF went through a traumatic shock but did not split.

It is ironic that during this period, as discontent in South Vietnam spread, the NLF, which had for so long stood as the only organized op-position to Diem, began to find its support dwindling. Suddenly every-one — intellectuals, Buddhists, students, the junior military — all were en-gaged in antigovernmental organization work, breaking the NLF monopoly on such activity. Those who had joined the NLF because it was the only viable anti-Diem organization found themselves surrounded by anti-Diem organizations. The result was defection from the NLF reaching almost mass proportions. Nearly 15,000 members of the NLF returned to the government under the amnesty program in the last half of 1963. It is estimated that NLF strength shrank from 300,000 to perhaps as low as 200,000, with the low point being reached in August 1963, at the moment when the Diem government's repressive measures were most severe.

The NLF leadership had probably anticipated a loss of popular support, for in early 1963 well-known old-line Communist cadres of the Viet Minh days, who had gone North, appeared for the first time at the provincial level and in August and September at the village level. Many were native to the villages to which they returned. They were frank with their old friends, freely admitting that they had been living in the North and had come South to help organize the Party at the village level and regularize the NLF. These cadres came not as VIP's but to stay and work, often at rather menial tasks;[9] in few cases could their activity be termed strategic. Usually they lived in the jungle around a village, or hidden by villagers when ARVN soldiers came. In some cases they acted as advisers to the provincial or district committees; in others they assumed a more authoritarian role, something like a political commissar. These precautions proved well advised, for the Diem demise placed terrible tensions and strains on the NLF. Its basic rationale had been "down with the U.S.-Diem clique." Diem, the NLF's personification of evil, was a theme of great strength but, because man is mortal, one of great weakness as well.

The regularization process — weeding out unreliables from the organization — was completed in practical terms in the first six months, but the effort continued and indeed at this writing in mid-1966 is still continuing. The successful take-over of the organization by Northern cadres, together with deeper American involvement, changed the face first of the NLF and then of the entire insurgency effort.

To summarize NLF organization building, first a skeleton was constructed, then flesh was added to the bones, then the muscle tissue was added, and finally the brain was installed; the blood of doctrinal belief was infused throughout the process. Surrounding this command-operational structure was the organizational structure, the system of liberation

[9] A Communist practice known in Vietnam as "sent to work at lower levels" (*ha tang cong tac*). The first appearance of Communist cadres at lower levels was regarded by Vietnamese observers as evidence of a power struggle within the Communist apparatus in which the losers were exiled to the hinterland. However, as the phenomenon increased in frequency and regularity, it became apparent that there could not have been that many losers.

associations running from the national Central Committee to the village. Within the structure was the People's Revolutionary Party, successor to the Lao Dong Party, the Communist apparatus, also running from the national Central Committee, apparently all the way to the village but certainly as far as the provincial level. To form a mental picture of this structure, imagine a broad-based pyramid, which was the people of Vietnam. Inside this pyramid was a second, narrower pyramid running from base to apex, the National Liberation Front. Inside this second pyramid was a third one, even more slender and also running, but as the core, from base to apex, the Communist apparatus — the PRP.

7

Communication of Ideas

The three basic means by which ideas are more or less systematically communicated are mass media, such as radio, television, newspapers, magazines, books;[1] the so-called informal channels of communication — word of mouth, rumor, gossip, itinerant peddlers; and social movements or social organizations, in which the organization itself — for example, a church or the Boy Scouts — acts as the channel, communicating not only ideas but also facts, data, and value judgments. The NLF used all three but relied on the third, the social movement, as its chief medium of communication.[2] It is with this phenomenon, together with one other Communist communication device — the agit-prop cadre — that we are chiefly concerned here.

In a sense it is false and misleading to treat the NLF's communication effort as a separate entity. In truth, almost every act of the NLF was con-

[1] See the author's monograph *Viet Cong Communication Techniques* (Cambridge, Mass.: Massachusetts Institute of Technology, Center for International Studies, 1966; No. C/66–11), which treats in some detail the methods employed by the NLF in communicating its ideas. For a much shorter version of this monograph see the author's *Vietnam: Communication Factors of Revolutionary Guerrilla War* (Cambridge, Mass.: Massachusetts Institute of Technology, Center for International Studies, 1965; No. C/65–16).
[2] NLF mass media are considered in Appendix B.

119

ceived as an act of communication. Its use of the communication matrix went beyond the normal social role as understood elsewhere. Its communication system not only communicated information, explained it in meaningful terms, and provided it with a value judgment based on individual relevancy — the more or less traditional communication function — but it also shaped a communication weapon and used it to strike at the vitals of the GVN. Its victories and defeats were essentially the result of successful or unsuccessful communication efforts.

Theory of Communication

The general characteristics of the NLF communication process were these:

1. The specially created social movements, such as the various liberation associations, became the primary vehicles for communication. Their activities were managed directly or indirectly by the agit-prop cadres and workers using both traditional channels, such as word-of-mouth and face-to-face communication, and mass media, the latter chiefly designed as a reinforcement.

2. Using this *apparat,* a theoretical formula was employed that first established a claim to truth in terms of basically rational appeals. This was not a full-blown ideology, Marxism or any other, so much as it was the conversion of specific ideas into actions and the transformation of abstract concepts such as nationalism into social levers. Second, using nonrational appeals, the emotions of the villagers were tapped, and passions, chiefly hatred (see Chapter 15), were generated. Third, a commitment to action was demanded, even if only a token act or gesture.

3. The Communist concept of communication predominated, with the Chinese rather than the Soviet experience serving as the model. As in China, great premium was placed on mass psychological techniques such as rallies, demonstrations, parades, movements (similar to China's "Back to the Countryside" movement), group criticism and individual denunciation campaigns, neighborhood and work meetings, and other forms of organizational communication, often with the mass social organizations acting as media.

4. The communication of ideas was viewed not as a separate act but as an integral part of the Revolution; communication was a seamless web. It was based on the orthodox Communist distinction between agitation and propaganda, derived from the famous Plekhanov (and Lenin) distinction between an agitator as one who presents only one or a few ideas to a mass of people and a propagandist as one who presents many

ideas to one or a few persons; this approach was necessary, it was held, because the masses could not be expected to understand Marxism-Leninism but nevertheless must be imbued with the proper spirit so that they would work and sacrifice for the cause. Propaganda thus consisted of theoretical indoctrination through which Party members were armed with scientific knowledge of the laws that govern society, or almost the exact opposite meaning of the word as used in non-Communist countries. In functional terms, agit-prop[3] activities were conceived as a servo-mechanism by means of which the rural Vietnamese were indoctrinated with a certain set of values and beliefs as the necessary first step, the formation of the masses into an organizational weapon. It was often reiterated in internal documents, as in the following PRP statement:

Agit-prop work is directed at the masses, for the benefit of the masses, and must involve the masses doing propaganda work under Party guidance. Thus the propaganda target is the masses, and the propaganda force is also the masses, but in the second case the masses are organized and educated by the Party in associations, groups, organizations, etc. . . .

5. Although communication efforts were conducted simultaneously on various levels and with differing and often contradictory themes, the key communicator at all levels was the agit-prop cadre. He was no mere technician but one who sat at the highest policy determining levels and who at the lower echelons tended to dominate all activities, not just agit-prop work. He was regarded as an instructor who explained NLF policies and programs in terms the ordinary rural Vietnamese could understand, using whatever arguments seemed most likely to be effective. Mass media, where they did exist, were never regarded as strong enough in themselves to convince the unconvinced.

---

[3] Originally the standard term for agit-prop in Vietnamese was *tuyen huan,* a contraction of *tuyen truyen,* meaning propaganda, and *huan luyen,* literally, training, but more precisely agitation in the Communist sense. Beginning in mid-1962 the NLF started using the term *tuyen van giao,* usually abbreviated as TVG, a contraction of *tuyen truyen* (propaganda), *van nghe* (meaning culture or letters and arts or literature and the fine arts, similar to the French *beaux arts et belles lettres* or *la littérature et les beaux arts,* but with a Confucian literary overtone), and *giao duc* (meaning education or, in the Marxist sense, indoctrination). After mid-1962 the NLF generally employed the TVG term, and the GVN continued to refer to these activities as *tuyen huan,* or agit-prop; at the same time the NLF continued to use the term *chinh tri* (political) *tuyen truyen* or, roughly, political propaganda. The significant difference is that TVG referred to communication activities within the NLF system, the liberated area, and among the masses, and *chinh tri tuyen truyen* connoted activities directed against the GVN. In order to maintain this distinction, the only important one to the reader, and to simplify reference as much as possible, the term agit-prop is used here to mean cadre TVG activities and the word propaganda by itself to mean those mass activities that are part of the struggle movement and designed to influence the enemy. Since at the lower echelons virtually all communication activity was in the hands of a single individual, the agit-prop (or TVG) cadre, this oversimplification of usage cannot be regarded as particularly serious. What must be borne in mind, however, is the distinction between the *agit-prop* (or TVG) work by the cadres seeking to motivate the masses and the *propaganda* work by the masses themselves as part of their struggle movement.

6. Although the successes of the communication program were not due to its Marxist content so much as to its pragmatic arguments, the appeals were rooted in fundamental Communist doctrine: the united-front concept, class consciousness, and the historically determined inevitable triumph of the cause. Contamination of the communication system was reduced by requiring cadres to use Radio Liberation and Radio Hanoi as basic sources of material and by postcommunication audits at higher levels.

7. The NLF communication system suffered from standard Communist communication weaknesses: obtuseness, formalism, irrelevancy, and ultraconformity.

This summary and the following sections on social movements as communication devices and on agit-prop work were taken from two key documents that fell into GVN hands in mid-1962. The first was an NLF document entitled *Directive on Information, Propaganda, Agitation, and Cultural Activities for 1961.* It was written at the Central Committee level for use at the provincial level and contained an analysis of GVN rural communication efforts, an assessment of the rural climate of opinion, a critique of NLF communication efforts during 1961, and a master plan for its communication work during 1962. The second, a PRP document entitled *Training of Propaganda, Cultural, and Educational Workers at the District and Village Levels,* was prepared for lower-echelon agit-prop cadres and dealt with specific agit-prop techniques and organization, the staffing of agit-prop and armed propaganda teams, and the use of culture and education (or indoctrination).

The first document was highly theoretical, the second concrete and practical. Taken together, they portrayed the full range of the NLF-PRP communication process; dozens of other documents, as well as more than 4,000 NLF propaganda leaflets subsequently collected, illustrated in detail the basic concepts outlined in the two major directives. Both documents stressed the importance of agit-prop work. The PRP cadre directive outlined it in specific terms:

> Daily the masses are oppressed and exploited by the imperialists and feudalists and therefore are disposed to hate them and their crimes. But their hatred is not focused; it is diffuse. The masses think their lot is determined by fate. They do not see that they have been deprived of their rights. They do not understand the purpose and method of the Revolution. They do not have confidence in us. They swallow their hatred and resentment or resign themselves to enduring oppression and terror, or, if they do struggle, they do so in a weak and sporadic manner. For all these reasons agit-prop work is necessary to stir up the masses, to make them hate the enemy to a high degree, to make them understand their rights and the purpose and method of the Revolution, and to develop confidence in our capability. It is necessary to change the attitude of the masses from a passive one to a desire to struggle

strongly, to take part more and more violently to win their rights for survival. Good or bad results in our Revolution depend on whether agit-prop action to educate and change the thinking of the masses[4] is good or bad. Every person in the Revolution therefore must know how to conduct propaganda. It follows that the [agit-prop] task is a very important one. During the Resistance, this task made the armed struggle possible. At the present time, with our struggle movement approaching, it is the unique weapon the Party and the masses use to strike at the enemy. Therefore a Party member must, in all circumstances — even when he has fallen into enemy hands — continue by all means to make propaganda for the Party under the slogan "Each Party member a propagandist."

Explaining the difference in approach between efforts during the Viet Minh war and the later period, the document declared:

During the Resistance our struggle approach was to arm all the people and have them engage in guerrilla warfare. At that time we had a slogan, "Propaganda action is half the resistance work." At the present time we pursue a political struggle combined with the armed struggle, which present to the world three faces: political struggle, armed struggle, and struggle among the enemy. . . . It is the present policy of the Party that after completing the indoctrination work in the Party, Youth League, and other mass-based revolutionary organizations, we begin to reach the masses by propaganda in depth, by meetings in hamlets and villages, word-of-mouth communication. In this, the first action is agit-prop work, . . . which serves two purposes: a means of persuading the masses to participate in the political struggle movement against the enemy and, second, it is a [propaganda] weapon we place in the hands of the masses in their political attack on the enemy. The masses themselves therefore must be trained in the use of propaganda arguments. What we must do is to influence public opinion so as to get the masses to stop the enemy and win over officials of the enemy administration and enemy troops.

The NLF Central Committee directive took a somewhat longer view:

In all phases of the Revolution, the Party's agit-prop effort is vital and must not be neglected. . . . Our programs and policies and our effort to develop Party leadership of the Revolution require that the Party make every effort to develop agit-prop potential and in this way develop and widen Party influence among the masses.

The end result of agit-prop activity, both documents clearly stated, was not to be passive belief or acceptance by the people but actions by them against the GVN in the form of propaganda activities, one of the several forms that the struggle movement could take. Said the NLF Central Committee directive:

If the masses take part in propaganda action it is because it will serve their interests. Because they want to keep their land, peasants persuade each other to take up the struggle. Because they want to protect their homes and prop-

[4] In Vietnamese, *chuan bi nhan tam,* literally, "preparing man's heart": to prepare the people for the coming drive, that is, to shape public opinion or win people's support.

erty and fight against regrouping [i.e., relocating], the masses take up the *binh van* movement.

Again the PRP cadre directive was more specific:

Agit-prop cadres must get the masses to invent propaganda arguments to use during struggle movements. . . . The masses already have developed many slogans such as "Struggle against shelling and bombing," . . . "Struggle against the strategic hamlet and agroville," . . . "Struggle against conscription," . . . "Struggle against looting," . . . and "Americans get out." During struggles, the masses themselves have invented many other arguments to deal with the enemy and stop terrorism.

The importance of agit-prop work was outlined succinctly in a document issued a year later by the Long An province central committee:

It helps the masses understand the Party's programs and policies . . . , assists in unmasking the U.S.-Diem plot to keep the masses poor and miserable, and helps them realize their condition is not due to their bad luck or ignorance, and thus causes the masses to hate the enemy and to sacrifice for the Revolution. . . . It promotes unity and helps organize the people in the struggle. . . .

The Social Movement as Communication Channel

With the social organization as a communication device we reach the heart and the power of the NLF. Here lay the solution to the mystery that for so long puzzled knowledgeable and thinking Americans: How could the NLF achieve success in the face of overwhelming GVN military superiority and massive inputs of American material resources for civic action programs to alleviate economic grievances? Not superior ideology, not more dedicated personnel, not because voluntary support of the villager had been won, but the social movement shaped into a self-contained, self-supporting channel of communication — that was the NLF's secret weapon.

Working from the fundamental assumption that if an idea could be rooted in the group it would become strong, durable, and infinitely more difficult to counter, the NLF created a communication structure far beyond any simple propaganda organization and plunged to depths far below mere surface acceptance of a message by an individual. In the hands of the agit-prop cadres the social movement as a communicational device made these contributions to the NLF cause:

1. It generated a sense of community, first, by developing a pattern of political thought and behavior appropriate to the social problems of the rural Vietnamese village in the midst of sharp social change and, second,

by providing a basis for group action that allowed the individual villager to see that his own efforts could have meaning and effect.

2. As an organizational armature, it mobilized the people, generating discontent where it did not exist, exacerbating and harnessing it where it did, and increasing especially at the village level the saliency of all the NLF appeals.

3. It altered to at least some degree the villagers' information input, perception of the world, attitude toward government, and daily actions in and out of the village. It changed underlying beliefs and even caused villagers to do things to their own disadvantage.

4. In a self-reinforcing manner it fostered integration of the NLF belief system, turning heterogeneous attitudes into homogeneous ones; the social facilitation or interstimulation that resulted canalized and intensified village feelings, reactions, and aims. Thus even when the NLF organization turned coercive as it finally did, members continued to hold imported and alien values and norms.

5. It greatly facilitated the NLF's efforts to polarize beliefs, stereotype anti-NLF forces, and generally shift villagers' attention in the directions chosen by the NLF leadership. As does any social organization, it caused the villager to rationalize more easily, being influenced by those around him. Since resistance to suggestion, that is, critical judgment, is lower within a group, it caused him to accept spurious arguments more easily and to succumb more quickly to emotional or personal appeals by the cadres and the village NLF leaders. Once critical judgment was impaired, the villager soon came to confuse desire with conviction.

6. Once momentum in the group was developed, the group itself tended to restrict freedom of expression to the sentiments acceptable to the NLF-created group norms. The individual became submerged, the group became the unit, and great social pressure was brought to bear against the deviant, thus achieving the ultimate NLF objective — a self-regulating, self-perpetuating revolutionary force.

7. Finally, because it helped cut social interaction and communication with the social system represented by the GVN, it isolated the villagers and heightened the sense of conflict between the two systems.

The significance of the social movement as a communicational device and the contribution it made to the NLF effort cannot be stated too strongly. Its essential importance was clearly grasped by the NLF from the earliest days, the result of lessons learned in the Viet Minh war. A 1961 document declared:

An enlightened people if unorganized cannot be a force to deal with the enemy. . . . Therefore organization of the masses is essential, it facilitates our cause in all ways. . . . The [social movement] provides a strong force to oppose the enemy, it makes the Party's task much easier, [and] it both provides an audience for the agit-prop cadre and facilitates further agit-prop work. The [social movement] is a measure of our physical and moral strength, it is a practical way of both serving the people's interests and guaranteeing Party leadership among the people, it is the decisive element in the Revolution.

What the NLF leadership realized — and was all too poorly understood in the United States — was that social organizations are especially potent communication devices in underdeveloped countries. Yet the process is in no way alien to Americans, with their proclivity for the voluntary organization. The Boy Scout movement, for example, transmits and inculcates a whole complex of beliefs, the scope of which is indicated by the twelve Scout laws. A college fraternity can heavily indoctrinate an impressionable youth, shape his political beliefs and economic values, even dictate what sort of a wife to choose. This is done not as a premeditated brainwashing scheme but simply as a byproduct function of the organizational essence or nature of its being. What the NLF did was deliberately to create such an organizational structure specifically to transmit information, data, ideals, beliefs, and values.

The Agit-Prop Team

The Communist institution of the agit-prop cadre is generally well known but little understood by Americans. Its utility to the NLF was so great that it has been singled out from other communication methods for special consideration here. Let us begin by inspecting the visit of a hypothetical NLF agit-prop team to a Vietnamese village.

The team approaches in late afternoon and has a rendezvous outside the hamlet with a Party member or sympathizer who carefully briefs it on developments in the village or hamlet since the team's last visit; he lists the local grievances, local animosities, the most disliked persons in the village.

At dusk the team enters the hamlet with a great deal of fanfare, shaking hands, greeting people, carrying with it an aura of excitement, a break in the village monotony. Villagers are asked to assemble voluntarily at some central location. One old man, known to be irascible and intractable, announces loudly he'll be damned if he'll listen to a bunch of agitators. The team chief ostentatiously excuses him. However, should a sizable number of villagers indicate reluctance to attend, the team chief grows stern and indicates by gesture and manner that it would be well to give the members of the Revolution at least an opportunity to present their message. So the villagers gather.

The session begins with a short talk by the team chief in which he mixes flattery of the villagers' spirit, sympathy for their plight, and the hint that he will present later a message of great importance.

An interlude of singing and quasi-entertainment follows. The team chief or one of the members leads the villagers in a traditional folk song known and loved by all South Vietnamese. When it ends, the song leader announces that he has written new words to the old melody that he would like to teach the villagers. He recites the verse, which carries a class consciousness and revolutionary message, and after the villagers learn the words, he leads them through it several times.

Then comes the main speech, lasting up to an hour. The team chief has previously received from the interzone agit-prop section a directive outlining current themes to be stressed; they are biological warfare and cholera in an anti-American context. These are carefully fixed to local grievances. He tells the villagers: "Your harvest this year was not so large as in years past. The reason for this is that the Americans are conducting in South Vietnam something called defoliation. Strange chemicals are sprayed from airplanes, killing crops and foliage instantly. It is true that no planes have been seen, for none has sprayed within fifty kilometers of the village. But these chemicals can be carried vast distances, even halfway around the world, by the wind. What has happened is that some of the noxious chemicals have drifted over the village and fallen on the crops, stunting their growth and causing a lower yield." It is also believed by the villagers that there is cholera in the village. "This isn't really cholera but a germ disease for which there is no cure, also spread by the Americans." He continues to recite local fears, grievances, and problems, ascribing them all to some action by the Americans or officials in Saigon. He recounts atrocities committed in nearby areas. As a closer, he tells the villagers that the only way they can fight this injustice, the only way they can survive, in fact, is to join with the NLF and work for a General Uprising, after which there will be peace, economic abundance, and freedom for all.

The general meeting breaks up and the submeetings begin. The farmers gather to be addressed by the team's Farmers' Liberation Association representative, women by the Women's Liberation Association representative, and the youth by the Youth Liberation Association representative. In these meetings appeals are further refined and pinpointed, and a theme employed in one group is often inconsistent with one employed in another. For example, farmers are told that all the NLF asks from them is a small financial donation; the women are told the NLF army will protect their village and provide complete security; the youths may be urged to enlist in the NLF army and may be told that they must be prepared to sacrifice even their lives for the Revolution.

The villagers then reassemble in a large meeting that becomes participational. Questions are solicited, including those critical of the NLF. The team chief, a master at handling the barbed comment or loaded question, handles these with ease. Some questions may be fed him by covert Party members living in the village.

In the midst of this question period the team chief, in a demonstration of omniscience, casually remarks that he knows there are enemy agents in the group. He points to Mr. Ba and says "I know he is an enemy agent and will report to the village chief tomorrow about this meeting." The villagers know this is true. But the team chief takes no action against Mr. Ba and simply goes on with the meeting.

Then comes the *pièce de résistance,* a dramatic skit presented by the team. It is a highly entertaining little drama set in Saigon, involving a taxi driver played by the team chief, a Vietnamese girl played by the woman team member, and an American played by another team member. The American accosts the young girl and makes an indecent proposal that is overheard by the taxi driver, who comes to her rescue. There is a lengthy dialogue between the taxi driver and the American — full of double entendres and ribald remarks at the expense of the American, which delights the villagers. The drama becomes a verbal contest between the Vietnamese and the American, and the American is thoroughly confused, deflated, shattered, and defeated. The taxi driver and the girl go off together.

Then the team departs, scattering leaflets in its wake or pasting them to trees and walls, and it hoists an NLF flag.

The Agit-Prop Cadre

Agit-prop activity rested on the fundamental NLF assumption that the personal intermediary was the most potent form of communication. On the agit-prop, he was constantly told, rested the burden of the Revolution. A steady flow of messages from higher headquarters constantly reminded him of the complexity of his task and the high degree of skill that he must employ daily, for the NLF knew what all professional communicators know: that the simple communication of facts is often ineffectual in changing men's opinions, majority opinion reinforced by social pressure counts for much more than expert opinion or leadership assertions, and people tend to misinterpret what they hear or read to suit their own preconceptions. And the NLF knew that, working within such complexities, technique counted for all.

Next to technique, the personality of the individual agit-prop cadre was of chief importance. The ideal cadre was a model of dedication, sobriety, skillfulness.[5] Agit-prop cadres were chosen, a directive noted, "from among those who have a clean past, who are virtuous in behavior, and who know how to arouse the masses." [6]

The previously cited Central Committee directive listed the duties of the agit-prop cadres in a general way:

To direct the masses toward political struggle, armed struggle, or action among troops [by] directing the thinking of the masses toward the Revolution; to arouse hatred for the enemy in the masses and at the same time to enlighten them about their interests; to consolidate their faith and generate revolutionary enthusiasm.

The cadre directive listed his duties specifically as to

(1) promote hatred of the enemy; (2) show the people it is in their interest to support the Revolution, for it serves them; (3) teach the people the meaning and techniques of the political struggle . . . ; (4) develop the people's faith and self-confidence in achieving revolutionary successes and maintain their enthusiasm.

As GVN battlefield interdiction began to take a heavy toll among agit-prop cadres and as the NLF grew in size, increased numbers of cadres were required, and infiltration by Northern-trained agit-prop cadres increased. Several of those who were captured gave interrogators a word picture of the training they had received in the North. It consisted of two parts: a session in political indoctrination and one in agit-prop techniques. The first, usually lasting two weeks, involved indoctrination in these major subjects: the world-wide advance of communism; socioeconomic progress being made in the DRV; the role of youth, a chief target in the task of building socialism and of liberating the South; the sociopolitical situation in the South; and the NLF and its successes. At the end of this period the inept were weeded out and

---

[5] A cadre directive noted that

the purpose [of agit-prop work] is to mobilize the people's thinking. This is an ideological struggle that is complex and hard to carry out. It requires time and painstaking efforts. A cadre should be patient, should follow up on each individual, and should repeat the same theme over and over. He should endeavor ceaselessly. He should build durable support and should not become discouraged. He should set an example for the masses, for unless we do how can we expect the masses to follow us? . . . He should behave modestly, listen to the people talk. . . . He should be humble. . . .

[6] The best cadres, it added, are those who

ceaselessly study [Party] directives and policies, consolidate their thinking, and improve their virtuous revolutionary behavior. At the same time they remain humble and listen to the judgment of the masses. . . . Cadres not only must know programs and policies but also must feel hatred when they witness killings and oppression of the masses. They must know the secret thoughts and interests of the masses, must share their joys and sadness, must be determined to work for the good of the masses, and must make every effort to influence the masses. They must suffer the hardships of the masses, for only in this way can they feel the suffering and sorrows of the masses. If cadres lack feeling, their propaganda will be emotionless and will not arouse the masses. Above all, . . . cadres must accept responsibility for the words they speak.

final selection of infiltrators made. The remaining group then received about ten days of further training in the specific techniques of agit-prop work.

The outer limits of accomplishment of the agit-prop cadres, in objective terms, appeared to be these: At best they hoped to shape villager opinion to such a degree that the villager would support the cause of his own volition; the least they tried to do, when greater achievement was not possible, was to confuse the opinions and emotions of the villager so that he became indecisive and thus ineffectual in providing support to the GVN. Within this range the agit-prop cadres sought to instigate strife along class lines. They dealt in misinformation, exaggeration, and distortion. They concealed or mistated Communist intentions. They drew attention to and inflated real or trumped-up village grievances.

Woolly-mindedness and lack of specificity were the major shortcomings of the cadres, who were instructed to allow their work to grow naturally out of the exigencies of the moment. Cadres were instructed to

study and understand both technique and policy. . . . Good technique does not consist of collecting materials about our policies and programs and then giving a "certified copy" to the masses. Neither does it mean picking up a megaphone and explaining general policies in a general way. It means ceaseless effort and taking detailed care to persuade the masses, to clarify their thinking. . . . Many cadres simply distribute slogans, and the result is that the masses know the slogans but do not know what actions to take.

Specificity of theme directed toward specific social elements was also stressed:

Among poor peasants it is necessary to stress the class-conflict viewpoint. . . . Among middle-class peasants, stress our agrarian policies, that peasants will be owners of land and rice fields. . . . Among religious groups, show how the Revolution will bring them concrete benefits in the form of religious freedom, and at the same time create class consciousness and strengthen the revolutionary struggle. . . . Among the intermediate classes, those between the worker-peasant class and the petite bourgeoisie and bourgeoisie, according to individual and group understanding about the NLF and the Party, conduct clever agitation to widen the Front and Party influence; for instance, stress and emphasize the just and correct policies of the Front and the Party. . . . Among the masses, popularize the Front and Party plans and programs, the successes scored in socialist and Communist countries. . . . When the enemy talks about famine in North Vietnam do not deny there is famine but talk about the unending increases in food production in the North. The enemy will say the Communists are bloodthirsty dictators. We should point to their crimes. . . . Maintain the upper hand in counterpropaganda. Meet the enemy's anticommunism charges by promoting class consciousness through the *dan van* movement.

An agit-prop cadre could operate in a team or alone. In the latter case he was told to take every opportunity for agitation. . . . On a busy train, in a bar, at a private party, make the subject lively and raise the level of the class consciousness of the individuals present according to the circumstances. . . . But be careful not to reveal yourself and avoid talking too much. . . . Here is a good example: Take a newspaper that carries a story about a certain man named A who committed suicide because he was unable to find a job. Bring up the subject of the newspaper story and then lead the conversation to the general subject of jobs, unemployment, the difficulties of earning a living, etc. In this way people are invited to complain about the hardships they face. From this seek an opportunity to incriminate American aid as a source of this state of unemployment and starvation.

Also commonly employed in the earlier days was the "root-and-link" device. A Party member looked for a prospective "root" whom he would meet, talk with, and win over, after which he would educate him. This root then became a "link" who looked for other roots, and thus a "chain" was formed. This did not necessarily involve Party membership or any form of formal organization. It was a transmission belt for propaganda, highly directed, specifically oriented, and very personal. The root-and-link device was an effort to make use of traditional channels of communication. NLF output referred to it and similar devices as word-of-mouth propaganda, which it described as

the principal medium of both covert and overt propaganda. It is direct. It enables us to present our views clearly and to understand immediately the response of the individual. We can by this means offer on the spot a solution to his problems and at the same time mobilize his thinking. . . .

Agit-prop teams also employed a vast number of psychological tricks, of which the following is an example. After the important NLF victory at Ap Bac in 1963, guerrilla units moving away from the battlefield passed through villages carrying, on a stretcher-like affair, a bulky item covered by a huge blue cloth. The band would stop for water in a village and the four bearers of the cloth-covered apparatus would set it down without comment. Villagers would gather around and exhibit curiosity about what was under the cloth. The guerrilla leader warned them not to get near it. Then, as their curiosity reached the bursting point, the leader would say: "Under this blue cloth is a new secret weapon. By means of it we shot down dozens and dozens of the enemy's helicopters at Ap Bac." The band would then finish its marching break, the four bearers would pick up the device, still covered by the blue cloth, and depart. Other techniques employed by agit-props included those that piqued the Vietnamese sense of humor:

It is possible to use riddles during such events [the incident that the agit-prop cadre is capitalizing on], such as this one we used in the [1960] presidential elections: "The head is fascist. The rear is colonialist. The hands and feet are feudalist. The mouth is republican. What is it? (Answer:

Diem)." Once these have been devised it is necessary to spread them to the towns and cities. . . . Ask [loaded] questions of the administration authorities or of soldiers and officers. One can pretend to be an ignorant farmer and ask an army officer in the market place: "What exactly have the people of Binh Ninh done to cause the killing of so many of them?" This technique can also be used in the *binh van* movement.

The individual behavior of the agit-prop cadres received close supervisory attention by the leadership, for the cadre was the NLF representative most often seen by the villagers, and their opinion of him to a great degree determined their attitude toward the more abstract aspects of the NLF.

Administrative Organization

Although the NLF Central Committee nominally controlled output, the highest working level — vested with great latitude in setting communication policy, determining general themes, planning and launching specific campaigns, managing the various ongoing programs, training and assigning agit-prop cadres — was the interzone agit-prop section, by far the most important element in the interzone headquarters. Some Vietnamese believed that the interzone level existed only for the purpose of managing agit-prop activity.

The interzone agit-prop section consisted of a section chief, a headquarters branch responsible for administration and housekeeping, and six operational branches: the *dich van* branch; the organization branch (social movement work and *dan van* activity); the *binh van* branch; a training and indoctrination branch; a liaison branch (working with functional liberation associations); and the security branch (concerned with countercommunication efforts as well as with general security matters among the agit-prop cadres). The section both administered the agit-prop teams, composed of an estimated 6,000 agit-prop cadres working out of the district level, and supervised, usually through the district TVG sections, the various communication programs at the village level. Parallel to this structure was the PRP communication channel, which consisted for the most part of indoctrination efforts and terminated as a separate function at the district level. The organization of the structure is illustrated in Chart 7-1.

As indicated earlier, the NLF placed the burden of communication on the shoulders of the people themselves. However, they were not left to their own devices but were closely supervised by the agit-prop cadre, who acted as a catalyst, or, as one Saigonese educated at a Midwestern United States university expressed it, "as a cheer leader." Nor in actu-

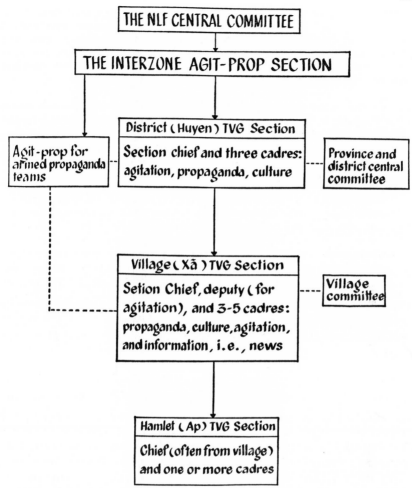

Chart 7–1 Organization of the NLF Communication Structure

ality did the efforts of the people consist of "propagandizing the enemy" so much as of convincing themselves, a form of self-agitation. As noted in the PRP cadre directive, "It is true that the masses do the agitation work, but it is necessary to educate them to perceive their agitation duties, to control their daily agitation activities, and to maintain the village [communication] organizations."

The district, or *huyen,* TVG section was small and contained the most professional of the agit-prop units. The NLF Central Committee directive stated: "It is led by a section chief and contains at least three other cadres, if possible selected from the villages (or the district), one each for agitation, propaganda, and cultural activities."

"The village [*xa*] TVG section," said the PRP cadre directive,

works under the guidance of the political cadre [of the village liberation
committee]. . . . It provides technical assistance to move, guide, and lead
the masses in TVG actions. . . . It reports experiences in the field of TVG
and popularizes [that is, publicizes] all good experiences . . . and trains
cadres . . . and correspondents for the provincial information bulletins and
newspapers. . . . It contains three to five persons. The chief of section should
be a Party or Youth League member or, if there are none present in the
village, an [administrative] liberation association member. . . . The chief of
section has all responsibility. . . . He guides the organization of the masses,
reports to higher echelons, and calls meetings in the village. The deputy chief,
if possible, is also a Party or Youth League member. . . . He is in charge
of agitation in depth and width . . . and of distributing printed materials
and taking an active part in the organization of all-village demonstrations
and meetings. . . . Also there is a cadre for education, to arouse the masses
to set up adult education classes in the evenings and to maintain schools for
children . . . , a cadre for culture who provides guidance for cultural shows
and productions, organizes dance groups, and, with the help of the Youth
League, aids and guides the children's groups. . . . In addition a cadre can
be put in charge of training hamlet correspondents to gather news about
the struggle of the masses and the U.S.-Diem clique crimes. . . . He will
either write articles or write down detailed facts to be sent to higher echelons
where articles will be written for the provincial newspaper.

The hamlet TVG section (often called simply the hamlet information
section), said the Central Committee directive,

will be organized in each hamlet . . . , to be headed by an information
chief who can be a village TVG cadre. . . . It is responsible for all TVG
activities in the hamlet. It guides the cells in reading aloud and commenting
on newspaper stories. It sets up information halls, gives news by means of
megaphones, organizes hamlet meetings, and guides the hamlet's dance
troupes and cultural activities. Special teams will read and comment on newspapers for other villagers [that is, illiterate villagers] and should be chosen
from among the younger members of the hamlet.

From an administrative standpoint the village and hamlet TVG
echelons were considered one. In general, the keynote was activism. A
Long An province memorandum instructed cadres in early 1962 to

start at once to form cells of the liberation associations, etc. into small study
groups and consider the duties and methods of agitation. . . . Cadres are
responsible for the review of individual agitation activities, give continuous
encouragement. . . . Some TVG sections [in the province] have demonstrated a spirit of eagerness and have conducted excellent work. They have
a high level of organization that all must make an effort to emulate. Each
village must [record] . . . how many persons take part in agitation actions,
how many have been reached by printed propaganda each month, and what
are the specific agit-prop problems.

The document went on to charge the village TVG sections with primary
responsibility:

Each month the village TVG sections must hold a meeting of all TVG personnel and representatives, to include the cadres and representatives of the hamlet and village groups and associations. At the meeting there will be a general review of the past month's activities, drawing out experiences and outlining the work for the coming month. . . . The TVG section must meet often and exchange ideas, divide the work load. . . . Every two weeks or at least once a month the TVG section chief must meet with all the TVG cadres to draw out experiences and to make assignments. Special attention must be paid to the cells that read aloud and comment on newspapers in the hamlets. At this meeting copies of the provincial [clandestine] newspaper will be given to cadres for distribution in their areas. . . . Each month the TVG section will make three reports: . . . TVG activities in the village and hamlet . . . , current events of the village that might be used by the provincial newspaper . . . , and agit-prop actions that specifically contributed to the struggle movement.

8

The Communist Role

As we have seen, the Communists[1] played the dominant but not exclusive role in the early years of the NLF, gradually extending their control until for all practical purposes they were managing NLF affairs at all levels from the national Central Committee to the villages. This was a gradual developmental process; the degree of control that the various Communist-controlled NLF organizations exerted over the villagers of course differed greatly from village to village.

From an administrative standpoint, the Communists had joined the National Liberation Front while keeping their own organization, at first as members of the Southern branch of the Lao Dong Party and later as members of the People's Revolutionary Party. There was no reason, however, why an individual Communist could not have dual membership in both the PRP and the regular Lao Dong Party in Hanoi.

The People's Revolutionary Party

The PRP was formally founded, as stated earlier, on January 1, 1962, and the first public announcement of its birth came on January 18, 1962

[1] For working purposes a Communist is defined here as a person who (a) claims to be a believer in Marxism-Leninism and (b) is loyal and obedient to the rulers in Hanoi.

in a Radio Hanoi broadcast quoting the Liberation News Agency. The announcement said that a new party had been formed by a "conference of Marxist-Leninists meeting in South Vietnam in late December under the guidance of veteran revolutionaries." Later it was learned that these were Vo Chi Cong, who became the chairman of the PRP Central Committee,[2] and Huynh Van Tam, who was named secretary-general. Tam was later replaced (and sent to Algeria as NLF representative) by Tran Nam Trung. There have been persistent reports that the DRV leader Le Duan came secretly to South Vietnam at this time and assisted in the formation of the PRP; this has never been substantiated.

The PRP consistently referred to itself in public statements as the "Marxist-Leninist Party of South Vietnam"[3] and thus never denied its Communist nature. Neither did it deny that it was more than simply an equal fellow member of the NLF; it was, it insisted, the "vanguard of the NLF, the paramount member." It did deny, however, that it had any official ties with the DRV or with the Lao Dong Party, its predecessor, beyond the normal "fraternal ties of communism." The PRP considered itself to be the reinforcing rods in the NLF structure.

A leaflet widely distributed in the South at the time explained that the organization had been founded because,

to fulfill their historic and glorious duty, workers, peasants, and laborers in South Vietnam need a vanguard group serving as a thoroughly revolutionary party. Held during the last days of December 1961, a conference of Marxist-Leninists decided to establish the Vietnamese People's Revolutionary Party. A platform and body of statutes were approved.

The People's Revolutionary Party is a party of the working class and

---

[2] The PRP Central Committee was frequently referred to in the U.S. press as the Central Office, South Vietnam (COSVN, or sometimes COSVIN). The implication of this usage was that the Central Office was organizationally and geographically separated from the Central Committee of the NLF, which was not the case. COSVN was the physical location, in Zone D of Binh Duong province, of certain elements of the PRP and the NLF, that is, of the individual officials; other elements of the NLF and PRP leadership were located in northern Tay Ninh province. The point is that the PRP at all times worked through the NLF and not independently of it. However, the PAVN units in South Vietnam apparently worked through neither the NLF nor the PRP but had a direct chain of command to Hanoi.

[3] The Communists in Vietnam, both North and South, eschewed public use of the word "communism" and employed extreme semantic dodges to avoid it. The Communist party in North Vietnam was the Vietnam Workers' Party (Dang Lao Dong Viet Nam); in the South, the Vietnam People's Revolutionary Party (Dang Nhan Dan Cach Mang Viet Nam). Likewise the youth groups, equivalent to the Komsomol in the Soviet Union, were the Labor Youth League in North Vietnam and the People's Revolutionary Party Youth League (PRPYL) in the South. Internal documents used the simple terms "Party member" (*Dang vien*) in the PRP and "League member" (*Doan vien*) in the PRPYL. In the same way the term "worker" (*lao dong*) was preferred to "proletariat" (*vo san*). The last time the word "Communist" was used in a party organization was in the Indochinese Communist Party, which was formed in 1930 and abolished in favor of the Marxist Study League in 1945.

laboring people in South Vietnam. It is also the party of all patriots in South Vietnam. The immediate task of the People's Revolutionary Party is to unite and lead the working class, the peasantry, the laboring people, and all compatriots in South Vietnam in struggling to overthrow the rule of the imperialists and feudalists . . . and liberate Vietnam; to set up a broad democratic coalition government that will achieve national independence and democratic freedom, improve the people's living conditions, give land to the tillers, develop industry, trade, culture, and education, bring a comfortable life to all the people, and achieve national reunification by peaceful means and contribute to protecting world peace. . . . The PRP warmly supports the declaration and program of action of the National Liberation Front and volunteers to stand in the Front's ranks. . . .

It was avowedly Marxist-Leninist and was so presented to the people. A PRP indoctrination booklet instructed cadres to use this approach in discussing the Party at NLF meetings and indoctrination sessions:

The Revolution our Party and all South Vietnamese people are carrying out is a national democratic revolution aimed at resolutely struggling to overthrow the ruling yoke of the U.S.-imperialist aggressors and their lackeys, to liberate South Vietnam, to set up a broad national democratic coalition government, to achieve national independence, freedom, and democracy, to improve the people's living standards, to provide land for the tillers, to develop industry, agriculture, culture, and education, and to advance toward peaceful national unification, thereby making a contribution to the protection of world peace. These are our urgent immediate tasks. . . . Our Party does not conceal its ultimate objective, which is to achieve socialism and communism. But our Party has not ceased pointing out that the path leading to that objective is long and that the objective cannot be achieved in a few years but several score years.

The Lao Dong Party, which the PRP replaced, had maintained itself largely in a covert fashion in the South after the end of hostilities in 1954 until it changed its name to the PRP and began an organizational buildup. Its membership in 1962 was estimated at not more than 35,000,[4] and the PRP membership was estimated in early 1966 at between 85,000 and 100,000. Members of the Lao Dong Party, chiefly Viet Minh who had been among the most important founders of the NLF, although never listed as Lao Dong Party members in published statements, in 1962 assumed PRP leadership positions. The Party as such had continued a sort of low-grade overt activity in the 1955–1962 period, mainly to remind people of its existence. For example, its members frequently scattered leaflets by night in Mekong delta villages; the leaflets, signed by the Lao Dong Party, usually called for the reunification of

[4] *Thu Do* (Hanoi), February 3, 1963, said that the Indochinese Communist Party was founded in March 1929 with seven members, that its membership in 1945 totaled 5,000, and that in February 1963 it stood at 500,000. Presumably this did not include the PRP membership. *Thu Do* listed this breakdown of membership: under eleven years of membership, 9 per cent; from eleven to fifteen years, 50 per cent; from sixteen to thirty years, 37 per cent; and over thirty, 4 per cent.

Vietnam. Covertly it continued its organization and penetration work, but this also was limited since most of the effort of its members was devoted to furthering the aims of the newly formed NLF. Not until late 1963 did the PRP begin to concentrate its efforts on its own internal organization.

For the first months of its existence the PRP continued to employ the liaison net and other channels of communication established by its predecessor, the Southern wing of the Lao Dong Party. Its pipeline into North Vietnam was the Lao Dong Party apparatus, which appeared to be its chief sponsor in Hanoi. In 1963, however, a special group was established in Hanoi, called the Committee for Supervision of the South, which had among its other tasks the administration of the PRP. This committee was headed by Le Duc Tho, a member of the DRV Politburo, and included Nguyen Van Vinh, chairman of the DRV National Assembly Committee for Reunification.[5] The Committee for Supervision of the South appeared to be chiefly a logistic and training unit; the Committee for Reunification appeared to be chiefly interested in substantive policy matters, such as stated political objectives of the NLF and the PRP. In addition the DRV National Defense Council and Ministry of National Defense concerned themselves with military activities in the South and represented the beginning of a direct chain of command to PAVN units operating in the South.

The PRP was more proletarian than the NLF in concept. A PRP cadre training manual described it as

the party of the laboring class that will lead the people of South Vietnam to final victory. . . . The Party serves the people and not private interests. Its aims are first to awaken the laboring class, then to awaken the poverty-stricken class, and finally to arouse the whole people, who together will revolt. . . . The Party uses the people's united-front policy [*chanh sach mat tran dan toc thong nhat*], based on agricultural and worker class distinctions. . . . The South Vietnamese proletariat as a class has several advantages: It controls the means of production; it is imbued with a highly developed collectivist spirit; it has a link with the people in the countryside who are struggling against local landlords, bourgeois moneylenders, and American imperialists; and its members are highly motivated, having nothing to lose and everything to gain from the Revolution.

A statement circulated among NLF cadres at the time of the formation of the PRP declared that the revolutionary movement in the South lacked organization and leadership and that the PRP was established as the paramount organization to provide both and to lead the people to victory.[6] Publicly the DRV treated the PRP as a purely indigenous

[5] See Chapter 18.
[6] It stated that

for over six years members of the Lao Dong Party have been working in the South and with the help of the people have struggled against the U.S.-Diem regime. . . .

Southern proletarian party.[7] To its own Lao Dong members it explained that the PRP was simply a continuation of the older party. A captured Lao Dong Party cadre document turned over to the International Control Commission (ICC) by the GVN in 1962 declared that the

creation of the PRP is a necessary strategy required within the Party and to deceive the enemy. The new Party must maintain the outward appearance of a separation from the Lao Dong [Party] so that the enemy cannot use it in his propaganda. . . . Within the Party it is necessary to explain that the founding of the PRP has the purpose of isolating the Americans and the Ngo Dinh Diem regime and countering their accusations of an invasion of the South by the North. It is a means to . . . permit the NLF to recruit new adherents and to gain the sympathy of nonaligned countries in Southeast Asia.

The PRP leaders handled the organization's formation with skill; they obviously had put a good deal of preparation into the public launching of the new party. Detailed instructions were issued to village cadres, and an intensive propaganda campaign was immediately set in motion throughout South Vietnam to acquaint the people with the existence of the PRP and to promote its acceptance. An internal document captured in the spring of 1962, dated January 1962, directed cadres (apparently Lao Dong Party) to hold special village ceremonies to mark the formation of the PRP (as cited in Chapter 5).

The Communist nature of the PRP, the document stated, was to be hidden from the general public, and it instructed cadres to hold study sessions within the Party apparatus and Front organizations and in general village assemblies. It then added: "In study sessions inside the Party and in Front groups, Party purposes [i.e., intentions] and slogans and the Party's platform should be discussed and understood. In public

---

The revolutionary movement has become stronger and has developed. But it continues to lack organization and leadership. At the lower levels especially the organization is not well formed nor is their leadership system adequate at the district level. For these reasons it is required that the Revolution in the South be placed under a unified leadership system. Only by this means can the Revolution be accelerated. . . . The PRP was established to assure that the Revolution in the South will have proper leadership. . . . No matter what circumstances develop, the Party has the means and policies to cope with and lead the people in overthrowing the enemy. The Party always is able to consider the situation at hand and devise correct countermeasures. . . . The Party is the highest organization. It is responsible for the leadership of all other organizations, the liberation associations, the mutual-aid associations, as well as for the leadership of all the people who will overthrow the old regime for the sake of the new. The Party is the paramount organization. It must always be progressive, knowledgeable, exemplary, and unselfish.

[7] A *Nhan Dan* editorial (May 5, 1964), for example, explained its formation in these terms:

The South Vietnam working class has clearly realized that to defend the people's, and its own, interests it must have a leading party, closely allied with the working peasants, broadly united with the other sections of the people. . . . The founding of the South Vietnam National Liberation Front and the birth of the Vietnam People's Revolutionary Party, a party of the South Vietnam working class and laboring people and at the same time of all patriotic South Vietnamese, are historic events on the road to victory of the national democratic revolution in South Vietnam.

sessions, only slogans and the Party declaration — but not the purposes — will be studied." The slogans used in the ceremony carefully avoided any reference to communism. They were

1. "Heartily welcome the establishment of the People's Revolutionary Party of Vietnam."
2. "Heartily appreciate the establishment of the People's Revolutionary Party of Vietnam, a party of workers, farmers, and all patriotic people."
3. "Vow to unite around the Party to liberate South Vietnam, to realize independence, democracy, and peaceful advance toward unification of the Fatherland."
4. "Realize freedom, democracy, improve living standards of the people by providing farm tenants [*dan cay*] with land."
5. "Suppress the domination of the U.S. empire and Ngo Dinh Diem and his clique, lackeys of the U.S. empire."

The PRP spelled out its specific program in a ten-point platform distributed in leaflet form throughout the Mekong delta, and also broadcast by Radio Liberation, during January 1962. The ten points were:

1. We will overthrow the Ngo Dinh Diem government and form a national democratic coalition government.
2. We will carry out a program involving extension of democratic liberties, general amnesty for political detainees, abolition of agrovilles and resettlement centers, abolition of the special military tribunal law and other undemocratic laws.
3. We will abolish the economic monopoly of the U.S. and its henchmen, protect domestically made products, promote development of the economy, and allow forced evacuees from North Vietnam to return to their place of birth.
4. We will reduce land rent and prepare for land reform.
5. We will eliminate U.S. cultural enslavement and depravity and build a nationalistic progressive culture and education.
6. We will abolish the system of American military advisers and close all foreign military bases in Vietnam.
7. We will establish equality between men and women and among different nationalities and recognize the autonomous rights of the national minorities in the country.
8. We will pursue a foreign policy of peace and will establish diplomatic relations with all countries that respect the independence and sovereignty of Vietnam.
9. We will re-establish normal relations between North and South as a first step toward peaceful reunification of the country.
10. We will oppose aggressive wars and actively defend world peace.

The Central Committee of the PRP issued what might be considered its foreign policy platform in April 1962. It vowed to pursue the NLF goals of peace, neutralism, independence, and unification; it denounced the United States for waging aggressive but undeclared war in South Vietnam; it thanked the Soviet Union, Communist China, and the other Communist nations for supporting the Vietnamese cause; it urged all peace-loving peoples of the world to support the Vietnamese Revolution; it urged the American people to show some concern for their government's policy in Vietnam; it asked Britain and the Soviet Union, cochairmen of the 1954 Geneva conference on Indochina, to implement the 1954 agreements; it denounced the British government for its stand on Vietnam; and it hinted that unless the Americans left Vietnam it would call on the DRV, China, and the Soviet Union to come to its aid.[8] In short, it was a classic Communist policy statement on Vietnam.

Gradually the emphasis on proletarianism gave way to fuller and more orthodox expressions of communism. And imperceptibly the national salvation theme as a goal began to merge with that of creating a collectivist society. This was apparent both in public output and in internal documents. A 1963 training manual for use by PRP cadres in working with NLF organizations instructed the cadres to emphasize that the PRP sought "to work through the NLF to achieve the liberation, neutralization, and unification of Vietnam through the establishment of a democratic coalition government." A similar training manual dated early 1965 said that the PRP was "the vanguard of Southern workers dedicated to achieving a patriotic, democratic, and national revolution in order to introduce socialism and then communism to Vietnam." The earlier manual stressed the national salvation theme: "The pressing task for the Party and the Front is to unite all South Vietnamese in the struggle against foreign domination." The later manual added that the Party also

must seek to do away with the deprivations caused by the imperialists and feudalists. Then we must abolish all deprivation whatever the cause. And finally we will then be ready to guide the workers, the artisans, and others along the road of collective production so they can come to live the life of people in other modern societies. Under socialism, the early stage of communism, there can be no economic deprivation, no individual poverty, no underdeveloped segments of the society. The workers become the rulers of the country, its industry, and its natural resources. The workers then exploit the natural resources and build up the nation's industry. Market cooperatives, formed voluntarily in the spirit of brotherhood, are created by the farmers, artisans, and retail traders. Intellectuals also cooperate, putting their talents to work for the benefit of the workers. To prevent a return of the parasitism and laziness that characterized the old regime, we will follow the socialist principle of reward — each according to his ability. We shall all live together intimately in the great socialist family. . . . Once Vietnam is reunited and socialism created, the Party will then lead the people toward the establishment of communism. Communism will be practiced as it is in the Soviet Union.

[8] Radio Hanoi, in English, April 24, 1962.

Factories, mines, fields, and all other land will be the common ownership of all the people. Automated machinery and electronic equipment will enable both industry and agriculture to grow at tremendous rates. Everyone will be able to reach the cultural level enjoyed today by engineers and doctors. The slogan "Each according to his work" will prevail. There will be houses, electricity, automobiles, and motion pictures for all. Life will be happy and civilized.

Another PRP cadre training manual, dated October 1965, also described Party policies and goals:

The Party [objective] . . . is to overthrow imperialism, colonialism, and feudalism, to build a life of peace, prosperity, and happiness without oppression and extortion. . . . Once independence is obtained, the next step is unification, constructed and consolidated in every way to make the country powerful and rich, a stronghold of peace. Then will come the social reorganization, along socialist-communist principles, without land demarcations, cooperating in rural electrification, re-education of individuals, nationalization of private property, cultural and scientific education for everyone, progressing day by day to better and better things in all fields. Also, helping other small weak countries to struggle against imperialism and rid the world of conflict and to help provide everyone with freedom, legality, warmth, food, and happiness. . . .

As noted earlier, PRP cadres were instructed to mute the socialism-communism theme should it be inappropriate in their areas, as, for example, where there was a heavy concentration of Catholic Vietnamese. Strangely, however, in outer trappings such as flags, the Communist imprint was firm. The PRP flag consisted of a red field on which was centered a white hammer and sickle. The PRP Youth League flag had a red field on which were centered three yellow stars, with a white hammer and sickle in the upper right-hand corner.

Since NLF propagandists up to 1962 had found it a successful gambit to be conspicuously silent on the whole business of communism in the South, it would seem that the leaders would consider the formation of a new revolutionary organization with overt Communist participation to be counterproductive. Certainly it would damage the NLF image presented abroad — and it did. But there were advantages that would far outweigh the drawbacks; and there were at least four reasons for the formation of the PRP.

First, there was the stated reason: The Revolution needed a better engine. It needed a tighter, more centralized organization and a more effective leadership. Countering the GVN's strategic-hamlet program especially required stronger organizational methods than previously had been necessary and called for the discipline, experience, and knowledge that Communists feel only they possess.

Second, there was a need for a stronger ideological content to help explain the Revolution to itself and help hold it together. Communism was the doctrinal cement, but communism without a Communist party was unworkable. Foreign communism, even of the Lao Dong Party brand, was strategically unsound; and the covert party had proved inadequate to the needs. It was not simply Marxism that was required but the larger body of Communist thought. The PRP leadership obviously felt that the NLF was jerry-built, chiefly because it lacked a strong sense of class consciousness, something that communism could inject. The PRP leaders also saw more clearly than the rank and file of the NLF the need to break out of the anti-Diem role and develop a broader xenophobic spirit of hate for the United States, what was usually expressed as "the movement for the salvation of the country against the Americans." This national salvation theme took as its model the Chinese Communist antifascist war against Japan. As the PRP influence developed and the Revolution became regularized, the effort did shift from the GVN to the United States. The PRP leadership saw as the task of the Revolution the neutralization of the Vietnamese army, chiefly if possible by proselyting activities, and then concentrating on the United States and its military forces.

Third, it was necessary to give Communist followers in the South better support. When talking in the 1960–1962 period with defectors who professed to having been Marxists, one frequently sensed in them a feeling of ideological isolation. Many indicated that they felt cut off from the mainstream of Communist thought, surrounded by nonbelievers, unable to suppress their doubts about the correctness of their actions, particularly those involving violence. Some even gave this as their reason for defection. At first, one cadre said, everything had been simple and understandable: Capitalism meant poverty and slavery; communism, abundance and freedom. Then he came South and found prosperous villages, more so than in the North, and people who seldom felt the touch of a governmental hand, unlike the omnipresent government of the North. Events swirled about him, and, with his inadequate grasp of Marxism, realistic explanations began to slip away. Uncertainty entered, followed by doubt, followed by a break in faith, followed by defection. Whether these feelings were endemic or deep we do not know, but probably they posed a serious enough problem to Hanoi to lead to orders to form a strong and overt party that would shore up the ideological underpinnings in the South and give the Party members a firmer platform on which to stand.

Fourth, there was the fear on the part of the DRV leadership and the Southern Communists that the Revolution might turn bourgeois, as it continually threatened to do, especially among the provincial farmers with their narrow range of interests that went little beyond land reform. The PRP formed an automatic pilot that would keep the Revolution on the track and go the whole distance. The entire thrust of the struggle in the early years was in terms of anti-Diemism. With the demise of Diem it was feared that revolutionary zeal would wane and the cause degenerate into simple reformism. Coupled with this was the fear that the war might be won but the subsequent peace lost. Indeed, as we have seen, something of this nature did take place. The golden aura of the Revolution faded, and the struggle continued not because of spirit but because of the organization that had trapped its followers and prevented their escape.

That the formation of the PRP meant in effect the creation of an alliance with an alien idea as well as with outside powers was not necessarily a detracting element. All Vietnamese political movements during the twentieth century, especially the militant nationalist ones, have allied themselves with outside forces or powers: the Japanese, the French, the Chinese, the Soviets, and the Americans. Independence itself has a special meaning for Vietnamese, carrying with it the connotation or the overtone of alliance.

PRP Organization

The organizational structure of the PRP closely resembled that of the NLF, a requirement imposed by the fact that the PRP was designed to be an integral part of the Front organization. There were two exceptions: The PRP developed the standard Communist cell structure to link together the individual members, and it developed a separate chain of command for urban areas, one similar to but separate from the rural chain of command. See Chart 8–1.

Under the PRP Central Committee (*Ban Chap Hanh Trung Uong Dang*) came the central committee of the interzone (*xu* or *bo*). Below the interzone the ladder split. The rural consisted of the zone (*khu*), province (*tinh bo*), district (*quan*), village (*xa*), and hamlet branch (*chi bo*); while the urban chain of command consisted of the special zone (*dac khu*), city (*thanh bo*), town or portion of city (*khu pho*), street zone (*kha pho*), and street branch (*chi bo*). At the bottom, in both rural and urban areas, was the three-man cell structure (*tieu to*). In addition there existed what was called the single-contact member (*dang vien don tuyen*), who was found at all levels from the zone to the branch and whose identity was not known to fellow PRP members; the leadership at the interzone central committee level often found it useful to have such an individual *sur place,* particularly if the organiza-

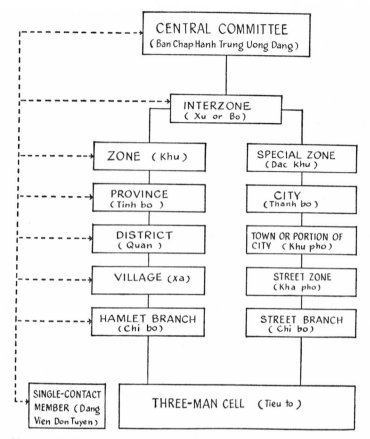

Chart 8–1   **Organization of the People's Revolutionary Party**

tion at his level were compromised or destroyed. He also acted as a top-secret courier and probably as a Party inspector.

Part or all of the headquarters for the PRP Central Committee, as noted, were in Binh Duong province, in the famed Zone D area north of Saigon but within easy reach of the city, although purportedly what existed there was the headquarters of the Saigon-Cholon-Gia Dinh Special Zone (of the NLF). (A part if not all of this headquarters complex was overrun by a joint GVN-U.S. military operation in January 1966, and some six thousand documents were captured; from this incredible haul came information to fill in many gaps in the GVN knowledge of the NLF and the PRP.) It was clearly established that although the NLF Saigon-Cholon-Gia Dinh Special Zone headquarters did exist, it was little more than a housekeeping unit for the PRP. Of course the leaders of the PRP did not remain long in any one place since the chance of betrayal increased with the passing of each day. Undoubtedly they spent much of their time in Laos, as did the NLF leadership. (There were also some persistent but never confirmed reports that the PRP Central Committee members spent much of their time in a second headquarters just inside the Cambodian border west of Hau Nghia province.)

The functions of the PRP Central Committee were threefold: military commissar work, manipulation of the NLF, and general administration. Chairman Vo Chi Cong was responsible for NLF activities as well as supervision of the proselyting program, the agit-prop and indoctrination work, and recruitment and organization building. Tran Nam Trung, the secretary-general, handled military affairs — that is, the NLF army — but, as far as could be determined, had little to do with North Vietnamese (PAVN) units operating in South Vietnam, which apparently maintained their own exclusive chain of command direct to Hanoi. The administrative work at the PRP headquarters was divided among a number of sections, including economic and financial, intelligence and counterintelligence, and communication and liaison.

The interzone central committee was basically a liaison and administrative echelon necessitated by the fact that geography and security needs prevented the complete centralization of leadership within the Central Committee. It consisted of some 21 members headed by a chairman, who according to the bylaws must have had five years of active Party membership. He was assisted by the presidium (also referred to as the standing committee or sometimes as the current affairs section) that consisted of the secretary-general, an assistant secretary, and the chairman.

The provincial central committee, or the city central committee, generally had from eight to ten members. It too was headed by a presidium (the chairman, secretary, and assistant secretary) and a series of section heads (for military activities, proselyting, agit-prop, finance and economic production, liaison and communication, and intelligence and counterintelligence). The bylaws stipulated that the provincial committee was to be elected at a convention held every two years. However, there is no evidence that such elections were held; captured memoranda on the subject argued that elections could not be held for security reasons, thus justifying the appointment of the committee by the Central Committee. At any rate, the central committee at all levels met only infrequently; hence affairs in effect were in the hands of the presidium.

The district level — the district central committee (*quan*) or town or portion of city (*khu pho*) — probably was the most important lower-level element of the PRP. It was responsible for overseeing all PRP activity within its area and had considerable latitude in its operations. It was the implementing arm of the Central Committee and prior to 1964 was the lowest operating level of the Party. Before this time Party members were frequently reported in villages, but as visitors and not as permanent operators. After 1964 the apparatus was extended to the level below the district; this was part of the general PRP organizational buildup that began at that time. The district central committee consisted of three to twelve members, most of whom were from the area and in fact after 1964 lived in the villages and served as village-level PRP officials.

The village (*xa*) or street zone (*kha pho*) was the lowest echelon with any significant amount of decision-making power at its command. It was the first echelon of the Party in specific geographic areas: villages, schools, rubber plantations, factories, or sections of cities. Its executive committee was composed of five to seven members, and it had under it from three to a dozen branches, or *chi bo*. Leadership generally was in the hands of a single full-time Party leader.

The basic PRP unit, to which all members belonged, was the *chi bo*, usually referred to in English as the hamlet branch group or the street branch group. It consisted of from one to seven three-man cells. The *chi bo* was the Party's "link with the masses" and was charged with the responsibility of extending and maintaining Party influence either directly with the people or through NLF and other organizations. It was also charged with the task of reporting upward local sentiment and of keeping the higher echelons informed of local conditions and situations.

The various levels of the Party appeared to be well integrated through the use of overlapping committee membership; that is, the central committee at each level was composed in part of top-ranking leaders from the level just below.

The PRP member was expected to remain activist at all times and beyond this to serve as an exemplary model of behavior for non-Party members.[9] "Party members must be carefully selected and well indoctrinated," declared the training manual. "They must be pioneers. . . . They must be able to win the people's confidence and must set an example for the people by being bold, energetic, fearless, able to suffer all hardships and misery, willing to make great sacrifices." [10] In early 1966 there were indications that the PRP was attempting to broaden its base into something resembling a mass political movement. Instructions went out to create what was called a "sympathizer group," which apparently was to be an element standing somewhere between the PRP and the

---

[9] See the PRP bylaws in Appendix C.
[10] An indoctrination booklet dated 1965 declared:

As militant members of the working class we must, when entering the Party, cast off our former values and thoughts and prepare to devote the rest of our lives if necessary to the Revolution. We must remain loyal to the working class, always understanding its sufferings and miseries, always loving it, and always struggling ceaselessly for its liberation.

NLF, closely allied to the PRP and a reservoir from which the Party could draw new members.[11]

The standard Communist principle of collectivist agreement reached through the mechanism of "democratic centralism" ostensibly prevailed in the PRP. "Democratic centralism" was defined in various documents as "decisions made at committee meetings by majority vote, which individuals must then obey. . . . The minority obeys the decision of the majority . . . , the lower echelons obey the decisions of the upper echelons, all elements of the Revolution obey the Central Committee. . . . There is one shout and a thousand echoes. . . ."

Criticism and self-criticism sessions were considered an integral part of Party life as were individual efforts by a member to promote his own "spirit of self-enlightenment, self-improvement, and voluntarism."

Discipline was apparently strict. Captured documents frequently cited disciplinary actions taken against individual members, usually because of immoral behavior or corruption. There were three forms of discipline: reprimand, official warning, and expulsion. Both individuals and Party units were subject to disciplinary measures. Said the training manual: "Discipline must be severe, for only by this means can order be maintained and progress assured. In addition to disciplinary punishment the Party seeks to educate its members to recognize their shortcomings in deed and thought."

The PRP required that an applicant for membership be sponsored by two Party members who had themselves been members for at least three months. Whereas Lao Dong Party members had to come from the workers' class, the PRP bylaws stipulated that a member must be "a worker; a peasant or a city proletarian; a middle-class peasant or petite bourgeoisie; a student or intellectual; a montagnard; or [an ARVN] deserter." Thus the chief requirement seemed to be that the individual had been actively supporting the cause and had a good record in this respect. His sponsors were responsible for both his indoctrination and his behavior during the probationary period, which lasted from four to six months depending on his social class. During his probationary period, when his application was being screened by higher headquarters, he was obliged to familiarize

---

[11] The instructions said:

[You are instructed] to investigate and discover persons who are sympathetic to the Party and who may be qualified for admission into the Party, that is, those who have made some achievement in the Revolution either in the liberated area or in the strategic hamlets, towns, or cities or those who have influence over a number of other people. Investigate these persons thoroughly — their past activities, their social class, their attitude toward the enemy . . . ; also investigate their relatives. Then indoctrinate them in communism and the Party's policies; heighten their sense of responsibility and correct any erroneous thoughts. Then indoctrinate them on the Party's bylaws. After being indoctrinated, the sympathizers may request admittance into the Party. . . . They may then become probationary Party members and, eventually, official members. . . . Absolutely do not admit a large number of sympathizers at any one time. . . .

himself with the Party bylaws, attend meetings (although he could not participate in them) and indoctrination courses, and pay dues.

There was little substantive difference between the Lao Dong Party and the PRP.[12] It was easier, especially for students, to join the PRP; the central committees met less often; and there were arrangements whereby elections could be, as they were, postponed.

Throughout, the Party seemed chiefly concerned with two major activities: political control of the military arm of the NLF, and implementation of the political struggle, which manifested itself chiefly in the form of military and civilian proselyting (*binh van*) work. Political commissars, undoubtedly all Party members, were found in all NLF army units. The task of the commissar was to ensure that the military unit commander did not deviate from the instructions from higher headquarters; he was also responsible for troop indoctrination work. Political activities, including the proselyting work, were administered through the NLF apparatus. The entire struggle movement also involved PRP cadres, but again the NLF served as the front for public activities.

The PRP was a Janus-faced organization. In the South it insisted to the Vietnamese people that it was not Communist but Marxist-Leninist, indicating philosophic but not political allegiance and implying some sort of national communism without outside ties, loyal only to the people of South Vietnam and their interests. In the North the DRV characterized the PRP as a vanguard Marxist-Leninist organization, indicating that it was in the mainstream of the world-wide Communist movement, both spiritually and materially connected to the North Vietnamese, the DRV government, and the Lao Dong Party.

Communist Youth

The PRP Youth League

The PRP's strong right arm was its Youth League (Doan Thanh Nien Nhan Dan Cach Mang), formed in mid-1962. Previously a Lao Dong Youth League had attached itself to the Southern branch of the Lao Dong Party but as far as can be determined amounted to little. *Quy chanh* stated that a Communist youth group existed but that the more effective and competent young people were utilized in the ranks of the Party itself, although not as official members. The PRPYL during the 1962–1964 period remained a rudimentary organization; however, fragmentary evidence indicated that it was well disciplined, highly dedicated, and well camouflaged. Apparently the line between the Party and its youthful arm was blurred.

[12] See the comparison of the PRP and Lao Dong Party bylaws in Appendix C.

A PRPYL indoctrination booklet, circa 1963, outlined the theoretical purpose and chief activities of the League:

The Party is the leading organization of the working class, responsible for providing the leadership for the Revolution. The Party needs mass organizations to carry out the Revolution, that is, it needs revolutionary groups. The Youth League is a mass organization of the Party. . . . Under the leadership of the Party, therefore, the Youth League leads the revolutionary struggle against the U.S.-Diem clique, seeking to set up a democratic government in South Vietnam, establish free trade between North and South as a means of working for unification of our Fatherland; also helping to consolidate the Democratic Republic of Vietnam, which is now progressing toward socialism, which is the first step toward true communism. . . . Our prime role is in the mobilizing of the masses. Our members also are in the vanguard — where the fighting is, in key communication tasks, carrying out the agit-prop duties, and protecting the secrets of the Party. . . . We have this special advantage: We are eager and courageous youths, ready to make great sacrifices; we are resolute, agile, full of initiative and progressive ideas; we are closer than others to the Party. . . . Therefore, when a difficult project is under way, the Youth League receives the assignment, which it carries out, after discussing the plan, regardless of the cost. Thus . . . the League is the special arm of the Party. The Party is the brain and the League is the great right hand holding the hammer ready to strike after the brain gives the order. . . .

In talking with defectors and studying the documents on the youth organizations one had the feeling that the Party was more interested in creating a strong youth apparatus than in using it, at that moment, for any specific purpose. The plans for the PRPYL were apparently long range; its day was yet to come.

The League served as the manpower pool for the Party, or, as one booklet put it, "the League is the melting pot for the supply of young members and worthy cadres to the Party itself." From the League the Party drew its volunteers for hazardous missions. Some of the most daring NLF sabotage acts were the work of boys in their mid-teens or younger. More than one grenade was tossed into Saigon cafés by persons later described as "about twelve years old."

Membership in the PRPYL was open to youths from 16 to 25, although defectors say these age categories were not strictly enforced. Girls particularly were encouraged to join. Membership was open to all social classes, although the most eagerly sought after were proletarian youths. A PRPYL learning document cited three criteria for membership in the League:

He must have a firm determination to fight a life-long struggle to attain the goals of peace, unification, in harmony with socialist doctrine and Communist ideals. . . . He must maintain close relations with youth masses, particularly farmer and worker youth. . . . He must be willing constantly to improve his political education and strictly to obey the directives of the Party and the League.[13]

Conditions of membership were essentially the same as for membership in the Party. The League bylaws, however, contained a clause not in the Party bylaws: "The League member shall take communism as the ideal of his life." A League candidate also was to affirm that he had never performed any act prejudicial to the interests of the masses. After a potential member was introduced by a member in good standing, his application went to the League's central committee, then to the Party's village committee. If approved, the candidate was inducted into the League in a formal ceremony, the highlight of which was the swearing of the oath. "The membership oath," said a learning document, "is a solemn pledge before the organization to remain faithful for all his life to the Revolution, to the Party, to the League. He swears he is ready to sacrifice his individual interests in the name of the Revolution. He swears he will overcome all difficulties and withstand all hardships in the cause of his new responsibility." A booklet used in indoctrinating organizers added this note: "The oath has a sacred significance and leaves a deep impression in the heart of the youth beginning a new life. The admission ceremony would lose its value if the oath were omitted or disregarded. . . ."

The idea that joining the League meant a new life or rebirth was stressed heavily in indoctrination sessions, which, defectors report, were long and arduous. One *quy chanh* said: "The Party was like an older brother or teacher, and the League was like a younger brother or pupil. Our older brother was brave and heroic, but we wanted to be braver and more heroic." League members prided themselves on the sacrifices that youth had made for the Revolution, and indoctrination sessions consisted largely of recounting the legendary exploits of revolutionary youths as far back as 1930.

The League did not have a nationwide hierarchic structure. It existed only at the village level and was directly responsible to the Party's village central committee. This was explained in a 1964 indoctrination booklet:

Under the present circumstances Youth League activities in South Vietnam are very difficult; liaison between units is often blocked and usually slow; the League organization is not yet large and strong. Therefore, the Party has not yet organized it top to bottom. At the present, the organization is being built from the bottom upwards, according to our requirements and according to the abilities of the cadres. At the correct moment, the League will be organized vertically up to the top central level, as stipulated in the League regulations.

[13] An untitled PRPYL study document for members of the NLF Youth Liberation Association.

Nor was there any autonomy or even "democratic centralism" at the village level.[14]

Within the village the League was organized at three levels. The League cell (*to Doan*) had three to five members and was the lowest unit. A village with more than three cells joined them into what was called a League fraction (*phan Doan*); at the same time the fraction became a League branch (*chi Doan*). As other fractions were formed in the village, they joined the same branch. The entire membership then met as the League branch, presided over by a secretary who had an assistant, both appointed by the Party's village central committee. League branch meetings witnessed a great deal of free-wheeling youthful debate, but there was little decision-making power.

The Vanguard Youth League

The PRP's Vanguard Youth League (Thanh Nien Xung Phong), an avowed Marxist-Leninist organization for youngsters between 12 and 15, was created in 1962. It was a sort of Young Pioneers and served as the junior member or suborganization of the PRP Youth League and as the youngest brother of the Party. It was open to children "regardless of social class, creed, or religion." Its avowed purpose was "to educate the youth to love their country and the masses; to hate the U.S. imperialists and their feudalist lackeys; to increase the ties of unity of youth in South Vietnam; and to guide youth in participation in the Revolution by offering them actions appropriate to their capabilities to contribute to the liberation of South Vietnam." The Vanguard Youth League existed as a single-level organization of 3 to 25 members within the village. It was administered by a leading member of the Youth League, who in turn was appointed by the Party's village central committee. Meetings consisted largely of educational activities and junior debates. The children paid nominal dues and elected their own chairman to "preside" over their meetings.

[14] Said the same document:

In the present circumstances in the unliberated South, the League must carry out its activities in secrecy, and so democratic rights have not yet been put into practice. . . . Therefore the Party's [national] Central Committee clear-sightedly chooses worthy young people to assume positions of League leadership.

9

The Course of the NLF

From an organizational standpoint the NLF passed through the three distinct phases discussed in Chapter 4. From an operational standpoint it also went through three phases: the social movement propaganda phase, completed by early 1962; the political struggle movement phase, which ended with the overthrow of the Diem regime in November 1963; and the legitimization-militarization phase, which ended with the decision by the United States to enter actively into the South Vietnam struggle and to begin air strikes on North Vietnam.

The Social Movement Propaganda Phase

The early years of the NLF were dominated by two major activities. The first was agit-prop work, which included informational and internal indoctrinational efforts designed to advertise the Front and indeed advertise the fact of the Revolution to the villager (propaganda) and counter his apathy by fanning his discontent into hatred and converting his grievances into hostility (agitation). The second major effort was

154

social organization propaganda work, utilizing the various specially created NLF groups and associations to mobilize the population. These two efforts met, and in fact became one, at the village level. During this first phase there also was a great deal of internal recruitment, formation of nucleus cadres, and training and indoctrination work within both the NLF and the Communist party in the South.

The early days of the first phase were devoted to gathering momentum. Cadres launched the ambitious organization-building program that served as the base for the struggle movement. Except to the youth groups, the NLF was portrayed to villagers as static, passive, or defensive in nature, akin to the traditional Vietnamese protective association. The organization was not so much sold by the organizers and agit-prop cadres at it was insinuated into the village. The villagers, though skeptical, saw in it an opportunity for political participation: The appointed officials would be driven out and the villagers would manage their own affairs as in pre-French days. Through the struggle movement, they were told, a great political change could be wrought. The village thus was conceived as militantly antigovernment, but only in a political and not in a military sense.

The NLF objective was to loosen the government's administrative hold on the village, which was often weak even without NLF pressure upon it. Civil servants were driven out. Troops were harassed when they conducted military sweep operations through the area. At the same time the NLF began to insinuate publicly that it was a quasi-government. It did this by blocking every effort on the part of the GVN to assert its legitimacy and by sabotaging every government effort to communicate, to adjudicate, to govern.

Thus the NLF goaded the government into increasingly repressive measures, and gradually the government found the gulf between it and the villagers growing wider. For the NLF response to government military action was to proclaim itself the protector of the people. The villager, to the degree that he perceived government action against his village as excessive and unwarranted, supported the NLF, which became to him a real and valuable thing protecting him and his village.

Government military action also provided the NLF with the rationale for its own use of force. A theme constantly employed in the early period was "The enemy brings violence; we wish only to struggle peacefully."

It was true that the leadership in the 1960–1961 period did not put much priority on the violence program, nor was there much direct appeal to any segment to employ terror techniques. This may have been a tactical move. To persuade a rural Vietnamese villager to go to the barricades or to run physical risks, real and legitimate grievances must be fanned; the injustices of a colonialist system, for example, can be converted into arguments for the use of force. But the Communists' chief grievance in the days when the Diem government was too weak to even make itself felt in the countryside was that Diem had refused to honor the 1954 Geneva accords, which he had not signed in the first place. How many rural Vietnamese would have been willing to risk their lives for this abstraction? However, the 1959–1961 period was not without bloodshed — far from it. In 1959, although no accurate records were kept, it is a sober estimate that one progovernment or government official was killed every other day. This figure rose to perhaps five a day by 1960 and climbed slowly during the year. But it did not begin to approach the figure reached after 1962, which included the Army of the Republic of Vietnam casualties, of 2,000 deaths a week. Violence was present during the period under discussion, but in scope and size it cannot be compared to the later stages.

It is important to understand the essentially political rather than military nature of the NLF's activities in the first period in order to appreciate the marked changes that followed in succeeding years. Virtually all effort was focused on the struggle movement, and the various acts of the violence program were designed to support that program, as, for example, the assassination of a village chief. The NLF leadership apparently believed that the shaky Diem government could be brought down through the deliberate creation of anarchy, and that this could be accomplished with the political struggle movement. At the end of its first nine months, clandestine newspapers summed up the NLF's accomplishments; these were expressed almost exclusively in struggle terms:

> In the light of the Front's program of action and due to the widened scale of the struggle, the struggle movements among the Southern people became more and more abundant; the slogans of the struggle manifested more and more clearly the deep political character of the movement. The struggle for livelihood and democratic rights was closely coordinated with the political struggle. . . . From complaints, petitions, and small demonstrations the movement advanced to big demonstrations, including thousands of people marching into the cities and towns, and uprisings that exterminated and gave warnings to "wicked agents," demolished agrovilles, and smashed the reactionary government. . . .[1]

Virtually no mention was made of violence; the language was in terms of the "peaceful struggle movement." The flavor of the period is described accurately, although exaggerated in detail. The article concluded the account of the first nine months:

> The situation that has developed in the South since the birth of the NLFSV proves that the struggle movement is the proper mass movement, having an "all the people" character, one that cannot be extinguished.

[1] *Nhan Dan*, August 28, 1961.

The end of the social movement propaganda phase was marked by the meeting of the NLF First Congress in February–March 1962. However, this was more symbolic than actual; what really marked the end of the period was the conclusion reached by the leadership, and spelled out at the congress, that the simple struggle movement in itself would never bring them to power. Diem was proving more durable than expected, at least in part because of American assistance. The leadership realized that it faced a protracted conflict for which it was well prepared. The fundamental organization building was completed.

The Political Struggle Movement Phase

Gradually the campaign grew more activist, from internally directed organizational meetings to outwardly directed demonstrations. In the second phase the NLF's objective was to complete the mobilization of the rural Vietnamese and concurrently to destroy the GVN administration in the rural areas. The instrument continued to be the struggle movement, but now increased priorities were placed on developing the armed struggle. The masses were to be the dynamite and the agit-prop cadre the detonator.

The period began in early 1962 and ended in late 1963. For the GVN it began with the launching of the strategic-hamlet program and ended with the overthrow of the Diem government. For the NLF the phase began with a complete but shaky structure of both administrative and functional liberation associations and ended with a firm organization and the launching in earnest of various activities in its liberated area. For the Communists it began with the formation of their new organization, the People's Revolutionary Party, and ended with the order to regularize the entire NLF machine. For the United States it was a period that began with the decision to supply all necessary aid to the Diem government and ended with the United States inextricably enmeshed in the war, supporting a far more popular but much weaker, greener government. In general it was a period in which the GVN grew in strength and diminished in popularity, then suddenly lost its strength but gained in popularity. For the NLF it was a period that began with high hopes and ended with disillusionment. Most significantly, for rural Vietnamese it was a time of disenchantment in the NLF, its cause, and its increasing use of repression and terror. In terms of strength of position, the two sides, GVN and NLF, reversed during the period, although the loss of strength on the GVN side was more temporary. In terms of popular support, positions were also reversed during the period.

Specifically the NLF sought to destroy the viability of the GVN administrative structure in the rural areas. It virtually achieved this goal at one point, in the days following the overthrow of the Diem government, but was unable to capitalize on events to the degree it had expected and in the end was cheated of the quick and final victory its followers had been led to expect. Most of the period's activity was devoted to the struggle movement, employing, where appropriate, a judicious use of violence. During this time American observers and many GVN officials tended to regard the situation as one of stalemate or deterioration for the GVN: The Army of the Republic of Vietnam could not "fix, find, and destroy" the NLF guerrillas; the strategic-hamlet program was encountering serious resistance. However, the NLF's perception of events was equally grim. Internal reports of the period stressed over and over the assessment that the Revolution was not moving with the necessary speed, that it had encountered far more resistance and hostility than anticipated, that the Diem government's counterinsurgency efforts, even if unpopular, might fatally injure the Revolution. Apparently there was little loss of long-range faith among the leaders and true believers, but they feared that the GVN might with short-run measures destroy the NLF structure and crush the insurgency. This attitude became strongest in April 1963, which conversely was the high-water mark of the Diem government.

In order to grasp the change we should begin with the earliest part of this second period, when hopes were high and idealism untarnished; the mood of the time is illustrated in these extracts from a secret NLF report on a Western Nambo Interzone Party conference in October 1961:

Our past effort has created for us the following: a strongly centralized organizational system echeloned from Anh Tam [code name] down to the cells;
good leadership; a united people's front that is increasingly expanding, has
gained much political prestige in rural areas, in the [Mekong] delta, the
highlands, and the cities. . . . We have won much support throughout the
socialist world. . . . Using many forms of self-defense struggle movements,
the heroic people have smashed the enemy's mopping-up operations and
upset his "pacification" scheme. The corrupt administrators have been weakened and their squeeze ended. . . . Their taxation policies have failed.
Thousands of soldiers have deserted. . . . Such important results have been
achieved thanks to the patriotism of our people, who, under the clear-sighted
leadership of our Party, have reached a high level of political understanding
and have acquired much experience through their valiant struggle against
the enemy.

This attitude of the late 1961 and early 1962 period gave way to grim pessimism a year later as a result of two developments: the advent of massive American aid, and the GVN's strategic-hamlet program. A

Central Committee memorandum dated July 1962 spoke of "a period of temporary difficulties for the Revolution," which was due, it said, to

the Americans . . . who are attempting to overcome the weakness of the Diem troops. . . . Their efforts have created a number of difficulties for the people's liberation movement so that at the moment a seesaw struggle of equilibrium exists between them and the Vietnamese people. . . . The basic approach and direction of the Revolution will not change, but owing to the American interventionists certain aspects are now somewhat changed.

One changed aspect was a realization that the NLF faced a "prolonged struggle full of hardships," a phrase that increasingly ran through the internal reports and directives of the period like the theme of a symphony. One of the leadership's most delicate problems was to inform both cadres and rank-and-file members that the road ahead was going to be long and hard, without destroying faith or diminishing zeal.

Typical of the tack taken is this example from an indoctrination booklet:

Each revolutionary fighter and patriot aspires to a speedy realization of the Revolution so that the people's misery may be alleviated. This desire is very legitimate. However, the Revolution must develop according to its own rules. . . . The revolutionary path in general is a long drawn-out one. For the peoples in colonial countries this long drawn-out character is clearly essential. The entire path of the Revolution is long and its stages long. This is particularly true of the first stage, in which the goal of the revolutionary struggle is to remove the imperialist and feudal forces. . . . Other colonialized nations' histories also clearly prove that to defeat aggression a long struggle is necessary. The revolutionary struggle formerly carried out by the Chinese people and more recently by the Algerian people eloquently proves this reasoning. . . . To achieve our goals the revolutionary forces must have the necessary time to realize the transformation of the masses. . . .

Loss of zeal was particularly dangerous to the PRP members. Said a PRP assessment report of March 1963,

A very important point relating to leadership should be thoroughly understood. It is that this is a long struggle, full of hardships. The long struggle full of hardships is an essential process in the Revolution. . . . It is a prolonged struggle because we are not yet in a position to defeat the enemy immediately but can do this only gradually, step by step. . . . Many comrades in our Party are not fully aware of this problem. Many are not adequately prepared morally to meet it. In providing moral leadership to the cadres, Party members, and the masses, we should educate them to understand that this is a prolonged struggle full of hardships but sure of success. We must stimulate and strengthen their fighting spirit, their courage, and their perseverance so they will never flinch, will constantly be cautious, and resolutely overcome all hardships and difficulties. We must preserve our military forces and avoid being foolhardy. We must teach all to win without arrogance, lose without discouragement, certain that eventually we will liberate the South and unify the Fatherland.

This document came about seventeen months after the October 1961 document previously cited. The change of tone is most apparent. It went on:

We must realize that we have many weaknesses and shortcomings. The Party has a well-established organization; cadres and Party members in general are adequate. But we are lacking in organization in certain areas. The quality of leadership is inadequate. The Party is not strong. The Front organization is not comprehensive. The army is still weak. The guerrilla movement is still limited. Our forces have not been adequately consolidated.

So the order went out to tighten loin strings and prepare for a prolonged struggle full of hardships. Caution became the watchword, consolidation the chief preoccupation. Specifically the orders were:

In view of the increasingly relentless measures carried out by the enemy, and in view of our shortcomings, especially in developing and consolidating our forces, we must . . . from the standpoint of general leadership, for a fairly long time, stick to the policy of consolidation of our forces. . . .

If the operational principle of conservation was to be practiced, the organizational principle to be followed was one of proliferation. NLF members and Party cadres were harangued to broaden the base of their particular organizations as well as of the NLF itself. A recruitment drive was launched on behalf of the NLF, and the more stringent bars of the earlier period were dropped. Cadres were instructed to recruit all except the "hard-core enemy," defined as "the Ngo Dinh Diem clique, servant of the U.S. imperialists, the most reactionary of the landowner class, feudalists and pro-American comprador bourgeois, those who lorded it over the people in the North and then fled South when peace was restored to Indochina, and . . . those who owe the Vietnamese people a debt of blood."

The year 1962 became largely a holding operation, and even the DRV's public assessment at the year's end was unenthusiastic. Said theoretician Nguyen Van Vinh,

Southern events during the year prove that the forces and the struggle movement of the Southern compatriots can be maintained . . . under very difficult circumstances. . . . Though not as intense or large as in the previous year, the struggle movement took place continually and more often. . . . Our valiant Southern compatriots are fully capable of achieving final success. . . .[2]

By the spring of 1963, faith in the myth of the General Uprising began to crumble. One internal memorandum to PRP cadres, dated April 1963, began to undercut the whole notion:

You will recall . . . that with regard to the Revolution in the South, Anh Nam [code name] had stated in *Revolution,* October 1961, that there was the

---

[2] Radio Hanoi, December 27, 1962.

great possibility that the Revolution in the South would result in a General Uprising. . . . Concerning the General Uprising, we should realize that in the present situation when the enemy keeps increasing his terror and destruction, when the U.S. imperialists are engaged in armed aggression, a General Uprising will be most difficult. . . . We face the possibility of a war quite similar to the Resistance. . . . The General Uprising idea was too rigid and simple an idea, and the possible developments that may have resulted from it have been disregarded. . . . At present we will carry out a military struggle that will accompany and stimulate the political struggle. Our aim remains to win step by step and eventually . . . cause a General Uprising. . . . But there are other possible outcomes. . . . Our struggle may compel the U.S. to discontinue intervention, to negotiate, to go back to the 1954 Geneva agreement, to withdraw troops from the South, or to stop the war . . . or . . . owing to the force of our struggle there may be big battles that thin out the enemy's ranks, after which we may combine with the people for a General Uprising, or a coup d'état. . . . Or, before a complete victory is achieved and a General Uprising staged, the threat of a collapse may compel the enemy to stop the war. . . . This may happen in the event the enemy suffers a heavy defeat having a decisive character and when the revolutionary movement is near complete victory.

The Legitimization-Militarization Phase

The NLF first organized its cause, then energized it, and then sought to legitimatize it. Part of the third phase was to have been the political take-over of South Vietnam. The phase began with the overthrow of the Diem government and ended, as noted, with the decision of the United States to put its full military power into South Vietnam.

The NLF attempted at all times to maintain a façade of legalism in its actions, partly to avoid the stigma of bandit and warlord that has characterized military forces in Asia since civilization began. (The Vietnamese word for soldier stems from the root word for bandit, just as the word for general stems from warlord.) NLF printed materials often employed legal language. When U.S. military men were captured and released, the NLF announcement on Radio Liberation spoke of their "arrest" and later of their "trial and conviction" on "charges of crimes against the people." When their "appeal for clemency" was granted, they were "released," the language seeking to convey the idea of due process. Assassinations were carried out following "trials in absentia," and great risks often were taken to pin a death note on an assassinated official. It was probably no accident that the chairman of the national Central Committee was a lawyer, or that the NLF carried on heavy correspondence with the international Communist lawyers' organization.

As early as December 1961 *Hoc Tap* referred to the ARVN as

"Diem's rebel troops." Later the NLF frequently asserted that it was the only legal ruler in South Vietnam and that the GVN forces were the dissidents. In a Radio Liberation commentary of May 30, 1964 on the GVN request to the U.N. Security Council for a fact-finding commission to visit the Vietnam-Cambodian border, the NLF said "The United States has sent its lackeys, the Saigon rebel authorities, to the Security Council. . . ." Then the assertion became an assumption. On December 28, 1964 Radio Liberation, in a statement on the border issue, declared:

Faced with the Cambodian Royal Government's decision to open negotiations with the NLFSV on the frontier problem . . . the Saigon puppet authorities on December 8 issued a communiqué aimed at distorting the negotiations and declaring arrogantly that only they themselves have legal sovereignty and competence to settle the Vietnamese-Cambodian frontier problem. . . . From the international viewpoint, the Front has the full prestige and power to represent 14 million South Vietnamese in dealing with foreign affairs for the benefit of the country and people. . . . On the basis of equality and free will, all that is signed, under whatever form, between the NLFSV and the Cambodian government will be valid.

By mid-1964 it was quite apparent from all of the NLF's behavior and public pronouncements that it meant to convert its latent political power into specific political achievements that would eventually mean NLF control of South Vietnam. This could come either through the third stage of revolutionary guerrilla warfare or by means of the conference table. Most of the effort during the period was such as to suggest that the NLF was in search of a negotiated settlement, a coalition government with NLF primacy. It spoke frequently of a "Vietnamese solution." It may have been that the leadership sought to pursue a dual course, as a hedge or a contingency. At any rate the balance from the political to armed struggle tipped late in the summer of 1963. In fact the exact moment can probably be fixed. It was the first week in September 1963, when the two DRV generals convened the "military conference," apparently held just inside the Cambodian border opposite the Darlac plateau, at which the NLF military units were reorganized and their development accelerated. The conference was followed in October by a series of two-week special training courses throughout the liberated area at which guerrilla units received retraining in conventional small-military-unit tactics, antiaircraft defenses, and techniques of sabotage.

Another indication was the appearance of guerrilla units wearing distinctive insignia, violating a fundamental rule of guerrilla warfare. Normally the guerrilla wore the black cotton two-piece pajama-like suit of the Vietnamese farmer, and although he might wear a helmet in actual combat, at other times there was nothing to distinguish him from other rural Vietnamese. In late 1963 the "red-scarf movement" began to spread in South Vietnam; members of guerrilla bands began wearing bright-red scarves around their necks, and the red scarf quickly became an NLF symbol; its appearance and the psychological significance of finding it necessary to distinguish soldier from civilian indicated the hand of the professional soldier.

The end of the Diem regime, it was determined later, was viewed by the NLF leadership as at best a mixed blessing. Diem had represented a serious threat to the insurgency, but also he had made an excellent symbol on which the struggle movement could be based. And since the struggle movement strategy required a militantly aroused population, a strong but repressive government was to be preferred over a weak but popular one. No long-run threat to the NLF loomed larger than the formation in Saigon of a popular, participational, democratic government.

The months of November and December 1963 in Vietnam were almost as incredible in their way as had been the last month of the Diem government. After the coup d'état, which South Vietnamese refer to as "the revolution," the country went on an emotional binge. The government went on a political holiday. Governmental administration broke down as three fourths of the country's 41 province chiefs were fired. Whole areas of the country were without any GVN officials. The Vietnamese felt that a long nightmare was over, that they were coming up from the depths. It was an exhilarating feeling for them, and they reveled in it. The military were the heroes of the day, and the new government, the liberating generals, would rule but would not govern; they would enforce no unpopular edicts, exert no governmental discipline. The resulting government was weak, but it was popular.

The Presidium of the NLF Central Committee met in extraordinary session on November 17 to assess the situation and to fix new policy for a radically changed situation. For the NLF it was both crisis and opportunity. The virtual anarchy in the countryside presented it with an unprecedented opportunity to extend its control. But it also faced a new enemy with new strengths, one far less vulnerable than the old government. In the massive NLF agit-prop and indoctrination campaigns, all of Vietnam's troubles had been personified in Diem, and when Diem collapsed, so did the campaigns. As a holding-operation measure the Presidium ordered cadres to begin a twofold campaign: to attempt to take credit for the overthrow of Diem and to vilify the new regime. The first effort was largely unsuccessful, in part because the new GVN conducted a massive information campaign in the countryside to counter the effort. Nor did the vilification campaign come to much; cadres simply lacked credible evidence with which to convince skeptical villagers of the new GVN's villainy.

The Central Committee had ordered the NLF army units to begin a maximum strike effort against the ARVN as soon as word was received that a coup d'état had taken place. In the first five days after the coup, NLF army military incidents increased 50 per cent. Two weeks later the weekly incident rate stood at 1,021, the highest ever recorded. The average for November was 745, double the monthly average for the first ten months of the year. Apparently the NLF sought chiefly to test the defenses of the new government. The ARVN was able to absorb all the NLF army could throw at it, and the offensive slacked off in tempo. But the new emphasis on military actions never ceased thereafter. In Communist terms, the armed struggle came to the fore.

The militarization of the effort, which included ordering thousands of North Vietnamese regular army soldiers to the South, had behind it various motives. First, the troops would deliver the *coup de grâce*, the final blow that would destroy the GVN and its armed forces. Second, the order was by way of anticipating a possible American response such as the dispatch of large numbers of American troops to South Vietnam. Apparently the NLF and DRV leaderships considered this a possibility but believed the United States could not and would not do so if it realized it faced considerable numbers of North Vietnamese regulars. Both assumptions were wrong. The third reason was the desire to have in South Vietnam a sizable number of troops loyal to Hanoi. This would prevent any separatist movement on the part of the NLF once it had assumed political control in the South.

In retrospect it appears that the NLF took the decision to militarize the struggle far too lightly, just as the DRV took too lightly its decision to send troops South. Both were convinced — as were many in the United States — that they were on the verge of total victory, that nothing could stop the collapse of the GVN and its armed forces, and only a small additional effort was needed to topple the Southern government. The DRV in particular was undoubtedly the victim of excessively optimistic reports from its cadres in the South. Equally important was the highly elusive morale factor in South Vietnam. The first American air strikes into North Vietnam and the announcement that large numbers of American troops had been ordered to Vietnam produced overnight a deep attitudinal change among South Vietnamese — among those within the government, members of the armed forces, and the general population. The South Vietnamese were convinced that at last the United States, the most powerful nation on earth, was coming to their rescue with full force. Obviously, to them, neither the NLF nor the DRV nor even Communist China was any match for such power. Their faith in easy American victory was, as events later proved, not justified. But at the time this widespread belief had the effect of snatching victory out of the Communists' hands.

The end of 1964 was the end of an era in Vietnam, and there would be no going back to the old revolutionary guerrilla warfare that had marked the previous five years. The Vietnam experience for the first time could be viewed in its totality. Clearly there emerged a beginning, a middle, and an end. The American escalation, the massive influx of American troops into South Vietnam, the air strikes against North Vietnam were all of a new order. An old war had ended and a new war begun, one with new rules and new participants, with new tactics and new strategies, and with new definitions of victory and defeat, whose outcome could more easily be surmised.

10

The Functional
Liberation Associations

Supporting the NLF, and in fact acting as the village base for the entire insurgency, was a clutch of functional liberation associations plus a host of other smaller but still vital social organizations.[1] As noted in Chapter 6, there were six functional liberation associations — farmers, women, workers, youth, students, and intellectuals or the culturally minded.

The essential importance of these organizations to the NLF leadership is quite apparent. What is less obvious is the reason why they were supported as strongly as they were in the early days of the insurgency by the villager himself. The answer lies chiefly in the fact that the individual villager considered that the liberation association had meaning to him personally. For the farmer, for example, the Farmers' Liberation Association meant land reform; for the village women the Women's Liberation Association meant status and more equal rights with men. Thus the individual villager saw in the liberation association, in terms of payoff, an opportunity for benefits that had not previously existed and so he voluntarily supported it. When the NLF began to turn coercive, begin-

[1] Consideration of these other organizations comes in Chapter 11.

166

ning in mid-1963, the individual villager began withdrawing his voluntary support from both the functional liberation association and the village administrative liberation association. But by this time he was enmeshed in a tangled web of NLF control and was obliged to continue his support even though it was no longer voluntary.

Farmers' Liberation Association (FLA)[2]

The FLA acted as the backbone of the NLF social movement program; it was the first organized, and it quickly grew to be the largest mass organization in the NLF. (In 1963 it claimed 1.8 million members.) Mao Tse-tung is credited as the author of the thesis that the peasant can be the main force in a Communist revolution, a thesis the NLF, as had the Viet Minh before it, accepted unreservedly. An early NLF document expressed the theme, constantly repeated throughout the era, that

the peasant is the main force of economic production, the most loyal ally of the working class; in alliance with the worker he is the main force of the Revolution. . . . The peasant is the axletree of the Revolution. . . . Control this axletree and one can move everything.

Within this context the FLA was the chief instrument and the mainstay of the political groups by which the Communists hoped to come to power. On the back of the farmer they placed the Revolution, for the drive was to make the farmer the "master of the countryside," and the process was to be the development of his "revolutionary struggle capability." But, because of past experience, the Communists both distrusted and feared the farmer. Like their Russian brothers of a generation before, they found him difficult to organize and discipline, unreliable with the revolutionary torch, most likely to lapse into indifference to the cause once he had achieved his own objective: land for himself. In the farmer the Communists saw their greatest opportunity and found their greatest threat. Like Communists elsewhere, the NLF theorizers struggled to transplant the Marxist industrial proletarian revolution into an agrarian setting. It was usually done by replacing the word "worker" with the word "farmer" or "peasant" in the indoctrination booklets. One such PRP booklet declared:

The proletarian peasant [*ban co nong*] class constitutes the most populous group in our society and the major force of production in Vietnam. It is brutally dominated, oppressed, and plundered by the imperialists and feudalists . . . and therefore is enthusiastic and firm in its support of the Revolution. It has a firm confidence in the leadership of the Party. . . . The peas-

[2] In Vietnamese, Hoi Nong Dan Giai Phong.

ant class is a major and most loyal ally of the working class. . . . The peasant class constitutes the main force of the Vietnamese people and of the Revolution, . . . and by close cooperation between the peasant and the worker we can move toward first the socialist and then the communist regime. . . . Above all . . . peasants must close ranks with the working class to form a solid group under the leadership of the Party. . . .

Outlining the relations between the PRP and the Farmers' Liberation Association, the same directive said:

It is Party policy . . . (1) to lead the peasant class to establish a peasant-worker alliance, . . . to eliminate feudalist and imperialist domination that takes the people's land from them, . . . to realize the slogans "Land to all peasants" and "One should have what one produces"; . . . (2) to guide the peasants gradually into cooperative programs to foster . . . the idea of the collective and thus to make them collectivist farmers; to improve production techniques, . . . including collective use of farm production machinery, . . . to build up a socialist and then a communist society in which there is no distinction between the countryside and the cities; . . . (3) to eliminate the landowners and make the peasants masters of the countryside under the leadership of the working class and the Party; (4) to incessantly raise the material and spiritual conditions of life of the peasant, . . . eliminating il-literacy and raising the cultural and scientific level of knowledge.

The same booklet set forth generalized and long-range goals, essentially the same as those being pursued in the DRV at the time, but also out-lined specific goals to be pursued: "(1) lower land rents for peasants; (2) assistance to peasants in protecting the land given them by the Resistance and struggling against infamous Ordinance Fifty-Seven of the GVN; (3) protection for peasants who have taken land on their own initiative [that is, squatters]; (4) opposition to the rice monopolists, the rice tax system, corvée labor, and the military draft, which dis-criminates against rural youth . . . ; (5) opposition to the enemy's terror campaign among the peasants and the Denunciation of Com-munism movement, and [at the same time] struggle for freedom of movement by peasants and the free election of village councils . . . ; (6) normalization of North-South relations with a view to eventual peaceful unification of the Fatherland." The heart of the cause was land and land tenure problems.

The NLF's image of the farmer was similar to the Communist's image of the worker elsewhere — one who produced the goods of the society but was not permitted to enjoy the fruits of his labor, one exploited, whose only hope was class warfare. The class struggle therefore became the dominant theme of the FLA. Vietnamese society, the farmer was told, was divided into three classes: the oppressors, the bourgeoisie (who may or may not be oppressors), and the oppressed. The oppressor class consisted of the feudalists (promonarchist Bao Dai supporters, most of whom also were landowners) and the commercial capitalists (rich farmers and landowners); the landowners[3] were of two types, the patriotic or progressive and the evil, with the former being less oppressive than the latter. The bourgeoisie consisted of intellectuals, students, and the petite bourgeoisie, meaning small businessmen, traders, and handicraft shop operators. The oppressed class included the workers or proletariat, "people's capitalists" (that is, national bourgeoisie), and the farmers. The farmers in turn were divided into three classes: landless farmers, poor or proletarian farmers, and middle-class farmers. Rich farmers, members of the oppressor class, were defined as "rural people's capitalists on the side of the enemy, who oppress the people. . . ." Capitalists, FLA documents added,

are of two types: the commercial capitalist Vietnamese with trade monopolies, who are valets of the U.S. . . . , and oppressed people's or pure capitalists, who support the Revolution. . . . In [the DRV] the people's capitalists work with the government . . . but once socialism is fully established there these people will disappear as capitalists and will become true workers.

The three types of farmers were classified as

the landless farmers, who must be given land . . . ; the poor farmers [*ban nong*], who own land but are poor because they are exploited; they must be helped . . . ; and the middle-class farmers who own land and love peace but who sometimes lend money for profit or even oppress poor farmers; they must be educated.

The organizational effort was pursued with great vigor. A typical directive began: "The Farmers' Liberation Association is a fundamental organization. It is the revolutionary group organization of the farmers, and it must have a large farmer membership. . . ." As a general rule organizers were told that they should seek a membership goal of up to 50 per cent of the villagers in areas where GVN control was slight; in nominally controlled villages the ideal membership figure would be about 30 per cent; "and in weak areas," the document concluded, "religious areas, villages along main roads, or agrovilles, or strategic hamlets, [membership] should be about 20 per cent." Excluded from membership were "rich farmers, spies, and farmers who have betrayed the Revolution."

The Phuoc Tuy province Farmers' Liberation Association bylaws listed six duties of each member: "(1) to carry out the directives of the association; (2) to agitate and propagandize farmers with a view to

---

[3] FLA study documents defined landowners as

those people with many large fields, plenty of money, vehicles, and houses. They do not farm but rent land at great profit. . . . However, there are patriotic and progressive landowners who reduce land rents and support the Revolution . . . and cruel and stubborn landowners who rent land at a profit, terrorize farmers, raise rents, and do not support the Revolution.

developing the association . . . and to develop solidarity and mutual-help programs within the hamlets and villages; (3) to lead the farmers in the struggle to protect their interests and claims; (4) to persuade farmer-soldiers and the families of soldiers to struggle against the U.S.-Diem clique and help build up the worker-farmer-military alliance to overthrow the U.S.-Diem clique; (5) to protect the association and its secrets and help prevent enemy spying and infiltration, . . . also to un-cover evil elements within the association; and (6) to take part in asso-ciation activities, pay association dues, and make other financial contribu-tions. . . ."

Each member was expected to be "influential with at least three persons outside the association . . . [and] if a member cannot be influential with any person he shall be expelled." Thus the FLA was designed as an influential instrument of communication. Members did propaganda work among the villagers for the purpose of "strengthening the Front, raising farmers' class consciousness, spreading the ideology of struggle. . . ." All these were communicational activities and were in addition to activities supporting the emulation campaigns, participating in struggle movements, acting as a mutual-support or cooperative organization, helping solve land tenure problems, and generally improving the economic conditions in the village. In the liberated area, members were also active in medical and educational programs and in efforts to increase farm production.

The basic unit of the Farmers' Liberation Association, the cell, contained from three to fifteen persons. It met every 15 days and held elections to choose a new cell chief (and deputy chief if there was one) every two months. Each cell member was expected to maintain close contact with three or four "sympathizers," relatives, or friends whom he could influence, thus widening the association's sphere of influence. Cell members were expected to join other village liberation associations and take part in all other community projects.

A village that had three or more cells formed a village Farmers' Liberation Association and elected, either by general membership vote or in a meeting of cell chiefs and deputy chiefs, an executive committee. This committee normally consisted of three officers, although it some-times had as many as seven in a large village: a chairman responsible for agit-prop work, indoctrination activities, the struggle movement, and the handling of the association's finances; a deputy or assistant chairman responsible for production work and what was called "crop protection," that is, diversion of the local rice production into NLF marketing channels; and a secretary responsible for organizational development and liaison with other liberation associations. If the village was large, say, more than 1,000 persons, the executive committee appointed a permanent secretariat, or what was called a management section (*ban can su*), made up of three to five managers (*can su vien*) in "weak" villages and five to seven managers in "strong" villages. The *ban can su,* which met weekly, was composed of cell leaders appointed on the basis of their good records; they worked as coequals with the village cadres, who also were appointed but by the village administrative committee. Hamlet and cell leaders were subordinate to both the cadres and the *can su vien.* The latter had such assignments as fund raising, popular culture work, medical care (administration of the village first-aid kit), security and counter-intelligence work, and sometimes served as inspectors for village officials.

The executive committee met on an average of twice a month. A day or so after its meeting the *can su vien* would meet, and a day after that the village cells would meet — an effort to ensure that committee decisions were quickly and efficiently implemented.

Monthly dues averaged about two piasters, and these, plus special project fund-raising campaigns, supported the organization. Any farmer who could prove himself indigent was absolved of all payments to the association. Funds were needed, according to a learning document, for "such expenses as the publication of documents, travel by association representatives, organization of indoctrination courses, office supplies, and assistance loans to farmers who have encountered accidents or natural disasters." The village chairman sent monthly financial reports, accounting for the village association's expenditures, through the district committee to the association's provincial headquarters. The chairman was prohibited from "spending money at his own will without the collective approval of the committee, nor can he lend money to anybody."

The FLA bylaws stipulated a system of rewards and punishments:

Any member who does not fulfill his responsibilities to association directives that we unite with the masses and carry out the struggle with the masses . . . , or who fails to pay his dues for three consecutive months . . . , or who misses three consecutive meetings without cause . . . shall be reprimanded, placed on probation, or temporarily or permanently expelled from the association.

The Farmers' Liberation Association bylaws prescribed that village associations send delegates to the district FLA congress once a year to elect a district executive committee, and that the same thing be done at the provincial level every 18 months. They also stipulated that similar congresses and elections be held at the zone and interzone, but not the national central committee, levels. However, no evidence was uncovered to indicate that the Farmers' Liberation Association existed as such above the provincial level. In at least some provinces a provincial Farmers' Liberation Association central committee managed association affairs within the province under the close control of the NLF provincial central committee. At the zone level and above, the affairs of the Farmers' Liberation Association were handled by the same section that had responsibility for all the functional liberation associations. Publicly, though, the image of a separate structure was maintained for the Farmers' Liberation Association. Radio Liberation, for example, frequently broadcast statements and support messages that it said had originated in the South Vietnam Farmers' Liberation Association. Listed as national chairman in this output was Nguyen Huu The, who in 1961 was described as a 53-year-old ex-teacher from Vinh Long province.

Inspection teams frequently visited the villages from the district and provincial levels, and a number of their reports fell into GVN hands; the reports indicated serious shortcomings and failures in the FLA system. For example:

The [organization] is regarded by the farmers as just another association; recruitment has not been standardized nor has it been careful; some people have even been recruited whose only purpose was to spy for the enemy . . . ; often only old people are recruited, and the young farmers are neglected. . . . The associations lack energy and aggressiveness. . . . There are poor operational policies, [and] the farmers are confused and do not understand the purpose of the organization. . . . Sessions are not attended. . . . There is no criticism and self-criticism work. . . . Leaders act like mandarins. . . . Funds are misspent for such things as building a Buddhist temple or holding feasts and festivals. . . .

But the FLA was an effective communicational instrument. That it was not more effective was not so much a reflection on the device as on the farmer himself. While he might be willing to support the organization in the short run, at all times the farmer was filled with distrust of the motives of the leadership.

Women's Liberation Association[4]

Women, frequently exploited by Asian social systems, represented a potent source of support, a fact not overlooked either by Asian Communists or by the NLF. Even at the risk of treading on masculine sensibilities, the NLF took a strong prowoman stand and maintained it consistently: "Women represent half the population and at least half of the revolutionary effort. If women do not participate in the Revolution,

[4] In Vietnamese, Hoi Phu Nu Giai Phong. Sometimes the term *lien hiep* follows *hoi*. *Lien hiep* means united with and implies politically universal or without class distinction. The term frequently appeared in connection with the women and youth liberation associations but not with the farmers' or workers' liberation associations, as the former were considered to be more broadly based than the more class-conscious farmers and workers.

it will fail. . . . Further, a society cannot progress if female members are retarded."

The Women's Liberation Association of South Vietnam was formed on March 8, 1961. It was open to any girl or woman over the age of 16 who met three requirements: "She must . . . agree to follow the precepts of the association; she must take an active part in the struggle movement aimed at overthrowing the U.S.-Diem clique; and . . . she must have a clean past and identity." Vietnamese women, the association documents stressed, possess such virtues as endurance, patience, willingness to work hard, and sacrifice and therefore make good revolutionaries. One document added that

because they boil with hatred, women struggle hard . . . , have fought with the [guerrillas], served in the agit-prop branches and as liaison cadres . . . , worked in the struggle movements, in meetings, demonstrations, face-to-face struggles . . . , have scored great successes in the *binh van* movement. . . .

Women's Liberation Association indoctrination materials frequently reminded women of their plight. For example,

During the hundred years of the French imperialist-colonialist regime, women were barbarously oppressed and exploited; not only did they share the state of slavery of all the people but as a class had to endure special oppression at the hands of society as well as within the family. They were despised, ill treated, without rights, regarded as private property. . . . Under the Diem regime they have been savagely violated, massacred, arrested, incarcerated, tortured, debauched, their thoughts poisoned, . . . and forced into prostitution.

If the Farmers' Liberation Association acted as the NLF's mass base and the Workers' Liberation Association as its connecting rod to historical legitimacy, the Women's Liberation Association might be termed the moral sounding board of the NLF. From the national central committee of the Women's Liberation Association came a neverending stream of appeals, statements, condemnations, manifestoes, and open letters sent to persons, organizations, and governments outside Vietnam, within the country, and within the NLF. In general this output assumed a prowoman character: that the women of South Vietnam, unlike their liberated sisters in the North, not only were obliged to endure the yoke of oppressive imperialism that hung around the necks of all Vietnamese but also were burdened with the "oppression of feudal society and the feudal family," as it was phrased in the Women's Liberation Association bylaws. "The bourgeois society," the bylaws continued, "considers women unworthy of respect and esteem and . . . seeks only to oppress and exploit them." With many Vietnamese women, particularly those in rural areas, this was true indeed.

To liberate the Vietnamese woman from the "life of the water buffalo" was one of the chief tasks of communism, and toward this end the PRP, as had the Lao Dong Party before it, took a far more intransigent posture than the NLF or even the Women's Liberation Association, possibly because these organizations were more aware of village male sensibilities. A PRP statement prepared for public consumption declared:

The Party is opposed to every injustice toward women . . . for women are a class that suffers the most from oppression and exploitation. . . . We stand for total liberation of women in every respect, . . . for economic equality, political equality, cultural equality, social equality, . . . and equality in the family.

Some of the passages would make the hackles rise on the neck of many a male Vietnamese:

Women are not only equal to men in society, they are also equal to their husbands. We will abolish inequality between husbands and wives . . . as we will abolish polygamy. . . . Family property is common property. . . . Women are equal to men in standing for elections. . . . Women must be free to choose their own professions. . . . Since they carry out the same work as men, women are to receive the same pay as men. . . . Female farmers will be allocated rice fields on the same basis as men. . . . In brief, we plan to liberate all women to be totally free and equal in society and in their families.[5]

The dominant theme in the Women's Liberation Association output was moral exhortation combined with fears based on sex. The future chairman, Mrs. Nguyen Thi Tu, reporting to the 1962 congress, used the word rape more than a dozen times in her speech. She described in intimate detail the fate of young girl students arrested, she said, for

participating in the struggle movement for disarmament, for building more schools, and for the use of the Vietnamese language in universities. . . . In torture rooms, the U.S.-Diemists use the most despicable torture methods — such as suspending victims on beams, cutting their breasts, exposing them naked to the sun, tying their undertrousers shut and dropping snakes inside, inserting rifle butts or bottles into their sexual organs, spreading grease on their naked bodies and letting German shepherd dogs bite them, sending an electric current through a wire connected to their sexual organs, and so forth.

Behind the shocked tone and indignant frown one catches the glimpse of an obscene smirk.

The Women's Liberation Association, which was to include at least 20 per cent of the women in the village, was expected to devote most of its effort to the struggle movement at the village level, and especially the *binh van* movement. Women were particularly effective in this latter role, being sharp tongued, quick witted, and frequently more than a

[5] Booklet entitled *Party Policy toward Women,* dated 1961.

match in a debate with a soldier or even a government official. Women were less vulnerable to repressive acts than men in similar circumstances. The association members conducted extensive letter-writing campaigns to ARVN soldiers, urging them to desert, and they helped deserters reestablish themselves in the village. Dramatic performances were presented by the association, with actors depicting the tortures and mistreatment allegedly experienced by women in the hands of the enemy. Social movement propaganda appeals by agit-prop cadres directed toward women emphasized those with a sexual overtone (chiefly sexual abuse and torture by ARVN troops); religious themes, Vietnamese women being much more religious than Vietnamese men; democracy that would include female participation; and promises of economic betterment, women generally being the keeper of the Vietnamese family purse strings. A serious effort was made to develop class consciousness among village women.

These activities were based on the NLF assessment of the weaknesses of Vietnamese women with respect to the Revolution; one inspection report listed women's shortcomings as:

They are not enlightened, especially about their class interests. Uneducated, they suffer from self-abasement, passiveness, lack of confidence. . . . The associations fail to meet norms, are loosely organized . . . , have lost prestige . . . , are too religious in character, and are not militant enough. . . . They are slovenly, weak, and of low quality.

Admission procedures were easy and simple: A proposed member was introduced by one regular member and approved by the branch central committee, with no probation period. The Women's Liberation Association, far from seeking to be a small, well-disciplined organization, sought wide membership. (In 1965 it claimed 1.2 million members.)

The basic unit of the organization was the branch, which operated in the village, the street zone, or at the market place. The rural market place, a natural social entity in Vietnam, served as the center of communal life; it was run primarily by women who operated fruit, vegetable, fish, and dry-goods stalls for customers who were mostly women. The market place afforded a superb center for clandestine political activity; couriers used it as a way station; food was purchased for guerrillas under secure conditions; gossip was translated into military intelligence; and the activities of the government and the ARVN were observed unobtrusively. The branch, generally of large size, that is, 15 or more cells, elected an executive committee of about seven members, which in turn appointed a three-woman standing committee or presidium. The latter usually consisted of a chairman, responsible for organization-building activities; a deputy, responsible for agit-prop work and indoctrination; and a secretary, responsible for finances. In the more secure NLF areas a section of cadres between branch and cells was appointed by the executive committee to work full time to administer affairs at the cell level. The association frequently operated as a clandestine organization, and the executive committee kept its identity secret.

The executive committee met monthly with the section of cadres and cell leaders. At this meeting the committee chairman would set forth the following month's program, explain directives received from higher headquarters, review the past month's activities, and lead the group in criticism and self-criticism.

Above the branch were four higher levels: the district central committee, usually located in the major market town of the area; the provincial central committee in the provincial capital; the regional central committee (equivalent to the NLF zone); and the ostensible national Women's Liberation Association central committee at the NLF headquarters.

The national chairman, Mrs. Nguyen Thi Tu, was listed as a former professor from Saigon. According to her NLF biographical sketch, she was active in social welfare work in Saigon until her arrest by the GVN in 1955, after which she was imprisoned at Chi Hoa prison, Phu Loi camp, and Poulo Condore until she was released several years later. Vice-chairmen were listed as Mrs. Buu Doan (sometimes Mrs. Mi Doan), a montagnard of the Jarai tribe and also vice-chairman of the Committee of the People for the Tay Nguyen Autonomous Zone; Mrs. Le Thi Lien, an NLF delegate from Eastern Nambo; and Mrs. Thanh Loan, a Saigon artist. The secretary-general of the association was Mrs. Nguyen Thi Thanh, a teacher. The wives of two prominent figures in the NLF — Mrs. Phung Van Cung and Mrs. Ma Thi Chu (Mrs. Nguyen Van Hieu) — were listed as permanent members of the national central committee. Mrs. Ma Thi Chu, a pharmacist, was also a member of the Afro-Asian People's Solidarity Committee. She was a member of a women's delegation, headed by one Mrs. Nguyen Thi Binh, that attended the June 1963 Women's International Democratic Federation (WIDF) congress in Moscow. She addressed the congress in the Kremlin conference hall on June 28, according to Radio Moscow, which said "most of her listeners' eyes were wet with tears when she exposed from her personal experiences the barbarities and unspeakable crimes of the South Vietnam fascist regime." [6] The delegation then went on to China for a three-week visit before returning home.

NLF organizers of women's groups faced a task that was anything but easy. A rural Vietnamese woman was apt to be a timid spirit in public matters, lacking aggressiveness and more inclined to endure than

[6] Radio Moscow, in Vietnamese, to Vietnam, July 5, 1963.

to strike back. Often she lacked social conscience and, as a consequence, revolutionary zeal. She was unused to organizational strictures and discipline. An internal document complained that,

although the women's movement grows each day, the political and revolutionary level is too low. Generally speaking, the Women's Liberation Association is slovenly, loosely organized, low in quality members. . . . It fails especially in its *binh van* and *chinh van* movements.

The Women's Liberation Association put market places, villages, and street zones into four categories: "the liberated area, the greatly effervescing area, the weak area, and the religious area." Organizers were cautioned to follow the principle of development of the organization as outlined in directives. Opportunism in organizational work, allowing an organization to move in the direction its members wanted it to go, was one of the NLF's primary problems, particularly with respect to women's groups. The Women's Liberation Association leaders seemed torn between the desire to develop a large and impressive mass organization and the fear that such an organization, once created, would become ponderous, unwieldy, and impossible to control. Responsibility for seeing that control did not slip was passed back to the overworked, ever-faithful cadre, with these organizational instructions:

Out of every 100 persons involved in a general struggle, select 20 for special struggle assignments and . . . on the basis of their behavior in the special struggle, select 4 of these for membership in the Women's Liberation Association. This means that among 100 persons involved in a special struggle movement, we would admit at most 20 per cent. . . . If we develop our organization beyond the 20 per cent figure, the "hard-core" nature of the association will lose its effect, and the membership will be so numerous that close leadership cannot be guaranteed. . . . All markets and villages must review their situation to see that developments conform to the 20 per cent ratio.

The arithmetic is tortuous but accurate. A Women's Liberation Association might begin with 500 women at a market place and involve them in some sort of protest meeting, for example, a drive to lower taxes. This would include nearly everyone in the market. Of the 500, the association would single out 100 of the more vociferous and organize them into a special struggle movement, say, a call on the district chief to demand that the GVN halt the military draft, and of this 100 a maximum of 20 per cent would be recruited into the Women's Liberation Association. The principle of selection was trial by fire. "Carry on your organizational development work," the instructions continued, "in a methodical and broad-scale way but not in a complicated and indiscriminate manner" — helpful advice indeed for the cadre. They added:

To strengthen the organization, it is necessary to educate the members about politics, the Revolution, and their duty to the Revolution. At the same time, put them to the struggle test and rely on this to strengthen the association and improve the quality of the individual member.

This was tempering by fire. The instructions concluded: "Respect the 20 per cent ratio. . . . In all areas cadres should fix a cell membership quota and see that it is fulfilled. . . ."

Thus the Women's Liberation Association differed from the Workers' and the Farmers' Liberation Associations in that greater effort was made to develop a uniform cell structure throughout the country and at the same time to create more of a mass movement. The women's group differed in other ways from the rest of the liberation associations. The benefits to accrue to Women's Liberation Association members were almost exclusively cast in terms of nonmaterial gains, just as the current deprivations of women were in psychic terms. The exhortatory passages of the bylaws and the training documents seldom spoke of raising standards of living or direct and personal economic benefits; instead their appeals were in terms of a morally uplifted society free from discrimination and degradation. One document, for example, admonished women to practice the five loves: love of country, love of work, love of equality, love of the masses, and love of peace. Women were called on to give to the association, not to expect something from it. Entwined in this abstract theme was a second, more tangible one: struggle, struggle, struggle. Vietnamese women were far harder workers than Vietnamese men. Knowing this, the NLF passed the burden of sheer drudgery to the most likely candidates in the name of idealism. The Vietnamese woman grew the vegetables, raised the chickens, and poled the sampans to deliver food to guerrilla bands; she ran the market struggle movement, unmasked the spies, and led the village indoctrination sessions; she made the spiked foot traps, carried the ammunition, and dug the crosshatch roadblocks. The woman was in truth the water buffalo of the Revolution.

Workers' Liberation Association (WLA)[7]

NLF activities in urban areas, chiefly the Saigon-Cholon area, were deeply clandestine and, especially among workers, of minimal effectiveness. The theory of revolutionary guerrilla warfare under which the NLF operated dictated that both organizational and communicational activities focus on the rural areas and that the cities be left to the end of

---

[7] In Vietnamese, Hoi Lao Dong Giai Phong, literally, Laborers' Liberation Association; *lao dong* can be translated either as a verb or as a noun; *worker* is used rather than *laborer* here in the interest of clarity and uniformity.

the struggle. The Workers' Liberation Association was most active among nonurban workers, chiefly the employees of the rubber plantations in the Massif Plain. Here they came into direct competition with the non-Communist trade-union movement from Saigon. Since the trade unions also offered the workers direct benefits of membership, such as higher wages and better working conditions, the Workers' Liberation Association met with little success in enlisting workers. It is an important commentary that the NLF could generate so little support among the great foreign-owned rubber plantations and in the textile and other factories outside Saigon. This was chiefly due to the intelligent and militant opposition presented by the trade-union movement in South Vietnam. Organized labor in South Vietnam, although stifled to a considerable extent by the Diem government, managed to maintain an integrity and worker identity that resulted in continued support by its membership. Moreover, its leadership was particularly skilled in battling the NLF in meaningful terms at the worker level.

The organization of the Workers' Liberation Association of South Vietnam (founded May 1, 1961) was neither along guild lines nor by industry but by geographic area, lumping together all of the workers in one district or industrial area. This resulted in concentrating the bulk of the association's activities in a few areas of the country: the Gia Dinh industrial strip and Saigon-Cholon, which contained virtually all of South Vietnam's manufacturing plants (textiles, food processing, chemicals); the rubber plantations, chiefly in the Massif Plain, the area between Saigon and the Cambodian border to the west and the highlands to the north; as well as the larger towns of Da Nang, Hué, Quang Ngai, Qui Nhon, Dalat, Can Tho, and Soc Trang.

A preliminary GVN labor survey taken in 1963 set the country's labor force at 60,930 rubber workers (on 710 plantations); 42,000 textile workers; 50,000 construction workers; and 150,000 transportation industry workers. In addition it listed 255,000 workers in 43,960 commercial and industrial firms, which would mean enterprises that averaged less than eight workers each. The total labor force therefore was slightly more than a half-million workers, but they did not fit the usual Communist stereotype of the worker as known in the Western world of the mid-nineteenth century. As an underdeveloped and almost entirely agricultural nation, Vietnam had few proletarians in the traditional Communist sense of the word. The country had no huge factories, no masses of workers. The industrial enterprises of size that did exist, such as the textile plants along the Saigon–Bien Hoa highway, presented NLF organizers with a difficult and generally unrewarding field of activity. Security problems were great, and the effort had to be entirely clandestine. Further, the vanguard function that Communist theory dictates be performed by the workers had been pre-empted (or, more correctly, assumed) first by the South Vietnam Lao Dong Party and later by the PRP.[8]

One almost gets the feeling that the NLF formed the Workers' Liberation Association because theory dictated that there ought to be a workers' group as the mass base for the Revolution. Clearly the NLF regarded the organization as important and spent a great deal of time, money, and effort in developing it. Part of the Workers' Liberation Association's objective was to associate the proletarians in Vietnam, such as there were, with the farmers so as to link the vast wealth of Marxist thought and literature with an agrarian revolution that had virtually no ethos at all. This resulted in constant use of the hyphenated term "worker-peasant" that appeared throughout all NLF literature, pretending that the two were equal. A typical expression of this theme came in the Workers' Liberation Association anniversary message of July 20, 1964, which declared: "Let the Liberation troops — vanguard combatants who deserve to be called a worker-peasant army — do their best to reduce the enemy's war potential, rush forward to deal deadly blows at the enemy. . . ."

The Workers' Liberation Association's initial organizing statement came on May Day, 1961; it declared itself an organization that would "unite tightly all the Southern working class and laboring people, both manual and intellectual workers, . . . and will work closely with the National Liberation Front of South Vietnam." Its avowed purpose, according to its bylaws, of which at least a half dozen slightly varying copies exist, was twofold: to bind the members together for mutual self-help purposes, and to overthrow the government of South Vietnam. "Worker" was not defined, although the bylaws stipulated that the term included handicraft workers (artisans in cottage industries) and vendors (keepers of market-place stalls, roving noodle-cart operators, and the like). Members had the right to discuss issues placed before the association and to vote on them, hold office and participate in elections, criticize ongoing policies and programs at association meetings, to take part in associational study groups, and to call on the association for financial and other personal assistance in times of need. Duties of membership involved participating in the political struggle movement, assuming leadership roles with respect to fellow workers, carrying out association directives

[8] "Led by the vanguard party [PRP] and following a correct line laid down in the political program of the South Vietnam National Liberation Front and closely united within the South Vietnam Workers' Liberation Association, the movement of the working class and laboring people in South Vietnam is powerfully developing." Thus declared *Nhan Dan*, implying that if you were a good proletarian you would join the PRP, for "the PRP is a party of South Vietnamese working-class and laboring people . . . and at the same time of all patriotic South Vietnamese." (*Nhan Dan*, May 5, 1964.)

without question, recruiting new members, paying dues, attending meetings, and protecting the secrets of the association. Workers were expected to pay monthly dues and contribute to several special funds that the organization maintained to finance its operations.

The basic Workers' Liberation Association organizational unit was the economic enterprise, such as the rubber plantation, the factory or workshop, the business enterprise, or, in a few instances, the social grouping such as the village or street zone. Any enterprise with three members could organize a cell and elect a cell chief; three or more cells combined to form a branch, which elected an executive committee and, if large enough, a permanent secretariat. Plantations and factories with 20 or more cells established an organizational layer between the cell and the branch, called the subbranch, consisting of five to seven cells plus a cadre appointed by the executive committee. Above the branch was the interbranch, corresponding to the district, and above the interbranch was the zone (five or more interbranches), roughly equivalent to the province. Membership control, even according to the bylaws, did not extend beyond the branch; the NLF's national Central Committee appointed the executive committees at both the interbranch and zone levels. Early Workers' Liberation Association documents stated that a national central committee for the association existed in the NLF headquarters and was headed by Chairman Phan Xuan Thai, described in 1961 as "age 44, member of the working class, native of Vinh Long province," and a secretary-general, 43-year-old Le Dinh Thu, from the village of An Son, Huong Thon district of Ha Tinh province, in what is now North Vietnam.

Early in its history the Workers' Liberation Association sought to develop close relations with international Communist labor organizations. A Workers' Liberation Association delegation attended the fifth World Federation of Trade Unions (WFTU) meeting in Moscow in December 1961. In January 1963 the executive committee of the WFTU admitted the Workers' Liberation Association as a formal member[9] and at the same time announced the formation of a group to be called the International Trade Unions Committee of Solidarity with South Vietnamese Workers and People. This committee held a conference in Hanoi in mid-October 1963, with Huynh Van Tam representing the Workers' Liberation Association. A delegation headed by one Tran Hoai Nam attended an Indonesian trade-union congress in Djakarta in September 1964.

Most of the Workers' Liberation Association as well as PRP activity among workers consisted of infiltration rather than outright agit-prop

---

[9] Under the name (WFTU translation) of South Vietnam Liberation Labor Union, a poor translation of *Hoi Lao Dong Giai Phong*.

work. Organizationally this took the form of so-called secret self-defense units *(cong tac tu ve bi mat)*.[10] The WLA, according to a 1962 study and indoctrination guide, considered its task to be "to unite the South Vietnamese working class and laboring people within a genuine organization, to struggle untiringly for democratic freedom and improvement of living conditions, and to join other patriotic organizations in struggling to overthrow the U.S.-Diem clique and liberate South Vietnam." [11]

The struggle movement and the strike formed its two major overt activities among the workers, and it treated all labor disputes in South Vietnam as if they were its exclusive domain. It sought to involve itself in all labor disputes and to take credit for any gains won either in negotiations by the legal trade unions or in strikes. Although in virtually all such cases NLF involvement and contributions were negligible, any benefit accruing from a strike or from negotiations with management was regarded as a victory for the Workers' Liberation Association. Its output never mentioned legitimate labor organizations in South Vietnam; news stories and radio broadcasts spoke only of strikers and workers, never of trade-union organizations. The WLA implied that all specific labor disputes were spontaneous eruptions by the workers, in which the Workers' Liberation Association achieved identification by association.

The themes employed in leaflets by agents and in mass-media output were the classic Communist appeals: anticapitalism and oppression of the worker.[12] The secret self-defense unit, a cellular structure, was de-

---

[10] Sabotage units that were to infiltrate the urban areas and hold themselves in readiness for the General Uprising.

[11] An October 1963 document listed a five-point program for the WLA:

1. To struggle for democratic rights and liberties, higher wages, unemployment insurance, free trade unions . . . , and an end to the infiltration of enemy agents into trade unions. . . .

2. To unite with the peasants to form a firm alliance that will unite with the people to overthrow the Diem government, form a national coalition government that advocates peace, neutrality, increased social welfare, . . . and unification. . . .

3. To work with the national bourgeoisie in pursuit of the above goals, working out through negotiations any divergence of views. . . .

4. To form an alliance with the military for the same purpose. . . .

5. And to support the world-wide trade-union movement.

[12] Said a directive to cadres of the secret self-defense units:

Show them how hard they are forced to work, from three o'clock in the morning until four o'clock in the afternoon, and for low wages, . . . are forced to attend "Denunciation of Communism classes" and other Diem-sponsored meetings, are drafted into the army. Workers have poor and miserable living conditions. . . . Secret police follow workers and sometimes threaten them. . . . Show them that the wealth of a society is produced by the workers and the farmers and then taken by the imperialists. Support the National Liberation Front and urge workers to join the Workers' Liberation Association. Show the great leadership role assumed by the Party in the NLF and describe its great prestige. Counter the distorting propaganda of the enemy against the Party and the Revolution. . . . Describe the successes of the socialist countries. . . . Use concrete details in talking with the masses. In rubber plantations point out the great burden of the workers in tapping up to 500 trees from early morning to noon and then having to carry ten kilos [22 pounds] of latex for five to seven kilometers

signed as an urban standby group that would, when the signal was given, rise in armed revolt within the factory or rubber plantation. The mission of each member while awaiting this day, said an internal document, was to

train himself to develop his revolutionary spirit and the techniques and tactics of protecting the Revolution and [when the time came] to fight the enemy . . . , to protect the organs of the Revolution and its cadres and maintain discipline within the organization . . . , to find out information about the situation of the enemy and report it to higher authorities . . . , to create the necessary conditions for fighting the enemy by all means when the order is issued . . . , to remain unsuspected by the enemy . . . , and to carry out all revolutionary missions assigned by higher authority. . . .

Youth Liberation Association (YLA)[18]

From the inception of their movement in Indochina, the Communists placed special burdens of responsibility on youth. Captured NLF documents frequently included indoctrination booklets on youth and its role in the revolutionary movement in Indochina and recounted the heroism of youthful revolutionaries. The first true Communist party in Indochina was the youth group, the Revolutionary Youth Association, formed by Ho Chi Minh in 1925, and the history of the revolutionary movement is studded with the names of similar groups: the Young Revolutionary Comradeship Association, the Communist Youth League, the Democratic Youth League, the Anti-Imperialist Youth League, the Youth League for the Salvation of Our Country, and the Vanguard Youth Group.

The NLF's chief strategic use of youth was to attack on a broad front all social *status quo* and traditionalism. In the words of one NLF document,

Youth has its own characteristics, which are not found in older people. Youth are growing physically and mentally — and so have a spiritual eagerness; . . . they are dynamic and progressive. Youth hate the old things and are fond of new things. They love their ideas and do not fear difficulty or danger. . . . The interests of youth lead them to oppose the old society, the old regime, all dark, evil, and undemocratic things.

A PRP document in mid-1963 added that

youth is the future of our society, nation, as well as Revolution. As Comrade Lenin once said, "The principal element of our Party is youth. Our Party

---

[3-4 miles], having to negotiate slippery slopes in the rain, and for which they are paid only 44 piasters [50 cents] a day.

[18] In Vietnamese, Hoi Thanh Nien Giai Phong, literally, Youth Association for the Liberation of South Vietnam.

holds fast to the future, and the future belongs to youth. Our Party is the Party of reformers, and youth are people dedicated to the reform of society." In the past three years [1961–1963] the [Party] Youth League has greatly expanded everywhere. It has become the shock force of the liberation movement.

The Youth Liberation Association was formed on December 25, 1961 at an organizing congress held in Zone D, near Saigon. The congress elected as chairman Tran Bach Dang, who was described in a 1961 document as age 36, a participant in the Viet Minh war, and active in veterans' organizations. Dr. Nguyen Xuan Thuy replaced him in 1962, but he retained his post as member of the NLF Central Committee Presidium. Elected secretary-general at the organizing congress was Nguyen Van Yen, but he was replaced a year later by Nguyen Ngoc Thuong, a teacher and one of the leading founders of the NLF. Active in Buddhist affairs and founder of the Afro-Asian People's Solidarity Committee of which he was chairman, Nguyen Ngoc Thuong also helped found the Radical Socialist Party and in all probability was a main-line Communist. Dr. Nguyen Xuan Thuy, about whom little is known, traveled abroad a great deal after assuming office, apparently with the assignment of developing support in Communist nations for the Youth Liberation Association and the NLF.

A leaflet widely distributed at the time of the YLA's formation declared that

the congress . . . set forth the responsibilities of members of the Association for the Liberation of the Southern Youth, which are to unite all strata of young people without distinction as to nationality, wealth, religion, and political party; to set up a large and strong youth front; . . . to lead the youth in time in its struggle in order to contribute to the liberation of South Vietnam.

The Youth Liberation Association was a hard-nosed group less likely to bow to traditional ikons than the other liberation associations. Its bylaws specifically mentioned the Communist (Lao Dong) party by name, the only liberation association to do so. It spoke more of discipline and less of democratic rights, more of duty and less of gain. It went right to the heart of the Communist thrust in Vietnam without any frills or extras. Said the bylaws:

The Youth Liberation Association was established to gather the South Vietnamese patriotic youths for the struggle against the Americans and Diem within the National Liberation Front of South Vietnam and under the leadership of the Party . . . and to contribute its part in the overthrow of the U.S.-Diem clique, restore peace to the countryside, and unify the nations.

These goals — overthrow the GVN and end ARVN operations in rural Vietnam, and unify North and South — represent the essence, the ultimate stripped-down objectives of the DRV in South Vietnam, stated as succinctly as they possibly can be.

Youth Liberation Association bylaws made no pretense of a democratically structured hierarchy running from the village to a national central committee. The basic Youth Liberation Association unit, the hamlet cell, contained three to five members in weak areas and seven to nine in more secure regions. Three cells combined to form a branch committee, which, when growth justified, named a standing committee or a secretariat to administer day-to-day activities. The size of the branch varied greatly but was roughly equivalent to the village in geographic area. Sandwiched between the hamlet cell structure and the branch committee was a section of cadres, as in the Women's Liberation Association. In effect a cell itself, the section had from three to five members who were appointed by the branch central committee and reported directly to it. Above the branch was a district committee, and above that a provincial committee. At the zonal, interzonal, and national levels Youth Liberation Association affairs were merged with those of other functional liberation associations, although, as usual, there existed a Youth Liberation Association "national chairman," which is to say an NLF national Central Committee staff official responsible for YLA affairs.

The Youth Liberation Association, its bylaws stated, was open to any male or female 16 to 25 years of age who pledged to work for the overthrow of the GVN, agreed to adhere to Youth Liberation Association bylaws, and promised to dedicate himself to the cause. Duties of membership included leading hamlet youth in "opposing the military draft, opposing American culture, developing unity in the hamlet, educating younger children, and participating in guerrilla activities." No other liberation association bylaws spoke of fighting or armed struggle or in terms of risking the lives of members in combat.

Organizational leadership in the Youth Liberation Association did not appear to have crystallized to the degree that it had in other associations, perhaps because upper-echelon leadership, or even guidance, was less necessary. The Youth Liberation Association's arena was the hamlet; its organization there was simple, almost elemental. A learning document outlined in specific and concrete terms for young organizers how they should proceed in creating a Youth Liberation Association. At the start, it told them, choose the most popular youths of the hamlet and form the organization around them. In the organization-building stage, district cadre teams would assist in the process and serve as acting branch officials. After a nucleus was formed, at least one three-man cell, cadres conducted a three- to five-day training session during which participants studied NLF policy directives on youth matters, background documents on the meaning of the Revolution, and the Youth Liberation Association bylaws. An intensive effort was made to entice the hamlet's most popular youths into attending the indoctrination sessions with a view to installing them as branch committeemen and, if they proved to be in sympathy with the deeper objectives of the organization, earmarking them for leadership positions.

In the more secure NLF areas the Youth Liberation Association also established a Village Children's Group (in Vietnamese, Doan Thieu Nhi Xa) as the junior element of the NLF. It was open to children of both sexes between the ages of 10 and 15. Originally the group was made up of children of liberation association officials and members, but it was gradually broadened to include all in the village who wished, or could be encouraged, to join. The organizational structure of the Village Children's Group consisted of six- to twelve-child cells, each cell electing its own leader but under the guidance of a Youth Liberation Association member. Activities included storytelling and memorizing revolutionary poetry, but the material used had less doctrinal content than that found in the PRP's Vanguard Youth study sessions.

At its inception the Youth Liberation Association stood second only to the Farmers' Liberation Association as a significant mass-based NLF organization, for it acted as the spiritual militant, the indomitable wave of the future. But gradually this function was transferred to the People's Revolutionary Party Youth League as part of the regularization of the NLF structure. The PRPYL members became the youthful elite, leaving behind in the Youth Liberation Association their less-dedicated friends. However, the Youth Liberation Association, particularly in remote rural areas, remained a viable and important organization that served the NLF as a source of manpower and as one of its most trusted liberation associations.

Student Liberation Association (SLA)[14]

NLF organizers carefully distinguished between youths and students and built a separate organization for each. This was a direct reflection of the Vietnamese social structure, which, like the Chinese, placed the scholar or student on a much higher plane than the farm youth. Student Liberation Association activities obviously were found only where there

[14] The full title is Association for the Union of Students and Schoolboys for the Liberation of South Vietnam (Hoi Lien Hiep Sinh Vien Va Hoc Sinh Giai Phong Mien Nam Viet Nam), variously translated as Union of Students for the Liberation of South Vietnam (international Communist translation) or Union of University and High-School Students for Liberation (DRV translation). In the South it was usually referred to as the Student Liberation Association or Student Liberation Union.

were numbers of students and did not exist at all in the more remote villages of the country where schooling ended after only three or four years.

The Student Liberation Association was formed on January 9, 1961, the anniversary of massive demonstrations in Saigon on that date in 1940 by students protesting the closing of their schools by French officials following the announcement of a student strike. The SLA never grew to particularly large proportions; its claimed membership in mid-1964 was 10,000. Membership was open to secondary-school and university-level students of both sexes as well as to students studying abroad.

The bylaws outlined its purpose:

1. To unite all students into a strong powerful bloc to support one another in study life and the struggle. . . .
2. To forge its members into a collective spirit of love for Fatherland and the righteous cause, to forge the spirit of the revolutionary and struggle ideal, to forge in its members the good and the beautiful. . . .
3. To struggle to obtain for students their legitimate demands, a secure future, the liberty to develop according to their intelligence and ability. . . .
4. To join with people of all strata and with other organizations to help break down the colonialistic and feudalist regime in South Vietnam and liberate Vietnam from the fetters of U.S. imperialism and its lackey clique . . . and advance toward unification of the homeland. . . .
5. To join with students in Asia, Africa, and Latin America in the interests of the preservation of peace, opposition to imperialism, and the strengthening of freedom, democracy, progressive culture, and education.

These were generalized goals. More specific purposes were contained in the manifesto issued shortly after the association was formed, which declared that the SLA stood for "opening more public schools, granting more scholarships, building more libraries and laboratories, government subsidies for private schools and the lowering of private-school fees, . . . financial help for students wishing to study abroad, . . . draft exemption for students, . . . guarantees of jobs upon graduation, . . . more sports in schools."

The appeals became even more specific each year during examination time, when the NLF took its place squarely on the side of the student in the ancient struggle with the final examination. Radio Liberation, in an editorial implying that the NLF stood for easier examinations, reported:

All candidates in the recent nationwide final examinations for junior-high schools were very angry because the questions were too difficult. . . . Candidates were faced with very difficult questions, especially in physics. At the Ban Co examination center many candidates left the room and refused to answer the questions, declaring they would not continue the examination in protest against the deceitful and deceiving examination policies of the U.S.-

Diemists. . . . It is clear that the U.S.-Diemists deliberately flunked the candidates . . . in order to drive them into a dead end. School children and students . . . will never forget these criminal actions by the U.S.-Diem clique.[15]

In search of a *cause célèbre* among students, the SLA took the examination issue to the sixth International Union of Students conference in Leningrad in August 1962. Its report, submitted to the conference, declared that the

imperialists deliberately flunk students to force them into the military, . . . and this proves the ugly reactionary nature of the imperialists. . . . They are very clever in their scheme of flunking. . . . They pick questions from the most difficult parts of the course. . . . They fix examination times close to one another so that students are always in a tense state. . . . They do not give enough time to write the examination.

The report concluded with a poem on the plight of the student, which, freely translated, reads:

> It is like a typhoon has passed, now, after the examination;
> Leaves have been plucked from the branches and scattered,
> And those remaining on the branches are bent and tired
> Still anxious about their fate.
> Let us now count to see how many are still alive.

The duties imposed on the SLA member were light and easy to carry out. Various internal documents indicated that a member was expected to implement the directives and instructions from higher headquarters, as were all members of liberation associations. Beyond that he was asked to

respect the organization, . . . make propaganda to develop the association, . . . maintain a sense of solidarity with other students, . . . study actively and unceasingly increase his knowledge of politics and culture [and] at the same time nurture a spirit of sacrifice and courage of revolutionary struggle, . . . and cultivate morality, . . . preserve association secrets, . . . hold fast to courage when encountering difficulties, . . . take part in association activities, . . . and pay monthly dues.

This sounded like a dilettante's notion of revolution, and to a large degree that was the attitude of the Vietnamese student, whom the Communists found to be flighty, unwilling to be disciplined, prone to try to "negotiate" his contribution to the Revolution rather than dedicate himself to it, too apt to adopt a "wait and see who will win" attitude with the intention of joining the struggle later when the sacrifices would not be so great. As a group, the students seemed softer and less idealistic than the members of the Youth Liberation Association.

[15] Radio Liberation, in Vietnamese, May 24, 1963.

The SLA geared its organizational structure directly to the educational institution attended by its members; the individual school was the basic unit of the association. The three- to five-man cell combined to form a subbranch by yearly class; the subbranches combined to form a branch, which included the entire school and was headed by an executive committee. The SLA had no cadre system but followed the usual liberation association policies concerning discipline, dues, and so on. If a number of schools existed in an area, the next higher level would be the interschool committee; if not, the branch committee reported directly to the SLA provincial committee. It appeared that at the national central committee level the Youth and Student Liberation Associations were treated as one and the same. For example, the national chairman was Nguyen Xuan Thuy, who, as noted, was also the chairman of the YLA. *Nhan Dan,* in its August 3, 1962 story on the WFDY (World Federation of Democratic Youth) meeting in Leningrad, described the organization that Dr. Nguyen Xuan Thuy represented as "the central committee of the South Vietnamese Union of Students and Union of Youth for National Liberation." Others active in the SLA at the central committee level were Luu Thanh Hai, a poet; Miss Nguyen Thi Binh, and Nguyen Ngoc Dung, all of whom traveled to conferences abroad in the name of the SLA.

The bylaws of the SLA called for elections at all levels, and indeed congresses and meetings were held frequently. A congress of SLA delegates from Eastern Nambo was held February 14–18, 1962 in the Zone D area. It was attended by Saigon University students and others and was convened for the purpose of drafting a program of action for 1962. The following September, representatives of the Western Nambo SLA gathered for a meeting in the Mekong delta.

On June 10, 1964 Radio Liberation reported the formation in Saigon of a new organization called the NLF Clandestine Youth Party,[16] composed, it said, principally of youths from Saigon and other large Vietnamese towns. The announcement came at a time of vast organizational ferment among students at the University of Saigon, and dozens of student groups with long and short names and with clear and uncertain purposes, ranging from militant anticommunism to strong neutralism, were busy organizing, staging speeches, issuing manifestoes, and sending letters to the American Embassy. The purpose of the Clandestine Youth Party was not clear, but apparently it was an effort to insinuate the NLF into this student activity as a legitimate student group. What is not clear is why the NLF leadership did not feel that the Student Liberation Association was the appropriate vehicle for such activity. The most probable reason is that it was an effort to overcome the antipathy on

[16] In Vietnamese, Dang Thanh Nien Bi Mat, more precisely translated as Secret Youth Party.

the part of university students in Saigon, Dalat, and Hué to the Student Liberation Association. This antipathy was apparent after the overthrow of the Diem government. Saigon University student leaders told the author in December 1963 that they had been approached by SLA cadres seeking to establish an alliance or hoping to recruit Vietnamese university students directly into the SLA; the leaders said they had rejected the offer because "we want to keep our movement free of adults [the SLA cadres had been in their thirties] just as we reject similar offers by [GVN] Ministry of Education officials."

The SLA effort was more successful among university students in Hué. In terms of organization and operation, the Student Struggle Committee (Uy Ban Tranh Dau Cua Luc Luong Thanh Nien, Sinh Vien Hue) formed in Hué and Da Nang in April 1966 was pure NLF.

Cultural Liberation Association (CLA)[17]

The Cultural Liberation Association was a frankly elite group made up of scholars, artists, and Vietnamese of learning whose backgrounds, the NLF felt, would make them uncomfortable in the more plebeian associations, reasoning that could be traced far back into Chinese historical sociology. The organization was formed in the Saigon area in early 1961. It originally consisted of only scholars, writers, and poets but gradually broadened its membership to include artists, musicians, and finally even entertainers, who served the cause by performing in rural areas. Apparently this activity was more a service of the association than an integral function. At an early meeting the group faced the problem of the role of the artist in a revolution and opted in favor of the school that believed an artist should produce only socialist realism. For example, the association declared that the poet was to produce "poems exchanging sentiments, poems relating combat examples, poems attacking the enemy, poems praising the indomitableness of our army and people, . . . poems promulgated from person to person, broadcast from information halls, copied in handwriting, printed in books and papers. . . ." The duty of the writer was to produce "stories in prose, short stories, tales, essays, reports, and descriptions. . . . The content of the creations always reflects men and facts in combat, in production, and in all social activities in the liberated area."

The CLA's first congress, held in May 1962, was attended by about 70 persons, apparently all of them Saigonese. Members drafted an open

[17] In Vietnamese, Hoi Van Nghe Giai Phong, literally, Association of Arts and Letters for the Liberation. The DRV translation is Artists' and Writers' Liberation Association, and it is infrequently encountered as Literary Association for Liberation. The association published several handbooks that are the source material for this section.

letter to Vietnamese artists and writers in the DRV informing them of the congress, which, the letter declared, "was held to mobilize all our artistic and literary forces, all our minds and souls to serve the second Resistance and lead it to a successful end." [18]

No copy of the CLA bylaws has ever been obtained, nor is it known whether any existed. The letter of the CLA central committee to the Northern artists, however, outlined the organizational structure and purpose of the CLA:

> The South Vietnam Artists' and Writers' Liberation Association — the center of unity of all patriotic literary and artistic forces — has its system organized at all zonal, provincial, district, and village levels and in all units of the Liberation Army. . . . Past activities [have included] seasonal artistic performances, training artistic cadres and workers, guidance of literary productions and artistic performances. . . . [The Association seeks to] make even greater contributions to the revolutionary cause, the liberation of South Vietnam, and the reunification of the Fatherland.

It is highly unlikely that the CLA did exist in all 2,500 villages of Vietnam as claimed. From observation it was clear that the organization was formed for two purposes: (1) as an externalization arm, and to this end the CLA sent a steady flow of messages to fellow artists and writers abroad, and (2) to encourage literary production, stories, and poems, published mainly in a weekly magazine called *Liberation Culture* (or *Liberation Arts and Letters*), and dramatic productions, including *hat boi*, the traditional semioperatic theatrical performance, in remote rural areas.

The chairman of the CLA national central committee was Tran Huu Trang, a Saigon playwright and founder of an organization called the Saigon Brotherhood. His play on French colonialism was presented in Hanoi in July 1964. Tran Huu Trang was one of the original founders of the NLF. Listed as vice-chairman of the CLA central committee were poet Van Tung and writer Tran Hieu Minh. The secretary-general was listed as Ly Van Sam, a writer and poet. Two other writers were listed as members of the central committee, indicating that the leadership was almost entirely made up of writers. From the standpoint of formal organization the CLA existed only in the Saigon-Cholon area, and the Saigon-Cholon central committee probably was the same as the national central committee, at least in terms of creative activity. The chairman of the Saigon-Cholon committee was Truong Vinh Tong, who wrote under the pen name Hoai Linh. (Virtually all Vietnamese writers use one or more pen names, making identification in many cases difficult if not impossible.) He was described in a February 1963 broadcast as a writer, former music teacher at Huynh Khuong Ninh Music School in Saigon,

---

[18] Letter to *Nhan Dan*, July 27, 1962.

and a playwright and dancing master for the Kim Chuong Theatrical Troupe. The secretary-general was listed as Nguyen Thi Loan, whose pen name was Thanh Loan, a former teacher and journalist on *Cong Ly, Nhan Loai, Tri Tan,* and *Mien Nam* newspapers and for the Song Moi Publishing House. She was arrested in 1960 and released in 1962, after which she joined the NLF and eventually became one of the vice-chairmen of the Women's Liberation Association.

The CLA conducted extensive public correspondence with the Afro-Asian People's Solidarity Organization's writers' group and was invited to send a delegate to the group's conference in Cairo in February 1962. There is no record that it did so, but it did send a delegate to the writers' meeting in Bali two years later. Judged by its output, the CLA did not share the general attitude of other liberation associations, who seemed to be greatly impressed with Soviet military strength and economic accomplishments, and was more sympathetic to the Chinese than the Soviets. In March 1964, for example, the CLA had a public exchange of poetry with Chinese poets, dealing of course with revolutions. The CLA affinity probably stemmed from the natural deference that Vietnamese scholars hold for Chinese literature and art.

When the General Uprising came, the workers were expected to be the shock troops in the city. Previous efforts were to have been made among other urban elements considered sympathetic to the cause. These other urban elements, listed as "intellectual [white-collar] workers, handicraftsmen, national intellectuals and bourgeoisie, and students and pupils," were considered chiefly valuable for the influence they wielded among the city middle class. Members and cadres of the Cultural Liberation Association as well as those from the various NLF special-interest organizations attempted to infiltrate their counterpart cultural and professional organizations in the cities. There were perhaps 1,200 creative intellectuals and artists in South Vietnam during the period, almost all in Saigon or Hué. Writers had more status than painters, and poets were the most respected of all; sculptors were not included in this group, for they were considered artisans. Artists lived precarious lives and generally were bohemian and unstable, uninterested in rural affairs. Aloof to farmers, Laotians, and Cambodians, they were inclined toward pessimism and cynicism and were fiercely independent. They regarded themselves as guardians of the culture and correctly believed that the great prestige that their group traditionally enjoyed had diminished in recent years. NLF agents infiltrated their organizations and attempted to develop public demonstrations; the primary communicational appeals employed were general hostility to the United States and the theme of peace.

A review of NLF internal documents concerned with worker and urban activities leaves one with the feeling that the effort was more reflexive than determined, that the NLF had neither faith in nor patience with such groups. This was due both to the assessment of the individuals involved and to NLF reluctance to associate itself deeply with groups and organizations over which it did not have deep and primary control. Documents captured in December 1964 indicated in guarded but definite terms that the NLF believed that the moment had arrived when a condition of permanent anarchy could be effected in Saigon. Great disorders did take place, but they soon fizzled. The NLF failed in its efforts to capture these movements and use them to deliver a *coup de grâce* to the GVN.

II

Other NLF Organizations

In addition to the six major functional liberation associations, and of course the Communist party itself, the NLF was composed of a host of other organizations, grouped here into three classifications: political parties, special-interest groups, and externally oriented organizations. Like the functional liberation associations most of these organizations did not exist before 1960 and were in fact created specifically as members of the NLF. Together they served to reinforce the other social movement activities of the NLF. Also like the liberation associations, they were seen by their members primarily as serving their interests and only secondarily as revolutionary institutions.

Political Parties

The two organizations publicly labeled as political parties were the Radical Socialist Party (Dang Xa Hoi Cap Tien) and the Democratic Party of South Vietnam (Dang Dan Chu Mien Nam Viet Nam).[1]

[1] P. J. Honey has noted in correspondence with the author that the Radical Socialist Party and the Democratic Party are exact counterparts of the Socialist and Democratic

194

The Radical Socialist Party (RSP) traced its lineage back to the Indochina Socialist Party, which was formed in the early 1930's by elements of the French Socialist Party but which fragmented in the 1940's into what were to become several obscure Vietnamese socialist groups of small size and smaller influence. The Radical Socialist Party was formed in July 1962 with Nguyen Ngoc Thuong, a 40-year-old former Saigon University professor, as chairman and Nguyen Van Hieu as secretary-general. The first public mention of the RSP came at the first regular NLF congress in 1962, when Nguyen Ngoc Thuong delivered a lengthy address about his new organization. He declared: "We were born just a year ago . . . and are an organization that unites all patriotic, freedom-loving, justice-loving, and peace-loving intellectuals who wish to struggle for the establishment of an independent, democratic, peaceful, and unified Vietnam." He outlined an eight-point program that closely resembled the NLF ten-point manifesto. He said the RSP had the following goals: "(1) toppling the U.S.-Diem regime . . . ; (2) establishment of a progressive and democratic regime that will guarantee freedom of speech, freedom of worship, freedom of business practice, freedom of association, and freedom of political association and activity . . . ; (3) development of an independent economy that will end unemployment, protect local industries, provide land for all peasants, exempt those who fight in the present struggle from paying taxes, . . . and end Vietnam's dependence on the United States . . . ; (4) establishment of a progressive social welfare service policy in which there will be care for the aged and disabled, unemployment compensation, intensive educational effort, etc. . . . ; (5) elimination of American cultural influence and the substitution of the people's progressive and popular culture; . . . abolition of foreign languages in the Vietnamese educational system; ending the unjust university and secondary-school examination system; . . . reduction of tuition in private schools; . . . forbidding the teaching of antiscientific material such as the "personalist" philosophy [of Ngo Dinh Nhu]; . . . elimination of the secret police infiltrating ranks of professors, students, and artists . . . ; (6) elimination of U.S. military bases and presence in Vietnam and a halt to the militarization now going on in Vietnam . . . ; (7) establishment of a peaceful and neutral foreign policy with diplomatic relations with all nations that respect South Vietnam's independence and sovereignty . . . ; (8) unification of Vietnam through peaceful means and by the implementation of the 1954 Geneva agreements." The speech studiously

---

parties of the DRV. The former caters to the non-Communist intellectuals who support the Lao Dong Party but are not eligible for various reasons for Party membership, and the Democratic Party caters to bourgeois elements of the same kind.

avoided use of the word "communism" and, ironically for an organization of socialists, used the word "socialism" sparingly.

The purpose and thrust of the RSP effort are apparent from a sampling of its announced activities. In June 1962, for example, it began a massive propaganda campaign over the Vinh case. Professor Le Quang Vinh and eleven Vietnamese students had been arrested in connection with the attempted assassination of American Ambassador Frederick Nolting. The RSP declared that "their bright example strengthens the intellectuals' will to participate in the Revolution . . . and indicates the way for those who still hesitate." On October 15, 1962 Radio Hanoi reported that the RSP had met in an extraordinary session for the purpose of endorsing an NLF memorandum of September 19, sent to the 17th session of the United Nations General Assembly, denouncing the "systematic interference of the United States in South Vietnam." The RSP statement declared that "the United Nations General Assembly is a competent organ to defend the peace and security of the various nations of the world . . ." (a stand reversed two years later by the NLF and all its organs). On June 18, 1963 Nguyen Ngoc Thuong opened a propaganda campaign that mounted steadily for a year. It aimed at sabotaging the GVN's efforts to encourage Vietnamese schoolteachers, particularly in the rural areas, to actively support the government's strategic-hamlet program. Other statements issued by the RSP supported the Buddhists in their struggle against the Diem government in mid-1963 and denounced the importation of military equipment into Vietnam by the United States; the party also made numerous world peace statements. In October 1964 one of its central committee members, Le Van Tha, issued in the name of the RSP a strong pro-Chinese statement.

The Radical Socialist Party served to attract to the NLF banner those Vietnamese philosophically inclined toward economic socialism as well as former members of the various Indochinese socialist parties. It also served as the NLF's intellectual platform, attracting teachers and university students; the RSP propaganda output clearly indicated its preoccupation with intellectuals and students, as did its efforts to establish closer relations with intellectuals outside Vietnam, working through Nguyen Ngoc Thuong's Afro-Asian People's Solidarity Committee. However, the RSP directed its appeal not only toward socialists, ex-socialists, and intellectuals but also at a broader segment of Vietnamese society. Saigonese familiar with the nuances of political thought among their countrymen asserted that the RSP connoted Western, particularly French-style, democracy. The party's name in Vietnamese, they maintained, had a distinct Western flavor to it.

Any "democratic" party in Vietnam, on the other hand, suggested to the Vietnamese not Western democracy but the so-called "new democracy" of Communist China. Intellectuals in Vietnam had followed Chinese political developments since the days of Sun Yat-sen, and the Chinese revolution and its achievements created a reservoir of admirers that the Democratic Party sought to tap.

Vietnam had known several political parties by the name of Democratic Party. The most illustrious was the party of that name formed in 1936 by the star-crossed Nguyen Van Thinh, who served briefly in the 1947 French-sponsored provisional government in Cochin China, trying to walk the middle ground between the French and the Viet Minh. (At mid-year he broke with the French, and in November 1947 he was found hanging from his bedroom window, an apparent suicide, although his death was never satisfactorily explained.)[2] A Vietnam Democratic Party was formed in Hanoi on June 30, 1944 by a group of Vietnamese nationalists. It, or its successor bearing the same name, continued to exist in North Vietnam, most recently headed by Nghiem Xuan Yem. There was the Vietnam Democratic Party, a non-Communist Vietnamese émigré organization based in Paris that also operated in Washington. It was founded by Nguyen Thai Binh and included General Thai Son and Tran Van Tung in its ranks. Perhaps the NLF hoped to benefit from this proliferation of democratic parties.

Whether the South Vietnam Democratic Party was intended to be a branch of the Democratic Party in the DRV is not clear. When it joined the NLF in late 1960, the Democratic Party's chairman was Tran Buu Kiem and its secretary-general was Huynh Tan Phat, both of whom went on to higher offices. The Democratic Party once described itself as "the party of patriotic capitalists and the petite bourgeoisie" and at another time as "the party of intellectuals, industrialists, and tradesmen." An analysis of its public statements and propaganda showed that its themes and interests ranged over the whole spectrum of social and political activity, indistinguishable in tone, emphasis, or balance from the output of the NLF itself. In January 1965 Radio Liberation reported that the Democratic Party had held a general congress "attended by many personalities, intellectuals, merchants, and industrialists from the Saigon-Cholon area . . . and other cities." It said the congress elected a 15-man central committee and listed 7 members: Huynh Tan Phat, Tran Buu Kiem, Lam Ngoc Chi, Duong Van Le, Ho Kim Son, Nguyen Van Lan, and Tran Van Huong, the first two being well known and the others almost totally unknown. Appeals issued by the congress

[2] See Donald Lancaster, *The Emancipation of French Indochina* (London, New York, Toronto: Oxford University Press, 1961), pp. 163–164, for an account of Thinh's problems as prime minister of the provisional Cochin-Chinese government and a "proof of suicidal intent."

were broad based and were directed at Vietnamese "intellectuals, workers, tradesmen, patriotic [military] officers, and civil servants," which indicated an urban orientation but little else.

Special-Interest Groups

The special-interest groups in the NLF included the *van hoi*, or professional associations, and religious, ethnic minority, veteran, and certain other organizations.

Van Hoi

A generic term meaning "association of those in the same profession," the *van hoi* bound together journalists, doctors, teachers, and businessmen sympathetic to the NLF cause in separate groups. These existed as independent chapters of 10 to 18 members in cities or towns but rarely in villages. Group activities consisted of self-interest and professional association work as well as contributing to the Revolution. The separate chapters were bound together in a nationwide organization that apparently was headed by a central committee but had no intervening administrative levels.

The most important of these organizations by far was the PDJA (Patriotic and Democratic Journalists' Association — Hoi Nha Bao Yeu Nuoc Va Dan Chu). It was formed in early 1962 by Nguyen Van Hieu, who in September of the same year represented the new association at the meeting of the International Union of Journalists in Budapest. He and Thanh Nho, who also attended and who later became director of the Liberation Press Agency, were listed at the conference as vice-chairman and chairman respectively of the PDJA.

Nhan Dan on April 26, 1963 described the journalists' group as

an organization to muster the combatants who have been and are using the press as a weapon to struggle for national independence, freedom, and democracy in South Vietnam. Those who have joined the association are the journalists who formerly took part in the anti-French Resistance and are now resolutely struggling to protect patriotic and democratic journalism, journalists who worked with the press in the cities but have now abandoned the enemy-controlled area to join the patriotic struggle of the Southern people. Another group of journalists that has joined the [PDJA] includes those who follow the line of the association even though they work for the papers published right under the censorship of the U.S.-Diemists. Journalists belonging to various tendencies, nationalities, and religions have joined the Patriotic and Democratic Journalists' Association, and this proves . . . it is attracting wide support. . . .

Apparently, however, the PDJA existed only as a paper organization, or as a group of journalists at the NLF Central Committee headquarters, until June 1963, when a provisional central committee of the PDJA was formed to make plans for an organizing congress. Leaflets announcing both the formation of the PDJA and the congress were distributed widely throughout the Saigon area. On August 26, 1963 the congress convened in a remote area of Tay Ninh province. Radio Liberation said it was attended by 150 delegates. Oddly, the provisional chairman of the new organization, Vu Tung, was not present; the broadcast said he was engaged in business elsewhere. Present as guests were NLF Chairman Nguyen Huu Tho, NLF Central Committee member Tran Buu Kiem, NLF youth leader Tran Bach Dang, Cultural Liberation Association Chairman Tran Huu Trang, and members of the NLF Central Committee. This high-level representation indicates, if nothing else, the importance the NLF leadership placed on journalistic activities.

The congress came at the height of the Diem government's efforts to repress the Buddhist movement, so the official statement of the conference dealt primarily with that. It said:

1. We denounce vehemently before public opinion here and throughout the world the crimes and plots of the U.S. imperialists and the Ngo Dinh Diem clique . . . and its bloody white terror aimed at suppressing the movement of the struggle for the freedom of belief of the Buddhist believers. . . .
2. We support resolutely the Buddhist people's struggle . . . and stand side by side with the students, youths, and intellectuals in the cities in their struggle against the U.S.-Diemists. . . .
3. We condemn the U.S.-Diemist fascist measures of strangling public opinion, destroying freedom of the press, and . . . [we] resolutely support journalists in Saigon in their struggle for freedom of the press. . . .
4. We earnestly call on the press and public opinion in the world to support positively the struggle of the Vietnamese people. U.S. aggressors — number one executioner in South Vietnam — go home.

The conference listed the major tasks that the NLF had set for the association. The PDJA was to "develop foreign propaganda, . . . increase propaganda activities among soldiers of the enemy, . . . raise the combativeness of the press (prolonged applause), . . . increase the accuracy of the press, . . . consolidate and broaden unity among journalists, . . . and make greater use of photography."

A 34-man committee was elected to administer the organization. The chairman was Vu Tung, chief editor of the NLF's "daily" newspaper in the Saigon-Cholon area, *Giai Phong* (Liberation). Three vicechairmen were named: Tan Duc, director of the Radio Liberation broadcasting station; Nhi Muc, described as the former editor of the newspaper *Saigon Moi* (New Saigon), and the well-known Nguyen

Van Hieu, already representing the NLF abroad. The secretary-general was Thanh Nho, director of the Liberation Press Agency.

In January 1963 the NLF announced the formation of a group called the Military and Civilian Medical Council. Radio Liberation reported that the organization would be headed by Dr. Phung Van Cung, and its purpose was described as to "strengthen and develop military and civil medical activities, to meet the medical requirements in the ever-broadening areas freed from U.S.-Diem control. . . ." Radio Hanoi in January 1964 reported that Dr. Phung Van Cung, acting as chairman of the NLF Central Committee's Health Committee, had sent a letter to "Nguyen Luu Vien, member of the Red Cross and Council of Notables of the South Vietnam puppet regime, urging the South Vietnam authorities to work out urgent measures to save the people, stamp out the epidemic, and supply medicines to the cholera-infested areas. . . ." In early February the station reported that the Health Committee had dispatched two doctors and 40 nurses to four villages in Zone D to help fight the epidemic. Nothing more was heard of the Medical Council until June 1964, when the NLF announced the formation of the Medical Liberation Association (sometimes referred to as the Liberation Doctors' Association), with the same Dr. Phung Van Cung as provisional chairman and Dr. Doan Thanh Trung as provisional secretary-general. Four doctors and a pharmacist were listed as members of the provisional committee, for which elections would be held later. The Medical Liberation Association was "open to all medical personnel who wish to serve the Revolution." In August 1964 Radio Hanoi reported that the original medical organization, with Dr. Phung Van Cung still chairman, had changed its name to Civilian and Military Public Health Council.

The South Vietnam Patriotic Teachers' Association (Hoi Nha Giao Yeu Nuoc Mien Nam) began as a local organization in the Saigon area. It was formed, said a learning document, when 50 Saigon teachers met outside Saigon on July 12, 1963, with Huynh Tan Phat, chairman of the Saigon-Cholon Special Zone NLF central committee, acting as host. Plans were made for a subsequent meeting, held in November 1963, attended by 115 teachers. The following May the teachers again met in a remote area and elected a 30-man executive committee headed by Le Van Uy, who was described as a former professor at Petrus Ky High School in Saigon. Elected secretary-general was Le Thuoc, described as a former schoolteacher in Can Tho. At the initial meeting Trung Van An, a member of the NLF Central Committee, outlined for the teachers the NLF philosophy on education:

Students must learn to benefit the people and serve the present task of saving the country from the U.S. invaders and to prepare for national construction in the future society. They learn not for the purpose of receiving a diploma or to promote their own personal interest, as is taught in the U.S.-Diem reactionary schools. The aim of our educational branch is to create a body of intellectuals who are qualified in all respects, who have skills and virtues and love the country and people, and who have the courage to make sacrifices for a just cause. Our educational branch is not aiming at training persons with cowboyish manners who forget their ancestry and who will readily cheat their masters and friends. Such men are being formed by the U.S.-Diemists to serve as their instruments.

Religious and Ethnic Minority Groups

The NLF regarded religion, as well as the efforts of the ethnic minority groups to achieve equal rights, as an integral part of its struggle and sought in every way to associate itself with such groups. Contrary to what might be expected, however, the NLF did little organization building among these people. Buddhists, sect members, Catholics, the montagnards, and the Chinese and Cambodian minorities were formed not into mass-based but into selective and for the most part *ad hoc* organizations. As a matter of policy NLF leaders avoided creating religious and ethnic organizations for fear they might not be fully controllable or might turn hostile to the NLF cause, as indeed happened with respect to the montagnards in 1962 and the Cao Dai in 1964. Extensive work was done among the religious and ethnic minority groups, of course, but every effort was made to incorporate the individuals into either the mass-based organizations or, preferably, into the PRP itself.

The general NLF policy toward religion was spelled out in an NLF document found in Kien Hoa province in May 1963, although apparently at least a year old at that time:

We must strengthen our actions among religious groups and increase our organizational work. Religious leaders should be won to our cause. Pay particular attention to Catholics, Cao-Daiists, and Hoa Hao Buddhists in Soc Sai. . . . Unmask the enemy scheme of using religion to divide the people. . . . Help the religious to maintain their principles, repair pagodas, temples, and churches. . . . Enable the people to carry on their prayers, attend mass and religious ceremonies. Absolutely do not use pagodas, temples, and churches for meetings and do not post slogans, slips, or banners inside or outside of them. . . .

In an address at the NLF's Second Congress, January 1964, Nguyen Huu Tho declared:

The struggle of the religious believers in South Vietnam is not separate from the struggle for national liberation but has become a component part of the revolutionary movement in South Vietnam. . . . The struggle for religious freedom cannot be waged separately from the struggle for national independence.

The initial NLF effort in the religious field concentrated on ethnic Cambodians living in Vietnam, most of whom were more ardent Buddhists than the average Vietnamese. One of the prominent early NLF leaders was a well-known ethnic Cambodian monk, Son Vong, who died in March 1963 and was replaced by Thuong Ba Phuong Long, who was elected vice-chairman of the Central Committee Presidium. In January 1965 Radio Liberation announced the formation in the Mekong delta of a new religious organization, the Patriotic Khmer (Cambodia) Monks' Solidarity Association, which it said had applied for NLF membership and had among its goals the strengthening of Cambodian-Vietnamese solidarity.

The Patriotic Buddhist Believers' Association[3] appeared to be most active in the Mekong delta and was mentioned in early 1961 NLF literature. An early document listed the group's leader as Thich Thien Hao, described as a native of Gia Dinh province (born in 1908), who served for many years in the Giai Ngan temple in Saigon and as president of the Luc Hoa Buddhist Association, one of the early Buddhist associations in Indochina. Thien Hao also served on the Afro-Asian People's Solidarity Committee and had the assignment of maintaining contact with Asian Buddhists. In July 1964 he went to Tokyo to attend the Second World Conference of Religious Believers in Peace, stopping en route in Hanoi and Peking. At the conference he delivered a standard NLF attack on the United States. Thich Nhan Tu, another Buddhist monk, was listed as an NLF Central Committee member. The Front employed the Patriotic Buddhist Believers' Association as a device for encouraging outside support for the NLF, and the association appeared to have been primarily foreign oriented. Its organizational structure therefore probably existed only at the national level; it is not even clear whether it pretended to be a nationwide organization.

The Cao Dai sect called the Foremost Cao Dai Sect (Phai Cao Dai Tien Thien) identified itself most closely with the NLF, although the official Cao Dai member of the Front was known as the Committee for Consolidating Peaceful Coexistence. The Hoa Hao member group was known as the Hoa Hao Morality Improvement Association (Hoi Chan Hung Dao Duc Cua Dong Bao Theo Ton Giao Hoa Hao). Many NLF Central Committee leaders were sect believers but not particularly identified as such. The chief sect spokesman within the NLF was the Reverend Nguyen Van Ngoi, who was born in 1897 in Vinh Long province, where he became a school principal and was active in the Tien Thien sect of the Cao Dai. He fought against the French in the Viet Minh war and said he had lost three sons and a son-in-law in

---

[3] In Vietnamese, Hoi Phat Tu Yeu Nuoc. The NLF Buddhist organization was sometimes known as the Buddhist Liberation Association.

the same struggle. Nguyen Van Ngoi was active in the NLF organization of Viet Minh war veterans and was also chairman of the Southern Central Interzone central committee, a key position. Although no announcement was made, he may have been replaced; after July 1964 his name was not mentioned, and Cao Dai statements were signed by Ngoc Ngoai Nghiep, about whom nothing is known.

Although the effort came to little, the NLF also attempted to develop its influence among the one million Catholics in South Vietnam. It assumed the public posture that the GVN even under Diem was antireligious and, although Diem himself was a Catholic, anti-Catholic.[4] The NLF in 1961 created the National Liaison Committee of Patriotic and God-Fearing Catholics (Nhung Nguoi Cong Giao Kinh Chua Yeu Nuoc), with Joseph Marie Ho Hue Ba[5] as chairman and guiding light. He was an ethnic Cambodian, born in 1898 in An Giang province and well known in the Mekong delta as an organizer of the NLF and an active member of various NLF peace movements. A 1961 NLF biographical sketch described Ho Hue Ba as a priest who had taught at the Cu Lao Gieng seminary until he was forced to flee because the police wanted to question him about his peace work. Apparently the committee was what it said it was, a liaison committee, and not a mass-based organization. Most of its activities consisted of sending letters to Catholics in North Vietnam. The DRV obliged by establishing a Catholic liaison group in Hanoi to forward this mail, and since most of the Catholics in South Vietnam were refugees from the North, the committee may have offered them a means of communicating with old friends and relatives there.

The thematic appeal of the NLF to religious believers was religious freedom, a freedom at no time in serious jeopardy in South Vietnam. Even the Diem-Buddhist struggle, as Buddhist leaders acknowledged, was essentially a political struggle. The NLF in the summer of 1963 attempted to turn the Buddhist movement to its own purposes. It did succeed in increasing its influence among Buddhist laymen, but no evidence was ever uncovered to indicate that it succeeded in penetrating the decision-making level in Hué or Saigon. Moreover, while no one could say with finality that such influence did not exist, there was little in

---

[4] According to Radio Liberation (August 28, 1964):

During the past few years the enemy has warred against all religious people, Buddhists and Catholics alike. The enemy has burned and destroyed pagodas, interfered with churches, and harmed and killed Buddhists, Catholics, and other religious people, . . . deprived all people of their freedom of religion. . . . Thus to protect freedom of faith and religion Buddhists, Catholics, and other religious people must struggle to oppose all fascist and dictatorial acts and the aggressive war of the U.S. imperialists and their lackeys.

[5] In French parochial schools in Indochina it was common for the teacher to affix a French name before the Vietnamese.

Buddhist policy that aided the NLF; and there was considerable evidence that the Buddhist hierarchy regarded the NLF as its ultimate enemy. After 1963 the Buddhists, moving in the direction of a third force, authentically neutral, were openly attacked by the NLF, which charged the Buddhist leaders with having sold out to the Americans. The Buddhist hierarchy in Saigon, known collectively as the Vien Hoa Dao, was split between the moderates led by Thich Tam Chau and the left wing led by Thich Tri Quang. The NLF mass media directed scalding verbal attacks against Tam Chau but only infrequently attacked Tri Quang.

Of the ethnic minority groups, the montagnards were wooed most strongly by the NLF in the early days. The overseas Chinese in South Vietnam were generally ignored, and the ethnic Cambodians usually were approached as Buddhists rather than as members of an ethnic minority group. There were no functional liberation associations within the NLF exclusively for ethnic minority groups. Instead they were incorporated directly into the major organizations.

The attitude of the NLF toward the montagnards was spelled out in a 1961 agit-prop directive:

In accordance with Article Seven of the Front's regulations concerning equality among all nationalities [reference here is only to the montagnards] and in accordance with our past experiences with respect to minorities at various stages of the Revolution, we should develop among the national minorities in South Vietnam the indomitable struggle tradition. This will conform to the earnest aspirations of the ethnic compatriots.

The most common method of NLF operation in the highlands was first to send in a penetration agent, either a member of the tribe or someone from a nearby tribe who spoke the dialect. After initial ground-breaking by this individual the agit-prop teams would arrive. If things went well and the agit-prop teams reported the montagnards receptive, a team of cadres would move into the village to begin directing montagnard activities, such as fighting or porter assignments with guerrilla bands. At the same time the cadres would recruit future montagnard leaders to be sent North or somewhere else outside their home area for training. The organizations formed were functional and usually had a paramilitary or supply mission. The only political organization was the Highland Autonomy Movement (Uy Ban Dan Toc Tu Tri Tay Nguyen),[6] which was formed by a congress of 23 montagnard tribal representatives on May 19, 1961 in the highlands. Ibih Aleo, a vice-chairman of the NLF Central Committee Presidium and a long-time activist in the highlands, was elected chairman. The organization seemed to have existed only on paper and hardly even there. It became dormant

[6] Variously translated; literally, Committee for the Autonomy of the People of the Western Plateau; the DRV's official translation was High Plateau National Autonomy Movement.

for a while, but following the disastrous summer of 1962, which saw a mass defection of montagnards from the Communists, the movement was resurrected. In a message on December 20, 1962 the NLF Central Committee encouraged the montagnards to establish an autonomous zone in the highlands. This may have triggered a more intensive NLF effort to influence the tribesmen and in turn may have been responsible for the so-called "revolt of the tribesmen" in the fall of 1964, in which militant Rhade defied the GVN, threatened secession, and finally were mollified through the good offices of American military with whom they had served. In general, Communist-montagnard relations were stormy, uneven, and not particularly successful.

Communicational work among the montagnards was almost exclusively personal. A Polish ship carried several thousand montagnards to North Vietnam during the 1954 partition; from these were selected agit-prop cadres to return to the South. The infiltrating teams generally were led by a Vietnamese, and all of them were hard working and dedicated. They came early, the bulk of the montagnard infiltration apparently having been in late 1959 and early 1960.

The montagnard is a simple person with a direct, nonabstract sense of loyalty; he is faithful to his friends and kills his enemies. It was this spirit that the NLF sought to harness, a fact of which more montagnards were aware than the NLF realized. When the test came, the NLF discovered that the montagnard was a devious animal, and that years of patient work did not pay off. American Special Forces teams started work among the montagnards in 1962. The montagnards found them helpful, honest, and more worthy of loyalty than the NLF Vietnamese, and so loyalty was switched. As American efforts swung whole tribes away from the NLF, the NLF tried a much harsher approach that in turn not only further alienated the montagnards but also drove an estimated 100,000 of them out of the highlands. The failure of the NLF to harness the deep and widespread resentment that the montagnards felt for the ethnic Vietnamese is attributed to the abstract nature of the NLF appeal, for example, the promise of autonomy after victory; the distrust the montagnards had for all Vietnamese, including NLF Vietnamese; and the highly exemplary work of the American Special Forces teams.

For reasons that were never clear the NLF tended to ignore the overseas Chinese in South Vietnam. Several internal documents dealing with agit-prop work among minority groups made no reference to the Chinese, listing only the montagnards, Cambodians, and Chams. NLF mass media likewise virtually ignored the Chinese. In the first four years of Radio Liberation output the author could find only four references to Chinese residents. These were appeals to the Chinese either not to serve in the

ARVN or to resist GVN efforts to recruit and form all-Chinese units within the ARVN. The NLF organization for the Chinese was called Vietnamese of Chinese Origin Association (Hoi Nguoi Viet Goc Hoa). It appears to have been small in membership and activity. In October 1964 the NLF began a propaganda campaign urging the Chinese in Cholon and elsewhere in South Vietnam to join actively in the Revolution, citing China as a model to follow. At the same time it announced the formation of the Provisional Committee of Chinese Students in Saigon-Cholon and other cities, which began issuing a series of manifestoes concerning labor disputes in the capital area.

Other Minor Special-Interest Groups

Beginning in 1961 the NLF organized a complex of veterans' organizations among the rural Vietnamese, which served two purposes: to augment and assist the military proselyting movement, and to develop a home-front link to the "hard hat" guerrilla units. The major organizations were:

Families of Patriotic Soldiers' Association (Hoi Gia Dinh Binh Si Yeu Nuoc), admitted to NLF membership in December 1962 and open to families who had a member serving in the Vietnamese armed forces. Ostensibly the purpose of the association, which consisted chiefly of women, was to work for a cessation to the fighting. Actually it became a major vehicle for pressuring soldiers to desert.

Former Resistants Association (Hoi Nhung Nguoi Khang Chien Cu), composed of veterans of the Viet Minh war. Nguyen Van Ngoi, the leader of the Cao Dai movement mentioned earlier, was listed as the chairman in 1962.

Vietnamese Fighters for Peace, Reunification, and Independence (Nhom Nhung Nguoi Dau Tranh Cho Hoa Binh Thong Nhut Doc Lap To Quoc Viet Nam). Behind this long and bland title stood one of the most deadly and secretive NLF organizations, the one concerned with clandestine operations within the Vietnamese armed forces; little or nothing is known about its structure.

Soldiers Returned to the People League (Nhom Binh Si Tro Ve Voi Nhan Dan), composed of ARVN deserters, whose chief purpose was to induce others to desert.

Disabled Veterans' and Heroes' Council (Hoi Dong Thuong Benh Liet Si), open to disabled veterans both of the Viet Minh war and of more recent guerrilla battles; it was described as primarily a mutual-protection association.

Soldiers' Mothers' Association, a gold-star mothers' group about which little is known.

Vietnam Mothers' Association, a veterans' auxiliary, consisted of 11-woman cells concerned chiefly with social welfare work, care of the indigent, helping families of guerrilla fighters, visiting the sick, and similar activities. The Mothers' Association was open to Women's Liberation Association members past the age of 50 who were "virtuous, possessing a clear understanding of the nature of the Revolution . . . and with a good record of activity in the revolutionary struggle." It was a sort of gathering of grandmother revolutionists.

Radio Liberation from time to time mentioned other special-interest groups. The Industrialists and Businessmen Against U.S.-Diem (Nhan Cong Thuong Gia Chong My Diem) apparently was not considered of much importance by the NLF leadership; at least no effort was made to communicate with the business community in the larger cities. It was not heard of after the end of the Diem regime, disqualified by its name if nothing else. Other NLF special-interest groups, which were probably paper organizations, noted by Radio Liberation or Radio Hanoi were the Vietnam Association for Scientific and Technical Dissemination, the Committee of Intellectuals for the Struggle Against Terror by the U.S. Imperialists and Their Henchmen in South Vietnam, the Liberation South Union, and the South Vietnamese Scientific Workers' Association (represented at a Peking conference by Nguyen Van Hieu in October 1964).

Externally Oriented Groups

The final clutch of organizations that made up the National Liberation Front of South Vietnam was concerned with affairs extending beyond the borders of Vietnam, mainly the dissemination of propaganda and maintenance of contact with world-wide Communist organizations. The largest and most important of these externally oriented groups was the Afro-Asian People's Solidarity Committee (Uy Ban Doan Ket Nhan Dan A Phi). Another major international organization was the World Peace Protection League of Vietnam, which was linked to the multitudinous Communist peace groups around the world; it apparently fell into eclipse.

Beyond these there were a number of minor externally oriented groups within the Front. The organization named Prominent Vietnamese Living Abroad (Nhan Si Viet Nam Ngoai Quoc) maintained contact with Vietnamese émigré groups abroad, chiefly those in Paris. The Young Patriotic Peace Lovers (Nhom Thanh Nien Nam Nu Yeu Nuoc Yeu Hoa Binh) was listed in early NLF literature but dropped from sight after 1962. The Liberation Red Cross Society (Hoi Hong Thap Tu

Giai Phong) began its career in 1963 by issuing appeals against the GVN's plant defoliation campaign. In September 1964 an NLF official, Nguyen Minh Phuong, toured China as a delegate from the association and was received by 1,000 members of the China Red Cross in Peking; Red Cross officials in Saigon of course deny that the organization is in any way connected with the International Red Cross movement.

The Afro-Asian People's Solidarity Committee (AAPSC) was formed in December 1961 primarily to link the NLF generally to the spirit of Bandung and specifically to the Afro-Asian People's Solidarity Organization headquartered in Cairo. Radio Hanoi announced its formation in a broadcast in English on December 9, 1961. The new organization was said to comprise "representatives of political parties, mass organizations, religious communities, and nationalities and prominent personalities who favor movements for self-determination by all peoples." The manifesto of the founding committee states that it was set up "to enhance the valuable and time-honored solidarity between the Vietnamese and Asian and African peoples so as to contribute to the latters' cause." At the same time the NLF began to distribute widely throughout South Vietnam a small 14-page booklet entitled *Declaration of the Afro-Asian People's Solidarity Committee of South Vietnam*. The booklet, which made no mention of the NLF, declared that

in order to tighten the bonds of unity between the peoples of Asia and Africa, we, the delegates, representing patriotic political parties, religious groups, etc., solemnly declare the formation of this Afro-Asian People's Solidarity Committee of South Vietnam as a member of the Council for the Unity of Afro-Asian Peoples.

Listed as the founding fathers of the AAPSC were Chairman Nguyen Ngoc Thuong, a teacher; Vice-Chairman Thich Thien Hao, Saigon Buddhist leader; and Secretary-General Huynh Cuong, a Cambodian intellectual. Committee members were said to be a woman, the active Mrs. Ma Thi Chu; a montagnard, Roches Priu; and a Cao Dai member, Ngo Tam Dao.

The AAPSC involved itself in all sorts of foreign-policy pronouncements: It signed a joint statement with the Indonesian Peace Committee in September 1962, declaring that the present state of the world was due to American imperialism, provocation, and aggressive schemes; it issued a statement in November 1962 backing the Chinese Communists in their border dispute with India; it condemned the British for "repressing" the people of Brunei; castigated the government of South Africa; and called for the return of Okinawa to Japan. Throughout, it kept up a steady exchange of good-will messages with the Afro-Asian People's Solidarity Organization in Cairo on the occasion of respective anniversaries and special days. It sent Mrs. Nguyen Thi Binh, then chairman of the Women's Liberation Association, to Moshi, Tanganyika, in February 1963 to attend the Afro-Asian People's Solidarity Organization conference, an act that resulted in an official note of protest to the government of Tanganyika from the government of South Vietnam. The Nguyen Thi Binh mission stopped in Cairo en route home and was received by the UAR Minister of Social Affairs as well as by Arab League officials. Its members attended a diplomatic reception given by the DRV mission and made arrangements for establishing an NLF mission in Cairo connected with the AAPSO headquarters. A short time later Nguyen Van Tien, a member of the NLF Central Committee, arrived in Cairo to assume the post of mission chief, accompanied by an assistant named Huynh Van Nghia. Together they formed, under the AAPSO umbrella, an organization called the Committee to Assist the South Vietnamese People. Included in its membership, in addition to the NLF, were China, the Soviet Union, Algeria, Guinea, Indonesia, Morocco, and Tanganyika. Apparently it was a fund-raising committee as well as a propaganda organ.

The World Peace Protection League (WPPL — in Vietnamese, Uy Ban Boa Ve Hoa Binh The Gioi) was an older organization, possibly one that predated the NLF. Some Vietnamese believed that the WPPL was the nucleus around which the NLF was formed, and the early roster of the League did suggest this. Active in it in about 1961 were Nguyen Huu Tho; Nguyen Van Hieu, its secretary-general; Phung Van Cung, its chairman; Son Vong; and Joseph Marie Ho Hue Ba. Nguyen Van Hieu went abroad for the League in July 1962, when he attended the Moscow disarmament conference, one of the first NLF missions abroad and one of the last references to the WPPL. It seems probable that the League was the early foreign policy arm of the NLF, a function taken over by the Foreign Relations Commission.

12

The NLF Command Structure

National Headquarters

The National Liberation Front headquarters consisted of the Central Committee; a Presidium, or Politburo, composed of select members of the Central Committee; a Secretariat, appointed by the Presidium and headed by the secretary-general, also a member of the Presidium and the Central Committee; and a staff responsible to both the Central Committee and the Secretariat. The Central Committee of the PRP, which was the Communist control mechanism, and the headquarters of the National Liberation Front army were also found at the national Central Committee headquarters. (See Chart 12–1.) Theoretically the Central Committee was elected by a congress made up of delegates chosen at the district level, but this process was manipulative rather than democratic. The Central Committee members originally numbered 35, a figure raised to 64 by the 1964 congress. The Presidium consisted of a chairman, who was also chairman of the Central Committee, and six vice-chairmen, of whom the sixth was secretary-general. The Secretariat had a total of five members, headed of course by the secretary-general. Thus the leadership breakdown as it stood in early 1965 was:

Officers of the Presidium	7
Secretariat (5 — 1)	4
Members of the Presidium	8
Central Committee members	34
Unfilled seats	11
	—
Total national Central Committee	64

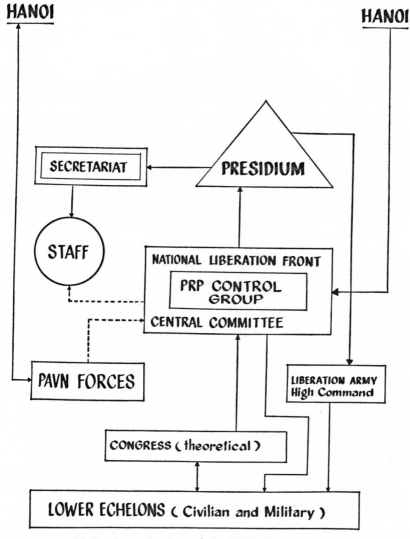

12–1 Organization of the NLF Headquarters

The actual headquarters of the NLF was believed to be in Laos, in the Attepo section east of the Se Kong River,[1] deep in Pathet Lao country. Periodically, from 1961 to 1964, the Central Committee convened in the sparsely populated area of northern Tay Ninh province. When the Central Committee was not in session, and this was most of the time, the NLF was managed by the Presidium and its Secretariat. The secretary-general undoubtedly was the most powerful individual in the NLF. The military high command, which was responsible for the violence program, reported directly to the Presidium. All other activity went through the Secretariat, dominated by the secretary-general.

The major tasks of the national headquarters were fivefold: supervise organization-building activity, that is, the creation of the liberation front committees and associations; direct the agit-prop work and supervise the preparation of mass-media output (although agit-prop policy guidance was a function of the interzone headquarters); manage the major socio-political programs of the NLF — the struggle movement, the army proselyting program, the creation of a governmental infrastructure; direct the violence program and encourage and develop military and paramilitary capability throughout the country; and assist in providing logistic support, money, food, war matériel, and manpower wherever possible.

The Foreign Relations Commission of the national Central Committee reported directly to the Presidium. The commission, which is described in detail in Chapter 17, was responsible for drafting NLF foreign policy statements, liaison relations with governments, organizations, and individuals beyond the borders of South Vietnam, and other duties, which made it a sort of embryonic foreign office.

A second office or function of the Central Committee headquarters also reported directly to the Presidium: the military command, responsible for the violence program, the armed struggle. Beginning in 1965, large numbers of regular army troops from North Vietnam (PAVN) were sent into South Vietnam. Their chain of command apparently was direct to Hanoi, not through either the Liberation Army high command or the NLF Central Committee.

The secretary-general's relations with the military command are not clear, although his seat on the Presidium would give him at least some control over the military apparatus. Some Vietnamese and some Americans believe that the NLF army was a separate and autonomous arm, independent of the Central Committee and its Presidium and perhaps reporting directly to Hanoi,[2] but there is little evidence of such a separa-

[1] Denis Warner, "Experiment in Neutrality," *The New Republic*, February 2, 1963.

[2] Colonel Edwin F. Black, "The Master Plan for Conquest in Vietnam," *Military Review*, Vol. XLIII, No. 6 (June 1963), asserts, without citation, that in November 1962 General Vo Nguyen Giap took over direction of the military affairs in South Vietnam, a move required, according to Black, because events were going badly in the South.

tion.[3] Communist governments traditionally fear the rise of a Red Napoleon and do not create autonomous military units. Instead they build into their system a number of devices to keep the military in check. Further, the military activity conducted in the name of the NLF was not military in the usual, or von Clausewitz, sense of the word but was a series of psychologically inspired acts of violence that, in addition to military assaults by guerrilla forces, included assassinations, harassing fire without infliction of casualties, terror incidents such as bombings and grenade throwing, and public executions. The decision to employ an act of violence in a specific case was a political decision based essentially on nonmilitary factors. In such an arrangement it would make no sense to have an independent military arm proceeding on the logic of military calculation. Finally, since the guerrilla unit did not have organic logistic support and was dependent on indigenous support, its "supply dump" in the field was the local liberation committee or the NLF central committee at whatever level the unit was operating. This tied the military unit directly to its organizational counterpart — the mobile column or battalion to the provincial committee, the company to the district committee, and so on. When such a pattern of total integration existed, it is unrealistic to believe that separate chains of command were maintained or that the military command was a separate entity. When the NLF regiment was formed, the military command that had existed as a headquarters and planning staff at the Central Committee headquarters assumed full military command. The NLF army then took on more of the shape of a regular or traditional army and no longer was a collection of loosely connected, self-contained guerrilla bands. Such a "militarization" did take place in late 1964; however, there is no evidence that its top control did not remain in the hands of civilians rather than with the military.

The Presidium thus was responsible for the violence program and foreign affairs. All other activity — directives sent down, reports going upward, appointments, and assignment of personnel — went through the Secretariat, dominated by the secretary-general.

The staff of the Secretariat comprised most of the actual manpower of the national Central Committee headquarters and had at least five major sections:[4]

[3] The NLF military organization is discussed in Chapter 13.

[4] The GVN at various times produced NLF organizational charts based on information from *quy chanh;* some of these charts were simple while others were extremely complex; some listed sections of the NLF national Central Committee headquarters in such vague terms as "rural section" or "political supervision section." Many of these entries were the figment of the imagination of the *quy chanh*, who was chiefly interested in impressing his hosts with his knowledge of the inner workings of the NLF but whose data were highly suspect.

The organizational activity section was concerned with personnel recruitment and organization building. Activists from this section in the early days actually went to the villages and created the organizations. As the Front grew, however, the job of organization building could no longer be managed from a central headquarters, and responsibilities had to be delegated to lower levels. This left the organizational activity section to devote itself mainly to the training, retraining, and indoctrination of the organizer cadres.

The permanent liberation association liaison section, the second major element of the Secretariat staff, actually managed the administrative liberation associations and appointed central committees at the lower levels. According to their bylaws, liberation associations were democratic structures with a congress electing a central committee at each respective level. However, no evidence exists that any liberation association congress was held above the provincial level. The permanent liberation association liaison section ran the six major and the sundry minor liberation associations. It also coordinated activities among the associations, acted as organizational troubleshooter, and arbitrated disputes among or within the associations.

The agit-prop section, the third element of the Secretariat staff, organized the various agitation and propaganda organs, including the all-important agit-prop teams. It supervised the most important of all NLF programs, the political struggle movement. Following the 1963 NLF reorganization, as noted, policy determination for the agit-prop teams, as well as agit-prop training and indoctrination of cadres, was transferred to the interzone level, which became virtually an independent agit-prop headquarters. The agit-prop section at the national Central Committee headquarters then confined its activities to a combination of public relations and external information service. From this office came a steady flow of messages to encourage the faithful.

The deadly *binh van* program, the NLF program aimed at the destruction of the nation's armed forces, was organized and administered by the fourth major unit, the military proselyting section, which was concerned with the destruction of the Vietnamese armed forces by nonmilitary means. A great deal of the proselyting work was done at the Central Committee level, probably in close conjunction with the NLF army high command. In addition to developing programs designed to reduce the effectiveness of the individual ARVN soldier, this section trained special agents who proselyted indirectly through the families of ARVN soldiers; it supervised the covert operations within the ARVN itself; and it set policy and supervised the handling of prisoners of war, including captured Americans.

The fifth major element of the Secretariat staff was the headquarters' administrative section, composed of four subsections: budget-fiscal, intelligence, security, and communication.

The Secretariat plus the National Liberation Front army high command, which was responsible for the armed struggle, acted as the fountainhead for all NLF activity in Vietnam. From a study of the Central Committee structure a clear picture of the leadership's scale of values can be obtained. The most important task, one that took precedence over all other activity, was organization building. Once created, the organization became the instrument for managing the social movement propaganda

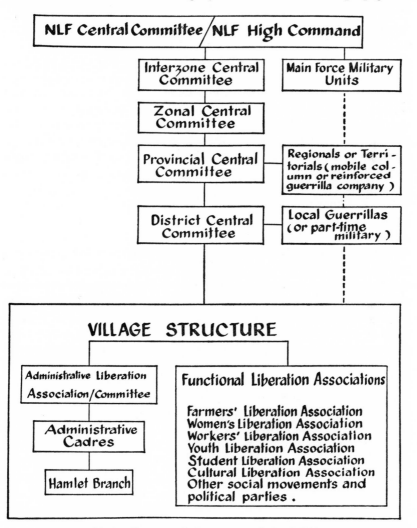

12–2 Command Structure of the NLF

work and the agit-prop activity to nullify the GVN administration (the political struggle) and to destroy the ARVN by a combined assault of persuasion (military proselyting program) and coercion (the armed struggle). The hierarchic organization of the NLF is shown in Chart 12–2.

National Leadership[5]

Little trustworthy information, which is to say non-Communist information, is available about the individuals who led the National Liberation Front. What is known has come almost entirely from Communist sources. As far as the author could determine, no Western or non-Communist newsman has ever interviewed the Central Committee chairman, Nguyen Huu Tho, although Vietnamese could be found in Saigon who knew him in his pre-NLF days. The Lenin of the NLF, Nguyen Van Hieu, talked with Western newsmen and others in Djakarta, Moscow, and East Berlin. Although more NLF leaders went abroad each year, most of them remained phantom figures slipping through the villages by night. Even the existence of some of the lesser figures was open to question, for example, some of the montagnard members of the Central Committee.

The best-known NLF figure in Vietnam was Central Committee Chairman Nguyen Huu Tho, who led the NLF from its inception. The secretary-general held the power reins in the NLF as frequently is the case in Communist nations: If the chairman is a figurehead, the secretary-general most certainly is not; if the chairman is not a Marxist, the secretary-general most certainly is. Phung Van Cung was the provisional secretary-general before the organizing congress in 1960. Since then, three persons have held this vital post: Nguyen Van Hieu, the skilled propagandist and organizational genius; Tran Buu Kiem, a cool, unemotional efficiency expert; and Huynh Tan Phat, architect turned theoretician.

In addition to the chairman and the secretary-general the Presidium membership included five vice-chairmen: Vo Chi Cong; Dr. Phung Van Cung (sometimes listed as Tran Van Cung); Tran Nam Trung; Thom Me The Nhem, an ethnic Cambodian and a Buddhist monk; and Ibih Aleo (or Y Bih Aleo; his name can be phoneticized in several ways), who represented the montagnards. The two ethnic minority representatives probably had little actual power in the NLF decision-making process and were regarded by the leadership as tools for use in manipulating the groups they represented.

Other members of the Central Committee included Thich Thien Hao,

[5] Biographical sketches and photographs of the NLF leaders are given in Appendix D.

Nguyen Van Ngoi, Le Van Huan, Ho Thu, Le Van Thinh, Tran Van Thanh, Nguyen Thi Binh, Joseph Marie Ho Hue Ba, Nguyen Van Tien, Nguyen Ngoc Thuong, Vo Dong Giang, Le Quang Chanh, Huynh Van Tam, and Vo Van Mon.

Several military figures were frequently mentioned in connection with NLF army leadership: Nguyen Don, Nguyen Chi Thanh, and To Ky. Quite obviously the NLF did everything possible to keep secret the facts about the military leadership, and therefore data on this subject are little more than speculation.

P. J. Honey has suggested that there existed in South Vietnam a still higher level of leadership than that just described, one deeply hidden and under the direct control of Hanoi. It was responsible for the actual top-level decision-making in South Vietnam. He said evidence of the existence of a four-man group was indicated to foreign correspondents at the Geneva conference on Laos in July 1962:

A leading member of this [the DRV] delegation inadvertently disclosed . . . that the published list of members of the Central Committee of the Workers' Party [in the DRV] was not complete. The identity of some members had been kept secret because "they are directing military operations in South Vietnam." He went on to name four such secret members of the Central Committee, but gave the impression that there are more than this number in the South. The four named are Pham Thai Buong, Nguyen Van Cuc, Pham Van Dang, and Le Toan Thu. . . .[6]

There is little doubt in this author's mind that the management of the NLF after 1963 was in the hands of the Hanoi-trained and -indoctrinated Communists, perhaps Southerners but responsive to the wishes of the leaders of the DRV. Existing evidence suggests that control was managed through the People's Revolutionary Party, successor to the Lao Dong Party in South Vietnam. The Honey report is consistent with this view. The four leaders to whom he refers could well be the top managers of the PRP, with direct control over the NLF national Central Committee, Presidium, and Secretariat.

Interzone, Zone, and Special Zone

Below the national Central Committee level lay the zonal command structure: the interzone, the zone, and the special zone. South Vietnam, the area south of the 17th parallel, was divided into six zones by the NLF: the portion below the parallel that once had been the Kingdom

---

[6] P. J. Honey, "North Vietnam's Workers' Party and South Vietnam's People's Revolutionary Party," *Pacific Affairs,* Vol. XXXV, No. 4 (Winter 1962–63), p. 383.

of Annam, an autonomous zone of the highlands,[7] three zones in what had once been Cochin China, and a special zone comprising Saigon and vicinity. This arrangement followed the Viet Minh organizational structure and even used the same numbering system employed by the Viet Minh.[8] Apparently the structure proved unworkable, for in May 1963 a new arrangement was devised and announced.

South Vietnam was divided into three interzones (*lien tinh,* literally, group of provinces): the coastal plain (Southern Central Vietnam Interzone — I), the highlands area (Western Highlands Interzone — II), and the vital area that once was roughly Cochin China (Nambo or Southern Area Interzone — III). The Saigon-Cholon-Gia Dinh area remained as a special zone. Under the three interzones were seven zones (*lien khu*), which were not command units but simply subdivisions of the interzone, established to facilitate communication and liaison procedures. The chain of command therefore ran from the Central Committee headquarters to the interzone committee to, via the zone committee, the provincial committee. The Central Interzone and the Highlands Interzone each had two zones, and the Nambo Interzone had three.

The Southern Central Vietnam Interzone consisted of the coastal plain from the 17th parallel down to Tuy Hoa province.[9] Within it were Zone Five, the "Northern Central Zone," which ran down the coast from the 17th parallel as far as Khanh Hoa province, and Zone Six, the "Deep Southern Central Vietnam Zone," roughly the provinces of Khanh Hoa, Ninh Thuan, and Binh Thuan.

The Western Highlands Interzone consisted of the highlands of South Vietnam. It was composed of Zone Seven, the "Zone of the Three Frontiers," [10] roughly the seven southernmost provinces in the highlands, and the "Western Highlands Autonomous Zone" (no number), the northern half of the highlands, including the border area adjacent to North Vietnam, where the separatist tendency was strongest.

The Nambo (Southern Area) Interzone, by far the most important in the organizational structure, was divided into three zones:

[7] The Western Highlands Autonomous Zone had a rudimentary form of administration consisting of the People's Autonomous Committee, which administered the entire area. Most of the zone was empty forest land; where the seminomadic montagnards were found the highly structured NLF committee system was not appropriate.

[8] The Viet Minh divided Vietnam into six zones, numbering from north to south; roughly zones one and two were in Tonkin, three and four in Annam, and five and six in Cochin China.

[9] Following good guerrilla warfare techniques, the NLF did not draw its administrative boundaries congruent to the GVN's provincial and district boundaries but deliberately included portions of two GVN administrative units into one of its commands so as to increase the GVN problem of coordination. The administrative areas of the two sides resemble each other closely enough, however, to allow the use of GVN administrative place names. See note in Appendix A for GVN changes in province names.

[10] That is, the frontiers of Cochin China, Annam, and Cambodia; not, as is often reported, Vietnam, Laos, and Cambodia.

Eastern Nambo — the area from the Cambodian border to the South China Sea above Saigon and below the highlands, approximately the nine provinces comprising the Massif Plain and the coastal lowlands.

Central Nambo — roughly the eight provinces below Saigon and above the Bassac River, running from Cambodia to the sea.

Western Nambo — the six provinces in the far south of South Vietnam, the Mekong delta area below the Bassac River.

NLF internal documents, as well as prisoners and defectors, occasionally referred to zone headquarters, but in all probability these headquarters were not command structures with a central committee but temporary headquarters established for the purpose of conducting indoctrination sessions or holding special conferences of members of provincial or district committees. The zone base existed as a clearinghouse for directives from higher headquarters, as a message center and way station for runners, but not as a decision-making entity. For it to have been so would have violated a cardinal NLF organizational principle: centralization in planning and decentralization in execution. A zone would have been too low in the hierarchic structure for planning and too high for operations. In mid-1964 captured memoranda indicated that the Central Committee had under active consideration a proposal to abolish the Nambo Interzone and elevate the three zones under it to interzones, raising the total number of interzones from three to five. This move was contemplated, it was indicated, so that the NLF would correspond more closely to the organizational structure of the PRP. There is no doubt that zonal activity was intensive; it was particularly useful for coordination work and conferences.

The city was of secondary importance to the NLF, following as it did the Chinese Communist guerrilla dictum: Capture the countryside and the cities will fall like ripe plums. Nevertheless the NLF was interested in an organizational structure within the only metropolitan area in South Vietnam, Saigon-Cholon and the surrounding suburban area in Gia Dinh province. The region was about 200 square miles in area and contained at least two million people. Hence the NLF established early the Saigon-Cholon-Gia Dinh (SCGD) Special Zone, which reported directly to the national Central Committee. The headquarters for the SCGD Special Zone was outside the zone itself, in the Boi Loi forest of neighboring Binh Duong province.[11]

---

[11] Its organizational structure followed the basic NLF concept, consisting of six sections: (1) a liberation front section, responsible for social movement and social organization activity, all of it clandestine; (2) an agit-prop and mass-media section, which included two primary subsections: a publications subsection since there was a great deal of handbill and leaflet activity in the area, and an entertainment subsection, a USO-type organization that recruited entertainers from Saigon for performances in the remoter sections

In January 1966, GVN and U.S. military units overran part if not all of the headquarters complex of the Saigon-Cholon-Gia Dinh Special Zone and captured some 6,000 documents. From this incredible haul came abundant evidence that the main purpose of the SCGD Special Zone was to serve as headquarters of the PRP. Previously this had been believed, but there had been little evidence to substantiate the belief. It had always been known that Huynh Tan Phat, chairman of the PRP, had been active in the SCGD Special Zone headquarters.

The SCGD Special Zone was divided into three operational sections: the city of Saigon-Cholon (in turn divided into eight districts following the same structural breakdown of the city as the mayor's office), the area north and east of the Saigon–Bien Hoa highway, and the area west and south of the highway. Captured NLF memoranda indicate that plans were under way in 1964 to create two other special zones: in the port city of Da Nang and in the old imperial capital of Hué in Central Vietnam.

Provincial Level

The provincial central committee was the NLF's all-important echelon in pursuit of its revolutionary guerrilla war, the command post from which the generalized directives from above were translated into specific operational orders and sent down to lower echelons. Below the provincial central committee there was no firm hierarchic structure but, depending on the development of the Revolution, a network of district, township, and village liberation committees, functional liberation associations, political parties and organizations, and special-interest groups, some closely linked with the NLF in a superordinate-subordinate pattern, others mere uneasy allies. The relationship of the provincial central committee to lower echelons thus varied greatly both in nature and in effectiveness. In perhaps as many as one third of the provinces in mid-1964 there was either no provincial central committee at all or only a phantom paper organization. Development of the committee was concentrated in key provinces, most of them in the Mekong delta or along the coastal plain below Da Nang.

---

of the country; (3) a military proselyting section that conducted activities among the large number of ARVN troops stationed in the Bien Hoa area; (4) a military section for the violence, or armed struggle, program; (5) an administrative section that was chiefly concerned with fund raising among Saigon-Cholon businessmen, purchasing supplies and materials in the city, and technical communication, including radio communication with Hanoi; and (6) a special section that devoted itself to military espionage for the zonal central committee. In addition to these six there existed some sort of a special liaison unit whose function is not clear, but it apparently dealt with clandestine liaison activities with individuals and groups in Saigon. Members of this group are believed to have negotiated the ransom of Japanese and other foreigners kidnaped by the NLF.

The committee's first task was to supervise the political struggle. This involved sending specific directives to the village liberation associations and the functional associations and groups. These were designed to keep them energetic, motivated, and moving in the correct direction. The bulk of the political struggle work involved agit-prop activities, and to this end the provincial central committee kept a steady flow of messages moving down to the agit-prop teams and cadres in the district and village committees. Its second major job was to administer the violence program, the armed struggle, and to make the decisions for assassinations and acts of sabotage and subversion as well as for military attacks by military and paramilitary units. Most of the technical military skills, for example, the demolition experts and the ordnance specialists, were found at the provincial level. Also found here were the individuals with special influence in ethnic and social groups and those with a high degree of dedication to the cause, who made up the special terror squads. The third area of primary concern to the provincial central committee was training and indoctrination work, part of the general administrative activity of the headquarters.[12]

Provincial leadership fell into certain patterns, admittedly amorphous. From NLF rosters captured by the ARVN in 1962 a limited-value study was made of the character of individual leaders. These rosters — crude affairs — listed basic information on the leadership in some 20 Mekong delta provinces and districts in the form of one- or two-word descriptions. A roster, for example, would list the provincial central committee chairman, vice-chairman, and secretary-general by name (or alias) and then note his social, ethnic, or class background. The study consisted chiefly of

[12] Provincial central committee headquarters organization charts captured by the ARVN indicated a wide diversity in actual organization structure, although after 1961 a pattern began to form: Charts dated later than 1961 contained a minimum of five identical sections. Under the provincial central committee and its secretariat were (1) an "action against the masses" (*dich van*) section, devoted to social movement organization and propaganda work; (2) a section dealing with agit-prop, cultural, and mass-media propaganda activities; (3) a section devoted to "action against the military," or the military proselyting section (*binh van*); (4) a section concerned with training and indoctrination of members from lower echelons; and (5) the Liberation Army provincial staff headquarters, which administered the violence program. Actual administration was vested in the secretariat, which consisted of a chief for organizational work, a chief for the violence, or armed struggle, program, a secretary charged with responsibility for the agit-prop, propaganda, and indoctrination work, and a secretary responsible for administration, including budget and fiscal matters. The secretariat therefore, under the supervision of the provincial central committee and its presidium, if a presidium existed, supervised or actually headed the five sections. It would appear that the provincial headquarters involved an elaborate hierarchic structure: a central committee, a presidium, a secretariat, and five section chiefs. Actually a few key individuals normally held down several posts simultaneously. The structure obviously was a copy of the national Central Committee and equally obviously was unnecessarily cumbersome. Why such a structure should be maintained, when in actual practice the same half-dozen persons performed all the work, was something of a mystery; it was suggested that the provincial liberation committee was a standby provisional provincial government.

translating and tabulating these data to provide something of a profile of the leadership. It showed as chairmen — 8 Marxists (defined here as cadres or officials of the Viet Minh organization; those so listed can be considered to be Communist or strongly pro-Communist), 5 Cao Dai, 5 intellectuals, and 2 notables (members of the traditional ruling group in the Vietnamese village, the Council of Notables); as vice-chairmen — 8 farmers, 4 Buddhist bonzes, 3 women, 2 teachers, and 1 each Marxist, Cao Dai, and businessman; as secretaries-general — 10 youths, 4 farmers, 3 workers, 2 Cao Dai, and 1 woman. These characterizations are not mutually exclusive; a central committee chairman, for example, could quite conceivably be a Cao Dai, a notable, an intellectual, and a Marxist; the criterion used by the roster makers apparently was what the individual was *primarily,* what his major image was to those who knew him. However, some inferences were possible. The chairman, where feasible, was drawn from the ranks of the Viet Minh and was either a Communist or a member of a non-Communist nationalist group so as to avail the NLF of his experience and background knowledge. It is surprising that this figure was not higher, for it indicated that 60 per cent of the leadership was not identified with the Viet Minh. The high percentage of Cao Dai is explained by the fact that the Cao Dai was the first major social group to begin actively opposing the Diem government as well as by the fact that most of the Cao Dai are found in the area covered by the study; there are few Cao Dai, for example, along the coastal plain or in Central Vietnam. Notables and intellectuals, which is to say teachers in most cases, are prestige or status positions within a Vietnamese village. Intellectuals were the second major group alienated by Diem. The vice-chairman was picked for the class or social group he represented, with farmers, Buddhists, and women comprising the largest categories. In terms of decision-making, the vice-chairman was probably less important than either the chairman or the secretary-general. The secretary-general was most apt to be a youth, but the next two categories, farmer and worker, would not have excluded the young man. The NLF placed heavy emphasis on youth, entrusting them with great responsibilities. In the secretary-general the NLF sought the eager, the zealous, the dedicated, the hard working, the young.

The same roster study tabulated the make-up of the provincial central committee general membership of approximately 150 persons. It showed that 32 per cent of the committee were identified with religious groups: Cao Dai, 13 per cent; Buddhists, 7 per cent; and Hoa Hao, Catholics, and Cambodian Buddhists, 4 per cent each. Young people formed the next largest bloc, with 12 per cent (youths, 7 per cent, and students, 5 per cent). Then came intellectuals with 11 per cent; women, 11 per cent; military, 7 per cent; farmers and Marxists each with 6 per cent; workers,

5 per cent; and "middle class," Democratic Party, Radical Socialist Party, notables, Chinese, refugees, and montagnards were represented by less than 3 per cent each. The obvious inference here was the effort to obtain a broad spectrum of representation. In an area almost totally rural, where proportionately the farmer would have been at the 90 per cent level, only 6 per cent of the committee membership was listed as rural.

The NLF made a great effort to portray itself as representing all the people of an area, offering them the right to participate in the governmental function. These themes — representation and participation — ran through all the output of the provincial central committees.

District Level

The last echelon to be formed, following creation of the command structure and the lower echelons (village and town level), the district committee appears to have been almost an afterthought. Some district committees acted as provincial committees, others simply as transmission belts from province to village, and still others as extensive village committees with a network of cells attached directly to them. The district level was created in mid-1962, almost a year after the installation of the provincial committee system. The over-all NLF organizational pattern was first to create the highest command structure, the national Central Committee, and at the same time form in "sympathetic areas" the more easily organized liberation associations and political groups; then to complete the command structure down to the provincial level; and finally to fill in the gap by establishing the district committees. In some areas, particularly the Massif Plain region, the district committee either was regarded as unnecessary and never created or had not been created by early 1964. *Quy chanh* from the Southern Central Vietnam Interzone maintained that no district committee existed in their area and that the village liberation committees reported directly to provincial headquarters. On the other hand, a strong district system existed in provinces along the Cambodian border (Tay Ninh, Kien Tuong, Kien Phong, An Giang, and Kien Giang); it was weakest in the coastal lowlands above Phan Thiet and nonexistent in the Western Highlands Interzone.

Two district organizational charts captured by the ARVN in 1963 indicate that the district committee structure was similar to that of the provincial committee.[13]

[13] Under the district liberation central committee and its secretariat were (1) a section for the organization building of functional liberation associations; (2) a section for liberation association operational activities, apparently composed of representatives of leaders of the actual village liberation associations; (3) an agit-prop and military proselyting section; (4) an administrative section concerned chiefly with financial and communication

In general the district concerned itself with three major functions: organization building, agit-prop work, and the violence program. However, it appeared that once the initial organization building was completed, with the agit-prop work directed by the interzone and the armed struggle directed by the provincial committee, the district would have little to do. Various Vietnamese suggested possible explanations for the continued existence of the district level: that it was a sort of headquarters, or even living quarters, for cadres working in the villages; that it was an *ad hoc* level established during the organization-building stage, later to be phased out; that it was the lowest level of the PRP, the Communist party in South Vietnam, and was therefore the operational level of the Party, with the district liberation association apparatus essentially a smokescreen behind which the PRP members could hide their activities.

The district committee profile, as indicated by a U.S. mission roster study, revealed the following: chairmen — Marxists, 67 per cent; farmers, 19 per cent; Buddhists and Cambodians, 5 per cent each; vice-chairmen — farmers, 17 per cent; Marxists, 14 per cent; women, 13 per cent; Cambodians, 12 per cent; businessmen, 12 per cent; intellectuals, 8 per cent; Buddhists, 7 per cent; and the rest divided fairly equally among Catholics, workers, and military, that is, deserters; secretaries-general — youths, 53 per cent; farmers, 28 per cent; Marxists, 11 per cent; and women, 8 per cent.

Village Level

Let us turn now to the village administrative liberation association. A GVN intelligence organization study of the NLF, dated 1962, quoted an NLF document describing the village committee's mission as

to conduct propaganda appeals and to stimulate the masses to denounce enemy schemes that seek to create enmity, and to develop the struggle against the enemy, to guide the masses in mobilization and motivation work, to take part in or lead the political struggle, military attacks, actions among the military, construction of combat hamlets, and in all ways protect the revolutionary potential. . . . Criteria for admission . . . should be based on the candidate's practical revolutionary achievements, his or her prestige among the people, the religious or political group he or she represents, . . . and the influence he or she has. . . . As to leadership it is advisable to allow members to select their own leaders . . . although key Party cadres should

---

matters; and (5) the violence, or armed struggle, section that controlled the local guerrilla units. One organizational chart showed the chain of command running from district to village but noted that at the moment no village committee existed; the implication was that the village association work in that district was being done by the district committee.

guide and obtain favorable representatives. . . . Avoid selection of young women who are simply popular . . . [and] avoid selecting former collaborators of the Diem government or members of the NRM.

To understand the NLF's work at the village level, let us consider the mythical village of Hoi Xa and its organizational structure. Hoi Xa, being a contested village in the struggle with the GVN, had a fairly well-developed NLF apparatus. To begin with, it had three functional liberation associations: the Hoi Xa Farmers' Liberation Association, the Hoi Xa Women's Liberation Association, and the Hoi Xa Youth Liberation Association. Virtually everyone in the village belonged to one of these three associations. Members were told that theirs was a democratic organization, each with its respective committees at the provincial, zonal, interzonal, and national levels, whose members were chosen by a congress of delegates elected by the villagers, even though no one in Hoi Xa had ever voted in such an election. To be sure, the district Farmers' Liberation Association held meetings from time to time to which the Hoi Xa Farmers' Liberation Association was invited to send a member. When the delegate returned from such a meeting he reported that it was devoted to criticism of the organization by its own members. The members of the three functional liberation associations met periodically to debate, and they elected their own officials from a previously prepared slate, but it seemed that most of the major decisions concerning the associations were made by the cadres, fellow villagers who did not engage in farming but worked full time at associational affairs.

Hoi Xa also had an all-village organization, the Hoi Xa National Liberation Front Association, which was composed of association representatives, including the three functional liberation associations, and members of local religious groups and political parties. Heading the organization was a central committee drawn from the ranks of the liberation association officers and appointed, the people were told, by the provincial central committee of the NLF. The central committee in the village will be elected, the people were told, "when conditions are proper."

The hierarchy of the NLF in the village was made up of three levels: the National Liberation Front village committee, the collection of functional liberation associations that actually were operational at the hamlet rather than the village level, and the individual liberation association cell. The structure varied greatly of course, depending on the security situation in the area. It must be assumed that the PRP committee within the village was an integral, although numerically small, part of the village committee.

The NLF village committee was headed by a chairman and vice-chairman, with representatives of the following:

village Farmers' Liberation Association

village Women's Liberation Association

village Youth Liberation Association

village troops' executive committee

other village liberation associations if they existed, such as workers' or students' associations

other political, ethnic, or religious organizations in the area that wanted to be part of the NLF, most commonly the Democratic Party, the Radical Socialist Party, Buddhist and Catholic groups, refugee groups, Cao Dai, and Cambodian minority organizations

the People's Revolutionary Party.

The specific tasks of the village committee, according to a document captured in 1963, were to implement the directives received from the provincial committee, develop and maintain highly motivated association groups, develop the political and military struggle, and provide money, men, and logistic support for higher echelons. Normally the village committee met at least every two weeks. It planned struggle movements, developed activities to keep villagers interested and active in the cause, and, where such activity was possible, it performed basic governmental duties such as collecting taxes, running schools, and redistributing land.

A word picture of NLF activity at the village level was obtained from a study of a number of ten-day reports sent by village committees to provincial committees, a number of which came into GVN hands. A typical report from either a village or district identified only by code (C–47), apparently in Binh Duong province north of Saigon, dated September 6, 1962, contained these entries:

During the ten-day period from August 25 to September 5, 1962 . . . motivation meetings were attended by a total of 1,719 persons. This included 850 persons at scattered propaganda sessions, five propaganda meetings attended by 585 persons, three armed propaganda sessions attended by 148 persons, and sixteen hamlet meetings attended by 136 persons. . . .

Master Sergeant Nghe from A/10 [code], a former Diem police officer, wanted to meet us. He asked for a reduction of rent. As a result his rent has been reduced from 1,200 liters to 400 liters of rice. He is now confident. . . .

At Phu Thanh Island at the end of August, 16 families had a struggle movement face to face with the district chief. They requested him to give permission for them to remain at their own homes until after harvest. As a result of this struggle movement the enemy gave in. . . .

At B/40 fifteen young men struggled against the corvée labor draft on the pretext that they needed to work the fields, and they were successful. . . .

We succeeded in achieving the desertion of two enemy soldiers. Soldiers Muc and Lao from Ben San Station stole away to their home village. They acted because of their relatives' attitudes toward the enemy scheme of demolishing houses, grouping people, and raping women. . . .

On the night of September 4 we planned a great unity movement to distribute leaflets and raise flags over the whole area and force the enemy to remain passive that night. However, the movement was not successful. Only Phuoc Long and Long Tan have submitted reports of success. At Phuoc Long, 515 leaflets were distributed, of which 275 were leaflets directed toward soldiers. . . . At Long Tan we attacked an enemy station. . . .

The functional liberation association was led by an executive committee consisting of a chairman, a vice-chairman, and a secretary, with membership divided among various hamlets of the village. Representatives of hamlet subsections sat on the executive committee. Since villages in Vietnam are often spread over a wide geographic area, the hamlet subsection became a sort of functional unit, the one with which the average association member had the most contact; the unit did not have any legal status within the NLF. At the hamlet level the association was usually represented by what was called a hamlet cadre committee, which in effect was also a subcommittee of the village committee. Often there would be only one hamlet subcommittee, representing the Farmers' Liberation Association, which would also be the arm of the village NLF central committee. At this point the functional and administrative liberation associations would merge.

Links with the provincial central committee included directives down and reports up, exchanges of messages, and periodic meetings.[14]

As in the imaginary village of Hoi Xa, the NLF maintained that the liberation association structure at the village level was democratic and involved free elections; typical of this assertion was a Radio Liberation broadcast of February 1, 1965:

Recently citizens in many villages in Tuy Hoa district, Phu Yen, eagerly went to the polls to elect liberation committees. During pre-election days all citizens held meetings to study the principles of balloting. They were elated to see democracy had been restored to them after years of perilous struggle. . . . On election day tens of thousands of NLFSV flags flew in the early morning sunshine. . . . Almost all voters went to the polls. . . . The people correctly selected those who deserved to be their representatives. . . .

[14] An NLF document captured in early 1963 illustrated the latter. It was addressed to one "Mr. Tam Lien, Liberation Front delegate" and stated:

The District Committee invites you to be present at the committee station on November 9, 1962 to prepare for the conference on November 10. In the past some persons were absent without adequate excuse. The committee hopes all those invited will be present at the designated time. Matters to be discussed will be (1) review of the activity status of the committee for the past three months, (2) review of two NLF Central Committee policies, independence and neutrality, and (3) assignment of new missions. . . . Note: You may come to the subordinate station of Mr. Ut at the barrier at My Loi-Thanh Hung. If traveling by the liaison path you may ask the way to My Loi and the barrier there; from this point onward, travel by sampan is most convenient.

Although listed only as an "NLF delegate," Tam Lien was probably a cadre.

How much democracy actually existed in the village liberation association was a question as difficult as it was important to answer. Apparently "democracy" varied from village to village. During Operation Sunrise, the start of the strategic-hamlet building program, villagers who had lived under a system of liberation associations revealed that they believed they had taken part in free elections; whether in actuality they had could not be determined. One NLF document advised cadres that it was wise to allow association members to select their own leaders but urged the cadres to attempt to "guide" the elections. An early document (circa 1961) specifically stated:

To ensure a large participation of the masses in the Front, the number of Party members in the Front committee must not exceed two fifths of the committeemen. The Party cell should lead the Front committee through Party fractions; that is to say, comrades who are members of the Front committee must undertake to educate the other committeemen so that the latter may understand their tasks, understand the purpose and utility of each operation, oppose those with bureaucratic attitudes and narrow interpretations that cause the organization to lose its initiative and its close identification with the masses.

In other cases directives from provincial headquarters on leadership at the village level outlined in imperious terms the requirements for the chairman of a village liberation committee:

. . . He must belong to the peasant class. . . . He must have a good political background. . . . He must have a good record in attacking the enemy in the three domains [i.e., the political effort or struggle against the masses, the military proselyting program or struggle against the military, and the armed struggle] and must have outstandingly fulfilled all his revolutionary assignments . . . , and he must have good and close relations with the villagers. . . .

These are not terms one would use if, as the bylaws stated, the election of the chairman was to be free and secret. In still other cases the village leadership was openly appointed by the provincial central committee; the cadres told the villagers that elections were not possible at the moment and quoted the clause in the village liberation association bylaws that read "When difficulties are encountered the central committee will be designated by the next higher level."

*   *   *   *   *

To summarize and rephrase the village organizational structure, in reverse order, in the interests of clarity:

1. The individual liberation association member was recruited into a particular functional association and was inducted into a three-man cell.

2. His cell was part of a hamlet subgrouping headed by a hamlet

cadre committee. The members of the cadre committee were members of the village functional liberation association, which was the lowest official level of the associational structure.

3. His particular functional liberation association at the village level joined other liberation associations to form the administrative National Liberation Front association in his village. This association "elected" a central committee, which guided the individual functional associations of the village, controlled the military activities in the area, and tied the village to the national structure through an upward chain of command.

4. The PRP overtly or covertly controlled the village central committee.

Cell Structure

Below the village and hamlet level came the lowest, most fundamental organizational unit, the liberation association cell, the same three-man cell structure that has served communism so well for the past fifty years. Referred to in various terms — the three-member cell (*to ba nguoi*), the glue-welded cell (*to keo son*), or the three-participant cell (*to tam gia*) — the unit was presented in terms of almost mystical unity: It "applies the principle of shared responsibility in fighting and performing all tasks." A Radio Liberation broadcast on March 9, 1965 declared that cell members must

build their cell into a three-member collective, glue-welded on the basis of comradeship and mutual life and assistance, stemming from a thorough revolutionary spirit, a noble class spirit, and good revolutionary virtues. To this end each cell member must tell his colleagues facts about his private life. . . . They must consider their [cell] as their home and their [cell members] as brothers. . . .

In those villages where the association was covert the cell was an all-important unit; when a village became more "secure" and the association regularized, the cell was maintained as a self-disciplinary device and a standby unit in the event that the association again was forced underground.

The cell in action was pictured in cadre notes taken at a Youth Liberation Association indoctrination session in typical Communist indoctrination style, the catechism technique of question and answer:

What is the mission of Cell M?

Cell M is the basic organization [of the village Youth Liberation Association] in the actual daily struggle in the hamlet. It works closely with all youth directly and leads youth in the daily struggle. It carries out faithfully the directives of the [village] committee. It reports on the enemy's situation and on the attitude of the hamlet youth regarding their feelings, desires, and hopes for life. It teaches revolutionary policy, the main ideas and purpose of the youth organization to all, . . . directs the struggle program among youth against the enemy, and constitutes the essential core in the movement of union and mutual assistance in the hamlets. . . . It carries out the programs and resolutions passed by the Youth Liberation Association and other youth organizations. . . .

What are the activities of Cell M?

To supervise the study work and the thinking and the spiritual life of the members. . . . To check our determination, to check on the cell spirit of unity and thus help each other. . . . Study directives, resolutions, policy statements, and the news. . . . To indulge in criticism and self-criticism. . . . To evaluate the attitude of youth toward the enemy and the schemes of the enemy toward youth. . . .

How does Cell M plan its activities?

Plans are based on the monthly directive of the [village] executive committee and on the actual situation in the hamlet. The cell plan is based on three factors: political duties, military propaganda [proselyting program], and security. On the basis of discussion, plans are made and then there is a discussion of ways of carrying out the plans and distributing the work. The cell leader then reports his action plan orally to the [association] headquarters that is in charge of the cell, . . . for approval of the headquarters is necessary in the interests of unity.

What is the mission of the headquarters cell control section?

The headquarters control section is a number of cell leaders who have been elected to inspect and supervise the various cells to ensure that they are executing headquarters directives properly and to report to headquarters the situation in each cell. The controller does not take initiative in a situation but reports the matter to the [village] executive committee.

The Cadre

A phenomenon of the Communist world, the cadre acted as combination priest, policeman, and editorial writer. He led the people in the struggle movement. He translated village committee plans and village management section (*can su vien*) programs into reality. He worked harder than anyone else, made fewer mistakes, served as the model of behavior and dedication. In general he was a native of the village, worked full time either for an administrative or functional liberation association (or in the Party itself), and was supported by the villagers and NLF or Party funds. The burden of the Revolution rested heavily on the cadre's shoulders. The scope of this burden is indicated in a series of notes outlining the subject matter considered at a five-day district cadre meeting. Among the assignments handed cadres at the meeting:

Consolidate the intelligence network, improve the logistic supply system, consolidate the communication network, and report improvements. . . . Provide greater leadership for the guerrillas in the armed struggle and specifically train them in combating airborne helicopter tactics. . . . Work with youth groups to encourage young people to join the guerrilla units. . . . Instigate greater sabotage efforts by members of the liberation associations, ensure better care for the wounded and proper burial for the dead, ensure that all persons know of the Front's policies toward captured soldiers or those who have surrendered, ensure that units do not use war booty for their own purposes, encourage Party members to study policy directives more carefully, hold meetings to discuss shortcomings and errors of members of the struggle movement or guerrilla units. . . . Improve Party relations with the Front organizations. . . . Motivate the peasants and solve all their personal problems. . . . Stimulate young people by using ideological arguments. . . . Encourage young men to increase agricultural production. . . . Work to win the support of ethnic Cambodians and combat the Khmer Serai. . . . Gain the support of religious groups, especially the Cao Dai in Tay Ninh. . . . Step up the *binh van* movement. . . . Start new indoctrination sessions for Party members. . . . Reconstruct the countryside, build up society, and win the support of the masses. . . .

On the cadre's shoulders fell the blame for all failure and error. NLF documents were filled with complaints about poor cadres. Typical was a handbook on cadre behavior captured in Kien Hoa province in September 1963. It asserted:

At the present time our cadres lack leadership capacity, and their contribution is poor from both a quantity and a quality standpoint. . . . All existing cadres lack capacity. They have the wrong ideology and the wrong concepts about lines of action and policies. They cannot work out programs or plan organizational activity. Some cadres, including members of the management section, are illiterate. This handicaps them in their political studies as well as in their daily activities. . . .

13

Violence

Introduction

The NLF until mid-1963 regarded the armed struggle as secondary to the political struggle and considered the primary duty of the military elements to be to support the struggle movement. This primacy of non-military activities, even within the military establishment, was clearly spelled out in an NLF indoctrination booklet dealing with the organization of of the Liberation armed forces. It declared that three organizational principles must be followed:

1. Organization must conform to political lines. . . .
2. The liberation army is a fighting army and therefore must be highly centralized, with inferiors obeying superiors. . . . There must be discipline. . . .
3. The army political tasks are fundamental: There must be unity between cadres and men, between army and people. . . .

It is of prime importance that these three principles be fully understood. They ensure that military action is subordinated to political action, that the army is united, and that the people are closely united with the army. They win over the members of the enemy, subvert enemy morale and organization, and ultimately completely annihilate enemy resistance.[1]

[1] A 64-page booklet entitled *The Glorious Experiences of the Liberation Army*, captured in An Giang province in May 1963.

The military as pictured in various NLF documents stands in sharp contrast to Western military establishments; not only the role but also the very nature of the military arm was regarded as unique by the NLF. For example, the indoctrination booklet just quoted described what might be called the myth of creation of the NLF army:

The people themselves had a hand in the birth of the SVN Liberation Army. The South Vietnam people were deeply resentful of the U.S.-Diem fascist regime. This resentment caused them to stage armed uprisings to crush the oppressive military might and liberate themselves and exterminate the U.S.-Diem regime. Hence the Liberation Army stems from the people and fights for the people. . . . The South Vietnam Liberation Army is a heroic armed force of the Vietnamese working people. The people have made many sacrifices and have fought gallantly in order to build up the present Liberation Army. The people themselves have killed enemy troops and seized their weapons in order to build up its strength. The people have fed and protected the army. The people have committed themselves to getting youngsters to enlist in the revolutionary forces. The Party organized the present Liberation Army, led it, trained and built up its human factors. The Party guided the Liberation Army in successive stages, in methods of work, fighting, and organization, all of which are bound to ensure success. The Party indoctrinated and trained the Liberation Army unceasingly and raised its present high level of political awareness. . . . It has stressed the five important factors of development, which are the rural population, fighting spirit, equipment and matériel conditions, quantity and quality of manpower, and cadres. . . .

The role of the Liberation Army was also considered subservient to the NLF in military-civilian terms. The entire army was directly bound up with the rest of the organization from the NLF national Central Committee to the village committee. Liberation Army representatives sat at all committee levels as an integral part of the organization. There was no such thing as NLF army autonomy; the military arm was totally integrated with the over-all operation. In addition, within the military apparatus the political officer, or political commissar, served as a further mechanism of Communist control over the officer corps.

Structure of the Armed Forces

The actual structure of the National Liberation Front army can perhaps best be made clear if it is approached from a functional standpoint. The over-all military structure in South Vietnam was the Liberation Army (*Quan Doi Giai Phong*), which in turn comprised one half of the total Communist armed force in all of Vietnam, the other half being the Defense of the Homeland Army, or People's Army (*Quan Doi Nhan Dan*), that is, the DRV army in North Vietnam, PAVN. Indoctrination work by the NLF stressed the difference between the Liberation Army and the People's Army:

In the North there is a regular and modern army. It is a matter of the difference in the stage of the Revolution. The liberation has come to the North while it is still going on in the South. The main duty of the People's Army in the North is to defend the territory of the North, the safe base. The main duty of the Liberation Army in the South is the liberation of the South.

From a functional standpoint the Liberation Army was clearly divided into (1) the paramilitary elements (*thanh phan ban quan su*), which were generally local, civilian, part time, and static and defensive, and usually not highly indoctrinated; and (2) the so-called full military, or Main Force, elements (*thanh phan quan su*), which were "military," full time, better trained, and more thoroughly indoctrinated.

Paramilitary Elements

The correct NLF nomenclature for the paramilitary force, considered collectively, was Popular Army (*Dan Quan*, literally, civilian troops), but because the paramilitary units engaged almost exclusively in guerrilla warfare, the term guerrilla (*du kich*)[2] was appended to the term, making it Guerrilla Popular Army (*Dan Quan Du Kich*).

The Guerrilla Popular Army unit was found at the hamlet level as a cell or half squad, or infrequently as a squad (that is, 3, 6, 12 men), and at the village level as a platoon of three or four squads (36 or 48 men). Here was the part-time guerrilla, the type the world knew best, who would peacefully plow his field by day and dynamite bridges by night. The rural Vietnamese regarded the *du kich* as local and civilian, not as outsider or soldier — both important distinctions in Vietnam. This guerrilla received little training, perhaps no more than a few lectures in the jungles outside his home village that were more indoctrination than basic military training. His weapons were primitive, often not even firearms but machete, spear, or bamboo spike. Indoctrination courses attempted to convince him that a spirit of revolution was vastly more important than a good weapon.

Members of the Guerrilla Popular Army were of two functional types: the village guerrilla (*du kich xa*) and the combat guerrilla (*du kich chien dau*). By mid-1965 they numbered around 85,000. The village guerrilla, the lowest man on the totem pole, was frequently an older Vietnamese; he was not militarily trained, he was poorly armed, and generally he was assigned to static defense of the village. His presence

---

[2] *Du kich* literally means strike and run; it is applied both to the individual guerrilla and to guerrilla tactics.

in the village was of more psychological than military value to the NLF. A band of village guerrillas served to put the village on the side of the NLF, but it was not expected to stand and fight if the ARVN conducted a military sweep through the village. This is not to imply that the village guerrilla was ineffectual or unimportant; quite the contrary, the fact that he was organized into a unit that had opted to fight for the NLF was of great political importance.

The combat guerrilla was less static and more likely to be used in combat missions away from his home village. Generally he was younger and better trained; his most frequent assignment was to aid the mobile column or other full military element on operations, usually as a bearer or runner or on propaganda and psychological warfare missions. A common institution in Vietnam was "the shouter," a combat guerrilla assignment. Prior to an attack on an ARVN outpost or a hostile village the NLF military commander would assemble a number of combat guerrillas who, on signal, would shout and beat sticks on trees in what was known as the "shout in unison" tactic, which was designed to convince the defenders inside the post or village that they faced a horde of attackers.[3]

The paramilitary units also served as a manpower pool from which the more talented could be drawn for assignment to the full military. Members of the Guerrilla Popular Army were described in a Main Force indoctrination booklet as

young people with revolutionary spirit, with some fighting experience. They are responsible for keeping close contact with the enemy, at all times surrounding enemy forts and barracks, disrupting enemy communication and transportation, serving with and improving the self-defense groups. When enemy forces conduct raids they shall stick to them and harass them, protecting the security of the villagers and identifying the enemy units that enter their village. At the same time members of the guerrilla force will perform armed propaganda, liquidate tyrants in their area, and subvert in all ways the enemy's hold on the people.

The basic unit of both the village guerrilla and the combat guerrilla force was the three-man cell. In GVN-controlled areas, where of course it was covert, it was known as the secret guerrilla cell (or unit—*du kich bi mat*). In addition to the secret guerrilla cell, there was a second type of cell that went by the bland name of special activity cell (*tieu to dac cong*); it was by far the most dangerous element in the entire paramilitary structure. Highly motivated, willing to take great risks, operating

---

[3] This tactic often resulted in a frantic radio message from the unit under attack to its higher headquarters to the effect that the attacking force was at least a battalion when in fact it might be only a dozen armed men; this in turn led to inflated internal reports and later to exaggerated newspaper stories misrepresenting the size of the NLF army attacks as well as its general military capability.

in territory they knew intimately, members of the special activity cell would strike anywhere at any time. From the roster of these cells were drawn the assassination teams, the volunteer grenade hurlers, the death or suicide squads. Most of the spectacular acts of sabotage, assassinations of province chiefs, or daring military escapades were the work of a special activity cell, sometimes working with demolition experts or other military specialists supplied by the provincial-level central committee.

The paramilitary units were also found in the so-called liberated area, but their role is not known. A brief NLF memorandum dated late in 1964 listed four types of paramilitary units in the liberated area: self-defense men (*tu ve*), self-defense combat men (*tu ve chien dau*), secret self-defense men (*tu ve bi mat*), and the people's self-defense men (*tu ve nhan dan*). Neither the nature of their activities nor how one type differed from another was ever indicated.

Full Military Elements

The term "full military" is likely to mislead, for the NLF was not an ordinary army using orthodox military tactics. The full military, or Main Force, continued to rely on guerrilla tactics; its elements were self-contained and not part of some broader military establishment; members thought like guerrillas, not like regular soldiers; the full military soldier was not in uniform; often his unit broke up between operations, and he lived with his family. Beyond these, differences between the NLF army and orthodox armies were in terms of infrastructure and logistics. The army of any modern nation is tightly hierarchic, running from the squad (or individual soldier) to the high command (or commander-in-chief) and tied together by a network of nonorganic support services: communication, transportation, supply; vertical services such as ordnance, medical, quartermaster; and horizontal services such as artillery, armor, and engineers. The guerrilla unit, on the other hand, was conceived as a self-contained element. If a guerrilla unit leader needed ammunition, he did not requisition it; he planned an attack on an enemy supply base. If the unit was attacked, there was no radioing for air strikes or artillery support; the unit got out as best it could. The resulting sense of isolation was what distinguished the mentality of a guerrilla from that of a regular soldier; the psychology of the two was profoundly different. For the guerrilla there was no home front; the enemy, more numerous and powerful than he, was everywhere. The sense of being a hunted animal was never far below his level of consciousness.

Just as the paramilitary element of the NLF army was of two types, so the full military element was composed of two basic entities: the

Regionals or Territorials (*Bo Doi Dia Phuong*), and the Main Force (*Quan Doi Chu Luc*), usually referred to as "hard hats" because of the distinguishing metal or fiberboard helmets, resembling American World War I helmets, that they and their predecessors, the Viet Minh, wore.[4]

Originally the Regionals were organized as armed propaganda teams with the task of propagandizing, using weapons only for defense and perhaps to hold an audience. Later they came to be known simply as "companies" (*dai doi*), serving at the district level and usually consisting of three or four platoons, and then "independent companies" (*dai doi doc lap*) to distinguish them from the company that was part of the Main Force battalion. The chief distinguishing characteristic of the independent company was that it took orders from the district or sometimes provincial central committee.[5] The independent company was described in an NLF army indoctrination booklet as

set up by the district committees, which provide them with their leadership, aided by cadres and guerrillas [that is, Guerrilla Popular Army] with good character and combat records. Their actions vary with geographic conditions and the enemy situation. They collect into units or disperse according to circumstances. They penetrate routinely into neighboring enemy territory. They stage armed propaganda meetings. They destroy strategic hamlets, kill tyrants who oppress the population. . . . The Regionals must have more political and class awareness than the [Popular Army] guerrilla. . . .

The independent company should be distinguished from the companies that made up the Main Force battalion. There were two types of full military companies: those that were autonomous and operated with instructions from the district level, and the companies that were part of a battalion of the Main Force whose orders came from battalion headquarters, which in turn got its orders from the provincial central committee.

The Main Force consisted of two types of battalions: the independent battalion (*tieu doan co dong*) and the concentrated battalion (*tieu doan tap trung*).[6] The Main Force battalions were either part of a structure of regiments (*trung doan*) or entities that would make up regiments to

---

[4] Categories of the NLF army are further obfuscated by the fact that the NLF, while considering its military forces to be of two basic types, in its public statements for propaganda purposes always addressed itself to three types, that is, "members of our Guerrilla Popular Army, our Regional Troops, and our Main Forces."

[5] The parallel structure of the NLF army and the NLF (and PRP) Central Committee was platoon and village committee; company and district unit; battalion and provincial committee; and regiment and interzone committee. However, as part of its effort to maintain "civilian" control, the political commissar of each military unit held the rank of the chairman of the political unit one step higher, so theoretically at least he outranked the military commander.

[6] In U.S. military parlance, the mobile battalion, sometimes known as the reinforced guerrilla band.

be created in the future. After 1965, when the entire nature of the struggle in Vietnam had changed, multibattalion or what could be called regimental operations were not uncommon.

The Main Force was described in the Main Force indoctrination booklet mentioned earlier as being

formed of young men with combat experience in the Guerrilla Popular Army or Territorial forces who have been indoctrinated in ideas of the Revolution and class struggle, in organizational methods, and in combat techniques; who understand the problems of coordination; who have high leadership skills on the battlefield; and who have high fighting efficiency; most of all, of those who are able to increase the political struggle movement.

Military activity, even guerrilla military activity, formed a relatively small percentage of the day-to-day work of the members of the NLF army, either of the paramilitary or of the Main Force units. Vietnamese officials estimated that a Main Force unit in the 1962–1963 period spent an average of one day a month on military missions. Much of the rest of the time was devoted to training and indoctrination work, agit-prop and other propaganda activities among the general population, or in what was called economic production — mainly the production of food. Most units had a dual responsibility for military action and food production, although certain units were excluded from the production work (*thoat ly,* literally, to be cut off, having no ties with). To be *thoat ly* was to be elite. The Main Force for the most part was *thoat ly,* although some members ostentatiously made a point of working in the fields at harvest time[7] in keeping with the Liberation Army motto, which was "We support ourselves" (*tu luc canh sinh,* or, literally, to increase the provision for one's livelihood by one's own strength). The guerrilla-unit spirit dictated self-support; if possible the unit depended on no outside help, and it paid its own way when necessary to purchase food or supplies. This too was a heritage from the Viet Minh. Defectors reported that their officers, in chastising them for wanting to depend on outside supplies, would quote General Vo Nguyen Giap's lectures to Viet Minh officers who waited for supplies from Communist China before planning an offensive.

The ARVN reported in early 1965 that the NLF army consisted of some 47 battalions, which it said were organized on paper into five regiments. The battalion was planned for 500 men but most had fewer, some as few as 250 men; the NLF Main Force company averaged about 85 men. There were an estimated 94 such companies as part of the 47 battalions. Of the total Main Force units in South Vietnam, approxi-

---

[7] An area that was *thoat ly* was considered by ARVN troops to be highly dangerous since it meant that the enemy guerrillas were not tied down during part of the year by farming work and were free to conduct operations.

mately one third was in the ARVN's First and Second Corps areas and two thirds in the Third and Fourth Corps areas.[8]

A characteristic of a guerrilla war is that the government side never knows how many of the enemy it faces — every cyclo driver, every Vietnamese who passes in the street could be a guerrilla — but by early 1965 at least 55,000 and perhaps as many as 80,000 "hard hats" were fighting in South Vietnam. Some of them had been fighting for more than a decade and were perhaps the toughest, most experienced guerrilla fighters to be found anywhere on earth. Standing behind them were fourteen infantry divisions of the Defense of the Homeland Army, the Red Army of North Vietnam.

In the 1960–1961 period, great emphasis was placed at indoctrination sessions on the need for individual initiative by Liberation Army soldiers. A legendary figure of the Scarlet Pimpernel type, the ideal hero of the people's guerrilla war, was one "Ba Bua," whose story was told in clandestine newspaper accounts of mid-1963 but apparently dating a year or so earlier.

"Ba Bua" is an ordinary young peasant. When a very young man he went with his father into the swamps of Camau to burn mangrove wood and make charcoal. There they were waylaid by bandits. He put up a valiant fight but received three slashes from the robber's ax. Since then he has been known by the nickname "Ba Bua," or "three ax slashes."

He had just been married and was living peacefully in a small house in Cai Cam hamlet when the enemy's troops launched a surprise mopping-up operation and captured Ba Bua's bride, who resisted with all her strength. Infuriated, the troops stripped her, tied her up, and took her back to their post, then raped her and took out her liver and ate, yes, ate it.

Upon hearing this Ba Bua almost went mad and could not sleep or eat for a week. . . . Then he joined a guerrilla band.

Ba Bua carefully learned the use of guns. . . . Then, one night, he and two others were called in and assigned the task of making a raid on a nearby enemy post. The enemy position was a stronghold surrounded by sharp stake fences and barbed wire. . . . There were spiked fields and deep moats bristling with sharp stakes. A single road led into the post, which swarmed with guards who always shut the gate at night.

One afternoon Ba Bua took a bath, dressed well, and entered the post before the enemy troops returned from a raid. He met the two others and they went to a café. He stopped in front and called "Mr. Kinh, please." Kinh was the notorious commander of a military unit in the post. Kinh came out of the café, a pistol strapped to his side. Ba Bua opened fire with his pistol and wounded Kinh in the arm. . . . Kinh ran back into the café and out the back door. . . . Ba Bua, hot on his heels, shot him again, . . . then took his pistol and got away. . . . The guns of the post quickly opened fire, but by this time Ba Bua was back in camp, where the commander smiled and hugged him, and both men could hardly keep back

[8] The ARVN divided South Vietnam first into three and later into four military corps areas, numbering from north to south.

their tears. . . . The news that Ba Bua had entered an enemy post and shot the commander thrilled the people of the entire region. . . .

Slowly, almost imperceptibly, the emphasis shifted from the heroic individual to the military team. Mass-media accounts of exemplary individual behavior were replaced by examples of unit dauntlessness. By late 1964 the Liberation Army rather than the heroic individual was making the most lasting contribution to the cause and in fact was the element on which victory depended. Said a late 1964 NFL clandestine newspaper editorial:

> We will be victorious because the Liberation Army troops — the beloved sons of the Fatherland, the working-class peasantry — have shown themselves extremely valiant in struggling against the aggressive, exploitative enemy because they have managed to endure thousands of shortages and difficulties and to struggle against egoistic, negative, and individualistic thoughts, and because they serve the people wholeheartedly and make sacrifices for the benefit of the Fatherland. . . . The longer we fight the stronger we become, the stronger we become the more victories we win. . . .

Collectively or individually, however, a premium was still placed on human superiority, on the man over the machine. Camp indoctrination lessons, *quy chanh* reported, always included Ho Chi Minh's observation, "During the Resistance we did not lose one tank or one plane." The scorn of the leadership for what it regarded as the GVN's masses of mindless conscripts was underscored in a July 1964 *Hoc Tap* article:

> What a rapid and marvelous change. Less than three years ago one side had 20,000 men and the other side 200,000. After a brief period of fighting the 20,000 figure has become 200,000, and the 200,000-figure side has been feverishly strengthening and supplementing its force in order to increase it to 600,000 men. . . . The above estimates made by the enemy itself can never represent a correct evaluation of our people's force. As for us, we do not make a comparison in such a manner. . . . Even the 10,000-man revolutionary force was invincible. . . . Politics, morale, and organization are the important factors in the strength of a revolutionary army. . . .

Categories of Violence

The acts of violence by the armed forces of the NLF consisted of five basic categories: military or paramilitary assaults, that is, the usual "guerrilla war," conducted either offensively against defended hamlets or U.S. military installations or defensively in the field against GVN military operations, chiefly the sweep or what the NLF called the "mopping-up" operation, a term widely used in the Viet Minh war; the ambush, so common and distinct an action in Vietnam as to be called *sui generis,* directed at military units or civilian officials traveling along roads or through canals; systematic harassing of villagers to coerce or intimidate but normally without taking life; sabotage and subversion; and acts directed against specific individuals such as kidnapings, assassinations, and executions.

Military and Paramilitary Assaults

The pattern of the assaults on the ARVN followed the Maoist dictum: "When the enemy advances, withdraw; when he defends, harass; when he is tired, attack; when he withdraws, pursue." Precision, speed, and, above all, deception characterized the NLF army attack. Targets were chosen at least in part for their psychological significance with respect to either ARVN soldiers or the villagers themselves. A typical incident personally investigated by the author took place on February 2, 1961 in Phuoc Trach village, Go Dau Ha district, Tay Ninh province. Guerrillas, numbering about a dozen, entered the village at dawn and killed at least three defenders, their target being the village's Cao Dai temple, where they found the object of their assault, 17-year-old lay priest Phan Van Ngoc, who had gained a reputation for his militant hostility in the pulpit to the NLF, charging that it was basically antireligious. He was stabbed to death and the guerrillas withdrew.

Such assaults intimidated not only the survivors in the village but others throughout the region. From time to time, rather than simply hit and run, guerrilla units would seize and hold a village or military installation for an entire day, usually on some politically important anniversary date. This happened from the earliest days: A provincial capital, An Loc (the capital of Binh Long province), was seized and held for a full 24 hours in mid-1960.

The basic purpose of violence in the village was the coercion of the general population. After an area-wide series of terroristic acts in Quang Nam province in October 1962, the following message began appearing on the walls of buildings and on trees surrounding the villages:

> To protect the life and property of the people, to assure order and security in the villages, the Quang Nam provincial Liberation Army issues the following order: (1) Don't obey severe U.S.-Diem orders such as shipping rice to the cities. . . . Don't fly the enemy flag. . . . (2) Remain where you are and continue to work. . . . If you want to leave the area, first get our permission. . . . (3) It is the duty of all to support the Revolution. . . . If you obey our orders you will be forgiven by the people and the Liberation Army. . . . If you work for the enemy you will be punished according to the law. . . .

The implication of this, and the fact of it, was that if a villager behaved himself and obeyed orders he had no reason to fear the guerrillas.

Even the military assaults on ARVN posts did not generally employ mass killing for its own sake, except for the highly motivated elite units such as the rangers and paratroopers, against whom the NLF was ruthless. Each soldier killed by the NLF created a pool of resentment among his comrades, family, and friends, and the NLF sought not to make this pool any wider or deeper than necessary. Early attacks primarily sought to capture weapons and supplies or to disrupt antiguerrilla operations. Later they concentrated on lowering soldier morale. But in almost all cases the military actions of the armed struggle movement pursued psychological rather than direct military objectives.

The NLF insisted in the early days — and later attempted to maintain the fiction — that there was no distinction between the Liberation Army soldier and the civilian in terms of military activities. An agit-prop cadre handbook, for example, declared that

> the war of liberation is fought by the people themselves, the entire people, who are the driving force. . . . The guerrillas, youth, the majority of the people including women and children and oldsters . . . are fighting the enemy. Not only the peasants in the rural areas but the workers and laborers in the city along with the intellectuals, students, and businessmen have gone to fight the enemy. . . . All these people form a revolutionary war by means of a worker-peasant-guerrilla alliance, a united people, attacking the enemy in all fields and surrounding it from all directions.

The Second Armed Forces and Guerrilla Forces Conference, held, Radio Liberation said, "somewhere in the liberated area" in June 1964, was attended by representative elements of the armed struggle, members of the NLF army, Regionals or Territorials, and the guerrilla bands as well as

> many South Vietnamese women [who] are very active and determined in their mission to destroy strategic hamlets and counter mopping-up operations and who have succeeded in killing a great number of aggressors and in protecting their native hamlets. . . . Children too [were present], for . . . they also make the nation's heroic traditions more brilliant. . . . In the defense of one combat hamlet, a children's unit killed 29 of the enemy. . . . Many children work closely with their fathers and brothers in annihilating the enemy, seizing enemy weapons, and assisting our troops intelligently and bravely. . . . The masses have found ways and means to kill the enemy. The display [at the conference] of locally made weapons revealed a great quantity of equipment that, although rudimentary, is skillfully made and easily used. Many rifles are so well made that it is hard to believe that they were produced by the blacksmith shops in villages and hamlets.

Although maintaining the fiction that all the people could and did engage equally in armed combat, the NLF leaders were of course obliged to develop technical military skill, competent leadership, discipline, and spirit within the Liberation Army ranks, as are the builders of any army.

They needed, and they sought to develop, a fully professional military force.

Most of the officers came from the ranks of the Viet Minh and, later, as battlefield actions began to cut these down, from North Vietnam. Most of the rank and file came from the more remote villages of South Vietnam — and they were almost always recruited young. The vast majority of the rank and file in the Liberation Army or in the NLF's special terror units were in their twenties. The reason is that the young were inclined toward greater idealism, more willing to take risks, physically more capable of the tasks assigned, less prone to question orders, and less likely to be or become double agents. The optimum age appeared to be around 18; some of the city sabotage, such as grenade throwing, was done by boys of 12 or 13; seldom were captured terrorists past the age of 25. NLF recruitment appeals were addressed to youth, and among the young the NLF attempted to portray the struggle essentially as that of the young.

A Radio Liberation broadcast in October 1964 expressed the image the NLF sought to create:

> In strategic hamlet C [code name] a 14-year-old lad was tending buffaloes when he saw a Liberation unit engaged in military operations. So thrilled was he that he asked other buffalo boys to take over his job, and he went to join the unit. . . . A large number of youths in various villages, refusing to listen to the advice of their families, have joined the Liberation Army. . . . Hundreds of girls have volunteered to take up rifles to kill the enemy. . . . Many villages have formed female guerrilla units.

The Ambush

The primary tool of any guerrilla (and a basic counterguerrilla tactic), the ambush,[9] as employed by the NLF army sought to inflict casualties on ARVN troops; restrict troop and vehicle movements, particularly at night, guerrilla war being largely a night affair; reduce the flow of military supplies; create a general condition of tension and a sense of insecurity in the minds of individual soldiers; demonstrate the isolation of the ARVN from the people, contrasting the fast-moving convoy (on a straight road it is most difficult to ambush a vehicle traveling sixty miles an hour) with the slow-moving farmers working in their fields; and in general lower the morale and efficiency of the military.

The ambush is an excellent psychological device. An attack on a village or outpost frequently was launched to decoy the relieving column, the primary objective. Such ambushes were carefully organized and re-

---

[9] For an excellent treatment of the ambush as employed in South Vietnam, see Malcolm W. Browne, *The New Face of War* (New York: Bobbs-Merrill, 1965), Chapter 6, "Ambush."

hearsed, often for weeks, in some remote jungle area. In addition to the deliberate ambush that struck at a particular target, such as the weekly shipment of medical supplies or a touring province chief, the NLF army also employed the random ambush, thrown across a major highway or canal before dawn and netting whatever happened to come along. An ambush force generally consisted of three parts: the actual ambush party, usually divided into two parts, one pinning down the ambushee and the second advancing for hand-to-hand engagement; a counterreinforcement unit that ambushed any relieving party that might be summoned by radio; and a screening force that covered the retreat of the first two ambushing the pursuit party.

A classic example of a politically motivated ambush came on March 22, 1961, when a truck carrying twenty girls, members of the Republican Youth Corps, was ambushed on the Saigon–Vung Tau road. The girls were returning to their home villages from a Trung Sisters Day celebration in Saigon, organized by the much disliked Madame Ngo Dinh Nhu. The ambush party opened fire on the girls, who were traveling unarmed in an unescorted truck, and killed nine. A Civil Guard post three miles away, hearing the gunfire, dispatched a squad to investigate. It was ambushed just before reaching the truck; then a large Civil Guard unit was dispatched, and the guerrillas fled, in apparent disorder, across open rice fields and into a mangrove swamp, pursued by the Civil Guard unit that had no sooner entered the swamp than it was ambushed. In all, six Civil Guardsmen and nine girls were killed. By this ambush action the guerrillas succeeded in inflicting losses on a military unit, presumably lowering the morale of its members and perhaps causing them in the future to be timid or overly cautious, demonstrated its prowess to villagers in the area, and cast a pall of gloom over the memory of the Saigon celebration.

Harassing of Villages

The most common form of village or small military post harassment was small-arms sniper-type fire. It seldom received much attention in the press or elsewhere because of its apparent inconsequential results. Strategic hamlets served as primary targets. Periodically during the night and day, guerrillas would approach a village and fire half a dozen random rifle shots into the village. This alerted the defenders, who could not be sure whether a full-scale attack was under way; word would be radioed to the nearby military headquarters, whose commander would be obliged to decide whether the action was harassing fire or an attack — and if an attack whether an ambush was its real purpose or whether the attack was actually a feint designed to draw the military unit away from the scene of an actual attack elsewhere. Any guess he made was apt to be the wrong one. The correct military decision usually was for the moment to do nothing and await developments; this caused the villagers to doubt that the unit would aid the village if it actually was attacked. The harassing fire would continue sporadically for weeks, generally accompanied by nocturnal megaphone taunts, threats, and appeals. Sometimes, after a few weeks of softening up, a full-scale attack would be launched. Harassing fire was cheap, costing only a few dozen bullets, and could be handled easily by even inexperienced guerrillas. It created a great sense of anxiety within the village, keeping villagers awake at night, impairing their farming and normal daytime activities. And it built up the guerrillas' confidence. (Armed propaganda team visits, another form of harassment, were described in Chapter 7.)

Sabotage and Subversion

Psychological objectives also dominated the various sabotage efforts. Guerrillas were under strict orders not to sabotage or interfere with permanent fixed economic installations. The huge Da Nhim Dam in the hills behind Dalat, for example, was built during this period by Japanese engineers as part of the payment of Japan's war reparations to Vietnam; at any stage of construction this hydroelectric project could have been destroyed, but, as one *quy chanh* expressed it, "we were told that it would someday be ours, so why destroy it?" Road and bridge sabotage was common as was destruction of telephone and telegraph communication equipment. Railroad trains were frequently dynamited to destroy the military cargo they carried, but also to put economic pressure on the GVN. Travelers boarding a train in Saigon or Hué often found, stuck between the boards of the seat, a leaflet that read:

The U.S.-Diemists use the trains for military purposes. . . . Compatriots are advised not to travel by train. If they are obliged to travel by train they must absolutely refrain from traveling on trains that carry weapons, military equipment, or soldiers and must resolutely protest against allowing army men to mingle with passengers. . . .

In the cities there seemed to be no end to the ingenuity employed in terroristic sabotage. The grenade was the most common instrument, often rolled into a café by a young boy who pedaled away rapidly on a bicycle. Sometimes the bicycle itself was the instrument of death, its hollow tubular frame packed with plastic explosive and the timing device located under the saddle. Terrorists would ride the bicycle into the area, lean it up against the building to be destroyed, set the fuse, and walk off.[10] Grenades lobbed into vehicles stopped for traffic lights; poison injected into bottles of wine with hypodermic needles; doors, drawers, or automobile motor engines booby-trapped — all formed part of the subversion effort. Often simply the threat of violence achieved subversion. In November 1964 a young Vietnamese girl typist in a U.S. aid program contractor's office in Saigon was caught with program plans in her purse. She told security officials that a man came to her apartment and told her that unless she stole the documents her family, living in rural Quang Tri province, would be harmed. Sometimes actions would be inexplicable. The author visited An Lac village in An Giang province in late 1960 and was shown an example of sabotage that had taken place the night before: Someone had entered the village school, piled up the benches and tables together, and set fire to them. Only the four bare walls remained. The villagers and the teacher maintained they had no idea why it was done.

In the liberated area extensive use was made of booby traps and mines. Hand-grenade traps would be set along jungle paths, on the hinge of a gate leading into a village yard, in fishing nets, fruit trees, chicken coops, and other places where troops might be curious or tempted to help themselves. A variation of this was called the horse gun, which usually consisted of a rat-trap shotgun-shell device set along a jungle trail with a trip wire that fired the shotgun shell into the chest of its victim; a similar device employed a bow and arrow for the same purpose. Mines, pressure or trip type or electrically detonated, were also common; generally they were placed on or near bridges, at stream fording sites, on narrow jungle trails in open rows between rubber trees, along the dikes of rice paddies, or at the entrances to villages. Spike traps, sometimes called *panji,* were used extensively by both sides. They were placed in rice fields, usually under water or wherever it was likely an enemy would step. Long trenches would be dug, the bottom lined with metal or bamboo spikes, and the trench then covered with grass. Long sharpened bamboo poles were set upright in open fields as an antihelicopter defense.

Violence Against Individuals

For the rural villager the forms of violence that struck home the hardest were the assassination, execution, and kidnaping. Turgid accounts

---

[10] Such explosive devices were employed in Saigon in May 1963, using a motor bicycle and a motorcycle to blow huge holes in the side of a U.S. military warehouse. A U.S. officer's billet in Saigon, the Brink, was dynamited, apparently by an explosive-packed vehicle that had been driven under it, on Christmas Eve 1964, and in the face of intensive U.S. internal security measures. The Pershing Sports Field explosion in Saigon involved burying under the grandstand a length of soil pipe packed with explosive and attached to a calendar-watch detonator. The Kinh Do Theater explosion in Saigon was the work of two NLF terrorists who dashed into the lobby carrying a pail of explosive with a lighted fuse, set it down, and dashed out.

of struggle movements or endless lists of statistics on military victories meant little to him. But when death struck in his village against someone he knew, a scar of fear formed in his mind. Here are three examples personally investigated by the author:

— On September 28, 1961 Father Hoang Ngoc Minh, a well-loved priest of Kontum parish, was ambushed by guerrillas at the edge of Kondela village. A roadblock stopped his car. He was taken from it, and the guerrillas drove bamboo spears into his body. Then the leader fired a *coup de grâce* into his brain. The driver, Huynh Huu, Father Minh's nephew, was seriously wounded.

— On September 30, 1961 a band of ten armed guerrillas kidnaped a farmer named Truong Van Dang, age 67 (of Long An hamlet, Long Tri village, Binh Phuoc district, Long An province), and took him to a nearby jungle clearing where in the presence of about fifty villagers he was put on "trial" before what was called a "people's tribunal." He was charged with purchasing two hectares of rice land and of ignoring NLF orders to turn the land over to the tenant who had been working it. He was condemned to death, taken to the rice fields he had purchased, and shot.

— On August 23, 1961 two schoolteachers, Nguyen Khoa Ngon and Miss Nguyen Thi Thiet, were preparing their teaching lessons at Miss Thiet's home when two guerrillas entered the house and forced them at gunpoint to go to their school, Rau Ram School, Phong Dinh province. There they found two men, named Oanh and Van, local farmers, to whom the guerrillas read an execution order. Oanh was then shot and Van decapitated. Although the teachers were not certain why they had been forced to witness the executions, they assumed that it was an effort to intimidate them and to discourage them from taking a pro-GVN attitude with their students.

Such incidents were recounted freely in the NLF mass media, where they always took on a moralistic tone. A typical assassination, told in typically Communist terms, was described by Australian Communist Wilfred Burchett and quoted in a Radio Hanoi broadcast, July 2, 1964:

In Mo Duc district, Quang Ngai province, was one Chau, a main Diemist agent responsible for the deaths of hundreds of former Resistance members. We sent a group of guerrillas disguised as Diemist officers to his house on the night of May 18, 1960. Our men persuaded him that since the next day was President Ho Chi Minh's birthday the Viet Cong would certainly make trouble, so action must be taken that very night. . . . Eventually he agreed and we set out with some of his agents. About one kilometer from his house he was executed, and his agents were arrested. . . .

The guerrilla interviewed by Burchett added:

Each village, each case was studied very carefully. . . . We compiled a detailed dossier of the various local despots. If someone merited the death penalty we sent a group to deal with him. Afterwards [loudhailers] were used to explain the crimes committed. . . . We posted names of other tyrants who would be dealt with if they did not cease their activities. . . . The executions . . . and the warnings . . . played a major role in breaking the grip of the enemy throughout the country . . . and created conditions under which we could move back into the villages, either permanently or on organizational visits. . . .

The common characteristic of this activity against individuals is that it was directed at the village leader, usually the natural leader — that individual who, because of age, sagacity, or strength of character, is the one to whom people turn for advice or leadership. Many were religious figures, schoolteachers, or simply people of integrity and honor. Since they were superior individuals these persons were more likely to stand up to the insurgents when they came to the village and thus most likely to be the first victims. Potential opposition leadership was the NLF's most feared enemy. Steadily, quietly, and with a systematic ruthlessness the NLF in six years wiped out virtually an entire class of Vietnamese villagers. The assassination rate declined steadily (as shown in Chapter 5, Table 5-1) from 1960 to 1965 for the simple reason that there was only a finite number of persons to be assassinated. Many villages by 1966 were virtually depopulated of their natural leaders, who are the single most important element in any society. They represent a human resource of incalculable value. This loss to South Vietnam is inestimable, and it will take a generation or more to repair the damage to the society. By any definition, this NLF action against village leaders amounts to genocide.

The assassination pattern appeared to be directed toward the very best and the very worst officials, against the highly popular and effective government civil servant and the most corrupt and oppressive local official; such a policy stimulated mediocrity among civil servants.

Especially in its assassinations the NLF attempted to maintain a façade of legalism, partly as a justification for its act; partly to convey to the villager that there was nothing whimsical or capricious about its actions, and that no villager therefore need fear the NLF so long as he understood what was "legal" and "illegal"; and partly to insinuate that the NLF held the status of a cobelligerent. Assassinations were carried out following a "trial," and a "death notice" was pinned to the victim, whose body was then placed, often at great risk to the guerrillas, where it would be viewed by villagers. A typical assassination "order" read:

In consideration of the fact that this man was a lackey of the U.S.-Diem clique, had been warned and educated twice by us, continued to work for the traitor [Premier] Duong Van Minh for whom he threatened the people and spied on them with a view to arresting them, thus harming both the people and the Revolution, we the Liberation forces have punished him, as we punish anyone who wickedly and stubbornly continues, after having been warned and re-educated many times, to change his ways. Signed: The Liberation Forces.

Internal documents frequently referred to shortcomings in the violence program, as discussed at criticism and self-criticism sessions. The chief criticisms, as indicated by the memoranda from such sessions, were foolhardiness in attack, which resulted in heavy casualties as well as failure of the mission, or, at the other extreme, timidity and unwillingness to take risks, particularly by individuals unwilling to expose themselves to enemy fire. Documents also cited cadres who were "too prone to regard the enemy strength as overwhelming and who adopted too passive an attitude toward revolutionary work." What was termed "localitis" also plagued the NLF; this was a tendency on the part of NLF units to deal willingly with the problem of opposition in their immediate area but very unwillingly to engage in any armed struggle in adjacent areas. Finally, there was a castigation of cadres for "laxity and indifference in carrying out assignments." A study of these documents presents a picture of a few zealous young men willing to perform any act of violence, regardless of the risk, and a vast majority insisting that any venture should be riskless and foolproof. The technique employed by the NLF — to rehearse armed struggle attacks until each team member was letter perfect — was probably a reflection of this attitude or shortcoming on the part of those engaged in the violence program.

The Uses of Terror

In his excellent essay on terror in internal war,[11] to which the author is indebted for many concepts in this section, Thomas Perry Thornton listed five proximate objectives of terrorism: morale building within the movement; advertising the movement among the general population; disorientation of the population, including psychological isolation of the individual through destruction of the structure of authority that was previously a source of security; elimination of opposing forces; and provocation, either forcing the incumbent toward more authoritarian means or causing him to take such elaborate precautionary defense measures that a general feeling of insecurity is communicated to the population at large. Thornton also distinguished between disruptive terror and suppressive terror, or what he called enforcement terror, usually by the incumbent, and agitational terror by the guerrilla.

[11] Thomas Perry Thornton, "Terror as a Weapon of Political Agitation," in Harry Eckstein, ed., *Internal War: Problems and Approaches* (New York: Free Press of Glencoe, 1964).

It would appear that the chief use of terror by the NLF initially was to advertise itself, and its chief use at all times was a means of eliminating opposition. Terror was used to immobilize those forces, including the GVN official, standing between it and its domination of the rural areas. For this reason there was little terrorism in Saigon and virtually none directed at top-level governmental officials. The NLF, for example, had ample opportunity to kill Diem or his family; as far as can be determined it never even made the effort.

We have no way of determining whether terror was employed by the NLF for internal morale-building purposes, but apparently it was not; the internal documents dealing with criticism and self-criticism of the violence program indicated a fairly widespread distaste for terror on the part of the NLF rank and file; successful acts of terror probably did boost morale among the cadres. Nor apparently was terror used by the NLF as provocation; at least no internal documents were ever uncovered that so instructed cadres; on the contrary, struggle movement cadres particularly were warned not to allow extremists in the crowd to commit any violent or terroristic act that would provoke the GVN or justify retaliation in force. Had provocation been a motive there would have been a greater use of terror in the cities.

Disorientation of the villager or individual psychological isolation was at least a by-product of the NLF violence program that did cause physical and psychological separation of the rural villager from the GVN. The assassination program, however, was chiefly directed at total elimination of the GVN apparatus in the village; thus the killings that resulted were cases more of murder than of terror. Nor did the NLF pursue terror in a random or indiscriminate pattern. On the contrary, the killing of individuals was done with great specificity, as, for example, pinning a note to the shirtfront of an assassinated government official, explaining the crimes he had committed. If a civilian was shot down in a market place, a few hours later an organized rumor campaign began asserting that the victim had been a secret GVN agent. The NLF made a concerted effort to ensure that there were no unexplained killings; sometimes it went so far as to issue leaflets denying the killing of individuals, asserting that they were killed by bandits masquerading as NLF army soldiers.

NLF cadres regarded the proper use of terror as terror applied judiciously, selectively, and sparingly. Terror, turned on and off, paradoxically produced both pro- and antiguerrilla feelings among villagers. On the one hand, of course, it engendered fear and hatred, usually the first predominating over the second. But when relaxed, as in an area-wide terror campaign, an exaggerated sense of relief spread through the villages, and the villagers would come to regard the guerrillas as being not nearly as inhumane as they were capable of being. Terror worked best in the liberated area and was virtually useless against the hard-core enemy. In general, however, the NLF theoreticians considered terror to be the weapon of the weak, the desperate, or the ineffectual guerrilla leader. They held that most objectives could be achieved without its use. *Quy chanh* reported that indoctrination sessions on the armed struggle cited the Malayan insurgency as a case where general indiscriminate terror was applied and failed. "We were told," said one of them, "that in Singapore the rebels on certain days would dynamite every 67th streetcar that passed along a street, the next day it might be every 30th, and so on; but that this hardened the hearts of the people against the rebels because so many people died needlessly."

The NLF also had before it the Viet Minh experience in which suppressive or enforcement terror was conceived as a holding action pending the buildup of Viet Minh strength among rural Vietnamese. As the Viet Minh's strength increased, its use of this form of terror diminished. Its use of disruptive terror, as pointed out by Brian Crozier, was to make repression by the French so costly that the French government would prefer to withdraw rather than to continue the struggle.[12] In general the experiences of the Viet Minh did not particularly recommend wide use of disruptive terror.

At least one monumental failure in the use of terror also conditioned the NLF leadership's attitude. This came in the highlands in the summer of 1962 and involved the montagnards. After years of patiently cultivating the montagnards, the NLF leadership apparently came to the conclusion that the policy had not paid off and that a harder line was in order. It was true that despite concentrated efforts the montagnards remained hostile to the NLF, especially Vietnamese representatives of the NLF. The GVN's resources control program in the highlands (where it was possible to starve to death) and the organizational work among the montagnards, chiefly by the American Special Forces teams, combined to create an inhospitable climate in the highlands for NLF cadres. When food became short the NLF cadre under the new policy did not hesitate to take the food of the montagnard and allow him to go hungry. The marked increase in the use of terror among the montagnards that resulted was designed to coerce them into supporting, feeding, and generally assisting the guerrilla bands operating in the mountains. The montagnard response to such use of force was a traditional gesture of discontent — sudden migration; the people of a whole village might vanish in a single night and reappear as refugees in GVN military and civilian centers. The total montagnard exodus may have reached 300,000 persons, perhaps a third of the total montagnard population in South

[12] Brian Crozier, *The Rebels: A Study of Post-War Insurrections* (Boston, Mass.: Beacon Press, 1960).

Vietnam. Eventually most of these people were relocated, and a number of them were recruited into antiguerrilla CIDG teams.

Beginning in February 1964 the NLF began a terror campaign against the Americans in Vietnam. It was random, indiscriminate, and closely resembled the Thornton proximate objectives. It probably did build up morale among the terrorists; the bombing of the American Embassy on March 30, 1965 most certainly was for morale-building purposes. The killing of American civilians, as in the theater or sports field explosions, obviously advertised the NLF in the United States. The terror also served to disorient Americans in Vietnam and create within them a sense of psychological isolation. Terror, however, was not used to the extent it might have been in eliminating American opposition; the casualty rate of American killings, for example, could have been much higher in the 1960–1965 period than it was. And finally, the protective measures — barricades and guards — taken at the American Dependent School and other civilian installations in Saigon did communicate a sense of insecurity both to the Americans and to the Vietnamese.

The initial burst of intensified violence in February and March of 1964 stopped almost as suddenly as it began. Within a ten-day period there were about two dozen major and minor terror-type attacks on Americans, some large and deadly in scope (had the Pershing Sports Field bomb not partly misfired and had all three lengths of pipe exploded rather than just one, the number of dead would have been in the hundreds and might have been as high as one thousand). But this campaign suddenly stopped, for reasons that were never clear. The author can offer one highly speculative explanation: The NLF leadership in the South, on its own, took the decision to launch an all-out terror campaign against the Americans to which the top leadership in Hanoi reacted with dismay — feeling that tactically it was unjustified — and ordered an immediate halt. The time lag involved tends to substantiate this thesis.

14

Bính Van: The Proselyting Program

In some ways the NLF's *binh van,* or proselyting, effort among ARVN officers and soldiers and GVN civil servants was the most deadly weapon in its arsenal. The *dich van* program and other activities in the political struggle movement might turn villagers against their government, and the liberated area with its various *dan van* programs might provide the NLF with a relatively safe haven and perhaps even with a rudimentary government, but so long as the GVN and its military establishment remained intact and viable the NLF could not hope for political status higher than mere pretender to the throne. The destruction of the nation's armed forces therefore became of overriding importance to the NLF leadership, and so it struck against the military and the civil servants in two basic ways: through its violence program, with armed attacks, assassinations, kidnapings, and other acts of terror designed not so much to eliminate as to paralyze, and through its proselyting program, called *binh van.*[1]

[1] Originally the NLF referred to this as its *binh* (military) and *chinh* (civilian), or B and C program; later *binh van* came to be used more loosely, to describe all proselyting activities, both military and civilian.

The purpose of *binh van* [a 1961 document stated] is to disorganize the enemy forces and build our support within the enemy's ranks [and] to undermine the last leg on which he stands. Efficient *binh van* efforts will reduce the difficulties we face and reduce bloodshed, . . . will move us closer to the General Uprising. . . . Another advantage of *binh van* is that it will cause enemy troops to disobey their officers and stop oppressing and extorting money from the people, stop drafting men into the army and into corvée labor units, and thus protect the lives and property of the people. . . . Still another advantage of *binh van* is that it keeps us informed of the enemy's schemes and daily activities, . . . helps us to capture military posts and installations, . . . and provides us with intelligence and information about the enemy's security activities so that we may cope with them. . . .

It is a strategic task, said a later document, "that must be carried out to the end of the Revolution. . . . Seek to destroy each individual enemy. This will disintegrate one element after another in the enemy's entire military organization. Seek to win the enemy over to our side. Infiltrate agents into the army for the day of the General Uprising. These actions must be done militantly or the *binh van* movement will not succeed."

Although the movement did not get under way until mid-1961, NLF media from the earliest days maintained a steady drumfire of reports on alleged military desertions. These examples[2] of such output indicate the milieu the NLF attempted to create:

—In the first six months of this year [1961] more than 4,000 men of the Diem army crossed over to the people's side. A great number brought arms with them and joined the people's self-defense forces. . . .

—Recently [November 1961] desertion has taken a collective character. In some localities whole units have changed sides. . . .

—In Ben Tre [Kien Hoa] province, awakened by the struggle movements staged by 300,000 people of the province, some 300 soldiers defected to the people's ranks. . . . [December 1961.]

—A Diem sailor in Quang Ngai province has crossed over to the people's ranks, bringing along two tommyguns and a rifle. . . .

—Cases of whole units deserting were recorded in the Yen Bai and Anti-Communist Alliance regiments, composed of members of the Hoa Hao religious community. . . . [January 1962.]

—One thousand minority nationals [montagnards], forcibly enrolled in the Ngo Dinh Diem army, deserted early this month [January 1962] from a training camp in Kontum province. . . .

—Soldiers at a post in Chau Thanh district, Ben Tre [Kien Hoa] province, on January 4 [1962] killed or wounded their commanders and brought their arms over to the people.

[2] The *binh van* examples cited in this chapter are for illustrative purposes only; any or all may have been figments of NLF imagination.

— Numerous troops stationed at five posts in Go Cong province on February 27 [1962] rose in revolt after being ordered to start a raid. They shot the Diem agents and left with 50 rifles to join the people's ranks.

— One unit refused to obey its commander's orders to repress the people, destroyed all of its munitions, . . . and deserted. [April 1962.]

— A whole company of marines of the Diem army deserted May 9 [1962], the day that U.S. Defense Secretary Robert McNamara arrived in Saigon. . . .

— Fifty-four Diem army men crossed over to the people's side with their arms on July 6 and 7 [1962] because they said they were disgusted with the barbarities committed by their colleagues under U.S. command.

— The criminal policy pursued by the U.S.-Diem gang to drive the people into "strategic hamlets" has met with increasingly severe opposition from just-minded soldiers. In Ben Tre [Kien Hoa] province [April 1963] more than 5,483 soldiers deserted and helped the people destroy their strategic hamlets. . . .

— Three officers of the Diem army, a field artillery captain, an infantry lieutenant, and an air force lieutenant, have deserted . . . and left behind a note denouncing the Diem repression of Buddhist monks, nuns, and laymen.

— Diem army unit 787 stationed in a village of Tra Vinh [Vinh Binh] province destroyed the Ba The Strategic Hamlet and went over to the NLFSV with all its weapons. . . . [October 1963.]

— In the first ten days of November [1963], 1,365 men of the U.S.-fostered puppet army in six provinces of the Mekong River delta left their ranks for the people's side. . . . After deserting many took part in demonstrations and struggle movements. . . .

— Patriotic soldiers of the U.S.-commanded South Vietnam army in Tra Vinh [Vinh Binh] province burned an enemy arms and ammunition depot [and] . . . 20 enemy barracks . . . [and] killed 27 soldiers . . . before deserting. . . . [April 1964.]

— In the first six months of 1964 . . . there were 91 cases in which U.S.-commanded soldiers rose up and in coordination with the people's patriotic forces annihilated outposts, burned gasoline depots, and attacked military strongholds of the enemy . . . , capturing 1,000 weapons, burned one million liters of gasoline . . . , and destroyed one hundred tons of munitions. . . .

The ARVN desertion rate (in the years 1960 through 1963), according to several independent sources, was about 0.1 per cent per month, or about 400 soldiers a month who either joined the NLF or returned to their home villages. This figure remained remarkably steady throughout the four-year period, so much so that American advisers concluded that the ARVN desertion rate was not the meaningful index to morale that it is in most armies. If this figure is correct, the desertions in the four-year period totaled at most 20,000 men.

Objectives

The general purpose of *binh van* was to destroy the GVN's military strength. The program, however, was directed along a spectrum of specific objectives that may be ranked in descending order of desirability to the NLF.

The highest achievement was to induce unit desertions, preferably accompanied by some final act of sabotage on the part of the departing element, which then joined the NLF army. For example,

In response to an appeal from the NLFSV and determined not to serve as cannon fodder for the U.S. aggressors and their henchmen, a squad of Civil Guards stationed at Kien Phuoc in Go Cong [Dinh Tuong] province . . . on December 21 [1964] while on night patrol shot dead two cruel agents of the puppet administration and crossed over to the people's side, bringing with them 12 guns, one field telephone set, one radio, 12 grenades, and 800 bullets. . . . They were warmly welcomed and rewarded. . . .

The next highest was to induce individual military desertion or civilian defection, preferably accompanied by a final act of destruction or theft of key documents, with the individual then joining the NLF: "At Thu Duc a cadet on August 2 [1962] changed sides, leaving behind a letter posted on the wall of the barracks calling on all his colleagues to follow him."

Then came inducing desertion or defection by individuals or groups without transference of allegiance to the NLF. In most instances the individual would return to his home village and resume life as a farmer. Radio Liberation (September 20, 1963), for instance, reported that "two officers and a noncom of the U.S.-Diem army, after crossing over to the people . . . , have returned to their home villages, where the . . . NLFSV is helping them to resume life as farmers. . . ." The NLF also encouraged what in effect were "third force" elements, that is, group desertions or defections that did not join the NLF but might associate with it in a loose way. Internal documents referred to these individuals as "partisans," apparently a category established by the NLF for the benefit of those who opposed both the GVN and the NLF but were willing to form a temporary and guarded alliance with the NLF.

The fourth highest was to induce major and significant opposition within the military or civil service, either covertly or overtly. Radio Hanoi reported this incident on February 16, 1963:

At Go Vap in the Saigon suburbs a private from a garrison unit ordered a meal in a restaurant and then molested the proprietress. When police arrived he pulled out a hand grenade and said: "This grenade is reserved for anybody who wants to arrest me. I would rather die here than pick up a bullet on a raiding operation." The district chief was called, and he said "Go back to your unit; no one will put you in prison." "But that's just it," he replied, "I want to be put in the clink." On thinking the matter over, the district chief solemnly promised, "All right, you may go to prison."

Strikes were also encouraged: "At Camau training center, 217 press-ganged youths held a hunger strike on May 19 [1962] in protest against the harsh training and bad treatment by their American commanders, declaring 'the food is worse than that given to dogs. . . .' Four were arrested, but the rest intensified the struggle and the . . . camp commander had to release the youths . . . and pledged to settle the trainees' demands. . . ." Radio Liberation also reported: "Besides desertion, an opposition movement in the army is also forging ahead. . . . Last month [November 1961] 300 soldiers in Phu Yen opposed the order to extend their enlistments, . . . 17 Catholic troops refused to go on military operations, . . . [and] a battalion in Thua Thien province went on strike against an order shifting it to another province to repress the people. . . .

Below this was any act that would drive a wedge between the Vietnamese military officer or civil servant and the U.S. advisers, usually involving an alleged act by an American at which the Vietnamese took umbrage: "At Quang Trung military training center a U.S. adviser forced the members of the Women's Paramilitary Corps to crawl under his machine-gun fire. He fired too low, and four trainees, exhausted by hard training, failed to crawl flat enough and were killed. Outraged, a South Vietnamese sergeant whipped out his pistol and brought the Yank down. . . . That night 20 women trainees fled the center."

Sixth on the scale was to induce low-grade pro-NLF activity among military officers or civil servants, who were often extremely vulnerable to NLF retaliatory measures, but in a covert fashion so that the individual did not jeopardize his position. In practice this became one of the most effective forms, and certainly the most insidious, of the *binh van* movement. Particularly in insecure areas and especially to low-ranking civil servants, the NLF would convey the idea that it would not harm a GVN representative providing he arranged that the programs for which he was responsible were not implemented in any effective way. This could be done by a slowdown, by snarling the pro-

gram in red tape, or by outright falsification of reports to higher headquarters. For instance, a strategic-hamlet chief could go through the
motions of creating a village security apparatus that only appeared to
have succeeded in separating the guerrillas from the villagers. Vietnamese Information Service posters and leaflets arriving from Saigon
could be distributed only superficially, in areas where district officials
would be likely to notice them, and the rest destroyed. A military patrol
leader could lead his patrol noisily down a well-traveled path and
after an hour return to the hamlet, never having made a serious effort
to determine whether guerrillas were in the area but with his superiors
being none the wiser. The effect was to place a premium on mediocrity
in low-level administration at a time when excellence was vital. A
civil servant would imagine he could enjoy the best of both worlds:
He could perform well enough not to arouse the suspicions of his
superior but not so well as to earn the hostility of the NLF. He might
even be in contact with the NLF so as to be certain that they understood
his position; many ARVN military operations were ruined by Vietnamese military or civil servants gratuitously passing on information
to NLF agents or persons they presumed to be in contact with the NLF,
simply in an effort to ingratiate themselves with the NLF — as a sort
of life insurance policy.

Finally, if nothing else was possible, any act was encouraged that
might serve to lower the morale of the military personnel or civil servants. The vast majority of the members of the GVN were loyal to the
cause. Some hated the NLF for what it was doing to Vietnam; some
feared what an NLF victory would mean to them personally; some were
enmeshed in family ties that automatically made them enemies of the
NLF; others fought it for doctrinal or religious reasons; opposition resulted from a vast range of motives. But all these individuals were
vulnerable to NLF attacks on their morale, and the NLF employed
against them the entire spectrum of appeals: certainty of NLF victory,
endemic betrayal, sympathy for the impoverished civil servants, patriotism, in short, any word or act that tended to cause the loyal cadre to
lose heart.

Adjuncts to *binh van* efforts were acts directed at those who might
become members of the enemy's administration, for example, by engendering hostility among rural youth for the military draft or careers
in the civil service. A typical example of this form of the *binh van*
program among draftees was described in a clandestine newspaper
article in December 1964:

An enemy ship carrying almost 2,000 youths drafted in the Vinh Long
area to serve as bullet shields . . . witnessed at Vinh Long city a struggle

movement by their relatives. One U.S. aggressor beat an old woman demonstrator. . . . Indignant at this, all the conscripted youths jumped from the ship, beat the U.S. aggressor to death, . . . and one thousand of them fled to the liberated area. . . .

Techniques and Methods

The *binh van* program was applied by the functional liberation associations, by the cadres themselves, indirectly through relatives, by means of mass-media appeals, and as a function of the NLF army. Specifically there were nine major *binh van* techniques:

1. Enunciation and constant restatement by all possible means of a liberal NLF policy toward recanting military and civil servants, including prisoners. In the early days NLF policy was stated in general terms:

The NLF applies a lenient policy toward military men and members of the enemy administration as well as toward captured foreigners, including Americans. . . . It pursues this attitude because the majority of the military men in the Southern army are workers, peasants, and laborers coming from the poor strata, who have been induced or forced to enlist. . . . The [policy] is proved by a letter from 90 military men captured during the Bac Ha campaign [June 1962] . . . , who wrote, "We have been well treated by the revolutionary soldiers. They appeared before us with a smile full of clemency and humanitarianism. . . . We, victors and vanquished, have been living together with fraternity and full of affection. . . ." [3]

[3] Later the policy was spelled out in more detail, as in the following Radio Liberation broadcast of October 27, 1963:

> The NLFSV once again emphasizes its unchangeable policy. . . . (1) Those persons or groups who rise up and fight the Americans, destroy enemy bases, and join the people . . . will be considered by the Front as partisan troops, . . . and the Front will commend their achievements, appropriately reward them for their feats, help them earn a living, or admit them to the ranks of the Liberation Army according to their wishes. (2) Those individuals or groups who refuse any longer to be pushed along the dark path of crime and seek to leave their ranks and return to their home villages to earn a living, the Front is ready to welcome. . . . (3) Those individuals, groups, or army units who wish to separate themselves from the U.S.-controlled military force and battle the enemy [on their own] the Front will provide with conditions to fulfill their wishes. . . . (4) Those individuals or political groups who hold political opinions differing from the enemy and who are terrorized and obliged to come to the liberated area, even though they do not totally approve of the Front's line of struggle, the Front is ready to protect and help on the basis of negotiations and equality. . . .

The categories thus appealed to were individuals who wished to join the NLF army or units that wished to integrate into the NLF army on an opportunistic basis; individuals who wished to withdraw their support of the GVN but not serve the NLF — primarily Buddhists; those separatist or "third force" military elements intent on anti-GVN efforts, chiefly the potential coup d'état elements in the ARVN; and those who sought to oppose the GVN from the safe haven of the liberated area while maintaining their own identity — chiefly political elements favoring a neutral settlement.

2. Wide and intensive use of selective terror and intimidation, chiefly of a psychological nature, against key functionaries and military units. Where possible, guerrilla forces would trap and ruthlessly eliminate to the last man elite ARVN units, such as rangers or paratroopers, although in general, as previously noted, the NLF army was not interested in killing Vietnamese military simply for the sake of killing.

Terror was often used against the families of soldiers in an effort to develop in the individual soldiers stationed in other parts of the country a sense of hopelessness in being unable to defend them. Blackmail was quite common: An enlisted man would be entrapped in a crime or some act of indiscretion, after which he was blackmailed into serving as a covert agent. Since duplicity played such a major role throughout, one of the most effective techniques was to release a captured prisoner almost immediately after capture and without explanation; the soldier returning to his unit would find his officers highly skeptical of his story that the NLF had simply turned him loose, and they would assume he had turned coat. He would be treated as an enemy spy, perhaps even discharged from the service, whereupon the NLF would find him receptive to its recruitment efforts.

3. Use of penetration agents to develop support within the military and the civil service. Infiltration was endemic on both sides. One internal NLF document listed the three major means of developing penetration agents: "contacting enemy personnel directly or through their relatives and converting them into penetration agents; use of existing penetration agents who contact members of their unit or service . . . and develop them as new agents; educating and training persons who are then placed in the enemy ranks. . . ."[4]

4. Use of family ties and friendships to induce or coerce military personnel and civil servants to desert, defect, or covertly serve the cause. In practice, most *binh van* appeals involved family and clan relationships. An early *binh van* memorandum instructed cadres to

mobilize the soldiers' dependents as the key spear with which to attack the enemy. The dependents must be fully motivated. Tell them about the crimes

---

[4] Another document called for intensive efforts to place servants in the homes of senior military officers, high-ranking government officials, and American advisers. This document added:

Develop agents for the purpose of preparing for the General Uprising. . . . Select only Party members, [Youth] League members, and those fully awakened to the Revolution, who are ready to make great sacrifices, and have fixed ideas. . . . Get them to realize the glorious task they have . . . , to dispel misgivings they may have or fear of death. . . . They should get at least ten days of training . . . and then take a sacred oath. Do not inform their relatives, although relatives may be used for liaison. . . . For contact work, use the liaison agent system. If this is not possible contact the agent by letter. Manage new agents carefully to avoid betrayal, for they may be double agents. If we are betrayed in an attack on a post by an agent on the inside, the liaison agent will be held responsible.

of the enemy against soldiers. Instill confidence in our *binh van* movement. . . . Awaken their sense of responsibility. . . . Hold intervillage meetings attended by all families of servicemen . . . [and] at the meeting organize those attending into individual cells. . . . Have deserters stand up and describe life in the army. . . . Develop letter-writing campaigns at the meeting. Each relative should be encouraged to write a letter to their soldier relative telling about their kin being rounded up, their houses burned, how they are miserable and sick, and so forth. The letters should also ask the soldier for assistance . . . and encourage him to write *binh van* slogans on his barrack walls and throughout the post. . . . Letters may be anonymous. . . .

The letter-writing campaign grew to massive proportions during 1963. Many such letters contained only subtle statements designed to undermine morale; others were filled with pitiful accounts of tribulations on the home front. Frequently cadres wrote the letters for the benefit of illiterate villagers. Within the village the Soldiers' Mothers' Association, later replaced by the Families of Patriotic Soldiers' Association, acted as the organizational base for the *binh van* campaign. Each village liberation association was expected to keep a roster of the names of families with sons or relatives serving in GVN ranks. The classification, said an instructional memorandum, "should be in three categories: those who sympathize with our cause, those indifferent to us, and those who are backward or prejudiced against us." The Families of Patriotic Soldiers' Association, it added, should be composed of members of the first category, grouped in units of five to ten families each, "who then will apply for membership in the Front. . . . Sympathetic families should convert those in category two. . . . Do not use force against those in category three, for if the family is not really conscious of the Revolution their efforts to convert their relatives will not be sincere. Establish an executive committee of the association, which should assume responsibility for assigning *binh van* work, organizing struggle movements, taking care of administrative matters, recapitulating and evaluating results, and in general providing leadership. . . ." A later document assigned a quota to the association: "Our goal for each province is one thousand families. . . . In villages where we are strong organize one half of the families of soldiers, in villages where we have only medium influence organize one third, and in villages where we are weak, one fourth. . . ."

The lunar new year (Tet) celebration in Vietnam, because of its sentimental overtones and because each Vietnamese traditionally was expected to return to his home village during the occasion, offered the NLF a particular opportunity to pursue the *binh van* campaign. A cease-fire was issued each Tet, and it was generally believed that any Vietnamese could travel with impunity anywhere in Vietnam, even into the liberated area, providing only that the NLF was convinced he was not a spy. "At Tet," said one provincial NLF internal document, "when soldiers come to their villages, organize meetings with their families, . . . point out to them that when they are in the village they are oppressed and exploited, . . . when they are drafted they are scorned and bullied by their officers, . . . when they are sent to the battlefield they may be killed and wounded, . . . but do not force families to summon home their relatives for us to educate as no lasting value will come of this. . . ." Village women were encouraged to send hand-kerchiefs, as Tet gifts to soldiers who could not return home, on which were embroidered the word "peace."

5. General struggle movements among civilians in the name of *binh van,* either defensively for use when troops came to the village or offensively, such as a demonstration at a military base. A variation of this form was the struggle movement within the military unit. Doctrine clearly dictated that the people themselves must carry the burden of the *binh van* effort. Said one PRP document:

> Experience has shown that *binh van* work involves not just Party members but the farmers and workers . . . and all the people. Specialized *binh van* cadres cannot be successful unless the masses by the millions participate in the program. The basic task of the *binh van* cadre is not to . . . subvert the military and civil service . . . but to educate the people in the program so they will pursue it. . . . The farmers and workers should win over the troops, the middle class should win over the officers, and the religious groups should win over troops belonging to their religions. . . .

A cadre directive outlined a typical *binh van* struggle movement that indicates the cleverness with which the technique could be endowed:

> A unit of the Liberation Army was [operating] outside a certain village in which there was a Catholic cathedral next to which some enemy troops were bivouacked. Agit-prop cadres had been in the village for some time attempt-ing to develop a struggle movement against the Catholic priest, during which he would be requested to ask the enemy officers to move the bivouac away from the cathedral area. . . . Liberation Army soldiers came to the village and talked about the successes of the political struggle in other places, and said that the Liberation Army always punishes the devils and helps the people. But they said if the Liberation Army attacks there will be many stray bullets and the cathedral will be destroyed, after which the enemy will return and build a stronger post, but if the masses take up the political strug-gle the enemy will depart for good. The masses took up the struggle and forced the enemy to withdraw from the cathedral. . . .

Another document outlined techniques for villagers to use against troops on military operations:

> Guide the masses in devising slogans. . . . The main purpose of the slo-gans is to win over the troops, not threaten them. For instance, do not put up a sign reading "Death zone"; instead put up a sign reading "Our brothers,

soldiers, and officers of the South, please go no farther, beware of spike boards, hand grenades, and traps set only for the purpose of fighting the U.S.-Diem clique," and so forth. . . . By means of indoctrination get the masses to understand proper *binh van* methods and techniques, including these: Making the NLFSV policies known to soldiers and officers; the masses must be used to put our literature into the hands of soldiers, officers, and officials of the enemy administration. . . . By [spreading news of our political and military successes] emphasize the political success that develops from military success [so as to sow disunity, deepen pessimism]. . . . By spreading information about hardships of enemy soldiers, such as stories about soldiers with low pay, hard training camp practices, oppression by American officers . . . ; for example, use the story of the enemy officer who committed suicide in the My Phuoc Tay Agroville . . . or stories of soldiers who refuse to pull down people's houses. . . .

Cadres used patriotic appeals and other themes calling for support of the NLF army as a means of inducing *binh van* appeals by the people. The guerrilla bands themselves, for obvious reasons, were interested in ensuring its success and frequently encouraged the people to press it, as indicated in this example from an internal report:

Our unit captured a large gun from the enemy and showed it to the people of a village and told them it would be used to level a nearby enemy military post. The people were impressed and gave many supplies to the unit. Then the enemy came and the people fled. Our unit also withdrew because the enemies were too numerous. When the people returned later they had many doubts. So our unit assembled the people and raised the question: What is the proper way to love the Liberation Army? Some said by contributing money. Others said by sending their sons to join the army. Others said by serving as intelligence agents. The cadres said these things were important . . . but said most importantly the masses must carry on the *binh van* movement and struggle to lower the prestige of the enemy and sow disunity among the enemy troops, . . . that only if they do these things can the enemy be defeated. If our unit fights the enemy, many in our ranks will be killed, and still we have not been able to protect the village. Thus the villagers themselves are to blame for the actions that result when the enemy comes to the village.

The various struggle movements often took some oblique tack, such as efforts to increase soldiers' pay and allowances, shorten the length of military service, or provide longer leave time. They were conducted in the name of the military and frequently took place at the front gate of smaller military posts where it was difficult, for example, for a post commander who himself may have been in grade for ten years to oppose a struggle movement favoring faster promotions. Village cadres working in the *binh van* program were instructed to

work through the liberation associations and the soldier family associations . . . to prepare "question-answer" check lists for study by the people, . . . the questions then to be put to soldiers in the market place or when they come to the village. . . . At meetings describe successful *binh van* techniques

. . . ; have defectors speak to the groups. . . . Proper indoctrination will build the people's confidence and encourage them to approach and solicit soldiers to desert and bring over their weapons.

The classic *binh van* struggle typically would involve a sharp-tongued old woman buttonholing a young and ignorant private in the market place of a small village, berating him because of the killing and destruction of the war, putting to him questions of military strategy, and in general making him feel alien, miserable, and unpatriotic. Struggle movements within the military, particularly the self-defense forces, were frequent. "Encourage the struggle movement within the army," said one document, "encourage troops to demand to be allowed to visit their families, demand early release from military service, . . . get them to refuse to obey orders, . . . and finally prepare them for the General Uprising. . . ."

6. Various types of appeals to the military and civil servants aimed to maximize damage to the GVN's military and administrative machine. Declared one of the original *binh van* instructions,

Because the U.S. imperialists are gradually turning [the ARVN] into an army of mercenaries . . . under direct U.S. officer control . . . it is necessary and possible to stimulate the feelings of nationalism, anti-U.S. feelings, the longing for peace, and the aversion to war in the minds of the troops, with the exception of the feudalists and evildoers. . . . The slogan "Coalition among farmers, workers, and troops" will not only demoralize troops but if used together with a strong political and armed struggle movement will also induce enemy units to oppose war and rebel. In order to be more effective the slogan should be made more specific: "People and troops and officers in the South Vietnam army should unite to oppose U.S. aggression." In addition, use other slogans aimed at stimulating nationalism, urging military men to oppose the U.S. and war, demand peace, and oppose U.S. military commanders.

Appeals took the form of letters from former comrades in arms or leaflets smuggled into military installations and left where they would be found. They also employed rumors, and some involved direct appeals by means of megaphones or loudhailers by guerrillas or women surrounding outposts at night. "When using megaphones," said one directive, "avoid provoking or angering the soldiers so they open fire. . . . Never use the word 'surrender,' for this hurts their pride. . . . Always follow up this type of propaganda by personally contacting the troops. . . ."

Officers came in for special attention. One directive noted that officers

come from the upper classes of society; so use the same methods with them as with upper-class civilians. . . . Officers usually are nationalistic and want an independent Vietnam. But they are suspicious about us, so we should educate them to understand that we offer them a chance to participate in a glorious task. . . . Concentrate on first and second lieutenants. . . . *Binh van* committees at the provincial level should include cadres who specialize in *binh van* against officers.

Beginning in 1964 the *binh van* movement increased its efforts toward civil servants. Leaflets left in government offices informed the civil servant that "you may think you are not guilty if you do not serve the enemy with a gun, but they are guilty who use only pens against us." One memorandum instructed cadres that "if a civil servant is sympathetic to us but unreliable, encourage him to defect; if sympathetic and reliable, encourage him to remain in his job and help us from the inside. . . . Many civil servants can be frightened into serving us." Appeals to civil servants took a heavily sympathetic tone:

You entered the civil service expecting to live a quiet life but instead find your life is one of fear and anxiety. . . . Your salaries are low. . . . You are under great pressure. . . . Your free time is stolen from you. . . . You are condemned by every new government for following the policies of the former government. . . . The NLFSV is aware of your plight, . . . value, and achievements . . . , and when peace is restored . . . be assured that you also will be able to lead a steady and plentiful life. . . .

With increased American *présence* among civil servants in the rural areas, the wedge-driving technique also came into play. According to a Radio Liberation broadcast of July 7, 1964,

the communiqué in late June [1964] by Nguyen Khanh openly recognized the right of the U.S. imperialists not only to send military advisers . . . but advisers to take hold of civil, administrative, economic, cultural, social, and agricultural branches in the provinces and districts. This means they will compel you civil servants to take off your robe of independence, bow your heads, and obey their orders. . . .

7. Tangible and intangible rewards for those who deserted or defected. Although it would seem to demean the cause by putting a price tag on anti-GVN actions, the NLF frequently and publicly spoke of monetary rewards for those who deserted or defected. Radio Liberation on April 19, 1964 announced that $2,000 was given to a group of deserters in Long An province as a "reward." It also claimed to provide financial assistance for "partisans" who wished to return to their native villages and resume life as farmers. (Although the GVN claimed that the NLF used beautiful women to lure Vietnamese military [and Americans] into supporting the NLF, the assertion has never been substantiated.) The NLF also made extensive use of commendations and citations, including the awarding of the Liberation Medal (first and second class), to worthy deserters:

The Quang Tri Provincial Central Committee of the NLFSV has awarded to the 38th Militia [Self-Defense Force] platoon . . . that rose up and killed cruel U.S.-Nguyen Khanh agents and joined the patriotic forces . . . the Order of Liberation to said unit and congratulatory certificates to several of its members.

8. Use of deserters, defectors, and prisoners. NLF treatment of prisoners was not nearly as generous as was publicly claimed. A villager or other person having a grievance against an individual prisoner could cause him to be tried by an NLF court, and *quy chanh* indicated that virtually all who were tried were convicted and executed.

The NLF frequently faced a dilemma with voluntary turncoats: Deserters and defectors often were undesirable types or "enemies of the people," yet treating them as such tended to undercut the *binh van* program, for word of executions spread quickly, and the execution of someone who voluntarily joined the NLF obviously had a pernicious effect on anyone contemplating the same move. Further, the NLF faced the problem that many of the apparent deserters and defectors were GVN agents on infiltration missions. An NLF army handbook instructed cadres to treat both captured prisoners and defectors and deserters (called returnees by the NLF) in the same manner: "They should be blindfolded and tied and their weapons removed. When traveling do not permit them to see the path you are taking. . . . Voluntary returnees must be treated in the same manner, even if they bring weapons with them."

Prisoners were classified as "captured prisoners," those actually taken in combat, usually wounded, and "surrendered prisoners," those taken during combat without a struggle or as the result of a roadblock action. Returnees who simply walked into the NLF-controlled area were regarded with greater suspicion than those who performed an overt act of commitment, such as killing an ARVN officer, before deserting. The two types of prisoners and the first type of returnee were watched closely although generally not incarcerated. All four were subjected to intensive indoctrination sessions and were frequently "tested" by cadres as to their changed political attitudes. All prisoners eventually were released, providing no one brought charges against them as an "enemy of the people." The handbook just cited ordered cadres to "release eventually even the most obstinate prisoners even if they refuse [both] to confess their guilt before the people and to ask for forgiveness . . . because this encourages others to return to the people, and it overcomes the enemy slander that we shoot all prisoners. . . . Officer prisoners, however, are not to be released but are to be sent to provincial head-quarters where their cases will be handled. . . ." The chief use of deserters, defectors, cooperative prisoners, and "partisans" was to further the *binh van* movement.

American prisoners (at least those released) received reasonably humane treatment. The author talked with four, including an American civilian, and all said that although life as prisoners was harsh it was not much worse than what the guerrillas themselves endured. NLF army unit commanders carried a supply of leaflets in English, one of which was to be handed to any American captured. It said that the NLF prisoner policy was fourfold:

1. Prisoners of war are not maltreated or insulted.
2. Prisoners of war shall receive sufficient food, receive care when they are ill or wounded.
3. They have occasion to understand that Liberation forces are not "rebels" but organized and disciplined patriots struggling for peace, independence, and democracy, for friendship with all the peoples in the world, including the American people, for a free and happy life without the U.S. monopolists and their valets in South Vietnam.
4. They shall be liberated.

In at least two instances American prisoners were shot shortly after capture, but apparently in both cases to prevent their rescue; one wounded American prisoner was shot because he could not walk, and the guerrillas were not willing to leave him behind. In early 1965 at least a half dozen Americans remained in NLF hands. Several of these were American Special Forces members who probably were treated more harshly than other Americans because of greater NLF fear and hatred of the U.S. Special Forces units. In 1964 the NLF attitude toward American prisoners hardened, and the outright execution of American prisoners may have taken place. There is also reason to believe that the NLF was interested in retaining a number of Americans for use as bargaining pawns in an NLF-GVN negotiation.

9. Various efforts among potential draftees to oppose the military draft. When the GVN announced plans in late 1964 to increase the size of the Vietnamese armed forces, the NLF launched a massive antidraft struggle movement. Cadres were ordered to "promote struggle movements to prevent the military draft. Organize meetings and demonstrations at which antidraft slogans are shouted. . . . Send petitions to enemy officials protesting the draft. . . . Encourage youths to dodge the draft by joining our self-defense forces and fighting the enemy. . . . Wives, children, and parents should be used to struggle, and cry when their kin are drafted. . . . Struggle particularly among the religious."

It is difficult to provide any over-all assessment of the success of the *binh van* movement. It would appear, despite the intensive effort mounted, that the campaign did not significantly affect the efficiency of the Vietnamese armed forces. As far as the author could observe, the average ARVN soldier, when properly led, was a tough, determined, and effective fighter. The apparent lack of greater success of the *binh van* movement was a tribute both to his sagacity and to his patriotism. It is also worth noting that no prominent South Vietnamese governmental official or well-known personage ever defected to the NLF.

15

The Liberated Area: Program

Introduction

The NLF leadership's regard for its "liberated area" grew directly out of the Viet Minh and Chinese Communist experiences: the need for a safe base from which NLF military forces could operate and to which they could periodically retire for restoration of psychic and physical energies; the need for evidence that the NLF was a permanent political-governmental entity and not simply a collection of guerrilla bands; and the need to begin making the fundamental social changes required for the creation of the new society it was to build someday. Vo Nguyen Giap's description of the Viet Minh liberated territory precisely fits the NLF model two decades later:

From the memorable year 1940, our people began to stand up, fighting to clear this country first of the French, then of the Japanese oppressors. . . . Secretly, but steadily, the revolutionary organizations of the Vietminh league have spread all over the land. From the heart of the jungle, from the depth of the forest, the fighting units of our guerrilla forces have developed into our present national Liberation Army.
A "Liberated Territory," comprising 6 provinces of North Vietnam, is being organized on new lines of administrative and social policy.

269

The present Provisional Government is embodying the will of the whole nation; it is not the representative of any political faction. . . .[1]

The liberated area was regarded as essential: "A study of the wars in Vietnam, Cuba, Korea, Algeria, and other countries shows that it was the combativeness of the people and their comprehensively consolidated rear areas that were the main factors of their victories over the imperialist aggressors," wrote Hoang Van Thai.[2] An early 1962 NLF document spelled out in specific terms the importance and value of the liberated area:

Revolutionary bases are most important. . . . They ensure our safety when we encounter difficulty, they enable us to build up our forces, to extend the Front movement, to carry out the armed struggle, . . . [and] they provide our [administrative] apparatus with a stable position from which to operate and provide the facilities for training and feeding elements of the Liberation Army. . . . Our goal is the establishment of a network of well-organized large, medium, and small-sized bases, all connected with each other and all economically, politically, and militarily strong. . . . Such a system will enable our [guerrilla] forces to move from one area to another, will facilitate communication and transportation, particularly from the highlands to the [Mekong] delta. . . . We must establish large and strong bases in the jungle and mountain areas. In these areas, when the enemy has been pushed out, we must establish good administration. Attention must be given to increasing the political consciousness of the masses in these areas; they also should serve as a [source] for recruiting people into the revolutionary organizations, . . . and [among them] the "secrecy preservation" movement should be intensified; production increased and self-sufficiency attained; and a social and cultural program for the people should be developed. . . . We should encourage agricultural production, handicrafts, [marketing] cooperatives, and trade. . . . A base is neither a temporary station nor a retreat . . . but is permanent, a flag flying for the Revolution.

The first public NLF references to the liberated area were in vague terms, for example, a report that the NLF's Central Committee had met "at a liberated area somewhere in South Vietnam." Later, specific claims were made, as by Radio Hanoi on January 9, 1964: "Two thirds of Ben Tre [Kien Hoa] province were liberated in 1963. . . . Today 430,000 people out of 636,000 in the province are living under the banner of the NLFSV." In the sense of an autonomous, inviolable region, which the term liberated area connoted, this claim was patently untrue; the NLF definition of a liberated area as used in these broadcasts was that the strategic hamlets of the area had been dismantled. Even then a numbers game was being played; Radio Hanoi on April 13, 1964, for instance, three months after its first report, said: "Within the past

[1] Message from Vo Nguyen Giap, September 2, 1945, quoted in Allan B. Cole, ed., *Conflict in Indochina and International Repercussions: A Documentary History, 1945–1955* (Ithaca, N.Y.: Cornell University Press, 1956), pp. 22–23.

[2] *Hoc Tap*, April 1964.

month 17 more villages in Ben Tre [Kien Hoa] province were liberated.
. . . The liberated area of Ben Tre now comprises 56 villages completely liberated and a large number partially liberated." Liberation, like
virginity, surely cannot be partial.

As early as 1962 both the NLF and the DRV claimed that "three
fourths of the country and half the population have now been liberated,"
and they continued to use the three fourths figure for the next three
years; the figure was also picked up and used without qualification by
segments of the press in the United States and elsewhere, as well as
by persons who, for their own purposes, sought to portray the GVN
plight as more dire than facts warranted. No portion of Vietnam and
certainly nothing approaching three fourths of the country was denied
to the ARVN during this period, and most of the country could be
entered in relative safety by company-sized units.[3] Yet the statement
that "three fourths of Vietnam and half the population have been
liberated by the NLF" continued to be bandied about by persons who
should have defined, but never did, their usage of the term "liberated."

Actually any debate over the liberated versus unliberated area as
an on-off, black-white categorization was unprofitable and unrealistic.
To the NLF a liberated area was an area where it exercised continuing
and predominant social control; this might or might not mean the
presence of GVN officials or military. The area need not be inviolable,
safe, or remote; a letter in Hanoi's *Thu Do* from the NLF's Saigon-
Cholon Special Zone central committee, for example, referred to "the
liberated area in suburban Saigon, . . . which is mopped up several
times each day by enemy troops." Usage of the term here conforms to
the NLF concept: The liberated area consisted of those villages, more
than safe havens for the guerrilla, where the NLF wrought deep and
significant social change.

In certain areas the Viet Minh, and then the NLF, controlled the
lives of the people for nearly two decades in something closely resembling a Communist state. Here and elsewhere — never more than
ten per cent of the villages of the nation — a unique social situation
was created, a quasi-Communist society within a non-Communist one.
Its aims, as indicated by a multitude of internal documents, directives,
and memoranda to cadres, were internal order, external security, mutual
welfare, and class justice, in that order; its economics: collectivism and
socialist competition; its political tools: custom and violence; its cloak
of authority: ceremony and symbolism. Where possible, it used the
strategy of persuasion and rational consent, but these probably would

[3] Partly this was due to the NLF army practice of keeping its guerrilla units, when
not on operations, broken down into small teams and scattered widely. Thus a guerrilla
unit normally would be in no position to oppose the sudden arrival of a good-sized
ARVN unit.

not have sufficed if coercion, or the threat of coercion, had not been ever present. Political obedience came because of villager self-interest and habit, but it also grew out of fear and force. Rural Vietnamese in these areas of long Communist control could remember no other government and regarded the NLF's administration variously with inertia, deference, sympathy, and numbed resignation.

Almost all Vietnamese, including leading Vietnamese sociologists in Saigon, were of the firm opinion that as the result of Viet Minh and then NLF activity, particularly in areas long under their control, deep, significant, and fundamental change had occurred in the social order — markedly in some villages and to some degree in virtually all villages. Unfortunately we know little about the scope and nature of this social change since no outsider, either foreigner or Vietnamese, was able to study objectively, at first hand, and at length a Communist-controlled South Vietnamese village. For that matter, even among GVN secure villages little sociological research has been done in the 1960's. The work by the Michigan State University group[4] stands as the lone exception. However, from talks with *quy chanh,* villagers freed from NLF control during the strategic-hamlet program, and village students coming to Saigon for higher education, it was possible to get a general perspective of the changes taking place, admittedly tentative and full of omissions.

Working in the NLF's interests were the social organizations specifically created by it, chiefly the cell, which provided a very broad and direct form of social control, and the functional liberation associations, which were instruments for launching various mutual-interest projects as well as self-regulating social control mechanisms; also working for it was its highly structured social arrangement, along with an absence of competing social influences. Working against the process were innate rural Vietnamese skepticism and cynicism, resistance to forced group cohesiveness, the constant agitation aimed at whipping up emotions and keeping them at fever pitch, factors common perhaps to all Communist societies; the ever-present threat of demoralization represented by Saigon as an alternative social arrangement; and finally, the rather alien nature of the entire experiment, which amounted to uprooting a whole social condition and replacing it with one transferred from another place and time.

The liberated area may be regarded as a rudimentary society, for it

[4] Whose work appeared for the most part in the form of monographs and preliminary studies, some available from Michigan State University, East Lansing, Michigan. Gerald C. Hickey's *Village in Vietnam* (New Haven, Conn.: Yale University Press, 1964), an excellent work, is virtually the only generally available recent sociological study of the Vietnamese village.

was an organized collection of persons working together and communicating with one another within the framework of a common culture. The community of interests, of course, did not differ greatly from that in villages not under NLF control. Group norms in the two areas apparently were rather dissimilar, although neither the exact degree nor nature was known. Probably it is safe to conclude that the group norm in the liberated area was characterized by a greater sense of equalitarianism, greater social mobility with individual merit counting for more and family for less, and a greater awareness of strata, class consciousness, or social solidarity; in a way, the people of the liberated area were more a social class than a society.

Strong social sanctions — physical, psychological, and economic — were employed to bring deviant members into conformity with the NLF's group norm. The degree of control varied widely; it was determined chiefly by the size of the village, the length of time the NLF had exercised influence, and the viability of the organizations created, largely a reflection of the skills of the cadres. Cohesion, with the possible exception of youthful elements, apparently was low, and group norms could not be maintained in the face of such a threat as the strategic-hamlet building program. Such cohesion as did exist grew from pragmatic or opportunistic reasoning, for example, the villager's conviction that the NLF's tenure in his village was going to be permanent.

To outsiders the NLF portrayed the liberated area as a sort of peaceful, tranquil Shangri-La, where not only hostility but even animosity had vanished. To those living in the area, however, it was a place of urgent tasks, a vast social construction site. There were combat hamlets to be built, food production to be increased, military units to be formed and trained, "national defense" taxes to be paid, and spies to be rooted out. "The liberated area," said one leaflet, "is a sea of flames surrounding the enemy."

The NLF clandestine newspaper *Red Flag,* which circulated in the Central Vietnam area, in October 1964 contained an editorial on the "four tasks to be performed in the liberated area":

1. The masses must be ideologically mobilized by means of education and . . . [agit-prop] activities. Particular attention must be paid to [land tenure] problems. . . . Unity must be strengthened and enlarged in order for the NLFSV to rally more and more people. . . . We must increase our patriotism and undauntedness. . . . The struggle must be heightened.

2. The NLFSV, the various liberation associations, and the PRP Youth League [note lack of mention of PRP itself] must be formed or re-formed so as to contribute to the effort to mobilize the masses. . . . Massively join the revolutionary organizations and consolidate them. . . . Strengthen the ranks of the basic patriotic organizations. . . .

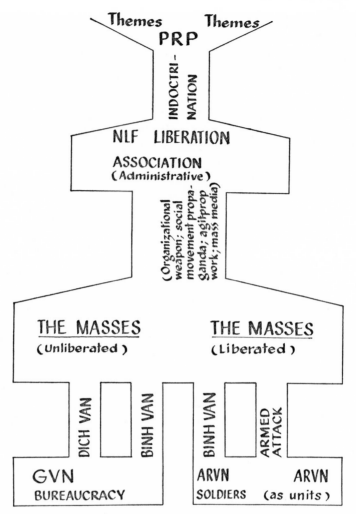

15–1   Functional Plan of the Communist Effort in South Vietnam

3. The combat hamlet system must be developed along with the guerrilla units designed to fight a war of movement. All of us patriots in South Vietnam must realistically take part in the guerrilla war with the most ardent determination to kill the enemies and save the country.

4. Efforts must be made to develop our economic base, as well as the cultural and intellectual life in the liberated area. . . .

It is to these *dan van* activities within the liberated area — the indoctrination system and the methods of organization and administration — that we now turn. (See Charts 15–1 and 15–2.)

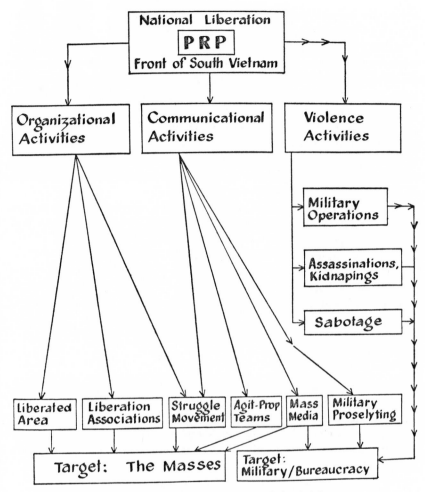

15–2   NLF/PRP Motivational Activities

Indoctrination System

The NLF's indoctrination system in areas under its firm control and in conditions of continuity took three basic directions:

1. The harnessing of social forces — once again, the organizational weapon. What the NLF brought to the Vietnamese village it controlled was order and system; it brought interpretation and the answers to questions, valuable especially to the young; it brought concern for people's problems — some merely apparent, but most of it real. Above all,

it brought organization, and, in the absence of any proper competition, this could not fail to have impact. The design was not an imposed organization as much as a self-imposed one, always rooted in individual self-interest. Each organization, horizontal and vertical, that cut through the village paid off in terms of the individual member, and he came to have a vested interest in it; superimposed on this was the propelling force of indoctrination.

2. Appeals to latent idealism, the traditional attractive element in communism, offering the rural Vietnamese a sense of mission, a means of getting in tune with history, a new path by which he could help the unfortunate of the earth, including himself. It mobilized his best impulses — unfortunately for the worst ultimate ends.

3. Rational appeals to self-interest. The NLF offered the notion that a recognizable relationship should exist between revolutionary zeal and reward, that personal achievement in the struggle for liberation should bring honor, prestige, and status, or more material gains. In many cases this amounted to a virtual bribe; the rural Vietnamese was offered the thing he wanted above all else: land. Around land and on the solution of land tenure problems, the NLF built its indoctrination system.

Land Tenure

"He should own the land who rubs it between his hands each season," runs an ancient Vietnamese proverb, expressing the great hunger that only the landless who work the land can ever fully understand. In a primarily agrarian society such as Vietnam, concern for land and land tenure problems is second only to concern for weather, and the NLF in those areas where land was a major issue, the Mekong delta and the coastal lowlands, made full use of it. Declared a *Red Flag* editorial, "satisfactorily solving the land problem of the peasants . . . is a way of mobilizing the people in the liberated area to participate in the struggle for, and protection of, the Revolution, . . . a means of mobilizing the masses in the oppressed areas to rise up . . . and liberate themselves." Cadres were instructed to turn every issue into land terms. The strategic hamlet was portrayed as a technique for depriving farmers of land (the land on which the village was built) or a means of swindling farmers out of good land in exchange for bad. Cadres asserted that the GVN represented the rich landlords and pursued a false land reform scheme; that GVN land taxes were unreasonable; that the "U.S.-Diem clique confiscated millions of hectares of the best rice land for military purposes such as building military bases."

The NLF began its administrative approach with respect to land by continuing the Viet Minh land redistribution program, which had caused some five thousand hectares (11,000 acres) of paddy land belonging to absentee landlords or to the French to be deeded to local Vietnamese.

The general direction and philosophy of NLF land administration policies were outlined in detail in a Long An province NLF central committee directive, dated May 1963 but apparently based on earlier NLF documents:

> Our policy is . . . to reduce land rents and ensure the ownership of land by the peasants, . . . to give back to the peasants land received during the Resistance and later stolen from them by the U.S.-Diem clique or reactionary landowners. . . . The Front does not consider rich peasants as landowners . . . but maintains a coalition policy toward them if they reduce rents for [their] tenants. . . . It respects the rights of middle-class peasants . . . , respects the lands of convents, pagodas, and temples . . . , respects the rights of landowners in the cities to collect rents in the rural areas, and, further, their ownership [title] is recognized. . . . With respect to land owned by the tyrannical and reactionary landlords who closely support the U.S.-Diem clique, we lead the peasants in their drive to refuse to pay land rent. With respect to those landlords who more or less support the Revolution we continue to recognize their ownership rights but lead the struggle of the farmers to obtain rent reductions according to a flexible rate that suits the present situation. . . . Rent . . . on good land whose output is 15 to even 30 bushels [per hectare] shall not exceed a maximum rate of $1\frac{1}{2}$ bushels. Just because the peasant works hard and increases his yield does not mean that a high rent charge is justified. . . . When yield is less than 15 bushels a reasonable rent rate to struggle for should be determined in discussion with the peasant involved. . . . If the rice field has been transformed into a garden the rent rate should be 10 to 25 per cent of the yearly yield or income. . . .

The program sought to serve the Vietnamese farmer by providing him with land, but under circumstances that were, by GVN standards, illegal. Thus the farmer accepting NLF land became enmeshed in the NLF socioeconomic structure. He came to have a vested interest in the NLF's success. In short, the land he worked itself became an indoctrinational device. The land distribution system was pressed until by the end of 1964 the DRV could claim that "the peasants in the areas under NLFSV control have become masters of more than 1.3 million hectares (3.2 million acres) of South Vietnam's total 3.5 million hectares (8.6 million acres) of cultivated land. . . ."[5]

Specifically the expropriation and redistribution of land consisted of, first, confiscation of "all land belonging to the imperialists and their

[5] The DRV's figures on South Vietnamese land totals appear to be in error. The GVN in 1964 reported that South Vietnam had 17,166,400 hectares of land, 40 per cent of which was in the Mekong delta and the Massif Plain, 32 per cent in the coastal lowlands of Central Vietnam, and 28 per cent in the highlands. Of this only 16 per cent, or 2,785,000 hectares, was under cultivation; and of the cultivated land 84 per cent, or 2,353,000 hectares, was rice paddy; rubber totaled about 100,000 hectares.

agents," a vague category subject to varying local interpretations, and subsequent distribution of such land to local farmers; or, second, the purchase from "patriotic" landlords of a portion of their holdings, "the amount left to them for cultivation to be determined by the local situation," with the land so purchased also turned over to local farmers. In either case the farmer received the land, usually at ceremonies during which impressive looking land "titles" were handed over, at no cost to him; obviously this was a better land reform system than the GVN system that required that land be purchased.

The first action — seizing land held by the enemy — presented the NLF with no internal problems; the second did. The "rich landowner" was an enemy, the "patriotic landlord" was not, and the effort to distinguish between the two often was not easy. The "patriotic landlord" was one with whom the NLF still hoped to do business; generally he was not an absentee landlord but a well-to-do farmer who worked some of his land and rented out the rest. Every effort was made not to alienate him; often he was allowed to keep all of his land, providing he charged only "reasonable" rents. Below him, economically, was the "average" farmer who owned and worked his own land, and below him was the "poor," or landless, farmer. Said an early NLF document on NLF land policies:

> The agrarian problem is very complex . . . and we must be careful and realistic in order to avoid mistakes. There must be close unity between the poor and the average farmers. While trying to meet the needs of the poor farmers, we must absolutely avoid encroaching upon the rights of the average farmer by taking his land for distribution to poor farmers. . . . In instances where the rights of average farmers have been encroached upon but not seriously, it is better not to try to readjust the situation but acknowledge the mistake and promise not to encroach upon their rights . . . again. If their rights have been seriously encroached upon, we should remedy the situation in a tactful manner with a view to consolidating the unity among the farmers. . . .

The instructions continued:

> With regard to poor farmers, in addition to the distribution of land in areas where feasible, we should help them improve their land and increase production. Promote solidarity and mutual assistance among farmers so they help one another with funds, seeds, and thus combat usury. Among average and poor farmers build up unity. . . . With regard to rich farmers, continue to protect their economic interests, . . . using indoctrinational means to lessen their apathy for our cause. . . . With regard to landlords who are not wicked agents of the enemy, we will continue to recognize their right to collect rent but will force them to reduce rents. . . .

The effort to drive rents down was aimed at increasing the NLF's influence among tenant farmers. It played a larger role in the early days when the NLF pursued its three-point land policy; reduction of rents, confiscation of land, and purchase of land, a policy largely supplanted after 1963 by the two-point policy just described — confiscation and purchase. On a local level the NLF arbitrated land disputes and attempted to "solve logically" the various problems raised by uncertain land titles, one of the most serious land tenure problems in South Vietnam, which resulted from originally inaccurate survey work, loss of landownership records because of war's destruction, or disputes among relatives following the death of a landowning member of the family.

The NLF did not challenge the right of rural Vietnamese to own and rent land, a fact that created among the more orthodox Marxists a belief that the policy was bourgeois, not sufficiently revolutionary, and a denial of the long-employed slogan "Land for the tillers." To meet such arguments the PRP issued a land policy statement, later republished by *Nhan Dan* on January 1, 1965, which argued that the NLF land policy was not nonrevolutionary and anyway was a necessary tactic:

Our Party's agrarian policy is to eliminate radically all oppression and exploitation in the countryside, liberate the peasant, and fulfill the slogan "Land for the tillers." This is the revolutionary position of the proletariat. . . . We still must rally the forces of various strata and classes of the people in order that the Revolution will succeed. Therefore the slogan must be fulfilled in accordance with existing circumstances and requirements of the Revolution. . . . However, certainly in the end, the slogan "Land for the tillers" will be fulfilled. . . . The alliance among the poor, middle-class, and wealthy peasants to destroy the landlord class . . . is just and rational.

An ominous indication of future collectivist land policies concluded the statement:

Due to the existing conditions of the resistance struggle, the South cannot yet organize the peasants for the collective mode of doing business on a large scale and under perfect forms. Yet this does not mean we cannot organize new modes of doing business that bear a collective character. . . . This is a major requirement in the countryside. . . .

However, if the rural Vietnamese were to benefit from the land programs, he was also expected to support the NLF by means of "rice taxes" that went directly to NLF cadres. Since increased production meant increased income for the NLF, an intensive effort was made to boost agricultural yields. The campaign that resulted, the well-known collectivist device called the emulation movement, not only fattened the NLF's coffers but also served as a second indoctrinational device to increase ideological support and commitment to the cause.

The Emulation Movement

An old Communist society device, the emulation movement was a short-run intensive mobilization effort for some specific purpose, developed chiefly among farmers, and designed to increase agricultural production, heighten revolutionary vigilance against spies, or to help solve any other specific problem faced at the moment by the leadership. An internal document described the emulation campaign as "an essential and patriotic means of producing achievements that accelerate the Revolution." It listed the major types of emulation in the liberated area as production, frugality, elimination of waste, fund drives, anti-illiteracy, guerrilla band enlistment, *binh van,* and training. The campaigns could pit individual against individual, cell against cell, village against village, organization against organization or, within the village, one liberation association against another liberation association, management section against management section, or executive committee against executive committee. The outcome was judged by a representative from the next higher echelon, who awarded proper public recognition and often more material rewards. *Quy chanh* indicated that one of the fastest means by which a cadre could increase status or win promotion was to perform some remarkable achievement during an emulation movement.

The first major emulation campaign was the Ap Bac emulation movement, named after the NLF army victory in the Plain of Reeds south of Saigon in January 1963. The movement began within the guerrilla units. The NLF Central Committee in March 1963 made the following announcement: "An Ap Bac emulation banner . . . will rotate among the outstanding guerrilla units, and at the end of the three-month campaign the unit that has accomplished the most exploits in emulating Ap Bac will be permanently awarded the banner." At the same time it announced that "a series of gifts have been reserved for organizations and individuals that accomplish political struggle movement exploits during the campaign, . . . struggles against the strategic-hamlet program, . . . the intensification and widening of the aggressive war, . . . and the spraying of poisonous chemicals. . . ."

An NLF publication called the *Military and Administrative Magazine* in November 1963 contained an article entitled "The Ap Bac Emulation Drive," written by one Le Truc, in which the NLF army goals in the second phase of the Ap Bac emulation movement were listed as:

1. All units must vie with each other in fulfilling the main tasks of the Liberation Army, . . . exterminating the enemy, destroying strategic hamlets, and stepping up the guerrilla war. . . .
2. It is necessary to single out and praise . . . the role and responsibility

of leading officers and unit commanders . . . who understand their missions, . . . correct their mistakes, . . . and overcome all difficulties. . . .

3. Special attention must be paid to the problems of thoughts. . . . Our combatants are good men. . . . They are credulous, activist, and receptive to new ways, and thus are easily mobilized. . . . However, because of their low political knowledge and changeable character, they must be carefully educated and constantly reminded. . . . If not, our work cannot be consolidated or long lasting. . . . Further, officers have often failed to mingle with the masses. . . . They must realize their responsibilities in this direction.

4. It is necessary to improve the technical capabilities of the basic cadres . . . who have not improved themselves during past drives, . . . who did not accept leadership roles, . . . who haphazardly took part in the emulation campaign. . . .

5. The emulation drive is the duty of all people and combatants. All persons in units or organs must join the drive. But, since our leadership capacity is limited, we must concentrate our activities on basic combat units . . . and on units that are relatively homogeneous, such as [manufacturing] workshops and construction sites, . . . and later expand the drive to include . . . emulation in study, . . . emulation in attending meetings, and finally . . . comprehensive emulation. . . . In short if we are to succeed in the emulation drive we must move step by step.

In tone, direction, phases of activities, statements of goals, ultimate rewards, in all ways, the NLF emulation campaign corresponded to the well-known Communist institution, the socialist competition campaign, such as the stakhanovite movement of the Soviet Union.

Education

Educational activities within the liberated area were distinguished from indoctrination in terms of organization but not content. "Education in the liberated area," said one directive,

differs completely from the enslaving and brain-clogging education under the U.S. and its henchmen. . . . Pupils . . . are educated to show industriousness in study and labor and to take an active part in the struggle movement. . . . Students are taught to love the Fatherland and to combine study with productive labor and class struggle. . . . Contributions to the Revolution are part of the class work. . . . In Can Tho province pupils in one school made 30,000 bamboo spikes, set 40 booby traps, laid two bamboo long-spike fields against helicopters, and planted 80 banana trees . . . as part of an emulation drive. . . .

The NLF opened or seized from the GVN numerous elementary schools, three to six grades; adult education classes usually called the mass education program; supplementary cultural schools; one normal school (established in September 1963 to train NLF teachers); and special cadre classes, as, for example, a six-month course in English for NLF representatives going abroad. Tran Thanh Nam, described as an "NLF member in charge of education in the South," possibly a DRV official, was quoted by Radio Hanoi in December 1963 as saying that "40 to 70 per cent of the children in the liberated area are now in school." The NLF claimed 1,500 elementary and adult education classes in operation in April 1963, and 3,000 (with 200,000 students) in April 1964. The Patriotic Teachers' Association of South Vietnam, headed by Le Van Huan, a former Saigon secondary-school teacher, was formed at what was called an educational congress in May 1964, with a 30-man executive committee named to administer the curricula in the liberated area and apparently also as a control device over the teachers. The committee also aided in the printing of textbooks, usually twenty- or thirty-page mimeographed texts, which were frequently found during ARVN operations into remote areas of the country. Elementary education consisted of the more or less standard Vietnamese reading-writing-arithmetic, with built-in revolutionary morality.

The GVN Ministry of Education (in 1964) estimated that 40 per cent of all Vietnamese, and probably 20 per cent of all rural Vietnamese, were literate enough to read a Saigon newspaper with ease. Adult education with primary emphasis on reading and arithmetic was therefore stressed as part of the NLF indoctrination program.[6]

A handbook dated mid-1961 said that "teachers are to be chosen from among the young men and women of the area, members of the Lao Dong Youth League, and others who understand the need to promote class consciousness. . . . When teachers cannot make their own living, that is, who teach full time, the people must be persuaded to support them." Another handbook for teachers of adult education courses, dated 1963, said the program consisted of three calendar years of study, with classes meeting six times a week, at night, for two to three hours per session. The curricula, it said, "must be clear and concise, for adults are busy and have many responsibilities. . . . The program should provide students, the majority of whom are farmers, with knowledge that will help them in their daily lives, will help them understand the views and policies of the Party and the Front, and will enable them to fulfill their political missions." The study of Vietnamese, or *quoc van,* formed 60 per cent of the three-year course (of this, 40 per cent was reading, 40 per cent political study, and 20 per cent composition); arithmetic 30 per cent; and history, geography, or hygiene the remaining 10 per cent. "In the *quoc van* course," said the handbook, "start with the *van quoc ngu* [the ABC

---

[6] Said Radio Liberation, June 30, 1964:

Compatriots attend classes and spend evenings in school. They get up very early the next morning and light torches and read over their lessons before returning to their fields. . . . In some cases, classes are held at siesta time in the fields. . . .

Book], . . . teaching up to 80 new words per lesson. Teach words that relate to daily work and our present revolutionary task, such as 'unity, . . . production, . . . struggle, . . . and so forth.' . . . Aim to teach correct and good writing. . . . By the end of the year students should be able to write short sentences. . . . In the second year teach how to read fluently and with correct accents. . . . At the end of the year students should be able to write short descriptions of persons and events, easy narratives, and short letters and reports. At the end of the third year, students should be able to write from dictation and should be able to write full reports, letters, and narratives." The 20 lessons, each of which was a small mimeographed book, resembled in content the GVN and Buddhist adult education courses except that they were more heavily interlarded with Marxist thought. The text for the third year *quoc van*, for instance, listed 20 types of writing that a student should be able to handle. The five chief ones were reports, letters, narratives (including chronological accounts, dialogue, and static scene descriptions), minutes of meetings, and poetry. Typical sample assignments that might be given the students for homework included these:

Recently you took part in a night assignment planting bamboo spikes along a river bank. Describe the event and your impressions. . . . You helped sabotage a road. Describe and give your impressions. . . . You participated in a successful struggle movement against a U.S.-Diem outpost. Describe . . . a typical military clash between the people's forces and some U.S.-Diem raiders. . . . Describe a May Day celebration in your village. . . . The barbarous U.S.-Diem have shot to death one of your compatriots. Subsequently you went to the victim's funeral. Describe your feelings. . . . Write a letter to an enemy soldier or civil servant who is your relative. . . . Write a report on a struggle movement, a popular education class meeting, or a visit by a district cadre to your village. . . . Write a typical minutes of a Farmers' Liberation Association meeting. . . .

"In mathematics," said the handbook,

teach only practical matters. . . . Lessons should be related to production, the economy, mutual assistance, and contributions to the Revolution. . . . Follow the rule: Learn little well, practice much. . . . History should stress the heroes of the Resistance, the origin of the Vietnamese people, the struggle against Northern [Chinese] domination, and the feudalist and colonialist periods. . . . Geography should deal with the local area, with Vietnam, and with the world, with special attention paid to Southeast Asia and the socialist countries.

The Utility of Hatred

If there was an essence of the NLF indoctrination effort, if there was an *élan vital* that permeated its system, if there was one emotion the leadership found of greater utility than all others combined, if there was any personality trait that differentiated the Vietnamese of the two camps, indeed if one were obliged to write the history of the NLF in a single word, it would be *hate*. Every NLF act was surrounded by an aura of hate. The struggle movement, with its unspoken theme that there were no neutrals, only friends and enemies, attempted to lash villagers into frenzies of hate. The indoctrination system decreed that the best cadres were those with the greatest capacity for hate. "To guide the masses toward the Revolution, the agit-prop arm must make the masses hate the enemy," declared a Central Committee directive, "building on the hatred that already exists." The cadre document added:

The American imperialists dominate the South in a new form of colonialism, vicious and cruel. The Diem regime is cruel, terroristic; it is responsible for killing, raping, looting, drafting people into corvée labor and the army. All this has fostered hatred among the masses. Agit-prop workers must further arouse hatred. . . . Promotion of hatred must be permanent, continuous, and directly related to the struggle movement as closely as a man is to his shadow.

Cadres were criticized for their failure to exploit the emotion:

In many areas the people have won victories and forced the enemy to be less repressive. Cadres in these areas have tended to be self-satisfied with their records and less eager to continue promoting hatred among the masses, and thus . . . the Revolution does not boil and remain violent.

Specific instructions detailed the basic approach:

Hatred can be promoted by rallies for the "denunciation of poverty." [7] Persuade victims to stand up and tell their stories in front of the masses in strong language. This method is very successful. At Vinh Ninh village, Cho Gao district, and at the Hau May and May Phuoc Tay Agrovilles we used the denunciation of poverty method to promote much hate and to induce tens of thousands of the masses to struggle violently against the enemy. . . . Denunciation of enemy crimes is another way to promote hatred, especially instances of pregnant women being raped or children and babies being killed. . . . Make a list of all the sufferings at the hands of the enemy suffered by one family or a hamlet or village during the past few years. The length of the list will impress the masses. . . . Specific objects are useful in promoting hatred. The objects left behind by the enemy, such as a mortar shell or bomb fragment that killed a family, can be displayed at rallies and will promote hatred to the utmost. A corpse is very good to demonstrate the unjust cause of the enemy. When using a corpse give the name, age, date of death, etc. of the victim; look for sad details of his life that can be put to good use. If possible, photograph the corpse so that the pictures can be shown throughout the country and abroad. . . .

[7] In Vietnamese, *to kho*, to denounce poverty, that is, the rich landowners and reactionary elements; apparently a direct copy of the Chinese Communist institution.

The only limitation placed on the use of atrocity themes to promote hatred was not to carry them so far as to induce fear. Said the cadre directive:

In promoting hatred, also praise the victories of the Liberation Army and the revolutionary abilities of the masses, for this shores up the will to struggle for revenge. Talking only about the crimes of the enemy may serve to frighten the people, and thus the effort will be betrayed.

Apparently the effort by the NLF was an attempt to copy the Chinese, who deliberately, efficiently, and effectively had put hate to work. Lucian Pye noted that "no other political culture places as much stress upon the emotion of hate as does the Chinese." [8] Pye found that hate had potency in China partly because of the country's historical evolution through modern times, that is, a China universally humiliated and taken advantage of; partly because of a peculiar pattern of Chinese political socialization in the last two generations; and partly for purely pragmatic reasons, for example, the Chinese Communist belief that nothing much could be accomplished in the way of nation building unless the passions of the people were stirred, or the leaders' use of hate as a temporary substitute for more positive policies. To some degree all of these factors were present in Vietnam; hate did serve as an energizer as did no other emotion or appeal.[9]

[8] Lucian W. Pye, *The Dynamics of Hostility and Hate in Chinese Political Culture* (Cambridge, Mass.: Massachusetts Institute of Technology, Center for International Studies, 1964).
[9] An illustration of the hatred theme is a short story by Che Lan Vien, entitled *Sparkling Fires in the South*, that was widely distributed in South Vietnam in pamphlet form. It is reproduced in Appendix E.

16

The Liberated Area: Administration

The indoctrination system, based on vested interest in land and given periodic adrenalin shots through the emulation movement and the generation of hatred, sought to create a self-ordered liberated area. That this was never achieved was abundantly evident from the leadership's preoccupation with those conditions and developments that it lumped together in internal memoranda as counterrevolutionary tendencies, by which was meant any deviation by individuals under NLF control or any internally generated or supported threat to the system, which represented the major administrative problems.

Administrative Principles

A number of NLF administrative practices were apparent in the NLF documents examined, the more significant of which were:

1. In policy determination and execution the principle followed was great centralization in planning and policymaking — almost all of it at

the national Central Committee level — and great decentralization in policy execution; great latitude was granted to provincial and even village committees in adapting general directives to local circumstances.

2. In division of labor the functional structure consisted of (a) the highest level for planning and supervision of the organization-building work; (b) the interzone level for training, indoctrination, and policy guidance for agit-prop activities, that is, determination of themes and appeals; (c) an administrative level at provincial headquarters that translated directives into operational plans and had at its call various specialists in fund raising, agit-prop campaigns, penetration of non-Communist organizations (such as the Buddhist groups), and experts in intelligence, sabotage, and terror.

3. The operational area was almost exclusively rural, following the Chinese model, with an administrative structure deliberately excluding the major cities of Saigon-Cholon, Da Nang, and Hué; even at the lower echelons, as at the provincial level, special units were set up to work in the larger provincial cities such as Can Tho and Nha Trang.

4. For recruitment the NLF was interested only in the young. Interviews with *quy chanh* indicated a strong pattern of recruiting the 16 to 20 age group first, the 21 to 25 age group second, and little interest was shown in those over 25 unless they demonstrated some special talent.

5. Administrative behavior was so structured as to suggest legality and legitimate government.

Administration in the liberated area, above all else, was an effort to create and maintain a population devoid of disenchantment, immune to GVN influence, and in fact hostile to any anti-NLF activity regardless of source. Beyond this, of course, the NLF was faced with the normal problems of government. The ideal toward which administrators were expected to dedicate themselves was spelled out in a 1962 document:

Our responsibility in the liberated area is to gather the people and rule them; to strengthen them politically, militarily, economically, socially, and culturally; to establish order and security; to improve the people's morality and material living conditions; to intensify the struggle against the enemy; . . . to mobilize manpower and resources so as to develop the revolutionary forces . . . and lay the foundations for a new political system. . . . The people will administer themselves in hamlets and villages, with no hierarchic form of administration used, for this is the most suitable administrative method in a political and armed struggle that is without delimited boundaries [that is, without a front line]. . . . In the delta the Front committee, or if there is no Front committee, the Farmers' Liberation Association central committee, is responsible for administration. . . . Party members within the associations will be cadres. . . . Avoid creation of unrealistic organizations.

The chief "unrealistic organization" was the hollow, *pro forma* village liberation committee made up of apathetic villagers, satisfied that their land tenure problems had been settled and indifferent to the Revolution, going through the motions of the struggle for the benefit of visiting cadres. The cadres themselves often were susceptible to the lure of inertia. A *Red Flag* editorial in October 1964 warned cadres: "It is necessary to develop strong organizations and not be content merely with 'beating the drums to call the masses to come and sign their names on a petition' as has so often been the case in the past." The villagers' attitude toward the administrator — and it was not confined to the villagers alone but ran well up into the ranks of the cadres — stemmed from the traditional Vietnamese attitude toward government: Bad government was hated, good government was regarded as somewhat better, but by far the best was no government, or government that never impinged on the individual's daily activities. When the cadres' "drums were sounded," the rural Vietnamese without too much pressure would come forward and sign a petition that someone else could deliver to the district chief. But any request beyond such a token gesture was likely to be greeted with indifference, well-reasoned excuses, or, even worse, hostility — in any case, counterrevolutionary tendencies.

One of the means employed by the NLF to overcome this attitude was to recruit as village liberation association committee chairmen the most prestigious persons in the village, around whom it would build, especially in the combat hamlet, a net of hard-core true believers. The village administrative liberation committee and those close to it were expected to act as "patriotic and vigilant citizens," that is, as watchers and informers on their neighbors, reporting heresy to the cadre section at the district level. The NLF during this period found it beyond its capability to establish a vast secret police system and so sought to use the committee to police the village; and through it insinuating to the rural Vietnamese that it was omnipresent, probably omniscient, and usually omnipotent.

Authority and Adjudication

An effort was made to handle questions of authority and later of adjudication with a degree of rationality — with more rationality in the latter than in the former. Authority assertion was essentially negative, denying the GVN access to the people, denying it had a right to access. A mid-1962 document described the NLF's perception of the threat to its authority and its response:

The enemy sends infiltrators to undermine the solidarity of the masses . . . [who] contact residual elements in the villages still supporting the enemy in a reactionary manner. . . . We must develop counterrevolutionary policies that are sound and specific, which aim at educating and reforming the backward and erring elements and chastizing their leaders. . . . But we should be very cautious in making arrests, . . . and people should have no misgivings or dissatisfaction with our method of arrest, investigation, and final judgment.

Another document, mid-1963, added:

Basically, the task of counterrevolutionary activities must be assigned to the village [administrative] liberation association or to the Farmers' Liberation Association. . . . But all the people must oppose the spies and enemies among us and not just the cadres or a few individuals.

Several internal documents listed the potentially dangerous elements of whom the villagers should beware:

former GVN officials, such as ex-village administrators and cadres still living in the villages, former members of the National Revolutionary Movement or the Can Lao,[1] former soldiers; . . . persons who have been in enemy jails; . . . those who are dissatisfied with the Revolution or have been punished by us in disciplinary actions; . . . those with relatives working with the enemy; . . . disloyal [ethnic] Cambodians; . . . people enamored of peace; . . . superstitious people; . . . erratic landowners; . . . people blinded by money, beauty, or offers of position; people with a grudge against the Revolution; vagrants, alcoholics, and thieves. . . .

The liberated area took on the character of a spy novel, filled with agents and counteragents and double agents. NLF documents warned cadres of an endless number of GVN stratagems and devices: Doctors, teachers, midwives, tailors, merchants, and others whose occupations took them into the countryside and were not generally molested by the NLF could be and often were GVN agents contacting anti-NLF persons. A sugar-cane cart, the Vietnamese equivalent of the "Good Humor" wagon, often was a police agent radio. Agents were infiltrated into strategic hamlets in the process of destruction; they then returned "home" with the villagers and became spies within the newly established combat hamlet. Letters and personal visits from pro-GVN relatives to rural areas were contact methods. Blackmail and outright threat were common. Villagers were bought off with money or by taking advantage of a weakness for gambling, alcohol, or women. One document cited the example of a landlord's daughter who attended a "spy school" in Saigon, returned to her village, and publicly "confessed" her error and pleaded forgiveness. She was "pardoned by the people," married an important NLF cadre, and was later caught dispatching a sheaf of her husband's secret documents to Saigon. The GVN often sent its agents into villages

---

[1] A quasi-political party, powerful during the Diem administration; it was semicovert, organized something like the Communist party (the three-man cell system was employed, for example); members reported directly to Ngo Dinh Nhu, the president's brother. It was disbanded in late 1963.

disguised as NLF cadres, and sometimes whole military units would go on patrol dressed as NLF army units. Villagers sold information to agents of both sides. Duplicity became the norm, distrust the rule for survival.

Beyond the secret agent, the NLF faced the activities of the indigenous enemy,

those villagers who cause division among us by creating disputes over land-holdings, who lie about the Front's religious policies, who revive old Viet-namese hatreds for the Cambodians, . . . who seek out a cadre's shortcom-ings and deliberately raise these at public meetings so that the cadre loses the confidence of the people, . . . those who spread false news, . . . who are defeatist and warn of danger of arrest or death during struggle move-ments, . . . who criticize work teams or indoctrination courses, . . . who sabotage the struggle movement by shouting extremist slogans to give cause to the enemy to take violent action against demonstrators, . . . who organize an underground village administration and speak of . . . an antigovernment, anti-Front government.

Increased indoctrination efforts, the cadres were told, were the chief defense against such activities. One village plagued by covert anti-NLF activities launched a six-point campaign "to counter the counterrevolu-tionaries." Study meetings were organized by the liberation associations at which "we explained the enemy's evil ways and bad motives." A series of dramas stressed the theme of class consciousness and the need for class solidarity. A secrecy preservation campaign was launched, which included plastering the village with "three no" posters (no knowing, no seeing, no hearing). A watch system was devised to follow all strangers coming to the village, and a secret system was established to "put all reactionary elements in the village under surveillance and help educate and reform them." A drive was launched against "cadres who are dis-satisfied or who show passiveness in their work"; they were "not per-mitted to express their grievances or complaints at meetings, . . . were boldly and determinedly criticized by fellow cadres, and were reminded daily of their bad actions. . . . This did not have any effect on some of them, and they were then reported to higher headquarters, which was asked to cope with them." Finally, a campaign was launched designed to persuade the villagers "to ignore false news about the defeats of the Liberation Army and other enemy lies about the Revolution." Another document outlined a "spy annihilation campaign." It said:

Along the paths through Thanh Son village antispy slogans are hung. In people's homes and in restaurants the slogan is posted: "The walls have ears: Guard classified information." . . . When any person reveals classified in-formation he is warmly and constructively criticized by others. When a stranger enters the village he is closely watched by the people. . . . In Ben Tre seven fishermen were arrested by the enemy and forced to turn spy, but when they returned to their village they immediately reported to local cadres.

A security section at the interzone level was responsible for counter-intelligence and security matters. It also acted as a sort of CID or detective division to handle crimes committed either within the NLF ranks, such as theft of funds, or within the areas closely controlled by the NLF. Two other law-enforcement systems helped to administer justice. At each provincial central committee headquarters, and possibly at other levels, a protection assistant (*tro ly bao ve*) policed the headquarters staff. He was concerned primarily with cases of malfeasance in office, corruption, and bribery. The village Farmers' Liberation Associations handled, on a quasi-judicial basis, what might be called civil cases — disputes over land titles, for example. The village liberation association in secure areas handled minor or petty crimes something in the manner of a police court, but crime of this sort was rare in the Vietnamese village.

Recruitment

Second in importance to security measures to the NLF administrative cadre were efforts to strengthen the organizational structure, including the continuous task of recruitment. The process of shoring up weak organizations and increasing membership rolls was outlined in a 1962 document:

First, the management section [*ban can su*] from the district or provincial central committee makes a census of the village, listing the names of the people and their motivations. (The census sheet should include: the name and age of each person by family; the class of each person, that is, very poor, poor, middle class, rich, landlord, or professional; the number of members in the Farmers' Liberation Association; village acreage, including total land, land under cultivation, and land not under cultivation; crop yields for the past year, including total rice produced, amount of rice sold, amount retained by farmers, total money earned, and, if appropriate, total rice purchased by villagers.) Then the management section establishes the proper ratio of association members to nonmembers, which should range from 20 to 50 per cent. Then it inspects the cell system. From these inspections will come a picture as to which hamlets of the village are weak. Recruitment will then be done in these hamlets. . . . A list of names based on a survey of sympathizers and potential new members will be drawn up by the cell leaders. Those selected will be contacted and, if willing to join, will first be given some task to prove themselves. Then a meeting will debate their actions, and those who performed well will be invited to join.

Recruitment, particularly recruitment into the guerrilla units, often, if not normally, involved manipulation of family ties. The sense of collective familial guilt common to Sinoized societies, in which all members of the family share the guilt of any member's act — and traditionally were so punished — served the NLF well. If one member of a family could be recruited, recruiting other members became infinitely easier. Most of the infiltrators from the DRV, especially in the early days of the NLF, returned to their home villages, contacted their relatives, and sought their support. Family loyalty almost always meant that the infiltrator would not be reported to the GVN; to do so would have brought disgrace upon the family, first because one member was disloyal, and second because the family itself was a betrayer. The avoidance of military draft delivered not only the draft dodger into the NLF ranks but his family as well. The young man had no place to go and hence remained with the NLF; over his family hung the constant threat that he would be turned over to the GVN. Most effective of all family manipulation devices was the double hostage system. A young man would be enlisted, often by force, in the guerrilla ranks and taken to serve in a distant part of the country. He would be warned that unless he served well his family would suffer reprisals by the NLF; his family was forced to serve the NLF in struggle movements or by supplying local guerrillas with food, shelter, information, and money on pain of punishment to their son. Only infrequently would the son and his family be able to contact each other and arrange for a joint, timed departure, he from his guerrilla unit and the family from the village, meeting at some secure rendezvous.

The Combat Hamlet

Since the liberated area had meaning only insofar as it was equated with NLF continuance and permanency, clandestine *présence* eventually had to be supplanted by a more concrete symbol. Such a symbol was the combat hamlet.

"Areas in which the enemy's oppressive administration has been smashed and in which the masses have been organized into associations," said a 1964 document, "but which have not yet constructed combat hamlets cannot call themselves 'liberated' . . . nor can a village that has [NLF] control but still is not a combat hamlet call itself 'liberated.'" The GVN, it said, must be denied entry, and this required defensive military measures, the combat hamlet, a strategic hamlet in reverse. The document continued:

The first task in creating a combat hamlet is to drive out the enemy's civilian agents and liberate the village. . . . The next task of the liberated village is to prepare for the return of the enemy so as not to fall under the enemy like a fish on a chopping block. . . . The two key activities of a combat hamlet are . . . forming liberation associations to support the armed struggle . . . and indoctrination. Together these two serve to lead the hamlet, guide each person in the defense effort, and raise his determination not to let the enemy wrest away our achievements. . . .

The document advised the establishment of a hamlet construction committee. It was to consist of a chairman; a military affairs representative, often a covert PRP member who would act as liaison with local guerrilla or NLF army units; a *binh van* cadre; and an administrative secretary. Added the document, "One cell in each village shall be keeper of the arms. . . . Each hamlet is to manufacture firearms, land mines, and foot spikes." The close liaison with the guerrillas was required, it said, because "guerrilla units have a major task in helping to construct combat hamlets."

The combat hamlet's defenses closely resembled those of the strategic hamlet. One memorandum reported that "the hearts of everyone are filled with grim determination as they prepare mantraps, sharpen bamboo spikes, lay mines. . . . The people realize their task is to defend the combat hamlet by . . . defeating enemy raids, working closely with the guerrilla units, . . . and, by working internally, to punish hooligans and spies in our midst. . . ." A fanciful description of a combat hamlet was provided by Radio Hanoi, September 24, 1963, apparently referring to a hamlet in the highlands:

The weapons and fortification may look simple, but they are dreadful in the eyes of the enemy. Outside the village is a thick fence with bamboo stakes planted everywhere. . . . It appears to have no defenses, nothing to divide it from the area around. Yet if the enemy takes a step toward it, . . . pointed lances will dart toward them. A rain of arrows follows. The frightened enemy jumps right and left to avoid stepping on spiked mantraps. A bunch of bananas on a tree looks tasteful to the hungry raiders, but if they touch them, dozens of spears fly into their faces. . . . There are 50 varieties of such traps, and each combat hamlet has many.

Administration in the combat hamlet carried one step further the semi-autonomous, multifaceted administrative system of the NLF command structure (described in Chapter 12). The village administrative committee, the functional Front organizations, and the paramilitary guerrilla teams were consolidated into a single administrative committee under which there were special committees for tending to the wounded, handling supplies, doing hygiene work, and carrying on educational and cultural activities. Distinctly a new organizational entity in the combat hamlet was the mutual-aid team, a sort of rudimentary collective described as a "voluntary labor brigade" suggesting the "red-ant" collectivization of Communist China. Radio Liberation claimed that "in some villages 80 to 90 per cent of the villagers have joined mutual-aid teams."

On December 20, 1964, *Nhan Dan* said that "collective farming is now practiced in the liberated area, enabling youths to enlist in the Liberation Army. . . ." Digging drainage and irrigation ditches represented another chief task of the teams: "In the first six months of 1964 compatriots dug over 200,000 yards of canals to drain off stagnant water and to bring fresh water to rice fields. . . . The canal digging plan is now ahead of schedule." This sort of collectivization represented by the mutual-aid team, one internal document stressed, should be gradual and voluntary; it added:

Gradually organize the people into collectives, first small and then large. . . . Collectives must indoctrinate and mobilize the people and develop their spirit for joint [cooperative] projects. Compulsion must not be used to force people to join collectives; they should be so exemplary that all people will wish to join them.

Cultural and athletic activities formed another side of life in the combat hamlet. Each hamlet was expected to develop theatrical, dance, and classical opera groups and to write and produce productions under the general supervision of the local Cultural Liberation Association. Information halls were also standard institutions in the combat hamlet but were essentially part of the communication pattern.

Medical Care

Medical care, an obvious morale factor, received considerable attention in the liberated area, although it remained a crude affair even by Vietnamese standards. Each combat hamlet was expected to maintain a medical-aid station, which consisted of an elaborate first-aid kit (valued at an estimated U.S. $50) manned by a first-aid cadre, usually a woman; the hamlet also maintained one or more midwives, a traditional figure in rural Vietnam.

The guerrilla bands in the early days even attempted to provide treatment and care for the wounded and sick but were handicapped by the lack of nearby fixed installations. Often a wounded man was left in the care of a sympathetic villager, who buried him if he died or sent him on to his unit if he recovered. Later, medical corpsmen (again often women) equipped with first-aid kits that included morphine, antibiotics, and amputation tools operated with the larger guerrilla units. Their medical training was gleaned for the most part from first-aid manuals, some 200 pages long, which prescribed treatment that was a blend of Western medicine and the traditional "Chinese doctor" treatment, that is, the application of exotic poultices and the administration of folklore herbs. Still later, more elaborate medication installations were created, usually clusters of thatch-roofed buildings that served as base hospitals for the guerrillas and sometimes for civilians. At least eleven of these were known to be operating by late 1964 in the Mekong delta and another two in the highlands behind the coastal lowlands of Central Vietnam. They were managed by medical doctors, including some from Hanoi, and staffed mainly by women. Working through the Liberation Red Cross, selected cases — children injured by napalm and serious military orthopedic patients — went to Hanoi, and in two known cases as far as East Germany, for specialized treatment (and to be exploited heavily by the Communist propaganda media).

International Communist-front organizations and private groups in and outside of the Communist bloc frequently announced the dispatch of drugs and medical instruments to the NLF via Hanoi;[2] the announced total value of these shipments came to well over half a million U.S. dollars in the 1963–1964 period. Drugs were obtained from ARVN and outlying civilian medical installations and leprosaria during raids, from medical supply convoys in ambushes, or by illegal purchases from such installations (five tons of medical supplies were stolen in mid-1964 from a U.S. medical warehouse in Nha Trang). Drugs and especially antibiotics were purchased in Saigon or Phnom Penh with ease, for in general the GVN made no serious efforts to halt the flow of medical material. Saigon doctors were occasionally kidnaped from their homes at night, blindfolded, and taken to some guerrilla base to operate or treat a patient, usually some high-ranking NLF official, and then released; the doctors seldom reported such incidents to the authorities. *Nhan Dan* on January 9, 1965 claimed that 3,000 medical cadres, 2,987 midwives, and 1,228 sanitation cadres were operating in the South.

Internal Communication System

Communication among the various levels of command within the NLF consisted of a primitive system of secret message drops and way stations linked by runners, bearers, or traveling sympathizers who could be trusted. Through this system passed directives downward, reports upward, and messages both ways. The administrative section at each central committee headquarters held the responsibility for administering this "jungle post office"; it also did the encryptographic work. At the national Central Committee and interzone levels and in the Liberation Army more sophisticated communication devices were used, chiefly radio. The ARVN captured a sufficiently large number of radios over the first four years of the struggle to indicate the types employed: old but serviceable Communist Chinese or East European radios; commercial sets manufactured in Japan or Western Europe; U.S.-made radios such as TR–20 transceivers seized in attacks on strategic hamlets, and walkie-talkies captured in military operations. The walkie-talkies were either put

[2] See Appendix F.

into use in the NLF army network or used to jam ARVN radio transmissions during field operations.

The DRV maintained that the NLF had a complete postal, telephone, and telegraph service operating in South Vietnam.[3] The DRV in early 1964 put on sale to postage-stamp collectors throughout the world a series of stamps that it said were in use in South Vietnam; they carried the inscription "National Liberation Front of South Vietnam." The first of these commemorated the NLF army victory at Ap Bac, South Vietnam, in January 1963 and portrayed an American helicopter being shot down in flames; the second pictured the heroic figures of a woman and child watching a burning strategic hamlet; the third, issued in English, French, and Spanish, bore the NLF yellow-starred flag and the NLF motto: "Independence, Democracy, Peace, and Neutrality." In actuality the NLF did not have any sort of a postal system that required postage stamps, nor did it have even the rudiments of a telephone or telegraph system.

Inspection System

We can piece together a description of the NLF inspection team by careful study of captured inspectors' reports. This means looking at the process only through the eyes of the inspector, for unfortunately we have no description of how it looked to the inspected, although it must not have been a pleasant experience. The general attitude the inspection team attempted to convey was one of constructive criticism. The team not only uncovered faults and lectured to the offending cadres about them but also attempted by means of indoctrination sessions to remedy them. Inspectors came from provincial or perhaps zonal headquarters. Their writing characterized them as tough-minded, no-nonsense, experienced organizers; undoubtedly they were dedicated, hard-core Communists, perhaps some of the best cadres available. Running through their reports, along with a notable lack of praise, were a sort of foot-tap-

---

[3] From "The P.T.T. System in the Liberated Area of South Vietnam Has Grown Up," *Nhan Dan*, January 6, 1964, quoting the Vietnam News Agency, which in turn quoted the Liberation News Agency:

> After almost three years of building, . . . the Postal Telephone Telegraph [P.T.T.] system in the liberated area of South Vietnam has [become] . . . a wide and steady network of communication and liaison from the 17th parallel to the Cape of Camau. This branch . . . has tens of thousands of employees. . . . The cadres and combatants of the P.T.T. branch of the Southern people have carried thousands of tons of postal matter according to the needs of all the battlefields serving the resistance. . . . The P.T.T. system in the liberated area [however] . . . is still trying to settle satisfactorily and develop the relay of normal correspondence of the people between one area and another, between the rear and front lines.

ping impatience and strong, universal criticism. Nothing short of perfection satisfied an inspector, and he never found it.

A typical team consisted of a team leader and two inspectors. It spent an average of two weeks in an area about the size of a district, two thirds of this time devoted to sessions with the district cadres and one third to liberation association meetings and conferences with functional association leaders. Whenever he had a free moment, an inspector would wander among the people of a village, chatting with them and attempting to assess their attitudes on various key subjects.

A standard inspection team schedule went like this:

On the first day the team heard a report from Comrade QUV [code designation] on the situation in AT [also code designation]. The next day the Party secretary-general reported on the situation in several townships. The third day the team met to review the missions of all individuals and organizations that were in dispute and to check on the relations of the cadres to the masses. . . . Three days were used for meetings with village leaders and village Party members, . . . during which time we also heard from the leaders of the popular associations. . . . Three days were spent in analyzing the situation, for which . . . the cadres were present. . . . One day was spent discussing meanings of directives from the central committee, and . . . the final day the team analyzed its experiences . . . and findings for the benefit of the cadres. . . .

In this particular case the final day must have been an uncomfortable one. The team found that

the cadres' organization was weak and they could not properly lead the struggle movement. . . . Relations between the cadres and the masses were weak. . . . Within the organizations there were many weaknesses, such as too many aged members and too many overly young persons. . . . The morale of members was low, . . . their knowledge of politics, duty, and their mission was poor, . . . the cadres lacked knowledge of their tasks, of the Party, and about communism, . . . they did not understand the principles of the struggle movement. . . . When we questioned the cadres about these matters we found their answers to be confused and imprecise. . . . Members of the investigation team became very tired. . . .

Some of this must be discounted as traditional Communist criticism. However, it does illustrate that the NLF in Vietnam found it easier to organize the people than to keep them organized and energized.

Fiscal Activities

Fiscal activity to the NLF leadership was, as was everything else, an instrument of motivation. If a rural family could contribute nothing else to the Revolution, it could donate a portion of its annual rice crop, a gesture important not only because food was needed by the guerrilla troops but because the donation was an act of commitment, a psychological identification with the cause. The importance of fiscal activity is indicated in this statement:

> In the present protracted struggle, great consideration must be given to economic leadership, because the economy is the material foundation and the decisive material sinew for developing our political and military forces. . . . In leadership it is necessary to hold firmly to production and thriftiness, which are the key basic tasks within the over-all economic and financial activities.[4]

By economic activities was meant production work, and by financial activities, fund raising. The following is taken from a 30-page untitled document captured in Kien Giang province in October 1962, apparently drawn up after a Western Nambo Interzone conference. The purpose of NLF economic activities was described as

> to boost the people's movement in food production and the movement for self-sufficiency of organizations; to oppose the economic blockade [GVN resources control program], the destruction [GVN strategic-hamlet program], and extortion [GVN tax collection] by the enemy; to maintain normal economic relations between base and outside areas. In the eastern areas of South Vietnam . . . we should oppose, boost, and protect production. . . . In northern South Vietnam we should eliminate unnecessary use and consumption of material. We should intensify economic struggle movements, protect and increase production to meet the economic needs of the people and the Revolution.

> • • • • • • • • • • • • • • • • • • •

> The purpose of financial activities is to increase income, economize, and improve financial management. Recently various echelons have not fully realized the importance of financial activities in providing for the needs of the Revolution. Action among the people to obtain contributions from them was inadequate; there were injustices and inconsistencies; national resources that could have been exploited were overlooked; financial management was defective. In the coming period we should make a survey to determine the potential income and the sources of income for each level; and we should cut down on expenditures that are not absolutely necessary.

The theme running through such statements was self-sufficiency and frugality. The rule of requisition in the military forces was if you want it, go get it from the enemy; within the civilian economy the rule was do without. The result was a smaller drain on the organization's economic resources as well as a somewhat simplified economic machine. Some expenses, however, could not be circumvented: the subsistence and maintenance costs for military units not engaged in production work; salaries or living expenses for full-time NLF leaders and cadres; and

---

[4] Radio Liberation, in Vietnamese, to South Vietnam, June 30, 1964.

military hardware, printing supplies, machine tools, and other materials that could not be obtained locally.

The NLF financial structure consisted of a series of linked finance committees running from the national Central Committee to the village. The most important level was perhaps the provincial finance committee, which did the budgetary planning, supervised all production work within the province, and handled the collection of taxes within the towns and urban areas.

To finance its Revolution the NLF had four sources of income. The first was the volunteer, or liberation, contribution, a system of fund raising in which social pressure but not force was applied. The NLF encouraged each rural family to make a donation to the cause, even a small token one, although generally it was indicated that the size of the contribution should be related to family income. In the early days of the NLF this voluntary contribution, plus perhaps some money from Hanoi, was the only source of the organization's income.

Beginning in mid-1965 the NLF began making increased use of the so-called Viet Cong War Bond. These were sold or forced on South Vietnamese as a means of raising additional money. The bonds were issued in VN $500 and VN $1,000 denominations (roughly U.S. $5 and U.S. $10) and were supposedly redeemable in five years. The redemption payment, it was promised, would be geared to the price of rice at the time they were cashed in, thus protecting the buyer from inflation. At least 50 per cent of the NLF income by early 1966 was coming from the sale of these bonds.

The second source of income was the liberation tax, or victory tax. This was conceived and presented to the rural people as a legitimate tax although in fact it was simple extortion. It was estimated that the NLF liberation tax in 1963 totaled more than three million dollars, although admittedly this is only an educated guess. The bulk of the tax came from levies on three economic activities: rice growing, about 30 per cent; rubber and tea production, about 25 per cent; and lumbering, about 15 per cent. The remaining amount came from the transportation industry, rice milling, and brick and charcoal making.

Two separate tax scales existed, one for agricultural revenues and one for business income; both were determined on the basis of income, amount of property held, and social class. Four tax brackets were established for the Vietnamese farmer. On the basis of his total harvest, he would pay, depending on his social class, from nothing to 20 per cent of the crop yield. In large areas of the Mekong delta in the 1961–1964 period this schedule was followed: The very poor farmer who raised less than 15 bushels of rice a season was exempt from the tax, the poor farmer (variously defined) paid 5 to 10 per cent, the middle-class farmer paid 10 to 15 per cent, and the rich farmer and absentee landlord 15 to 20 per cent. Crop failure meant automatic exemption, and generally there was no tax on manioc, corn, or sweet potatoes. A former district cadre responsible for NLF finances in Binh Phuoc district of Long An province, one Cu Khac Quy, defected in June 1963 and told newsmen that the NLF agricultural tax in Long An was 130 *gia* per hectare (44 pounds per 2.5 acres), or the farmer could pay in cash at the rate of about 70 cents per *gia*. This amounts to about 20 per cent of the total yield and seems rather high. Mr. Quy said the business tax was 10 per cent of the yearly net profit as estimated by the NLF. He added:

Village cadres must report anyone who does not pay his taxes after three calls at his home. Those who do not pay but demonstrate no ill will or rebellious action against the Viet Cong will be jailed in the Plain of Reeds. Those who do not pay and report the tax collection to the legal government authorities are liquidated. . . . Several farmers have been liquidated by the Viet Cong, but most of those arrested try to sell their properties to pay the taxes and avoid prison and possible death.[5]

The tax structure, like other NLF activities, was based primarily on sociopolitical considerations. For example, an NLF tax directive stated that "the main objective of the tax system is to cause the people to recognize their duty to the Revolution. . . ."

The farmer was the main economic support of the NLF. Even the Front's slogan, used in fund-raising drives, proclaimed "Agricultural revenues — lifeblood of the struggle for liberation of the South." Small businessmen, such as noodle vendors and women operating market-place stalls, paid taxes based on estimated yearly gross income. In the Camau peninsula this schedule was followed: individual entrepreneurs 2 to 5 per cent; businesses that employed others 5 to 10 per cent; larger businesses, the directive frankly stated, would be assessed on the basis of what the traffic would bear, but the amount should not be less than 10 per cent of the annual net profit; lumber firms were to be taxed the equivalent of U.S. 30–50 cents per cubic meter of lumber shipped; trucking firms paid as much as 5 per cent of the value of the shipment. In late 1964, when increased financial burdens were placed on the NLF machine, the tax rate in certain parts of the Mekong delta jumped astronomically — to as high as 50 per cent in some local areas.

As a corollary effort to its own revenue gathering the NLF prevented GVN tax collections wherever possible, even to the extent of assassinating tax collectors in the villages. When the GVN failed to collect taxes, the NLF would assert itself as the only "legitimate" tax collector in the area.

[5] Vietnam Press Agency, *Bulletin* (in English), June 24, 1964, p. 1.

The third source of NLF income was money extorted from the wealthy or the vulnerable. Methods included shakedown, ransom, blackmail, levies on large firms subject to sabotage, or simple robbery at gunpoint. In practice the NLF collected money from every economic activity it could at least partially control. How widespread their control was, no one knew for sure. French rubber and tea plantation owners, Chinese rice millers, and truckers employed by American petroleum firms were all universally believed in Saigon to be paying the NLF to permit them to continue business. Understandably, since such payments were illegal under GVN law and violators subject to stiff fines, these business-men vehemently denied the allegations. Whenever a public bus was dynamited on an open highway, killing innocent people, the rumor quickly spread that the bus company had missed its weekly payment to the NLF; the rumor of course could have been started by NLF sym-pathizers as an effort to explain or justify the killing of innocent bus-riding civilians. In this sort of activity no pretense to legitimacy was made; the NLF took what it needed or wanted in the name of the Revolution. French, Australians, Japanese, Filipinos, and Americans were kidnaped and ransomed by the NLF, but details of the transactions were lacking. Malcolm Browne, Associated Press correspondent in Saigon, reported that the average ransom for French plantation owners rose from $7,000 to $41,000 between January and October 1962.

Another form of extorted income was confiscation, or what was called the "necessity ration," in which the guerrilla band took what it needed, usually food, and offered in exchange either a receipt or payment in script to be cashed in after victory. One GVN provincial official said farmers in one district of his province had so much NLF necessity ration script that they had a vested economic interest in an NLF victory. Still another form was loot or booty taken during military operations. Goods and money captured were to go into the NLF coffers and not remain with the military unit. Declared one directive on the subject:

The people lose much blood in the Revolution and in the process of seizing booty from the enemy. Therefore the booty must be protected and . . . must be used to reduce the people's contributions.

Still another form of extorted income was the highway holdup in which money was taken from passing motorists. This effort also served as a propaganda tool. Cars were stopped, their occupants marched a mile or so to a jungle clearing where they were forced to listen to a lecture, and a collection was taken. One Saigon Vietnamese described being stopped on the road to Vung Tau:

First we were told we could leave anytime we wished, but the guns of the guerrillas said otherwise. Then the leader said to us that they were not bandits and that when we returned to our cars we would find nothing stolen, and he added: "Would you dare leave your car open like that in Saigon?" Then we were told that the Liberation donation was a duty of all patriotic Vietnamese, and that if we loved Vietnam we would make a donation to the cause. Then a guerrilla came around with a helmet into which we could drop our donations. He came to me, looked at me carefully, and said "one hundred dong" [about $1.25].

Production enterprises constituted the fourth major source of NLF income. Rural people in areas not under GVN control were harnessed into various economic activities, mainly farming on a collective basis. This practice was known as the "daily work exchange" (*hoi doi cong*).

The combat hamlet served as the economic base of this production effort. A 1963 internal Central Committee document stated that while the main source of income would remain contributions from villagers, cadres should seek to develop various economic enterprises in the liberated area:

The purpose of economic activities in the liberated area is to boost the people's food production capabilities and make them more self-sufficient, . . . to oppose the enemy's economic blockade program. . . . Food we do not have in abundance should be stockpiled, and sale to outside areas should be limited. . . . However, production of food, lumber, charcoal, and so forth should be increased and sold to provide income for our activities. . . .

If the demands for direct contributions and "taxes" were reduced, demands in terms of production goals and norms were increased. The rationale for this continued to be the GVN's resources control program, its defoliation program, and its other efforts designed to reduce the amount of food available in the rural areas. This campaign to raise more food apparently was pressed for several reasons: to increase revenues, to stockpile food against bad crop years, in preparation for feeding a larger military force, as an excuse for emulation movements and indoctrination work, and to deny rice to Saigon, which was badly needed for export to earn foreign credits.

From the earliest days of the liberated area the avowed NLF economic goal was self-sufficiency. The manner in which economic self-sufficiency was to be achieved was indicated in an NLF directive instructing production cadres to

ensure that in the economic sphere . . . : (1) Production and economic leadership involve specific planning. . . . Do not sit at your desk and invent unrealistic figures or plans for self-sufficiency and issue general plans. . . . Planning must be specific and simple and not unrealistic and superfluous. . . . (2) The people are led in the proper manner. . . . Be patient with them in educating them and persuading them to carry out the production plans. . . . (3) The liberation associations remain the backbone organization of the production movement. . . . (4) The emulation movement is utilized fully. . . . Praise the leading individuals and units in the production movement, . . . elect production heroes, . . . give prizes and other recognition, . . . mobilize the people in production by use of propaganda, cultural and artistic activities, the press, motion pictures, information, radio broadcasting, and education. . . . (5) You strengthen the leadership of the production and the economy, . . . store food for the protracted resistance. . . . On the question of capital . . . if the people need money to buy tools, salt, and cloth . . . , public funds may be used for this purpose . . . if they later pay back their debts out of the crops they produce. . . . In the delta where there is much capital, . . . educate the people and imbue them with the proper spirit so they form credit cooperatives to make loans at low interest.

Another document instructed cadres to

develop food sources equal to present and anticipated needs. Develop the "production emulation" spirit, for it is a main task. At the same time, be thrifty, eliminate bribery and corruption among us, be frugal in expenditures, take from the enemy wherever possible. . . . Use these slogans: . . . "Production is everyone's job." . . . "Work hard for full stomach." . . . All organizations are responsible for contributing to the production effort. . . . In guerrilla units the executive officer will head the production section. . . . In other Front organizations, the logistic section chief is responsible, and his section should include persons with practical production experience. . . . Production should equal last year's consumption. . . . Recapitulate the situation each month. . . . Rewards and discipline should be part of the production campaign. . . . Planning should be done thoroughly at all levels. . . . During the four-month growing season concentrate on producing and gathering crops, but be ready at the same time to fight or carry out emergency tasks if they arise. . . .

Should self-sufficiency be achieved, of course, then the liberated area could cut all economic ties with the rest of the country without damage to its own economic system. Radio Liberation stated this baldly in a February 15, 1964 broadcast that listed the year's production tasks as

to step up thriftiness and production, reinforce our finances, reduce people's contributions, and create material wealth with which to fight the enemy economically. . . . If production is developed, we will no longer be dependent on the enemy for the supply of goods, . . . will gradually build an autonomous and independent economy. . . . That is our objective. . . .

July 1964 broadcasts asserted that good progress was being made in this direction:

Weaving, sugar making, papermaking have been restored or developed. One hundred new sugar mills have been built in one province. . . . Markets in the liberated area have been expanded. . . . Thanks to the development of production and handicraft activities, the purchasing power of the people has increased. . . .

The economic program took on the overtones of a full-blown Communist society. The Long An monthly newspaper *Quyet Tien* in July 1964 declared:

After three months of positive activities the 98 farmer households of An Ninh village, Duc Hoa district, Long An [province], fulfilled their financial norms for all of 1964. . . . On May 12 the hamlet organized a noisy meeting to rejoice over successes . . . and to pledge to exert further production efforts, step up revolutionary activities, and score further achievements.

The NLF budget for 1964 was estimated at one billion piasters, or about U.S. $75 million. As far as could be determined, income raised in the South represented only about 80 per cent of the total expenditures, with the deficit being made up by the DRV. Tax moneys at first stayed in the areas in which they were generated. Since much of Vietnam had a barter economy, payments to the NLF often were in the form of produce that was turned over to cadres as payment in kind. In general about 10 per cent of the liberation tax money collected stayed at the tax source level, about 30 per cent went to the cadres at the district level, and the remaining 60 per cent went to the provincial central committee, where it remained. From time to time, as needed, the national Central Committee would place special support levies on the provincial committees. Expenditures, as noted, were directed for the most part by the provincial financial committees. One provincial financial committee prepared a list of rules for use by cadres: "Spend money only on urgent and necessary activities. . . . The political struggle movement activities should be organized so as to avoid excess loss of time in production work by the people. . . . Wage constant economic self-criticism efforts. . . . Guard always against corruption. . . ."

A financial report captured by the ARVN described the expenditures for an unnamed Mekong delta village:

Two thirds of our [monthly] expenses were for the armed struggle movement, for military expenses, workshop projects, medical treatment of the wounded, and for sampans and communication-liaison work . . . and one third was for printing, propaganda, and administrative expenses. . . .

The budget for Rach Gia (Kien Giang) province listed as its yearly expenses for 1962:

village workshop projects, VN $70,000; propaganda activities, VN $15,000; medical expenses, VN $12,000; transportation, VN $12,000; office expenses, VN $1,200; allowances for district cadres when in the area [at VN $3 per day], VN $3,600.[6]

Another directive on proper budget planning urged the lower echelons to

[6] The official exchange rate during most of this period was between 60 and 73 piasters per one U.S. dollar; a special 30 to 1 rate applied for the import of goods under an American economic aid agreement; the free-market rate ranged from 80 to 110 piasters per dollar.

plan and coordinate financial activities. . . . Use funds to speed up the construction of combat hamlets and to support the guerrilla forces. . . . Develop and strengthen the revolutionary organizations and increase the political awareness of the people, cadres, and Party members through increased indoctrination activities. . . . Visit liberation associations and other groups so as to keep informed of their financial situations.

17

Externalization: Projecting the NLF Image Abroad

An examination of the National Liberation Front's efforts to advertise itself and extend its influence beyond the borders of South Vietnam immediately plunges one into a muzzy world of the pseudo-event that logic dictates should be dismissed at once and out of hand as the figment of a collective imagination. Shortly after its formation, the NLF assumed the public posture that it was the true government of the people of South Vietnam, and, although it might be a government in hiding, it not only represented but also controlled most of the 14 million Vietnamese living south of the 17th parallel. For five years the leadership worked tirelessly to develop this image and by 1965 felt that it could assert that it was capable of dispatching envoys and legally assuming the obligations of treaties. It brushed aside the Saigon government as a mere pretender to the throne, as a "rebel authority."

In its early days the NLF leadership hid in mangrove swamps, its "diplomats" fleeing at the approach of any sizable Vietnamese army force. Even later it had none of the appurtenances of a government or a foreign ministry. Therefore on one level its assertions were preposterous. As a governmental organization conducting foreign affairs it existed

306

only in the minds of its planners and of those outside the borders of Vietnam whose own purposes were served by playing out the pretense. Yet the externalization effort could not so easily be dismissed. What had been asserted, however patently untrue, after five years of effort became real, or at least relevant, because men and governments acted as if it were reality. In attempting to expose what at initial glance appeared to have been a gigantic hoax, one was bogged down first in semantics and then in metaphysics, asking first the question "What is truth?" and then "What is reality?"

Early Efforts

However, an examination of the NLF externalization effort can serve two worthwhile purposes. First, it can indicate the international orientation of the NLF and demonstrate more graphically than any other means its highly Communist nature. In seeking support abroad the NLF, from the start, did not turn to liberal non-Communist individuals, organizations, and nations as an authentically prodemocratic revolution might have done. Instead it established and maintained bonds with international Communist-front organizations and Communist-bloc nations and with such countries as Cuba, Indonesia, and certain African nations whose foreign policies served the Communist cause in virtually every way. Second, it can throw light on official NLF attitudes toward various proposals for a negotiated settlement in Vietnam. In the United States particularly one frequently heard the call for a negotiated settlement from persons who quite obviously had no idea of the NLF position on the matter. A review of the NLF's words and actions with respect to external relations will aid in evaluating such calls as well as in understanding the NLF responses to them.

Announcement of the NLF's formation in December 1960 was met by general world indifference, even in Communist nations whose assessment apparently was that the Front probably would fade into obscurity. Only the DRV understood its significance, but Hanoi noted the birth in muted tones, undoubtedly because it sought to be neither the first nor the loudest. Cambodian newspapers carried the first stories about the formation of the NLF on January 26, 1961 as the result of the work of NLF agents in Phnom Penh, who on January 25 circulated the NLF manifesto to the local press, embassies, and foreign correspondents in the capital. In the next month items appeared in the back pages of newspapers in France, Britain, the United States, and eventually throughout the world. NLF activities continued, and support statements began emanating from Communist-bloc capitals. In October 1961 the DRV Na-

tional Assembly called on the "parliaments of all countries to support
the Vietnamese people's patriotic struggle"; on November 29, 1961 the
Chinese Communists issued a statement pledging support for Vietnam
in its "liberation struggle"; the North Korean National Assembly Presidium the same month called for an end to hostilities and for the withdrawal of U.S. forces in South Vietnam; a resolution supporting the
"liberation effort in South Vietnam" was adopted in November 1961 by
the World Peace Council (WPC) meeting in Stockholm. But these
were referenced vaguely, and often it was not clear whether they were
directed toward Hanoi or the NLF; many did not distinguish between
North and South, and few mentioned the NLF by name. The first clear-
cut recognition came when the Afro-Asian People's Solidarity Organization met in Cairo in December 1961 and announced that it was "recog-
nizing" the NLF and had invited it to attend its third congress, to be
held the following year.

The need and value of increased externalization efforts were stressed
in a Vietnam Fatherland Front report quoted on April 21, 1961 in
Nhan Dan:

> The more our just struggle wins the strong support of the people of the
> world, the more we will have the ability to demand the implementation of
> the Geneva agreements, including the implementation of the most impor-
> tant of all clauses, the one on national reunification.

In late 1961, probably December, the NLF Central Committee decided
to launch a major externalization effort. On its first anniversary, December 20, 1961, the provisional Central Committee sent identical messages
to the cochairmen of the International Control Commission (Britain
and the Soviet Union), the World Peace Council, and the AAPSO
meeting in Cairo. The message "drew attention" to U.S. intervention
in South Vietnam and the repressiveness of the Diem government and
declared:

> We are of the opinion that the Soviet Union and Great Britain in their
> capacity of, and responsibility as, cochairmen of the Geneva conference . . .
> should take urgent and special measures to stop the bloody hands of the
> U.S. imperialists and compel the United States and the Southern government
> to respect the Geneva agreements.[1]

A study of the first year's external public output indicated that the
NLF pursued a threefold objective: to introduce and advertise itself to
as wide a world audience as possible; to remove as far as possible its
stigma of illegality; and to become accepted and treated as an authentic
part of the world diplomatic scene.[2]

---

[1] Radio Hanoi, December 22, 1961, which at this time was acting as the radio medium
of the NLF.

[2] For a detailed listing of NLF activities with specific bloc and nonbloc countries see
Appendix F, "NLF Externalization Efforts."

Initially the effort consisted in loosing a flood of unsolicited communications — congratulatory, denunciatory, and explanatory — to Communist-bloc nations and the more amenable non-Communist ones. The reader may raise the question of authenticity in this activity. An effort has been made to corroborate the reports, taken chiefly from clandestine NLF newspapers and from Radio Liberation. However, fantasy not fact ruled. Whether, for example, the NLF actually sent a message to the U.N. Security Council did not matter; what mattered was that the South Vietnamese would be convinced that the NLF had the authority to dispatch such a message or that the Communist press and, hopefully, the non-Communist press would report what it said it had done. Not the act but the appearance of the act counted. Efforts to this end were reported dutifully by Radio Liberation. A typical example came in February 1962:

The provisional Central Committee of the NLFSV has cabled thanks to the governments and parliaments of the socialist countries for their support of the South Vietnamese people's struggle for liberation. Cables were sent to the Soviet Union, China, Mongolia, the Democratic People's Republic of Korea, and the German Democratic Republic. The messages pointed out that the countries' statements, demanding an end to U.S. interference in South Vietnam and supporting the South Vietnamese people's struggle for liberation, constituted a great stimulus for them.

Where possible, communiqués were geared to a specific event. For example, when the United States announced plans to raise its military mission in Saigon from a group (MAAGV)[3] to a command (MACV),[4] the NLF dispatched notes to various Communist countries advising them of the action and asserting that "the veneer of national independence maintained by the U.S.-Diem clique for nearly eight years now has been stripped off. . . . The United States has formally begun a policy of using Vietnamese to fight Vietnamese."

Nguyen Van Hieu Mission

On June 21, 1962 Radio Liberation announced that the Central Committee had appointed a delegation to make friendship visits to a number of countries and attend conferences of world organizations. The delegation was headed by Nguyen Van Hieu, secretary-general of the NLF Central Committee, also representing the Radical Socialist Party, the South Vietnam Peace Committee, and the South Vietnam Afro-Asian People's Solidarity Committee. The delegation included Mrs. Ma Thi Chu, a pharmacist and member of the NLF Central Committee and the

[3] Military Advisory Assistance Group, Vietnam.
[4] Military Assistance Command, Vietnam.

Women's Liberation Association (and Hieu's wife), and Le Thanh Nam, a journalist and member of the presidium of the South Vietnam AAPSC. This was the famed Hieu mission responsible for "introducing" the NLF to the world. It went abroad as a "delegation of the people of South Vietnam" so as to keep ambiguous the matter of whom it represented. The journey is worth tracing in some detail for the light it throws on the NLF's communication techniques in projecting an obscure organization into the media limelight of the world.

Although the mission passed through Hanoi and Moscow, its first public stop was Prague, where the delegation arrived on June 26, 1962 and was greeted by the DRV ambassador, Pham Thieu, and resident Vietnamese.[5] In Moscow, where it arrived July 5, the mission was the guest of the Soviet committee of the Afro-Asian People's Solidarity Organization. Hieu was interviewed on July 18 by newsmen from Australia, Bulgaria, Hungary, Cuba, Romania, Japan, the Soviet Union, and the United States (including *The New York Times*). He told them that the NLF consisted of 20 political parties and religious and ethnic organizations, that its chief aim was the establishment of a coalition government with a neutral foreign policy, that it stood for "step-by-step" negotiations to achieve reunification with North Vietnam, and that it followed a policy of clemency toward captured American military personnel. The delegation attended the Communist-sponsored World Congress for Disarmament and Peace in Moscow. It toured the Soviet Union, stopping in Yerevan in Armenia, Tbilisi in Georgia, and Leningrad.

The next stop was Budapest on August 5, where Hieu attended the Fifth Congress of the International Organization of Journalists, international communism's front organization for newspapermen. From Hungary on August 14 the delegation went to East Berlin, then to Potsdam, Leipzig, and Dresden. On September 13 the delegation flew from Moscow to Hanoi, to Peking, and then to Indonesia, and for the first time an NLF representative set foot officially outside the Communist world.

The ten-day visit of the Hieu mission to Indonesia was a milestone. The leader of the Indonesian Communist Party (PKI), Chairman D. N.

[5] Hieu was to write later: "We spent the first day of our historic journey in a friendly country: Czechoslovakia." Hieu broadcast (in French) over Prague Radio, "introducing the NLF platform to the Czechs and outlining our ten urgent policies to save South Vietnam." On June 29 Hieu and Mrs. Ma Thi Chu visited a collective farm ("there were 1,800 people, 1,000 cattle, 1,500 swine, and 5,000 chickens") and talked to local people. ("We were surprised to see how well informed local people were on the situation in our homeland. . . . One farmer showed us a map of Vietnam with all the U.S. military bases located on it. . . .") The delegation went on to Lidice, which Hieu described as "a place of sweet-scented roses" and compared it to "Duy Xuyen, Huong Diem, Mo Cay, Phu Loi, and other scenes of U.S.-Diem massacres in South Vietnam." Nguyen Van Hieu, *Ban Be Ta Khap Nam Chau* [Friends on Five Continents] (Hanoi, 1963).

Aidit, greeted the group. The delegation met with representatives of the Indonesian Peace Committee, the Indonesian Afro-Asian People's Solidarity Committee, women journalists, and cultural associations; and on September 17 it was received by Indonesian Foreign Minister Subandrio. The highlight of the visit, and what proved to be the most valuable moment of the entire trip, came on September 20 when President Sukarno received the Hieu mission formally at Merdeka Palace. Sukarno was subsequently reported in the world press as declaring to the visitors:

The National Liberation Front of South Vietnam's struggle is a just struggle. That is why this struggle will surely succeed. There are many similarities between the struggle of the South Vietnamese people and that of the Indonesian people for the liberation of themselves from colonialism.

It was a priceless statement for the NLF and was quickly and widely disseminated throughout South Vietnam. It also brought a diplomatic protest from the GVN. On September 22 Foreign Secretary Vu Van Mau handed Abdul Moels, the Indonesian consul-general in Saigon, a note that characterized the NLF as a "rebellion movement taking orders from Hanoi. . . . Therefore, any support given to it constitutes an intolerable interference in the internal affairs of South Vietnam."

To this the Indonesian newspaper *Eastern Star* replied "That is their own opinion. On our side we see the quite obvious fact that there is now a great force rising up in South Vietnam. The people, under the banner of the NLFSV, are determined to chase out the ruling imperialism." This was precisely the sort of statement the delegation sought in non-Communist countries; the editorial was widely distributed by the NLF. At the end of the visit the NLF and the Indonesian Afro-Asian People's Solidarity Committee issued a joint statement:

The South Vietnam delegation admires the close cooperation in a common front of Indonesian nationalists, Communists, and religious groups against colonialism, old and new. . . . The Indonesian people express their profound sympathy with and unreserved support for the just struggle of the people of South Vietnam for national liberation. . . .

From Djakarta the Hieu mission on September 23 flew to Peking, where, in a planeside statement, Hieu declared:

The NLFSV proposes the setting up of a neutral zone, covering South Vietnam, Cambodia, and Laos. This proposal conforms to the feelings of the people of the southern part of Vietnam. Peace in South Vietnam can be restored, provided the U.S.-Diem clique is willing to comply strictly with these proposals. But the essential condition is that the U.S. imperialists get out of South Vietnam.

The statement set the theme for the visit: The NLF stood for neutralism; the Chinese Communists approved of its stand. In China the delegation received a more outwardly enthusiastic reception than in any of the seven countries visited, although it was peculiarly ritualized. All forms were observed. The proper hosts were chosen. The delegation was received by Chairman Mao Tse-tung, Chairman Liu Shao-ch'i, Premier Chou En-lai, Vice-Premier Ch'en Yi, and the chairman of the National People's Congress, Chu Teh. Tours were made, and at each stop the proper-sized crowd appeared. (In China, apparently, visiting dignitaries rate various-sized crowds, depending on their status; the NLF mission rated 1,000- and 2,000-person crowds.) Peking had a crowd of 2,000. In Shanghai (before a crowd of 2,000) Hieu said the city reminded him of Saigon; he met with local Communist Party officials and greeted a number of old-line Vietnamese revolutionaries who had retired in China, including Quach Mat Nhuoc, Lieu Thua Chi, Tran Thuc Thong, and Mrs. Ly Duc Toan. The delegation also visited Foochow, Fukien, and Canton, where Hieu laid a wreath at the grave of the legendary Vietnamese revolutionist Pham Hong Thai.[6] A joint statement issued by the mission and its hosts, the China Peace Committee and the Chinese Afro-Asian People's Solidarity Committee, marked the end of the visit. According to the joint statement:

1. Both sides strongly condemn the aggressive war that U.S. imperialism is now conducting in South Vietnam on an ever larger scale and at an ever quicker tempo. Both sides denounce the majority members of the International Control Commission in Vietnam for their slander about the carrying out of so-called subversive activities in South Vietnam and their allegations that distort facts. The NLF side makes it clear that in order to settle the present situation in South Vietnam, U.S. imperialism must . . . stop its armed aggression, . . . withdraw its troops, weapons, and war materials. . . . A national democratic coalition government embracing all political tendencies must be established; a foreign policy of peace and neutrality must be realized, and South Vietnam must be prepared to form a neutral zone together with Cambodia and Laos. . . . The Chinese people always endorse and support the struggle of the people in South Vietnam to save their country and their homes. . . .

2. The NLFSV delegation fully supports the just stand of the Chinese people to liberate Taiwan, . . . strongly condemns the continuous intrusion by U.S. imperialism into the territorial waters and airspace of the Chinese People's Republic [CPR], . . . extends hearty congratulations to the Chinese people on their great achievements in the past 13 years, . . . which are an important contribution to the reinforcement of world peace and an inspiration to the struggle for national liberation of the people of various countries in Asia, Africa, and Latin America. The NLFSV delegation completely supports the CPR proposal for the conclusion of a treaty of peace and mutual

---

[6] The patron saint of Vietnamese nationalists. He tossed a bomb into a banquet attended by Indochinese Governor-General Martial Merlin, visiting in Canton, on June 19, 1934; Merlin escaped, but five of his companions were killed. Each June 19, ceremonies are held by Vietnamese in Canton at his tomb.

nonaggression in Asia and the Pacific area, to include the United States of America, and for the establishment of a nuclear-weapons-free zone covering the same area.

Although the visit to China had been properly enthusiastic and all protocol observed, Nguyen Van Hieu, writing about it later, could not hide a sense of empty formalism and lack of genuine hospitality with which the visit left him. His description of China was cold and stilted.

From China the group flew to Hanoi for what was probably the most important but least publicized stop of the entire trip. The visit was announced in Hanoi on October 17, only two days before the mission arrived. It is possible that the visit was a crash affair, hastily organized by the DRV, alarmed at being upstaged by the Chinese Communists. An unprecedented welcome campaign was generated, geared to what was called the Great Kith and Kin Emulation Movement, which was designed to increase the North-South sense of identity in the minds of the Northerners. Arriving with Nguyen Van Hieu was poet Luu Thanh Hai of the Youth Liberation Association and Cultural Liberation Association central committees. At the Hanoi railway station the pair were met by Xuan Thuy, secretary-general of their host organization, the Vietnam Fatherland Front, and various representatives of quasi-official DRV groups including the "regrouped" Vietnamese Association (South Vietnamese living in the North), the Vietnamese Journalists' Association, and the Vietnam Artists' and Writers' Union. *Nhan Dan* described the welcome as "the largest crowd ever assembled in the railway station." Hieu declared: "The NLF delegation is very happy and moved to be able to visit the northern half of our beloved Fatherland after eight long years of separation." Xuan Thuy replied: "The Vietnam Fatherland Front regards the birth of the NLFSV as a major historic event and holds that its political program has met the present aspirations of the people." The DRV was careful to treat the mission as a private and foreign group and to note that it had arrived in Hanoi after visits to six other countries. That evening the Fatherland Front held a reception for the mission, attended by diplomats from the Soviet Union, China, Bulgaria, Czechoslovakia, the German Democratic Republic, Hungary, North Korea, Mongolia, Poland, Romania, Cuba, Indonesia, and Laos. On October 20 Ho Chi Minh "met and warmly embraced these two sons of the suffering but undaunted South." Nguyen Van Hieu presented him with a bound copy of the NLF's 1960 manifesto and a vase made of a U.S. artillery shell. Luu Thanh Hai presented him with a book of poetry written by "a patriotic liberation fighter who died in a U.S.-Diem prison." Ho Chi Minh was shown some photographs of the "struggle in the South, . . . to which he responded by placing his hand on his heart and saying 'I carry here a picture of South Vietnam.' " The visit ended with a tearful meeting of the delegation with some 500 regrouped Vietnamese.

Then it was on to North Korea, where Hieu acted much like a tourist. He later wrote:

We visited much and came to feel a sense of real identification with the Korean people. [On November 14] we visited the Korean Revolutionary Museum and stood for a long while before exhibits of the art of the revolutionary activities of Marshal Kim Il Sŏng . . . and I wrote in the museum guest book: "We saw articles and materials associated with the undaunted struggle of the Korean people against colonialism and imperialism. . . . The heroic Korean people, with such a glorious tradition, will surely unify their country by repulsing the U.S. imperialist aggressors." [7]

At the Hungham Fertilizer Factory, Hieu seemed more impressed by the snowdrifts than by the factory. A birthday party held for Hieu on November 19 was attended by members of the North Korean National Assembly, the Korean National Peace Committee, the foreign diplomatic community, and, as ranking guest, the North Korean vice-minister of foreign affairs. The mission attended a photographic exhibit in Pyongyang. Hieu described it as "160 pictures exposing the U.S. aggressive policy against South Vietnam and the atrocities committed by the U.S. imperialists and their stooges. . . . [It was] opened officially on November 21 by Paek Nam Un, vice-president of the Presidium of the Supreme People's Assembly." A joint statement signed by Hieu and the deputy chairman of the North Korean National Assembly was issued at the end of the visit. It confined itself to expressions of solidarity.

Upon his return to South Vietnam Hieu broadcast a series of commentaries on the trip, aimed at exploiting in South Vietnam the results of the mission. The Sukarno statement and the reception received in Indonesia were given the most intensive treatment, followed by the reception of Mao Tse-tung and the Chinese; Eastern Europe and the Soviet Union received less attention. NLF memoranda to cadres at the time directed that the "victories" of the Hieu mission and other missions to Indonesia, Cuba, Algeria, and China be emphasized:

Information about the above-listed achievements should be widely disseminated in the villages to encourage the population. Especially it should be directed toward the government officials, military forces, and the middle classes. . . . Reports should be made by cadres on the reactions of the various classes, officials, and military forces after they receive this information.[8]

[7] Nguyen Van Hieu, *op. cit.*
[8] NLF communiqué dated October 1962. A typical result of this directive was the following editorial in a clandestine NLF newspaper dated April 1963:

An NLF delegation during 1962 brought the voice of justice and fellowship from the

The Hieu mission was viewed by the Saigon press as "an attempt to deceive international opinion and to try to conceal the Viet Cong crimes in South Vietnam that the government continually has denounced to the ICC." [9]

In the first year of its externalization effort, NLF delegations were dispatched to seven international meetings and conferences[10] and to nine countries.[11] It should be noted that the NLF delegates always were guests of a Communist organization in the host country, never of the government itself.

Formal Relations Abroad

At the beginning of 1963 the NLF created a more formal organization to handle foreign affairs. The Foreign Relations Liaison Committee was upgraded to the Foreign Relations Commission. The NLF entered its golden era in externalization, exploiting the Diem-Buddhist diffi-cuities, the consequences of which were incalculable in Buddhist countries. After the fall of Diem the commission concerned itself less with public relations activities and more with matters of foreign policy. The

---

South to Czechoslovakia, the Soviet Union, the German Democratic Republic, China, Cuba, Indonesia, Algeria, and North Vietnam. Our banner appeared at many international conferences. At these conferences many resolutions were adopted to support our just struggle and to condemn the U.S.-Diem clique's barbarities. NLFSV delegates were elected to the executive committees of many international organizations. . . . Many countries, such as the Republic of Cuba and the Republic of Algeria, have approved the establishment of permanent NLFSV representatives in their capitals. . . . All this testifies to the fact that the NLFSV has unceasingly grown during the year to become the genuine representative of the South Vietnamese people.

[9] *Saigon Moi*, July 5, 1962.

[10] The World Congress for Disarmament and Peace (sponsored by the World Peace Council) in Moscow, July 9–14, 1962 (Nguyen Van Hieu); the Fifth International Organization of Journalists meeting in Budapest, August 5–13, 1962 (Nguyen Van Hieu); the executive committee meeting of the World Federation of Democratic Youth (WFDY) in Budapest, August 5, 1962 (Mrs. Nguyen Thi Binh); the Sixth World Federation of Democratic Youth General Assembly in Warsaw, August 10–16, 1962 (Truong Van Loc); the Sixth International Union of Students (IUS) Congress in Leningrad, August 18–29, 1962 (Truong Van Loc); the Afro-Asian Lawyers' Conference (sponsored by the International Association of Democratic Lawyers — IADL) in Conakry, Guinea, October 15–22, 1962 (Nguyen Van Tien); and the third Afro-Asian People's Solidarity Organization conference in Moshi, Tanganyika, February 11, 1963 (Mrs. Nguyen Thi Binh).

[11] Czechoslovakia, June 25–July 4, 1962 (Nguyen Van Hieu mission); the Soviet Union, July 5–August 4, 1962 (Nguyen Van Hieu); Cuba, July 1962 (Le Van Thinh); East Germany, August 14–18, 1962 (Nguyen Van Hieu); Indonesia, September 13–21, 1962 (Nguyen Van Hieu); Chinese People's Republic, September 23–October 16 (Nguyen Van Hieu); Algeria, November 1, 1962 (Huynh Van Tam); Democratic People's Republic of Korea, November 13–24, 1962 (Nguyen Van Hieu); and the United Arab Republic, February 18, 1963 (Mrs. Nguyen Thi Binh).

Foreign Relations Commission acted like a foreign office,[12] issuing diplomatic notes and official statements, publishing communiqués and appeals, and dispatching emissaries abroad.

Within the Communist bloc the commission worked most closely with the World Peace Council and the Afro-Asian People's Solidarity Organization. Relations with non-Communist nations consisted chiefly of exchanging letters and unilateral statements. A statement was issued in May 1964, for example, after President Johnson had asked the Congress for a supplemental Vietnam appropriation; the commission continued to issue statements following each Honolulu defense conference and any other time the United States took official note of Vietnam in international diplomacy. Some of the personnel sent abroad probably were actually from the DRV Ministry of Foreign Affairs; for example, Dang Quang Minh, the NLF representative in Moscow, almost certainly lived and worked in Hanoi throughout the 1960–1965 period. Press conferences by its representatives abroad were a common method by which the NLF communicated with the non-Communist world. Nguyen Van Hieu held a press conference in almost every country he visited during his 1962 tour. The commission also sent individuals abroad for the specific purpose of conducting information activities,[13] and it arranged "guided

[12] The NLF "foreign service" as of late 1965 consisted of the following, in order of arrival:

Country	Representative	Date Arrived
Algeria (Political Bureau of FLN)	Huynh Van Tam Chung Van Ngoc (LPA)	February 3, 1963
Afro-Asian People's Solidarity Organization (Cairo)	Huynh Van Nghia Nguyen Van Tien	May 1963– January 1964
Cuba	Vo Dong Giang Le Van Minh	July 20, 1963 October 1963
Czechoslovakia	Dinh Ba Thi	February 1964
East Germany	Nguyen Van Hieu Duong Dinh Thao (LPA)	March 14, 1964– mid-1964
Indonesia	Nguyen Thi Binh Le Quang Chanh	mid-1964 early 1965
Communist China	Tran Van Thanh Nguyen Minh Phuong (deputy)	September 11, 1964
Soviet Union	Dang Quang Minh (five-man delegation)	April 22, 1965
Poland	Tran Hoai Nam	October 30, 1965

[13] Huynh Van Tam, in an interview published in the *Alger Républicain*, March 26, 1963, said:

The presence of the NLFSV delegation in Algeria has no objective other than further strengthening the long-existing friendly relations and mutual assistance between the peoples of the two countries and making the Algerian people more clearly understand that the South Vietnam people are waging a just and heroic struggle full of sacrifice. . . .

tours" of South Vietnam for Communist journalists such as Australia's Wilfred Burchett and France's Madeleine Riffau. To facilitate its efforts, Radio Liberation reported on April 28, 1964 that "the commission conducted a six-month course in English, . . . and the first class was graduated last week in special ceremonies." By late 1964 the Foreign Relations Commission in word and deed had assumed the overt position of a foreign office. Radio Hanoi in a broadcast on December 15, 1964, for example, reported that Nguyen Van Hieu had gone to Phnom Penh to "negotiate" the frontier problem with Cambodia, and in late December 1965 it gave a progress report on the NLF's efforts to establish itself abroad as a quasi-government:

[By the end of 1965] the Front maintained eight permanent representations in the socialist countries of Asia, Africa, and Latin America. . . . The NLF and its organizations had sent 75 delegations to foreign countries, as follows: 1961, 1 (East Europe); 1962, 10 (East Europe, 3; Asia, 5; Africa, 1; and Latin America, 1); 1963, 16 (East Europe, 3; Asia, 7; Africa, 4; Arab countries and Latin America, 1 each); 1964, 21 (East Europe, 8; Asia, 11; Latin American, 2); 1965, 27 (East Europe, 5; Asia, 7; Africa, 5; Latin America, 3; Arab countries, 2; and West Europe, 5). . . .
From 1961 to November 1965, international conferences. . . . : trade-union delegations, 11; women's delegations, 6; jurist delegations, 3; Buddhist delegations, 2; youth delegations, 11; Afro-Asian People's Solidarity Organization delegations, 7; journalist delegations, 2; scientist delegations, 2; student delegations, 5; peace committee delegations, 7; economic delegations, 2; cinematographic delegations, 1 (1961, 1; 1962, 7; 1963, 14; 1964, 21; and 1965 to November, 23).[14]

[14] Radio Liberation, December 20, 1965.

18

NLF Foreign Relations

Context

In NLF terms the effort to take political control of South Vietnam could be pursued by three basic means: military, the three stages of revolutionary guerrilla warfare or possibly even a limited conventional war; political, the struggle movement culminating in the General Uprising; or diplomatic, the establishment of a coalition government with Saigon elements, which of necessity could be brought about only if outside forces, chiefly the United States, would because of diplomatic and other outside pressures agree to such a development. External support was most important if the NLF pursued the first or third choice and least important if it pursued the second. By early 1965, of course, the choice no longer was in the hands of the NLF but rested chiefly with the DRV and Communist China, although the NLF retained a certain residual veto power since it could sabotage any arrangement not satisfactory to it.

The specifics of the NLF's policy relations outside Vietnam must be viewed in the perspective of its association with the major powers that had a vested interest in South Vietnam, namely, the United States, the DRV, Communist China, the Soviet Union, and, to a lesser degree,

Britain and France. The basic objectives of these powers in mid-1965, when the narrow-based revolutionary guerrilla war had phased into a broader struggle, appeared to be the following.

The United States. Its objective from the start was to prevent Communist domination of South Vietnam. Although the United States saw this effort as one requiring military force, that is, as a counterinsurgency effort, it never ruled out the possibility of achieving its objective by negotiation. Full support was offered the South Vietnamese long before the start of revolutionary guerrilla warfare. America was dedicated to the aid of South Vietnam and indicated by word and deed in early 1965 that no force on earth could turn it away from this objective.

The DRV. North Vietnam's chief objective and interest in the South was reunification. Hanoi leaders felt they had been cheated out of the victory won in the Viet Minh war and were determined to gain control over all of Vietnam. The time element in reunification was never indicated, probably for tactical reasons. The DRV pressed for reunification as soon as possible and was reluctant to consider any proposal that would postpone it, such as the "two Vietnams" proposal or the various "Southern neutralization" ideas. Reunification would greatly strengthen the Northern regime. Success in achieving reunification would demonstrate that the faith Vietnamese placed in the DRV was justified; it would mean increased viability, for the rice lands of the South would appreciably reduce the DRV's economic problems and lessen its dependence on Peking; and reunification would be the first step toward what was probably the DRV's ultimate goal, a federation of Indochina that would include Laos and Cambodia, with Vietnam as senior member. Reunification promised a host of side benefits: It would erase the shame of agreeing to the 1954 partition, help relieve desperate economic pressures on the North, redeem the pledge given to the Southerners regrouped in the North, and remove a rival center for Vietnamese loyalties, a standing threat to the Northern regime. However, the DRV did not want escalation and had the most to lose from it; the fact that its actions triggered the massive American involvement was the result of miscalculation on its part.

Communist China. The overriding Chinese Communist objective in South Vietnam appeared to be the elimination of U.S. military force, part of its general objective of eliminating American military power around its perimeter. Conceivably this goal lost some of its importance as China developed a nuclear warfare capability. Although it cannot be documented from public statements, logic suggests that the Chinese did not particularly welcome the idea of a unified Vietnam, preferring two Vietnams with a Southern regime either pro-Chinese or at least willing to consult with Peking before making any major moves. As the Sino-Soviet dispute deepened, the Chinese of course became prisoners of the doctrine of liberation wars, involving Chinese leadership efforts throughout Asia.

The Soviet Union. The Soviet Union's chief concern quite clearly was that events in Vietnam should not force it into a position where it had either to confront the United States in a military showdown or to abandon North Vietnam. As a reflection of the Sino-Soviet dispute it also sought a diminution of Peking's influence primarily in Hanoi but also within NLF ranks. With respect to South Vietnam, the Soviet Union appeared deeply interested in an end to the fighting and the withdrawal of U.S. military forces, preferably under the cloud of defeat but also under conditions that would not be regarded as a clear-cut victory for the Chinese Communist thesis of revolutionary guerrilla warfare. Both interests could be served by the establishment of a nonaligned but pro-Soviet government in South Vietnam. In general, however, the Soviet Union seemed to focus its efforts on Hanoi and not on the NLF.

Relations with the DRV

No aspect of the Vietnam problem was subjected to more debate, most of it uninformed, by the U.S. press and others than the nature of the relationship between the DRV and the NLF. Usually it revolved around the question, how much help does Hanoi give the South? As thus phrased, the question was neither very meaningful nor in context with the frames of reference employed by either the NLF or the DRV. For the answer to that question could be either that the North supplies only minimal assistance or that the North supplies all necessary assistance. Both answers would be factually correct. Nevertheless the nature of the relationship was widely depicted and interpreted. At one extreme was the flat assertion by the GVN of a one-to-one relationship, that is, the NLF cadres were main-line agents of Hanoi and, beyond that, of Peking. The GVN stated this position in a white paper issued in July 1963.

The policy of the Communists of North Vietnam has not varied since 1954. . . . What they seek is to absorb South Vietnam by force or subversion in order to extend Communist domination over all of Vietnam, sacrificing the interests of the Vietnamese people to those of Red imperialism. . . . Most certainly the war of aggression against South Vietnam continues only because the Communist powers, particularly the Peking regime, continue to provide military aid to their satellite, North Vietnam. Without this aid the Vietnamese people would soon see the end of Viet Cong guerrilla warfare. . . . We draw world attention yet again to international Communist plans for expansion in Southeast Asia and to the danger these Communist ambitions pose to world peace.[1]

At the other extreme was the DRV's assertion, abroad though not domestically, that it wished the NLF well but aided it in no material way. Ho Chi Minh, when interviewed by the Australian Communist Wilfred Burchett, was asked about DRV support for the NLF and he replied:

The struggle of our compatriots in the South has the full sympathy and support from all the Vietnamese people, north and south of the 17th parallel. As for material support, the government and the people of the DRV strictly abide by the Geneva agreements. . . . [The NLF consists of] representatives from all sections of the [Southern] population who have rallied in a front of national liberation which now coordinates and directs the resistance activities.[2]

Between these two extremes were a vast number of gradations, generally fixed not by facts but by individual international political orientation. It is the thesis of this book that the DRV was indeed the godfather of the NLF, that its support over the years was developmental, from lesser to greater, that until mid-1964 this aid was largely confined to two areas — doctrinal know-how and leadership personnel — and after mid-1964 it supplied antiaircraft weapons and certain other types of military hardware not available through capture, but at all times from 1960 on *it stood ready to help the NLF in any way that was absolutely necessary.*

To a certain degree the argument is a semantic one. From a vast outpouring of DRV statements on the NLF and South Vietnam it is possible to extract a paraphrase of the mystique of this relationship. The DRV held thus: Vietnam is one. The South is the Brass Citadel of the Fatherland. Just as what happens in one organ of the body affects the entire body, so what happens in South Vietnam of course involves us Northerners. Vietnam is in the midst of a Revolution. It began in August 1945 and it continues today. The Revolution has progressed at varying rates throughout the country. In the North it is in the socialism stage, working toward communism. In the South the stage of the Revolution is not this advanced. Each Vietnamese, regardless of where he lives, has a responsibility to contribute to the Revolution; each must perform his own revolutionary task. Because each Vietnamese has his own revolutionary tasks it is unfair to ask him to assume the burden of others. Each must be self-contained. Each must be self-supporting. None of us should expect those from other parts of the country to perform his tasks. We in the North have our revolutionary tasks; they in the South likewise have theirs. We morally support each other. We exchange messages of

---

[1] Republic of Vietnam, *A Danger to World Peace* (Saigon, 1963).

[2] Interview as broadcast by Radio Hanoi, in English, August 8, 1963.

encouragement. We develop a sense of unity and solidarity. But, because each must be self-supporting, we do not demand material aid from one another. However, when the demands of the Revolution are such that aid is required, we will give it unstintingly. If, for instance, the needs of the Revolution were such that we Northerners were needed to fight in the South, we would do so without hesitation.

Early DRV statements indicated support of a type that was not denied, that is, know-how and techniques of management. Le Duan, a member of the DRV Politburo and first secretary of the Lao Dong Party, for example, said at the September 1960 party congress, meeting in Hanoi: "We must constantly intensify our solidarity and the organization and education of the people of the South — especially the workers, peasants, and intellectuals — and must uphold the revolutionary fighting spirit of all strata of the patriotic compatriots." He called for the formation of a "broad national united front, directed against the U.S.-Diem clique in South Vietnam." [3] An early NLF document spelled out for Southern Lao Dong Party cadres how this effort would be tailored for the South:

For victory in the South under the leadership of the workers' class . . . the people must establish a worker-farmer-soldier coalition and set up an anti-U.S.-Diem united front . . . comprised of all patriotic classes and social strata and both Vietnamese and ethnic minority peoples, patriotic parties, and religious sects as well as everyone who opposes the U.S.-Diem clique. . . . The operation of the front must be flexible. It must further the solidarity of the people, steadily struggle to protect peace . . . with its basic task to liberate the South from imperialist and feudal domination. . . .[4]

The statement went on to justify the approach in terms of Communist ideology:

The struggle in the South in its various forms is entirely harmonious with the policy of the National Congress of the Vietnam Workers' Party and with the declarations of the Communist party conference in Moscow dealing with revolutionary periods and the differing ways colonies achieve their national independence. The struggle also is entirely suitable to the real situation in South Vietnam, based on many years of experience. It is a peaceful movement, because it avoids war in South Vietnam and seeks to abolish the military bases of the American imperialists there. It is also a national movement that is struggling for the liberation of our people and for the abolition of the American colony in South Vietnam. It is furthermore a democratic movement, because it struggles for freedom and democracy in favor of the South Vietnam population and against despotism and fascism.

Radio Liberation on May 8, 1961 issued a progress report on the implementation of the Lao Dong Party congress instructions:

---

[3] At the Lao Dong Party Third Congress, September 1960, in the committee report published in *Nhan Dan*, September 6, 1960.

[4] Unsigned memorandum entitled "On the Struggle for the Unification of Our Country," dated December 29, 1960.

In general the above-mentioned decision of the congress . . . concerning the Revolution to be carried out in South Vietnam has been correctly executed by the Party in South Vietnam and the different echelons of the Party. . . . In order to meet the exigencies of the Revolution and to meet the new situation that the Revolution faces, all of us — cadres and members of the Front as well as those who love their Fatherland and the Revolution in South Vietnam — must strictly execute the basic and immediate mission as determined by the [Lao Dong] Party. . . .

At a Lao Dong Party congress in September 1961, delegates heard a report that specifically outlined the stages for the liberation of the South: (1) overthrow of the Diem government, (2) establishment of a coalition government, and (3) open negotiations with the North for reunification.

Instruction on revolutionary guerrilla warfare, as described in Chapter 2, was generally available, as it is in books in any American bookstore. From Hanoi came the original Mao-Giap doctrine as well as specific directives that adapted earlier experiences to the changed setting of the South.

No very meaningful line could be drawn between doctrinal instruction and personal leadership, between smuggling in a memorandum or a textbook and sending down an observer, adviser, or administrator. At the Ho Chi Minh trail, certitude vanished. Virtually no one in the later days denied there was traffic in personnel along the trail. By mid-1963 Northern-trained cadres were being captured in numbers. Discussion did center around the role of the infiltrators, whether commissars or assistants, and around the magnitude of the DRV effort. Both the GVN and the United States issued a series of reports, white papers, and letters to the ICC on the role and nature of the DRV assistance, which the reader, if interested, is invited to review.[5] No purpose would be served by detailing or even summarizing the data they contain. The author could supply additional data: He saw Chinese-made weapons still warm from combat, and he talked to NLF army prisoners who freely admitted they had come from the North. He collected at least 200 internal NLF documents that referred again and again to Lao Dong Party memoranda and to the

---

[5] These include the following documents issued by the GVN: *Violations of the Geneva Agreements by the Viet-Minh Communists, 1954 to June 1959: A White Paper* (Saigon, July 1959); *Violations of the Geneva Agreements by the Viet-Minh Communists, July 1959 to June 1960* (Saigon, 1960), particularly Section III, "Problems of Subversion"; *La politique agressive des Viet Minh Communistes et la guerre subversive Communiste au Sud Vietnam, periode de mai 1961 à juin 1962* (Saigon, 1962); *Report to the International Control Commission*, October 24, 1961 (a series of case histories); *A Danger for World Peace: The Communist Aggression Against South Vietnam, June 1962–July 1963* (Saigon, July 1963), case histories of individual infiltrators, photographs of captured equipment, translation of captured documents; and by the U.S. Department of State, *A Threat to the Peace: North Vietnam's Efforts to Conquer South Vietnam* (Washington, D. C., 1961) and *Aggression from the North: The Record of North Vietnam's Campaign to Conquer South Vietnam* (Washington, D. C.: 1965).

key role of Party cadre leadership. To detail these data would largely duplicate the material published in the documents cited and would contribute little to the credibility of the assertion of DRV leadership centrality in the South. In the final analysis one's conclusion must amount almost to a matter of faith, whether or not one accepts the DRV assertion that it supplied only spiritual help and that all "evidence" to the contrary was fabricated.

It is a truism in counterinsurgency that a guerrilla organization is most vulnerable with respect to leadership. Lost weapons can be replaced, and the rank-and-file manpower pool is seldom ever emptied. But loss of an experienced leader does damage to an organization that can never be completely repaired. The NLF suffered such severe cadre damage in late 1962 and early 1963 that by mid-1963 the DRV was obliged to make up NLF leadership shortages. These were chiefly of three types: first, those with technical skills and actual experience in leading men in struggle movements and combat, who were needed largely to replace battlefield casualties; second, those who could maintain a disciplined organization, since the GVN's strategic-hamlet program put severe strains on NLF organization; and third, those who because of long indoctrination believed firmly that the cause inevitably would be successful and were immune to blandishments of a compromise, including the GVN's *Chieu Hoi,* or returnee, program. Beyond this was the need to regularize the system (described in Chapter 6) and screen out cadres with separatist tendencies whose interests it was feared might eventually conflict with those of Hanoi. From a number of sources it was possible with some extrapolation to assemble the statistics given in Table 18–1 on the number of cadres who came South. (The author believes these figures are accurate within plus or minus 10 per cent.) In the early years almost all of these were Southerners; but as of 1965 it was estimated that at least half of the 35,000 civilian NLF cadres were either "regrouped" Southerners or "pure" Northerners. Many of these were killed in the years before 1965; therefore, of those still alive in 1965 (a total cadre strength of about 35,000), half were from the North. The estimates in Table 18–1 are probably conservative. U.S. Defense Secretary

Table 18–1 NLF Cadres from the North, 1954–1965

Year	Number
1954 through 1960	1,900
1961	3,700
1962	5,800
1963	4,000
1964	6,500 (at least a third Northerners)
1965	11,000 (almost all Northerners)
	32,900

McNamara in April 1965 said that Pentagon intelligence officers set the total infiltration figures from 1960 to April 1965 at 39,000.

Material aid by the DRV in the period before mid-1964 probably was minimal, not because the DRV respected the Geneva accords but because it did not consider such aid necessary. But with the launching of the NLF army buildup in mid-1964 and with the advent of increased air operations, more weapons, including those for antiaircraft purposes, were required, and they were promptly sent down from the North. In the earlier days, when the NLF Main Force numbered about 10,000 and the paramilitary about 30,000, probably the units had sufficient weapons for at least 10,000 men. With the buildup to at least a 30,000-man Main Force and perhaps as many as 80,000 paramilitary, obviously additional weapons were needed. A fiction of the Vietnam struggle was that the NLF army could take weapons in any number required from ARVN units and outposts anytime it wished. It was not nearly as simple as this, and never as successful as generally believed. In the 1960–1965 period the NLF army captured an estimated 39,000 weapons; at the same time it lost approximately 25,000. In general the quality of the captured weapons was better than that of the lost weapons. But this still leaves a net gain of only 14,000, which, added to the approximately 10,000 usable weapons the NLF recovered from caches hidden at the end of the Viet Minh war, amounted to only 24,000 weapons for a force of at least 110,000 men. Arms for the remaining 86,000 had to come from somewhere else; they came from the North.[6]

Perhaps the best means of portraying the early DRV-NLF relationship is to use a father-son analogy: After a son has reached maturity, completed his education, married, and begun a career, to what degree does his father assist him from then on? Perhaps from time to time the son may be faced with a personal crisis and the father will advise him on what course to take. If he is having financial troubles perhaps the father will loan him money. Perhaps he will do nothing because nothing is required. What is relevant is the potential. The father stands ready to help his son in massive terms; he himself might not know the extent to which he would go to aid his son if the situation required. So too with the DRV, father of the NLF. If material aid was marginal, its willingness potential was virtually unlimited, stopping just short of survival of the DRV. It follows from this that the two were separate entities with

[6] Indicative of the scope of later assistance was the Cape Varella case: A 115-foot ship was sunk in Vung Ro Bay, north of Nha Trang, in shallow water on Feburary 16, 1965. The cargo salvaged later included 100 tons of ammunition and explosives (including a million rounds of ammunition); 3,000 weapons, including large machine guns; and 500 pounds of medical supplies. Also aboard were Haiphong (DRV) newspapers dated January 23, 1965. The evidence was sufficiently damning that the North Vietnamese News Agency in a Radio Hanoi broadcast on February 22, 1965 officially denied it was a DRV vessel.

separate lives. The NLF was not an independent, indigenous organization as it asserted. But neither was it simply a hammer in the hand of the long arm of the DRV. If the NLF-DRV in the early days appeared monolithic and inseparable it was because no serious effort was made to split them.

Another worthwhile approach to DRV-NLF relations is to inspect the assessment of events in the South by the Northerners. In general, Ho Chi Minh and the Northern leadership believed

the revolutionary struggle in our country presents a miniature picture of the revolutionary struggle throughout the world. The two great revolutionary tides in our age, which are the socialist revolution and the revolution for national liberation, are also the two great tides of the Vietnamese Revolution. The revolutionary struggle constitutes a profound manifestation of revolutionary relationships . . . and the contradictions among the reactionary influences.[7]

The Northerners consistently suffered from excessive optimism about the manner in which events in the South were proceeding, a not uncommon tendency of the "reverse slope," as the U.S. military would say. The launching of the NLF itself followed the attempted coup d'état against the Diem government by elements of ARVN paratroop units in November 1960; the formation of the NLF was ordered because the DRV believed massive dissatisfaction existed within the Vietnamese armed forces and signaled imminent disintegration. The overthrow of the Diem government in 1963 again was regarded by the DRV as the threshold of victory. The instability that followed Diem seemed to confirm this belief. Hanoi's *Cuu Quoc* (National Salvation) on February 4, 1964 expressed the belief that the end had arrived:

The [GVN's] present crisis is developing amidst the patriotic movement of our people [who are] fighting the aggressors and traitors in all areas, politically and militarily. . . . Serious deterioration is developing in the army, the central and the local governments. Uprisings and secessional activities are developing. . . . The United States cannot even find a Vietnamese traitor to unite the counterrevolutionary forces. . . .

Gradually the euphoria again faded, and in fact serious doubt apparently entered the ranks of the Northern leadership. In July 1964 Hanoi publications contained a rash of arguments seeking to prove that the NLF was winning, that without question it was destined to win. Angry diatribes were leveled against unnamed doubters. "Anyone who shows indifference to or does not support the just struggle of our compatriots in South Vietnam will commit no small crime," warned Nguyen Van Vanh ominously in the July 1964 issue of *Hoc Tap*. The DRV began to return to its earlier policy position: to declare publicly that there must be

[7] *Hoc Tap*, July 1964.

a negotiated settlement in the South among the Vietnamese themselves, and privately to encourage the NLF to increase its armed struggle movement, at the same time supplying the necessary leadership and material to enable it to do so. The DRV National Assembly on July 5, 1964 issued a statement that set the return to earlier policy. It said in part:

1. The U.S. government as well as the governments of the countries that took part in the 1954 Geneva conference on Indochina must live up to their commitments, respect the sovereignty, independence, unity, and territorial integrity of Vietnam, and refrain from interference in its internal affairs.

2. The U.S. government must put an end to its aggressive war in South Vietnam, withdraw all its troops and weapons from there, and let the South Vietnamese people settle by themselves their own internal affairs in accordance with the program of the NLF.

3. The peaceful reunification of Vietnam is an internal affair of the Vietnamese people. It will be solved in accordance with the spirit of the political program of the Vietnam Fatherland Front and the NLF.

In late 1964 DRV optimism was again revived and its settlement line hardened. General Vo Nguyen Giap indicated in an interview with a Japanese journalist on November 1, 1964 that the price asked of the United States had been raised. He was asked about a settlement and, after replying with the standard answer ("withdrawal of U.S. troops, . . . material, stop aggression, . . . let the South Vietnamese settle their own destiny . . ."), he added this sentence:

At the same time it [the United States] must also respect the Geneva agreements on Laos and Cambodia and put an end to its policy of intervention and aggression in the Kingdom of Laos and respect the sovereignty, independence, and neutrality of the Kingdom of Cambodia.[8]

In March 1965, again in an interview by a Japanese journalist, Vo Nguyen Giap declared:

The United States government must stop at once its acts of provocation, sabotage, and aggression against the DRV and immediately [stop] the aggressive war in South Vietnam, withdraw U.S. troops and weapons from there, and let the South Vietnamese people settle their own affairs by themselves in accordance with the program of the NLFSV.

He had thus dropped the conditions for Laos and Cambodia and added the condition of a halt in American air strikes.

The original organizational base for DRV-NLF relations was the Fatherland Front, the DRV's broad-based united front mentioned earlier. In April 1961 the national congress of the Fatherland Front met and

---

[8] Quoted by Radio Hanoi, November 1, 1964.

took cognizance of the NLF in a resolution welcoming its formation; the NLF, however, did not join the Fatherland Front. In late October 1962 NLF representatives and Fatherland Front officials met in Hanoi, and on October 30 they issued a communiqué:

The 16 million North Vietnamese will continue to give their positive support to the liberating struggle of the compatriots of South Vietnam [who are] struggling to make of the NLF a strong base for the struggle and with a view to reunification of the Fatherland.

A Fatherland Front conference communiqué, September 29, 1964, described its association with the NLF as one designed to "develop North-South friendship activities, tighten North-South union, and go all out in supporting the patriotic struggle of our compatriots in the South."

The climax to the DRV's externalization effort on behalf of the NLF came in Hanoi, November 25 to December 1, 1964, when the Vietnam Fatherland Front, the Vietnam Peace Committee, and the Vietnam Afro-Asian People's Solidarity Committee sponsored the International Conference for Solidarity with the People of Vietnam Against U.S. Imperialist Aggression and for the Defense of Peace.

Among the countries and international organizations represented were the Soviet Union, China, the United States (Radio Hanoi listed as delegates Mr. and Mrs. Robert Williams, Sidney Rittenberg, Frank Coe, William Worthy, and Anna Louise Strong), the WFDY (Indonesian and Venezuelan delegates), the AAPSO (a six-man delegation made up of two Chinese, two from Cameroun, a Japanese, and a Southern Rhodesian), the WPC (Chile, Algeria), the Afro-Asian Journalists' Association (Indonesia), the Peace Liaison Committee for the Asian and Pacific Regions (New Zealand, Indonesia, and Japan), the International Association of Democratic Lawyers (France), the World Council Against Atomic and Hydrogen Bombs, World Religious Believers for Peace (Japan), Albania, East Germany, Korea, Sudan, Malaysia, Thailand, Yemen, Nigeria, Somaliland, Chad, Zanzibar, Argentina, Bolivia, Chile, Colombia, Ecuador, Haiti, Peru, Uruguay, Venezuela, Cambodia, Canada, Poland, Bulgaria, Cuba, Mongolia, Czechoslovakia, Romania, and Hungary.

The largest NLF delegation ever to attend a foreign event was present: Tran Van Thanh, Central Committee member and chairman of the executive committee of the Workers' Liberation Association; Nguyen Van Tien, Central Committee member, secretary-general of the South Vietnam Afro-Asian People's Solidarity Committee (deputy); Huynh Van Tuan, executive committee member of the Youth Liberation Association and the Student Liberation Association; Mrs. Le Thi Cao, teacher, member of the executive committee of the Women's Liberation Association, Saigon-Cholon section; Mrs. Nguyen Thi Thai Nga, member of the Trung Bo section of the Women's Liberation Association; Doctor Tran Thanh Van, NLF Thua Thien provincial central committee member; Vian, Bahnar montagnard, member of the Gia Lai provincial central committee; Mrs. Cham Kim, Sedang montagnard, representing the Tay Nguyen provincial Youth Liberation Association; and Ho Van Bot, Ben Tre schoolboy injured by napalm.

On the surface the conference was a standard Communist and fellow traveler solidarity meeting. The ostensible theme was anti-Americanism, that is, U.S. aggression and repression in South Vietnam, Laos and Cambodia, Japan, the Congo, Cuba, and Latin America and racism within the United States. Actually the purpose was twofold. First, to "internationalize" the struggle in the South by developing a broad base of foreign support, backing was sought against escalation of the war by the United States by indicating to the United States that a large number of nations supported the DRV. An effort was made to convince the delegates, and through them those they represented, that the United States lacked resolution with respect to South Vietnam, the Americans present being held up as the true voice of the American people with respect to Vietnam. The second purpose was to put the final stamp on the DRV's regularization of the NLF. Out of the conference came a quasi-formal structure for the conduct of NLF affairs within the DRV framework, a transition from a Southern private to a Northern quasi-governmental apparatus, and a culmination of the NLF's externalization efforts.

Following the conference the DRV announced the establishment of an international conference bureau with the task of "maintaining liaison with organizations and individuals participating in the conference, carrying out its resolutions, and providing members with information about the situation in the South." The bureau became the major NLF organ in Hanoi for the conduct of diplomatic relations with the world and the chief DRV check on such activities. Its formal name was Bureau of the International Conference for Solidarity with the People of Vietnam Against U.S. Imperialist Aggression and for the Defense of Peace. It was composed of four indigenous Vietnamese organizations: the NLF Central Committee, the Fatherland Front Central Committee (DRV), the Vietnam Peace Committee from both North and South, and the Afro-Asian People's Solidarity Committee from both North and South. On January 17, 1965 Radio Hanoi announced that the headquarters of the bureau had been established in Hanoi. As chairman it named Hoang Quoc Viet, Presidium member of the Fatherland Front Central Committee; vice-chairman, Tran Van Thanh of the NLF Central Committee; and secretary-general, Nguyen Duy Tinh, secretary-general of the DRV Vietnam Peace Committee. Members were listed as Mrs.

Nguyen Thi Luu, assistant secretary-general of the Central Committee of the Fatherland Front; Nguyen Xuan Tram, secretary of the DRV Afro-Asian People's Solidarity Committee; and Huynh Tan Vam, member of the executive committee of the NLF's Youth Liberation Association.

While the DRV attempted both to tighten its direct controls in the South in its regularization drive and to systematize the NLF's externalization efforts through the bureau in Hanoi, it continued to assert publicly that the NLF was the only representative of the South Vietnamese people, a position, as we shall see, at least in part the result of subtle competition between the DRV and Communist China within the NLF ranks.

Hanoi's relations with the NLF were also complicated by a number of internal factors. For example, the DRV was irrevocably and totally committed to the support of the struggle in the South. The DRV had bound itself to the NLF with hoops of steel that could not be loosened. A typical expression of the bond of sentiment it had created came in this Radio Hanoi broadcast of December 20, 1962:

> The relations between North and South are relations between two parts of the same country. . . . To regard relations between the two parts of our country as though between two different countries is to recognize U.S. imperialism's neocolonialist regime, which was illegally established in the southern part of our country and is an illegal thing. Our compatriots in the South do not recognize that regime and are determined to topple it, for that is their inviolable right. . . . We Vietnamese may not, after achieving liberation in the North, seek only to build up the North. . . . The resistance for national salvation of our Southern compatriots is obligatory, necessary, and essential.

Not only had it committed itself to the South but the DRV leadership had staked its prestige on the goal of reunification. The Southern struggle had been regarded as an excellent internal motivation tool. It became an instrument to develop socialist enthusiasm among the Northern people. March 19, 1963, for example, was a nationwide anti-American day, and a massive effort was made to arouse anti-American, pro-Southern feelings among the people. During the Geneva agreement anniversary in July 1963 an anti-American week was also staged, coupled with an intensified effort to raise the Kith and Kin Movement to new heights. On July 15, 1963 Radio Hanoi said:

> We achieved new victories in our campaign to support our Southern compatriots. Letters were sent from 600 intellectuals to colleagues in the South. . . . The engineering section of the Hai Phong cement plant raised its productivity from 43 to 110 per cent; . . . tanker unloading at Hai Phong port was reduced from 15 to 7 days, saving the state 80,000 dong [piasters]; . . . plowing, harrowing, and planting at the Nghe An agricultural cooperatives was done 1.5 times faster than previously. . . .

On December 30, 1963 Radio Hanoi reported the conclusion of the "Struggle Against the U.S. Imperialists and Their Henchmen Week," during which "a million dong, equivalent to 2,500 tons of rice, was collected and sent to our Southern compatriots. . . ."

The result of this campaign was to put the NLF and its activities very much to the forefront of the consciousness of the average DRV citizen; any effort by Ho Chi Minh to extricate himself was fraught with the probability of intolerable psychological losses among his own people. And, because in the inner councils the leadership had put the matter of reunification so much to the fore, virtually equating it with victory, success came to be measured not simply in terms of an NLF victory in the South accompanied by U.S. withdrawal but in terms of reunification. An NLF victory at the price of continued partition would not have been regarded in the North as a victory at all. During the same period the DRV faced internal economic difficulties chiefly because the leadership had been unable to solve its agricultural problem, which has been exacerbated by a population increasing steadily at 3 per cent a year. In addition, any loss of enthusiasm or any show of timidity on the part of the DRV leadership would endanger DRV relations with China; like other neighbors, the DRV knew it must never show weakness to the Chinese. If it is assumed that the basic Chinese goal with respect to South Vietnam was to force out the Americans, even at (or *especially at*) the price of continued partition of Vietnam, the DRV's dilemma increased.

When the struggle broadened and American air strikes began against the North it was no longer necessary to maintain the posture of separation. Vietnam was one, and all of it was being attacked. After December 1964, for example, General Vo Nguyen Giap felt free to send messages of commendation to the NLF army on victories it had won and encouraged it to increase its militancy and intensify its armed struggle. On February 5, 1965, on the fourth anniversary of the founding of the NLF army, he sent this message:

The North Vietnamese army and people are infinitely grateful and moved by the NLF. . . . They call on the South Vietnamese troops and people to strike hard blows at the heads of the U.S. aggressors and their henchmen in an attempt to safeguard North Vietnam. . . .[9]

NLF messages were of the same tone. For instance, the NLF Central Committee on February 8, 1965 issued a statement condemning U.S. air strikes in North Vietnam:

The Vietnamese people are one. Any aggressive act of the U.S. imperialists against North Vietnam constitutes a challenge to all Vietnamese people. The

[9] *Nhan Dan*, February 16, 1965.

Presidium of the Central Committee of the NLF calls on the troops and people of South Vietnam to unite to heighten vigilance . . . and to step up all political and military activities.

Relations with Communist China

From its inception the best foreign friend the NLF had in its externalization efforts was Communist China. Unequal as they were in size and power, the two forces had a maximum of common interests and virtually no conflicting interests. For the NLF, China was a power on the move from whom it could derive prestige and assistance and whose umbrella, if not nuclear, at least was the most protective in Asia. China, in turn, found the NLF valuable as an example of the success syndrome in the Sino-Soviet dispute; a vehicle for undercutting America's position and influence and for engendering anti-American feeling, not just in South Vietnam but throughout Asia; a device for denigrating the United Nations; and a showpiece example of the unswerving support it stood willing to supply any groups in any nation interested in a revolutionary guerrilla war.

At the outset the Chinese did not distinguish South from North Vietnam, accepting the DRV orientation that Vietnam was one nation. The visit of the Chinese military good-will mission to North Vietnam in December 1961, for example, was marked by the statement of Marshal Yeh Chien-ying on his arrival that "China and Vietnam are 'lip and teeth neighbors,' an intimate comradeship in arms binding together our struggles against aggressive imperialism." Marshal Yeh also did a certain amount of saber rattling, which was invaluable for NLF internal use; widely quoted in NLF leaflets was his statement that

U.S. imperialist intervention in and aggression against South Vietnam have become extremely serious. The Chinese people will never be indifferent to this adventurist action. . . . The Chinese absolutely cannot ignore this adventurist conduct.

The first NLF delegation to visit China was the Nguyen Van Hieu mission described in Chapter 17. It was followed by the arrival of Huynh Van Tam, a member of the executive committee of the NLF's Workers' Liberation Association en route home from a visit to Moscow. He was presented at a Peking press conference at which

he introduced to the press the contents of the program of the NLF, which aims at the overthrow of the Diem clique . . . and the realization of peace, independence, democracy, and improvement of the people's life . . . and the attainment of reunification.

This was the text of his statement as broadcast on January 16, 1962; whether he or Radio Peking substituted the goal of "improvement of the people's life" for what was usually the third (or sometimes fourth) NLF goal of neutralization is not clear. At any rate it indicated the Chinese effort to play down the idea of neutrality for South Vietnam. To set the record straight, the NLF Central Committee, upon Huynh Van Tam's arrival home, sent a telegram to Peking, broadcast by Radio Liberation on March 8, 1962, thanking the Chinese for "the warm support demonstrated by the Chinese people for the NLF in its just struggle for independence, democracy, peace, neutrality, and unification." But the Chinese were not to be deterred; *People's Daily* on December 20, 1962, in a direct misstatement of fact wrote of the NLF: "In 1960 this organization raised a platform that it stands for independence, democracy, food and clothing, and peaceful unification of the Fatherland." From time to time, particularly in its more official statements prepared for foreign ears, the Chinese included neutralism as an NLF goal, continuing to ignore it at home. The Chinese also lost enthusiasm, beginning early in 1964, for the idea of an international conference to settle the Vietnamese problem. This coincided with its disenchantment with the United Nations and its active support of Indonesia's "confrontation" with Malaysia. Early Chinese statements echoed the DRV in the call for implementing the Geneva conference; by late 1964 China had dropped this theme, apparently favoring a more direct NLF route to power.

The externalization effort continued unabated. Huynh Van Tam was put on tour in China, attending a rally in Peking (2,000 persons), one in Shanghai (1,000 persons), and one in Wuhan (1,000 persons). Le Viet Hung of the NLF's Youth Liberation Association arrived on March 4, 1963 as a guest of the All-China Youth Federation and the All-China Student Federation. He told a rally in Peking (1,000 persons) that the "U.S.-Diem armed forces pursue a three-all policy: kill all, burn all, and loot all," a phrase picked up and used extensively by the NLF in its internal output. Radio Peking said an NLF Workers' Liberation Association delegation attended the 1963 May Day celebrations in Peking but mentioned no names. Mrs. Nguyen Thi Binh and Mrs. Ma Thi Chu arrived in Peking in July 1963 and, according to Radio Peking, told a rally on July 15:

Finally let us affirm resolute support for the just struggle of the Vietnamese people for the peaceful unification of their Fatherland. (Applause.) U.S. imperialism get out of South Vietnam. (Applause.) Victory will go to the heroic Vietnamese people. (Applause.) Long live the militant friendship between the Chinese and Vietnamese people. (Prolonged applause.)

A month later Le Thanh Nam and Thanh Hai arrived to attend a series of anti-Diem, pro-Buddhist rallies. This delegation was later joined by Mrs. Nguyen Thi Binh, and the troupe toured China as guests of the China Peace Committee and the Chinese Afro-Asian People's Solidarity Committee. The delegation was received on August 29 by Mao Tse-tung. Radio Peking in a domestic broadcast on August 30 reported that

on the occasion of receiving the NLF delegation on August 29 Chairman Mao Tse-tung issued a statement against the U.S.-Diem clique for aggression and persecution in South Vietnam. . . . On behalf of the Chinese people he voiced his full support of the struggle of the South Vietnamese people and called on people of the world to stand resolutely on the side of the South Vietnamese people.

Mrs. Nguyen Thi Binh replied to Mao with a comment on nuclear testing:

Basically the partial nuclear test ban treaty signed recently in Moscow by the United States and the Soviet Union and others in no way restricts the United States from conducting nuclear tests. . . . It definitely will not reduce the threat of nuclear war for peace-loving peoples . . . and definitely will not weaken the will of the South Vietnamese people to struggle against the United States.

Tran Hoai Nam arrived on January 6, 1964, representing the NLF's Workers' Liberation Association; he too toured China, and he delivered a violently anti-American address at the Memorial Hall of the February Seventh (1923) Railway Workers' Strike in Wuhan (1,000 persons). A large and impressive NLF delegation headed by Nguyen Minh Phuong (plus Youth Liberation Association representative Huynh An Tuan and staff members Le Xuan Ninh and Trinh Van Anh) arrived on July 14, 1964, attended the tenth anniversary of the signing of the Geneva accords as guests of the China Peace Committee and the Chinese Afro-Asian People's Solidarity Committee, and departed on July 28. Also in Peking at the same time was the chairman of the Luc Hoa Buddhist Association of South Vietnam, Thich Thien Hao, who was en route to a religious conference in Tokyo; he issued a singularly un-Buddhist-like statement: "No matter what officers the United States may send or what weapons it may use, U.S. imperialism will never defeat a nation that has risen in resistance and is fighting for its liberation."

The NLF's permanent delegation in Peking, Tran Van Thanh (chief) and Nguyen Minh Phuong (deputy), arrived on September 11, 1964, and they were welcomed by Vice-Premier Ch'en Yi. It was a significant moment for the NLF:

Banners waved at the station. . . . The delegation got off the train amid the noise of gongs, drums, and applause. Officials walked toward them and warmly shook hands. Flowers were presented to all members of the delegation by young girls. . . . Also welcoming them were envoys and diplomats of the socialist, Asian, and African countries to China.[10]

The delegation was received on September 23 by the foreign minister, reported Radio Liberation, to whom "the delegation presented its credentials." The Chinese explained that the delegation was in China "under an agreement between the NLFSV and the China Peace Committee and the Chinese Afro-Asian People's Solidarity Committee." DRV reportage on the arrival of the permanent delegation was singularly terse: Radio Hanoi reported only that it had arrived and was given a reception by the DRV ambassador in Peking; Hanoi evidenced mixed feelings about the idea of a permanent NLF delegation in Peking.

The delegation began at once behaving like an embassy: On October 1, according to a Radio Peking report of that day, it had met with President Modibo Keita of Mali, who was visiting China; on October 11 it said it had "received" a delegation of the Zimbawe African National Union; on December 21 it had a "conference" with the Chinese premier.

Chinese public statements to and about the NLF tended to be militant and highly purposive. The primacy of hate for the forces opposing the NLF was an overriding characteristic. In vitriol and violence the Chinese statements exceeded all others. In imaginative use of the atrocity theme, it was unequaled. And the NLF served as text for the Chinese on various aspects of the anti-imperialism campaign. Mao Tse-tung issued a statement on September 29, 1963, when the Diem-Buddhist troubles were at their height. After listing the various trials the South Vietnamese were undergoing he declared:

The people of South Vietnam should not base their hopes for liberation on the wisdom of the American imperialists or Diem. On the contrary, victory can be achieved only by a unified, persistent struggle. . . . We Chinese are determined to support this struggle for righteousness and justice by the South Vietnamese people.

Liao Ch'eng-chih, chairman of the Chinese Afro-Asian People's Solidarity Committee, on August 30, 1963, spelled out clearly the Chinese contention that the NLF's friend certainly was not the Soviet Union:

The modern revisionists [that is, the Soviet Union], however, are not only pouring cold water on the South Vietnamese people's just struggle and trying their utmost to disparage its world significance but are trying to make a very despicable deal with the U.S. imperialists at the expense of the South

[10] Radio Hanoi, September 12, 1964.

Vietnamese people. . . . As it will thwart their dream of colluding with U.S. imperialism they hold, according to their logic, that the South Vietnamese people should lay down their arms and act the part of the conquered people, . . . thus betraying Marxism-Leninism and selling out the South Vietnamese people and the people of the world. [Stormy applause.] If only the South Vietnamese people will unite around the NLFSV with the support of the people of North Vietnam and the whole world, they will most assuredly be able to surmount all difficulties and win final victory.

For the Chinese, the NLF served as an admirable exhibit in its dispute with the Soviet Union. Here is proof, they said, that revolution is the way. Radio Peking on December 27, 1963 declared:

Their victories show that the oppressed peoples and nations must not make their liberation dependent on the "sensibleness" of imperialism and its running dogs. They can win victory only by closing ranks and persisting in militant struggle.

Ch'en Yi at an NLF reception on December 19, 1964 in Peking said "the struggle and victory of the South Vietnamese people once again prove that in the face of an awakened people, U.S. imperialism, although armed to the teeth, is a paper tiger."

There were in general two types of Chinese messages directed toward Vietnam: those addressed to the "Vietnamese people," sent to Hanoi and signed usually by specific Chinese officials; and those directed specifically toward the NLF, which would refer to the Southern struggle and seldom mention the DRV and would be signed by "the leaders of the Chinese People's Republic." It was a subtle form of wedge-driving between the NLF and the DRV.

The NLF exploited the messages to the fullest. Nguyen Huu Tho, for example, replied to Mao Tse-tung's statement of September 29, 1963, noted earlier, in a Radio Liberation broadcast on September 30, in which he said: "His statement constitutes great encouragement for our people, contributing to the increase of our combat potential and our confidence in final victory." The Vietnamese ambivalent attitude toward the Chinese, however, crept into even the Radio Liberation output; shortly before, for instance, on July 17, Nguyen Huu Tho in a speech on the struggle movement in South Vietnam said "We consider it an honor to continue the glorious traditions of our ancestors, who valiantly fought against such Chinese invaders as Han, Wu, Sung, Tang, Yuan, and Ming."

China's successful nuclear test in mid-October 1964 brought a round of applause from the NLF. Tran Van Thanh, acting for the NLF Foreign Relations Commission, sent a note to Ch'en Yi on October 19, congratulating China on the test and declaring,

China's possession of nuclear weapons can mean only further consolidation of world peace, a new guarantee for nations struggling for self-liberation, and another strong impetus to the world revolutionary movement. The successful nuclear test by China . . . will increase the strength of the world's revolutionary forces and encourage the national liberation policies.

Ten Chinese organizations were frequently listed as carrying on some form of correspondence or relations with the NLF. In general, however, the major organizations involved in the NLF externalization effort were the China Peace Committee, the Chinese AAPSC, and the All-China Federation of Trade Unions; of somewhat lesser rank were the Chinese National Women's Federation, the All-China Youth Federation, and the All-China Students' Federation.

Chinese support also took more tangible forms. The Chinese Red Cross on July 14, 1963 announced that it had donated 100,000 yuan to the NLF's Liberation Red Cross Society. This was followed on July 19 with the announcement of another donation by the same organization of 100,000 *jen-min-p'iao* (JMP), or 3,000,000 South Vietnamese piasters, worth of medicines and medical instruments. Semiautomatic carbines made in China began showing up in South Vietnam in July 1963; although this type of weapon (first produced in 1944 in the Soviet Union) was manufactured in several bloc nations, each one carried a chop near the trigger housing to identify the factory, and those captured in South Vietnam undoubtedly had been manufactured in China in 1960. At least 20 were captured during 1964. By late 1964 Chinese 90-mm rocket launchers, 60-mm mortars, and 75- and 57-mm recoilless rifles, carbines, pistols, and flares were being captured in quantity in South Vietnam.

Chinese support abroad for the NLF was full scale and militant. Ch'ien Ta-wei, the Chinese delegate to the International Union of Students Committee for Solidarity with South Vietnam meeting in Budapest, on February 13, 1964 delivered a militant speech that ended with a call for the IUS to

1. Actively unfold extensive activities in support of the struggle of the South Vietnamese people and students; expose the crimes of the U.S. imperialists in South Vietnam and their slaughter of the South Vietnamese people.

2. Mobilize the students of all countries to render to South Vietnamese students substantial political and material help, including weapons.

3. Intensify propaganda and publicize the development of the struggle of the South Vietnamese people and students, their experiences and heroic deeds, the significance of their struggle, and the contributions of their struggle to the defense of world peace.

4. Unfold extensive mass struggles for students in all countries against the U.S. imperialists, thereby giving powerful support to the patriotic anti-U.S. struggle of the South Vietnamese people and students.

5. Resolutely condemn the U.S. criminal act of sending a [U.N.] inspection team to South Vietnam, which was an infringement of the sovereignty of the South Vietnamese people and an insult to the people of South Vietnam and Asia.

The GVN on August 1, 1964 claimed that Communist Chinese advisers had been seen in South Vietnam. It sent a note to the ICC stating that Communist Chinese officers had led the 514th and 261st battalions (which it said were made up of DRV army soldiers) in an attack on July 20 on Sung Hieu in Cai Be. The note said their commands in Chinese could be heard during the battle; it added that of the 42 enemy bodies left on the battlefield, 8 had been decapitated and their heads taken away to prevent identification as Chinese.

Radio Hanoi as early as September 4, 1964 hinted at the possibility of Chinese "volunteers" for action in Vietnam. It said

The DRV foreign ministries [embassies] abroad have received tens of thousands of telegrams and letters voicing support for the South Vietnamese people's struggle. . . . The letter from the workers at the Peking Metal and Electromechanical Plant states that "all of us are ready to respond to the call of the Fatherland and will not hesitate when necessary to go to the front line, in Vietnam or anywhere else."

Hanoi said it had received offers for volunteers from youths in China, East Germany, and Hungary.

Vying with the Soviet Union, the Chinese Communist statements of support for the NLF steadily grew more militant and less equivocal in the early part of 1965, culminating in the open offer of troops and matériel on March 25, when *People's Daily* declared:

We now solemnly declare that we Chinese people firmly respond to the NLFSV statement and will join the people of the world in sending all necessary material aid, including arms and all other war materials, to the heroic South Vietnamese people who are battling fearlessly. At the same time we are ready to send our own men, whenever the South Vietnamese people want them, to fight together with the South Vietnamese people. . . .

Although Chinese good faith in this offer was open to question, Peking was seriously interested in building up the NLF externally. Reliable reports in early April 1965 said that the Algerian United Nations delegate had relayed to Secretary-General U Thant a message from Premier Chou En-lai that any negotiations on peace in Vietnam must be undertaken directly with the National Liberation Front. This represented another major victory for the NLF in its externalization efforts.

However, there were indications that the Chinese were somewhat less than fully satisfied with the NLF's approach to the struggle in South Vietnam. The most significant evidence for this was contained in the famous Lin Piao document on Maoist strategy,[11] in which Lin Piao seems to be saying to the NLF and Hanoi that they made a bad mistake in 1964 by getting off the "national salvation" thesis and concentrating on the more military route to victory. The Chinese appeared to believe that the NLF should have used as its model the Chinese people's antifascist war against Japan and felt that many of its actions — the use of terror, for example — tended to turn Vietnamese against Vietnamese rather than to unite them against what China considered the sole enemy — the United States. There seems to be little doubt that the Chinese Communists were appalled by many of the NLF activities and techniques.

What can we conclude about Chinese-NLF relations during the 1960–1965 period? China had everything to gain and nothing to lose by fully supporting the NLF. The overriding Chinese goal with respect to South Vietnam was the elimination of the U.S. military force. It sought a government in South Vietnam that, if not under Chinese domination, would at least "check with Peking" before making any major decisions. And China sought control of at least one major political force or organization in the South, preferably the NLF. The Chinese probably were at least mildly opposed to the reunification of North and South Vietnam and may have been strongly opposed to it; the issue was never tested. In general, the Chinese acted as if South Vietnam should be their natural sphere of influence, which they meant to get sooner or later.

Relations with the Soviet Union

The NLF image of the Soviet Union was that of a rather remote big brother, powerful and successful; yet chiefly because of the geographic and psychological distances involved, it was an image that did not impinge deeply on NLF consciousness. The relationship was classic, a sort of doctrinal reflex action. The Soviet revolutionary experience was regarded as the great model for the NLF, despite the lack of similarities. Radio Liberation on November 7, 1963, for example, said:

From the October Revolution the South Vietnamese people have learned many significant lessons. First of all it was a national liberation revolution. It showed oppressed and colonized peoples the path of struggle for self-liberation. It revealed the weaknesses of a backward nation, but when the

[11] Lin Piao, "Long Live the Victory of People's War! In Commemoration of the 20th Anniversary of Victory in the Chinese People's War of Resistance Against Japan," *Jenmin Jih-pao*, September 2, 1965, and *Peking Review*, Vol. VIII, No. 36 (September 3, 1965), pp. 9–30, also in William E. Griffith, *Sino-Soviet Relations, 1964–1965* (Cambridge, Mass.: The M.I.T. Press, 1966), Document 30.

people united solidly, they had surprising strength and incomparable intelligence and thereby were able to deter the capitalists and imperialists who banded together armed with modern weapons. The October Revolution is a shining example of how the spirit of enduring pain, the spirit of self-sufficiency, heroic sacrifice, and unshakable faith can combine to create faith and an example for all oppressed peoples.

Nguyen Huu Tho's message to the Soviet Union in October 1964 echoed the same theme:

Having the sympathy of and strongly supported by the Soviet Union, . . . studying carefully the revolutionary struggle spirit of the heroic examples of the Soviet Union's people in the October Revolution and war to protect the Fatherland, the South Vietnamese people are determined to move forward steadily . . . , to liberate the Fatherland completely.

In Soviet mythology, the 1905 Russian Revolution started the Indochinese on the road to social consciousness; World War I set them on the road to partisan warfare in the name of nationalism; the popular front in Europe in the 1930's aided the movement in a practical sense; the Soviet war against Japan set the stage for the Viet Minh war; and in general there was a prevalence of Marxist tone to all events in Indochina from 1930 onward. Events of the post-1954 period in South Vietnam were due largely to the ineptitude of the GVN and to GVN tyranny, plus the exacerbating efforts of the United States. Such was the way the NLF thought the Soviet Union viewed it, a view reinforced by such Radio Moscow commentaries as the following:

Implementing Lenin's teachings, the Soviet Union during its 46 years of history has always resolutely supported the liberation of colonies and dependent countries, has always been a faithful friend of countries engaged in a tenacious struggle for national independence. What is taking place in South Vietnam cannot but cause just concern among the Soviet people. . . . At the United Nations the Soviet delegation expressed its concern, issuing a statement condemning the infringement of human rights in Vietnam. The Soviet Union demands that the South Vietnamese people be allowed to settle their domestic affairs themselves. . . . The Soviet people once again declare their admiration for the courage and heroism of South Vietnamese patriotic fighters who are carrying on a just struggle under the NLFSV banner, aimed at establishing a unified, peaceful, independent, democratic, and prosperous Vietnam. . . .[12]

In the earlier days of the NLF the Soviet Union tended to regard all of Indochina as a whole, treating the Cambodian situation and the wars of liberation in Laos and Vietnam as a single entity. The first NLF representative to visit the Soviet Union and the first to go abroad was Huynh Van Tam, who spent a week in Moscow in December 1961, a trip given little attention at the time by either the Soviet Union or the NLF. It was the Soviet Union that actually launched the NLF on

[12] Radio Moscow, December 17, 1963.

its externalization program with the Nguyen Van Hieu mission's attendance at the World Congress for General Disarmament and Peace in Moscow in July 1962. The three-man delegation (Hieu, his wife Ma Thi Chu, and Le Thanh Nam) were joined in Moscow by Xuan Thuy, representing the Youth Liberation Association. The Soviet Union sponsored an NLF exhibit in Moscow during the conference and arranged a luncheon at which the NLF delegates were introduced to the Japanese delegation. The major message that Hieu brought to the conference on behalf of the NLF was that events in South Vietnam represented a threat to world peace, that the NLF was engaged in a liberation struggle, and that

our Front holds that the struggle for national independence is inseparably linked to the struggle for general disarmament and peace. . . . Our aims are entirely compatible with the aims and tasks of the World Congress for General Disarmament and Peace. . . .[13]

The NLF also backed the Soviet position on the nuclear test ban, a decision it was to reverse in less than a year.

The Soviet Union acted with extreme caution in its statements on South Vietnam. The Soviet chief at the United Nations, Valerian Zorin, at a New York press conference on February 26, 1962 told newsmen: "Americans are getting bogged down in a very disadvantageous and politically unjustified war which will entail very unpleasant consequences. . . . The United States should be very careful." [14] This obscurely phrased statement was generally interpreted at the time as a vague warning to the United States, although some interpreted it simply as a growing concern on the part of the Soviet Union over the sharpening conflict in South Vietnam. For the most part the Soviet Union with respect to the NLF confined itself to bland "faithful friend" utterances. On July 20, 1962, for example, Radio Moscow broadcast to Vietnam:

From the distant capitol of Moscow, the Soviet people's powerful voice flies to South Vietnam. They always sympathize with and follow the struggle of their distant brothers in South Vietnam. The Soviet government resolutely condemns U.S. intervention and demands that the United States stop its acts of interference in South Vietnam's internal affairs.

The replies were equally bland. Nguyen Huu Tho in a message noting the forty-fifth anniversary of the Russian Revolution cabled Premier Khrushchev: "We frankly thank the Soviet government and people for their support and assistance in the struggle for the liberation of South Vietnam, . . . support manifested especially in the recent first visit to the Soviet Union of an NLFSV delegation led by Professor Nguyen Van Hieu. . . ." Radio Liberation in December 1963 said that the NLF had

[13] Article by Nguyen Van Hieu, *Pravda*, July 13, 1962.
[14] *The New York Times*, February 7, 1962.

received 100,000 rubles worth of medicine, including 5,000 doses of antitetanus serum and medical equipment, the gift of the All-Union Central Council of Trade Unions of the U.S.S.R.; the Soviet Red Cross and Red Crescent Societies issued an antidefoliation statement in February 1963; Nguyen Huu Tho published a letter in *Pravda* (May 7, 1963) calling for an end to the Diem government and the establishment of a national democratic administration. He said the struggle "still can be settled peacefully" and that the NLF stands ready to explore such a solution with all parties; he listed as the primary condition for negotiations the ending of the "aggressive war" by the United States. Hieu was back in Moscow on December 20, 1963 and was received at the Kremlin. In December 1964 Le Van Thinh went to Moscow to make arrangements for the establishment of a permanent NLF delegation there.

In 1964 the Soviet Union revived its effort to increase its influence in Vietnam, although primarily with respect to the DRV. Khrushchev, on July 8 at a reception in honor of Soviet military academy graduates, was quoted as saying (by Radio Moscow, Radio Hanoi, and then Radio Liberation):

For many years now the United States has carried on a bloody aggressive war in South Vietnam. Playing the role of an international gendarme, it is scheming to suppress the South Vietnamese people's national liberation movement. . . . The South Vietnamese people have the perfect right to take up arms to struggle for their liberation and interests. They are waging a sacred struggle for freedom and independence, and we support them in this struggle.

The chief Soviet instrument for dealing with the NLF was the Soviet Afro-Asian People's Solidarity Committee, the Soviet Peace Council, and the All-Union Central Council of Trade Unions of the U.S.S.R. Its most valuable effort to support the NLF was the formation of the Permanent Bureau of the International Conference for Solidarity with the People of Vietnam in Hanoi in November 1964, described earlier, although its motives then seemed divided between providing a way of channeling funds and supplies to the NLF and refuting Peking's statements that Soviet efforts to help the revolutionary struggles in Asia were feeble and hypocritical.

The Soviet Union in late 1964 began directing more of its attention directly toward the NLF; on November 17, 1964, for example, Premier Kosygin sent a solidarity message directly to the NLF Central Committee, something that, as far as can be determined, had not been done by Khrushchev.

In January 1965 the Soviet Union announced that a permanent NLF delegate had been accredited to Moscow, following discussions with Nguyen Van Tien of the NLF. Three months later Dang Quang Minh arrived to take up duties as NLF chief of mission in Moscow, accompanied by at least four other Vietnamese, to make the mission in the Soviet Union the largest that the NLF maintained. The NLF delegation presented its "credentials" to the chairman of the Soviet Afro-Asian People's Solidarity Committee on April 30, 1965. An interview with Dang Quang Minh appeared in the Soviet publication *New Times*, in the edition dated May 26, 1965.

During this period the Soviet Union began asserting in increasingly direct terms the primacy of the NLF in South Vietnamese affairs. Radio Moscow, for example, on April 19, 1965 declared:

The NLFSV has already obtained wide international recognition. It has permanent representation in the Soviet Union, Czechoslovakia, the German Democratic Republic, China, Cuba, Indonesia, and other countries. Everything goes to show that the NLF is obviously a real expression of the will and desires of the people of South Vietnam, its only legitimate representative.

Unlike China, the Soviet Union had a great deal to lose and nothing much to gain in a continuation of hostilities in South Vietnam, even in an NLF victory. Fighting in Vietnam mitigated against détente with the United States. The Soviet Union was interested in a primacy of influence in some Southeast Asian country, but in its eyes Burma would serve as well as Vietnam. Nothing was to be gained in having to choose between accepting U.S. punishment of the DRV or military confrontation with the United States. In short, the Soviet Union would have gained from any settlement in Vietnam short of a GVN and United States victory.

The Sino-Soviet dispute did not impinge particularly on the covert NLF externalization effort. The NLF, like many earlier Vietnamese organizations, could maintain a Janus-faced policy, presenting two visages to the world: one toward Peking and one toward Moscow. It could assume the hard, unsmiling face of pure Marxism-Leninism of the Chinese and speak of its militant struggle; or it could assume the blander Soviet visage of peaceful coexistence and emphasize neutrality and the peaceful reunification of Vietnam. The use of the term "peaceful reunification" implied adherence to the Soviet thesis that small countries can be wrested from the imperialist camp by many means, including peaceful ones; its call for liberation and stress on the armed struggle obviously was a bow to China. Reports from rural Vietnam on the activities of agit-prop workers indicated that the NLF did what the DRV was able to do for so long a time — walk the line between the two powers, evading every effort to be forced to opt for one. A *quy chanh* during interrogation was asked about the attitude of the NLF toward the Sino-Soviet dispute, and he replied graciously that China was his mother and Russia his father.

19

NLF Policy and Goals

Policy Statements

As its first public act in December 1960 the NLF issued its "Ten-Point Manifesto," listing what it described as its "action program." This manifesto in slightly amended form was reproduced and distributed by the thousands throughout South Vietnam and later throughout the Communist world. If it came to power, said the NLF, it would do the following:

1. *Establish a coalition government.* "The present rule is a disguised colonial regime set up by the U.S. imperialists. The South Vietnam ruling clique is a servile administration carrying out U.S. imperialist policies. Such a regime and administration must be overthrown and replaced by a broad, national, and democratic coalition government composed of representatives of every sector of the population, various nationalities, political parties, religious communities, and patriotic personalities. The people's control of the economic, political, social, and cultural interests must be recovered, and independence, democracy, im-

344

provement of the people's living standards, peace, and neutrality achieved for the attainment of a peaceful national unification."

2. *Promote democracy*. "[We will] abolish the present constitution of the Ngo Dinh Diem dictatorial government and with universal suffrage elect a new National Assembly. Freedom of expression, press, assembly, association, travel, religion, and other democratic liberties will be promulgated. Religious, political, and patriotic organizations will be permitted freedom of activity regardless of beliefs and tendencies. There will be a general amnesty for all political detainees, the concentration camps dissolved, and fascist Law 10/59 and other antidemocratic laws abolished. Persons who fled the country because of the U.S.-Diem regime will be free to return home. Illegal arrests, illegal imprisonment, torture, and corporal punishment shall be forbidden. Those who terrorized and massacred the people and do not repent shall be punished."

3. *Develop the economy*. "[We will] build an independent and sovereign economy and improve the people's standards of living. The monopolies established by the U.S. and their lackeys will be abolished, properties of the U.S. imperialists and their agents confiscated and nationalized, and an independent and sovereign economy and financial system built to serve the nation's interests. Industry will be encouraged by limiting or halting importation of foreign goods that can be manufactured at home and by reduction of import taxes on raw materials and machinery. Handicraft and cottage industries will be encouraged by the abolition of taxes on their products. Farming, fishing, and cattle raising will be encouraged, new land will be opened, wasteland reclaimed, agricultural productivity promoted, crops insured, and sale of farm goods guaranteed. Trade will be encouraged between the cities and the countryside, between the delta area and the highlands. Trade with foreign countries will be without regard for politics, on the basis of equality and reciprocity. An equitable and rational tax system will be established; arbitrary penalties will be abolished. Labor legislation shall be promulgated, and arbitrary dismissal and mistreatment of employees shall be forbidden. Workers' living conditions will be improved. Child labor laws, covering health measures, working conditions, and minimum wages, shall be implemented. Social assistance shall be organized: jobs for the unemployed, assistance for orphans, aged, and invalided persons, aid for victims of fighting, the result of the war of the U.S. imperialists and their henchmen. There will be assistance for victims of crop failure, fire, or natural calamities. Those from North Vietnam who wish to return home shall be permitted to do so. Jobs will be provided for those who wish to stay. Forcible relocation, destruction of homes, the concentration of people in special centers shall be prohibited. Security will be provided both farmers in the rural areas and workers in the cities."

4. *Institute land reform.* "[We will] reduce land rental costs as the first step in land reform. Farmers will be guaranteed the right to till their present plots of land; land reclaimed will be guaranteed to those who reclaim it; farmer ownership of land already distributed will be ensured. Agrovilles, prosperity zones, and land development centers will be abolished. Those who have been forced to settle in these camps will be free to return to their native homes. Land belonging to the U.S. imperialists and their henchmen will be confiscated and distributed to the landless. Communal land will be redistributed in an equitable and rational manner. By means of negotiation and by paying an equitable and rational price the state will purchase land from landowners having more than a certain amount of rice fields, the amount to be determined according to the land situation in each locality. This land will be distributed to landless or land-lacking farmers. The farmers receiving the land will pay nothing and will not be bound by any conditions."

5. *Promote education.* "A national democratic cultural and educational program will be launched. The depraved U.S. culture and education will be eliminated; a progressive culture and education will serve the Fatherland and the people. Illiteracy will be wiped out by building more schools, universities, and professional schools. Teaching will be in the Vietnamese language. Tuition will be reduced and eliminated in the case of poor students. The examination system will be reformed. Science, technology, literature, and art will be developed. Intellectuals, writers, and artists will be encouraged by providing them with the necessary conditions for expanding their abilities in the cause of serving the Fatherland. A program to develop the people's health will be begun, and a physical-culture movement will be launched."

6. *Develop the armed forces.* "A national army to defend the Fatherland and the people will be developed. The present system of U.S. military advisers will be abolished. Compulsory service will be abolished. Soldiers' living conditions will be improved, and they will be provided with political rights. Mistreatment of soldiers is condemned. Assistance will be given to the families of poor soldiers. Officers and soldiers who perform well against the U.S.-Diem clique will be rewarded. Leniency will be granted to former U.S.-Diem clique agents who committed crimes against our compatriots if they repent and serve the people. All foreign military bases in Vietnam will be eliminated."

7. *Protection of minority rights.* "[We will] realize equality among the different nationalities and between men and women. National minorities will be ensured the right of autonomy in zones created as part of the family of Vietnam. Equal rights will prevail, and all nationalities will be free to use their own language and script and maintain or change their customs and habits. The U.S.-Diem clique policy of persecution,

oppression, and assimilation of minorities will be abolished. The minority groups will be aided in economic and cultural development; cadres will be trained. Equality between men and women will be realized; women will be entitled to the same rights as men in all fields — political, economic, cultural, and social. The legitimate interests of foreign residents in Vietnam shall be protected. The interests of overseas Vietnamese shall be protected."

8. *Pursue a nonalignment foreign policy.* "A foreign policy of peace and neutrality shall be carried out. All unfair agreements violating national sovereignty, signed by the U.S.-Diem ruling clique, shall be abolished. Diplomatic relations shall be established with all countries, regardless of their political regime, in conformity with the peaceful coexistence principles stipulated at the Bandung Conference. [We will] closely unite with the peace-loving and neutral nations and develop friendly relations with Southeast Asian nations, especially Cambodia and Laos, not participate in any military alliance, and will receive economic aid from any nation if it is provided without conditions."

9. *Work for reunification.* "The peaceful reunification of the Fatherland is the earnest yearning of our compatriots throughout the entire country. The National Liberation Front stands for step-by-step reunification by means of negotiations between the two zones under conditions beneficial to both sides. Pending unification the two sides should pledge to refrain from using propaganda or violence against each other. Economic and cultural intercourse should be established, and there should be freedom of movement for commercial activities, tourism, and freedom of correspondence."

10. *Condemnation of war.* "[We shall] oppose aggressive wars and all forms of imperialism's slavery. War propaganda is opposed and general disarmament and prohibition of nuclear weapons supported; atomic energy for peaceful purposes is supported. The struggle movements for peace, democracy, and social progress throughout the world are supported and [we will] . . . actively contribute to the defense of peace in Southeast Asia and the world."

On its first anniversary, December 20, 1961, the NLF issued a list of "immediate action" demands, which it said did not supplant its earlier Ten-Point Manifesto but was a series of interim demands. The NLF called for

1. Withdrawal of all U.S. military personnel and weapons from South Vietnam and abolition of the Staley Plan.[1]

[1] The Staley Plan, written in 1961 by a group headed by American economist Eugene Staley, had as its major recommendations increasing the size of the Vietnamese armed forces and launching the strategic-hamlet program.

2. End to hostilities.
3. Establishment of political freedoms.
4. Release of political prisoners.
5. Dissolution of the National Assembly and election of a new assembly and president.
6. Ending the resettlement program.
7. Solution of Vietnam's economic problems.
8. Establishment of a foreign policy of nonalignment.

The only significant addition to the original manifesto was the demand for an end to hostilities. The most significant omission from the second list was reunification, a theme that began to taper off about this time. The DRV in this same period listed the NLF objectives as "peace, independence, democracy, a comfortable life, and the peaceful unification of the Fatherland . . . through the overthrow of the U.S. imperialists and the Ngo Dinh Diem clique," [2] indicating a divergence of stated views between the DRV and the NLF leadership on the question of unification.

The initial policy statements were the result of actions taken at the NLF organizational congress in December 1960 and subsequent decisions by the national Central Committee. At the organizing congress plans were announced for the convening of the first regular NLF congress within a year. After several postponements it finally met in northern Tay Ninh province from February 16 to March 3, 1962.[3] It was attended by approximately 150 persons representing the provisional Central Committee, the NLF interzones and zones, the PRP, the Radical Socialist Party, and the Democratic Party and central committee members of the functional liberation associations and the *van hoi* groups within the NLF.[4]

[2] Ton Duc Thang writing in *Hoc Tap*, December 1961.

[3] The NLF news media reported in detail on the congress; the essential facts were later confirmed by GVN penetration agents who attended the sessions.

[4] A somewhat romanticized but essentially accurate description of the meeting place for the first and last day of the session was described in a clandestine newspaper:

> A large house, covered with latania leaves, was built in the fresh shadowy forest. Two rows of benches provided sufficient seats for hundreds of delegates. Multicolored silk banderols, bearing slogans, and a vase of multicolored wild flowers placed in the middle of the conference room made it gayer and more beautiful. . . . Some delegates, hands all calloused, came to the conference with the pride of a young mother who practices thriftiness to build her family's future. Others, after victoriously fighting enemy raids, slipped stealthily between enemy posts to arrive with faces showing gallantry and diligence. . . . Others came still smelling of the gunpowder of victories. . . . The delegates shook hands and asked about each other's achievements. Cables poured in from everywhere, asking for the delegates' health and wishing the conference success. . . . Military units in the area sent delegates fish they had caught . . . or stags they had killed. . . . Among the gifts presented were flags inscribed with the words "Welcome Front's Congress" and "Welcome 1962 Congress." A number of Chinese working people presented the congress with a silver-embossed map of a united Vietnam bearing the words "Chinese and Vietnamese laboring people pledge solidarity for struggle."

Actually this conference, as were all NLF conferences, was a deeply clandestine one and as mobile as a floating New York crap game. Americans in Vietnam, hearing daily Radio Hanoi reports on the progress of such conferences, were puzzled as to why the Vietnamese air force did not bomb the meeting sites. The answer was that the meetings were as ephemeral as the morning mist, that the NLF, like the Viet Minh before it, had well-developed techniques for conducting what might be called the mobile conference. One *quy chanh* described the process basically as follows: After the day's meeting each delegate (or subgroup of delegates) would be given privately a jungle mail-drop location and instructed to go there the next day at precisely 7:00 A.M. There might be as many as 25 such mail drops for 150 delegates. Then the delegates would scatter, melt into the countryside. Some might sleep in a nearby village at a friend's house; others might sleep in the jungle or down river in their sampans (if in the Mekong delta). The next morning the delegate went to the jungle mail drop and found a message (placed there shortly before his arrival) giving him the location of the day's meeting. This might be a few miles away or as much as three hours' travel by foot or sampan. When all arrived at the meeting place, the session would convene. Should a delegate not arrive, the conference would immediately adjourn for the day. No one was permitted to leave the conference area while it was in session. About mid-afternoon the conference would end, and the delegates would be given the location of the next day's jungle mail drop and again would scatter for the night. Under this system no one except the top leadership knew in advance the location of the following day's meeting, thus effectively preventing ambush. A delegate had to proceed at once from his jungle mail drop to the conference site; if he delayed, detouring to leave a message with GVN officials, he would be missed and the alert sounded. (There was also the possibility that he was being shadowed by an NLF security agent.) Since the actual gathering lasted only a few hours — usually from about 10:00 A.M. to 3:00 P.M. — even if word was gotten out to an ARVN unit, it was virtually impossible for the unit to arrive before the delegates had departed. During one Eastern Nambo regional meeting in 1962 a GVN penetration agent walked all night to meet a fellow agent and get from him a portable radio transceiver, which he lugged back to the jungle mail drop. He then read the location on the message and radioed it to headquarters. Airborne troops were in the area by noon. As they buzzed in to land they saw the delegates, warned by air-raid wardens, scattering from the meeting hut. A few of the delegates were captured, but the majority of them, given a five-minute head start, vanished into the scrub jungle.

The theme of the first regular congress was one of unity and certainty of victory by means of the General Uprising. Declared the newly elected chairman, Nguyen Huu Tho:

Only with a broad and firmly united bloc, struggling in accordance with a program consistent with the interests of the masses, can we defeat the U.S. imperialists and their followers. . . . A General Uprising of the South Vietnamese people to overthrow the U.S.-Diem regime is natural and inevitable. . . .

Reiterated were earlier basic policies of the Front. An official statement was circulated throughout South Vietnam after the congress. It listed NLF objectives as the establishment of "a broad national democratic coalition administration in South Vietnam, realization of national independence and democracy, democratic freedoms, improvement of the people's living conditions, . . . defense of peace, carrying out the policy of neutrality." The version broadcast by Radio Hanoi on April 13, 1962 added "advancing to peaceful reunification of the Fatherland."

The rest of the official statement added nothing new to the NLF domestic program. In general the statement was reasonable in tone, conciliatory, and vastly different from those issued a year later.

One of the major organizational acts of the congress was the establishment of a 52-man Central Committee, of which 31 seats were filled; the 21 other members were were to "be chosen by the Central Committee at a later date." This was bait for other groups interested in joining the NLF. The congress declaration stated:

The congress is of the view that at the present time a number of mass organizations, parties, political groups, and personalities of good will, at home and abroad, do not yet have favorable conditions to contact and join the NLF. The congress has . . . sincerely called on the mass organizations to seize the earliest opportunity to share actively the responsibility of paramount importance that the people in South Vietnam have entrusted to the National Liberation Front.

On the July 20, 1962 anniversary of the signing of the Geneva accords, the NLF issued a "four-point manifesto":

1. The U.S. government must end its armed aggression against South Vietnam, abolish its military command, withdraw all its troops and personnel, as well as the troops and personnel of U.S. satellites and allies, and withdraw all weapons and other war equipment from South Vietnam.
2. Concerned parties in South Vietnam must stop the war, re-establish peace, and establish conditions throughout South Vietnam to enable the South Vietnamese to solve their own internal affairs. The South Vietnam authority [that is, government] must end its terror operations.
3. There must be established a national coalition government, to include representatives of all political parties, cliques, groups, all political tendencies, social strata, members of all religions. This government must guarantee peace. It must organize free general elections in South Vietnam to choose a

democratic National Assembly that will carry out the urgently needed policies. It must promulgate democratic liberties to all political parties, groups, religions; it must release all political prisoners, abolish all internment camps and all other forms of concentration [camps], and stop the forced draft of soldiers and the military training of youth, women, public servants, and students. It must carry out economic policies aimed at safeguarding free enterprise, economic independence. It must abolish monopolies and improve the living conditions of all people.

4. South Vietnam must carry out a foreign policy of peace and neutrality. It must establish friendly relations with all nations, especially with her neighbors. It must not enter any military bloc or agree to let any country establish military bases on her soil. It must accept aid from all countries [if] free of political conditions. A necessary international agreement must be signed in which the big powers of all blocs pledge to respect the sovereignty, independence, territorial integrity, and neutrality of South Vietnam. South Vietnam, together with Cambodia and Laos, will form a neutral area, all three countries retaining full sovereignty.

A new theme introduced at this time was the idea that the South Vietnamese should settle their own affairs, which replaced the policed neutralism idea suggested by the first regular congress. The July 20, 1962 statement declared:

The Central Committee of the National Liberation Front of South Vietnam believes that in the spirit of Vietnamese dealing with Vietnamese solving their own internal affairs, with the determination to put the Fatherland's interest above all else, the forces that oppose U.S. imperialism in South Vietnam will, through mutual concessions, be able to reach a common agreement for united action to serve the people.

The NLF in late 1962 also began referring to the possibility of a cease-fire, separating it from the demand for withdrawal of American troops and matériel. These references ceased in early 1963.

The Presidium of the NLF Central Committee met periodically throughout 1962 and 1963. Its October 6–7, 1962 meeting was concerned with the "question of autonomy for the people of the highlands" and came in the face of a mass exodus of the montagnards caused by the increased hostile activity of the NLF cadres. The Presidium also discussed "the methods of winning over the support of the Diem soldiers," which marked the beginning of a serious *binh van,* or proselyting, program, and it approved the joint NLF–Chinese Communist and joint NLF-DRV statements signed earlier in Peking and Hanoi by visiting NLF representative Nguyen Van Hieu. The Presidium met on December 19, 1962 to mark the NLF's second anniversary; on January 7–8, 1963 to discuss "external recognition progress and the . . . matter of a cease-fire at Tet"; on March 6–8, 1963 to hear "a report by Tran Buu Kiem on foreign affairs and . . . a report on the American defoliation and chemical warfare scheme . . . and on contradictions in the ARVN"; and again on April 17, 1963 to discuss "U.S. defoliation plans." The Buddhist struggle with the Diem government broke out at this time (May 8, 1963), but the NLF paid singularly little public attention to it. Its half-year report, broadcast by Radio Liberation on July 6, 1963, for example, ran to more than 5,000 words but devoted less than two paragraphs to what at the moment was the dominant political crisis in South Vietnam; even that was little more than a statement of the Buddhist position. When unrest in Vietnam reached a critical stage on September 4, 1963, the Presidium met in extraordinary session, after which it issued a communiqué condemning the Diem government's actions against the Buddhists but asserting that primary responsibility rested with the Americans:

The conference found that the origin of the present and extremely grave situation in South Vietnam is the criminal interventionist and aggressive policy of U.S. imperialism and the dictatorial and cruel regime of the Ngo family that the United States set up, which is thoroughly rotten and hated and scorned by all Southern people. Unable to learn, the warlike U.S. clique, headed by Kennedy, is advancing further and further into the endless tunnel. It is trying to find means to dominate South Vietnam.

This tack was in anticipation of the end of the Diem government, whose overthrow virtually all Vietnamese by this time regarded as inevitable. Emphasis was shifted from the GVN to the United States:

Running-dog Ngo Dinh Diem has been isolated to such a degree that he can do nothing and has become an obstacle to the implementation of the aggressive policy of the warlike U.S. clique, headed by Kennedy. . . . To pursue its aggressive policy in South Vietnam, the Kennedy Administration is applying a new program: on the one hand it uses political pressure and aid to force the Ngo Dinh Diem family to docilely obey its orders; on the other hand it deceives public opinion, mustering other faithful lackeys, and using all measures — including military measures — to overthrow the Ngo Dinh Diem family and replace it with new lackeys.

On September 11, 1963 the NLF issued a "three-point peace plan," which it sent to the United Nations. It called for "an end to American military assistance, withdrawal of American forces, and a coalition government of political and religious organizations. . . ." Coming at the time it did, the statement had a curiously irrelevant quality about it. Diem and the Buddhists were locked in a death struggle, the Americans looking on helplessly and the NLF suggesting U.S. withdrawal as a solution. In the weeks that followed, the NLF voice muted itself on internal developments. Radio Liberation carried stories on specific incidents involving the Buddhists, but these were basically factual and without comment. Policy statements dropped off almost entirely. Attacks on Americans mounted in intensity and hysteria. Radio Liberation acted as though the Buddhists did not exist. Nor, as had been anticipated, did the NLF agit-prop teams flood the countryside with anti-Diem leaflets in the name of Buddhism. The leadership appeared unwilling or unable to capitalize on the most significant struggle movement in Vietnamese history. An effort was made to infiltrate some of the Buddhist demonstrations, but even these appeared to be halfhearted; the NLF tailed after the Buddhists.

Had the NLF leadership wished to do so, it could have used its impressive struggle machine to launch in the name of the Buddha a nationwide struggle movement that conceivably could have ended with its long-pursued General Uprising. The NLF's reluctance to involve itself deeply in the Buddhist struggle was somewhat puzzling. Knowledgeable Vietnamese attributed its refusal to act to an unwillingness to involve itself in an alien struggle movement. The NLF and the Communists, ran the argument, avoid mass activities over which they do not exercise total control; they wish to conceive, organize, launch, and at all times master a struggle movement, and they hesitate to join movements tending to violence over which they do not have mastery. The Buddhist leadership made it clear it did not seek NLF help since it wished at all costs to avoid the Communist stigma. Another popular explanation for the NLF's "sit-tight" policy during the Buddhist troubles was that the NLF was going to allow the bourgeois revolutionary forces to succeed in toppling Diem, after which it would capture the Revolution, as the Kerensky government was captured in the Russian Revolution. No such effort, however, was made by the NLF. A slanderous but widely bandied explanation among Vietnamese at the time was that the NLF did not want Diem removed, that he and his brothers and sister-in-law were far more valuable to the NLF in office than out. In truth the NLF posture during this period remains something of a mystery.

Radio Liberation was an uncertain trumpet in the days immediately following the overthrow of the Diem government. It characterized the Saigon street celebrations as anti-American demonstrations (a patent absurdity) and managed to imply that the NLF deserved credit for the overthrow. Two days after the coup d'état Radio Liberation began a series of commentaries on the "correct path to national salvation." The major themes were that the change of government meant increased American involvement in Vietnamese affairs and that social forces were loosed that would result in increased American-GVN contradictions.

Five days later (November 7) the NLF issued its first post-Diem policy statement, a list of "eight demands," which were:

1. Destroy all strategic hamlets and quarters and other disguised concentration camps.

2. Release all political detainees, whatever their political tendencies.

3. Promulgate without delay democratic freedom — freedom of assembly, expression, the press, worship, trade, and so on.

4. Root out all vestiges of the fascist and militarist dictatorial regime.

5. Stop all persecution and repression and raiding operations.

6. Dissolve all nepotist organizations, all forms of control, Republican Youth organizations, and other paramilitary organizations of youth, women, students and pupils, and public employees.

7. Immediately stop forcible conscription and militarization of youth, women, and public servants.

8. Cancel all kinds of unjustified taxes.

Since the new Duong Van Minh government already was in the process of doing all but one of these (halt the draft), the demands, which appeared later in leaflet form, were an obvious effort to take credit for changes in GVN policy when they were made.

As noted earlier, the NLF leadership believed that the end of the Diem regime would almost certainly lead to NLF assumption of power. By mid-November its hopes were beginning to dim, but they had not yet been dashed. It was at this moment (November 17) that the Central Committee issued its first serious official statement since the end of the Diem government. The statement again advanced a series of demands, this time numbering six:

1. *Eliminate the vestiges of the Diem regime.* "Unconditionally abolish the dictatorial and fascist regime of Ngo Dinh Diem as a whole, including the U.S. dependent lines, the anti-Communist policies that mean antipeople policies, the dictatorship in general in internal and external affairs, the reactionary political organizations under such labels as 'Labor and Human Dignity Organization,' 'National Revolutionary Movement,' 'Women's Solidarity Movement,' 'Association of Victims of Communism,' 'Association of War Martyrs' Families,' 'Republican Youth and Women,' the network of policemen and secret agents, and so on, which constitute the tools to manipulate, control, and suppress the people; the 'strategic hamlets, quarters, and sectors,' the policies of militarizing youths and women, the antipopular laws such as Law 10/59, the fascist law controlling the press, the emergency order, the order on mobilization and requisition, and so on. Release all political detainees regardless of tendency, bringing into the open the crimes of the U.S.-Diem regime, and bring to trial and duly punish those who have perpetrated bloody crimes against the people."

2. *Establish democratic freedoms.* "Carry out without delay real and broad democracy, including freedom of thought, expression, the press, organization, assembly, demonstrations, trade unions; freedom to set up political parties, and social, cultural, and professional organizations; freedom of movement, trade, religion, and worship; corporal liberty; and

guarantee by law nondiscrimination for all the people; stop the persecution, arrest, and detention of patriots and opposition individuals and parties; cancel the barbarous prison regime, especially torture, penitence, brainwashing, and ill treatment of prisoners. Refrain from setting up in South Vietnam any form of dictatorial regime, either militarist or of a group or party, and from carrying out a policy of monoparty or monoreligion, a policy of dictatorship concerning thoughts, politics, religion, and economy."

3. *Eliminate American influence.* "Put an immediate end to the U.S. aggression in South Vietnam, withdraw all U.S. advisers from the Republican army units and military and civilian branches in an advance toward withdrawing from South Vietnam all U.S. troops and military personnel, including the military command of Paul D. Harkins, weapons, and other war means. The U.S. imperialists must respect South Vietnam's independence and sovereignty and must not interfere in its internal affairs. The U.S. Embassy must halt spying activities to foment trouble in South Vietnam. South Vietnam must enjoy complete sovereignty in all political, military, economic, and cultural fields, in internal as well as in foreign relations. It must not be dependent on any country whatsoever and must enjoy an international position on equal footing with other countries. Only on such a basis can the relations between South Vietnam and the United States be normalized and the interests and honor of the latter in South Vietnam be guaranteed."

4. *Make social and economic reforms.* "Carry out a policy of [building] an independent, democratic national economy; gradually raise the people's living standard in an advance toward eliminating unemployment and poverty. Cancel all harsh economic laws; recognize freedom of business and trade; abolish completely all kinds of exacting taxes, supplementary taxes, and forcible money collections; reduce other taxes and cut fines. Guarantee and encourage the national economy; check the influx of foreign goods that upset the South Vietnam market. Abolish the monopoly of the U.S. imperialists and the Diem family. Increase wages of workers, army men, public servants, and private enterprise employees."

5. *Halt the fighting.* "Stop at once terrorist raids, strafings, and operations and the use of chemical poison, toxic gas, and napalm bombs; generally speaking, end the war; restore peace and security and stabilize the situation in the countryside and the other part [nonliberated area] of South Vietnam; stop bloodshed among the Vietnamese people. Halt press-ganging; demobilize the soldiers of the Republican army whose military terms have expired and let them return to their families and earn their living. We loudly declare that 18 years of war is more than

sufficient! There is no reason to drag on the state of mourning on our soil merely because of the ambition of the warlike U.S. imperialists and their followers."

6. *Establish a coalition government*. "The parties concerned in South Vietnam should negotiate with one another to reach a cease-fire and solve the important problems of the nation, to stabilize the basic internal and external policies, with a view to reaching free general elections to elect state organs and to form a national coalition government composed of representatives of all forces, parties, tendencies, and strata of the South Vietnamese people."

The statement also contained a return to the unification theme, although this was not listed as one of the "demands." It declared:

Concerning the reunification of Vietnam, as was expounded many times by the South Vietnam National Liberation Front, the Vietnam Fatherland Front, and the DRV government, it will be realized step by step on a voluntary basis, with consideration given to the characteristics of each zone, with equality, and without annexation of one zone by the other.

These demands represented nothing new in either substance or emphasis from the September statements. One almost had the feeling they were a sort of holding action, pending the Presidium's clarification of the situation.

The NLF Second Congress, originally slated for February 1963 but postponed several times by the Central Committee because "conditions were not favorable," finally met January 1–8, 1964 in northern Tay Ninh province with about 150 persons in attendance. Represented were NLF regional and provincial committees, the Democratic Party, the Radical Socialist Party, the People's Revolutionary Party, the Highland Autonomy Movement, the Women's Liberation Association, the Youth Liberation Association, the Farmers' Liberation Association, the Cultural Liberation Association, the Patriotic and Democratic Journalists' Association, the Patriotic Teachers' Association, the Student Union, the Veterans' (former Resistants Fighters) Association, the Liberation Red Cross Society, the the Liberation armed forces, North Vietnam refugees (including Nungs), overseas Vietnamese, montagnards (specifically Ede or Rhade, Sedang, and Bahnar), Mahayana and Hinayana Buddhists, Catholics, Protestants, Chams, residents of Ap Bac, the Committee for Consolidation of Peaceful Coexistence in Tay Ninh (Cao Dai), the Defense of World Peace Committee, the Union of Chinese Residents, the Cao Dai Resistance Army, ARVN defectors, and persons involved in the abortive November 11, 1960 coup d'état.

The mood of the meeting, judging by the speeches, was one of supreme confidence. One speaker characterized it as a meeting of "unity and indomitability, a boiling enthusiasm for victories, and an iron-clad confidence in final victory." Declared Chairman Nguyen Huu Tho, "It was a congress of great unity, a congress of great victory, a congress of determination to fight and triumph. . . . This was a congress of winners."

The key statement in the congress was an address by Tho. He called for a negotiated settlement clearly and unequivocally by

a halt to the war and the withdrawal of American military forces, and negotiations by all forces and parties in South Vietnam to find a rational solution for the achievement of a policy of peace and neutrality. The U.S. government has poured into its war in South Vietnam nearly two million dollars a day, as much as the French colonialist expenditure during the crucial period of their war in Indochina. . . . The U.S. imperialists have brought to South Vietnam 25,000 troops, . . . 700 aircraft, 20 warships, including 4,000-ton warships and one aircraft carrier, 500 motorboats, hundreds of amphibious vehicles, thousands of armored cars, and dozens of thousands of tons of ammunition. They have built 110 airfields, several naval bases and ports, numerous military bases, and strategic roads. . . . The United States wants to:

1. Suppress the patriotic movement in South Vietnam so as to consolidate its defense line from the Mid-East to northern Asia.
2. Threaten the national liberation movement in general.
3. Draw experiences to cope with the revolution of colonial peoples. . . .

[Our] great successes stem from the following causes:

1. The heroism of the South Vietnamese people. . . . We began with empty hands. . . . Violence has battled justice, and justice has won many glorious victories not because we had more guns but . . . because of our patriotism and our heroic mettle. . . .
2. The solidarity and the unity of our people. . . . Even large numbers of Chinese in Vietnam have joined us . . . as have overseas Vietnamese, and people of many political ideas. . . .
3. We have determination to win. . . .
4. [We have] the ever broader and stronger support and sympathy of the people of the world, . . . who regard our struggle as part of the struggle of progressive mankind for independence, social progress, and peace. . . .

In its December 20, 1964 anniversary message the NLF reiterated policy statements it had enunciated earlier. Nothing was added; no change of emphasis appeared. Its formula for settling the issues remained the same:

The NFL once again reiterates its stand that the United States must get out of South Vietnam, and the South Vietnam problem must be solved by the South Vietnamese themselves. If the U.S. ruling circles refuse to face reality and instead stubbornly plunge headlong into the adventure of intensifying and expanding the aggressive war in South Vietnam, then the logical result awaiting them will be ignominious and a complete failure.

On March 22, 1965 the North Vietnamese government issued its famous "Four-Point Statement on Vietnam," which it said must be the basis for any political settlement of the war in Vietnam. The statement was repeatedly endorsed by the NLF and was also reiterated by DRV officials in interviews with foreign newsmen during the months that followed. As of mid-1966 it remained the avowed basic policy of both the DRV and the NLF:

1. Recognition of the basic national rights of the Vietnamese people: peace, independence, sovereignty, unity, and territorial integrity. The U.S. government must withdraw from South Vietnam all U.S. troops, military personnel and weapons of all kinds, munitions and war materials, dismantle all U.S. military bases there, and end its policy of intervention and aggression in South Vietnam. The U.S. government must stop its acts of war against North Vietnam [and] completely cease all encroachments on the territory and sovereignty of the DRV.

2. Pending the peaceful reunification of Vietnam, while Vietnam is still temporarily divided into two zones, the military provisions of the 1954 Geneva agreements on Vietnam must be strictly respected, the two zones must refrain from joining any military alliance with foreign countries, there must be no foreign military bases, troops, and military personnel in their respective territories.

3. The internal affairs of South Vietnam must be settled by the South Vietnamese people themselves without foreign interference, in accordance with the program of the National Liberation Front of South Vietnam.

4. The peaceful reunification of Vietnam is to be settled by the Vietnamese people in both zones without any foreign interference.[5]

NLF Goals

A great deal of the NLF's stated purpose is common to any government. It said it sought, among other aims, to establish democracy, develop the nation's economy, promote education, build an armed force, and give equal rights to minority groups. Scarcely any government does not claim to embrace these objectives. Three elements of NLF policy, however, are critical and should be examined separately. They are the issues of coalition government, neutralization, and reunification.

Coalition Government

The NLF's public definition of a coalition government was one that represented "every sector of the population, various nationalities, political

---

[5] Slightly varying versions of the original statement have been issued by the DRV, possibly due to changes in translation. In December 1965 the DRV again issued its "Four-Point Statement," this time in English. This quotation therefore at least presents an official DRV translation. This version was broadcast by Radio Hanoi, International Service, in English, December 9, 1965.

parties, religious communities, and patriotic personalities." [6] In short, the NLF specifically excluded the GVN because, it said, "the present rule is a disguised colonial regime set up by the U.S. imperialists . . . [and] a servile administration. . . . Such a regime and administration must be overthrown. . . ." [7]

This does not suggest coalition government in any meaningful sense. The term coalition government employed here means an arrangement in which the NLF would share with the GVN and would not hold exclusive political decision-making power in South Vietnam. Throughout the years Vietnamese in Saigon have felt that the basic political problem involved in bringing peace to the country consisted of eliminating the DRV-loyal elements from the NLF and bringing the remaining indigenous elements back into the political decision-making arena. Ultimately perhaps this will be the outcome. Certainly political stability cannot develop in Vietnam so long as the NLF as a sociopolitical force remains segregated from the rest of the society. But neither can the NLF be integrated in any form until it no longer stands for or represents DRV interests.

Considerable evidence is available that the NLF leadership has at times seriously considered authentic coalition government. A secret internal NLF document dated August 1962 spelled out the leadership's attitude at that moment toward the idea of a government that would include elements of the Saigon bourgeoisie:

Owing to our persevering struggle, the enemy may get bogged down, unable to win. The more protracted the struggle, the more of a disadvantage they will face. Therefore they may be forced to negotiate and compromise. The nature of the negotiations will vary, depending on the relative strength of ourselves and the enemy. The result could be similar to that now seen in Laos. Or the outcome could be similar to the Algerian defeat of the French, whereby the enemy would be obliged to recognize our sovereignty and independence.

Along the coalition spectrum of course there were many gradations. In September 1963 the NLF asked the United Nations for help in establishing a coalition government in South Vietnam similar to the one established in Laos the year before. In a letter to the General Assembly on September 11 Nguyen Huu Tho called for (1) an end to U.S. participation in Vietnamese affairs, (2) withdrawal of U.S. military forces, (3) an armistice, and (4) the establishment by South Vietnamese of a national, democratic, peaceful, and neutral coalition government. No mention was made of reunification. Probably at that moment the NLF

---

[6] National Liberation Front, "Ten-Point Manifesto" of December 1960, quoted earlier in this chapter.
[7] *Ibid.*

proposal was serious, for at the time it still looked favorably on the United Nations.[8]

Some of the original NLF leadership, such as the Cao Dai element, genuinely favored a true coalition government in which power would be shared; these people saw as their enemy a limited group of Saigonese, whose elimination, along with the launching of certain social and political reforms, would have satisfied them. These elements in the leadership have since been themselves eliminated. Among the true believers, however, and especially among the regulars who controlled the NLF entirely after mid-1964, a coalition was only a transitory arrangement that must give way to full Communist control. Even as a tactic it was considered dubious after mid-1964, probably because the leadership did not feel it was necessary. *Hoc Tap* in July 1964 contained a significant statement on the matter of negotiation. It declared:

> The aim of the Revolution and liberation of our compatriots is to defeat the aggression and frustrate the warmongering policies of the U.S. imperialists and their lackeys. To that end, it is necessary to smash the reactionary administrative machinery and the imperialists' mercenary army. This Revolution can and should be settled only by the use of revolutionary acts and the force of the masses to defeat enemy force. It absolutely cannot be settled by treaties and accords. . . . Laws and accords consistent with the basic interests of the people and country can be achieved only through a long and acute struggle of the people against the enemy. It is illusory to hope to persuade the cruel enemy of the people to comply with accords. The contradictions between the people in South Vietnam and the U.S. imperialists and their lackeys are antagonistic. The correct solution is not to reconcile the contradictions and the classes but through revolution to eliminate the contradictions. It is impossible . . . to count on "talks" and "negotiations" with [the imperialists] as advocated by the modern revisionists. . . . The liberation of South Vietnam can be settled only by force.

Obviously this was an anti-Soviet statement, but it indicated the dim prospects for any sort of negotiated settlement with the NLF, including negotiation of a coalition government.

The NLF asserted after the end of the Diem government that hostilities continued in Vietnam only because of the United States efforts and that the post-Diem governments remained viable only because of United States support. The NLF therefore demanded the withdrawal of American forces as the prerequisite to any settlement. Nguyen Huu Tho in a Radio Liberation broadcast on February 10, 1964 spelled out the NLF policy that remained in force throughout all the subsequent events:

> The United States [must] . . . end its aggressive war in South Vietnam, and the various parties and forces there [must] negotiate with one another to find a reasonable settlement in the interests of the Fatherland on the basis

---

[8] For evidence of its sharp change of attitude toward the United Nations see Appendix F.

of peace, independence, and neutrality. . . . The source of the present serious situation is the U.S. imperialist aggressive war and the dictatorial policy of their lackeys. . . . The only obstacle to stabilization and the ending of bloodshed is U.S. imperialism.

Early NLF statements on the subject of coalition implied that the NLF must dominate any coalition government since it represented all the "people's elements," in fact everyone except the Diemists. The change in language suggested that the NLF leadership recognized significant political forces outside the NLF, chiefly Buddhists, with which it could do business and to which it was making a serious proposal. Said the July 20, 1962 declaration:

The National Liberation Front of South Vietnam is ready to collaborate on an equal basis with all forces, parties, cliques, groups, associations, and individuals to oppose the aggressive war of U.S. imperialism in South Vietnam, even if these forces do not completely approve of the basic principles of the National Liberation Front. This extends to forces existing inside the country or abroad and even to those who in the past have collaborated with the U.S. imperialists but who now oppose such imperialism. It extends to those political, cultural, social, and professional groups or armed organizations that heretofore have opposed the Revolution in South Vietnam, or are still part of the South Vietnam government or army, but now seek to rise to save the country. The National Liberation Front wishes to contact all these forces to exchange ideas, seeking a mutual understanding of viewpoints, and to discuss concrete methods to save the country. The basis for negotiations will be the above policies or specific parts of these policies.

Nothing came of these offers, and therefore it is impossible to determine whether they were sincere. The offers did serve the NLF well, for they helped set the stage for the third phase of NLF development, in which a major objective was to attempt to legitimatize the apparatus.

The NLF in mid-1964 put forth feelers for a proposal for what appeared to be an authentic coalition government. It was to consist of 18 ministers, 6 of them members of the PRP, including Nguyen Van Hieu and his wife Ma Thi Chu; 8 ostensible non-Communists from among the Paris émigrés closely associated with Tran Van Huu; and 4 from the GVN. In typically involuted Vietnamese organizational fashion, the 18 would be not cabinet ministers but vice-ministers or assistant ministers, "sitting behind" a cabinet made up of prominent Vietnamese non-Communists; the five vice-ministers whose "assistants" would be Communists would hold the posts of defense, interior, foreign affairs, economy, and rural affairs — all the key offices. Part of the settlement also would involve de facto partition of South Vietnam, with the NLF having exclusive control over the five southern provinces adjacent to the Cambodian border: Tay Ninh, Kien Tuong, Kien Phong, An Giang, and Kien Giang. It was never clear whether this proposal actually came from the

NLF as a serious offer or whether it was merely a divisive effort. At any rate, a rumor circulated later to the effect that the proposal had fallen through because the "proper" Vietnamese could not be recruited in Paris. It is doubtful that the offer of participation in a coalition government at any time appeared promising to non-Communist political elements in Vietnam, and certainly not after mid-1963. Even at the time of the NLF's formation the professional politicians, government officials, and religious leaders throughout the country correctly assessed the NLF as a Communist-dominated front group seeking exclusive power for the Communists. By 1964 all were aware of the regularization effort that had taken place within the NLF, and none, with the possible exception of the Buddhists, thought themselves equal in size and power to risk entering into a coalition, fearing that if they did the whale would swallow the minnow. Coalition government with a strong NLF could not be sold within South Vietnam, although it was a useful product for the NLF to market abroad.

Neutralization

True neutralism in the sense of foreign policy nonalignment should be distinguished from the anti-imperialist neutralism in Marxist thought that is regarded simply as a step on the road to communism. Vietnamese scholar Nguyen Xuan Tho has said [9] that he found evidence that the neutralization of Vietnam in the true sense was ancient, and that China in 1883 proposed as a counter to French colonialism the neutralization of the entire Indochinese peninsula. To the South Vietnamese in the 1960's neutralism was a powerful appeal, for it was the appeal of withdrawal, of escape from tension and strain in the Cold War. For many it was the golden panacea. It meant peace and the elimination of all military forces from the country. It meant a third alternative, a compromise that all could accept.

The NLF played skillfully on the neutralization sentiment, as indicated by this statement taken from a leaflet distributed in 1963 in Long An province, the scene of much military action:

No one is unaware of or not grieved to see the South Vietnamese people suffering from twenty years of ruinous, protracted war, an irrational war formerly imposed by the French colonialists, now by the U.S. imperialists. This war has stolen many lives, much property, and has slowed down the nation's advance. . . . While our country suffers in an atrocious war, in neighboring Cambodia the people peacefully and joyfully build up their country and live a happy life, applying a domestic and foreign policy of independence, peace, and neutrality.

[9] In a statement to the author.

The NLF at its 1962 congress issued a statement on a neutralized Vietnam and possibly Indochina:

[We will] continue to respect the Geneva accords and demand that U.S. imperialists stop their armed aggression and withdraw weapons, military advisers, and troops from South Vietnam and give up the bloody Staley, Taylor, and Nolting plans.[10] [We demand] immediate restoration of peace in South Vietnam, halting at once the war against the people. . . . [We propose] carrying out a foreign policy of peace and neutrality . . . , that [we] set up an Indochina neutral zone, to include South Vietnam, Cambodia, and Laos, but with full sovereignty and independence for all three countries.

It even indicated willingness to accept policed inspection:

The proposal for a neutral zone comprising South Vietnam, Cambodia, and Laos is proof of the sincerity and uprightness of the Front's program. Such a zone can be created only with the agreement of neighboring countries, which, as a matter of fact, are concerned with the implementation of obligations freely consented to. Better still, this neutrality, to be valid, should be guaranteed. Then the Front's sincerity would be beyond doubt.

This seemed to suggest that the NLF was agreeable to an arrangement in which world powers would establish a neutral zone and then undertake the task of enforcing the neutrality. Such an arrangement was considered advantageous to the NLF, since it would tend to exclude undue influence by either the DRV or China but would not preclude establishment of a national Communist government.

The critical factor in any such proposal lay in the definition of the word "neutral" and beyond that in the matter of good faith. Ho Chi Minh, when asked whether the Gaullist proposal for the neutralization of Indochina was acceptable to him, replied with an answer that could be interpreted as yes, no, or maybe:

There is only one solution, pointed out by the NLFSV, . . . to respect the will of the people of South Vietnam . . . and settlement of the South Vietnam question by the people of South Vietnam themselves on the basis of national independence, democracy, peace, and neutrality, with . . . the first condition the withdrawal of U.S. forces. . . . President de Gaulle's suggestions on the neutralization of this part of Southeast Asia, including South Vietnam, . . . deserve serious attention.[11]

In Communist terms the theoretical base for Communist-style neutralization was spelled out in an early (1961) document that argued thus:

After the re-establishment of peace [1954] the people's Revolution in Vietnam entered a new phase: the Northern part of our country began the transition to socialism, while in the South the people continued to struggle to fulfill the tasks of the people's national democratic revolution, . . . [which]

---

[10] These so-called "plans" were various recommendations made to Washington on pacification activities.

[11] Radio Hanoi, in English, April 21, 1964.

is characterized by a stage of neutralization, . . . [marked] by pursuit of a neutral attitude in foreign affairs . . . and collaboration with the Northern compatriots to achieve national reunification.

To the PRP leadership neutralization was a tactic and was not to be confused with nonalignment. Said an agit-prop memorandum on neutralism, dated July 1963:

The peaceful neutrality proposed by our Party is quite different from the neutralism of capitalism in a nationalistic country. Our neutrality is a new form of struggle and a part of the international proletarian revolution. Thus in reality there is no neutrality but the choice of the socialist side and the determination to fight back imperialism, especially U.S. imperialism. . . . A peaceful policy of neutrality does not hinder the democratic national revolution. . . . If the leadership of the Party is correct and knows how to exploit circumstances to broaden the anti-U.S.-Diem force, the Revolution will advance easily. The term "peaceful neutrality" exploits favorable circumstances to hasten the national democratic revolution and hasten the reunification of the country.

The PRP obviously believed that a neutralized South Vietnam would mean a virtual political vacuum in which, through the highly organized NLF, it would find great opportunity. Neutralism was a means of bypassing American military strength. It was also a powerful public opinion and diplomatic weapon to bring to bear against the United States. Said the same document:

International opinion watches the situation and especially the armed intervention of the American aggressors. Neutrality for the South often is mentioned in international circles. . . . The neutrality drive, strongly supported by international opinion, will divide imperialism, isolate U.S.-Diem, and create better conditions for the Revolution.

Within South Vietnam, however, the neutrality theme was muted since it tended to undercut the NLF's efforts to develop the militant and all-out struggle movement against the GVN; neutralism too easily could be seized upon by the population as a third force, a way out, and thus work against the NLF's efforts to arouse the rural population.

As an external theme after mid-1962 the NLF's Foreign Relations Commission treated neutralism as its chief foreign policy instrument. Nguyen Van Hieu broached the idea in an interview with *The New York Times,* July 9, 1962; the World Peace Council took up the cry, as did its individual peace committees in bloc nations and in Burma, Indonesia, and Cambodia, often referring to neutralism as "Diem's nightmare." Cambodian Prince Sihanouk as early as 1961 suggested the creation of an Indochina neutral zone to include South Vietnam, Laos, and Cambodia, to be guaranteed by a big-power conference. In advance of the July 20 anniversary in 1962 the NLF issued a four-point manifesto in which it called for a "foreign policy of peace and neutrality." On August 18, 1962 the Central Committee of the NLF issued a "Fourteen-Point Statement on Neutrality." Summarized, the points were:

1. South Vietnam will not join and will not accept the protection of any military bloc or treaty.

2. All foreign military personnel will be withdrawn from South Vietnam.

3. South Vietnam will follow an independent, sovereign foreign policy.

4. The Bandung spirit of peaceful coexistence will be followed in relations with all countries.

5. An army will be built but with the sole aim of safeguarding South Vietnam's sovereignty, independence, territorial integrity, and security.

6. South Vietnam will thoroughly realize democratic liberties for the people, and freedom of thought, worship, opinion, and organization will be guaranteed to all citizens, political parties, mass organizations, religions, and nationalities.

7. Economic aid without political conditions will be accepted from all countries.

8. Economic and trade policies will be democratic and independent.

9. Foreign nationals will be allowed to reside and earn their living in South Vietnam, and foreign capitalists will be permitted to do business, and their interests will be guaranteed provided they respect South Vietnam's laws.

10. South Vietnam will carry out cultural exchanges and broaden cultural cooperation with all countries.

11. In view of the fact that Vietnam has been divided into two zones with different political regimes, due concern will be shown the question of reunification. Adequate consideration will be given to the characteristics of this situation and the two zones. This question will be decided by the people of the two zones on the principle of equality, nonannexation of one zone by the other, negotiations between the leaders of the two zones, and step-by-step reunification. Priority will be given to the consideration of the question of restoration of normal relations between the zones. The future political regime of unified Vietnam will be decided by the people of both zones.

12. South Vietnam will stand ready to form a peaceful and neutral zone with Cambodia and Laos.

13. South Vietnam will actively unite with all states and organizations and work for peace and friendship among nations.

14. South Vietnam's independence and neutrality will be respected and guaranteed by the countries and parties concerned in the 1954 Geneva agreements on Vietnam.

Sihanouk, the most (and probably only) sincere advocate of Vietnamese neutralization, in December 1963 proposed the creation of a neutralized federation of Indochina, to consist of Cambodia and South Vietnam. He asserted that unification of Vietnam was at the moment premature if not impossible and that federation would serve as an interim settlement. The foreign affairs of the two countries, he said, would be conducted jointly; each would act as a check on the other. Through neutralization would come peace and through federation would come economic advantages to both. Such an arrangement, he maintained, would be acceptable to Hanoi — a most debatable point — and once accomplished would tend to favor the non-Communist world. The NLF as far as can be determined never commented publicly on the federation idea.

The GVN at all times was hostile to the idea of the neutralization of South Vietnam or even of negotiations with the NLF.[12] The post-Diem government of Duong Van Minh declared that neutralization

is but a glaring maneuver of the North Vietnamese authorities aimed at encouraging their schemes to enslave the South Vietnamese people for the exclusive benefit of international communism regardless of the Vietnamese people's deep aspirations toward territorial reunification in peace and through really free and democratic elections.[13]

On March 1, 1965 the GVN issued a statement on its position with respect to negotiations in general:

The Republic of Vietnam cannot rally itself to a solution that would have the effect of rewarding armed aggression. A cease-fire without prior withdrawal of troops and Communist cadres would amount to the pure and simple capitulation of our side. . . . The Republic of Vietnam deems that negotiations to restore peace could have a chance of success only if the Communists show their sincere desire to put an end to the war of which they are the authors by withdrawing beforehand their armed units and their political cadres from South Vietnamese territory. . . . Any international settlement [must] pay attention to the legitimate aspirations of the Vietnamese government and people under the principle of self-determination. . . .[14]

One of Vietnam's most brilliant intellectuals, Dr. Tran Kim Tuyen, as early as 1961 predicted that the NLF would use the neutralist vehicle

[12] Persistent reports circulated in Saigon in October 1963 that the Diem government, in the person of Ngo Dinh Nhu, was in secret negotiations with the NLF and the DRV through the Polish representative on the ICC in Saigon; ARVN Major General Ton That Dinh, Minister of Security in the Duong Van Minh government in December 1963, at a press conference in Saigon said he had documentary evidence to this effect, but it was never released.

[13] Note to the ICC dated January 4, 1964, quoted by Vietnam Press Agency the same day.

[14] Vietnam Press Agency, April 14, 1965.

in its drive for power. In a private memorandum circulated at the time among friends, he predicted how this would be done:

First, they will establish what they will call the liberal democracy stage. . . . All restrictions on political actions will be removed. The people can be stirred to rise and struggle for this liberal democracy without any particular explanation [that is, ideology] or . . . anything about what democracy means. The country will become a state of anarchy, because people will be acting in a political manner without any clear knowledge of politics. . . . Political struggles will not be over doctrine or policies but will be fights by individuals and groups for their own interests. . . .

Then will come the coalition government stage. . . . It will be argued that since there are too many political groups in the country a coalition be formed of all of them, including the Communists, and a coalition government organized. . . . But this will merely be a division of portfolios, . . . what I call a basket-of-crabs arrangement, that is, all the political parties will be in one basket like crabs and will kill off one another. . . .

Since the only policy that this coalition government will be able to agree on will be . . . neutralism . . . they will go to the people with the doctrine of new external relations [*chu truong doi ngoai*], that is, they will say to them: "Neutralism must be created and once we are free of outside influence, then we can make progress in the field of social welfare. . . ."

While the members of the government are busy with the task of neutralization, which will raise many disputes among them, there will come the shift of alignment. Communist cadres will be penetrating and taking over the lower administrative organs of the country, . . . and the reports from the rural area lower administrative organs, on which the government must depend for making decisions, will be submitted by Communist cadres. These reports . . . and other actions . . . will suggest to the central government that the people want a further shift of alignment, from the "neither pro-American nor pro-Communist" policy to the "anti-American, proneutralism" policy. . . .

Once this is achieved, the country will be isolated and an easy target for the fifth Communist phase, the . . . take-over stage.

In sum there is no evidence to indicate that the Communists themselves believed in the prospect of a "neutral" Vietnam in the Cambodian sense. And after the 1960–1961 period few Vietnamese on either side, with the possible exception of a few Buddhist leaders in the South, entertained the idea seriously.

Reunification

NLF policy with respect to reunification was developmental, from strongly favorable in the early days to serious doubt after 1963. Three distinct attitudes toward the subject appeared to exist within the NLF ranks: There were those who maintained that it must be pursued at all costs, those who favored it in principle but asserted that it was impossible to achieve, and those who opposed it on the grounds that it would mean absorption by the Northerners. As Northern cadres began to fill the ranks of the NLF (by mid-1966, for example, half of the 35,000 civilian NLF cadres were Northerners) strong support built up for the idea of reunification, but this did not necessarily mean that prospects for reunification were any brighter.

In the North, and among those in the South deeply loyal to the North, unification carried a mystic quality that Ho Chi Minh expressed frequently.[15] The Lao Dong Party Central Committee had a Reunification Committee, with Nguyen Van Vinh, a Hanoi lawyer, as chairman, which existed as early as 1960 and made yearly reports to the Party. On May 1, 1963 a parallel 18-man group was formed in the government — the DRV National Assembly's Reunification Committee, headed by Tran Huy Lieu, director of the Vietnam Institute of History and a member of the Assembly's Standing Committee. *Nhan Dan* on May 1, 1963 reported that it had been charged with the

task of helping the National Assembly adopt an attitude and resolutions on, and issue statements and appeals about, the reunification problem . . . ; to encourage the South Vietnamese compatriots' struggle . . . ; and to call on the people of the world to support the struggle for unification. . . .

Throughout its history the NLF publicly vacillated and temporized on the question of unification. References in its output varied from daily to none at all for months. In mid-1963 its output switched from the theme of unification by means of free elections in North and South, under the Geneva accords, to unification by means of what were called "step-by-step negotiations of representatives of the two zones." This was an NLF effort to separate neutralization from unification — two terms that previously had been closely linked, even hyphenated. It obviously was based on the NLF's assumption that unification of a North-South neutralized Vietnam was totally unlikely, for while Hanoi might accept

[15] For example: "Our compatriots in the Southern area are citizens of Vietnam. Rivers can dry up and mountains wear away, but this truth stands." [Letter to Southerners, May 3, 1946.] "Each day the Fatherland remains disunited, each day you [of the South] suffer, food is without taste, sleep brings no rest. I solemnly promise you, through your determination, the determination of all our people, the Southern land will return to the bosom of the Fatherland." [October 23, 1946.] "National reunification is our road to life. Great unity is the power that will surely triumph. Thanks to this great unity, the Revolution was successful and the Resistance victorious. Now, with great unity, our political struggle will certainly be victorious, our country will certainly be reunified." [July 6, 1956.] "South Vietnam is our flesh and blood. . . . Vietnam is one country. South and North are of the same family, and no reactionary force can partition it. Vietnam must be reunited." [September 2, 1957.] "Every hour, every minute, the people of the North think of their compatriots in the South. The South Vietnamese people relentlessly have fought for nearly twenty years, first the French colonialists, then the American-Diemists. They are indeed the heroic sons and daughters of the heroic Vietnamese nation. South Vietnam truly deserves the name: Brass Citadel of the Fatherland." [May 9, 1963.]

neutralism as a temporary condition in the South, it would never accept it in the North. *Nhan Dan* in a February 11, 1964 editorial flatly ruled out neutralization of the DRV: "Our people will never accept the neutralization of North Vietnam." Such a move would have amounted to decommunizing North Vietnam, and no one thought this within the realm of possibility. Therefore the NLF sought to separate reunification from neutralization in an effort to deal with each more realistically.

The PRP, loyal to Hanoi above all, remained strongly committeed to direct and immediate unification. Vo Chi Cong, the PRP chairman, declared in a July 23, 1963 Radio Liberation broadcast:

Loyal to the view that Vietnam is indivisible and the Vietnamese nation indivisible, the PRP never abandons struggling for a unified Vietnam. The first task we face is liberation of South Vietnam and . . . establishment of a neutralist foreign policy. . . . In liberating the South our people will also create practical conditions for unification . . . for then unification will become an internal problem. . . . The PRP feels this stand is opportune and necessary . . . and in accordance with the spirit and the words of the 1954 Geneva accords [that is, reunification by means of elections]. Marxist-Leninists in South Vietnam are happy to pursue this correct struggle line.

The NLF moderates, those who desired reunification but held that it was impossible to achieve, apparently dominated the NLF at least in this period. The indigenous Southern elements in the NLF who opposed reunification on any basis of course were not vocal about their fears. After the Cao Dai elements, originally among the chief supporters of the NLF, defected *en masse* following the end of the Diem regime, some of their members told the GVN that at least the majority of the NLF rank and file opposed reunification since they felt that it would amount to turning South Vietnam into a vassal state of the North.

The division grew increasingly apparent in late 1964 and early 1965, when Radio Liberation spoke constantly in terms of "U.S. withdrawal and the establishment of neutrality" while Radio Hanoi spoke constantly in terms of "U.S. withdrawal, negotiation, and reunification." In the same sense, Radio Liberation spoke of "Southerners settling their own problems" and Radio Hanoi of "all Vietnamese discussing their various problems and settling them."

The American air strikes into North Vietnam paradoxically both strengthened the case for unification and made it even more remote. On the one hand the strikes tended to weld the DRV and NLF into a more common or joint cause. The NLF had long maintained that part of its duty was to assist in the protection of the North. With the launching of the air strikes it had no choice but to announce its undying support of the North. On the other hand, since it resulted in deeper American involvement in the war, it injected a new element into the unification question and made it less likely at least in the short run. The Gulf of Tonkin incident in August 1964 brought from Radio Liberation on September 19 an NLF army high command "communiqué," which declared:

We the NLFSV Army High Command . . . are extremely indignant and we severely warn the U.S. aggressors that in the future if they dare bomb and strafe or provoke North Vietnam recklessly, all the NLF armed forces will close with the North Vietnamese people, double the fighting tempo, increase the vigor of attacks, and annihilate more U.S. aggressors and their hirelings on all battlefields. . . .

After the second raid, Radio Liberation on September 21, 1964 declared:

The NLFSV Central Committee states that it energetically condemns and denounces before world public opinion these extremely dangerous plans of the U.S. imperialists to broaden the war. . . . If the U.S. imperialists and their hirelings foolishly and recklessly embark on a dangerous military adventure . . . the South Vietnamese people, as one, with their Liberation troops, armed forces, and paramilitary forces will cooperate closely with their 18 million compatriots in North Vietnam and the brother Vietnam People's Army in resolutely resisting to the end in order to annihilate the U.S. imperialists . . . and to protect the North. This is our unshakable iron will. . . .

This position certainly doomed any possibility of unification at the conference table. Since the United States came to look with total disfavor on any move to join North and South, nothing short of sheer military force would achieve unification, and such was beyond the capability of either the NLF or the DRV. The prospect was doubly unlikely if the assessment of the Chinese view, noted earlier, was correct — that is, if the Chinese in actuality were opposed to reunification.

Summary

Study of NLF policy statements, inspection of its externalization efforts, and measuring its actions against its words leave one with a subjective impression of the general design of NLF goals and the parameters of those goals. These appear to be the following:

1. To achieve operative political control of South Vietnam; a willingness, but reluctance, to settle for some political power rather than all if it were clearly demonstrated that the alternative to some political power was either stalemate or total defeat.

2. To seek a South Vietnamese governmental policy of nonalignment in foreign affairs (but under a definition that would classify the DRV as domestic rather than foreign), one that in operational terms would permit the reduction of American troops in exchange for the

withdrawal of PAVN forces from South Vietnam but with the proviso that this arrangement must be agreeable to the DRV.

3. To work for reunification of the two Vietnams through a step-by-step process, the time limits of which would be negotiable.

4. To forge a broad base of world support, one principally rooted in Communist-bloc nations and not tied too closely with any one foreign country. (Again, in NLF terms, relations with the DRV would be internal, not external.)

5. To vilify the United States, mobilize world opinion against it, and heighten its feelings of frustration and futility in its efforts in South Vietnam.

6. To exploit every American and GVN weakness abroad regardless of how insignificant or transient any instance might appear to be.

7. With respect to the Sino-Soviet split, to contribute what little it could to healing the breach but not be forced into a position where it had to choose sides.

8. With respect to the DRV, to prevent itself from being submerged by Hanoi and to retain a bargaining position. Undoubtedly a schism existed: The majority of the politically acute NLF supporters realized that Northern and Southern interests were not identical. The cadres and the PRP members within the NLF shared the DRV goals; they grew progressively stronger and virtually monopolized the hierarchy by 1965. The most divisive issue in this respect was reunification. The indigenous elements maintained that reunification meant annexation by the DRV and at any rate was opposed by too many forces within and outside of Vietnam ever to be possible; the loyalists maintained, as did the DRV, that reunification must remain the central long-range goal.

9. To strive for the withdrawal of American forces from South Vietnam, based on the calculation that the United States could be persuaded to accept a coalition neutral government if its position in South Vietnam became sufficiently untenable.

10. To avoid a "negotiated settlement" at an international conference on the ground that it would almost certainly amount to a sellout of the NLF. (But this did not preclude acceptance, as a tactic, of a coalition government.) In the event that a negotiated settlement might be required because complete victory was impossible or because outright defeat was a growing prospect, the conditions it hoped to achieve included (a) an authentic coalition government that would include elements of the NLF at the cabinet level; (b) an understanding that South Vietnam would pursue a nonaligned but China-leaning foreign policy on the model of Cambodia; (c) closer economic ties with the DRV; (d) amnesty for its followers, or opportunity for them to move to the DRV; and (e) withdrawal of most, but not necessarily all, American military forces.

20

Mystique

To those outside Vietnam there was a general perception, one shared neither by Vietnamese nor by foreigners within the country, that South Vietnam was a place of terror and sudden death, of coups d'état and bombings, of alarms and excursions by night. These things did exist. Yet somehow they remained in perspective and did not dominate the lives of either Americans or Vietnamese, in or out of Saigon. Tolstoy, although writing of another time and place, described exactly how it was:

The tales and descriptions of that time without exception speak only of the self-sacrifice, patriotic devotion, despair, grief, and the heroism. . . . But it was not really so. It appears so to us because we see only the general historic interest of that time and do not see all the personal human interests that people had. Yet in reality those personal interests of the moment so much transcend the general interests that they always prevent the public interest from being felt or even noticed. Most of the people at that time paid no attention to the general progress of events but were guided only by their private interests. . . .[1]

Thousands of Vietnamese villagers lived through the entire 1960–1965

[1] Leo Tolstoy, *War and Peace* (New York: Simon and Schuster, 1942), pp. 1045–1046.

period without being involved in, and hardly ever being inconvenienced by, either the NLF's armed struggle or the GVN's military operations. Although subjected to great NLF organizational and political attention, the average rural Vietnamese was seldom if ever a direct victim of its violence program. The mental picture held by most Americans of rural Vietnam as a vast, boiling battlefield, of innumerable military engagements by day, of villages again and again torn apart by ARVN-guerrilla clashes, of a people in the midst of constant fighting and bloodshed, with no place to hide, living in a sort of no man's land between two contending armies — that picture simply does not hold up under scrutiny.

A villager of course would be monumentally affected if his village found itself under guerrilla attack, was the scene of a battle between ARVN troops and the guerrillas, or, if in a liberated area, was bombed or napalmed. But the odds of this happening in the 1960–1964 period were not much greater than the odds of being hit by lightning. If, on a statistical basis, a single rural villager was selected at random and studied in terms of how much the war impinged on his life, how often he witnessed combat or even saw combatants, it is most likely that he never would have been directly affected to any degree. The author talked to innumerable villagers in all parts of Vietnam, and most of them spoke of the effects of the war on others but admitted that it had never fallen on them.

The average rural Vietnamese could plant his rice, watch it grow, harvest it, and begin the cycle again, placidly unconcerned, unaffected by the swirl around him. The result was that he did not perceive the situation in Vietnam as a "war" in the same way that Americans regard the Vietnam "war." Thus the frequently stated observation that the Vietnamese peasant "has known nothing but war for twenty years," although technically accurate, is also misleading. An American reading this formed a mental picture of the peasant in "war" under circumstances quite different from reality.

The Organizational Weapon

The basic characteristics of the NLF and its activities were the use of a united-front organization to establish a mass base of support; organization of the rural people, employing both rational appeals to self-interest and coercion, and then using the specially created social movements in antigovernmental activity; heavy use of various techniques for the communication of ideas to foment social strife; use of specialized military actions, selective in nature and psychological in intent; use of the Communist party *apparat*, and Communist doctrine among the leaders and full-time cadres, to establish orthodoxy and maintain discipline. The goal was control of the population and, through this control, organization of the people as a weapon against the government. But it was more than this. It was more than simply the inculcation of new beliefs or differing attitudes. The NLF's ultimate objective taken together with other activities was to create a new socialization pattern.

The NLF was concerned with the deepest social values. It sought to create a new system of formal and informal groupings by which the socialization was to be accomplished and behavior regulated. It manipulated economic activities, the base for all human activities, in such a way as to increase the degree of communalism or collectivization and thus to some degree alter the village means of production; it introduced a new political structure to keep internal order and to regulate contact within South Vietnam, particularly with respect to villagers hostile to the NLF; it manipulated educational and other intellectual activities within the village. It apparently attempted to substitute a disguised brand of Marxism for traditional religious beliefs, although in an oblique manner; and it introduced new language terminology, social mythology, and folklore. In short, it attempted to work within the totality of village life and provide a new cultural focus.

Understanding sociopolitical developments in Vietnam involves cataloging the various social and political groups, organizations, cliques, and clans — some of them covert and almost all of them parochial or regional in nature — and then mapping the interrelationships among these various forces. Political infighting consists not so much of open confrontation with one's opponent (or even directly and forcibly destroying him) as it does of drowning, absorbing, splintering, fragmenting, discrediting, turning him aside, or, if necessary, joining him and working at his side to eliminate him. The immediate goal is usually status or prestige more than pure political power. The NLF was superior in this type of political struggle — especially in the rural areas — chiefly because success in this effort depends on good organizational ability and skilled management of social movements. Therefore the secret of NLF success in the early years — and they were many — was organization. Probably the NLF expended more time, money, and manpower on organizational activity than on all other activities combined. Further, this effort was concentrated in what was an organizational vacuum.

In those areas of the country where it had firm and continuous social control the NLF was in effect a society within a society, with its own social structure, values, and coercive instruments. The NLF cadres made a conscious and massive effort to extend political participation, even if it was manipulated, on the local level so as to involve the people in a self-contained, self-supporting revolution. The functional liberation associations at the village level attempted to serve each individual member in terms of his own personal interests while at the same time developing a deep revolutionary consciousness. Ironically, as the result of increased coercion on the part of the NLF, as its popular support dwindled, its actual authority increased. What had been essentially a persuasive mechanism became basically a coercive one, not so much because of the failure of the original NLF social organization pattern as because of the arrival of Northern cadres who were unwilling to trust the original form because they felt in the long run that it would not serve the interests of the Party and indeed might become a threat to it. Once again, the not unfamiliar story of the revolution betrayed. But the organization at all times, whether persuasive or coercive, remained the central NLF activity in the village.

That the leaders of this enterprise were professionals must be evident from the structure they created. It is difficult, however, to estimate the number of NLF leaders and cadres who were professional revolutionaries. Most of them were vastly experienced, some by choice, some by circumstance. The initial NLF leadership corps was made up of the ex-Viet Minh. Many of these, probably the majority, were professionals such as doctors, lawyers, and teachers. They were competent and enjoyed high status among their followers. Most of them had been in the movement, either Viet Minh or NLF, for most of their lives, although generally the guerrilla leaders had served longer than the civilians. Within the NLF these early leaders came to hold the main-line administrative posts or became the commanders of the Main Force units. They were inclined to be more nationalistic and less doctrinal than those who came after them, and they were far less pro-DRV. Those who rose in prominence after the launching of the NLF, that is, in the early 1960's, were more politically oriented, less apt to have a professional background, and therefore of somewhat lower status in the eyes of the rank and file. They were more doctrinal, more anti-GVN, pro-DRV, and pro-Communist. With the regularization came both cadres and top leaders from the North; their great social trauma had been the Viet Minh war. Most had been young cadres during the Viet Minh war and had climbed the status ladder in the North according to DRV standards, which meant they excelled in Communist virtues, technical competence, zeal, discipline, and unwavering faith in the cause. They had a vested interest in victory through following orders from Hanoi, for it was there that their homes were located, their families lived, and their careers were rooted. Their motivation was quite different; it was North Vietnamese whether or not they had originally come from the South. Above all, these Northern-trained leaders, and they were found chiefly in the NLF military apparatus, were professionals, less marked by the self-righteous puritanism that characterized the earliest NLF leadership group or the individual initiative and revolutionary consciousness that marked those who rose in the ranks during the early stages of the insurgency. They were less moved by the deep sense of frustration that drove the earlier leaders, and their devotion to the cause stemmed more from career building than from ideology or hatred.

One of the most persistent questions asked about the NLF follower was "Why did he join?" The implication in the question is that for one or more rational or emotional reasons the individual Vietnamese decided to enlist in the cause, did so, and thus entered as a believer. As must certainly be apparent from the preceding chapters, almost the reverse was the case. The Vietnamese youth was first surrounded by a social organization that he had no hand in creating but to which he somehow belonged. Through a process of insinuation the youth came to realize that he was part of the NLF, never quite sure of how this happened and never with any overt choice presented to him. The process of glacially slow recruitment came first, the mystique was developed later. Or, as it has been aptly put, conversion followed subversion. Therefore not motives but circumstances must be considered in understanding the recruitment pattern and its contribution to the NLF mystique.

The most common answer given by a *quy chanh* to questions concerning the circumstances under which he became part of the NLF indicated that he was initially drawn into the organization and later recruited. He might first be asked to act as a messenger, or to take part in a struggle movement, or to deliver leaflets to an agent in the provincial capital. Then he would be urged to join his friends in a study group that might also be a literacy class. Then he would be asked to commit some act of violence; at this point, whether he knew it or not, he was in the net. When handled skillfully, subtly, and gradually, a teen-aged youth did not realize that he was involved until he was already enmeshed. This technique succeeded, for the most part, not in areas where the GVN was exerting itself but in the remote villages where the NLF and the Viet Minh before it were the only visible "government" the youth had ever known. And so the *quy chanh* would say, "Everyone seemed to think it was the correct thing to do," often adding plaintively, "There didn't seem to be any danger. The Saigon government was so far away I didn't think they would ever know about me." Of course a small minority actually sought out and joined the NLF. These included draft dodgers, military deserters, those who hated the government for some personal reason, opportunists, the ambitious who were seeking status, the rejected, the adventurers, and all the others in Eric Hoffer's categories of the True Believer.[2]

---

[2] Eric Hoffer, *The True Believer: Thoughts on the Nature of Mass Movements* (New York: Harper & Row, 1951).

For the most part, however, the supporters were recruited under circumstances where there was no alternative. Most recruitment was from among social groups such as the religious sects, with grievances against the government, and less effort was placed on the recruitment of individuals at random. At the same time the NLF sought to create situations that would give rise to grievances among such groups so as to facilitate recruitment. Once the youth was recruited, the training and indoctrination work supplied the rationale for belonging.

Americans and others often assumed that the NLF army members were fanatics. Because they performed well in combat, it was argued, they were highly motivated, which meant dedication to an ideological cause. Thus the search was for the essence of this belief. It proved elusive, largely because it did not exist. The best of the military units — the Main Force units — were highly effective because they were composed of professionals. These were not green young Vietnamese farmers, only recently introduced to the rifle, but experienced guerrillas who had been fighting most of their adult lives. What impelled them was not ideology so much as professional competence, much like the United States Marine or the French Foreign Legionnaire. The men in the best of these units were very good; their discipline was superb; they knew how to use camouflage well, a requirement for survival; they were well skilled in small-unit tactics, especially the ambush in its many variations; they trained hard, rehearsed, and practiced attacks until letter perfect, and then they fought hard. Their mystique should be attributed chiefly to a unit *esprit de corps* that stemmed from the consensus that each man in the unit was a superior and vastly experienced professional.

Doctrinal Cement

The strength of the NLF was the result of careful organization building, not the product of some unique spirit or élan. The mystique, to the degree that it existed and bound together the separate building blocks of the movement, resulted from indoctrinational efforts, shared social myths, and leader-led relations. The mystique's functions were, first, identity, stemming from the doctrinal course of the Revolution, the ideology of communism, and the recruitment pattern; and, second, unity, resulting from the nature of the leadership, the indoctrination itself, and individual self-motivating standards of behavior.

Course of the Revolution

The various pseudoscientific laws that the leadership regarded as governing the Revolution were at no time themselves challenged by the

NLF followers, nor was the principle that such definitive laws existed, as asserted in these terms in an early NLF document:

A revolution develops according to objective laws, which exist independently of man's wish. The revolutionary should not rely on his subjective wish but should rely on objective reality, on the objective law of social development, to act and promote the development of history. To lead the Revolution correctly is to act in such a manner that under concrete historical conditions one can mobilize and organize all forces that can be mobilized in order to bring the Revolution to victory. . . .

The leadership considered its chief doctrinal task to be the translation of abstract theory into the setting of a traditional society. It did this by placing prime value on loyalty, as perhaps all such groups must. The Revolution assumed a pragmatic, not greatly intellectual, cast, and it was characterized by an absence of agonizing. It lacked the depth of thought marked by, say, the Russian Revolution and far more resembled the Chinese revolution. To both the NLF and the PRP, determinants of success were twofold: revolutionary capability, including the proclivity for revolution by the Vietnamese people themselves, and PRP leadership, which is to say Communist leadership. The people's revolutionary capability was more asserted than proven, and the Party's monopolistic leadership imposed rather than prescribed. Both developed into articles of faith, a mystic belief in the power and loyalty of the people and a sense of trust in the omniscience of the Party. What was then required was to put the formula to work: The people would support the Revolution if only the cadres would show them that their interests were identical to the cause, would constantly agitate them so as to prevent loss of ardor, and would develop them into creatures of initiative who would act and not merely react.

No evidence was ever uncovered to indicate that schisms existed in the early years on the proper course of the Revolution. The quarrel that did develop, as we have seen, lay in writing the final act of the revolutionary drama — whether it should consist of the General Uprising, the Mao-Giap third stage, or negotiated settlement. The dispute was resolved in favor of the Mao-Giap thesis, not through discussion or by successfully decimating the two other alternatives but because the new supraleadership in Hanoi concluded that it represented the correct course to pursue and used its Northern-trained and Northern-loyal cadres to force acceptance of its decision.

However, even in the days when it was the dominant doctrine, the leadership consistently overestimated its progress and several times erroneously believed that the moment of the General Uprising had arrived. Internal documents from a Lao Dong Youth League conference in June 1961, for example, stated that speakers at that time asserted flatly that the

General Uprising would take place in the first three months of 1962 and that all cadres must plan accordingly. After the overthrow of the Diem government and again in the spring of 1965 the leadership apparently believed the moment had come, only to have their hopes again dashed. These failures undoubtedly contributed to the decision to "militarize" the struggle and pursue victory by means of the Mao-Giap third stage. But this triggered a new level of American response, which meant that from a doctrinal standpoint it had failed as much as had the General Uprising thesis.

In sum, from a standpoint of mystique the General Uprising served the NLF well through the golden days of the Revolution. It was not mere window dressing but the justification and rationalization for the insurgency, the cement that held the effort together, and a powerful tool for agit-prop team use in working with villagers. In the end it failed because it was not sufficiently rooted in reality, because it could work only if the Communists' assessment of the social milieu in the South was correct, which it was not.

The NLF and the people it influenced lived in a muzzy, myth-filled world of blacks and whites, good and evil, a simplistic world quite out of character with the one to which the Vietnamese was accustomed. But it created a powerful external image for the Vietnamese immersed in the cause, restructuring his reality, providing him with a new identity and a boundless sense of unity. The elements of this mystique were fourfold.

First, it was characterized by great moralism and was far more moral than ideological. Virtue was the golden word. The cause consisted of moral duties based on moral absolutes, guided by moral imperatives; duty itself, under a virtuous leadership, was the highest value. Preoccupation with law and legality was not simply an effort to establish legitimacy but a justification of the moral correctness of the cause. Because he was virtuous, the NLF supporter was morally superior to the enemy and hence politically and militarily superior. The moralism manifested itself in a spirit of sincerity; the NLF surrounded its words and actions with an aura of sincerity.

Second, it was characterized by extreme romanticism. The NLF leaders, like Mao Tse-tung and Ho Chi Minh before them, were romantic rebels who saw themselves as idealists. Idealistic appeals abounded: the promise of the good life in utopian terms; the opportunity to revolt against all the evil, injustice, and inequity of this world; the chance to be part of a great crusade. But behind these was the romantic lure of the struggle itself; the means not the ends counted. There was more glory along the road than at its end. The clandestine organization made up of multitudes of inner groups, cults, and secret arrangements played on the Vietnamese individual's romantic love of the devious, and like

Kim along the Grand Trunk Road he played The Game. (A psychiatrist visiting in Vietnam said it was actually a latent homosexual fear of penetration.) Yet in general the NLF mystique was less a positive cause than a negation. But this too had lure to the romantic — the lure of anarchy, beyond which, if it failed, lay the lure of martyrdom. The NLF in creating its mystique was acutely sensitive to the age-old Asian attitude of fatalism.

Third, its mystique was imitative and therefore militantly defensive, which probably should be counted as a weakness. The NLF leader was driven by a compulsive search for answers from elsewhere, anywhere. Examples were taken from other places and they were forced, and from other times and they were distorted. If the NLF was not slavishly copying Mao Tse-tung on the Long March, it was employing the Viet Minh's analysis of French Maginot Line thinking as it applied to the Americans, or calling on all cadres to repeat in a literal manner some victory scored a few months earlier in another part of Vietnam. The constant scanning of the horizon was part of a preoccupation with contemplation and self-analysis. Cadres, in a curious form of intellectualism, would explain the Revolution over and over to their most disinterested students — the rural Vietnamese. Copied though it was, it provided the supporter with a worldview that might not be understood but was satisfactory. Through indoctrination and even socialization he received needed psychological support and release from cultural tensions. (The same psychiatrist said the NLF was a father image led by Ho Chi Minh.)

And finally there was a will to believe, perhaps a characteristic of any mystique. It grew from the sense of universality of a movement representing Vietnam, the world, excluding not even a full social class (the enemies in Saigon and Washington). It was based on an assessment of the world environment that the NLF believed made Revolution in Vietnam irresistible and doomed GVN and U.S. prowess to steady deterioration. It was based on faith in the Vietnamese people's revolutionary capability, faith in the doctrinal approach, faith in revolutionary guerrilla warfare consisting of the combined armed and political struggle, and the infallible wisdom of the Party's leaders, who from long experience could divine the laws of history.

The Role of Communism

Marxism-Leninism as filtered through first Chinese and then Vietnamese thought contributed much to the NLF mystique. After the regularization efforts not only Communist thought but the communist-society goal was proclaimed openly, as previously it had been asserted internally. For example, the PRP asserted in a Radio Liberation broadcast, December

9, 1964, that its ultimate objective was a communist state, and the only question was whether this would come early or late:

> The [enemy] slanders us saying that our Party monopolizes the Front and that our Party's solidarity policy is nothing more than a trick for the present. . . . It says the Party's strategic objectives are against those of the Front, such as national independence, democracy, peace, and neutrality, and they say that our Party cannot pursue a sincere and lasting policy of solidarity with the Front. This argument proves that the enemies of our people do not understand anything about our Party of Marxism-Leninism. . . . The general Marxist-Leninist principles of the working class are aimed at rallying the majority of the forces into a united national front, a worker-peasant alliance led by the working class. . . . Our Party does not conceal its ultimate objective, which is to achieve socialism and communism. But our Party has never ceased pointing out that the path leading to that objective is long, and that the objective cannot be achieved in a few years, but several score years. . . .

A Communist condition had prevailed within the NLF from the start and was assumed as a matter of course by Vietnamese of all political shadings. With respect to the mystique the matter of communism's paramountcy became somewhat more complex. Partly it was a matter of definition.

If a Communist is one who believes that man's future is shaped by his tools of production, that history is dominated by a class struggle for control of those means of production, that capitalism must grow increasingly evil, and that a brotherhood of workers and farmers swearing allegiance to an international ideal must unite to seize power and build its own society led by the vanguard, the proletariat, and in turn by the vanguard of the vanguard, the Communist party — if this is a Communist, then there were few Communists among the NLF. If, however, a Communist is one who swears blind allegiance to the world movement whose loci of power are Moscow and Peking, from which in this instance via Hanoi he draws through a political umbilical cord sustenance and strength that he cannot, and does not want to, supply himself, then most of the NLF's leaders, cadres, and true believers were Communists.

It was the difference between philosophic communism and alliance communism. For, in the first instance, to be a Communist meant mastering Marxism-Leninism, which NLF Vietnamese found notoriously difficult to understand since it is distinctly un-Vietnamese in nature and at variance with their most deeply ingrained views of the universe. (For example, it must have been indeed a Herculean task for a cadre to convince a Vietnamese that matter and not God or Spirit is the ultimate reality, or that nothing is inherently unknowable.) The second instance meant simply establishing identity and achieving unity in which an NLF supporter had only to approve of the powerful foreign forces that stood behind him and his cause. Only among the higher-echelon cadres, and even here not with total acceptance, was communism regarded as a new body of wisdom to be learned, understood, and put to use.

Thus the NLF was Communist not because it incorporated Communist doctrine but because it linked itself to foreign states that did. This distinction, or weakness, meant that the strengths that hold Communists and Communist movements together during dark days elsewhere were largely absent in Vietnam.

Final Word

There can be little doubt that the combination put together by the NLF was a potent one. However, the fundamental question it raised — to which we have no final answer — is whether victory, that is, seizure of complete political power, could be achieved by means of the social-political-military techniques devised or perfected by the NLF. In NLF terms, to go almost the whole route to victory, to go up to the actual portals of victory, and then see one's forces either recede or be pushed back could mean only that the whole venture was futile and a failure. As in sports, it is the final score that counts. Using the General Uprising thesis the NLF came perilously close to victory — it was standing at the gates in December of 1963 and again in the spring of 1965 — but both times victory somehow eluded it. The conclusion of the Northerners, who by 1965 dominated the NLF, was that the General Uprising thesis could carry the movement along the path toward victory but could not carry it the entire route. And so the order came to switch doctrines and pursue the effort in the pattern of the Viet Minh war. Some Southern NLF members believed this was a disastrous mistake, that only the General Uprising thesis could win — but we will never know whether they were right. The possibility of the NLF returning to the General Uprising thesis was regarded by Vietnamese as remote. Said one *quy chanh,* "to return to the *khoi nghia* would be to slow down a typhoon; there is no such thing as a slow typhoon, for when a typhoon slows down it breaks up."

In the final resolve perhaps the Northerners were right. The NLF's functional liberation associations were highly effective, yet its organizational efforts among important ethnic and religious groups were far less successful. The social changes brought to the liberated area were perhaps more apparent than real. The NLF administrative liberation association was more manipulated than participational, and such an arrangement usually carries with it the seeds of its own doom. The great emphasis on communication of ideas failed to achieve its principal goal: The rural

Vietnamese, lacking informational background, often failed to under-stand in context the meaning of the message. The rural Vietnamese knew little about the social forces loose in his country and even less about the outside world, and he greeted NLF efforts to remedy this deficiency with indifference — the condition of parochialism in which the next village is in the other world dies hard in Asia. Finally, the effort mounted by the NLF required a type of cadre — talented, skilled, dedi-cated, an almost superhuman person — that did not exist in sufficient numbers to ensure success.

Yet the principles involved remain intact. The deeper one plunged into the study of the NLF the stronger became the feeling of being on the edge of a future social morass, only dimly seen. Here, one felt, was to-morrow's society, the beginning of 1984, when peace is war, slavery is freedom, the nonorganization is the organization.

NLF Accounts of *Dich Van* Struggle Movements

An impressionistic but by no means statistically accurate indication of the importance the NLF placed on the struggle movement can be found in the following results of a random sample survey of NLF mass-media accounts of specific *dich van* movements.

No doubt these figures were inflated — inflated by the organizers reporting to higher headquarters, inflated by each level as they passed up the line, and further inflated by the mass media. Inflation of crowd figures was endemic in Vietnam (a GVN rally at which foreign newsmen counted 2,000 persons was reported in the Saigon press as 100,000). But this misses the point: Numbers did not count; they were used like dabs of color in an impressionistic painting: One dab might be wrong, but it was the over-all color that struck the eye that counted. In the struggle not the numbers but the spirit mattered. Further, NLF statisticians did not distinguish between an NLF and a non-NLF-organized demonstration, a Buddhist or a student demonstration. In fact it would admit no distinction; it was all one, the people struggling.

385

Note: Both the NLF and the DRV refused to recognize the changes in province names ordered in Presidential Decree No. 153–NV of October 22, 1956, and both continued to refer to the provinces by their former names. Some of the changes effected by the GVN combined several provinces into one; others divided a province into several provinces. The following list gives the former name of an area, either province or district, and the new name of the province in which it is located.

Former Name	*New Name*
Thu Dau Mot	Binh Duong
Ham Tan and Tanh Linh	Binh Tuy
Duc Hue	Nau Nghia
Xuan Loc	Long Khanh
Cholon and Tan An	Long An
Long Xuyen	An Giang
Camau	An Xuyen
Soc Trang	Ba Xuyen
Vi Thanh	Chuong Thien
My Tho	Dinh Tuong
Rach Gia and Ha Tien	Kien Giang
Ben Tre	Kien Hoa
Phong Thanh	Kien Phong
Moc Hoa	Kien Tuong
Can Tho	Phong Dinh
Tra Vinh	Vinh Binh
Vinh Long and Sadec	Vinh Long
Ba Ra	Phuoc Long
Ba Ria and Vung Tau	Phuoc Tuy

One of the earliest records of full-scale *dich van* was contained in a report from Chau Thanh district of Dinh Thuong province concerning events there beginning on December 25, 1960:

The enemy shelled the village of Phu Phong, killing a woman and a child. As soon as the shelling was finished, 200 compatriots immediately marched to the village office to struggle for compensation for the deaths and for a halt to the shelling and killing. Village officials heard the request earnestly and promised to report to their superiors.

On December 26 the struggle moved a step further. Four hundred people, including families of Diem's soldiers, carried the two victims and the shell fragments to the village officials. The frightened assistant village chief tried to soothe their anger and accepted more than 100 petitions.

After the funeral of the victims on December 27 the struggle continued. One thousand one hundred people of the four villages of Phu Phong, Bai Long, Binh Trung, and Huu Dao . . . carried the petitions in an orderly march to the Chau Thanh district chief. . . . A rally was then held at the Ba Lon crossroad. One hundred cars were stopped, and the occupants, . . . when told about the matter, expressed their agreement with the people. . . . When the struggle demonstration continued to move down the road toward the Nhi Binh military post the enemy sent their commandos and fire engines. Even though tens of persons were killed, wounded, and arrested, the demonstration, which consisted chiefly of women and children, continued to move courageously onward. When 16-year-old Truong Thi Bay, carrying the sheaf of petitions like a banner, was killed by an enemy bullet, Nguyen Thi Be, 28 years old, immediately took her place. And when she fell, another woman replaced her, carrying the sheaf of petitions onward. The people moved forward, boiling with anger, shouting slogans: "Down with the terrorists." "Down with the Ngo Dinh Diem fascist and dictatorial regime. . . ."

The tide of anger rose higher and higher. Continually during January 29–31 thousands demonstrated on the road to Giua market. . . .

On the morning of February 8, a unified struggle began: Five rallies of 6,300 people struggled against district officials in Chau Thanh. . . . The district chief had to accept petitions. . . .

Then there was a grand demonstration numbering 15,000 people . . . to demand a halt to the U.S.-Diem repression and terrorism, and to demand improved standards of living and democracy.

Massive turnouts were not necessarily the most effective *dich van* methods. One person, in this case a woman, became a hero-martyr in a lone struggle with the governor of Ben Tre (Kien Hoa) province:

Woman: How many kinds of Americas are there in the world?
Governor: Only one kind, the United States of America. It has granted aid to Vietnam and belongs to the Free World.
Woman (in a firm voice): In my opinion there are two kinds of America. Disinterested America is good. But the America that has brought bombs and guns to South Vietnam and spread noxious chemicals to massacre the South Vietnamese people is as bad as a mad dog.

Hardly had she finished when other demonstrators shouted "Down with America for spraying poison chemicals."

This woman participated in many demonstrations in her village and province and even in Saigon. From 1960 to May 1963 she took part in 380 such struggles. . . . She was arrested and beaten by the enemy 26 times. The last time they tortured her to death. Gathering her remaining strength, she told her friends, "If you love me please take my corpse to the governor to struggle. . . ." Her determination stimulated her compatriots to continue the struggle.

Another homely example is given in an indoctrination booklet:

An old man asked a soldier stealing his chicken the name of his native village. The soldier told him and the old man said "My son is also a soldier of the national army. At this very moment he may be engaged in a clearing operation, arresting and terrorizing the people of your village. Perhaps the government is afraid to allow you to stay near your own village because you would not have the heart to terrorize your own people and take the chicken of your neighbor. Therefore the government sends you to our village and my

DATE	PLACE[1]	NUMBER OF PERSONS	STATED PURPOSE
1960–1961			
December 26–January 31	Chau Thanh district (My Tho)	15,000	against artillery shelling
December 26–January 22	Cai Lay, Chau Thanh district (My Tho)	tens of thousands	against terror, for democracy
1961			
January 11	Ben Tre	2,000	against terror and repression
January 11	Tan An	2,000	against terror and repression
January 17	Duc Hoa	5,000	against terror; for standard of living rise, democracy
January 19	Vinh Long	8,000	against shelling
January 19	Can Tho	tens of thousands	against terrorism
January 20	Can Tho	6,500	against shelling
January 20, 21	Trang Bang district, Tay Ninh	6,000	against draft and terror
January 22	Trang Bang city	—	market-place strike
1962			
January 19	Quang Nam province	300	against U.S. base
January 21–28	Area of Bien Hoa province along Highway 15	—	against defoliation
January 21–28	Tay Ninh province	—	against U.S., terror, strategic hamlet
January 31	Tra Vinh province	500 Cambodians	against bombings
January–February	Quang Ngai province	—	110 demonstrations, meetings
February 26	Ba Ria	300	against airport runway extension
February 26	Gia Dinh	300	withdrawal of U.S. troops

[1] Further complicating the matter of province names is the fact that in 1964 the GVN re-created some of the old provinces. Usage here is the name of the province at the time of the usage in the mass media.

1962 (continued)

Date	Place	Number	Description
February	Western Nambo	11,600	388 struggle movements—release 61 political prisoners, return VN $102,000, 11 tons of seized paddy
March 1–20	Western Nambo	720,000	20,000 meetings
March 1–20	Central Vietnam	148,000	3,700 meetings (37,000 flags, 80,000 leaflets)
March 6	Cai Lay district (My Tho)	8,000	against terror, repression (4,000-signature petition to district chief)
March 13	Ben Tre	8,000	———
April 25	Liberation Press Agency said that 3,000,000 persons demonstrated during first quarter of year in central provinces		
April–May	South Vietnam	1,000,000	against U.S. aggression and Diem terror, strategic hamlet, and draft
May 1–10	Tan An	60,000	30 meetings
June 1–10	Tay Ninh province	———	100 struggles: against U.S. aggression, ICC
January–June	3,500 struggles involving 12,500,000 people		standard of living rise
July, early	Hiep Hoa sugar refinery	1,000 workers	100 struggles: against strategic hamlet; for standard of living rise
July, early	Two districts of Long Xuyen and Chau Doc provinces	6,000	70,000 meetings
July–September	Central Vietnam	1,800,000	754 meetings (60,000 NLF manifestoes)
July–September	Long Xuyen and Chau Doc provinces		9,500 struggles: against military operations, strategic hamlets
August, September	Central Vietnam	134,000	against strategic-hamlet program
September 1	Central Vietnam	96 families	pro-NLF
September	Central Vietnam	10,000	31,000 signatures on 870 NLF resolutions
September	Ben Tre province	———	against military operations
September, October	My Tho province	60,000	
October 8–15	Camau	1,000 students	against draft

Date	Place	Number of Persons	Stated Purpose
1963			
January–March	Central Vietnam	2,230,000	against military operations, strategic hamlet, chemical warfare, Diem repression
January–March	Central Vietnam (liberated area)	2,900,000	anti-U.S., anti-Diem
July 10	My Tho province	8,000	market strike and pro-Buddhism
July 11	Chau Thanh district town	2,000	Buddhist support
July 15	Can Tho, Soc Trang, Tra Vinh province capitals	25,000	against strategic hamlet
July	South Vietnam	73,000 (10,000 Buddhists)	against U.S.-Diemists
September 18	Tan An	4,000	against strategic hamlet (petition to province chief)
September 20	Cai Lay District	3,000	against military operations
September 20	My Tho city	3,000	petition to province chief
September 23	Can Tho	6,000	prostudent, anti-Diem
September 23	Camau province	4,000	release political detainees
September	Camau	10,000	anti-Diem
September	South Vietnam	5,000,000	against strategic hamlet, military operations, repression; pro-Buddhism
November 2	Camau	3,000	anti-U.S.
November 3	Phung Hiep district, Can Tho province	300	anti-U.S.
November 4	Tan Chau district, Chau Doc province	3,000	anti-Diem remnants
November 5	Camau province	3,000	against strategic hamlets
November 6	Bac Lieu town	6,000	anti-U.S.
November 11	Tay Ninh	5,300	against U.S., military operations
November 12	Camau	11,000	against strategic hamlet and U.S.
November 16	My Tho city	28,000	against U.S., strategic hamlet, and military operations

1963 (continued)

Date	Location	Number	Description
November 16	Chau Doc province town	5,000	against strategic hamlet and U.S.
November 16	Can Tho	9,000	anti-U.S. (stoned Americans, tore down U.S. flag)
November 17	Tra Vinh and Go Cong provinces	13,500	anti-U.S.
November 17	Long Dinh district, My Tho	500	refugees wanting to return North
November 18	Can Tho	4,500	against strategic hamlet and U.S.
November 21–25	Cai Lay district	20,600	against U.S. puppet army
November 24	Gia Dinh	1,000 students	anti-Diem remnants
November 25	Ben Tre province	10,000	against strategic hamlet and military operations
November 25	Camau	1,000	anti-U.S.
November 27	Quang Tri, Quang Nam provinces	10,000	anti-Diem remnants
November 29	Ben Cat district, Thu Dau Mot	2,000	against strategic hamlet
November 30	Long Dinh district	1,500	against strategic hamlet and military operations
December 2	Ben Tre city	8,000	anti-U.S.
December 12	Cao Lanh	8,000	against strategic hamlet and U.S.
December 12–19	South Vietnam	100,000	against draft, strategic hamlet
December 16	Tra Vinh capital	5,000	anti-U.S.
December 19–20	Tay Ninh capital	—	anti-GVN
December 23	Phung Nghiep	2,500	anti-U.S.
December 26	Long Phuoc strategic hamlet, Ba Ria	1,000	against artillery shelling
December 27	Long Xuyen capital	4,000	release political prisoners
December 28	Camau	4,000	against strategic hamlet, military operations
December 29	Chau Doc town	150	antidraft

1964

Date	Location	Number	Description
January 1–7	Soc Trang	8,000	release political prisoners
January 5	My Tho province	6,000	release prisoners
January 16	Phung Nghiep township, Can Tho province	2,500	anti-U.S.
January 22	Tan An	6,500	against U.S. and military operations

Date	Place	Number of Persons	Stated Purpose
1964 (continued)			
January 27	Camau	5,000	against U.S. and chemical warfare
January 29	Go Cong province	6,900	29 meetings (release prisoners)
January	Duc Pho district, Quang Ngai province	—	62 demonstrations (against strategic hamlet)
February 5	Ben Tre city	6,000	against military operations and U.S.
February 5	Ben Tre province	8,000	anti-U.S.
February 6	Qui Nhon	1,000	peace and neutrality
February 11	Cho Long province (6 villages)	1,200	release prisoners
February 16	Ben Tre province village	40 women	against shelling
Mid-February	Sadec (19 villages)	10,000	anti-U.S.
March 13	Ben Tre province	10,000	anti-U.S.
April 4	Can Tho	5,000	antidraft
April 4	Phong Dieu	100	against mortar shelling
April 5	Can Tho	4,000	anti-U.S.
April 5	Chau Doc province	Cambodians	against bombing
April 10	Ha Tien province	500 Buddhist monks and nuns	against strategic hamlet
April 11	Tra Vinh province	10,000 (1,000 ethnic Cambodians)	Cambodian-Vietnamese solidarity
April 13	Phu Tho hamlet, Quang Ngai	1,000	anti-U.S.
April 16	Go Cong province capital	2,500	against U.S. base
April 17	Ben Tre province capital	2,000	anti-U.S., pro-NLF
April 17	Mo Cay district town, Ben Tre province	—	pro-NLF
May 15	Saigon	20,000	30 struggles in various forms (strikes, demonstrations for wages, working conditions)
January–June			
July 13	Ben Tre city	3,000,000	anti-U.S., pro-NLF
July 13	My Tho and Go Cong provinces	20,000	anti-U.S.
		30,000	anti-U.S., pro-NLF

1964 (continued)

Date	Location	Number	Description
July 13	Cai Be	500	anti-U.S.
July 13	Moc Chau	5,000	anti-U.S.
July 15	Long An province	2,000 women	against artillery shelling
July 15	Tan An city	5,000	anti-U.S.
July 17	Camau province capital	40,000	anti-U.S., pro-NLF
July (month)	South Vietnam	214,200	anti-U.S., pro-NLF
August 4	My Tho province	20,000	against U.S., bombing, and shelling
August 12	My Tho city	13,000	anti-U.S.
August 12	Cai Lay township	4,000	anti-U.S.
August 12	Hoa Dong	2,000	anti-U.S.
August 2	Thanh Hoa village, Can Tho province	4,000	against bombing
August 15	Bac Lieu city	7,000	anti-U.S., antidraft
August 20	Bac Lieu city	8,000	anti-U.S., antidraft
August 21	Bac Lieu city	17,500	anti-U.S., antidraft
August 24	Da Nang	30,000	anti-U.S.
August 25	Rach Gia city	4,000	anti-U.S.
August 20–30	Bac Lieu province	30,000	anti-U.S., antibombing, antidraft
August 27– September 16	Go Cong and 5 adjoining provinces	60,000	anti-U.S., antidraft
September 6	Tan An city	1,500	anti-U.S. (demonstrations before 2 U.S. military compounds)
September 15	Hoa Dong township, Go Cong province	2,500	anti-U.S.
September 15	My Tho city	6,000	against chemical warfare
September 25	Quang Ngai province capital	30,000	against artillery shelling
September	Mekong delta	1,000,000	anti-U.S., antiwar
September	Ben Tre province	53,000	1,400 struggles
September	Tra Vinh province	26,000	300 struggles

son to your village, both to terrorize. . . ." The soldier bent his head and pondered for a while, then looked into the face of the old man and uttered a curse against the vicious U.S.-Diem plot. . . .

Nor did massive input that yielded slight output dishearten the NLF cadres. A struggle movement reported in an internal document dated November 8, 1962, which in American eyes probably would be regarded as a failure, was regarded by NLF officials as quite successful:

We used 15 militants . . . from five cells, including two cadres, two Cao Dai, and four Buddhists. We had six petitions, four demanding the resignation of Ngo Dinh Diem and two denouncing Diem's repressive measures. . . .

At 2:00 A.M. we left S. Village [code name] for Ben Tre city. By 7:00 A.M. we had reached Nam Loi sawmill and there met our first obstacle. The police guard stopped our group and would not allow us to go to the market place. . . .

So the struggle was launched there. The militants vehemently denounced the barbarous acts of murder, rape, robbery of the U.S.-Diem clique. . . . We said "In the rural areas we have endless suffering and injustice. Our life is miserable. We come today to present petitions to the province chief with the hope he will help us. Your families are also in rural areas. . . . Helping us will help them." The policemen agreed to take our petitions and promised to send them to the province chief. . . . One policeman said privately "My family is from the country. I know well your miserable situation." The situation thus was favorable, for one of our comrades had used persuasive words to win the policeman to our cause. . . .

The struggle group left Ben Tre at 10:00 A.M. and arrived back at S. at 5:00 P.M. A large crowd greeted the militants. . . . A big meal was served and we were all satisfied and encouraged. . . . The following day a tea party was organized to celebrate the victorious struggle. . . .

The cadre's poststruggle assessment made this comment:

The struggle group fought with great courage and determination. They won a policeman to our cause. . . . Comrade T. C. was most distinguished in the struggle. He courageously denounced the murderous acts of the U.S.-Diem clique. He used wise methods in the struggle. He was reasonable and moderate with his words to convince the policeman and win him to our side. Comrade T. C. should be rewarded. . . . The remaining comrades of the group were not very bright in the struggle. They need more study and training. The struggle was a complete success. . . . I therefore submit this report to the executive committee [of the village].

The petitions undoubtedly wound up in the river. The policeman gave no real indication that he had been influenced; more likely he simply wanted the group to leave quietly. Such effect as was created, if any, was on the militants themselves. A considerable effort had been made and there was little to show for it. This was a common NLF (and Communist) experience, but they were not surprised that a massive effort to change people's opinions had only minimal effect, even if the change obviously was for their own good. Americans would approach such an effort believing that a small manipulation must produce immense results; otherwise it has failed.

The anatomy of one struggle movement is worth examining in some detail:[2]

On October 15, Diem's troops in the Dam Doi subsector came to the village with plans to build a strategic hamlet. They came first to Tan Diem hamlet of Ta An Khuong village, in two groups. The first group, composed of 22 (including a man named Lau, widely known for being cruel) fired at the Cay No people, destroyed their hamlet gate, and burned the information office. Our Self-Defense Force attacked and wounded one of them. Before withdrawing they captured three old men and took them back to Nga Tu post; that afternoon they released two of them but held Mr. Pham, 67 years old. . . . The second group arrived by landing craft at Lung Xinh at 8:00 A.M. There were 97 in the force, including the district chief; they had three radios and four police dogs. They arrived and fired many shots. Then they divided into two groups. One group went with the district chief to study the layout of the former Non Truong post [of the NLF army]. The other group went into the hamlet, fired into people's homes; they wounded and captured two men (Mr. Rang, 43, and Ho, 23). They also looted the home of Duong Thi Tat and stole one phonograph, two bags of clothing, and some jewelry. When leaving they shot Mrs. Tat, who died with a bullet in her chest, still holding her five-month-old baby. Then they withdrew.

Tat's family and relatives assembled to mourn. At the same time the village liberation executive committee met and decided to launch a struggle. The victim's family was consulted and agreed to a plan to use the woman's corpse. However, they were all afraid, and only one man, her uncle, dared join the struggle movement. So, the executive committee decided to refrigerate the body and send runners in sampans to other hamlets to gather people for the struggle. Five persons were used in this assignment. . . .

At 1:00 A.M. [October 16] the sampans were ready to leave for Camau city. At the last minute, Tat's mother, mother-in-law, father-in-law, her aunt, one uncle, and three other persons joined the group. . . . The delegation was accompanied and protected by some young men.

At 4:00 A.M. finally the group left in three sampans, one carrying the corpse and the other two each carrying six people including guards. They were towed by a motor boat, which took them near the Camau market.

At 6:00 A.M. the corpse and the group from the hamlet arrived at Camau wharf, where they were joined by 22 supporters, so in all there were 30 people.

At 6:30 A.M., when the enemy's radio called on the population to be ready for the "salute the colors" ceremony, the sampan with the corpse was moored near the bank, and the body covered with a grass mat. Tat's mother then began to cry very loudly. Boats and people began to gather. Soon there were 40 boats and about 500 people from the city . . . soon joined by 200 from the market who had been told of events. . . .

The mother, in her lament, explained to the crowd what had happened: "My daughter was a good person but the soldiers from Dam Doi district shot her to death. They also stole her clothes and jewels. . . . She had five

[2] Cited here is a case history based on a "Report to the Camau [An Xuyen] Provincial Central Committee" by the Ta An Khuong village committee on a mid-October 1962 struggle.

young children and her baby who is only five months old and who was fed by her mother. How can I survive this injustice?"

Accompanied by a woman and two children (ages 3 and 5) who lived in Camau city she went to the [government] office and handed in a petition asking the authorities to deal with this injustice. . . .

The clerk in the government office accepted her petition, and his attitude indicated he was panic-stricken. . . .

Meanwhile, from 6:30 to 8:00 A.M., the corpse was displayed in Camau market. The wound in the chest was shown. . . . The spectators clicked their tongues in a sign of pity. . . . A cyclo driver said "Nowadays life is unbearable." One merchant said the soldiers were sadists for having killed the woman and stolen her money and jewelry. . . .

Some 30 or 40 policemen came to suppress the demonstration. . . . They arrested two people and clubbed others. . . . Tat's mother said to them "Murder and looting in our hamlet, but we come here to complain and instead of helping us you mistreat us more. . . ." The police seized the boat and the body and towed the boat away. They arrested three adults and four children. . . . Later the police came back and asked for the leaders of the demonstration by name. . . . They had been told the names by the persons they arrested. . . .

That evening the corpse was buried behind a pagoda. (We know this because one of our people managed to follow the corpse and watch it all day.)

We continue to spread the news of this U.S.-Diem massacre and . . . it is causing great dissatisfaction among the people.

This is followed by an appraisal of the struggle, apparently written by a cadre from the district level:

Although the enemy succeeded in stealing the corpse, we were able to impress a total of about one thousand people about the atrocity. The corpse was on display for about two hours. . . . A large number of people came to view the spectacle (so many climbed on the boat deck house that they almost sank the boat). . . . All activity in the market ceased. . . . The salute to the colors ceremony was not attended. . . . The enemy showed signs of worry and panic. They blocked off the center of town and would not allow people to enter. Identification cards were checked. . . . However, they did not disperse the crowd at the market or suppress the struggle movement. . . . The soldiers showed sympathy and did not strictly obey their superiors' orders to break up the groups of people. Some of them said to the people "This was a shameful thing for soldiers to do. . . . Now the people will blame all soldiers." . . . Soldiers' wives shed tears. . . .

The strong points of the struggle were these: There was good leadership; the village executive committee acted quickly . . . ; the struggle was well planned, and no difficulties were encountered in getting the body to the market place . . . ; the timing was correct; early morning in the market place was the correct time for the struggle . . . ; there was [follow-up] . . . ; when the hamlet people returned to their village more demonstrations were held. . . . Medical care was given to those injured during the demonstration. . . .

The weak points of the struggle were these: The executive committee was not prepared for an immediate struggle but had to send people to other hamlets for assistance. . . . When the police came to suppress the demonstration, those from the village did not stand up and admit they were from the village, but in fact they denied it. . . . Unfortunately the only member of the victim's family at the market-place struggle was the girl's mother; the rest got "cold feet" when approaching Camau and turned back. . . . It was necessary therefore for us to supply a "make-believe sister and children" to accompany the mother. . . . No one argued when the police came to take away the body. . . . They just all stood and watched. . . . The petition to the officials only asked for the correction of this injustice and did not include other demands, such as an end to the strategic-hamlet program. . . . There was a lack of firmness in requesting the release of those arrested during the demonstration. . . .

To this report, which apparently was reproduced and distributed to cadres at the village level, the provincial central committee appended the note:

This is a report on a face-to-face struggle using a corpse . . . to protest the enemy's terror acts. You are requested to study this report and to discuss it . . . including the weak and strong points of the struggle.[3]

[3] Radio Hanoi, October 5, 1963; essential details were later confirmed by Americans living at the time in Soc Trang.

Mass-Media Communication

With a population generally unconditioned to mass-media appeals and having a mass-media system in only a rudimentary sense, it was evident to the NLF leadership that such media as clandestine newspapers and radio broadcasting could at best serve as reinforcements to other more direct means of communication or as channels for use when other means were blocked as, for example, communication with Americans in Vietnam. Throughout the era mass media were used, but definitely in a secondary role.

Communist and nationalist publications marked the Indochina scene from the beginning of revolutionary activities, among the earliest being the Communist Youth League's *People's Friend,* a newspaper published in the early 1930's in the Hanoi area; in 1937, when the Communist Youth League became the Democratic Youth League, the paper split into two operations and became *The Gioi* (The World) in Hanoi and *Moi* (New) in Saigon. The Viet Minh press in the 1950's consisted of about 150 periodicals, including 49 published in what was then Cochin China (of these two were in French and one each in German and in English), all supervised by the Viet Minh Director General of Information, Tran

Van Giau. Three of these 49 publications were major newspapers: *Cuu Quoc* (National Salvation), the organ of the Lien Viet, which by late 1951 had published a total of 22 issues with an average circulation of 160,000 copies; *Nhan Dan* (The People), organ of the Lao Dong Party, supervised by Truong Chinh, with an average run of 24,000 copies in the South and 27,000 in the North; and *Su That* (The Truth), edited for Party members. In addition, the Viet Minh operated a system of provincial newspapers and a series of periodicals for social groups such as the army, farmers, students, women, and Catholics. The Director General of Information supplied reprints of both *Cuu Quoc* and *Nhan Dan* to the provincial newspapers, which consisted of editorials or news stories and commentaries broadcast at dictate-speed by Radio Viet Minh. The Viet Minh also had a representative in Bangkok to do liaison work with foreign news agencies and correspondents; for a time that office published a news bulletin and distributed it around the world. Claude Guigues described the Viet Minh press as

dull, printed on newsprint the color of wrapping paper . . . with a tone of military cockade, filled with clumsy drawings, puerile poems. . . . There are no advertisements, no pictures. The Viet Minh newspapers smell of gloomy propaganda. In fact it is impossible to distinguish information from propaganda. . . . But they are read because they are the only newspapers available [in rural areas].[1]

Although the NLF regarded mass media as only reinforcements, it did consider mass media, as well as news itself, to have great utility. The Central Committee directive on agit-prop work declared:

We can help achieve these [revolutionary] goals by using news for indoctrinational purposes. Current news can be used by agit-prop cadres to develop enthusiasm and confidence of the masses for the Revolution, to portray the various defeats of the enemy, to show the victories being achieved in socialist countries [and] in peace-loving and democratic independent nations of the world, to inform the people of the victories of our forces throughout the country. . . . Some cadres have failed to understand the value of current news in agit-prop work, have failed to make use of newspapers, information sheets, radio broadcasts, and have failed to popularize these media among the masses.

Newspapers and Periodicals

The NLF newspaper system went through three phases from 1960 to 1965: the provincial newspaper period, which lasted from early 1960 to early 1963; the regional newspaper period during the rest of 1963 and lasting until late 1964; and the Communist-style press after late 1964.

[1] Claude Guigues, "The Viet Minh Press," *Indochine Sud-Est Asiatique*, October 1952.

After the 1954 partition, Viet Minh cadres, before moving North, buried at least a dozen small-sized printing plants, including type and ink; these were later resurrected by NLF cadres — cast-iron letter presses and printing ink being practically indestructible — and put to work. Newspapers and other printed materials were also produced by NLF cadres on mimeograph machines both at NLF bases and secretly in the cities. Newsprint was purchased in Saigon, smuggled in from Cambodia and the DRV, or made locally from bamboo. The NLF in the 1960–1961 period attempted to launch a newspaper in all provinces, and newspapers did appear sporadically in about one third. Usually these bore the name *Giai Phong* (Liberation); the most frequently encountered were *The Quang Ngai Giai Phong, The Binh Duong Giai Phong, The Can Tho Giai Phong* (Phong Dinh province), and *The Ba Ria Giai Phong* (Phuoc Long province). Less frequently encountered publications of this period included *The Quan Giai Phong* (Liberation Troops) serving the guerrillas, the *Western Nambo Anti-American, Liberation Women,* the *Khmer Bulletin* (published in Vinh Binh province, in Cambodian), and the *Mien Nam Chien Dau* (Southern Struggle or, as it was frequently translated, Fighting South) printed in English under the imprint of the NLF Foreign Relations Commission, with Le Van Tha as director. NLF internal documents occasionally mentioned the *Ma Bec* in Darlac province and *Vuong Le* (or sometimes *Vuong Len*) as "newspapers of the Tay Nguyen nationalities," supposedly published in Rhade and Jarai, but the author was never able to obtain copies of either. Because of the low literacy rate and the large number of mutually unintelligible dialects in the highlands it is doubtful that printed materials played much of a part in the NLF communication efforts among the montagnards. Newspapers probably averaged one edition every six weeks. Approximately five copies of each edition of the provincial newspaper were sent to each hamlet, and each copy was expected to serve 20 to 30 families.

In mid-1963 the NLF Central Committee abolished the provincial newspaper system as a failure. A memorandum at the time noted their chief shortcomings:

Lower-echelon cadres did not supply [editorial] materials because they were busy or because writing was difficult for them. The result was that a few specialized [provincial] cadres did the writing, and the articles lacked richness. Those lower-echelon cadres who did write articles did not grasp proper writing techniques, there was no criticism or self-criticism, and gradually no one wanted to write any more. . . . The materials were always too high-flown, such as an editorial entitled "Supporting the Declaration of Comrade Khrushchev at the United Nations Plenary Session," . . . or flat articles such as "Gather New Successes." . . . Articles consisted of what people did not like to read, such as editorials or general commentaries that were long, hard to read, and complicated. People like to read articles about people, arts, or articles criticizing something. . . . Jargon was used that is common in the Party but that the people did not understand, such as "the struggle policy is to combine political struggle and armed struggle." . . . The masses like beautiful, ingenious, and colorful newspapers, but ours lack this because of our poor printing abilities. . . . There was a time lag of a month and a half from the time the newspaper was published till it was placed in the reader's hands. . . . In summary, the standard of knowledge of province cadres is insufficient for publishing newspapers. Because of this situation the Central Committee has decided that the province should no longer publish any newspapers, either Party or Front newspapers. . . .

The NLF replaced the provincial newspaper system with a series of regional newspapers supplemented by one-page mimeographed news-sheets produced by the provincial agit-prop section. The NLF claimed that all the provinces produced these newssheets in addition to at least 17 regional newspapers with an average run of 80,000 copies — claims that seem grossly inflated.

The *Giai Phong* appellation was continued in the regional newspapers, and there emerged *The Western Nambo Giai Phong, The Central Nambo Giai Phong, The Eastern Nambo Giai Phong, The Zone Five Giai Phong,* and *The Saigon-Cholon-Gia Dinh Giai Phong. The Western Nambo Giai Phong* appeared as early as December 1961, apparently as the chief organ of the Central Committee. Its format was somewhat smaller than an American tabloid newspaper, running four to eight pages per edition, and supposedly issued monthly; Radio Liberation in July 1964 said that 30 issues of *The Western Nambo Giai Phong* had been published. These newspapers contained a mixture of news, commentary, and such nonnews as poetry, fiction, and official Central Committee pronouncements. They carried endless and usually meaningless statistics on the struggle, the result of information supplied by lower echelons; a 1962 Central Committee directive instructed village cadres to supply the agit-prop newspaper cadres with data of this sort:

We request you to submit monthly reports on U.S.-Diem crimes, including number of women raped (exact figures); number of people detained or killed (if there are no exact figures take one hamlet as an example and give population ratio of hamlet to village); number of houses demolished; paddy land destroyed; paddy stolen or burned; crimes toward workers; crimes toward farmers (in first report also give total from 1954 to date); crimes toward religions, such as temples burned or priests killed; crimes against ethnic minorities, including names. . . .

After 1964 the NLF concentrated its newspaper efforts on three papers: *Giai Phong, Nhan Dan,* and *Trung Lap,* although in some areas the regional newspapers continued to be published.

Giai Phong was first published as the official NLF Central Committee newspaper in early 1962, with Duong Van Vinh listed as publisher and

Le The Thoi as editor. It became dormant for more than a year and was revived in December 1964, with Huynh Tan Phat listed as director, Truong Son as editor-in-chief, and Ky Phuong as editor. The first issue of the revived series, a twelve-page tabloid, declared that

on the political and ideological front *Giai Phong* will resolutely uncover and crush all aggressive plots of the U.S. imperialists and their lackeys . . . ; gather and mobilize all patriotic forces in the rural areas, cities, mountains, and delta and pursue the political and armed struggles to counter the aggressors and save the country . . . ; will reflect the activities of the [liberated] area . . . ; contribute to national construction in the fields of military matters, politics, medicine, culture, education, economy, trade relations, etc. . . . It will present the activities of the NLFSV . . . and on the international front the achievements scored by various friendly countries and popular movements throughout the world struggling for peace, independence, the proletariat, and social progress.

Nhan Dan, the PRP's tabloid weekly, patterned after the Lao Dong organ of the same name in Hanoi, was first published in October 1964. It described itself as

the ideological struggle organ of the Party . . . , the Party tribune faithfully reflecting the aspirations and desires of Party members, liberation combatants members of all revolutionary organizations, and patriotic people of all walks of life, aiming at the union of all parties and peoples in the struggle for the interests of the Fatherland. . . . As an organ of the Party, *Nhan Dan* will popularize the line and policies of the Party as well as the experiences gained in the various political and armed struggles in building the Party and other revolutionary organizations. . . . While our country is temporarily divided, *Nhan Dan* . . . introduces to Southern compatriots the results of socialist construction in the North.

The first issue contained an editorial exhorting Party members to make greater sacrifices; a news story on the September 18, 1964 Gulf of Tonkin incident in which U.S. planes struck at DRV naval installations; an article on the fifteenth anniversary of the founding of the Chinese People's Republic, which "sincerely thanked" the Chinese for their support of the struggle in South Vietnam; a commentary on "U.S.-lackey internal contradictions"; an official NLF Central Committee statement on Saigon political events; a biographic sketch of "the guerrilla Tran Huu who destroyed one hundred of the enemy"; a column in which Party members were urged to stand and understand Party regulations; a poem, "To the North"; and the words and music to a popular song, "The Pointed Bamboo Stick."

Trung Lap (Neutrality) first appeared in February 1963, although newspapers of this name had been published in Indochina in previous years; for example, a *Trung Lap* was published in Phnom Penh in Vietnamese as early as January 1962 and copies circulated secretly in Saigon. Whereas *Nhan Dan* was left of *Giai Phong, Trung Lap* was right of it. Ostensibly it was published by a group affiliated with the NLF and dedicated to a "neutral solution to the Vietnam problem." Most of its editorial opinion pursued the neutralist theme.

The NLF provincial newssheet in the form of one-page mimeographed sheets continued to be published during 1964 in at least a third of the provinces. These contained, or were intended to contain, regional and local news, usually material copied from dictate-speed Radio Liberation, nonpolitical content such as serial fiction and poetry, and words and music for revolutionary songs. News consisted chiefly of stories dealing with NLF army victories, the strategic-hamlet program, land tenure problems, the military draft, and of course the struggle movement. Various journalistic forms were employed, including the news story, the memoir, the interview, letters to the editors, and in some cases submissions by correspondents. Apparently both NLF and PRP policy directives were meant to apply to editorial matter, for one memorandum on provincial newssheets instructed that "news of the Front must be written in accordance with the Front's policies, whereas general news of the day should be written from the viewpoint of the Party." The newssheets were sent to district cadres who pasted them on the walls of village information halls, and read them at nightly newspaper reading sessions. The higher-echelon leaders apparently thought little of the medium, which came in for heavy and frequent criticism. A typical memorandum declared:

The news stories [in them] are written without consideration of the situation with respect to the masses' struggle and therefore do not serve the cause. . . . Facts are not checked, and the news bulletins contain more errors even than do the newspapers . . . [and] take up to 20 days to reach the readers. . . . They contain news that is not indispensable or includes unnecessary details. . . . For example, one province reported that the farmers in the North were now planting rice. . . . Another talked about Major Gargain traveling some megameters around the world, when it was certain that none of us understand the word "megameter," including the person who wrote the news story.

According to the minutes of a provincial-level agit-prop conference one agit-prop cadre was asked about the villagers' opinion of the newssheet. He replied "We print them and deliver them, just as we burn votive papers, so we don't know whether or not the gods appreciate them."

Among the more prominent NLF periodicals were *Co Giai Phong* (Liberation Banner), which bore the masthead slogan "Revolutionary Struggle Is the Path to Follow to Liberate the Cities" and described itself as the "fighting organ of the Southern city dweller"; *Tien Phong,* the "political and theoretical organ of the PRP"; *Artists' Review,* published as early as 1962 by the NLF Cultural Liberation Association; and *Thoi Su Pho Thong* (Current Events), which appeared in early 1965, with its first edition containing articles on Liberation Army victories, floods in Central Vietnam, and the liberation movements in Venezuela and the Congo, the purpose of the magazine being unclear. The NLF also published a number of books, usually small 40–60-page works of fiction with innocuous false covers, containing stories of heroic revolutionary efforts by resplendent and flawless revolutionaries against overwhelming odds.

The Leaflet

The traditional communicational tool of the revolutionary, the clandestine leaflet, was the major mass medium of the NLF in its earliest days. Leaflets collected by the GVN in the 1958–1960 period were usually signed "Liberation Forces of the South" or Lao Dong Party. Typical titles were "Letters from Long An Lao Dong Provincial Committee to Rural Compatriots on the Thirty-Ninth Anniversary of the Founding of the Party" and "An Appeal by the Lao Dong Party South Vietnamese Executive Committee to Compatriots in the South." Many of these contained Ho Chi Minh's picture and at least one was issued to mark his birthday. Apparently they served chiefly to advertise the fact that the Lao Dong Party continued to exist in the South.

The NLF leaflet program reached its zenith of utility in mid-1963, after which it declined. The leaflets usually took the form of a two- or four-page tract containing several thousand words of text; a small leaflet (about 3 by 5 inches) containing a much shorter message; or a slogan slip, which was a strip of paper on which a single slogan was written. The leaflets were usually the work of cadres. The slogan slip was the work of the people themselves, usually as part of a struggle movement, and was a device highly prized by the leadership. The cadre directive on agit-prop work declared that

the slogan is a form of agitation that concentrates the determination of the masses to struggle, expresses the attitudes and actions of the masses to make revolution, and lowers the prestige and power of the enemy. . . . They are of three types: those that praise our policies; those that express hatred, especially for the U.S.-Diem crimes; and those that support the *binh van* movement.

It went on to say that slogans could be written on paper, on wood panels, carved into tree trunks, lettered on walls or on large banners to be hung across roads leading into villages, in addition to being shouted during struggle movements. The directive added:

Slogans may be written in the form of poetry, in verses of six to eight words, or in the form of words to popular songs. . . . But all slogans must be written in serious and dignified form and not scrawled. Many slogans now used are disorderly. These must be improved. The masses must be taught to write slogans properly, hang them in public places, and protect them from enemy soldiers during [mopping-up] operations.

The directive gave an example of villagers protecting their slogans:

In one village the people wrote slogans on the bark of tree trunks. The enemy soldiers came to the village and saw the slogans on the trees and said "We think we should cut down these trees with these offending words." The people replied to them: "If the Liberation soldiers had written the slogans on bridges would you blow up the bridges?" The enemy soldiers were forced by this logic to withdraw, without cutting down the trees.

The tract and the miniature leaflet were usually written at the inter-zone agit-prop section and sent to the district or village where they were reproduced and distributed by local cadres. It is difficult to determine the scope of this leaflet activity; a *quy chanh* who had worked in the Kien Hoa provincial agit-prop section said that in September 1961, probably the high point of the NLF leaflet program, the provincial agit-prop section issued 500,000 leaflets of ten different types. An NLF internal report said that the Central Nambo zonal central committee produced three million leaflets dealing with the GVN's April 1961 elections.

The cadre directive stated that leaflets were to be

used in areas where we are not able to organize demonstrations. They have the purpose of causing the masses to stand up and struggle. They are used in areas where we have no organization or only a weak one, such as a provincial capital. Butterfly leaflets create a willingness among the people to struggle against the enemy and heighten the prestige of the Revolution. In the areas where we are organized but the enemy still is in control we can use leaflets to make propaganda for our organizations. This should be the main objective in the use of leaflets. But also they should arouse public opinion, create confusion among the people, and give the masses subjects to discuss. . . . Leaflets disseminate only general policies. Detailed treatment of a subject should be done in face-to-face agit-prop work. Do not rely too much on leaflets.

Leaflets were scattered by hand at night by agit-prop teams. They were surreptitiously placed in women's shopping baskets in small-town markets or left in public places, on buses and trains, in schoolrooms, or sent through the mail. Kites and balloons were flown over towns and military posts, carrying leaflets that were scattered by the wind when a mechanism released them from their airborne conveyors. In cities and towns cadres at night would soak leaflets in water and secretly spread them on the roofs of the taller buildings; the morning sun would dry them; they would come loose from the roof tiles and blow over the town. The NLF also employed a special hand grenade that exploded without injuring anyone and scattered leaflets over a wide area.

NLF cadres estimated that in a random leaflet-scattering operation in a GVN-controlled area only 10 per cent got into the hands of the population. Leaflets became less important as the organizational structure developed. A 1964 memorandum noted,

> When we started [the NLF] we had no firm foundation and therefore needed many tracts and leaflets. Now we do not need as many. We need not distribute them in all places, only in the towns and in areas where the enemy is in firm control, in army posts, in refugee villages, and among religious groups. We do not need them in the liberated area . . . except when enemy troops come through.

News Media Organizations

The chief association of NLF news media personnel was the Patriotic and Democratic Journalists' Association, whose chairman was Vu Tung, editor of *Giai Phong*. The vice-chairman was Tan Duc, director of Radio Liberation, and the secretary-general was Thanh Nho, director of the Liberation Press Agency (LPA).

The Liberation Press Agency was founded in February 1961. It described itself at the time as "the official organ and information agency of the NLFSV . . . entrusted with the task of disseminating news about and the rich experiences of the struggle of our compatriots in all parts of the country." The LPA maintained correspondents abroad; Nguyen Van Hieu's first trip to Moscow was under the ostensible sponsorship of the LPA; Duong Dinh Thao served in East Berlin.

Unlike most insurgents elsewhere, the NLF made no effort to contact Western foreign correspondents in Vietnam and in fact normally rebuffed the efforts of such newsmen to establish contact. Radio Liberation in 1964 began to refer to "press conferences" that it said were being held outside Saigon for the benefit of Vietnamese newsmen on Saigon dailies. In late 1964 the NLF claimed that the Australian Communist Wilfred Burchett and the French Communist Madeleine Riffau of *L'Humanité*, the French Communist Party's newspaper, toured the liberated area of South Vietnam. Radio Hanoi in December 1964 said that an NLF delegation had visited the Tran Phu Printing House in Hanoi, which "has brotherhood relations with the Tran Phu Printing House operated by the NLFSV Central Committee."

Radio

Radio Liberation went on the air on February 1, 1962 as the "Voice of the National Liberation Front." Previously, clandestine radio broadcasts had been heard sporadically from the Mekong delta, from a station billing itself as the "Voice of Liberation." The signal source changed frequently, giving rise to a belief that the transmitter was aboard a barge that kept moving to prevent GVN destruction. In late 1961, after the tail of a typhoon lashed the southern part of the delta, the station went off the air and was never heard again; speculation in Saigon at the time was that the barge had sunk.

Radio Liberation's first broadcast declared that the purpose of the new station would be to

report the arduous and complex struggle of the South Vietnamese people, to denounce the barbarous crimes of the U.S. imperialist aggressors and the Ngo Dinh Diem clique, and to inform compartriots of the policies of the NLFSV, together with the Front's experiences in the struggle, with a view to contributing to the struggle of the Southern compatriots until final victory.

Initially broadcasting (on 7,393 kilocycles) consisted of a total of ninety minutes of air time per day — a half hour in Vietnamese and fifteen minutes each in English, Cambodian, French, and Chinese (alternating Cantonese and Szechwanese). In July 1963 the programing in Vietnamese increased to two and a half hours per day, and by late 1964 the station was on the air an average of five and a half hours a day, although some of the programs were transmitter repeats of earlier programs. The signal at the start was weak and irregular and in later days averaged only about 60 per cent intelligibility in Saigon, even using the most expensive receivers. The station was jammed by the GVN, and it is doubtful that more than 10 per cent of the programing was intelligible to a listener in the rural areas using an ordinary transistor receiver. A typical day of broadcasting in Vietnamese in the early period consisted of a sign-on song, "The Heroic South Vietnamese People Stand Up to Overcome All Storms March" (replaced in October 1964 by "The Southern People Rise Up and Engage in the War of Resistance for National Salvation under NLFSV Leadership March"); a five-minute reportage on a recent election of the Women's Liberation Association central committee, and a list of the new officers; a five-minute commentary entitled "U.S.-Diem Crimes"; a ten-minute talk on the "Recent Formation of the PRP"; and a ten-minute feature, "Daily Topic," a two-voice program on the "High Cost of Living in Saigon Today." Later the station's format was standardized into half-hour segments (in late 1964 Radio Liberation was averaging nine half-hour segments in Vietnamese daily). These consisted of three types of programing, interspersed by music: news and commentaries; features and background-type programs; and cultural and aesthetic programs. Typical features were the "Ap Bac Trumpet" (discussion of the NLF army and its prowess) on Tuesday, "Review of the Southern Press" on Thursday, and "Life in the Liberated Area" on Saturday. The titles of typical cultural programs were "Stories of the Valiant South" (serials of the soap-opera type but read rather than acted), "Combat Poems," and traditional Vietnamese musical programs. Important announcements, such as a statement by the NLF Central Committee, would be repeated as often as a dozen times a day in an attempt to ensure that the message got through.

Radio Hanoi (the Voice of Vietnam) broadcast by medium wave on a three-network system: Network I was directed to the general population of North Vietnam; Network II, about five hours a day of broadcasting, was directed to South Vietnam; and Network III was directed to both audiences but primarily to the North. It consisted chiefly of cultural and intellectual programs, modeled after the BBC's Third Programme. Hanoi also broadcast by short wave to Southeast Asia and to Europe in English, French, and other languages. In September 1964 Hanoi Hannah went on the air broadcasting a half-hour program daily in English to American servicemen in South Vietnam. Radio Hanoi also broadcast, on separate frequencies, dictate-speed news to South Vietnam. This program, and in fact much of the Radio Hanoi and Radio Liberation programing, was not for the mass audience so much as for communication with the NLF leadership at the village level. An NLF memorandum dated mid-1964 noted that

dictate-speed broadcasts are the fastest means for transmitting the best-quality news items that have the greatest value for agit-prop cadres. . . . Provincial central committees are requested to urge village organizations to disseminate widely bulletins with material [copied] off the air. . . . Material should also be used for word-of-mouth propaganda.

Radio Hanoi also broadcast daily what it called its "document copying program," which consisted of Party directives and official statements read at slow speed so that they could easily be copied by cadres; although this program was apparently aimed at DRV cadres in the North, some of the directives had applicability or interest in the South. Radio Hanoi claimed a large audience in the South; a July 3, 1964 broadcast, for example, asserted:

The people of Tan Phu village listen daily to the Voice of Vietnam broadcasts on agriculture, how to defeat drought or too much water on the land, and so forth. . . . They particularly follow broadcasts on agricultural science and technique . . . and learn how the people of North Vietnam have overcome difficulties brought about by the vagaries of nature.

In addition to jamming the Communist broadcasts, the GVN used other counterradio devices; Radio Liberation on August 9, 1962, for example, warned listeners that

the enemy recently set up a false self-styled Radio Liberation using our frequency and sign-on music, . . . and it has been broadcasting false news and distorting arguments about the struggle of the South Vietnamese people.

Motion Pictures

In mid-1963 NLF output began referring to what was called the Liberation Film Studio, which, it said, "started with only a little equipment, one camera, and some floodlights and now has grown and has numerous centers." It said that the studio had produced 13 reels of film "recording the historic events of the people of the South . . . , which have been sent to the people in the North." It also claimed that each provincial agit-prop section had a motion-picture projector for showing motion pictures and that film audiences in South Vietnam averaged 40,000 persons a month during 1963. Huynh Van Tuan, listed as the head of the Liberation Film Studio, went to Djakarta in April 1964, where he entered two films in the Third Afro-Asian Film Festival. These were "Heroic South" and "We Must Take Up Arms." "Heroic South" is perhaps the best-known NLF film about South Vietnam and was shown widely in the United States as well as throughout the world. Others purportedly made by the Liberation Film Studio and shown abroad were "Flames of the Second Front," "On the Banks of the Demarcation River," and "White Smoke," all feature films, and three documentaries: "New Vietnamese Women," "Struggle of the Courageous South Vietnamese People," and "Blooming Season."

In all probability these films were the work of DRV film-makers, possibly using footage shot in South Vietnam. "Heroic South" was perhaps the most indigenous, but it contains scenes that are distinctly Northern. The documentaries used footage that indeed was shot in the South by the GVN's newsreel-making teams and probably obtained by the DRV in Paris. Certainly the editing, printing, laboratory processing, and sound and music mix work were done in Hanoi.

Cultural Activities

Although the NLF lacked motion-picture capability it made up for this handicap by extensive use of cultural activities at the village level, including drama, traditional opera, ballet, music, and storytelling. The cadre agit-prop directive declared:

Culture is a form of education, indoctrination, and agitation that has great impact on the masses because it involves emotions. Cadres must promote a cultural movement. Those who fight and live the revolutionary life have the best materials for the creation of good cultural productions. Members of the [guerrilla] forces should be encouraged to produce dramas. . . . Do not be too severe in your criticism about their [dramatic] techniques, only if the political content is wrong. . . . Scripts of productions should be sent by [village] cadres to the provincial committee for criticism and improvements. . . . Themes should support the Front's policies and programs, promote hatred and resentment, mobilize the masses for the struggle. . . . It is necessary to view cultural works as having the purpose of promoting strong hatred. All cultural activities must promote hate continuously and permanently. . . . In one area the play "Opposing Disastrously Cruel Manslaughter" was performed. Thousands of people shouted "Down with manslaughter," and others wept. Plays have great educational effect.

Particularly in the Central Vietnam area, the NLF made extensive use of drama. Each village was expected to develop its own cultural team, which would provide both entertainment and indoctrination for the villagers. The provincial agit-prop sections organized five- to ten-man drama teams that traveled in the safer areas presenting skits and dramas that were basically entertainment but had a heavy moralistic overtone.

A villager in Quang Ngai who lived for several months under NLF control described to the author the use of drama as a tool of indoctrination:

Performances were held in open fields. There was a round wooden stage about [three feet] from the ground with black curtains in front and a Liberation flag on the back curtain. There were [butane] gas lights and a [public address] system that operated from storage batteries. Cadres were in the audience to maintain order and to defend against [ARVN] attack. The first play was about a new Viet Cong recruit who found life with the Viet Cong too difficult so he deserted. He went home and was scolded by his father. He repented and joined the Farmers' Liberation Association and worked in the village to turn it into a combat hamlet. Then came a talk by a cadre on the strategic-hamlet program and some songs and traditional dances. Then came the second play, about an American army officer and an [ARVN] officer who led a band of soldiers in searching peasants' houses and oppressing people. The play showed how rude and cruel the enemy was, especially the American. The third drama was like a [traditional Vietnamese] opera, with music and dances and spoken dialogue. It was about an American adviser who came to help a hamlet chief. The American insulted the chief by throwing away the gifts given him and by raping the hamlet chief's daughter. The chief then schemed with the Viet Cong to turn the hamlet over to the Viet Cong.

Music, too, was extensively employed. The traditional *vong co,* or folk music, was rewritten with new words appended. Songs from the Viet

Minh war were revived, also with new words. A cadre agit-prop directive instructed that

> songs, music, and dances must be used in accordance with our policies, and only correct songs should be used. Some songs praise peace and do not cause the masses to hate the enemy deeply or to struggle. Some laud the Liberation troops as during the Resistance but with the idea that the troops are at the front fighting and the masses in the rear supporting them . . . and thus the masses don't realize we are in a war that involves all persons. Music should not be peaceful or happy because this is injurious to efforts to stir up wrath. We can praise peace but we must appeal to the people to fight. . . .

Other Media

In late 1961, when communication efforts in the villages still were rudimentary, the NLF Central Committee began to establish village information services to act as news disseminators at the village level. Information halls were built, and cadres, usually youths, were placed in charge of them. The cadres read newspapers aloud at night, arranged photographic displays received from the district level, and distributed leaflets and other printed materials.

The NLF flag consisted of two broad horizontal bars, red over blue, the red symbolizing revolutionary spirit and the blue signifying peace. Superimposed on the field was a gold (for the Vietnamese people) star representing the five elements supporting the Revolution: peasants, farmers, workers, soldiers, and student-intellectuals. Flags were flown openly in the liberated area, although constantly destroyed by ARVN units. They were raised clandestinely in the cities; children made them out of paper and distributed them; and they were often sent aloft by means of kites, balloons, or birds.

The stele, called the "crime stone" or "mourning altar," also was common. A cadre directive declared:

> In order to promote hatred in the villages, it is necessary to build steles on which are engraved the crimes committed by U.S.-Diem in the village, specifically listing how many people were killed, looted, how many homes were burned down, etc. Separate steles can be erected for each instance. . . . Before the home of a person killed by enemy artillery fire, a stele may be erected, which says: "On the ___ day of ___, U.S.-Diem forces, using American guns, shelled the house of Mr. ___, killing ___ persons, including Mrs. ___, a child named ___, age ___, and a woman named ___, who was pregnant. The U.S.-Diem clique must pay for this act with their blood." In front of a house burned down by the enemy, erect a stele with this incription: "This burned debris is the result of the national policy of equalitarian social progress of the U.S.-Diem strategic hamlet. The house of Mr. ___ was burned by Diem soldiers on the ___ day of ___ in order to regroup people into the strategic hamlet."

The use of effigies also was common. Dogs and monkeys were dressed up as ARVN soldiers or U.S. advisers and turned loose in the market place. Declared a cadre directive,

Use effigies to attack the U.S.-Diem clique. . . . Guide the masses and even children to make effigies of clay. They need not be beautiful. But do not make these humorous, as, for example, in some places [people] have made effigies of Diem and [Madame Nhu] making love. Instead make the effigies with ugly features, such as a fat face, a hunched back, etc., to incite the masses to feel hatred and resentment to such a degree that they desire to beat and curse the effigies.

Effigies labeled with the name of the current American ambassador were often burned on a river bank across from GVN-controlled villages.

People's Revolutionary Party Bylaws

Article 1 — Membership: Membership in the PRP was open to any Vietnamese, 18 years of age or more, who accepted the Party's guiding principles, directives, and bylaws, who pledged to remain active in at least one Party organization, who agreed to work wholeheartedly to achieve Party goals, who agreed to subject himself to Party discipline, and who paid his membership dues.

Article 2 — Duties of Members: A member obeyed Party resolutions and directives, took part in Party activities, made propaganda, and did the necessary organizational work. He was to be absolutely loyal and honest toward the Party; at all times he served the people in the name of the Revolution and struggled with perseverance, determination, and courage. He accepted Party discipline, worked to increase Party solidarity, and was constantly vigilant in the protection of Party secrets. He was to remain close to the masses, mixing with them, teaching them, and learning their aspirations and opinions. He was to regard himself as a leader of the masses. He studied Marxism-Leninism and official Party directives with a view to increasing his own political knowledge, improving his own capabilities, and continually setting an example for others. And he indulged in criticism and self-criticism.

Article 3 — Rights of Members: According to the bylaws each member had the right to participate in Party debate and decision-making, be a candidate, and vote in Party elections. His rights also allowed him to criticize Party members, organs, or policy at open meetings, although he was required to accept Party directives from higher headquarters without question; should he disagree with a directive, he had the right to present his views to the Presidium of the Party Central Committee from which it came.

Article 4 — Admission to Membership: An applicant for membership was sponsored by two regular Party members; his application was approved by the local Party cadre *(chi bo)*, after which he began a probationary period.

Article 5 — Categories of Probationary Membership: Persons with questionable social backgrounds served a longer probationary period: For workers the period was three months; for poor farmers or children of poor farmers, four months; for middle-class farmers and secondary-school students, six months; for university students, nine months; and for what were called "revolutionary intellectuals," [1] one year. All other social classes served two-year periods. Provincial committees were allowed to determine the probationary period for what were called "special classes," which included ethnic minorities, ARVN deserters, and those who had been active in non-NLF political or religious organizations. This was a regulation aimed at admitting to membership, but under conditions of tight control, members of the Cao Dai and Hoa Hao religious sects. Correspondingly, to sponsor a person of questionable social background, one's own membership had to be longer. For example, to sponsor a worker one needed to have been a Party member only three months; to sponsor a university student, nine months; and so on.

Article 6 — Duties of Probationary Members: Probationary members were required to study Party learning documents and attend special indoctrination classes. At the end of the probationary period the cadre examined the candidate and passed on his admission. An unqualified probationary member could be granted an additional period (up to twice the length of the regular probationary period) in which to prepare himself; if he again failed, he was excluded from the Party.

Article 7 — Transfer: A Party member moving from one area to another took with him a letter of introduction to his new Party organization, signed by the chairman or cadre of his former unit. Frequently,

[1] By which was meant those associated with the various non-Communist dissident groups in Vietnam and those involved in the unsuccessful attempt to overthrow the Diem government in November 1960. (Those involved, including paratrooper command officers, fled to Cambodia.)

stringent security requirements were added to this article to reduce the possibility of a GVN penetration agent joining the NLF.

Article 8 — Isolated Members: A Party member isolated from his organization or out of contact with other Party members but who continued actively serving the Party was permitted to count that period in determining his Party age. (This article as well as security aspects of Article 7 differed from the DRV Lao Dong Party bylaws, which contained no such clause, since they were not required.)

Article 9 — Loss of Membership: A member who failed to pay his dues or ceased Party activity was considered to have left the Party voluntarily.

Article 10 — Organizational Principles: The principle of "democratic centralism" governed the Party. The Party apparatus was to be elected, with the highest authority being the Party Congress, which theoretically elected the "central level" (*trung uong*), or Central Committee. Below the national Central Committee were the interzone central committee (*xu* or *bo*) and the five intermediate levels of organization down to the three-man cell, as described in Chapter 8: Below the interzone the structure split into two separate chains of command, one for urban and one for rural areas. Thus below the interzone were the zone (*khu*) for the rural areas and the special zone (*dac khu*) for the urban; below them, in order, were the province (*tinh bo*) and city (*thanh bo*), the district (*quan*) and town or portion of city (*khu pho*), the village (*xa*) or street zone (*kha pho*), and hamlet branch group (*ap chi bo*) or street branch group (*chi bo*) of one or more cells. Beneath this was the standard three-man cell (*tieu to*). As an operating principle, all Party problems were to be solved at the lowest feasible level. Congressional resolutions required only simple majority for passage and were immediately binding on all members. Policy determination and propaganda themes were to be determinated by higher levels, and lower levels were warned not to take this prerogative upon themselves. Public pronouncements were to reflect Party policy.[2]

Article 11 — Leadership in GVN Areas: In enemy-controlled areas, stated the bylaws, organizational leadership would not be elected but would be appointed after consultation with the membership.

Article 12 — Types of Organizations: The bylaws stipulated that the Party units were to be based on "administrative [rural], production [urban], or operational [military] units," which is to say, in the rural

---

[2] The faithful could get the word from *Tien Phong* (Vanguard) and *Chien Dau* (Struggle), two theoretical journals infrequently published in South Vietnam. *Tien Phong* described itself as "the theoretical organ of those who follow the doctrines of Marx and Lenin in South Vietnam" and after July 1962 maintained that it was the official organ of the PRP. *Chien Dau,* launched in April 1962, stated that it was "the official political and theoretical organ of the PRP." A monthly newssheet, *Nhan Dan,* for PRP members was started in October 1964.

area the functional unit was the village, in the city it was the factory or economic enterprise, and in the ARVN it was the military unit. With respect to the NLF army the bylaws simply stated that "special regulations apply," apparently meaning the commissar system.

Article 13 — Day-to-Day Authority: Decision-making authority rested with the Party Congress and, when it was not in session — it usually was not — with the Central Committee; the same principle applied with respect to congresses and central committees at all lower echelons.

Article 14 — Convening of Congresses: The congress of members at any level was ordered (or postponed under "extraordinary" circumstances) by the central committee. One half of the membership could cause the convening of a congress with the approval of the next higher central committee. The central committee determined delegate responsibility, enforced parliamentary procedure, and examined credentials. It could appoint up to half of its own membership as delegates to the congress and could appoint delegates from areas that had not yet been able to elect delegates (up to a total of one third of the congress). A quorum consisted of half the membership. The central committee, in turn, elected the congress.[3]

Article 15 — Special Congresses: A special-session congress was composed of the central committee members and certain other congress members selected by the central committee to attend; apparently the special congress was in the nature of an emergency session group, although its purpose is not clear. Decisions taken by the special-session congress required approval of the next higher level central committee.

Article 16 — Central Committee Staffs: The central committees at all levels were authorized to establish subcommittees and special agencies for administrative and operational purposes.

Article 17-19 — The Basic Organization: The basic organization was regarded as the foundation of the Party and its direct link to the masses. The basic organization was the branch group (*chi bo*), formed of one or more three-person cells at the hamlet (*ap*) level in the rural areas and the street zone (*khu pho*), equivalent to a precinct, in the city, or infrequently in economic enterprises such as a factory or in governmental organizations such as a bureau or military unit. The branches were subdivisions of the village (*xa*) or the street zone (*khu pho*); in actual usage Vietnamese employed the term *chi bo* to describe all Party organizations up to the provincial level, although usually with a suffix: *chi bo xa* (village), *chi bo quan* (district), *chi bo khu pho* (street zone), and so on. The

---

[3] No hard information is available about election practices in the PRP. Several defectors and *guy chanh* who maintained they had been PRP members said there were no elections at any level. There is no reason to believe that genuine elections were any more a part of the PRP than they are a feature of other Communist organizations or societies.

executive committee for the *chi bo* was called the *chi uy* (a contraction of the term *uy vien chi bo*).

Article 20 — Duties of Basic Organizations: The basic organization associated the Party with the masses; advanced Party ideas in conformity with Party directives; reported to headquarters; propagandized, educated, organized, and led the masses in the struggle movement; indoctrinated Party members; distributed assignments; led the cadre criticism and self-criticism effort; collected dues; recruited new members; disciplined Party members; protected the security of the Party by maintaining "revolutionary vigilance"; discussed Party directives and drafted resolutions that contributed ideas to higher headquarters; and maintained close liaison with higher echelons.

Article 21 — Probationary Cadres: Probationary cadres were established in areas with fewer than three Party members; their rights, however, were limited.

Article 22 — Branch Conferences: A branch meeting was held at least every three months and called by the secretary or by half of the branch central committee. Decisions taken by the conference, including the election of the branch central committee secretary, were approved by the district central committee.

Article 23 — Branch Officers: If a branch had three members it elected a secretary; five to seven members, a secretary and assistant secretary; more than seven, a central committee, which in turn elected a secretary and if necessary an assistant. This committee stood for election every six months.

Article 24 — Special Membership: Under certain circumstances it was permissible to establish a category of membership called the single-contact Party member (*dang vien don tuyen*), which existed at all levels and reported to the central committee that appointed it.

Article 25 — Basic-Unit Congresses: Congresses at the basic-unit level met every six months, providing the unit had at least two branches.

Article 26 — Duties of Basic Organization Central Committee: It conducted all Party activity in its area, carried out instructions from its congress and higher echelons, managed Party finances, and organized, administered, and guided the Party membership.

Article 27 — Central Committee Meetings: The central committee of the village, street zone, and enterprise met at least every two months; its leadership consisted of a secretary and if necessary an assistant secretary; also, if necessary, it named a one-man presidium of the central committee. Officers of the central committee had to have been Party members for one year before their election.

Article 28 and 29 — Higher-Level Organizations: District and rural town congresses met every eighteen months; province, city, zone, and special zone congresses met every two years. Central committee meetings followed this schedule: district and rural towns every three to four months, province and city every three to six months, zone or special zone every six to nine months. Half the membership of any central committee could convoke a special-session congress.

Article 30 — Central Committee Leadership: Central committees at the district and rural town level and up elected a permanent secretariat, which consisted of a secretary and an assistant secretary; officer requirements were at least three years of Party age for district and town and five years for province, city, zone, and special zone; elections in all cases were approved by the next higher headquarters. The secretariat had complete authority to take decisions involving Party matters when the central committee was not in session.

Article 31 — The Central Organization: The Party Congress ordinarily met every four years, its Central Committee every six months. The Congress elected the Central Committee, which in turn elected a Presidium, a Secretariat, and a central control section, as well as its own officers, a chairman, and an assistant. The staff assignments at the central level were filled from the ranks of the membership of the Central Committee.

Articles 32 and 33 — The Party Group: The Party established Party groups (*dang doan*) in mass and other organizations, including the member organizations of the National Liberation Front. Party groups were appointed by the central committee at the appropriate level. Their duties were to work within the organization to influence its policies and decisions, increase Party influence among individual members of the organization, and report to their respective central committees on important events within the organization. The Party group, if large enough, was headed by a secretary and an assistant, appointed by the central committee and responsible to it. These groups could be clandestine if necessary.

Article 34 — The Party and the Youth League: The People's Revolutionary Party Youth League was regarded as the Party's right arm, charged with conducting agit-prop campaigns among villagers and providing feedback on public opinion. The League was under the direct control of the Party and reported both to the Party central committee on its own level and the League central committee on the next higher level (up to the district). Party organizations, in turn, were required to aid the League in its organizational, ideological, educational, political, and theoretical activities and in its efforts to maintain close relations with the masses. The Party had prime responsibility for developing League leadership. Dual membership in the two organizations was prohibited.

Articles 35–39 — Discipline: The bylaws stated that Party discipline was

Table C-1 Comparison of PRP and Lao Dong Party Bylaws*

Item	Lao Dong	PRP
Categories for admission	1. Workers, peasants of many generations, poor peasants, poor urbanites 2. Middle-class peasants, petite bourgeoisie, intellectuals	1. Workers, peasants, and poor in cities 2. Middle-class peasants and petite bourgeoisie 3. Students and intellectuals 4. Montagnards 5. ARVN deserters
Probationary period, members of category 1	6 months	4 months
Sponsors, category 1	2 members, in Party 6 months	2 members, in Party 3 months
Probationary period, category 2	one year	6 months
Sponsors, category 2	2 members, in Party one year	2 members, in Party 6 months
Village central committee meetings	once a month	every 12 months
District central committee meetings	once a month	every 3 to 4 months
Provincial congresses, meetings	each year	every 18 months
Presidium, central committee zone meetings	every 3 months	every 3 to 6 months
Zone congress meetings	18 months	every two years
Party Congress	every three years	every four years

*Early copies of the bylaws used the term Workers' (Lao Dong) Party. After 1960 the bylaws used the term "Party" only, while after January 1962 the terms PRP or Party were used. Yet all were remarkably similar.

necessary to maintain unity, purpose, and aggressive spirit. Discipline was strict, just, carried out in the spirit of corrective education. Individual discipline consisted of reprimand, official warning, removal from Party office, probation (up to one year), and expulsion. Discipline of a Party unit took these forms: reprimand, official warning, and dissolution. Party age did not increase during probation, nor could a member on probation take part in elections. An individual member facing disciplinary charges would appear before a branch meeting or village congress; a decision on probation or expulsion required approval by the next higher echelon. A branch official or cadre could be reprimanded or officially warned by the congress or central committee meeting at the same time as the congress. Expulsion could be ordered only by the congress or by one half the central committee and later referred to the congress, and in all cases it had to be approved by the next higher headquarters. Discipline of a Party organ in the form of a reprimand or official warning was carried out by the central committee at the next higher level. A central committee could be dissolved by the next higher central committee, providing the central committee above the committee taking the action approved the order. A Party organization could be dissolved only by the Party congress at the next higher level with the approval by the national Central Committee or its agencies. Caution was urged in discipline, particularly expulsion. Generally the charged person was to be present to state his case and hear his form of discipline explained. Appeals could be made up to the national Central Committee, and there was to be no delay in sending cases forward.

Article 40 — Finances: Party income consisted of membership dues, collections taken at Party meetings, and donations by sympathizers. One third of the money collected was retained at the basic organization and the remainder sent upward. Fund raising required prior permission from the next higher headquarters, and a uniform procedure for handling funds was practiced throughout the Party.

Article 41 — Amendments: Only the national Central Committee had the power to amend the bylaws.

Biographical Notes

The reader must realize that some of the biographical data contained here is highly suspect; it is included chiefly because of the overwhelmingly important role individuals play in revolutionary movements, leading to the belief that even tinged or questionable data are of more value than none at all and because, as Lasswell has observed, political science without biography is a form of taxidermy. The following are the major figures of the NLF with such biographical data as were available. These are in alphabetical order with the first name encountered, the family name, being alphabetized. The names of individuals whose photographs are reproduced in this appendix are followed by an asterisk (*).

Dang Tran Thi

Dang Tran Thi was born in Central Vietnam, date unknown. He has been associated with the Workers' Liberation Association, first as an official and then in January 1965 as its vice-chairman. Little is known of him.

Ho Hue Ba*

(Joseph Marie)[1] Ho Hue Ba, purportedly the Roman Catholic representative on the NLF Central Committee, was born in Sadec in South Vietnam in 1898. He taught, according to his biography, at a seminary in An Giang province and served during the Viet Minh war as the vice-chairman of the Long Xuyen Catholic Association and was active in peace movements in the 1954–1960 period. It is probable that he is a "regrouped" Southerner, that is, a South Vietnamese who moved to North Vietnam in 1954. The NLF maintains that he was a member of the hierarchy of the Catholic Church, but Church officials in Saigon state that there is no record of such a person ever having held a Church office.

Ho Thu*

Ho Thu, a pharmacist, served as both assistant secretary-general of the NLF Central Committee and secretary-general of the Democratic Party. He was born in Phan Thiet, Central Vietnam, in 1910, the son of a mandarin family. He was graduated first in his class, Prix Bailly in Paris, in 1933 as a pharmacist. He served as a *fonctionnaire* under the French and was active in cultural organizations in Saigon. He wrote articles for Saigon newspapers under the name Truong Son Chi and during the later stages of the Viet Minh war, from 1951 to 1954, served as editor of the Democratic Party's organ *Doc Lap*. He was also active in programs to aid Viet Minh prisoners held by the French, for which he was, according to his biography, arrested several times. He appears to have confined his aid to the Viet Minh to a noncombatant role, and apparently his chief usefulness to the NLF was his connection with the Democratic Party of South Vietnam. He became a member of the NLF Central Committee in January 1963. Radio Hanoi (August 21, 1964) listed him as vice-chairman of the Liberation Red Cross Society, an organization that had no connection with the international Red Cross. He is considered one of the NLF's leading intellectuals. Apparently he has chief responsibility for the administration of NLF medical facilities.

Huynh Tan Phat*

Huynh Tan Phat, the chief NLF theoretician, the Liu Shao-ch'i of the NLF, was born in 1913 near My Tho, studied at Hanoi University in

---

[1] Vietnamese, particularly those educated in Catholic schools, often append Western names.

the 1930's, and was graduated as an architect. His biography reports that he was active in anti-French movements in Northern Vietnam in the 1930's and served in 1944 and 1945 as editor of the newspaper *Thanh Nien* (Youth), a clandestine anti-Japanese publication. During the early years of the Viet Minh war Huynh Tan Phat worked in Southern Vietnam with an organization called the Vanguard Youth, a combination activist revolutionary and social welfare group. He was remembered by some Vietnamese in Saigon as having been active in the Democratic Party, an ostensibly anti-Communist party actually controlled by the Communists after 1946, and in its anti-illiteracy campaigns. During the late 1940's he worked his way up through the ranks of the Democratic Party, eventually to become a regional committeeman and a member of the Party's central leadership, maintaining at all times his anti-Communist posture. He was jailed twice by the French, serving a total of two years in Saigon prisons. In the last stages of the Viet Minh war he worked with Nguyen Van Hieu in the South Vietnam Propaganda Bureau. After the war ended, Huynh Tan Phat opened an architect's office in Saigon with his brother and resumed his Democratic Party activities. In 1958, when the Diem government instituted repressive measures against the Democratic Party, Huynh Tan Phat suddenly vanished, to reappear at the first NLF organizational congress in late 1960. He was listed in NLF documents at that time as secretary-general of the Democratic Party and was appointed chairman of the Saigon-Cholon-Gia Dinh Special Zone central committee, which in actuality was the PRP in South Vietnam; therefore he was one of the leading Communist officials in the South. In mid-1964 he became secretary-general of the NLF Central Committee. Persistent rumors in Saigon in the period 1961 to 1963 maintained that the NLF regarded Huynh Tan Phat highly because of his contacts high within the Diem government and with key members of Vietnamese émigré groups abroad. It was even reported frequently that he was on good terms with Ngo Dinh Nhu and had on occasion met him secretely.[2] None of this was ever substantiated, although there is evidence that Ngo Dinh Nhu had been in contact with NLF members just prior to the coup d'état that overthrew the Diem government.

Huynh Van Tam

Huynh Van Tam was born in Saigon in 1919 of working-class parents. He was active both against the Japanese during their occupation of Indo-

---

[2] See Robert Shaplen, *The Lost Revolution: The Story of Twenty Years of Neglected Opportunities in Vietnam and of America's Failure to Foster Democracy There* (New York: Harper & Row, 1965).

china and during the Viet Minh war. He was a member of the NLF Central Committee and in this capacity visited the Soviet Union in December 1961 and Communist China in January 1962. In mid-1962 he was sent to Algeria as the NLF representative there. Western newsmen who have interviewed him describe him as personable, clever, and a dedicated Marxist. Vietnamese police officials list him as one of the founders of the PRP. Some of these police reports list him as the first secretary-general of the PRP.

Ibih Aleo*

Ibih Aleo,[3] a Rhade montagnard, was born in 1901 near Banmethuot in what is now Darlac province in the central highlands. He was converted to Christianity by a Protestant missionary in 1946. Ibih Aleo served in the French highlands military organization during the early part of the Viet Minh war but later deserted and joined the Viet Minh, serving in the Darlac area along the Laotian and Cambodian borders until late 1946, when he was taken prisoner and sentenced to death, a sentence later commuted to life imprisonment. Released by the French in 1952 from Di Linh prison, Ibih Aleo returned to Banmethuot, where he was arrested by the Diem government in 1958 for antigovernment activity, the nature of which was never made clear. He was freed a year later, and he dropped from sight until his appearance with the NLF in 1961 as chairman of the Autonomy Movement for the Western Highlands. He was an original member of the NLF Central Committee and was prominent as the NLF's montagnard representative. It is generally believed that he had little actual power in the NLF decision-making process but was used by the NLF leadership as a tool to manipulate the groups he represented.

Le Quang Chanh

Le Quang Chanh[4] was a relative latecomer to the NLF ranks. He was first mentioned in NLF mass-media output in early 1964, when he went to Djakarta as a member of an NLF good-will team. Le Quang Chanh was born in An Xuyen province in 1924 and was educated as a teacher. He was active in youth groups in the Mekong delta during the Viet Minh war, and it is believed he moved to Hanoi during the armistice period after the Viet Minh war. The mission to Djakarta was in the company of Mrs. Nguyen Thi Binh, the delegation leader, and Huynh Van Ba. Le Quang Chanh later was named NLF permanent

---

[3] The name can be phoneticized in several ways: Ibih Aleo, I Bih Aleo, or Y Bih Aleo.
[4] Sometimes listed as Le Quan Chanh or Le Cong Chanh.

representative to Indonesia. He has been a member of the NLF Central Committee since 1964 and was probably a Hanoi appointee.

Le Van Huan

Le Van Huan was named assistant secretary-general of the NLF Central Committee in 1964. He was born in 1906 in Nhan Ai village in Phong Dinh province in South Vietnam. He taught school in Saigon throughout the Viet Minh war and actively entered politics in 1954, when he became a founding member of the Saigon-Cholon Peace Committee. Before his election to the NLF Central Committee he served as chairman of the Patriotic Teachers' Association, a member group of the NLF. He became a member of the NLF Central Committee in 1963 and was a member of an NLF delegation on a good-will visit to Cuba in January 1964.

Le Van Tha

Le Van Tha was born in Tay Ninh province in 1914 and educated in French schools as an electrical engineer. Reportedly he lived in France during much of the Viet Minh war and was deported back to Vietnam near the end of the war. His official biography says he was jailed by the Diem government during the late 1950's and was released in 1961, at which time he joined the NLF. He became a member of the NLF Central Committee in 1963 and a vice-chairman of the PRP Central Committee in early 1964. Radio Hanoi (August 31, 1964) listed him as editor of *South Vietnam in Struggle,* an English-language magazine of the NLF Foreign Relations Commission. Beginning in 1964 he has taken an increased public interest in the Radical Socialist Party. Vietnamese police officials believe he manages Radio Liberation, but this has never been substantiated.

Le Van Thinh

Le Van Thinh was born in the vicinity of Hanoi in 1920 and was active throughout the Viet Minh war in the central and northern parts of the country. The first mention of him in NLF output came in March 1963, when he was listed as a member of NLF Workers' Liberation Association on a good-will visit to Cuba. In mid-1964 he returned to Havana as the NLF's permanent representative in Cuba and served there until mid-1965. There is no evidence that he ever lived or worked in South Vietnam. He appears to be a DRV official sent to Cuba in the name of the NLF.

Mrs. Ma Thi Chu*

Mrs. Ma Thi Chu was born in Quan Long in An Xuyen province of South Vietnam in 1924 and was educated as a pharmacist. In the early 1950's she taught pharmaceutics at Saigon University. She was one of the original members of the NLF Central Committee and has made frequent trips abroad as a representative of the NLF. In June 1963 she was named a member of the NLF permanent delegation in Prague. She is the wife of Nguyen Van Hieu, one of the most prominent figures in the NLF.

Nguyen Huu The

Nguyen Huu The was born in Vinh Long province in 1908 and taught there for many years as an elementary schoolteacher. He was listed in July 1961 as the chairman of the central committee of the Farmers' Liberation Association, an important post; a January 1965 report by the NLF indicated he still held that post. He became a member of the NLF Central Committee in December 1961. Little else is known of him.

Nguyen Huu Tho*

Nguyen Huu Tho is probably the best-known NLF leader, serving as the chairman of the NLF Central Committee from its inception to this writing. Nguyen Huu Tho was born on August 10, 1910 in Vinh Long province in Southern Vietnam (one biographic sketch said he was born in Cholon), the son of a rubber plantation manager who was killed during the Viet Minh war, apparently by non-Communist guerrillas. Nguyen Huu Tho went to France in the 1930's, studied law in Paris, received his *licence,* returned to Saigon, and began practicing law. There is no evidence of political activity on his part during the 1930's, during the Japanese occupation, or during the early years of the war against the French. His first open act of hostility toward the French came in 1949, when he led an anti-French demonstration by a group of Saigon intellectuals. He came into prominence in South Vietnam in 1950 by leading a protest demonstration against the good-will visit to Saigon of three United States warships. For this he was arrested by the French and sent to Lai Chau prison in North Vietnam, apparently without trial, where he remained for two years. Midway during his imprisonment he went on a prolonged hunger strike, which did not secure his freedom but did bring him considerable notoriety, and he emerged from prison rather well known throughout the Southern Vietnam area. He later said that he led the 1950 demonstration, as well as the one in 1949,

Ho Hue Ba (Reverend Joseph Marie) member, NLF Central Committee

Ho Thu assistant secretary-general, NLF Central Committee

Huynh Tan Phat secretary-general, NLF Central Committee, 1964 to date

Ibih Aleo vice-chairman, NLF Central Committee

Mrs. Ma Thi Chu member, NLF Central Committee; member, Women's Liberation Association central committee

Nguyen Huu Tho chairman, NLF Central Committee, 1960 to date

Nguyen Thi Dinh deputy commander, NLF army

Mrs. Nguyen Thi Tu chairman, Women's Liberation Association central committee

Nguyen Van Ngoi Cao Dai member,
NLF Central Committee

Nguyen Van Tien NLF representative,
AAPSO in Cairo

Dr. Phung Van Cung vice-chairman,
NLF Central Committee

Thich Thien Hao member, NLF Central Committee

Thich Thom Me The Nhem vice-chairman, NLF Central Committee

Tran Buu Kiem secretary-general, NLF Central Committee, 1963–1964

Tran Nam Trung secretary-general, PRP

Vo Chi Cong vice-chairman, NLF Central Committee; chairman, PRP

Ho Chi Minh (center in white suit) and members of NLF army. Caption reads: "President Ho Chi Minh takes walk in Presidential Garden with delegation of heroes and model fighters of South Vietnam Liberation Army." (*Vietnam Courier,* January 1, 1966.)

Ho Chi Minh embracing Nguyen Van Hieu, 1960–1963 secretary-general of NLF Central Committee, on Hieu's arrival in Hanoi, October 1962.

Mao Tse-tung (left) greeting NLF visitor to Peking, Nguyen Minh Phuong, at mass rally. (Nguyen Minh Phuong remained in Peking as member of NLF delegation.)

NOTE: Unless otherwise noted all photographs are from *South Vietnam on the Road to Victory,* Liberation Publishing House, South Vietnam, October 1965 (sold by Peace Book Company, Hong Kong, enterprise owned and operated by Chinese Communist government).

Women making *panji* for use in deadfalls and foot traps around villages. Longer sharpened stakes at left probably for use in mantraps. (*Vietnam Today* [Hanoi], February 2, 1966.)

Placing *panji* in mantrap (also known as spike trap or Malaya tiger trap).

Member of the NLF army firing a Chinese Communist-made 60 mm. mortar

Members of paramilitary unit in Mekong delta. Weapons are U.S.-made carbines. (*Vietnam* [Hanoi], No. 102 [March 1966].)

Adult education class being conducted by NLF cadre in liberated area. Arithmetic lesson on blackboard. (NLF places great emphasis on adult education; mixes education with indoctrination.)

NLF army unit passing through a village behind an NLF flag. (Much of the clothing worn is North Vietnamese.)

This photograph appeared in various DRV publications during 1966. In some the caption said it showed a Liberation Army unit passing through a village in the South; others described it as a picture of villagers seeing young men off to enlist in NLF army.

Typical struggle movement in South Vietnam organized by the NLF. Caption declares that women are protesting bombing and artillery shelling of their villages by carrying the body of a dead infant to the office of a district chief. Location not given; dated early 1966. (*Vietnam* [Hanoi], No. 102 [March 1966].)

because he wanted to force the French to negotiate an end to the war, not because he sided with the Viet Minh. After the establishment of the Republic of Vietnam Nguyen Huu Tho stayed in Saigon, engaging in teahouse politics and working in a group called the Saigon-Cholon Peace Committee, most of whose members later joined the NLF under the name of the World Peace Protection League.

In 1958, for reasons that are not clear, he was arrested by GVN officials and jailed in Tuy Hoa and Cung Son prisons in Phu Yen province. According to the NLF biographic account he was "liberated by a daring guerrilla raid on the jail in 1961." The author could find no one in Phu Yen who remembered a guerrilla raid on any jail in the province in 1961 or later. Nguyen Huu Tho was provisional chairman of the NLF and was elected Central Committee chairman at the organizing congress in December 1960. He went to Hanoi via Cambodia in April 1962, his only trip outside Vietnam so far as can be determined. In its printed output the NLF made no particular effort to identify Nguyen Huu Tho as a Marxist, and Vietnamese who knew him did not regard him as doctrinaire. The general image he projected was that of a statesman, a man of vision, a man of peace, a man who would make a good president, precisely the image the NLF sought to project. Japanese journalists who have interviewed him describe him as something of a dandy in dress and somewhat pompous in manner. Probably he was without much actual power in the NLF and was more of a figurehead projecting a father image than a policymaker. The strongest evidence of this is the fact that Nguyen Huu Tho's public figure throughout was static, motionless, one dimensional. He did not "build" in the theatrical sense but remained what he was at the outset. No effort was made to develop him into a dynamic, charismatic leader.

Nguyen Ngoc Thuong

Nguyen Ngoc Thuong, a leading Radical Socialist Party representative on the NLF Central Committee, was born in Cholon in 1923 of a mandarin family and educated in Hanoi. He taught school for several years in the Saigon area. He has no record of activity during the Viet Minh war but was an original member of the NLF Central Committee. In July 1961 Radio Liberation listed him as secretary-general of the Youth Liberation Association and editor of a magazine aimed at Vietnamese high-school and university students, called *Justice*. Public announcements in the period after 1964 linked him chiefly with the Radical Socialist Party as assistant secretary-general and with the Afro-Asian People's Solidarity Organization as chairman of the NLF's AAPS Committee,

Mrs. Nguyen Thi Binh

Mrs. Nguyen Thi Binh was listed as having been born in Saigon in 1927, the daughter of Vietnamese nationalist Phan Chu Trinh, who led anti-French demonstrations in the years before World War I. Her biography says she was active against the French beginning in 1950 and was jailed by them for several years in the early 1950's for her activities among clandestine women's groups. It is believed that she moved to Hanoi in 1954. In 1963 she was listed as chairman of the Women's Liberation Association, succeeded in 1966 by Mrs. Nguyen Thi Tu, and has been a member of the NLF Central Committee since 1963. Since 1962 she has traveled abroad extensively in the name of the NLF, chiefly attending Communist-sponsored international conferences: Peking, Moscow, and Cairo in 1963; Indonesia and North Korea in 1964; North Africa in 1965; and Moscow in April 1966.

Nguyen Thi Dinh*

Nguyen Thi Dinh first received public mention in mid-1965, when *Pravda* listed her as the deputy military commander of the NLF army. A Soviet correspondent, Nikolai Shchedrev, reported he had met her while he was on a secret visit to the NLF.[5] He said she told him she was born in the Mekong delta in 1920 and had been engaged in revolutionary activities since she was 17. Her photograph, with caption identifying her as deputy military commander of the NLF army, has appeared several times in Hanoi publications. Very little is known of her, and many Vietnamese doubt that the second in command of the Liberation Army is a woman.

Mrs. Nguyen Thi Tu*

Mrs. Nguyen Thi Tu was born in Can Tho in 1923 but was raised in Cambodia, where her father was a businessman. She returned to Vietnam in about 1950 and became active in Saigon women's organizations, particularly labor unions of women workers. Apparently she took no direct part in the Viet Minh war. Some reports list her as a schoolteacher. She was jailed by the GVN in 1955. She was named chairman of the Women's Liberation Association in February 1966, succeeding Mrs. Nguyen Thi Binh. Some Vietnamese police reports list her as a devout Marxist. Probably she is the most powerful woman in the NLF.

[5] *Pravda*, July 12, 1965.

Nguyen Van Hieu*

Nguyen Van Hieu was the best-known NLF figure outside Vietnam. One of the most colorful of the NLF leaders, he stood in sharp distinction to the flat, one-dimensional figure of Nguyen Huu Tho. As secretary-general Hieu traveled a great deal, and NLF publications were filled with details of his actions and speeches. His 1962 NLF good-will visit resulted in a book, *Friends on Five Continents,* published in Hanoi in 1963. Later, as the NLF representative in East Berlin, he talked with American scholars visiting in East Berlin, appeared on East German television, and wrote an article for an American periodical. Born on Camau peninsula in 1922, Nguyen Van Hieu became a revolutionist at the age of 23, participating in the original outbreak of violence against the French in 1945 in the far south, in what his biographers call the "General Camau Uprising." During the Viet Minh war he headed an organization called the South Vietnam Propaganda Bureau, which encouraged the formation of local propaganda groups throughout the Mekong delta. At the end of hostilities he took a series of jobs on Saigon newspapers, writing under the pen name of "Khai Minh"; he is remembered by former colleagues as an energetic, eloquent, flamboyant, and well-dressed man. He left Saigon in 1958. While NLF secretary-general, Nguyen Van Hieu also held the post of secretary-general of the Radical Socialist Party and was active in the World Peace Protection League. His wife, Ma Thi Chu, was also active in NLF affairs.

Nguyen Van Ngoi*

Nguyen Van Ngoi, a member of the Tien Thien Cao Dai sect, was born in My Tho province in South Vietnam in 1900 and at an early age became a schoolteacher in Vinh Long province. He joined the Cao Dai (Tien Thien sect) in 1927, served with the Cao Dai forces during the Viet Minh war in Vinh Long province, and remained active in Cao Dai affairs in the province during the late 1950's. He served as a GVN Ministry of Education official. He joined the NLF in 1960 and was named to the NLF Central Committee in 1961. As of mid-1966, NLF mass media had made no mention of him for more than two years.

Nguyen Van Tien*

Nguyen Van Tien appeared to be the NLF's most important official abroad, with the possible exception of Nguyen Van Hieu. He was born in North Vietnam in 1919 and taught school in the Hanoi area for several years. He was named a member of the NLF Central Committee in 1962 and has been abroad most of the time since then: the Afro-Asian Lawyers' Association meeting in Conakry, Guinea, in November 1963; the Communist world conference on Vietnam in Hanoi, December 1964; in Moscow in early January 1965 to arrange for the opening there of a permanent NLF delegation; in Cuba in late January 1965; the CPSU Twenty-Third Congress in Moscow in April 1966. His permanent base has been in Cairo, where he is the NLF delegate to the Afro-Asian People's Solidarity Organization. He is believed to be a Northerner who has never served in the South. Little is known of him.

Phan Xuan Thai

Phan Xuan Thai was born in Vinh Long province in 1917. He was listed as chairman of the NLF's Workers' Liberation Association in 1961, and a 1966 NLF statement indicated he still held that post. Little is known of him. He became a member of the NLF Central Committee in December 1961.

Phung Van Cung*

Phung Van Cung,[6] one of the founders of the NLF, was born in 1909 in Vinh Long province in South Vietnam and was educated at Hanoi University, where he received an M.D. degree. He practiced medicine in Kien Giang province and in Saigon for many years. He apparently sat out the Viet Minh war and joined the Diem government in 1955 in the Ministry of Health. Vietnamese who knew him in the pre-1960 period describe him as nonpolitical but of a rigid personality. He practiced medicine in the Hué area. Then, in 1960, quite suddenly, for reasons that are not clear, he took his family and joined the guerrillas in the jungle of Central Vietnam. One explanation for his action is that he had been a secret French collaborator and that the NLF had blackmailed him into joining them. There is no evidence of political activity on his part prior to 1960. On the other hand, he was reported authoritatively to be a strong believer in extensive terror as a revolutionary device, one who insisted at top-level council meetings that terroristic measures be increased. *Quy chanh* described him as a fanatic, deeply feared by his associates. Obviously there is an inconsistency between the reluctant and the fanatic revolutionary. Early Vietnamese police reports listed him as the chief supervisor of the NLF's *binh van*, or proselyting, program; other reports listed him as the chief of the NLF

---

[6] Also listed as Tran Van Cung.

intelligence network. Radio Liberation on June 11, 1964 listed him as chairman of the NLF Civilian and Military Public Health Council and as chairman of the NLF Central Committee Health Subcommittee. It is probable that he is the leading NLF figure concerned with health and medical care in the NLF ranks. Phung Van Cung was a member of the provisional committee that predated the NLF Central Committee and was one of the original Central Committee vice-chairmen.

Thien Hao*

Thich Thien Hao, in addition to membership on the NLF Central Committee, was listed as the chairman of the Luc Hoa Buddhist Association, vice-chairman of the Afro-Asian People's Solidarity Committee, and member of the central committee of the Central Nambo Zone. He was born in 1909 in Gia Dinh, near Saigon. He was active during the Viet Minh war, after which he returned to Saigon, where he was associated with the Giac Ngan pagoda. In 1963 he attended a Buddhist conference in Peking, where he met Mao Tse-tung; later that year he went to a Buddhist conference in Tokyo as a member of what was called the South Vietnam Patriotic Buddhist Believers' Association. Apparently he was the "kept" Buddhist in the NLF hierarchy.

Thom Me The Nhem*

Vice-Chairman Thom Me The Nhem, an ethnic Cambodian and a Buddhist monk, acted as leader of the Cambodian minority in Vietnam as well as the chief NLF liaison figure with the Vietnamese Buddhist organizations. He became vice-chairman of the Presidium in 1964, when he replaced Thich Thuong Ba Phuong Long, who in turn had replaced Thich Son Vong who died on March 26, 1963. Thom Me The Nhem was born in 1925 in An Xuyen province in South Vietnam of Cambodian parents. He became a Buddhist monk at an early age, according to his biography, and served during the Viet Minh war in Buddhist organizations supporting the war effort in the Mekong delta. After the war he remained in South Vietnam in Bac Lieu province, although little is known of his activities. He joined the NLF in 1964, or possibly in 1963, "because of religious persecution," according to his biography. His appointment as a vice-chairman of the NLF Central Committee probably was part of the NLF leadership's effort to involve itself more deeply in Buddhist activities in South Vietnam. On August 16, 1966 Radio Liberation reported that Thom Me The Nhem had died "from the rifle bullets of the U.S. aggressors and their lackeys on July 19, 1966 while fulfillnig a mission in an area in Western Nambo." Saigon newspapers reported he was killed during an air strike.

Tran Buu Kiem*

Tran Buu Kiem, the second person to hold the NLF secretary-general-ship, was described as a precise and efficient man with the ability to hone an organization, particularly a youth group, into a sharp-edged weapon. He was born near Can Tho in the Mekong delta in 1921. Little is known about his early life or education, although he was reported to be well educated and was regarded in NLF ranks as an intellectual. During the Viet Minh war and in the early days of the NLF he organized the most difficult activity of the Front, the clandestine student groups in government-controlled areas. He also held several important Viet Minh positions in South Vietnam. When the NLF Central Committee's Foreign Relations Commission was organized in 1963, Tran Buu Kiem, then a Central Committee member, was named chairman. The announcement of his appointment as secretary-general in August 1963 (Radio Hanoi, August 7, 1963) said that he would continue to hold the commission post, and when he was relieved of the secretary-generalship in 1964 he continued to serve on the commission. Since the Foreign Relations Commission was a post of ever-increasing importance, the NLF leadership may have felt that Tran Buu Kiem could best serve there, preparing himself to become foreign minister in the government the NLF hoped to establish. At any rate, his removal from office remained something of a mystery. Tran Buu Kiem, however, apparently has been a doctrinaire Communist since his student days. He was one of the founders of the NLF and was listed in early NLF records as a member of the NLF Central Committee.

Tran Bach Dang

Tran Bach Dang was born in 1925, reportedly in the Mekong delta. He was listed in early NLF documents, circa 1960, as chairman of various youth organizations and in 1961 became chairman of the Youth Liberation Association and a member of the NLF Central Committee. He was also associated with various NLF-sponsored veterans' organizations. Some Saigon Vietnamese believe he is a key figure in the PRP's indoctrination and agit-prop programs, but this has never been substantiated.

Tran Huu Trang

Tran Huu Trang was chairman of the NFL Cultural Liberation Association and an early member of the NLF Central Committee. He was born in 1906 near My Tho, the son of a scholar, and he himself became a scholar. In 1922 he began writing drama and produced a large number of plays with revolutionary themes. One of his plays was staged in Hanoi in 1964. He is regarded as the NLF's chief nonpolitical intellectual.

Tran Nam Trung*

Tran Nam Trung,[7] PRP secretary-general, was probably the single most important figure in the entire *apparat* in South Vietnam. He was born in 1913 in Quang Ngai province. His official biography says simply that he served as a militant revolutionary throughout the 1930's and 1940's, was jailed several times by the French, and served in the Viet Minh. He is a latecomer to NLF and PRP activities. Tran Nam Trung was not listed on any rosters before 1964 (that is, on the lists of officials published following the Second Congress in January 1964). At that time he was listed as a vice-chairman of the NLF and as "representative of the Liberation Army and People's Armed Forces." GVN police officials maintained that Tran Nam Trung spent the 1954–1963 period in the DRV as an officer in the North Vietnamese army, which is probable. It is possible, as some Vietnamese claimed, that he is the top military commander in the Viet Cong forces in the South, but it is more likely that he was the DRV's political commissar for all NLF military forces. At any rate the evidence is strong that he was a high-ranking military officer from North Vietnam with a record of commissar-type activity and was relatively new to South Vietnam.

Tran Van Thanh

Tran Van Thanh, the NLF representative in Peking, was also active in the Workers' Liberation Association. Born in 1921 in Vinh Long province, he was jailed during World War II by the French and released in 1945. He was reportedly active in the trade-union movement in Saigon in the period from 1954 to 1960, but this could not be verified. He appeared at an international conference of Communist trade unions in Hanoi in October 1963 and then went on to Peking in December. He went to Cuba in July 1964 and then returned to Peking to take up duties with the NLF permanent mission in Communist China. Most likely he is a "regrouped" Southerner who moved to the DRV in 1954 and has not been in the South since that time.

[7] U.S. and Vietnamese news media in 1965 reported that Tran Nam Trung was in fact Tran Van Tra, a member of the Lao Dong Party Central Committee in Hanoi and deputy chief of staff of the PAVN, who had been ordered South in 1963 to take command of the insurgency. Although entirely possible, no satisfactory evidence is available to substantiate this assertion.

Ung Ngoc Ky

Ung Ngoc Ky, one of the NLF's chief intellectuals, was born in 1920 in Can Tho, the son of a government civil servant. He was educated at the University of Hanoi and worked for several years on newspapers and magazines in Saigon. There is no record of his activity during the Viet Minh war other than occasional articles with a nationalistic tone written for *Doc Lap,* the journal of the Vietnam Democratic Party. He was an early member of the NLF and an original member of the NLF Central Committee. In January 1964 he was named assistant secretary-general of the NLF Central Committee.

Vo Chi Cong*

Vo Chi Cong, chairman of the PRP Central Committee, was the Anastas Mikoyan of the NLF, the indestructible old-guard revolutionary who began clandestine revolutionary activity in Southern Vietnam in 1930, opposed the French throughout the 1930's, violently opposed the Japanese during their occupation of Indochina, and began anew his opposition to the French upon their return after World War II. Unlike most Southerners, Vo Chi Cong stood for militancy in revolution. Born in Quang Nam province in 1912, he was an associate of such early Vietnamese revolutionaries as Phan Boi Chau and Phan Chu Trinh. From 1935 to 1940 he was involved in various organizations dedicated to the expulsion of the French and the overthrow of the royal court of Annam. Late in the 1930's he became active in an organization known as the Anti-Fascist Democratic Front. In 1942 he was arrested by the French and sentenced to house arrest in Central Vietnam,[8] where, his NLF biography stated, he continued to act as adviser to the revolutionary groups in the South. After joining the NLF in 1960 he organized the People's Revolutionary Party. He was one of the major founders of the NLF, as vice-chairman, and probably the key figure in the formation of the PRP. He served as the security chief in the newly formed NLF and as a sort of inspector-general of the NLF's organizational work and political struggle activities. He was in effect Hanoi's ranking political commissar in the NLF Central Committee. Vietnamese who have known Vo Chi Cong describe him as a thoroughly indoctrinated Marxist, a person who has throughout his life stood for militancy and terror in revolution.

[8] Other reports say he was sentenced to life imprisonment on Poulo Condore, Vietnam's prison island off the southern coast.

Vo Dong Giang

Vo Dong Giang became a member of the NLF Central Committee in mid-1963 and a year later was named as the NLF delegate to Havana. He was born in Tam Ky, Quang Nam province, in Central Vietnam in 1921. He worked in the highlands as a civil servant and is believed to have gone to North Vietnam in 1954. He has appeared abroad as an NLF representative since 1963. On April 8, 1965 Radio Havana reported that he had attended a farewell party in his honor in Havana, but it was not clear whether his departure was temporary or permanent.

Vo Van Mon

Vo Van Mon,[9] the Binh Xuyen sect representative on the NLF Central Committee, was born in Cholon in 1918. He joined the Binh Xuyen early, rose to the rank of colonel in the Binh Xuyen armed forces, and became commander-in-chief after the 1954 accords. After his sect was smashed by the GVN army in 1956 he went into hiding. He joined the NLF in 1960, apparently bringing with him elements of his former military force. He was made a member of the NLF Central Committee in 1962.

Military Figures

While it is possible that Tran Nam Trung was the top military commander of the NLF forces it is more likely that the leading military figures of the NLF were deeply covert, operating behind code names and therefore unknown to anyone in the South except a few leaders.

Among the names of military leaders that have appeared most regularly in published reports in the past several years are the following:

Cau Dang Chiem. Purportedly a general officer in charge of DRV intelligence operations in South Vietnam directed against the Americans.

General Dong Van Cong. Vietnamese newspapers in November 1965 reported him as the commander of NLF forces who had been recalled to Hanoi, the result of a political struggle in the DRV Politburo in which his faction had been defeated.

Lt. General Lam Van Dong. Also encountered as Bay Quan, Bay Quang, Cao Thanh Tra, and Cao Van Tra (some Vietnamese have sug-

[9] Vietnamese police records list this name as an alias for Bay Mon, operator of the famous Big World gambling center in Cholon in the pre-1954 days.

gested that he is actually Tran Nam Trung). Purportedly he is the top military official in South Vietnam, on assignment from Hanoi, and commanding all Liberation Army forces in the South.

General Nguyen Chi Thanh. Also encountered in the South as Major General Hai Hau and Vo Van Hau. Beginning in late 1965 he was widely reputed to be the ranking PAVN general officer commanding all NLF military forces in the South. He is a former teacher who at one time headed the political commissar office of the PAVN. He accompanied Ho Chi Minh to Moscow in 1960 and was generally considered by foreign diplomats in Hanoi as being strongly pro-Chinese. There is no doubt that such a person exists, but there is no evidence that he was in South Vietnam commanding the NLF military forces.

Major General Nguyen Don. Perhaps the most frequently encountered name of the "top military commander of the NLF armed forces." As in the case of General Nguyen Chi Thanh there is no doubt that a Major General Nguyen Don did exist. He was born in Quang Ngai province of Central Vietnam in 1914 and joined the Communist movement at an early age. He served with distinction throughout the Viet Minh war and and by 1954 had risen to the rank of major general commanding an entire zone. General Nguyen Don would be a logical person to command the NLF armed forces, but evidence that this was the case could not be developed.

Brigadier General To Ky. A name that has appeared from time to time since 1960 as the commanding officer of the NLF military forces. Such a person did exist and served as a leading Viet Minh military commander in the Saigon area from 1945 to 1951, when he dropped out of sight. He appeared in 1958 in North Vietnam as commanding officer of the PAVN 338th division. Given his intimate knowledge of the terrain in South Vietnam and his military experience in the area he would be a logical appointment to the post of top military commander. Confirmation, however, has never been available.

Lt. General Tran Van Du. Purportedly the chief of staff of the NLF army.

Still other names encountered are Brigadier General Van Muoi, Muoi Cua, Tran Luong, Pham Van Dang, Nguyen Van Suc, Le Toan Thu, and Pham Tai Buong.

Sparkling Fires in the South[1]

Che Lan Vien

Through a paradox of history and the evil plots of the U.S.-Diem clique the peaceful Hien Luong River, the river of my childhood, which flows along the 17th parallel, has for eight years played the role of a sword, splitting the country asunder. My parents, who live south of this river that I know so well, who live in a house only a stone's throw from the river, have for years given me no sign that they are alive and well. But let us not blame the river.

The "clever" Americans are using the river and the barbed wire running along it to accomplish more than physical separations. They want to split the human heart as well, to make wives fearful of showing love for their husbands, to drive parents to repudiate their children, and to force friends to avoid each other, to make fellow countrymen bitter antagonists. . . .

Awaiting those [in the South] are strategic hamlets, prisons, napalm bombs, chemical defoliants, poisoned food, American planes and guillo-

[1] *Sparkling Fires in the South,* by Che Lan Vien, if read with empathy, will provide the reader with an insight into the worldview of the NLF true believer. This was the cause, and its nature, as he saw it. The sketch also represents a typical example of the sort of material fashioned by the NLF for the manipulation of Vietnamese emotions, especially hatred.

tines, American paratroops, arson, rape, and police dogs. The nationalists [that is, the GVN] are showered with such American treasures as liquor, clothes, automobiles, and even an American "God" when needed. . . . An American gun is pushed into his hands and he is separated from his fellow men whom he hunts for his American master. This separation is incomparably more terrifying than any barbed wire along a peaceful river.

Even more terrifying is American lust. This is apparent everywhere. You have probably heard about the U.S.-Diem troops indulging in cannibalism, disemboweling a man, and eating his liver raw. Talking to newsmen when he paid a visit to a joint security post north of the demilitarized zone, a young Diemist officers calmly said that cannibalism was hardly a novelty to him and that, although he had never tasted human flesh, all cadets at the officers' school had eaten human liver more than once. This must be the officers' school with American-type training, where young men eat human liver in a sophisticated manner during an evening dancing party or a fishing trip. Training is dispensed in a cruder manner at lower levels. Back from his tour of sentry duty a new recruit asked for his meal. He was shown a huge pot of soup, and he fainted when he saw human skulls in it. Not only did no one help to revive him but fists rained upon him and he was threatened with being shot on the grounds that Viet Cong blood must be running in his veins, making him faint at the first whiff of Viet Cong flesh. Then these commanding officers — who bear likeness to the image of Christ and pray "Thou shalt not kill, thou shalt love they neighbor as thyself" — forced the recruit down on his back and made him swallow the flesh of his own kind. Now whether this young soldier soon forced human soup into others, committed suicide, or turned his rifle against the U.S.-Diemists, I cannot tell. Suffice it to say this is how to turn men into fiends, lesson one.

A man named Ty was captured at Ben Tre by the U.S.-Diemists, eviscerated, his liver taken out, and then turned loose. Blood streaming all over, he ran aimlessly, shrieking with pain, stumbled a few meters, and dropped dead amid the enemy's merry laughter. They raped a pregnant woman and then beat her stomach until she aborted to their great jubilation. A seven-year-old boy suspected of serving as a Viet Cong sentry was caught and tied to a tree and burned alive. His mother, forced to watch, screamed helplessly and then fainted, much to the amusement of the U.S.-Diemists. This — the fact that they are trying to make man unfit for society — is what hurts me most about my country's partition. . . .

Why do the Americans scheme so? They want the sun to rise and set according to their whims. Do they not plan to turn heroes into slaves?

To turn the people into prisoners and Vietnam into an American land? . . .

A certain hamlet was the target for bombing by 50 U.S.-piloted planes for six hours; one hundred tons of bombs were dropped on one thousand persons. Each received one hundred kilograms of explosives, but they did not have even one kilogram of rice. The Americans may lack humanity and intelligence, but they do not lack bombs. . . .

This is why men smile on their way to the firing squad, why a patriot sacrificed himself trying to prevent the enemy from tearing up a national flag and died eviscerated and with his skull crushed, why a young man whose stomach was slashed open by the enemy took out his bowels and with his own hands held them up to the enemy.

NLF Externalization Efforts

NLF Ranking of Foreign Countries

In an effort to measure the relative ranking that the NLF accorded the various countries of the world, an analysis of NLF internal output (Radio Liberation, leaflets, and clandestine newspapers) was made for the years 1963 and 1964. A random sampling, which amounted to about 8 to 10 per cent per year, was taken from the total NLF output available. It was screened for all news stories, NLF statements, communiqués, exchanges of greetings, commentaries, and other items that involved NLF relations with governments, private organizations, and individuals abroad. The DRV, China, and the Soviet Union were excluded, since references to them permeated the NLF output. The results, which should be considered as impressionistic rather than definitive, are indicative of the thrust of the NLF externalization effort. The spread was great: In all, 38 countries were contacted in some way during the two years. And the intensity was high: About 13 per cent of the total NLF communication effort was devoted to communications abroad to those other than the major actors, namely the DRV, Communist China, the Soviet Union, and the United States. Indonesia, Cuba, and Japan, all non-Communist in the minds of most Vietnamese, dominated the scene. Only North Korea and East Germany, and to a degree Albania, received any special attention. Britain, totaled with Lord Russell, exceeded all other countries in 1963 but dropped off sharply in 1964. See Table F–1.

Table F–1 NLF Externalization Wordage Study, 1963–1964

	1963	1964
Indonesia	3,600	10,800
Cuba	3,600	7,500
Japan	1,500	3,000
North Korea	2,120	2,820
East Germany	1,140	1,860
Lord Russell	3,020	1,800
Great Britain	2,100	1,500
Africa*	960	1,490
Algeria	1,360	1,200
Burma	1,140	1,200
Latin America†	1,120	1,080
Albania	540	1,020
New Zealand	0	900
Ceylon	0	900
Bulgaria	0	780
United Arab Republic	660	660
Czechoslovakia	540	600
Mongolia	0	540
France	1,020	300
Poland	240	300
Morocco	190	180
Pakistan	180	180
Romania	0	180
Yemen	0	60
Nepal	0	60
Philippines	120	0
Hungary	940	0
Laos	300	0
India	100	0
Total	26,490	40,910

* Below the Sahara.
† Excluding Cuba.

Non-Communist Countries

Indonesia

The first nonbloc country to associate itself publicly and officially with the NLF was Indonesia, and by early 1965 a virtual alliance existed between the two. In July 1962 several Indonesian women's organizations sent anti-U.S., pro-unification messages to the NLF; in January 1963 Nguyen Huu Tho cabled congratulations to President Sukarno "on the occasion of your hoisting the rightful Indonesian national flag over West Irian"; in late November 1963 Indonesian and Vietnamese trade-union leaders issued a statement condemning U.S. imperialism and aggression in South Vietnam; and in August 1964, on the nineteenth anniversary of Indonesian independence, Nguyen Huu Tho addressed a message to President Sukarno, which read: "The NLFSV reaffirms its resolute support of the just, patriotic, and certain victorious struggle of the peoples of Indonesia and North Kalimantan to smash the Malaysian Federation."

A rally sponsored by the Indonesian Afro-Asian People's Solidarity Committee was held on December 20, 1962 in Djakarta to mark the second anniversary of the NLF and "to shout such slogans as 'Imperialism is a paper tiger.'" On July 20, 1963 some 1,500 persons attended an anti-U.S. rally sponsored by the Vietnamese-Indonesian Friendship Association. Radio Liberation reported on August 30, 1963 that a delegation of Indonesian Buddhists had prepared an "anti-Diem statement that . . . was sent to the Foreign Ministry [in Djakarta] asking that it be handed to the consulate-general of the Diem clique in Djarkarta . . . expressing our condemnation of the cruel persecution of Buddhists in Vietnam. . . ." On July 20, 1964 a rally was held in Djakarta, attended by some 2,000 persons, to mark the tenth anniversary of the signing of the Geneva accords. Sukarno sent an anti-imperialism message that was read; the Indonesian Communist Party (PKI) leader D. N. Aidit was there and spoke.

The Hieu mission (described in Chapter 17) was the first diplomatic intercourse between the NLF and Indonesia; it was followed in December 1963 by the arrival of a second delegation (Mrs. Nguyen Thi Binh, NLF Central Committee member; Huynh Van Ba of the Youth Liberation Association (YLA); and Le Cong Chanh of the Workers' Liberation Association), which attended special events in Djakarta as part of the Support the Patriotic Struggle of the South Vietnamese People Week that began on December 23. The sponsors were Indonesian trade unions, youth groups, and the Afro-Asian People's Solidarity Committee. President Sukarno met the delegation at a reception on December 23 and was quoted in the world press as saying "I hope the struggle of the South Vietnamese people will be victorious. I hope the day will come when I will have the opportunity to visit liberated Saigon." This brought a second strong reaction from the GVN. On December 29 the Foreign Ministry in Saigon called in the Indonesian consul-general and handed him a note, which declared:

President Sukarno's statement was an intolerable interference in Vietnam's internal affairs and . . . amounts to open encouragement of an aggression prepared and directed against the Republic of Vietnam by the Hanoi authorities, whose so-called National Liberation Front is but a mere stooge.

A farewell party for the NLF delegation on January 12, 1964 was attended by representatives of the Indonesian National Front, Indonesian Communist Party Politburo members, members of the Indonesian Moslem Scholarship Association, the Indonesian Party, the Murba Party, and the Perti Party. Before leaving for home the delegation toured Java, Bali, and West Irian. The Indonesian Communists led the support campaign for the NLF in Indonesia. The president of the All-Indonesia Central Trade Union, interviewed on August 18, 1962 by *Lao Dong,* the DRV trade-union publication, was quoted as saying that "the Indonesian working class energetically condemns armed U.S. intervention in South Vietnam and Ngo Dinh Diem's persecution of the people there." In July 1963 *Harian Rakjat,* the PKI organ, conducted an editorial campaign against the "deadly and cruel campaign of terror and chemical warfare by the Americans in South Vietnam." The PKI conference in July 1964 adopted a resolution entitled "Support the Struggle of the South Vietnamese People to Drive Out U.S. Imperialism."

The original Indonesian organization dealing with the NLF was the Vietnamese-Indonesian Friendship Association, which was founded on July 6, 1959 as an Indonesian-DRV group and later broadened to include the NLF. In July 1964 the Committee for Solidarity with and Support for the Struggle of the South Vietnamese People was formed, with membership drawn from the ranks of the Indonesian People's Committee, the Afro-Asian People's Solidarity Committee, the Vietnamese-Indonesian Friendship Association, the Afro-Asian Journalists' Association, and the Afro-Asian Film Festival Committee. The new group sponsored a Support Vietnam Week, marked by film showings and special exhibits in Djakarta and Bandung. Huynh Van Tuan, described as the chief of the NLF's Liberation Film Studio, was in Djakarta for the week. Indonesia's "confrontation" with Malaysia found the NLF stoutly behind it. Nguyen Huu Tho dispatched a message to President Sukarno in November 1963 expressing support for "the measures taken by Indonesia in its confrontation against Malaysia. . . . The South Vietnamese people will spare no effort to support the struggle of the Indonesian people until final victory. . . ." The NLF Central Committee on January 12, 1965 issued a statement hailing the Indonesian decision to leave the United Nations. On April 20, 1965, press reports from Djakarta quoted Antara as saying that visiting DRV Premier Pham Van Dong discussed with R. Kartawinat, the Indonesian parliament chairman, the possibility of dispatching Indonesian "volunteers" to Vietnam. The NLF sought in all ways to forge a mystic bond between itself and the government of Indonesia and between the South Vietnamese and Indonesian people. "The day will come," declared Radio Liberation in late 1964, "when the South Vietnamese people will welcome President Sukarno, our patient and heroic comrade in arms, to a free Saigon, as the president has stated is his wish."

Japan

The NLF took virtually no public notice of Japan until mid-1963, when conditions within the Japanese Communist Party made it feasible to begin serious intercourse. The first action came in Havana on August 12, 1963, when the Japanese Communist Party and the NLF issued a joint declaration of mutual support, solidarity, and condemnation of the United States:

The Japanese Communist Party wholeheartedly supports the political and armed struggles of the South Vietnamese people under the NLF. . . . The delegation of the NLFSV expresses its conviction that the heroic struggle of the Japanese people will win final victory under the leadership of the Communist Party of Japan.

The statement was carried in the Japanese Communist Party newspaper, *Red Flag*, but as far as could be determined it was not disseminated in South Vietnam. A joint statement was also signed by the NLF and the Japanese Communist Party at the WFTU (World Federation of Trade Unions) congress in 1963.

Japanese Communists exploited Diem-Buddhist troubles. The Vietnam-Japan Friendship Association, headed by Tokumatsu Sakamoto, basically a Japanese organization for relations with the DRV, issued a series of anti-Diem statements. Youth groups in Japan demonstrated outside the GVN embassy in Tokyo on August 31, 1963 and sent in a note to GVN officials, calling for freedom of religion and withdrawal of U.S. bases in South Vietnam; the U.S. base issue was particularly salient among left-wing Japanese. The Vietnam-Japan Friendship Association, the Vietnam-Japan Trade Association, the Japanese Peace Committee, and the Japanese Afro-Asian People's Solidarity Committee sponsored a rally on July 20, 1963 in Tokyo at which Diem was castigated for his actions against the Buddhists.

The Japanese Communist Party sent the NLF a support message in December 1963; the Free Workers' Trade Union of Japan delegation in Havana presented Vo Dong Giang, the NLF representative in Havana, with a resolution of support on May 17, 1964; Thanh Hai, representing the NLF's YLA and SLA (Student Liberation Association), signed a joint statement with a Japanese youth delegation in Peking on May 2, 1964. It was anti-imperialist, propeace, opposed to the extension of the U.S.-Japan Defense Treaty, and called for the return of Okinawa to Japan. A similar statement was signed on October 4, 1964 by the NLF delegation in Peking and Fujiwara Tohoziro, who is listed as chairman of the Japanese National Council Against the U.S. Security Treaty and for Defense of Peace and Democracy. The Japanese Peace Committee on April 2, 1964 announced plans to join with the Vietnam-Japan Friendship Association to launch a drive to collect ten thousand signatures and one million yen for relief work among the South Vietnamese people. In May 1964 the committee announced the formation of a new mass organization in Japan to support the NLF cause. It was called the Japanese Working Committee in Support of South Vietnam and was composed of 45 organizations, including the Japanese Communist Party, several socialist parties, the Vietnam-Japan Friendship Association, the General Council of Trade Unions, and the Japanese Afro-Asian People's Solidarity Committee.

Africa below the Sahara

Among the African nations with which the NLF communicated were Kenya (June 1963 and February 1965), Zanzibar (December 13, 1963), Guinea (May 30, 1964), Chad (May 30, 1964), Ghana (May 30, 1964), Malawi (July 11, 1964), and Mali (September 26, 1964). Among the African organizations with which the NLF exchanged solidarity or support messages were the African National Union of Kenya, the African National Congress of South Africa, the Pan-African Congress of South Africa, the Basutoland Communist Party, the Zimbawe African National Union, the South West African National Union, the People's Organization of South West Africa, the Bechuanaland People's Party, the Swaziland Progressive Party, the Progressive Party of Patriotic Mozambique and South Africa, the Mozambique National Democratic Union, and the Mozambique Liberation Front.

Nguyen Van Tien, Central Committee member, toured West Africa in November 1963, spending most of his time in Ghana as guest of the Ghana Convention People's Party and the Ghana Trade Union Congress. The NLF and the Ghana Trade Union Congress and the NLF and the Federation of Revolutionary Trade Unions of Zanzibar in March 1964 signed joint statements calling for the withdrawal of U.S. troops from South Vietnam. Mali in December 1964 issued a postage stamp bearing the words "solidarity of the Mali workers with the workers and people of South Vietnam," becoming the first African government below the Sahara to take official note of the Southern struggle. Internally the NLF treated Africa as a bloc, expressing its solidarity with Africa largely in terms of mutual aspirations and common interests; Vietnamese knowledge of African geography precluded a broader approach.

Great Britain

No individual within the Communist bloc or without was of more value to the NLF in its externalization efforts than Bertrand Russell, the British philosopher. In terms of total media output by the NLF within South Vietnam, he ranked sixth. That this eminent searcher after truth should have wanted to carry on a dialogue with the NLF is perhaps understandable; that he should have become such an unthinking transmission belt for the most transparent Communist lies; that he should have thrown over all objectivity and accepted on an unsubstantiated basis virtually all statistics and statements supplied him by the NLF is one of the great intellectual tragedies of our times. He did a disservice to the cause of peace, to his own country, to the Vietnamese people, and, in the end, to himself. Lord Russell was led to write of events in South Vietnam in the grossest stereotypes; perhaps for the same reason he was led to believe that America was the chief danger to world peace.

In letters to *The New York Times* (April 8, 1963), the *Washington Post* (March 22, 1963), *The Times* of London (August 26, 1964), and in at least three to the NLF he charged that

the United States government is conducting a war of annihilation in Vietnam. . . . The purpose of this war is to retain a brutal and feudal regime, . . . exterminate all those who resist dictatorship, . . . and invasion of the North. . . . [It does so] to protect economic interests and prevent far-reaching social reforms in that part of the world. . . . [The U.S. effort has resulted in] eight million people in barbed-wire concentration camps, surrounded by machine-gun turrets and patrolled by dogs, . . . 50,000 air attacks on villages in 1962, . . . [has] killed 160,000 people, maimed 700,000, and imprisoned 350,000. . . . [It is] reminiscent of warfare as practiced by the Germans in Eastern Europe and the Japanese in Southeast Asia.

His letters followed the Communist line, adhering to every zigzag, every tortuous rationalization, using all the phony statistics; the language was the same; even the order of condemnation of events was the same. During the Diem days his major themes were U.S. intervention and Diem repression; after the Diem regime fell he switched back to the U.S. violation of international agreements, exactly as did the output of Radio Peking, Moscow, Hanoi, and the NLF. He described the NLF as an "avowedly neutralist and national movement, the aim of which is independence and the removal of a brutal dictatorship supported by the United States." This was written not about the Diem regime but in April

1964, when the GVN at the time could perhaps have been described in several unflattering terms, weak and chaotic as it was, but "brutal dictatorship" was not one of the terms. Lord Russell's correspondence with Nguyen Huu Tho, Nguyen Van Hieu, Truong Cong Quyen of Hanoi University, and Nguyen Xien, a Hanoi engineer, were seized by Radio Liberation and the Liberation Press Agency and widely disseminated throughout South Vietnam. At first the coverage consisted of selected quotations such as "war of annihilation in South Vietnam" or "purpose of invading North Vietnam"; later the NLF news media took to reprinting his letters verbatim. Later, when he began to sound like a broken record, his usefulness to the NLF diminished and its exploitation of him began to taper off.

The NLF directed to the British government in its capacity as co-chairman of the Geneva conference a steady flow of messages that were ignored. The rest of its British dialogue was with a relatively small number of British organizations and individuals. Nguyen Huu Tho sent a telegram to the British Labour Party on May 31, 1962:

The Central Committee of the NLFSV notes that the actions of many British Labour MP's are timely and constitute valuable contributions to the cause of peace in South Vietnam. . . . We call on the British people and the Labour MP's to make use of their competence and prestige to compel the U.S. imperialists and their henchmen to implement the 1954 Geneva agreements and withdraw all U.S. troops and weapons from South Vietnam.

Hilda Vernon of the British-Vietnam Committee visited Hanoi in July 1962 and was quoted by Radio Hanoi as saying "the [government of Great Britain] know there is not a shred of evidence of the so-called subversive activities [in the South] on the part of the DRV"; the same organization sent a letter to the British Foreign Office proposing a settlement identical to the NLF proposal: "cease-fire, withdrawal of U.S. troops, negotiations seeking peace and independence by the Vietnamese themselves"; Nguyen Van Hieu wrote an article, "Defending Our Right to Live," in the November 1962 issue of *Vietnam Bulletin,* the organ of the British-Vietnam Committee. Other Britons visited Hanoi during the period, but generally their remarks tended toward understatement and for the NLF lacked impact value.

Algeria

The warmest reception received by the NLF in the Middle East and Moslem world was in Algeria, whose anticolonial experiences paralleled those of the Vietnamese. Radio Liberation reported on October 15, 1962 that the NLF Central Committee had "voted to send a sum of money to Algeria as a token of the South Vietnamese people's sympathy with their brother Algerian people in their difficult days of starting economic construction"; Huynh Van Tam arrived in Algiers on February 3, 1963, was received by President Ben Bella, and established a permanent delegation, technically accredited to the Political Bureau of the FLN; he was followed a few months later by Chung Van Ngoc, who established a Liberation Press Agency bureau to operate in the African area. Nguyen Huu Tho and President Ben Bella exchanged various greetings: Algerian National Day, November 11, 1962; the convening of the FLN congress on April 17, 1963; the second Algerian anniversary, July 3, 1963; Ben Bella's election in December 1963 and his reappointment as secretary-general of the FLN in April 1964; and the tenth Algerian National Day, October 27, 1964. The messages consistently spoke of "our common heritage of the struggle against French colonialism . . . and our iron-like friendship." NLF organizations also exchanged greetings with fellow Algerian organizations. In August 1963 Truong Van Loc attended the fifth congress of the Algerian Moslem Students' Union, where he delivered an anti-Diem speech. In April 1965 President Ben Bella presented Huynh Van Tam with a check for 100,000 dinars for use by the NLF.

Burma

NLF externalization relations with Burma were conducted for the most part through the Burmese Peace Committee; the general themes were anti-Americanism and the need to observe the Geneva accords. NLF clandestine newspapers reported that writers and journalists in Rangoon had translated into Burmese two volumes dealing with South Vietnam: *From the Fatherland Front* (originally published in Hanoi, a collection of letters purportedly from South Vietnamese to Northern relatives) and *Hell on Earth*, written by Nguyen Xuan Tram, a member of the DRV Vietnam Peace Committee. The newspapers *The People* and *Vanguard* took up the chemical warfare charge in mid-1963; the *Burman* also carried articles favoring the NLF, which were reproduced in South Vietnam.

Latin America (Excluding Cuba)

The most prominent incident involving the NLF and Latin America came in October 1964 in Caracas, Venezuela. The National Liberation Front (NLF) of Venezuela kidnaped and threatened to kill U.S. Air Force Lt. Col. Michael Smolen, who was in Venezuela as a U.S. military adviser, unless the GVN released Nguyen Van Troi, a 24-year-old Vietnamese convicted in Saigon of attempting to mine a bridge over which U.S. Defense Secretary McNamara's car was slated to pass. Troi was executed and Colonel Smolen later released, but the value to the NLF was considerable. Radio Liberation reported:

Venezuela is a Latin American country where the armed struggle movement against the U.S. imperialists is in full swing. The Venezuelan people have closely followed the heroic struggle of the South Vietnamese people. . . . On hearing of the Nguyen Khanh clique's decision to execute Mr. Nguyen Van Troi, Venezuela became very angry and immediately cautioned the U.S. imperialists over the aforementioned act. This clearly and touchingly reflects the close fighting friendship between the two peoples. . . .

The NLF had begun a long-distance public dialogue with the NLF of Venezuela in December 1963, when the Central Committee dispatched a message, declaring that, "standing on the same front against the North American imperialist, the South Vietnamese people fully approve and support the just and victorious struggle of the Venezuelan people." The two Fronts, on November 14, 1963 in Havana, had signed a joint statement declaring that their "peoples will support each other in the just struggle against the common enemy, U.S. imperialism and its lackeys." Radio Liberation reported that

the representatives of the two Fronts entered into extensive talks recently and exchanged views on the developments in the patriotic revolutionary struggles waged by each . . . and decided to set up a Committee of Solidarity with South Vietnam in Venezuela and a Committee of Solidarity with Venezuela in South Vietnam . . . [and] to organize a day of solidarity with Vietnam in Venezuela and a day of solidarity with Venezuela in South Vietnam to acquaint the peoples with each other's revolutionary struggle. . . .

In February 1965 the NLF announced the formation of an *ad hoc* group called the South Vietnam Committee for Solidarity with Latin American Peoples, whose task, it said, was the strengthening of NLF–Latin American ties.

Panama ranked second in NLF interest among Latin American nations. Mrs. Nguyen Thi Binh spoke on behalf of Panama at a rally in Djakarta on January 19, 1964, where she said "imperialism is the world's number one enemy and the Panama Canal is the symbol of that enemy"; Nguyen Huu Tho sent a message on January 12, 1964 to the president of Panama, in which he linked the NLF with the "valiant struggle of the Panamanian people to defend their national sovereignty against savage terror acts and the brazen aggression of the U.S. imperialists." The NLF Foreign Relations Commission issued a statement on January 21, 1964 declaring "it is necessary to return the Panama Canal to the Panamanian people, as the Suez Canal was returned to the Egyptian people, so that peace can be preserved." The Liberation Press Agency correspondent in Havana reported via Radio Liberation on April 1, 1964 that eight Panamanian youth organizations had adopted resolutions declaring that "the

Panamanian people turn their thoughts with admiration and deep sympathy toward the South Vietnam brother people's valiant struggle."

Nguyen Huu Tho sent a message of congratulations to Jamaica when it proclaimed its independence in August 1962. The chief of the Peruvian National Liberation Front, Salmon Bolo Hidalgo, was quoted by Radio Hanoi (October 29, 1963) as saying in a telegram to the NLF: "In the capacity of one of the chairmen of the Peruvian NLF in South America I convey to you our full moral support for the struggle of your people against American imperialism, our common enemy." The NLF Patriotic and Democratic Journalists sent a cable on April 16, 1964 protesting the "illegal arrest [on spy charges] of Chinese [Communist] journalists and trade-union officials by Brazilian officials in Rio de Janeiro." The NLF delegation in Peking received a Mexican women's delegation on October 4, 1964.

France

Hostility for the French remained a real and vital factor among the NLF as a result of the Viet Minh experience, although for tactical reasons support was sought from the French government. The NLF assessed the abortive November 11, 1960 paratrooper coup d'état as a French effort to establish in power South Vietnamese sympathetic to France. An NLF internal learning document entitled "Situation after the Coup," and apparently issued in mid-1961, declared:

We now realize that the coup was the result of antagonisms between the United States and France, and that it was concocted by the French and not by the Americans as we believed earlier. Coup leader Dong was a French stooge. . . . Further evidence lies in the fact that after the coup failed the leaders fled to Cambodia and there were taken care of by local Frenchmen. These people have set up a new organization to continue their activities in South Vietnam, particularly among the Hoa Hao in the western provinces, whose leaders are still loyal to the French. . . . France has never ceased planning the reconquest of South Vietnam. . . . Although evicted from here France still has economic and cultural interests and continues to wield political influence among the bourgeois intelligentsia and religious sects. . . . Many in the armed forces are still loyal to France. . . . There are many French lackey factions. . . . France is losing ground to the United States and seeks to convert countries that are being occupied by the Americans into neutralist countries, as in Cambodia and Laos, the better to move in and develop and maintain their holdings. France wants South Vietnam to be pacifist and neutralist, less friendly to America, so she can develop her interests. . . . Therefore our immediate strategy is to win the cooperation of the pro-French factions, . . . to use Enemy Two to fight Enemy One. . . .

NLF traffic with France consisted mainly of communication with the French Communist Party and French student and peace groups. French efforts to enhance France's influence in Vietnam as a matter of pride and national honor largely went unnoticed by the NLF. French business remained powerful during this period in South Vietnam, with holdings in the South totaling an estimated $200 million, chiefly in rubber and tea plantations, banking, insurance, breweries, and smaller businesses. Owners and operators of these enterprises were subjected to blackmail efforts by the NLF to pressure them to force policy changes from their government. The National Union of Students in France, made up of a number of Vietnamese émigrés, from time to time held rallies, meetings, and press conferences at which, chiefly, the GVN was denounced. French Communist Party Political Director Jacques Duclos on October 4, 1963 addressed a Paris rally, attended by some 400 persons, and said that the French Communist Party magazine *New Democracy* had launched a campaign to "mobilize public opinion in France to oppose the U.S. aggressive war in South Vietnam." The National Council of the French Peace Movement and the French Women's Union during 1964 issued a series of calls for a negotiated settlement. In general the French organizations tended to ignore the NLF and addressed themselves to the proposal for an international conference attended by all interested parties to write a peaceful settlement to the Vietnamese problem.

Cambodia

A special relationship always existed between the NLF and the government of Cambodia. Relations between Cambodia and the GVN under Diem were poor, marked by frequent border incidents and exchanges of recriminations. The NLF sided with Cambodia in these disputes and in early 1962 distributed leaflets in villages along the border, condemning the GVN for "provoking its neutral neighbor Cambodia with the aim of creating enmity between the South Vietnamese and the Cambodian people." Both the leaflets and Liberation Radio broadcasts asserted that

the U.S. imperialists scheme to destroy the independence and neutrality of Cambodia. The U.S. imperialists during the past two years have set up many centers in South Vietnam to train rangers and mercenary soldiers among traitorous Vietnamese-Cambodians and members of the treacherous Khmer Serai [Free Khmer] organization . . . with a view to seizing the Cambodian government. . . . The NLFSV Central Committee recently ordered its armed units to increase vigilance in order to exterminate in time the treacherous forces of the Khmer Serai under U.S. command.

GVN officials estimated that in the 1961–1964 period two thirds of the Communist-bloc shipments to the NLF went through Cambodia, going first to Sihanoukville, then to Phnom Penh, then down the Mekong River into the canal system of the delta. In several instances GVN officials seized shipments of tons of nitrates. Captured NLF army bases in the border area often contained week-old Cambodian newspapers, tinned Cambodian food, and Cambodian cigarettes. In part this reflected a traditional trading pattern in the area; during the days of French control residents in the Mekong delta would shop as often in Phnom Penh as in Saigon, there being no customs restrictions or travel barriers.

In early 1964 Nguyen Huu Tho and Prince Norodom Sihanouk, Cambodian chief of state, began exchanging messages. In early March the NLF sent the prince a message denouncing "American imperialism" and praising the "growth of Cambodia under . . . a policy of neutrality." In his reply Prince Sihanouk said he was "deeply affected" by the Front's support of Cambodia. Prince Sihanouk on October 27, 1964 announced that he would grant diplomatic recognition to both the DRV and the NLF; a few days later he added the qualification "if there are any more border incidents." This was followed in November by the Cambodian suggestion that the NLF and the Cambodian government meet and discuss the border question. Radio Liberation on December 28, 1964 stated:

> The Cambodian government . . . has therefore proposed negotiations with the NLFSV to provide a definite and lasting solution to the frontier problem. This act demonstrates the friendly relations between the Cambodian royal government and the NLFSV. . . . The NLFSV has agreed to negotiate with the Cambodian government on the frontier problem between the two countries in order to improve mutual understanding, further consolidate the existing friendly relations between the two peoples, and defend the peaceful and friendly border line between South Vietnam and Cambodia. . . . The NLFSV considers it fully rational to carry out negotiations with the Cambodian royal government concerning the frontier problem. . . . The Front and its armed forces actually control the major portion of the Southern territory, including almost all the border area between South Vietnam and Cambodia.

This marked the beginning of a period of close NLF-Cambodian relations as well as the launching of the so-called "Cambodian solution" to the Vietnam problem. Sihanouk suggested the establishment of a loose, truly neutral Indochinese federation that would include the two Vietnams, Laos, and Cambodia — in all, nearly 40 million persons. The chief requirement for its establishment, he felt, was to persuade the United States that neutralism was possible.

In mid-February 1965 a preparatory meeting for the Indochinese People's Conference was held in Phnom Penh; it was attended by organizations representing nonofficial organizations from the four countries: the Fatherland Front (DRV), the Neo Lao Hat Xat and the Laotian True Neutralist Forces (Laos), the Kampuchea Krom Struggle Movement and the Sangkum Reastr Niyum (Cambodia), and the National Liberation Front of South Vietnam. Also present was Tran Van Huu, representing the Committee for Peace and Amelioration of South Vietnam, a Paris-based organization that had often served as a mouthpiece for the NLF and the DRV but was not considered Communist. Tran Van Huu was one of the best-known Cochin-Chinese politicians, active since 1915; he and his organization stood for the neutralization of South Vietnam and the ultimate federation of the Northern and Southern portions of the country.

After a postponement due to an internal Cambodian political fight, the Indochinese People's Conference met in Phnom Penh from March 1 to March 8, 1965; it was attended by 38 organizations from the four countries. Huynh Tan Phat, NLF Central Committee vice-chairman, was the NLF delegation chief, but Tran Buu Kiem of the NLF's Foreign Affairs Commission appeared to have equal authority. Also attending under the NLF banner were Madame Le Thi Huong of the Women's Liberation Association and Thich Thien Hao representing an *ad hoc* NLF Buddhist organization (three separate Buddhist organizations from South Vietnam were represented); in all, 20 South Vietnamese organizations were supposedly in attendance, but the NLF spoke for all of them. Tran Buu Kiem called on Sihanouk and presented him with a revolver that he said had been seized by the NLF army while attacking a Free Khmer training center in South Vietnam in November 1963; the prince said he was very moved and would put the revolver in the Sihanouk museum in Phnom Penh.

At the opening of the conference Sihanouk issued a statement listing the principles he hoped would be followed:

> The conference shall be open to groups and organizations that have a program, statute, and a past struggle consistent with the objectives of the conference and benefiting from support of the masses . . . and are in harmony with the conference aims, which are solidarity, independence, and peace. . . . That these working principles shall be observed: unanimous agreement through negotiations of differences arising at the conference, avoidance of raising internal questions of specific countries, avoidance of raising pending problems among the countries or questions likely to create discord, . . . and an agenda that will consider (a) means of reinforcing friendly and mutual understanding of the four countries through cultural and commercial agreements . . . and (b) creation of a permanent organization to ensure contact and coordination of efforts among the participants.

In a speech the same day Sihanouk called on the conference to allay American fears that the neutralization of Indochina even with some form of international controls was impractical if not impossible. Disengagement and international controls, he said again, should be the basis of the settlement, and they should apply to all four countries involved. Once the settlement was reached, he added, it would then be ratified by the Big Powers at a reconvened Geneva conference.

The prince's hopes came to little at the conference. The DRV, although irked that the NLF was treated as an equal, swallowed its pride and used the conference as a platform to condemn the U.S. air strikes on southern North Vietnam. The NLF reiterated its position on settlement, unchanged from earlier statements. Huynh Tan Phat in a major address on May 8 declared that the "most basic solution [of the Vietnam problem] to ensure independence, peace, and neutrality for South Vietnam is that the U.S. imperialists must withdraw from South Vietnam and let the South Vietnamese people settle their internal affairs by themselves." The conference resolution on Vietnam attacked the United States for its activities, which it said endangered peace in Southeast Asia. It concluded:

The conference demands a halt to the U.S. aggressive war, the withdrawal of armed forces, military personnel, and war matériel of the United States and its allies; the liquidation of U.S. military bases and the restoration of peace; and approves the principle that the South Vietnamese people settle their own affairs on the basis of independence, democracy, peace, and neutrality.

In short, the terms were precisely the same as before the conference. Sihanouk's formula of "disengagement and international control" was pushed aside and not even mentioned in the final communiqué. Neither was his call for a permanent organization of those attending. Sihanouk in a speech at Olympic Stadium on March 9 noted there had been differences at the conference "as to ways and means leading to peace, but only on a plane that I call technical." Noting that Western observers had already termed the conference a failure, he said "At no conference would one find all the participants expressing an identical point of view. . . ."

In terms of the federation of Indochina the conference achieved nothing. But it helped establish the NLF as a quasi-government, more so perhaps than any other event in the four previous years.

Other Non-Communist Countries

Nguyen Huu Tho sent a spate of messages of good will to rulers and nations throughout the world: to Laotian Prince Souphanouvong of the Neo Lao Hat Xat, and (on December 20, 1963) the prince replied: "We fully support the demands of the NLFSV"; to Laotian Prince Souvanna Phouma congratulating him on the formation of the Laotian National Union government; to Abdullah Sallal on the founding of the Arab Republic of Yemen, October 1962; to Habib Bourguiba on the occasion of Tunisian National Day, March 1963; to King Hassan on the eighth anniversary of the kingdom of Morocco, March 1964; and to King Mahendra of Nepal on National Day, March 1964.

The strongest messages of support came during late August and September 1963, when Diem and the Buddhists were locked in their death struggle. Rallies in or statements from Laos, the Philippines, Thailand, and Cambodia all denounced Diem; their denunciations were broadcast and published throughout the South. Other incoming messages included ones from the Ceylon Trade Union Federation, December 20, 1963; the Ceylon-Vietnam Solidarity Association, July 20, 1964; UAR Premier Ali Sabri thanking the NLF for its message of greetings; the Pakistan Federation of Trade Unions supporting the NLF Workers' Liberation Association in May 1964; the Finnish Women's Federation, April 29, 1964; and the Belgian Communist Party, July 22, 1964. Virtually no intercourse was conducted with the Indians. Nor was there much traffic with the Canadians; the Canadian Peace Congress in April 1964 declared that "the struggle in Vietnam is the cruelest war in history." The New Zealand Communist Party, one of the most militant and pro-Chinese Communist parties, provided considerable grist for the NLF mill. Editorials from *The People's Voice* (the party organ) were reprinted extensively, as were various appeals from the New Zealand Peace Council.

Communist Countries

North Korea

Of all the satellite nations, excepting the DRV of course, North Korea developed the closest relations with the NLF. The North Korean Foreign Ministry took official note of the NLF in a statement issued on June 11, 1964, quoting NLF policy statements and adding: "The demands and propositions of the NLF are just, and the entire Korean people and the DPRK (Democratic People's Republic of Korea) government fully support them." North Korean newspapers were particularly vitriolic in their denunciations of the United States. The Hieu mission visited Pyongyang in 1962; in July 1964 it was followed by a second mission, led by Mrs. Nguyen Thi Binh, which took part in the tenth-anniversary observance of the Geneva accords. The Korean Committee for Support of the Struggle of the South Vietnamese People (part of the WFTU), the Korean Afro-Asian People's Solidarity Committee, and the Korean National Peace Committee were the groups closest to the NLF. A large number of messages were exchanged, which militantly stressed the theme of unification. Struggle-solidarity weeks were exchanged; North Korea staged such events in December 1963, July 1964, and again in December 1964. Radio Pyongyang, for instance, reported on December 21, 1964:

[North] Korea shook during the past week with the resounding voices of the people throughout the country expressing warm militant solidarity with the South Vietnamese people and their heroic struggle for national liberation. . . . Led by the Korean Committee for Support of the Struggle of the South Vietnamese People, the Fatherland Front, the General Federation of Trade Unions, the Korean Democratic Youth League, the Korean Democratic Women's Union, the Korean AAPSC, the Korean National Peace Committee. . . . The Pyongyang Textile Combine issued a statement. . . . Tae Dong Mun Cinema House had special films of Vietnamese. . . . The Korean Central Broadcasting station and provincial stations presented special programs. . . . Dailies in the capital and provinces issued special editions . . . with banner headlines such as "Militant Solidarity with the South Vietnamese People." . . . Taking up much space in the press were stories of the glorious path traversed by the NLFSV and the growth of the might of the South Vietnamese people's armed units . . . and the new life for the people in the liberated area.

The NLF said it staged a Day of Struggle for the Korean People on July 19, 1964, which was attended by 500 people "in the liberated area" for the purpose of "supporting the South Korean people in their struggle against U.S. imperialism." It said the meeting approved a five-point demand:

1. the United States withdraw from the peninsula and stop sabotaging the Korean cease-fire agreement;
2. Pak Chong Hui administration to stop repression and terror of Korean people . . . ;
3. establish North-South economic and postal exchanges;
4. oppose Japan-ROK talks and the order sending South Korean technicians to South Vietnam;
5. step up the anti–United States movement and smash the [United States] plan for expanding the war. . . .

On January 31, 1965 the NLF Central Committee issued an official statement on the dispatching of Republic of Korea troops to South Vietnam:

The U.S. imperialists are forcing a number of their satellites, including South Korea, to send mercenaries to South Vietnam. . . . The NLFSV declares solemnly that the U.S. imperialists and their lackeys are fully responsible for the unforeseeable consequences of their criminal and aggressive actions. . . .

Cuba

The NLF took little notice of Cuba until July 1962, when it sent Le Van Thinh and Ly Van Sau to Havana to help the Cubans observe Geneva Agreement Day, July 20. The following year the NLF delegation doubled in size (consisting of Vo Dong Giang of the NLF Central Committee; Nguyen Minh Phuong of the Workers' Liberation Association; Major Nguyen Van Luong, NLF army battalion commander;

and Mrs. Nguyen Ngoc Dung of the Women's Liberation Association).
Radio Hanoi reported on August 3, 1963 that Fidel Castro received the
delegation and said to them that "the government and the people of the
Republic of Cuba consider the NLFSV as the only and genuine representative of the South Vietnamese people. . . . We will spare no effort
in supporting the heroic struggle of the South Vietnamese people against
the U.S. imperialists."

From this time on relations between the NLF and Cuba took on an
intensive and serious nonceremonial character unique in the NLF's externalization efforts. Vo Dong Giang remained in Cuba as the permanent
NLF representative until mid-1965 and was extremely active. After the
overthrow of the Diem government he held a press conference in Havana
in which

he pointed out acute contradictions among the U.S. imperialists and their
henchmen . . . to 50 newsmen, including correspondents of the U.S. paper
The Worker and the Canadian newspaper *Vanguard* and representatives of
television agencies and mass media in Cuba, Latin America, Europe, and
Asia.

In May 1964 Radio Liberation reported that he "visited Cuban labor
teams in rural Cuba. He went to the fields and helped the teams cut
sugar cane, . . . then spoke over a local radio station." He signed, with
the NLF of Venezuela, a statement of mutual support in November 1963,
and a month later he signed a similar statement with a visiting delegation
of Japanese Communists.

Nguyen Van Hieu spent 17 days in Cuba in January 1964 and met
with Ernesto "Che" Guevara, "who eagerly inquired about the fighting struggle of the South Vietnamese people . . . and warmly praised
the achievements of the people against a common enemy." Nguyen Van
Tien was in Cuba in January 1964; Nguyen Minh Phuong returned in
June and the Nguyen Van Tien mission returned in January 1965. This
heavy influx of NLF personnel, perhaps the most intensive in any
country, led to persistent speculation about joint NLF-Cuban efforts to
promote a series of wars of liberation in Latin America. The chief overt
Cuban organization with which the NLF dealt was the Cuban National
Committee for Solidarity with the South Vietnamese people, led by Mrs.
Melba Hernandez. One of Vo Dong Giang's coups was a statement extracted from a group of American students visiting in Cuba in the summer of 1964; their statement and their names were widely reproduced
throughout South Vietnam. It began:

We, the undersigned young Americans visiting Cuba, wish to offer this
statement in support of the people of South Vietnam in their just struggle to
rid themselves of imperialist oppression directed by our government. Today

our government is waging one of the most brutal and criminal wars in history. In this war American poisons are ruining Vietnamese crops, killing livestock, and crippling and killing the people of Vietnam. . . .

The Cuban government announced in February 1965 that one and a half million pieces of clothing were being sent to South Vietnam as a gift from the Cuban people.

A particular saliency marked NLF-Cuban relations, as exemplified by this editorial in a clandestine NLF newspaper dated April 1963:

The South Vietnamese people are greatly honored to receive a gift of an American rifle — booty obtained by the Cuban people at the Bay of Pigs — from the Cuban people, as the Cuban people received a crossbow — from the highland compatriots through their representative in the NLF. . . . In honor of these exchanges NLF poet Le Cao Phuong has written:

How can the imperialists in the White House
Understand a heroic people
Seven million persons are seven million combatants who,
Holding firm their weapons in their arms, are ready to defend their country.
Our Cuba is never alone.
It has friends and brothers across the four seas,
Millions of hands together defending Cuba as they support my native land, the southern part of Vietnam.

Within South Vietnam the externalization effort with respect to Cuba was pressed over all others save the DRV. April 17, 1963 was observed by the NLF as Cuban Solidarity Day, and during the day Radio Liberation said:

Friends, you have us and we have you. This is the voice of seven million Cuban people from the Western hemisphere and of 14 million South Vietnamese people on this side of the Pacific. . . . Our comradeship in the fight against U.S. imperialist aggression binds us together. The South Vietnamese citizen feels very proud when speaking of Cuba. . . . The shouts from the green island in the Caribbean sea . . . "Down with U.S. imperialist aggression spraying poisonous chemicals in South Vietnam" mingle with the cries of elation when the Cuban people learned of the Ap Bac victory. . . . The Cuban citizen daily follows every forward step of the South Vietnamese Revolution. . . . In his surroundings of boiling water and burning fire, the South Vietnamese citizen is moved when learning that a Cuban woman doctor wishes to be foster mother to a South Vietnamese child, that a Cuban female nurse requests that she be allowed to serve in South Vietnam, and that brother Domingo Martinez, a Cuban officer, volunteers to fight against the Americans in South Vietnam.

At the July 29, 1963 NLF Central Committee meeting, a letter to Havana was drafted, which read in part, "The NLF is deeply moved by the Cuban government's decision to name a Cuban village after Ap Bac, which was the scene of a resounding victory of the people's armed forces over the U.S.-Diem troops in South Vietnam." The Front's military high command then announced that an NLF army unit had been named the Bay-of-Pigs (or Giron) Liberation Unit. A captured cadre handbook for use in indoctrinating members of the unit instructed cadres to stress these indoctrination themes: Members of the unit must be worthy of the name so as to honor heroic Cuba, they must maintain internal unity and discipline "as does the Cuban army," and they must become better Party members, for "thanks to the Marxist-Leninist Party, the Party of the proletariat, the Cuban Revolution has succeeded. In the light of Marxism-Leninism, the Cuban Party has built a strong army with a valiant spirit. . . ."

The German Democratic Republic

The Hieu mission arrived in East Berlin on August 14, 1962 as guests of the German Southeast Asia Society; they were met at the airport by Max Sefrin, Minister of Public Health and the society's president. A reception and the issuance of a joint declaration stressing the reunification theme followed. Hieu held a press conference in East Berlin on August 25 stressing the same theme. Nguyen Huu Tho cabled Walter Ulbricht on July 1, 1963, his seventieth birthday. The East German Red Cross on July 20, 1963 announced a donation to the NLF of 52,000 marks worth of blankets, medicine, and medical equipment. The GDR National Front of Democratic Germany the same month offered to provide medical treatment for twenty NLF army personnel, including their transportation to and from East Germany. It also announced that twenty crates of medical equipment were being shipped to South Vietnam. Late in the month the Free German Trade Union Federation (GDR) told Duong Dinh Thao, the NLF Liberation Press Agency chief in East Berlin, that it had donated 50,000 marks worth of medical equipment and was prepared to defray the costs of medical care for five NLF army personnel. Nguyen Huu Tho sent greetings on the fourteenth anniversary of the founding of the GDR, October 7, 1963, to which the GDR replied, in a message signed by Walter Ulbricht and Otto Grotewohl, "We sympathize with the South Vietnamese people's just struggle to achieve peace, independence, freedom, and reunification. . . ." In December 1963 the Afro-Asian People's Solidarity Committee of the GDR announced that it had donated 135,000 marks to South Vietnam and agreed to underwrite medical care for 25 NLF army personnel; at the same time the GDR itself announced the donation of one half million marks to the NLF as a solidarity gift; the GDR delegation of trade unionists in Hanoi in September 1964 announced another gift of 500,000 marks in cash and 320,000 marks worth of medicine. In March 1964, when the NLF established a permanent delegation in East Berlin, the National Front Council of Democratic Germans sponsored a photographic exhibition officially opened by K. Schneidewind of the GDR Foreign Ministry. Radio Liberation reported on October 7, 1964 that

the German Democratic Republic's people have collected hundreds of thousands of marks to buy cloth and medicine for the South Vietnamese people. In the liberated area everyone is familiar with the Hoang Le Kha Hospital, sponsored and equipped mainly by the GDR people.

The day was observed, said Radio Liberation, as German Solidarity Day in South Vietnam.

The Central Committee held an enlarged meeting at a revolutionary base. Two large NLFSV and GDR flags were hung together under a white parachute. . . . Tran Buu Kiem, chairman of the NLFSV Foreign Relations Commission, . . . spoke of the struggle of the German people against the revanchist West German warmongers . . . and their struggle for unification.

Albania

Newspapers in Tirana in July 1963, on the anniversary of the signing of the Geneva accords, carried editorials describing the NLF's activities. Nguyen Huu Tho sent nineteenth-anniversary greetings to Albania on November 26, 1963, stating: "We highly value the wholehearted support of the Albanian government and people and consider it a valuable encouragement for our patriotic and just struggle." Albanian journalists issued a statement in February 1964 "protesting . . . the crimes of the U.S. imperialists against the textile workers in South Vietnam." The Central Council of Trade Unions of Albania sent a solidarity message to the NLF's Workers' Liberation Association on May Day 1964. Nguyen Van Hieu arrived in Tirana on May 28, 1964, was received the following day by First Secretary Enver Hoxha, and that evening attended a mass rally sponsored by the Tirana Committee of the Democratic Front. During the tenth-anniversary celebrations of the Geneva accords on July 20, 1964, the Albanian press issued statements of support for the NLF, closely following the Chinese Communist themes. A Support South Vietnam Week was held July 14–20, sponsored by the Albanian Afro-Asian People's Solidarity Committee. In October 1964 the Central Council of Albanian Trade Unions announced that it was sending one million leks to the people of South Vietnam. And in November 1964 Huynh Van Tam went to Tirana to attend the observance of the twentieth Albanian National Day.

Czechoslovakia

The Hieu mission was the first NLF delegation to visit Czechoslovakia, arriving in Prague on June 26, 1962 as the guest of the Czechoslovak National Front. For about a year (1963) Hieu was the NLF permanent representative in Prague. He issued a series of statements in late 1963 and was interviewed by GDR and other Communist-bloc television newsmen after the fall of Diem. Radio Liberation reported on March 14, 1964 that workers of the Vigony Blanket Factory in Czechoslovakia held a mass meeting on March 5 to "protest against the U.S. imperialists . . . spreading toxic chemicals in South Vietnam." It also said the NLF Central Committee had received a letter from the dean of the economics faculty at the university in Prague, which said: We [the faculty] declare our support for the struggle of the South Vietnamese people for their legitimate interests; we demand that the U.S. imperialists put an immediate end to their savage acts in South Vietnam." Radio Liberation took note of the nineteenth anniversary of Czechoslovakia's liberation on May 9, 1964. On May 12 the Liberation Press Agency reported receiving a letter and some medicines from a Czech woman. "Though living far away, she understands the suffering of the South Vietnamese people due to the war waged by the U.S. aggressors." Throughout the summer a Czech letter-writing campaign developed. Said Radio Liberation, "We have received a large number of letters, resolutions, and cables." Tran Hoai Nam of the NLF visited Prague in December 1964 as guest of the Czech trade unionists. In April 1965 the Czechoslovak National Front Central Committee announced that it was sending "millions of crowns worth of gifts to the South Vietnamese people."

Other Bloc Countries

The Central Council of Mongolian Trade Unions presented 57 cases of medicine worth 170,000 tughriks as a solidarity gesture in March 1963. Nguyen Huu Tho sent a message to Ulan Bator on July 14, 1964 congratulating Mongolian leaders on Mongolia's forty-third National Day. In the following December Mongolia replied with its thanks, as it did in February 1965. The Central Council of the Bulgarian Trade Unions issued a statement denouncing U.S. actions in South Vietnam on July 20, 1964. Nguyen Huu Tho sent the NLF's condolences, May 5, 1964, on the death of the chairman of the Presidium of the National Assembly of Bulgaria. The Hungarian International Committee for the Defense of World Peace sent a letter to the ICC in May 1962 calling for implementation of the Geneva accords and the unification of Vietnam. The Hungarian Committee for Solidarity among Independent Nationalities announced in September 1963 that it was sending a gift of clothing and medicine to South Vietnam, for which Tran Buu Kiem sent a message of thanks. In October the Hungarian Red Cross said it was donating 100,000 florins to "help the South Vietnamese people overcome diseases caused by the noxious chemicals airdropped by the U.S.-Diemists." The Hungarian trade unions' central council in December 1963 announced it was donating 100,000 florins worth of medicine to the NLF. Poland's twentieth anniversary was hailed by a telegram from Nguyen Huu Tho in July 1964, as was Romania's the following month. The Peace Council of Poland announced in March 1964 that it had sent a letter to President Johnson and the United Nations charging the United States with chemical warfare in South Vietnam.

International Communist-Front Organizations

The NLF trafficked with seven of the twelve major international Communist-front organizations and with the Afro-Asian People's Solidarity Organization, which, although technically not a Communist-front organization, is indistinguishable from one. An impression of the relative rank of these organizations in the minds of the NLF leadership can be gained from the results of a word-count study, similar to the one described earlier, covering the 1962–1965 period and totaling about 57,000 words.

1. World Federation of Trade Unions (WFTU): 19,200 words, of which 7,200 were devoted to the WFTU Solidarity Committee meeting in Hanoi in October 1964.
2. Afro-Asian People's Solidarity Organization (AAPSO): 12,960.
3. World Peace Council (WPC): 10,800.
4. International Association of Democratic Lawyers (IADL): 7,980.
5. International Organization of Journalists (IOJ): 4,320.
6. International Union of Students (IUS) and the World Federation of Democratic Youth (WFDY), which were usually treated collectively by the NFL: 1,200.
7. Women's International Democratic Federation (WIDF): 600.
8. Organization of International Radio and Television (OIRT): none.
9. International Federation of Resistance Fighters (FIR): none.
10. World Federation of Scientific Workers (WSFW): none.[1]
11. World Congress of Doctors (WCD): none.

[1] A total of 300 words was devoted to the Peking Scientific Symposium, August 1964.

12. International Medical Association (IMA): none.
13. World Federation of Teachers Union (FISE):[2] none.

In addition the NLF communicated with a large number of regional groups and associations; Radio Liberation in December 1962 said that during the year the NLF had communicated with 67 international and mass organizations.

The World Federation of Trade Unions

The oldest (formed in February 1945) and largest (it claimed a membership of 100 million, of whom 90 million were from the bloc countries) of the international Communist-front organizations, the WFTU strongly supported the NLF from its inception, although, since Vietnam was an agrarian country and trade unionism played little part in the NLF efforts, its support tended toward the formalistic. During the first years the WFTU confined its activities to standard messages of support: December 20, 1961 (failure of the ICC); July 8, 1962 (U.S. aggression); March 4, 1963 (chemical warfare in South Vietnam); August 28, 1963 (pro-Buddhist statement); July 13, 1964 ("expanded" U.S. war in South Vietnam); and October 24, 1964 (a solidarity statement from the thirteenth WFTU General Council meeting in Budapest). These were all nominal efforts. The main WFTU contribution came through a section of the organization called the ITU International Trade Union (ITU) Committee for Solidarity with the Workers and People of South Vietnam, formed in Prague in March 1963, which in turn established in at least 32 countries, under local WFTU sponsorship, what were called the ITU Committees for Support of the Struggle of the Workers and Peoples in South Vietnam.

The 14-man presidium of the new group called a conference in Hanoi in October 1963. It was attended by Tran Van Thanh and Le Van Thong for the NLF, and the delegation was at stage center during the month of sessions. The Solidarity Committee, as it was called, was also a stage on which scenes of the Sino-Soviet competition were acted out; the DRV tried to maintain parity between the two powers, especially in matters of protocol, as exemplified by this *Nhan Dan* description of brimming proletarian internationalism at the opening session on October 3:

> The delegates all stood and cheered when the delegates of the All-Union Central Council of Trade Unions of the U.S.S.R. and the All-China Federation of Trade Unions presented to the South Vietnam Workers' Liberation Association a portrait of Lenin and a banner embroidered with the words in Chinese "Final Victory in the Struggle of the South Vietnamese Workers and People Against U.S. Imperialism and the Ngo Dinh Diem Clique."

[2] From its French designation, Fédération Internationale Syndicale des l'Enseignement.

A permanent presidium or secretariat was then named; it was chaired by Renato Bitossi of Italy, also president of the WFTU, and was designed to provide a broad geographic spread to include representatives from the WFTU (Kang Yung-ho of China, member of the WFTU secretariat), the DRV, the NLF (Tran Van Thanh), Asia (Indonesia's SOBSI), Europe (France's CGT), Latin America (Cuba), and Africa (National Union of Trade Unions of Mali). Radio Hanoi said that 35 delegations were in attendance, including 3 trade unions and 169 persons from 32 countries: Albania, Algeria, Australia, Brazil, Bulgaria, Ceylon, Chile, China, Cuba, Czechoslovakia, France, the GDR, Ghana, Hungary, India, Indonesia, Italy, Japan, Korea, Laos, Mali, Mexico, Mongolia, Morocco, New Zealand, Poland, Romania, South Vietnam, the Soviet Union, Tanganyika, Zanzibar, and the DRV.

The committee announced as its tasks and aims

1. To mobilize the workers and trade unions of the world to take all possible steps for the immediate end of the armed intervention by the government of the United States in South Vietnam and the withdrawal of all American troops, military personnel, and war matériel from South Vietnam; the immediate, strict, and integral application of the 1954 Geneva agreements on Vietnam so as to let the Vietnamese people decide their own affairs; an end to the repression perpetrated by the American-Diemist clique against the patriotic movement conducted by the workers and people of South Vietnam, a powerful support for the NLF and for its official recognition by various countries.

2. The organization of maximum moral and material solidarity of the international trade-union movement with the patriotic struggle of the South Vietnamese workers and people.

3. The promotion of the broadest unity of action possible among trade-union organizations of all tendencies to achieve the above-mentioned aims.

Among the means of action listed were:

Expose and condemn among the workers of all countries and to world public opinion the criminal acts perpetrated by American imperialism. . . . Increase publicity activities among the workers and trade unions of the whole world on the growth and successes of the patriotic struggle waged by the workers and people of South Vietnam. . . . Observe national or international days or weeks of solidarity. . . . Help the Workers' Liberation Association extend its international relations. . . . Organize the collection of funds, medicines, and materials to help the workers and people of South Vietnam. . . .

A large number of good-will messages from WFTU units around the world were read, but only the Cuban message specifically mentioned the NLF by name. Among the messages, said Radio Hanoi (in English October 23, 1963), was one from

the American Negro women and children of Birmingham, who cabled . . . "We condemn the heathen atrocities being committed against the patriots of

South Vietnam by the racist U.S. government in its bid for world conquest and aided by local political prostitutes. . . ."

The Solidarity Committee met the following March 20–21, 1964 in Prague.

Afro-Asian People's Solidarity Organization

The AAPSO was highly valued by the NLF — even above the WFTU, which tended to represent more industrialized nations — because of its links with the Chinese and nations more receptive to playing the externalization game. It served the NLF well. Within South Vietnam the South Vietnamese Afro-Asian People's Solidarity Committee, headed by Nguyen Ngoc Thuong, was responsible for the specific externalization efforts. The AAPSO, formed in Cairo in December 1957, maintained that its spiritual forebear had been the Bandung Conference. Actually several paths led out of Bandung, including the seventeen-nonaligned-nations movement, which was active in 1965 in attempting to negotiate a settlement in Vietnam; the NLF was not associated with this group. The AAPSO was more broadly based than the nonaligned nations, was somewhat more cohesive, and was far more subject to Communist, especially Chinese Communist, control. The AAPSO may not be an international Communist-front organization, but its stand and statements on Vietnam differed in no way from those of the NLF, the DRV, or Communist China; such nuances of difference as did exist simply reflected varying attitudes of the three Asian elements. As far as South Vietnam was concerned, the AAPSO, for working purposes, was an international Communist-front organization. Its value to the NLF was not in terms of influencing foreign policy but as a vehicle for gaining legitimacy and recognition and for developing solidarity. The AAPSO's Moshi conference was a major NLF externalization victory. Originally scheduled for January 1963 at Dar es Salaam, Tanganyika's capital and principal seaport, it was switched at the last moment to the small Tanganyika town of Moshi on the slopes of Mount Kilimanjaro. The third Afro-Asian People's Solidarity conference was attended by some 400 delegates representing 60 nations.

The NLF sent a three-man delegation led by Mrs. Nguyen Thi Binh and including Nguyen Van Tien. Great coverage of the conference events was given within South Vietnam by the NLF, which managed to imply that the entire purpose of the conference was to consider South Vietnam; actually the conference passed 27 resolutions, of which one dealt with South Vietnam. Nguyen Huu Tho, in the name of the NLF Central Committee, sent the conference a message, which declared the conference must pay attention to U.S. aggression in South Vietnam as it endangers peace in Southeast Asia and in the world and is in opposition to the national liberation movement of Asian and African countries. We demand the withdrawal of U.S. troops from South Vietnam, a demand not only of the Vietnamese people but also of the peoples of Asia, Africa, and the world.

Because of its status, ambiguously Communist rather than overtly so, the GVN decided it must take cognizance of the presence of the NLF delegation. GVN Foreign Minister Vu Van Mau sent a note to the Tanganyikan government, stating:

I would like to call your attention to the Communist maneuvers aimed at establishing a new form of imperialism and particularly to the attempt by the so-called DRV to present at the conference the candidacy of the so-called NLF of South Vietnam as a member of the AAPSO. I believe it should be underlined that the NLFSV is solely the creation of the Communist regime in Hanoi, with the sole policy of carrying out aggression and subversion in South Vietnam. The above-mentioned Front has nothing to do with the South Vietnamese people, who on the contrary for many years have suffered an untold number of atrocities at the hands of Communist agents.[3]

This note was ignored, and not only was the NLF admitted but it was given a seat on the 14-man presidium of the conference, an action that brought from Radio Liberation, February 22, this statement:

The AAPSO has bestowed an exceptional honor on the NLF and the people of South Vietnam. Our election . . . proves that the Afro-Asian people have highly esteemed the struggle of the South Vietnamese people for liberation and against imperialism . . . and that these people fully support the revolutionary movement against the U.S. and the Diem lackeys. . . . The protest message issued by Vu Van Mau was only laughed at by the conference. . . .

Independent reports from the conference at the time indicated that it was marked by a series of splits among delegates, not all of whom were Communists. The Indian delegate, Congress Party member of Parliament D. Chaman Lal, left the floor, incensed at the presidium's decision to shelve an Indian resolution on Sino-Indian border troubles; delegates from Malaya and Singapore were denied admittance to the conference; two African delegations engaged in abusive recriminations; there were walkouts and an excessive amount of tumult, shouting, arrests, and expulsions.

The language of the conference resolution on South Vietnam and others was distinctly Maoist. One resolution called for the creation of a united national front in every country not liberated from colonialism. The conference statement on South Vietnam read in part:

The conference . . . salutes and entirely supports the South Vietnamese people in their just cause of national liberation against U.S. aggression. The

[3] Vietnam Press Agency, *Bulletin,* February 9, 1963.

patriotic struggle waged by the South Vietnamese people under the leadership of the NLFSV is an important contribution to the cause of the peoples of Asia and Africa and the world for independence and peace, and against imperialism and colonialism. . . . The conference strongly urges that the U.S. government renounce its policy and activities of aggression . . . [and that] the Ngo Dinh Diem administration stop its massacres and other barbarous crimes.

Nguyen Van Tien assessed the Moshi results in an interview in Moscow, March 6, 1963:

First . . . the NLFSV was officially recognized, its membership application approved, and . . . it was appointed to the presidium of the conference. . . . The second victory was that throughout the conference the South Vietnamese people's struggle was highly publicized . . . as a torch blazing the way for freedom-loving nations of the world. . . . The third victory was that the conference adopted a special resolution on South Vietnam demanding an end to American aggression . . . and the Diem administration's repression . . . and approving the NLFSV's policies and line. . . . The final and major victory was that the conference unanimously elected South Vietnam to the permanent secretariat of the Afro-Asian People's Solidarity Organization.

In the months that followed, the NLF sought to solidify its victory at Moshi. The NLF permanent delegation at the AAPSO headquarters in Cairo, Huynh Van Tien and Nguyen Van Nghia, extended contacts and collected support statements from member nations. The AAPSO issued a statement after the fall of the Diem regime in which it

reaffirmed its firm and total support for the struggle of the South Vietnam National Liberation Front for liberating South Vietnam from U.S. armed intervention . . . [and condemned] the statement of the new U.S. President Johnson on the day after the death of Kennedy in which he declared he will continue his predecessor's aggressive policy in South Vietnam.

And in November 1964 the AAPSO "congratulated" the NLF army for its attack on the Bien Hoa airfield, in which a number of American aircraft were destroyed: "The AAPSO expresses its admiration for and extends congratulations on the victory scored by the South Vietnamese patriots over U.S. imperialist forces." On March 22, 1965 the permanent secretariat sent a note to all of its affiliated organizations calling on each to "start broad mass movements in support of the Front's [NLF] demands, give it both material and moral support, including weapons, and initiate a youth and army man's movement to volunteer to go and fight in South Vietnam. . . ."

The World Peace Council

The World Peace Council, generally considered the most influential of the international Communist-front organizations — at least in the

1950's and early 1960's — worked closely with and was regarded by the NLF chiefly as a link to the Soviet Union. Just as the NLF sought to harness nationalist, anticolonialist, and anti-imperialist sentiment by means of the AAPSO, it used the WPC to engender support among those preoccupied with peace. And just as the South Vietnam Afro-Asian People's Solidarity Committee's work (through the AAPSO) was identified most closely with China, so the activities of the South Vietnam Peace Committee (headed by Phung Van Cung) were most closely identified with the Soviet Union. Anti-imperialism belonged to the Chinese, peace to the Soviets. However, the primacy of the Chinese and the saliency of anti-imperialism over peace as a theme made the WPC somewhat less useful than the AAPSO. The South Vietnam Peace Committee generally dealt directly with individual peace committees and not with the parent organization; it was particularly active with respect to committees in Indonesia, Burma, Ceylon, and Laos. Phung Van Cung in mid-1962 dispatched a series of messages to various countries and organizations attacking the Indian and Canadian members of the ICC; Radio Liberation said that the message "exposes the erroneous tendency of the Indian and Canadian delegations to tune in to the U.S. slander that the NLF is involved . . . in aggressive and subversive activities." The message also "expressed the hope that, in the name of the World Peace Council, [ICC] members will urgently check their incorrect and fallacious conclusions."

The WPC's World Congress for Disarmament and Peace, held in Moscow in July 1962, provided a platform for the NLF (Hieu mission) to link the NLF to the WPC's efforts. Hieu also attended the WPC meeting in Warsaw in December 1963. A WPC-sponsored signature campaign entitled "Petition for Peace in South Vietnam" started in mid-1963; it maintained that peace could be restored only if Vietnam adopted a two-point program: withdrawal of the American military forces and implementation of the Geneva accords, both of course adaptations of NLF goals to the peace theme.

In 1964, as the peace theme became less prominent in Communist output and as the NLF's armed struggle intensified, there was a drop-off of activity by the South Vietnam Peace Committee, related perhaps to the increased control the DRV and Communist China were exerting over the NLF. The last significant report on its activities was the trip by a Buddhist monk, Thich Thien Hao, to Tokyo in July 1964 for the tenth meeting of the World Council Against Atomic and Hydrogen Bombs; he stopped en route in Peking and was received by Mao Tse-tung.

International Association of Democratic Lawyers

Although international Communist-front organizations of professional people are by their nature not mass based, and hence were of limited value to the NLF, they did serve as sounding boards and therefore were useful. The IADL (founded in 1946) was particularly valuable for helping the NLF to increase its image of legality. The Afro-Asian Lawyers' Conference held under IADL sponsorship in Conakry, Guinea, October 15-22, 1962 was attended by an NLF delegate and for the first time took note of the Vietnamese situation:

The conference warmly supports the patriotic and just struggle of the South Vietnamese people under the leadership of the NLFSV for . . . the cause of national independence, democracy, peace, and neutrality.

A general resolution, presented by IADL Vice-President Yoshitaro Hirano of Japan, continued the Leninist thesis on just and unjust wars, adding that "all struggles for complete independence for the restoration of their territories including armed struggle conducted by the peoples are entirely legal."

At the *WFDY* meeting in Warsaw in January 1963 the organization established a Committee of Support for the Patriotic Struggle of the South Vietnamese People; members included representatives of the DRV, the United States, France, Japan, Algeria, and Hungary. Nguyen Huu Tho, himself a lawyer, sent greetings to the meeting, declaring that "South Vietnamese lawyers welcome with gratitude any initiative by the world's lawyers to halt U.S. interference in South Vietnam, a prerequisite for restoring peace there." The conference in turn adopted a resolution supporting the NLF and asserting that "U.S. armed intervention is inconsistent with the 1964 Geneva agreements."

The IADL executive committee meeting of November 23, 1963 in Conakry was attended by NLF representative Nguyen Van Tien, who was also received by Guinea President Sékou Touré. Tien addressed the committee on the subject of "NLF sovereignty," after which the committee issued a statement holding that

the struggle of the South Vietnamese people must be considered as a legal self-defense struggle against aggression. . . . All lawyers in all countries must denounce the aggressive war and scheme of the United States.

Nguyen Van Hieu attended the IADL meeting in Budapest in March and April 1964 and, although not a lawyer, was elected to the presidium of the IADL congress. He addressed the meeting on "the illegality of U.S. napalm and chemical warfare activities in South Vietnam." The congress adopted a statement condemning GVN Decree 93, issued by the post-Diem government, which prohibited Communist or neutralist propaganda or activity in South Vietnam; the statement held that the decree was a violation of the U.N. declaration on human rights. In March 1965 the IADL secretariat in East Berlin issued another pro-NLF statement and called for implementation of the 1954 Geneva accords.

The International Union of Students and the World Federation of Democratic Youth

Although separate within Vietnam, these two organizations were treated jointly by the NLF in its externalization efforts, probably because of a shortage of representative manpower abroad and because the WFDY and the IUS often sponsored joint activities, including the mammoth World Youth Festivals.

The WFDY, claiming 107 million members, held its sixth assembly in Moscow, August 10–16, 1962, during which a statement was issued citing GVN repression of youths and calling on all governments to support the NLF. Its executive committee met in Budapest in February 1963 and established the International Youth Committee for Solidarity with the Struggle in South Vietnam. The session was attended by an NLF delegate, Truong Van Loc, a member of the NLF's YLA executive committee. He then went on to Algiers in May to the IUS executive committee meeting and the first session of the newly established Youth Solidarity Committee. The committee also met in Budapest in February 1964. During both of these sessions as well as in between, the committee issued militant appeals to the youth of the world to support the NLF. It also conducted a spirited exchange of messages with Tran Bach Dang, chairman of the NLF's Youth Liberation Association. Truong Van Loc went to Moscow on September 27, 1964 to attend the World Youth Forum, where he concentrated on collecting signatures of American youth on an NLF support petition. The same petition, circulated extensively by the IUS during 1964, had been launched in February at the Budapest meeting, attended by a major NLF delegation — Vo Cong Truong, Nguyen Thi Binh, and Nguyen Van Hieu. Several thousand names were gathered during the meeting, including those of three African students who announced rather naïvely that they were sending to South Vietnam for relief work fifty yuan, the currency of Communist China. In Prague, the following June, a World Students' Committee for Solidarity with the Students and People of South Vietnam was established, identical to the solidarity committees of other international Communist-front organizations. The committee announced at once that it was sending medicine and medical equipment to the NLF in South Vietnam, and it collected signatures for an anti-United States petition "from students from Ceylon, Indonesia, Iraq, Yemen, Cameroun, Congo, Guinea, Kenya, Somali, Sudan, Mexico, Peru, Venezuela, Italy, and other countries," carefully listing only non-Communist countries. The NLF's Student Liberation Association representative at the Prague meeting was listed as Le Phuong, probably an alias; it is very likely that he was not from the South but from Hanoi.

International Organization of Journalists

Partly perhaps because its chief representative abroad, Nguyen Van Hieu, was a journalist, but chiefly because of the benefits to accrue from associations with Communist news media personnel, the NLF carried on considerable activity with the IOJ as well as with the Organization of International Radio and Television (OIRT), although its activities with the latter were internal for the most part. Nguyen Van Hieu attended the Fifth IOJ Congress in Budapest in August 1962 and made arrangements for National Liberation Front news representatives to visit the various Communist countries. When the Afro-Asian Journalists' Organization (AAJO) came to the fore in 1962, the NLF tended to work through it rather than through the IOJ. It sent a representative to the AAJO congress in Djakarta on April 30, 1963; the GVN also sent two journalists, but they were refused admittance to the conference, which then went on to pass a resolution condemning the GVN's strategic-hamlet program. The IOJ in December 1963 issued a resolution calling on the United States to "(1) stop its aggression and withdraw its troops, . . . (2) ensure democratic freedoms in South Vietnam, and (3) abide by the 1954 Geneva agreements. . . ."

Woman's International Democratic Federation

World communism in 1962 began to make increased efforts to gain the support of women. The NLF, however, did little with the WIDF compared to its work with other international Communist-front organizations. There were exchanges of messages between the Women's Liberation Association and the WIDF. Mrs. Ma Thi Chu attended the WIDF congress in Moscow, June 1963, at which she heard some children recite poems, one of which was entitled "We Do Not Want the South Vietnamese Mothers to Cry." But in general the NLF, for reasons that are not clear, did not exploit fully the possibilities of international women's organizations. On October 26, 1964 the WIDF, at its plenary session in Sofia, attended by Mrs. Nguyen Thi Binh of the Women's Liberation Association, announced that it had established a Committee for Solidarity with the South Vietnamese People.

Non-Communist International Organizations

In its early days the NLF used the International Control Commission and to some extent the United Nations as means of projecting itself into the world's consciousness. It apparently believed that the International Control Commission and the United Nations might be of service to it, a belief dropped in 1962. On May 28, 1961 the NLF sent its first message to the ICC, and it was typical of the dozens that followed in the next few years: "We call your attention to the current situation in Vietnam and the crude aggressive attempts by the United States, which render the situation serious and threaten peace. . . ." A year later, on May 24, 1962, the NLF tone had changed:

The South Vietnamese people will not recognize any partial and erroneous conclusions reached by the majority votes of the ICC. . . . It is regrettable that the ICC has, in many cases, drawn unscrupulous and nonimpartial conclusions . . . busying itself with the so-called subversive and aggressive activities of North Vietnam, a product of the imagination and slander.

In June 1962 the Indian and Canadian majority of the ICC (the Poles dissenting) issued a report on the source of the armed struggle in South Vietnam:

The Committee has come to the conclusion that in specific instances there is evidence to show that armed and unarmed personnel, arms, munitions, and other supplies have been sent from the Zone in the North to the Zone in the South with the object of supporting, organizing, and carrying out hostile activities, including armed attacks, directed against the Armed Forces and Administration of the Zone in the South. Those acts are in violation of Articles 10, 19, 24, and 27 of the *Agreement on the Cessation of Hostilities in Vietnam.* . . . The Committee has come to the further conclusion that there is evidence to show that the People's Army of Vietnam [the North's regular army] has allowed the Zone in the North to be used for inciting, encouraging, and supporting hostile activities in the Zone in the South.[4]

Nguyen Huu Tho, for the Central Committee of the NLF, replied:

The National Liberation Front of South Vietnam Central Committee formally declares that this conclusion is completely contrary to the truth, unlawful, and dangerous. . . . We request [the Commission] reject this erroneous, illegal, and completely invalid conclusion of the Indian and Canadian delegates. . . .

The NLF's flow of messages to the ICC continued, but they appeared increasingly to be simply for their externalization value. From mid-1963 on, the NLF virtually ignored the ICC.

The NLF took a positive attitude toward the United Nations in the

[4] *Special Report to the Co-Chairmen of the Geneva Conference on Indo-China,* issued in London as a White Paper (Cmd. 1755), June 1962, cited from a U.S. State Department release.

early days, encouraging the United Nations to take note of events in South Vietnam and making frequent references to the U.N. human rights declaration. On September 29, 1962 Nguyen Huu Tho sent the U.N. General Assembly a message detailing the NLF interpretation of events in Vietnam since 1954, but asking for no action. A year later, on September 11, 1963, he sent another message to the General Assembly, in which he said:

> On behalf of the Central Committee of the NLFSV I draw the Assembly's attentions to the particularly grave situation created by the U.S. government in carrying out an aggressive war here. . . . We hope the United Nations . . . will take urgent measures to compel the United States to respect the 1954 Geneva agreements and the U.N. Charter to end the war.

Correspondence with the United Nations ceased abruptly in mid-1964, when, on June 8, the U.N. Security Council announced, on the basis of a Cambodian complaint of border violations by South Vietnam, it was sending a two-man team on a 45-day visit to the border area; the move raised in the NLF leadership's mind the real possibility of U.N. involvement in South Vietnam. Said Radio Liberation on May 30, 1964:

> The U.S. imperialists and their lackeys grind out their obsolete propaganda. They utter slanders about the patriotic forces of South Vietnam committing encroachments on the Cambodian frontier. Now in the United Nations . . . they have sent their lackeys, the Saigon rebel authorities, to the Security Council . . . to cover up the true facts . . . and have announced their aim of sending many units of foreign troops under the label of the United Nations to the Cambodian border area to infringe openly upon the sovereignty, independence, and territory of South Vietnam. . . . We hope that responsible men in the United Nations will take a positive attitude and check in time the schemes and illegal maneuvers of the United States. . . .

A commentary two days later denied the right of the United Nations team to enter Vietnam and warned that the NLF would oppose the team physically: "Our troops and our people will not allow anyone to come to our country without the consent of the Front. . . . The South Vietnamese people know only their legal representative, the NLFSV, and listen only to the Front's orders." On June 14 Radio Liberation said:

> This indicates that the United Nations has begun to intervene officially in the Southeast Asia question, particularly in the Vietnamese problem. To say it another way, the ICC is becoming a thing of the past and the 1954 Geneva accords are becoming a relic.

The NLF seemed to reject even the concept of the United Nations as inimical to its purposes:

> In the light of events in Korea and the Congo, the peoples of the world have come to realize what the so-called intervention of the U.N. organization

474   *APPENDIX F*

really means and will never forget the monstrous crimes committed under its flags by the U.N. imperialists. . . .

This was followed by a detailed statement of the NLF's attitude toward the United Nations. It seemed to go the whole length and deny that it could then, or in the future, be influenced in any way by the United Nations, ruling out any possible role the United Nations might play in the Vietnamese situation:

In view of the aforementioned situation, the NLFSV, in the name of 14 million South Vietnamese people, solemnly makes the following statement to public opinion at home and abroad:

1. The fact that the U.S. imperialists take advantage of the U.N. Security Council's resolution to pursue their interventionist and aggressive policy in South Vietnam and Cambodia is contrary to the 1954 . . . agreements. . . .

2. There is absolutely no basis for any organ of the United Nations to intervene in the internal affairs of the South Vietnamese people, or of any people of the Indochinese countries. All direct or indirect activities of the United Nations aimed at carrying out the U.S. imperialists' policy to intervene . . . will constitute violations of the sovereignty of these countries and threats to their security, independence, and territorial integrity. It will be held fully responsible for the grave consequences ensuing from these activities.

3. Because it actually controls and administers nine tenths of the South Vietnamese territory along the South Vietnamese–Cambodian border, the NLFSV will not allow any U.N. organ to come to its liberated area for investigations. The U.S. henchmen in South Vietnam cannot represent the South Vietnamese people nor are they qualified to express, in the name of the South Vietnamese people, views at the United Nations. . . .

4. For both the present and the future, the NLFSV will neither recognize nor accept any responsibility for or task contained in any conclusion drawn by the U.N. Security Council's fact-finding mission. . . ." [5]

[5] Radio Liberation, June 19, 1964.

Name Index

Subject Index